UMI ANNUAL COMMENTARY

PRECEPTS FOR LIVING®

MISSION STATEMENT

We are called
of God to create, produce, and distribute
quality Christian education products;
to deliver exemplary customer service;
and to provide quality Christian
educational services, which will empower
God's people, especially within the Black
community, to evangelize, disciple,
and equip people for serving Christ,
His kingdom, and church.

Urban Ministries, Inc.
The African American Christian Publishing
& Communications Co.

UMI ANNUAL SUNDAY SCHOOL LESSON COMMENTARY
PRECEPTS FOR LIVING® 2012–2013

INTERNATIONAL SUNDAY SCHOOL LESSONS
VOLUME 15

UMI (URBAN MINISTRIES, INC.)

Melvin Banks Sr., Litt.D., Founder and Chairman
C. Jeffrey Wright, J.D., CEO

All art: Copyright © 2012 by UMI.
Bible art: Fred Carter

Get the Precepts for Living® eBook!

Are you among those joining the digital revolution by reading books using a Kindle, iPad, NOOK, or other electronic reader? If so, there's good news for you! UMI is keeping up with the latest technology by publishing its annual Sunday School commentary, *Precepts for Living®*, in the leading eBook formats: Kindle (Amazon), NOOK (Barnes & Noble), and iBooks (Apple).

To buy an eBook copy of Precepts for Living®, visit our website at urbanministries.com/precepts to find download links and step-by-step instructions.

If you've purchased *Precepts for Living®* for your e-reader, be sure to leave a rating and a review at the iTunes, B&N, or Amazon store sites to tell others what you think. Also, spread the word on your favorite social networking sites, and follow *Precepts for Living®* on Facebook and Twitter (with the handle @precepts4living).

PRECEPTS FOR LIVING®

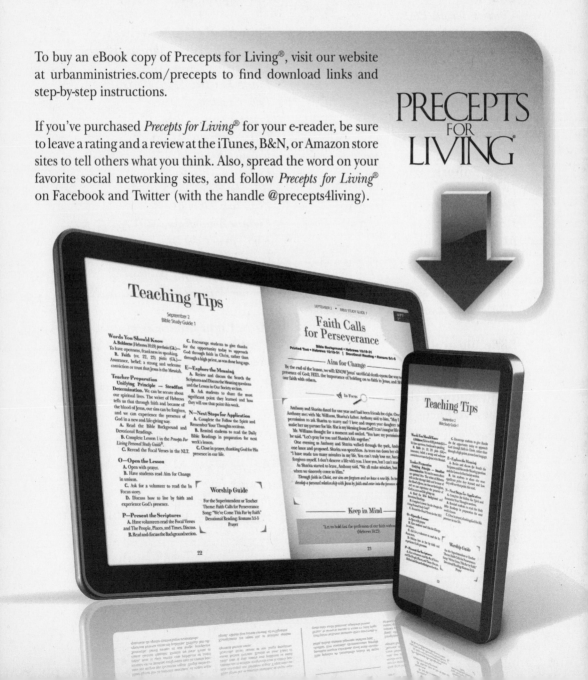

CONTRIBUTORS

Editor
Vincent Bacote, Ph.D.

Vice President of Editorial
Cheryl Price, Ph.D.

Developmental Editors
Evangeline Carey, M.A.
DeVona Alleyne, B.A.

Copy Editors
Joyce Garcia
Eric Gwinn
Pamela Graves
Mary C. Lewis
Marjorie Vawter

Cover Design & Layout
Trinidad D. Zavala, B.A.

Bible Illustrations
Fred Carter

Contributing Writers
Essays/In Focus Stories
Evangeline Carey, M.A.
Lisa Crayton, B.A.
Rukeia Draw-Hood, Ph.D.
Judy St.Clair Hull, Ph.D.
Barbara Carr-Phillips
Bertram Melbourne
Rosa Sailes, Ed.D.

Kyle Waalen, M.S.

Bible Study Guide Writers
Allyson D. Nelson Abrams, Ph.D.
Evangeline Carey, M.A.
Judith St.Clair Hull, Ph.D.
Lisa Crayton, B.A.
Jay D. Ganger, B.S.
Jean Garrison, M.A.
Jennifer King, M.A.
LaTonya Mason, M.A.
Beverly Moore, M.S.
Frederick Thomas
Evonne Thompson, M.B.A.
Kim Varner, M.Div.
Faith Waters, M.Div.
Christanthenopia Watkins
Jimmie Wilkerson-Chaplin, M.B.A.

More Light on the Text
J. Ayodeji Adewuya, Ph.D.
Evangeline Carey, M.A.
Moussa Coulibaly, Ph.D.
Clay Daniel, M.Div.
Richard Gray, Ph.D.
Kevin Hrebik, D.Min.
Judith St.Clair Hull, Ph.D.
Beverly Moore, M.S.
Keyonn Pope
James Rawdon, Ph.D.
Philip & Jerii Rodman, M.Div.

Dear Precepts Customer,

It is our privilege to present the 2012–2013 *Precepts For Living*®. As you encounter God's Word through these lessons, we anticipate that you will find this resource to be indispensable.

Precepts For Living® comes to you in three versions: the Personal Study Guide (the workbook), the CD-ROM version, and a large print edition. You will also notice that the biblical text for each lesson includes the New Living Translation in addition to the King James Version. This contemporary translation will enhance your textual understanding when you compare it side by side to the classic English translation. It is very helpful in illuminating your understanding of the text.

Precepts For Living® is designed to be a witness through our learning and sharing more of the Bible. Our intent is to facilitate innovative ways for pursuing a deeper understanding and practice of God's Word. One of the ways we strive to do this is by highlighting the larger narrative of God's work in salvation as a key part of understanding each biblical passage. We believe it is important to help you understand not only the particulars of the text but also the broad extent of God's revelation to us as well. This panoramic approach enhances our ability to witness to others about the saving power of Jesus Christ.

This year we explore the themes of faith, Jesus as Lord, hope, and worship. Each year of Bible study offers great potential for a more intimate and transformative walk with God.

We want to continually refine *Precepts For Living*® as we endeavor to meet our customers' needs. We are always looking for ways to enhance your study of the Bible, and your comments and feedback are vital in helping us. If you have questions or suggestions, we encourage you to please e-mail us at precepts@urbanministries.com or mail your comments to UMI, *Precepts For Living*®, PO Box 436987, Chicago, IL 60643-6987.

May God draw you closer to the fullness of life with Him through this book.

God's blessings to you,

Vincent E. Bacote, Ph.D.

Vincent E. Bacote, Ph.D.
Editor

Uncovering the Benefits of Precepts

It is a great privilege to participate in Christian education and play a significant role in the spiritual formation of fellow Christians in our churches. *Precepts for Living®* is a resource that is designed to help you lead others toward greater knowledge and practice of following Jesus Christ. To that end, please take full advantage of the substantive offerings provided to you in this year's commentary. From the standpoint of your vocation as a teacher, it is very important to be aware of the great responsibility that goes along with your position. James 3:1 reminds us that we have such a great opportunity in front of us that we run the risk of greater judgment if we are derelict in our duties. This is a strong word that helps us understand the great influence we have when we help our students learn about God's Word. Being a teacher means participating in one of the church's greatest tasks, one that the ancient church called "catechesis." While this word is often associated with particular denominations and with a form of teaching that relies upon a systematic question-and-answer format, the central meaning of the word is teaching. It carries with it the idea of imparting the entirety of the faith to Christians. While many Sunday school teachers might not be familiar with this word, the truth is that every time we help other learn about God's Word and ways, we are participating in this great task of the church that has been with us from the beginning. Our participation in catechesis is central to the life of the church. Unfortunately, though, this gets lost amid other concerns. As a teacher, you have an opportunity to energize or revitalize this aspect of your church's ministry. Reflect on how you have prepared for the challenge.

What is the goal when you use *Precepts for Living®* to open up the riches of the Bible to your students? It is beyond the mere acquisition of "spiritual data." Certainly we want our students to grow in knowledge, but the knowledge we seek to pass on does not solely comprise Bible facts but includes a larger sense of comprehension where the information and doctrine conveyed is oriented toward a faithful life of discipleship. The People, Places, and Times; Background; In Depth; and More Light on the Text sections are there to help you provide insight and understanding of the text. But the sections include more than a simple compilation of information. In each lesson, you will also see In Focus stories and Lesson in Our Society and Make It Happen sections serving as catalysts for applying the biblical text to life situations. It is very important that we as teachers pass on knowledge that will enable our students to deepen their devotion to God in an upward focus and encourage them to better embody that devotion in a way that makes their lives a living witness to the world. Our hope from every lesson should be to inspire students to become the best living examples of the Scriptures with the understanding that their lives may be the only Bible some people ever read.

To best take advantage of this commentary, utilize the essays highlighting notable African Americans to emphasize quarterly themes and enhance the classroom experience.

We believe this commentary is a great tool to help form fully devoted followers of Christ, and we invite you to wholeheartedly partake in all of the resources provided here. May God be glorified as you play your part in this great task of the church!

Creative Teaching

• **Energizing the Class.** If the class does not seem as enthusiastic or energy is low, after you open with prayer, have everyone stretch to the sky or outward. Then tell the class to shake off the low energy, and open up their hands to receive the love of God that is right there. You can always have a 30-second meet-and-greet time. This usually helps to wake people up so you can begin class on a higher energy level.

• **Two Teachers in One Class—Bring Out the Best in Both.** Taking turns works in some classes, but in others it creates tension and favorites. Encourage teachers to study together, and then divide the segments of the lesson. Perhaps one will teach the introduction while the other teaches a section of the text. Encourage them to also become a true team with each contributing throughout the lesson.

• **Remember.** Everyone cannot read or write on the same level. Use different teaching techniques and styles when teaching. How you learn affects how you teach, so be open and willing to learn and teach through various media.

• **Avoid Study in Isolation.** People often "get it" when they are involved with more than talking about the lesson. Why not allow the class to see the connections themselves? Try using a chart to have adult students work in pairs or groups to compare and contrast Bible persons such as David and Solomon or Ruth and Orpah, Naomi's daughters-in-law. To help the students get started, suggest specific categories for comparisons such as lifestyles, families, or public ministry. As class members search the Scriptures, they will learn and remember much more than if you told them about either person.

• **Group Studies.** Have the class form groups, and have each group read the Scripture lesson and a section of the Background for the text. Have each group create a two-minute skit about the Scripture to share with the class. Encourage the groups to use their imaginations and energy. You may want to have at least one "leader" in a group if you have more than two or three reserved persons in your class.

• **Volunteers.** Many classes begin with reading the lesson. When class members have studied, this activity is more "bringing minds" together than about the actual lesson. Still some classes can benefit from dramatic and creative reading of Bible passages at any point in the lesson. When the passage under study lends itself, assign parts to volunteers. This need not be formal—standing up isn't even critical. This strategy works best in passages that have a story such as the conversation between Moses and his father-in-law, Jethro, or Paul confronting the merchants in Thessalonica. Assign one person to each speaking character in the Bible text. Feel free to be creative with giving the class roles as "the crowd." Make sure to assign a narrator who will read the nonspeaking parts. It is fun, it is fast, and it makes for memorable Bible reading.

• **Alternatives.** Select one or two persons from the class to read the Scripture lesson with enthusiasm and drama. Ask a few persons to develop a newspaper or magazine headline with a brief story that explains the headlines. Have another group write the headlines and a story that will be used in a cell phone video. (Let the class know that they should bring their cell phones—with video recording—so that most people can share in this activity.)

- **Materials.** You may want to have large sheets of paper, markers, glue or tape, newspapers, and magazines available on a weekly basis for the various activities.

- **Additional Methods.** Write the theme on a large poster board or sheet of paper, and ask each person to write a word or draw a picture that best describes the theme. Read the themes aloud, and discuss any of the pictures before you begin your class discussion or activities. If you have a very large class or time is limited, only select a few words and/or pictures for discussion. You can either lead the discussion or invite members of the class to do so.

- **Web sites.** Connect with on by logging on to www.urbanministries.com. E-mail us at precepts @urbanministries.com, and send us some of your favorite Teaching Tips for ages 18 and older that you want to share with others. If yours is selected, we will post them under our Teaching Tips sections for Precepts. If you have ice breaker activities, please submit them as well. Your submissions should be no longer than 125 words.

- **Closing.** At the end of the lesson, give your class the assignment of looking for scenes from films or television, advertisements, or parts of songs that either demonstrate the coming week's In Focus story, Lesson in Our Society section, or Make It Happen section. Encourage them to be creative and to come up with an explanation of how their contribution helps make the truth of the lesson come to life.

- **Prayer.** Have a Prayer Request Board for people to write their prayer requests on each Sunday. You may want to make this a weekly activity. Have someone read the prayer request and let the class decide which prayer requests they will pray for during the week. One Sunday school teacher has his class write their prayer requests on sheets of paper and place them in the middle of the floor once a year. He then shares with the class that he will write them all down in a prayer journal that he keeps and prays over them at least once a week. Be creative and create your own prayer journal or prayer tradition(s) within your class.

Questions Related to the Heritage Profiles:

1. Why are some people chosen over others to be recognized for their achievements?

2. When reading the Heritage Profiles, what contemporary person comes to mind? A family member or friend can be a part of your decision.

3. Have you ever been recognized for a special achievement? How did you feel, and who have you lifted up to receive a special award in your church, community, or family? Why?

4. List three things you believe are important that someone else knows.

5. What similarities do you see between the historical figure and your life? If there are none, share ways the person's life may have made an impact on your life and on future generations.

6. List three characteristics that stand out about the Heritage Profiles that you think are either positive or negative. List three characteristics about your life that you believe are either positive or negative. Compare the lists and write a short paragraph about the similarities and/or differences.

Remember that creative teaching can maximize your students' learning experience.

TABLE OF CONTENTS

2012–2016 Scope and Sequence—Cycle Spread

	FALL	WINTER	SPRING	SUMMER
YEAR ONE 2012–13	FAITH **A Living Faith** Psalm 46 1 Corinthians 13:1–13 Hebrews Acts	GOD: JESUS CHRIST **Jesus Is Lord** Ephesians Philippians Colossians	HOPE **Beyond the Present Time** Daniel Luke Acts 1, 2 Peter 1, 2 Thessalonians	WORSHIP **God's People Worship** Isaiah Ezra Nehemiah
YEAR TWO 2013–14	CREATION **First Things** Genesis Exodus Psalm 104	JUSTICE **Jesus and the Just Reign of God** Luke James	TRADITION **Jesus' Fulfillment of Scripture** Zechariah Malachi Deuteronomy Matthew	COMMUNITY **The People of God Set Priorities** Haggai 1, 2 Corinthians
YEAR THREE 2014–15	HOPE **Sustaining Hope** Jeremiah Habakkuk Ezekiel Isaiah	WORSHIP **Acts of Worship** Psalm 95:1–7 Daniel Matthew Mark Luke John Ephesians Hebrews James	GOD: THE HOLY SPIRIT **The Spirit Comes** Mark John Acts 1 Corinthians 12-14 1, 2, 3 John	JUSTICE **God's Prophets Demand Justice** Amos Micah Isaiah Jeremiah Ezekiel Psalms Zechariah Malachi
YEAR FOUR 2015–16	COMMUNITY **The Christian Community Comes Alive** Matthew John 1 John	TRADITION **Sacred Gifts and Holy Gatherings** Leviticus Numbers Deuteronomy	FAITH **The Gift of Faith** Mark Luke	CREATION **Toward a New Creation** Genesis Psalms Zephaniah Romans

THE KING OF GLORY [JESUS] WAS PIERCED FOR YOU AND ME !

by Evangeline Carey

Before we explore the themes of *Faith—A Living Faith* for the fall quarter, *God: Jesus Christ* for the winter, *Hope Beyond the Present Time* for the spring, and *Worship—God's People Worship* for the summer, let us reflect on the cover of this commentary. You will notice first the crown of thorns that bring to mind the suffering of Jesus on the cross. The crown points us to the nails that represent the "5- to 7-inch-iron spikes" that were used to secure our Lord and Savior Jesus Christ on that old rugged cross at Calvary (John 20:25; Wycliffe, 1173). These nails were meant to prolong the agony of the one who chose to hang on the cross. Yes, I said chose, for Jesus Christ being fully God and fully man did not have to die; but out of His unconditional, authentic love for us, He chose to do so. As a vintage song by the late singer, arranger and composer James Cleveland proclaims, "[Jesus] would not come down from the cross just to save himself. He decided to die just to save me." Jesus could have called 10,000 angels to rescue Him, but He decided to die for you and me. It was through this gruesome death that "God canceled the certificate of debt consisting of the Mosaic decrees against us" (Wycliffe, 1174). Therefore, our sin penalty was paid in full by the only one who was and is sinless. First Peter 2:21-22 tells us we should follow Jesus' steps because He "did no sin, neither was guile found in his mouth."

As you imagine those nails, consider the passion of our Lord and let your faith rest on what He did for you. And then there is the blood—oh that blood, His precious blood that was shed so that we might have a right to the tree of life, so we might have eternal life, and so we might forever and ever live with a Holy God! Colossians 1:13-14 tell us the Father "hath delivered us from the power of darkness, and hath translated us into the kingdom of his dear Son: In whom we have redemption through his blood, even the forgiveness of sins."

Verses 20-21 explain further: "And, having made peace through the blood of his cross, by him to reconcile all things unto himself; by him, I say, whether they be things in earth, or things in heaven. And you, that were sometime alienated and enemies in your mind by wicked works, yet now hath he reconciled." When we believe on the Lord Jesus Christ and accept Him as Savior, His blood covers our sins (from John 3:16). We are no longer enemies but are now the children of God, joint heirs with Christ—sharers in the inheritance of the King of kings and Lord of lords (Romans 8:17).

There is *no other way* that we can be saved. There is *no other one* who can save us. When Adam and Eve sinned in the Garden of Eden (Genesis 3), their disobedience brought sin into God's perfect world. Thus, you and I were born into sin. It was imputed (attributed) to us because of what Adam and Eve did. First Corinthians 15:22 (KJV) conveys that "For as in Adam all die, even so in Christ shall all be made alive." Therefore the second Adam, Jesus Christ, came and brought His righteousness to replace what the first Adam's disobedience caused: sin and death, or eternal separation from a Holy God.

In Isaiah 53:5-6, the prophet draws a vivid picture of what Jesus did at Calvary when he says: "But he was wounded for our transgressions, he was bruised for our iniquities: the chastisement of our peace was upon him; and with his stripes we are healed. All we like sheep have gone astray; we have turned every one to his own way; and the LORD hath laid on him the iniquity of us all."

Then in the New Living Translation, these same verses tell us: "But he was pierced for our rebellion, crushed for our sins. He was beaten so we could be whole (represented by the dove in the picture). He was whipped so we could be healed. All of us, like sheep, have strayed away. We have left God's paths to follow our own. Yet the LORD laid on him the sins of us all."

Let the images of those nails and blood trickling down penetrate your heart and mind. Then take the time to appreciate the dove that represents the peace He brought us, reflect on the passages of Scriptures, and then allow them all to help you worship God, who is worthy of our adoration and praise! Thank God that by Jesus' death on the cross, our sins have been paid for in full and we are now in right relationship with Him! As you study the cover, remember this church sign declaration: "The key to heaven hung on a nail." That key is Jesus Christ. The King of Glory took those iron spikes (nails) for you and me!

Sources:

The Holy Bible: King James Version. Logos Research Systems, Inc.: Oak Harbor, WA. 1995.

http://www.lyricstime.com/rev-james-cleveland-he-decided-to-die-lyrics.html. Accessed December 27, 2011

Pfeifer, Charles F., Howard F. Vos, John Rea, eds. Wycliffe Bible Dictionary. Peabody, Mass., Hendrickson Publishers. 1975. 1173-1174.

Evangeline Carey was the Developmental Editor for *Precepts For Living®* and held a Master of Arts degree in Biblical Studies from the Moody Bible Institute in Chicago, Ill.

A Living Faith

The study focuses on faith. The first unit uses passages from Hebrews to move participants toward a definition of faith, while the second and third units continue the study of faith through the lens of the early church.

UNIT 1 • WHAT IS FAITH?

These lessons engage learners in responsive obedience to God's love that is revealed in Jesus. This response is an act of faith.

Lesson 1: September 2, 2012
Faith Calls for Perseverance
Hebrews 10:19–31

We can be secure about our spiritual lives. The writer of Hebrews tells us that through faith and because of the blood of Jesus, our sins can be forgiven and we can experience the presence of God in a new and life-giving way.

Lesson 2: September 9, 2012
Faith Is Assurance
Hebrews 11:1–3, 6; Psalm 46:1–3, 8–11

Because of all the conflicts in the world, people may lose hope for positive change. According to the writers of Hebrews and Psalms, because God is with us, we can be rescued, and then change can take place by our belief in God's strength.

Lesson 3: September 16, 2012
Faith Is Endurance
Hebrews 12:1–11

People know that to win a race, we sometimes have to suffer some pain but that we must keep our eyes on the goal. The writer of Hebrews introduces us to a huge crowd of witnesses of the faith who have trained well, kept their eyes on God in Christ Jesus, and have grown in grace and character.

Lesson 4: September 23, 2012
Faith Inspires Gratitude
Hebrews 12:18–29

People fear many things, especially judgment and death. The writer of Hebrews says God, in Christ Jesus, brought us forgiveness and the promise of eternal life.

Lesson 5: September 30, 2012
Faith Requires Mutual Love
Hebrews 13:1–3; 1 Corinthians 13

People search for a workable and reliable definition of love. The writers of Hebrews and 1 Corinthians define love and tell us that it is greater than faith and hope.

UNIT 2 • WHO UNDERSTANDS FAITH?

The first two lessons focus on Stephen's message and martyrdom. The third lesson explores the repercussions for those who treat faith as a commodity. The fourth lesson looks at the faith that guides both Philip the evangelist and the Ethiopian seeker to examine the Scriptures together.

Lesson 6: October 7, 2012
Stephen's Arrest and Speech
Acts 6:8–7:2a

People need a bold and perceptive leader to articulate truth in times of uncertainty Stephen, in the face of opposition, demonstrated the power and wisdom of the Spirit to speak the truth of Christ.

Lesson 7: October 14, 2012
Stephen's Martyrdom
Acts 7:51–8:1a

When strong leaders confront traditional ideas, their words may incite anger and violence. Stephen's criticism of the religious establishment and his exaltation of Christ enraged the religious leaders, so they stoned him to death.

Lesson 8: October 21, 2012
Simon Wants to Buy Power
Acts 8:9–24

Some people try to buy power. When Simon the magician tried to buy the power of the Holy Spirit, Peter plainly laid out the fatal consequences for those who think the Spirit can be bought or sold.

Lesson 9: October 28, 2012
Philip and the Ethiopian Eunuch
Acts 8:26–39

When it comes to membership in certain groups, some people want to prescribe who is in and who is out. Philip's sharing of the Good News about Jesus and the baptism of the Ethiopian demonstrate the universal availability of the gospel message.

UNIT 3 • WHAT DOES FAITH COST?

This unit is a four-lesson study of Paul's faith and ministry. The first lesson examines Paul's speech before King Agrippa. The second lesson goes with Paul aboard the ship to Rome.

The final two lessons focus on Paul's ongoing ministry even though he is a prisoner.

Lesson 10: November 4, 2012
Paul before King Agrippa
Acts 26:19–32

It is difficult to stand by our convictions when other people think we are crazy. Confident that he spoke the truth, Paul did not back down from sharing the story of his faith in Christ.

Lesson 11: November 11, 2012
Paul Sails for Rome
Acts 27:1–2, 33–44

In times of crisis, our panic can lead us to behave irrationally. Paul's confidence in God's faithfulness enabled him to act calmly and assure all the ship's passengers that they would survive the storm.

Lesson 12: November 18, 2012
Paul Ministers in Malta
Acts 28:1–10

Often we can tell something about the character of people by observing how they respond in difficult situations. Because through Paul's faith in Christ a man was healed, the people of Malta recognized something extraordinary about him.

Lesson 13: November 25, 2012
Paul Evangelizes in Rome
Acts 28:23–31

It is a paradox of human nature that even when we have good news to share, some will ignore or reject it. Paul persevered in faith, preaching the Gospel and bringing salvation to those who would listen, even though there were many who refused to believe in the Lord Jesus Christ.

PAYING THE PRICE!

"And they stoned Stephen
(one of the first deacons)
calling upon God,
and saying, Lord Jesus,
receive my spirit"

(Acts 7:59, KJV).

Christian Education in Action

Book	Author	Audience	Purpose	Key People
Matthew	Matthew (Levi)	The Jews	To prove that Jesus is the Messiah, the eternal King	Jesus, Mary, Joseph, John the Baptist, the disciples, the religious leaders, Caiaphas, Pilate, Mary Magdalene
Mark	John Mark—not one of the 12 disciples— joined Paul on his first missionary journey (Acts 13:13)	Christians in Rome, where he wrote the Gospel	To present the person, work, and teachings of Jesus	Jesus, the 12 disciples, Pilate, the Jewish religious leaders
Luke	Luke—a doctor (Colossians 4:14), a Greek, and Gentile Christian; he was a close friend and companion of Paul	Theophilus ("one who loves God"), Gentiles, and people everywhere	To present an accurate account of the life of Christ and to present Christ as the perfect human and Savior	Jesus, Elizabeth, Zechariah, John the Baptist, Mary, the disciples, Herod the Great, Pilate, Mary Magdalene
Psalm	King David wrote 73 psalms; Asaph (12); the sons of Korah (9); Solomon (2); Heman (with the sons of Korah); Ethan and Moses each wrote one; 51 are anonymous	Often parallel Jewish history	Written to provide poetry for the expression of praise, worship, and confession to Almighty God.	David

Book	Author	Audience	Purpose	Key People
1 Corinthians	Apostle Paul	The church in Corinth and all believers	To identify and offer solutions to problems in the Corinthian church and to teach believers how to live holy, godly lives	Paul, Timothy, members of Chloe's household
Hebrews	Biblical scholars have suggested Paul, Luke, Barnabas, Apollos, Silas, Philip, Priscilla, and others	Perhaps second-generation Hebrew Christians	Written to show the sufficiency and superiority of Jesus Christ	Jews who were evaluating Jesus and who were struggling with their faith
Acts	Luke (a Gentile physician)	Theophilus and all believers	Written to give an accurate account of the birth and growth of the Christian church	Peter, John, James, Stephen, Philip, Paul, Barnabas, Cornelius, James (Jesus' brother), Timothy, Lydia, Silas, Titus, Apollos, Agabus, Ananias, Felix, Festus, Agrippa, Luke

Life Application Study Bible, New Living Translation. Wheaton, IL: Tyndale House
     Publishers, Inc. 1062, 1766, 1867, 1936, 2120, 2261, 2444.

Pfeifer, Charles F., Howard F. Vos, John Rea, eds. *Wycliffe Bible Dictionary.* Peabody, Mass.:
     Hendrickson Publishers, Inc. 1998. 713.

Note: Matthew, Mark, and Luke are known as the Synoptic Gospels because of their close resemblance to each other in content and in viewpoint. Although they differ in many respects, they follow the same general order of events and deal largely with the ministry of Jesus in Galilee (Wycliffe, 713).

STEADFAST LOVE!

"And now abideth
faith, hope, charity (love),
these three,
but the greatest of these
is charity (love)"

(1 Corinthians 13:13, KJV).

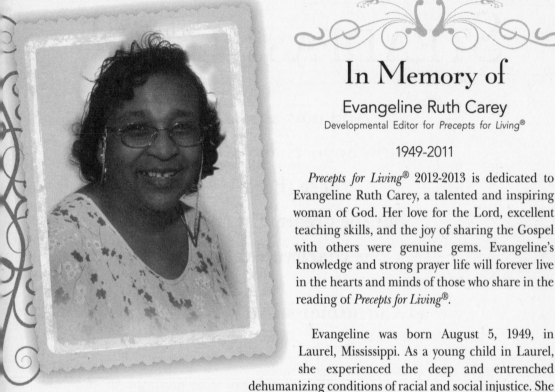

In Memory of

Evangeline Ruth Carey
Developmental Editor for *Precepts for Living*®

1949-2011

Precepts for Living® 2012-2013 is dedicated to Evangeline Ruth Carey, a talented and inspiring woman of God. Her love for the Lord, excellent teaching skills, and the joy of sharing the Gospel with others were genuine gems. Evangeline's knowledge and strong prayer life will forever live in the hearts and minds of those who share in the reading of *Precepts for Living*®.

Evangeline was born August 5, 1949, in Laurel, Mississippi. As a young child in Laurel, she experienced the deep and entrenched dehumanizing conditions of racial and social injustice. She would recall what was it like to ride in the back of the bus, stand in lines that were marked by signs that read "colored only" and "white only," and experience the poor educational conditions that permeated the lives of Black people. At an early age, she was determined to receive an excellent education, fight injustice, and create opportunities for others to learn. Evangeline lived this resolve through her faith and her willingness to encourage others to strive for excellence!

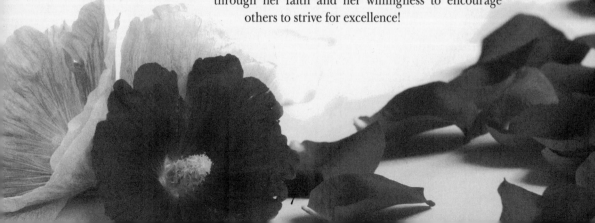

Evangeline and her family relocated to Gary, Ind., when she was about 12 years old. She attended Beckman Middle School and graduated with honors from Gary Roosevelt High School in 1968. When she was 15, she met the love of her life, Winston Carey. Their courtship continued throughout high school and they married in March 1969. They were blessed with three children and seven grandchildren during their 42 years of marriage.

Evangeline received a bachelor of science degree in sociology with a minor in psychology from Indiana University Northwest. Her pursuit for additional higher education was delayed by her failing health, and she was not able to finish as quickly as she wanted. Yet, she did not give up. Even when her doctor said she would die from her health issues, she did not stop working toward her educational goals.

Evangeline was a fighter who believed that her strong faith in God, continual prayer, and the support of her family and friends allowed her to press toward the mark of her educational prize. In May 2012, Evangeline received a master of arts degree in biblical studies from Moody Bible Institute.

While pursuing her master's degree, Evangeline tutored her grandchildren, assisted other students with papers and research, wrote poetry and books, and counseled those who needed her wisdom and kindness. Whenever she met someone who thought that a high school level of knowledge was as far as they could aspire, she would promptly let them know that God had more for them, but they had to step out in faith, want to learn more, and do more.

In addition to writing more than 300 published works, including UMI's Direction and Adult Vacation Bible School Series, Evangeline wrote and co-authored numerous articles, poems, books, and lessons. Her writings often praised and celebrated God's work. Additionally, she developed research work for various research pieces. Her printed work and words of inspiration motivated many to pursue their educational dreams and find encouragement during difficult times.

Evangeline's deep love and appreciation for God's Word was expressed in her meticulous and diligent work as Developmental Editor for *Precepts for Living*® at UMI. It was her ultimate dream to work for a Christian publishing company. UMI gave Evangeline the opportunity to write and teach God's Word to thousands of people. She often said: "I want God's Word to reach the masses!" God allowed her to achieve her dream and to bring the Good News to many people in a variety of places.

Evangeline accepted Christ at a young age and believed that she should serve God's people in the church and the community. She worked in the church as a Sunday School teacher, as vice president of the Women of the Church of God (WCG), and as a member of the board of Christian education. She taught various workshops, preached, and donated school supplies and gifts to children and teens who were in need.

Evangeline's love for Christ, people, and especially for children in need will always be remembered and cherished.

Teaching Tips

September 2
Bible Study Guide 1

Words You Should Know

A. Boldness (Hebrews 10:19) *parrhesia* (Gk.)—To have openness, frankness in speaking.

B. Faith (vv. 22, 23) *pistis* (Gk.)—Assurance, belief; a strong and welcome conviction or trust that Jesus is the Messiah.

Teacher Preparation

Unifying Principle — Steadfast Determination. We can be secure about our spiritual lives. The writer of Hebrews tells us that through faith and because of the blood of Jesus, our sins can be forgiven, and we can experience the presence of God in a new and life-giving way.

A. Read the Bible Background and Devotional Readings.

B. Complete Lesson 1 in the *Precepts For Living Personal Study Guide®*.

C. Reread the Focal Verses in the NLT.

O—Open the Lesson

A. Open with prayer.

B. Have students read Aim for Change in unison.

C. Ask for a volunteer to read the In Focus story.

D. Discuss how to live by faith and experience God's presence.

P—Present the Scriptures

A. Have volunteers read the Focal Verses and The People, Places, and Times. Discuss.

B. Read and discuss the Background section.

C. Encourage students to give thanks for the opportunity today to approach God through faith in Christ, rather than through a high priest, as was done long ago.

E—Explore the Meaning

A. Review and discuss the Search the Scriptures and Discuss the Meaning questions and the Lesson in Our Society section.

B. Ask students to share the most significant point they learned and how they will use that point this week.

N—Next Steps for Application

A. Complete the Follow the Spirit and Remember Your Thoughts sections.

B. Remind students to read the Daily Bible Readings in preparation for next week's lesson.

C. Close in prayer, thanking God for His presence in our life.

Worship Guide

For the Superintendent or Teacher
Theme: Faith Calls for Perseverance
Song: "We've Come This Far by Faith"
Devotional Reading: Romans 5:1-5
Prayer

Faith Calls for Perseverance

Bible Background • Hebrews 10:19-31
Printed Text • Hebrews 10:19-31 | Devotional Reading • Romans 5:1-5

——————— Aim for Change ———————

By the end of the lesson, we will: KNOW Jesus' sacrificial death opens the way to the presence of God; FEEL the importance of holding on to faith in Jesus; and SHARE our faith with others.

———————  In Focus ———————

Anthony and Sharita dated for one year and had been friends for eight. One Saturday, Anthony met with Mr. Williams, Sharita's father. Anthony said to him, "May I have your permission to ask Sharita to marry me? I love and respect your daughter and want to make her my partner for life. She is my blessing from God! I can't imagine life without her."

Mr. Williams thought for a moment and smiled. "You have my permission, Anthony," he said. "Let's pray for you and Sharita's life together."

One evening as Anthony and Sharita walked through the park, Anthony knelt on one knee and proposed. Sharita was speechless. As tears ran down her cheeks, she said, "I have made too many mistakes in my life. You can't truly love me, because I have not forgiven myself. I don't deserve a life with you. I love you, but I can't marry you!"

As Sharita started to leave, Anthony said, "We all make mistakes, but God forgives us when we sincerely come to Him."

Through faith in Christ, our sins are forgiven and we have a new life. In today's lesson, we can develop a personal relationship with Jesus by faith and enter into the presence of God.

——————— Keep in Mind ———————

"Let us hold fast the profession of our faith without wavering"
(Hebrews 10:23).

"Let us hold fast the profession of our faith without wavering"
(Hebrews 10:23).

Focal Verses

KJV **Hebrews 10:19** Having therefore, brethren, boldness to enter into the holiest by the blood of Jesus,

20 By a new and living way, which he hath consecrated for us, through the veil, that is to say, his flesh;

21 And having an high priest over the house of God;

22 Let us draw near with a true heart in full assurance of faith, having our hearts sprinkled from an evil conscience, and our bodies washed with pure water.

23 Let us hold fast the profession of our faith without wavering; (for he is faithful that promised;)

24 And let us consider one another to provoke unto love and to good works:

25 Not forsaking the assembling of ourselves together, as the manner of some is; but exhorting one another: and so much the more, as ye see the day approaching.

26 For if we sin wilfully after that we have received the knowledge of the truth, there remaineth no more sacrifice for sins,

27 But a certain fearful looking for of judgment and fiery indignation, which shall devour the adversaries.

28 He that despised Moses' law died without mercy under two or three witnesses:

29 Of how much sorer punishment, suppose ye, shall he be thought worthy, who hath trodden under foot the Son of God, and hath counted the blood of the covenant, wherewith he was sanctified, an unholy thing, and hath done despite unto the Spirit of grace?

30 For we know him that hath said, Vengeance belongeth unto me, I will recompense, saith the Lord. And again, The Lord shall judge his people.

31 It is a fearful thing to fall into the hands of the living God.

NLT **Hebrews 10:19** And so, dear brothers and sisters, we can boldly enter heaven's Most Holy Place because of the blood of Jesus.

20 By his death, Jesus opened a new and life-giving way through the curtain into the Most Holy Place.

21 And since we have a great High Priest who rules over God's house,

22 let us go right into the presence of God with sincere hearts fully trusting him. For our guilty consciences have been sprinkled with Christ's blood to make us clean, and our bodies have been washed with pure water.

23 Let us hold tightly without wavering to the hope we affirm, for God can be trusted to keep his promise.

24 Let us think of ways to motivate one another to acts of love and good works.

25 And let us not neglect our meeting together, as some people do, but encourage one another, especially now that the day of his return is drawing near.

26 Dear friends, if we deliberately continue sinning after we have received knowledge of the truth, there is no longer any sacrifice that will cover these sins.

27 There is only the terrible expectation of God's judgment and the raging fire that will consume his enemies.

28 For anyone who refused to obey the law of Moses was put to death without mercy on the testimony of two or three witnesses.

29 Just think how much worse the punishment will be for those who have trampled on the Son of God, and have treated the blood of the covenant, which made us holy, as if it were common and unholy, and have insulted and disdained the Holy Spirit who brings God's mercy to us.

NLT continued

30 For we know the one who said, "I will take revenge. I will pay them back." He also said, "The Lord will judge his own people." **31** It is a terrible thing to fall into the hands of the living God.

The People, Places, and Times

Holy of Holies. It was located in the innermost sanctuary of the temple. Separated from the other parts of the temple by a thick curtain, the Holy of Holies was specially associated with the presence of Yahweh, God. In the early years of the existence of the temple, the Holy of Holies contained the Ark of the Covenant, which represented God's presence with the people of Israel.

High Priest. He was the one in charge of the temple worship. It was a hereditary position based upon descent from Aaron. Normally, the high priest served for life. Only the high priest could enter the Holy of Holies and only on the Day of Atonement.

Hebrews. Because there are references to religious sacrifices and ceremonies, the book of Hebrews was probably written before the destruction of the temple in Jerusalem in A.D. 70. The name of the author is not given, but the person is a "brother" of Timothy (Hebrews 13:23). The setting for the book is a period when Jewish Christians underwent severe persecution from the Romans and Jews, both socially and physically. It's clear that the author was knowledgeable of the Old Testament because there are direct quotations from it as he argues the superiority of Jesus Christ and faith.

Background

Sacrifices were practiced from the earliest of times in the Old Testament. Sacrifices from the produce of the land and firstborn of the flock were offered by Cain and Abel; Noah built an altar and offered sacrifices after he left the ark. The Mosaic sacrifices were prior to Christ's ultimate sacrifice on the Cross. Animals were imperfect sacrifices that could not completely purify and atone for the sins of the people. If they could, they would have ceased. The annual sacrifice on the Day of Atonement was a visible reminder of the sins of humanity.

The writer expressed the importance and superiority of Christ's priesthood and the New Covenant to the Levitical priesthood and the Mosaic covenant. The Levitical high priest could only enter the Holy of Holies, which was the most holy place (inner sanctuary of the temple) one day a year, the Day of Atonement, the 10th day of the seventh month of the Jewish calendar (September-October). On the Day of Atonement, the high priest made reconciling sacrifices for the sins of the entire nation. The images that the writer revealed about the Day of Atonement emphasize the superiority of the priesthood of Christ.

In Chapter 9 of Hebrews, the writer explained that the *diatheke*—the Greek word for agreement, covenant, or arrangement—was placed into effect when Christ died (Hebrews 9:11-12, 24-28). The new covenant, which was initiated when Christ died, frees believers from the bondage of the first covenant. God took away the Levitical sacrificial system, which was the first arrangement, when He established the perfect sacrifice—Jesus Christ.

At-A-Glance

1. The Priesthood of Christ Is Superior
   (Hebrews 10:19-21)

2. The Priesthood of Christ and Our
   Profession of Faith (vv. 22-25)

3. The Priesthood of Christ and
   Knowledge of the Truth (vv. 26-27)

4. The Priesthood of Christ and How God
   Will Judge His People (vv. 28-31)

In Depth

1. The Priesthood of Christ Is Superior (Hebrews 10:19-21)

In chapters 5 through 10 of the book of Hebrews, the writer has explained that the priesthood of Christ is superior to the Levitical priesthood, which was made at Mount Sinai. The Levitical priesthood could not bring the people to perfection. There was no permanent reconciliation between the people and God through the temporary animal sacrifices. The people needed the perfect sacrifice, Jesus Christ, who gave His life once to restore the people to a relationship with God. The Levitical high priests atoned for all sins of the people on the Day of Atonement. Every year, the high priest entered the Holy of Holies where he made a sacrifice for the nation's sins. A curtain prevented anyone from seeing the inner sanctuary. When Jesus died for the sins of humanity, the curtain was torn open, permitting anyone to enter the holiest of all—God's presence. The high priest was no longer required for believers to be forgiven. By a "new and living way" (Hebrews 10:20), believers can go directly to God through faith in Christ.

During biblical times, the high priest passed through a veil to enter the inner sanctuary where God's presence existed. Because of Christ's sacrificial death on the Cross, believers can now personally come before God. Christ shed His blood to give humanity the ability to come before God's presence by faith. Our High Priest is Jesus Christ, who experienced the pain, temptations, and trials that we experience as believers. By the righteousness of Christ, the Superior Priest, we can approach God with "boldness ... by the blood of Jesus" (Hebrews 10:19). Through the shed blood of Christ, we can come before our Creator by faith. Have you accepted Christ by faith and experienced a relationship with God that is only available through Christ, the Superior Priest?

2. The Priesthood of Christ and Our Profession of Faith (vv. 22-25)

Through Christ, we can freely enter into the presence of God. Through faith in Christ's work on our behalf, we have "full assurance," or certainty, that our sins are forgiven. There is an allusion to Christian baptism when the writer refers to "our hearts sprinkled" and "bodies washed with pure water" (Hebrews 10:22). Because of the eternal efficacy of the blood of Christ, our consciences are cleansed. When the high priest entered the "holy place . . . He shall put on the holy linen coat ... the linen breeches ... a linen girdle ... these are holy garments" and he must be cleansed; therefore "shall he wash his flesh in water" (Leviticus 16:3-4). Likewise, the believer must be cleansed before he or she can come before the Holy One. While we are declared "not guilty" because of the work of Christ, we need to cleanse ourselves daily by turning away from sin and turning to God to experience the fullness of relationship with Him. We must give ourselves completely

14

to God and maintain a personal relationship with Jesus.

The writer encourages believers to "hold fast the profession of our faith without wavering" (Hebrews 10:23). God reveals His promises and truths through His Word; thus, we must embrace God's Word and resist temptation and opposition. His promises are our treasures that we believe with a confident expectation. The foundation of our faith, therefore, is based upon the integrity and righteousness of Christ. We have hope because "God is faithful" (1 Corinthians 1:9). Although the Jewish Christians were experiencing persecution, the writer urges the believers to resist the temptation to apostasy. He wants to reassure the believers by calling them to remember, "He (God) is faithful that promised"; God will do what He has promised (Hebrews 10:23).

The writer instructs the believers to "consider"—which means to observe or contemplate—each other (Hebrews 10:24). Believers must provoke or stir up the qualities of love and good works toward each other (Hebrews 10:24). The writer knew believers could have an impact on one another by loving and doing good deeds for each other.

Because of the fear of persecution, some of the believers had stopped attending worship services; therefore, the writer encourages believers to pull together to stir up loving and active faith. The fellowship of believers is a source of encouragement; it is an opportunity to share faith and grow stronger. The writer urged the believers to get involved in encouraging or "exhorting one another" with the truth (Hebrews 10:25). The fellowship of believers promotes accountability; it is the opportunity to worship and pray with others.

As you fellowship with the body of believers, encourage someone today!

3. The Priesthood of Christ and Knowledge of the Truth (vv. 26-27)

The writer of Hebrews reminds believers that if they "sin wilfully" they deliberately reject Christ (Hebrews 10:26). It is a conscious rejection of God after receiving the truth and the guidance of the Holy Spirit. The writer does not refer to an occasional act of sin. God sent Jesus to die for our sins; "If we confess our sins, He is faithful and just to forgive us our sins and to cleanse us from all unrighteousness" (1 John 1:9). Believers should not willfully rebel against God's provisions after receiving and fully understanding the "knowledge of the truth," which is Christ's offer of salvation (Hebrews 10:26).

The consequences of rejecting God are "judgment and fiery indignation, which shall devour the adversaries," and there is no hope of forgiveness (Hebrews 10:27). Thus, those who reject Christ and disobey God are His adversaries. There is one certain judgment, death and destruction, for obstinate apostates. The apostates will experience the wrath of God because there is no other help for sinners who reject their only remedy—salvation through accepting Jesus Christ as Lord and Savior.

4. The Priesthood of Christ and How God Will Judge His People (vv. 28-31)

The Old Testament refers to the sin of idolatry that requires "two witnesses, or three witnesses ... (to) be put to death" (Deuteronomy 17:6). The judgment for idolatry was death by stoning, but there is a worse punishment for someone who rejects the word of Christ. If someone considers the "blood of the covenant ... an unholy thing," the person grieves the "Spirit of grace," the Holy Spirit (Hebrews 10:29). The person that rejects the Spirit of God will receive a punishment greater than a physical death.

Judgment belongs to God for "the LORD shall judge his people" (Deuteronomy 32:36). There is no other sacrifice for sin except Christ's sacrifice on the Cross. If someone rejects God's mercy, he or she will receive God's judgment. The writer of Hebrews states, "It is a fearful thing to fall into the hands of the living God" (Hebrews 10:31). The apostate will experience an eternal punishment from God's hands. Believers, who have received the mercy of God through Christ, are saved and have nothing to fear.

Search the Scriptures

1. What is the "Holy of Holies" (Hebrews 10:19)?

2. What is the "new and living way" that Jesus has prepared for believers to come into the presence of God (Hebrews 10:20)?

3. Explain the difference between a "willful sin" and an "occasional sin." (Refer to the "knowledge of the truth" and the effects of deliberately rejecting "the truth" that are discussed in Hebrews 10:26.)

Discuss the Meaning

1. How can we draw near and remain in the presence of God each day? How can we truly experience God's presence?

2. When we accept Christ, He responds, "henceforth, I call you not servants ... I have called you friends" (John 15:15). What should be our response to Christ as believers? Does your relationship with Christ reveal that He is your friend?

Lesson in Our Society

Faith is effective when we depend on God and rest in what Christ has done on the Cross. The writer of Hebrews urged believers to recognize the superiority of our faith and live in obedience to God each day. Through Christ, we have an eternal reward and significant privileges that we can experience through our new life in Christ. Through Christ, we can experience God's presence and develop a relationship with Him. We can grow in faith and experience a deeper relationship with God when we trust and believe without doubts and concerns that the world presents. The world is temporary, but our life with God is eternal. Each day we must trust God and hold on to our faith and then share our faith with others. When we share our love for God, we can encourage others and introduce them to a new life through Christ.

Make It Happen

The world focuses on tangible rewards, promotions, and recognition with financial bonuses. The world encourages the pursuit of tangible endeavors and earthly wealth with retirement plans focused on life in the world. Retirement plans can be important, but as Christians, our focus is greater. Because we have accepted Christ by faith, we are friends of Christ with a purpose to share our love for Christ through faith. Consider local ministries that allow you to share your faith in God. Volunteer your time to share your love for God with people who do not know Him, or share your faith and encourage believers who are homebound or sick. Help others to remain faithful and experience the presence of God each day. Make a daily affirmation to share your faith. Finally, ask God for boldness to share your faith with others. God will give you the opportunity and bless your desire to be faithful.

Follow the Spirit

What God wants me to do:

_____

_____

_____

_____

Remember Your Thoughts

Special insights I have learned:

_____

_____

_____

_____

More Light on the Text

Hebrews 10:19-31

19 Having therefore, brethren, boldness to enter into the holiest by the blood of Jesus, 20 By a new and living way, which he hath consecrated for us, through the veil, that is to say, his flesh;

The writer of Hebrews has now concluded the doctrinal section of his epistle and has fully shown the superiority of Christ in all areas. He is superior to all men and angels, His priesthood is superior to that of Aaron and his successors. His blood, unlike that of the animal sacrifices, is efficacious in reconciliation of humankind to God. In the following verses, the writer of the epistle proceeds to show the practical implications of his teachings. This is an allusion to the case of the high priest going into the Holy of Holies. He went with fear and trembling, because, if he had neglected the smallest item prescribed by the law, he could expect nothing but death. Nadab and Abihu died while offering incense (Leviticus 10:2), and it had become the custom for the high priest not to linger in the Most Holy Place on the Day of Atonement, lest people be terrified. But Christians can approach God confidently, completely at home in the situation created by Christ's saving work. We now enter "the Most Holy Place" (Hebrews 10:19, NLT), which, of course, is no physical sanctuary but is, in truth, the presence of God "by the blood of Jesus" (v. 19, KJV), that is, on the basis of His saving death. We can come even to the throne of God with confidence, as we carry into the divine presence the infinitely meritorious blood of the great atonement.

"By a new and living way" (v. 20)— It is a new way because the death of Jesus on the Cross has created a completely new situation. The way by the old covenant neither gave life nor removed the liability to death. The way to peace and reconciliation, under the old covenant, was through the dead bodies of the animals slain; but Christ is living, and ever lives, to make intercession for us. Therefore, He is a new and living way.

"Through the veil" (v. 20)—The high priest lifted up or drew aside the veil that separated the holy from the Most Holy Place that he might have access to the Divine Majesty, and the veil of the temple was rent from the top to the bottom at the crucifixion of Christ to show that the way to the holiest was then laid open. Likewise, we must approach the throne through the mediation of Christ and through His sacrificial death. His pierced side is the way to the holiest. Here, the veil—His humanity— is rent, and the kingdom of heaven opened to all believers.

21 And having an high priest over the house of God;

The function of the priest was to build a bridge between man and God. This means that Jesus not only shows us the way to God, but also when we get there, He introduces us to His very presence. The house or family of God is the Christian Church, or all true believers in the Lord Jesus.

22 Let us draw near with a true heart in full assurance of faith, having our hearts sprinkled from an evil conscience, and our bodies washed with pure water.

The consideration of what Christ has done should move Christians into action. First, we are to draw near to God "with a true heart." The word "true" suggests what is genuine, sincere, and faithful. The heart stands for the whole of the inner life of man, and it is important that as God's people approach Him, they be right inwardly. It is the "pure in heart" that see God (Matthew 5:8). All hypocrisy (pretending to be what we are not or using Christian vocabulary when in reality our experience is mostly defeat) must go. In view of what Christ has done for us, we should approach God in deep sincerity. The "full assurance of faith" stresses that it is only by trust in Christ, who has performed for us the high priestly work that gives access to God, that we can draw near at all (Hebrews 10:22).

The references to the sprinkled hearts and the washed bodies should be taken together. The washing of the body with pure water is most likely a reference to baptism. Baptism is the outward sign of an inward cleansing, and it was the latter that was the more important. So here it is mentioned first. The sprinkling of the hearts signifies the effect of the blood of Christ on the innermost being. His shed blood cleanses believers within (see the sprinkling of the priests, Exodus 29:21; Leviticus 8:30).

23 Let us hold fast the profession of our faith without wavering; (for he is faithful that promised;)

The second exhortation is to hold fast to the profession of faith; although, the NIV translation "the hope we profess" is more appropriate. The verb translated here as "hold fast" (Gk. *katecho*, **kat-EKH-o**) has been previously used by the author for the readers to "hold fast" to their confidence and their glorying in hope (Hebrews 3:6) and the beginning of their confidence (3:14). Now, he wants them to retain a firm grasp on "the confession of *our* hope" (10:23, NKJV). Christians can hold fast to their hope in this way because behind it is a God in whom they can have full confidence. As Luke Timothy Johnson states, "Holding to the confession is not a matter of grim determination, but of active and mutual commitment and up-building" (Johnson, 259). God is thoroughly dependable. When He makes a promise, it will infallibly be kept. He has taken the initiative in making the promise, and He will fulfill His purposes in making it. He who cannot lie promises the eternal life to you that is the object of your hope. As He who has given you this promise then is faithful, hold fast the profession of your hope.

24 And let us consider one another to provoke unto love and to good works: 25 Not forsaking the assembling of ourselves together, as the manner of some is; but exhorting one another: and so much the more, as ye see the day approaching.

This is the only place where the author uses the expression "one another" (Gk. *allelon*, **al-LAY-lone**), though it is frequently found elsewhere in the New Testament.

He is speaking of a mutual activity, one in which believers encourage one another, not one where leaders direct the rest as to what they are to do. Our danger is that we become so involved in this world that we forget the other. The word "provoke" is actually a noun (Gk. *paroxusmos*, **par-ox-oos-MOS**) that is often used negatively as causing "irritation" or "exasperation." It is used here in a positive sense to suggest "urging" or "stimulation." Christians are to provoke one another to "love" (*agape*), and to do good works.

Corporate worship is important. We must worship together with other believers. There were some among those in the audience of the Hebrews writer who had abandoned the habit of meeting together. There may be some who think it is still possible to live the Christian life while abandoning the habit of worshiping with God's people. This should not be the case. Donald Guthrie notes, "The New Testament lends no support to the idea of lone Christians. Close and regular fellowship with other believers is not just a nice idea but also an absolute necessity for the encouragement of Christian values" (Guthrie, 216). The exhortation takes on a sense of urgency "as ye see the day approaching" (v. 25). The "day" here has eschatological overtones that derive from the Old Testament prophetic tradition that spoke of a day in which God would judge (Joel 1:15; 3:14; Amos 5:18-20), a tradition that is maintained in the New Testament (1 Corinthians 1:8; 5:5; 1 Thessalonians 5:2). The day of the Second Coming is approaching; when things as we know them will end. The early Christians lived in that expectation. So must we. In the time we have, it is our duty to do all the good we can to all the people we can in all the ways we can.

26 For if we sin wilfully after that we have received the knowledge of the truth, there remaineth no more sacrifice for sins, 27 But a certain fearful looking for of judgment and fiery indignation, which shall devour the adversaries.

It is clear that the writer has apostasy in mind. He is referring to people who "have received the knowledge of the truth" (Hebrews 10:26), where "truth" (Gk. *aletheia*, **al-AY-thi-a**) stands for "the content of Christianity as the absolute truth" as it frequently does in the New Testament. Receiving the knowledge of truth means entering into the community that is defined by the true God; in Hebrews, the comparison is often with the nation of Israel where we find those in the community who turn away from the covenant through unbelief or idolatry. The people to whom the epistle was written, then, know what God has done in Christ. Their acquaintance with Christian teaching is more than superficial just as Israel was well acquainted with God and His covenant. If, knowing this, they revert to an attitude of rejection—of "sin(ning)" or continual sin (Gk. *hamartano*, **ham-ar-TAN-o**, meaning "keep on sinning")— then there remains no sacrifice for sins. An important word here is "wilfully" (Gk. *hekousios*, **hek-oo-SEE-ose**), which can be translated as deliberately. It suggests that their action is voluntary. Such people have rejected the sacrifice of Christ.

The sin that is freely chosen couldn't be considered as a minor transgression, but apostasy, a deliberate turning away. "Only a fearful expectation of judgment" awaits such people (v. 27, NIV). The nature of this expectation is not defined, and the fact that the fate of these evil persons is left indefinite makes the warning all the more impressive. The Greek adjective *phoberos* (**fob-er-OS**), meaning "fearful" is unusual; it occurs elsewhere only in verse 31 and 12:21 and conveys the idea of "frightening."

In Hebrews 10:27, the NIV text describes it as "raging fire," an echo of Isaiah 26:11, which is a vivid expression for the fire of judgment that is intent on devouring God's adversaries. In Hebrews 10:27, the word "adversaries" (Gk. *hupenantios*, **hoop-en-an-TEE-oos**) shows that the apostates were not regarded as neutral. They have become the enemies of God.

28 He that despised Moses' law died without mercy under two or three witnesses: 29 Of how much sorer punishment, suppose ye, shall he be thought worthy, who hath trodden under foot the Son of God, and hath counted the blood of the covenant, wherewith he was sanctified, an unholy thing, and hath done despite unto the Spirit of grace?

The author now adopts an argument form of the lesser to the greater. Jews held the Law of Moses to be divinely given: Anyone who rejected it also rejected God's direction and was killed without compassion. There was no place for mercy. He must be executed (Deuteronomy 17:6; 19:15). The author of Hebrews invites the audience to work out for themselves the worst punishment someone would deserve for rejecting the gift of God in Christ. Because Jesus is greater than Moses, it must be more severe than under the old way (Hebrews 3:1-3); the new covenant is better than the old, founded on better promises (8:6) and established by a better sacrifice (9:23).

The grievousness we experience when we "deliberately continue sinning" (10:26, NLT) is elaborated in three phrases of 10:29. First, such a person has "trampled under foot the Son of God" (NASB). The verb "trampled" is found in the NASB (Gk. *katapateo*, **ka-ta-pa-TEH-o**), used with a personal object. "Trampled under foot" is a strong expression for disdain. It implies not only rejecting Christ but also despising Him. This is more than falling from grace; it is a mockery of the giver of grace.

Another characterization of the apostate is that the person takes the shedding of covenant blood lightly. "The blood of the covenant" is an expression used for the blood that established the old covenant (Exodus 24:8; see Hebrews 9:20) and also of the blood of Jesus that established the new covenant (Matthew 26:28; Mark 14:24; see also Luke 22:20; 1 Corinthians 11:25). The apostate regards that blood as "a common thing" (Hebrews 10:29, NKJV). That is to say he treats the death of Jesus just like the death of any other man. The word "common" can also be understood as against the holy or "unhallowed." This stands out more sharply with the understanding that this blood has "sanctified" him. To go back on this decisive act is to deny the significance of the blood, to see it as a common thing.

The third indictment of the apostate is that he or she has done this spitefully or has "insulted the Spirit of grace" (v. 29, NIV). In the Greek, the writer's word for "insulted" is *enubrizo* (**en-oo-BRID-zo**), an intensified form of *hubris* (**HOO-bris**), which means to reduce the honor that is due to another person. Willful sin is an insult to the Spirit, who brings the grace of God to humanity.

30 For we know him that hath said, Vengeance belongeth unto me, I will recompense, saith the Lord. And again, The Lord shall judge his people.

The author calls God "him that hath said" words of Scripture. He uses the Greek word for "said" (*epo*, **EP-o**) six times, four with quotations from Scripture. He is sure that God speaks to men. The author's first quotation here is from Deuteronomy 32:35.

Vengeance is a divine prerogative. The emphasis here is on the certainty that the Lord will act. The wrongdoer cannot hope to go unpunished because avenging wrong is in the hands of God. The second quotation from Deuteronomy 32:36 leaves no doubt about the Lord's intervention, for He is named and so is His activity. The word "judge" in Hebrews 10:30 may mean "give a favorable judgment" as well as "condemn." The latter is intended here. Claiming to be one of God's people does not exempt a person from judgment. God judges all. Let not the apostates think that they, of all people, can escape.

31 It's a fearful thing to fall into the hands of the living God.

A simple statement carries a chilling effect. "Falling into the hands" of someone means to come under his power (Judges 15:18). Usually "falling into (God's) hands" means reassurance, but it is not so here. To fall into the hands of God is to fall under His displeasure, and He who lives forever can punish forever. How dreadful to have the displeasure of an eternal, Almighty God to rest on the soul forever! Apostates, and all the persecutors and enemies of God's cause and people, may expect the heaviest judgments of an incensed deity; and these are not for a time but through eternity.

Sources:
Bruce, F. F. *The Epistle to the Hebrews, Revised: New International Commentary on the New Testament.* Grand Rapids, MI: Eerdmans. Reprint, 1988.
Guthrie, Donald. *Tyndale New Testament Commentaries: Letter to the Hebrews.* Grand Rapids, MI: Eerdmans, 1983. 216.
Holman Pocket Bible Dictionary. Nashville, TN: Holman Bible Publishers, 2004. 762-764, 773.
Johnson, Luke Timothy. *Hebrews: A Commentary.* The New Testament Library. Louisville, KY: Westminster John Knox Press, 2006. 259.
Keener, Craig S. *The IVP Bible Background Commentary: New Testament.* Downers Grove, IL: InterVarsity Press, 1993. 647-650, 670-671.
Lane, William L. *Hebrews 9-13. Word Biblical Commentary, Vol. 47B.* Dallas, TX: Word Inc., 1991.
Life Application Study Bible, King James Version. Wheaton, IL: Tyndale House Publishers, Inc.,1997. 2154-2155, 2170-2172.
New Testament Greek Lexicon. Bible Study Tools.com. http://www.biblestudytools.com/lexicons/greek (accessed September 6, 2011).
Radmacher, Earl D., ed. Nelson's New Illustrated Bible Commentary: Spreading the Light of God's Word into Your Life. Nashville, TN: Thomas Nelson Publishers, 1999. 1648-1653.

Say It Correctly

Abihu. uh-BAHY-hyoo.
Nadab. **NAY**-dab.

Daily Bible Readings

MONDAY
A Great Faith
(Matthew 8:5–13)

TUESDAY
A Saving Faith
(Romans 10:8–17

WEDNESDAY
A Justifying Faith
(Galatians 2:15–21)

THURSDAY
An Examined Faith
(2 Corinthians 13:5–10)

FRIDAY
An Enduring Faith
(Romans 5:1–5)

SATURDAY
An Exemplary Faith
(1 Thessalonians 1:2–10)

SUNDAY
The Full Assurance of Faith
(Hebrews 10:19–31)

Teaching Tips

Words You Should Know

A. Faith (Hebrews 11:1, 3, 6) *pistis* (Gk.)—Belief with the predominant idea of trust (or confidence); assurance.

B. Refuge (Psalm 46:1) *machaceh* (Heb.)—A shelter from rain, storm, or danger; hope.

Teacher Preparation

Unifying Principle—Steadfast Confidence. According to the writers of Hebrews and Psalms, because God is with us, we can be rescued and change can take place by believing in His strength.

A. Pray for lesson clarity.

B. Read and study the entire lesson.

C. Complete Lesson 2 in the *Precepts For Living Personal Study Guide®*.

D. Read the Focal Verses in a modern translation.

O—Open the Lesson

A. Before the students arrive, write on the board, "How do we experience the presence of God?"

B. Open with prayer.

C. Discuss the question.

D. Ask the students to share times they have experienced the presence of God in their lives.

P—Present the Scriptures

A. Focus on God's presence and the awareness that God is always with us.

B. Read and discuss the Focal Verses, The People, Places, and Times and Background sections.

E—Explore the Meaning

A. Discuss the Lesson in Our Society and Discuss the Meaning.

B. Share the most significant points from today's lesson.

N—Next Steps for Application

A. Read the Keep in Mind verse in unison.

B. Complete the Follow the Spirit and Remember Your Thoughts sections.

C. Close in prayer, thanking God for the miracles that He has already revealed.

Worship Guide

For the Superintendent or Teacher
Theme: Faith Is Assurance
Song: "Blessed Assurance"
Devotional Reading: Psalm 27:1-6
Prayer

Faith Is Assurance

SEPT
9th

Bible Background • HEBREWS 11:1-7; PSALM 46:1-11
Printed Text • HEBREWS 11:1-3, 6; PSALM 46:1-3, 8-11 | Devotional Reading • PSALM 27:1-6

———— Aim for Change ————

By the end of the lesson, we will: KNOW the meaning of faith and its implication for our lives; FEEL God's constant presence; and DEVELOP a practice of relying on God for positive change.

———— In Focus ————

Because Angela was selected to manage the IT upgrade project for a new client in New York, she could not join her family when they traveled to Japan. The family talked and laughed as Angela drove her parents and sister, Simone, to the airport.

Her mom said, "This is the first family trip without you."

As Angela hugged her mom, she said, "I will see you in one week."

While Angela was in a project meeting, she received an important call from her director. As Angela held the phone to her ear, she stood expressionless; then she fainted. Moments later, the project team heard the news: a massive earthquake occurred in Japan. A secretary explained that Angela's family was in Japan.

As the days slowly passed, Angela did not hear any news about her family. Each day, she had to trust and rely on God.

In today's lesson, we learn that faith is necessary in order to believe and rely on God's strength. When we are waiting for news or we experience conflicts in life, we can trust God by faith. God will not leave us; He is always with us.

———— Keep in Mind ————

"Now faith is the substance of things hoped for, the evidence of things not seen" (Hebrews 11:1).

"Now faith is the substance of things hoped for, the evidence of things not seen" (Hebrews 11:1).

Focal Verses

KJV **Hebrews 11:1** Now faith is the substance of things hoped for, the evidence of things not seen.

2 For by it the elders obtained a good report.

3 Through faith we understand that the worlds were framed by the word of God, so that things which are seen were not made of things which do appear.

11:6 But without faith it is impossible to please him: for he that cometh to God must believe that he is, and that he is a rewarder of them that diligently seek him.

Psalm 46:1 God is our refuge and strength, a very present help in trouble.

2 Therefore will not we fear, though the earth be removed, and though the mountains be carried into the midst of the sea;

3 Though the waters thereof roar and be troubled, though the mountains shake with the swelling thereof. Selah.

46:8 Come, behold the works of the LORD, what desolations he hath made in the earth.

9 He maketh wars to cease unto the end of the earth; he breaketh the bow, and cutteth the spear in sunder; he burneth the chariot in the fire.

10 Be still, and know that I am God: I will be exalted among the heathen, I will be exalted in the earth.

11 The LORD of hosts is with us; the God of Jacob is our refuge. Selah.

NLT **Hebrews 11:1** Faith is the confidence that what we hope for will actually happen; it gives us assurance about things we cannot see.

2 Through their faith, the people in days of old earned a good reputation.

3 By faith we understand that the entire universe was formed at God's command, that what we now see did not come from anything that can be seen.

11:6 And it is impossible to please God without faith. Anyone who wants to come to him must believe that God exists and that he rewards those who sincerely seek him.

Psalm 46:1 God is our refuge and strength, always ready to help in times of trouble.

2 So we will not fear, even if earthquakes come and the mountains crumble into the sea.

3 Let the oceans roar and foam. Let the mountains tremble as the waters surge!

Interlude

46:8 Come, see the glorious works of the LORD: See how he brings destruction upon the world.

9 He causes wars to end throughout the earth. He breaks the bow and snaps the spear; he burns the shields with fire.

10 "Be still, and know that I am God! I will be honored by every nation. I will be honored throughout the world."

11 The LORD of Heaven's Armies is here among us; the God of Israel is our fortress.

The People, Places, and Times

Sons of Korah. Psalms 42 through 49 were written by the sons of Korah, who were temple musicians and assistants. The Korahites were among the chief Levitical families; they were listed as "gatekeepers." Korah was a Levite who led a rebellion against Moses. Although Korah was killed, his family remained faithful to God and continued to serve in His temple. King David appointed men from the clan of Korah to serve as choir leaders.

Later, the choir leaders continued to serve as temple musicians for hundreds of years.

Psalms. The book of Psalms is a series of five collections: Book 1 (Psalms 1—41), Book II (Psalms 42—72), Book III (Psalms 73—89), Book IV (Psalms 90—106) and Book V (Psalms 107—150). Several authors wrote the collections, and some are anonymous. David wrote at least 73 psalms, and Asaph, sons of Korah, Moses, Solomon, Ethan, and Heman wrote others. Psalms was written over a period of more than 1,000 years, which included the time of Moses (around 1440 B.C.) to the time of captivity in Babylon (around 586 B.C). The majority of the books were written during Israel's wilderness experience and time in Israel, Judah, or Babylon. The title "Psalms" was first used in the Septuagint. The traditional Hebrew title is *"tehillim,"* which means "praises" but most of the psalms are *"tephillot,"* which means "prayers."

Background

The readers of the book of Hebrews knew Scripture and professed faith in Christ. Because of doubt, persecution, or false teaching, the believers, who were Jewish Christians, considered giving up Christianity and returning to Judaism. The writer emphasized the superiority of faith to encourage the Christians of the first century to stand by faith.

Christians were demoralized and discouraged because centuries of tradition were replaced with spiritual freedom based upon faith in Christ. As a result, the believers experienced the wrath of the Jewish religious establishment because they believed in God's greatest promise—Jesus Christ—the Messiah, who fulfilled the prophecies of the Old Testament. The writer wanted to prevent believers from rejecting Christianity and returning to Judaism.

The writer explained the superiority of faith by examples of people who demonstrated greater faith. The heroes of faith were intended to encourage the power of faith as the believers adhered to their profession of true religion. Through examples in biblical history, faith is revealed through assurance in God's future promises with the implications that inspire believers to persevere. Through the summary of Jewish history, the heroes of faith challenge believers to grow in faith and live in obedience to God.

Psalm 46, which was written by the sons of Korah—who were temple assistants—was a celebration of God's deliverance. The psalm may have been written when the Assyrian army invaded the land and surrounded Jerusalem. As the psalm speaks to ancient Israelites, it speaks to believers today. We need not fear if we trust God. Through faith we can give thanks for God's constant presence in our lives. Because God is with us, we can be rescued. The writer refers to a "river" (Psalm 46:4), which is the tunnel that King Hezekiah built to guarantee a continuous water supply for Jerusalem during times of war. Like the tunnel, God's presence is constant for believers.

At-A-Glance

1. Faith Is Confidence and Certainty (Hebrews 11:1-3)
2. Faith Is Necessary (v. 6)
3. Faith Is Trust in God as Our Refuge (Psalm 46:1-3)
4. Faith Is Trust in God Whose Presence Is Constant (vv. 8-11)

In Depth

1. Faith Is Confidence and Certainty (Hebrews 11:1-3)

The writer of Hebrews begins chapter 11 with a description of faith as "the substance of things hoped for, the evidence of things not seen" (Hebrews 11:1). The reality of faith is what is "hoped for." Our prayers and hopes are based upon the promises of God. With a firm persuasion and expectation, the writer encouraged the believers to trust that God will perform what He has promised through Christ. We cannot see the future nor do we know what will happen tomorrow, but our confidence is based upon the certainty of God's trustworthiness.

To encourage struggling believers to hold to the superiority of their faith in Christ, the writer refers the believers to the elders of the Old Testament (Hebrews 11:2). The "elders" received a "good report," which was the evidence that they would receive the promise of participating in God's kingdom when it arrives in its fullness. Their actions revealed a genuine faith that will bring honor to the ancient believers.

Many Jewish teachers believed the material universe was created based on God's invisible pattern exemplified in His Word or wisdom. By faith, we believe God created everything out of nothing. Moses detailed the story of creation in Genesis chapter 1; there was a majestic display of power and purpose. With each creation, God "saw that it was good" (Genesis 1:4, 10, 12, 18, 21). By faith, we believe God spoke and created the entire universe. Our faith is based upon who God is; our response should be confident and certain hope in God because He is ever present. Do you have certain and confident faith in God?

2. Faith Is Necessary (v. 6)

Faith reveals the reality of God. "It is impossible to please God" without faith because faith is necessary to have an active relationship with God; it is necessary to walk with God (Hebrews 11:6, NLT). By faith, we believe in God and trust with certainty the future promises that He has revealed.

The heroes of faith believed and obeyed regardless of the consequences. In the same way, we can believe with a willing trust and please God. Our steadfast confidence is based upon who God is—the creator of the universe. God will recognize and reward our faith because we "diligently seek him" (Hebrews 11:6). By faith, we realize our own insufficiency and depend on God to work within us and through us. By faith we have confidence in the continual promises of God.

3. Faith Is Trust in God as Our Refuge (Psalm 46:1-3)

The sons of Korah were temple assistants who wrote Psalm 46. The psalmists recognized God as their source of help; they realized God's complete power and ability to rescue His children. As believers, we do not need to fear because God's presence is constant. God is our refuge; therefore, we can flee to Him and find security.

Life presents temporary destruction, doubts, and uncertainty, but God's presence is constant; "therefore will not we fear" (Psalm 46:2). We can appreciate God's constant presence because He is our mighty fortress. The earth swallowed up Korah, but the psalmists did not fear. We can be fearless with God as our present help, too.

God is not a temporary resource; instead God is our eternal refuge. The psalmists remind believers, "Though the waters thereof roar and be troubled, though the mountains shake," God's power is complete and victory in Him is certain (Psalm 46:3).

27

We should not be troubled when the earth is unstable because our confidence is not found in the earth. Our confidence is based upon God, our sound eternal footing.

4. Faith Is Trust in God Whose Presence Is Constant (vv. 8-11)

The psalmist urges the believers to "behold the works of the LORD" (Psalm 46:8). Recognize the presence of God and His ability to save His children. He is the creator who cares for nature and all living things. As believers, we can trust in God's strength and His constant presence. Those who oppose God will experience desolation and face His judgment. But believers can stand in awe of God's power.

The psalmist encourages believers to respond with a generous heart. We can, as the psalm states, "Be still, and know that I am God" (Psalm 46:10). Even though war, destruction, and famine are a part of the world, God is still in charge. He is sovereign. Final victory belongs to Him, and He will be exalted. Therefore, we can rest assured and know with comfort that He is Lord.

Search the Scriptures

1. How did the writer of Hebrews describe faith (Hebrews 11:1)?

2. Who received a "good report" (Hebrews 11:2)?

3. Why is faith necessary to "understand that the worlds were framed by the word of God" (Hebrews 11:3)?

Discuss the Meaning

1. The writer explains that faith is required to understand that God created the universe where nothing existed. Genesis 1 details the awesome creation of the universe that was formed by God's Word. Faith is the beginning of our relationship with God.

What qualities of faith are necessary to continue to grow and strengthen our relationship with God?

2. When Korah, Dathan, and Abiram led 250 princes against the priesthood of Aaron and Moses' general authority, God punished the leaders by allowing their challengers to be swallowed up by the earth. A fire consumed 250 of them. The psalmist, the sons of Korah, reiterates God's presence and encourages readers not to fear. How can we maintain a quiet confidence in the midst of economic turmoil, natural disasters, and continual wars?

Lesson in Our Society

If we watch the news, listen to the radio or interact with others, we hear about the current state of the world. Many people are homeless, unemployed, or on the verge of both. Natural disasters occur, and the number of fatalities grows. War and destruction are continually reported by the news. Peace seems impossible. While positive change seems nonexistent, we must not lose hope. God is ever present. If we trust God, we will be rescued and change will occur through God's strength. We can rely on God for positive change as we realize our faith will be tested. How has your faith in God become stronger or weaker in light of world events, catastrophes, and unrest? How much do you think the world dismisses the constant help of God as a result of abundant negativity, catastrophe, and unrest?

Make It Happen

To remain faithful with steadfast confidence and certainty, we must keep our eyes on God through continual prayer. We must remain hopeful for positive change, as we believe that God is in control. We can have faith in God's constant presence even today because we know He is our refuge in times of trouble. Make a commitment to regularly attend Bible study and Sunday school to increase your awareness of God's power in troubling times. Join ministries that actively build the community and encourage people who are suffering or do not know God. Allow God's presence to be evident through your actions and words.

Follow the Spirit

What God wants me to do:

_____

_____

_____

_____

Remember Your Thoughts

Special insights I have learned:

_____

_____

_____

_____

More Light on the Text

Hebrews 11:1-3, 6; Psalm 46:1-3, 8-11

1 Now faith is the substance of things hoped for, the evidence of things not seen.

Faith, the author of Hebrews tells us, is the substance of things hoped for. The Greek word *hupostasis* (**hoop-OS-tas-is**), translated "substance" (KJV), has previously been used with the same meaning in 1:3. In other contexts, it may be regarded as "confidence," a subjective meaning, as in 3:14.

The translation "substance" is preferred here. Understood this way, it means that faith authenticates the things believers hope for as though things already exist. Faith lays hold of invisible realities. The word "evidence" (Gk. *elegchos*, **EL-eng-khos**) usually signifies a proof or test. Faith is the evidence or proof for things unseen. It then acts on those unseen things as if they are visible or easily identified by the senses.

2 For by it the elders obtained a good report.

With the use of the conjunction "for" (Gk. *gar*), 11:2 goes further to explain how faith is the "substance" or "proof" because "the elders" (Gk. *presbuteros*, **pres-BOO-ter-os**), a term that may be used of age or dignity, attested. These men had witnesses borne to them (Gk. *epimartureo*, **ep-ee-mar-too-REH-o**), or were held up as good examples on account of their faith. In agreement with the author's usage of bearing witness or testifying in 2:4; 7:8, 17; 10:15, and elsewhere, it is clear that God is the one who bore the witness to or gave affirmation to the faith of the elders.

3 Through faith we understand that the worlds were framed by the word of God, so that things which are seen were not made of things which do appear.

"Through faith" runs through the chapter with compelling emphasis. For the most part, it is attached to the accomplishments of the great ones of previous generations. Here, however, the writer speaks not only of the ancients or elders but also of "we" in the present, claiming a close tie between himself and his hearers. Faith is a present reality, not exclusively the property of past heroes. Faith gives us convictions about creation. For the author, the visible universe is not sufficient to account for itself. But it is faith, not something material, that assures him that the universe originated with God. His view is nonetheless certain because it is based on faith, and he does not qualify his statement as though any doubt were possible. This world is God's world, and faith assures the author that God created it. Faith's understanding that the universe is framed or fashioned by the word of God changes the human perception of all things: "So that things which are seen were not made of things which do appear." Without a doubt, this is the most indispensable of all insights, the one that distinguishes believers from the atheists. The world is not self-derived, self-contained, nor self-sufficient.

11:6 But without faith it is impossible to please him: for he that cometh to God must believe that he is, and that he is a rewarder of them that diligently seek him.

In this verse, the author draws out the implication of Abel and Enoch's examples (Hebrews 11:4-5) with a general proposition concerning faith itself. He moves directly to faith as an appropriate way of responding to God. Though the Old Testament does not say that Enoch had faith, the author goes on to explain why he can speak of it so confidently. It is impossible to please God without faith, and Enoch pleased God. Thus, it is clear that he had faith. The author issues a flat denial that anyone can please God apart from faith. He does not say simply that without faith it is difficult to please God; he says that without faith, it is *impossible* to please Him! There is no substitute for faith. Whoever approaches God must first believe that He exists. This is basic. Without it, there is no possibility of faith at all. But it is not enough. There must also be a conviction "that he rewards those who earnestly seek him" (11:6, NIV). Only if God is all-powerful Creator can He reward

those who seek Him. As Barclay puts it, "We must believe not only that God exists but also that he cares" (Barclay, 139). Without that deep conviction, faith in the biblical sense is not a possibility.

46:1 God is our refuge and strength, a very present help in trouble. 2 Therefore will not we fear, though the earth be removed, and though the mountains be carried into the midst of the sea; 3 Though the waters thereof roar and be troubled, though the mountains shake with the swelling thereof. Selah.

Psalm 46 has been popularized by Martin Luther's rendition in the hymn, "A Mighty Fortress Is Our God." It is said that he wrote it at that moment in 1529 when the Turkish army retreated to the Balkans after besieging the walls of Vienna in vain. The psalm is an expression of confidence in God. It begins with a confession of faith and presents God in a very personal way to Israel. The "times of trouble," in which God offers protection, are times when chaos attempts to reassert its primacy over order, both in the natural world and in the world of nations and human affairs (46:1, NLT). The affirmation of God's presence in a protective capacity is the basis for the confidence in the community's words: "We will not fear …" (v. 3, NIV). This great God is "ever-present" with His people. His presence in protecting the people of God is described by three words—"refuge," "strength," and "fortress"—that designate the source and effectiveness of Israel's strength. God is their strength (see Psalm 29:11; 68:35; 71:7; Isaiah 26:1). As their strength, He is like a refuge where one finds rest and asylum (see Psalm 14:6; 61:3; 62:7-8; 71:7; Isaiah 25:4; Jeremiah 17:17). His strength is also evident when they find protection in Him as a fortress. The fortress was an isolated, elevated place where people built a stronghold against the enemy (see Psalm 9:9; 18:2; 48:3; Isaiah 33:16). Each of these descriptions relates to a people in need. Only when they are in distress do they need His special protection (see Psalm 22:19; 27:9; 40:13). They always need Him, but they experience the power of His presence particularly in periods of anguish and distress (see 23:4). Then He is close to them—"very present" (46:1; see Deuteronomy 4:7). God had always been their strength—including when Moses led them out of the clutches of Pharaoh in Egypt. Consequently, He could now be trusted to remain even if the mountains, wonderful symbols of permanence, below the ocean were to quake, consequently causing an unheard-of flood. For God is Immanuel, meaning, "God is with us." Thus, if God is not moved, then, because our refuge is in Him, we shall not be moved either.

46:8 Come, behold the works of the LORD, what desolations he hath made in the earth. 9 He maketh wars to cease unto the end of the earth; he breaketh the bow, and cutteth the spear in sunder; he burneth the chariot in the fire.

The psalmist exhorts the godly to be wise and discerning by considering the works of God. The announcement is applicable to almost any occasion when the people of God were delivered from a pressing peril. For Israel, the "works of God" include all acts of God in the history of salvation: Exodus, conquest, the period of the judges, and the monarchy (see Psalm 66:5-7). Reciting the mighty acts of God plants evidence of His care, protection, and providential rule deep in the memory of God's people. Those who are wise enough to remember and see the world around them have tokens of God's constancy toward His

people. The deliverance of Israel from its threat occurs by "desolations," which God accomplishes among the nations (46:8). But there is another side to the story. Every victory, every subjugation of a hostile nation, and every stroke on the canvas of the history of redemption clarifies that the Lord's very plan for humankind includes cessation of wars for an era of peace. His judgments of the nations will result in removal of evil instigators, troublemakers, rebels, and expressions of hostility in every form. The God of peace will make "wars cease" (46:9; see Isaiah 2:4; Ezekiel 39:9; Micah 4:3; Zechariah 9:10). The instruments of warfare described in Psalm 46:9, symbolized by the bow, the spear, and the chariot, will become inoperative (see Isaiah 9:4; Ezekiel 39:9-10; Hosea 2:18; Micah 4:1-4). Yet, to do so, in the end, God must surely cause great convulsions—for evil is a serious power to be reckoned with. Consequently, He breaks the bow and shatters the spear and burns the chariot in the fire.

46:10 Be still, and know that I *am* God: I will be exalted among the heathen, I will be exalted in the earth. 11 The LORD of hosts *is* with us; the God of Jacob is our refuge. Selah.

Verse 10 begins with a common invitation in Christian spirituality. In its context, as John Goldingay rightly observes, the verse "issues an important challenge to the superpower to stand still and recognize that God is God and that the superpower is not" (Goldingay, 73). Israel, like the nations, must stop looking after its own destiny and acknowledge that God is God— therefore God is its refuge and strength. Yet, the verse speaks to us to learn to cultivate the habit of silence. Second, the psalmist encourages the godly to "know" that the Lord is God. Though it was tempting to ally themselves with foreign powers, to rely on military strength, or to give themselves over to idolatry and pagan ways, the godly had to learn to persevere to the end by trusting in God. Throughout the history of Israel and Judah, severe national distress brought the temptation to abandon true religion for the short-lived security of political alliances, military strength, and worldly paganism. Instead of choosing a negative option, the people of God distinguished themselves by their pursuit for godliness: "Know that I am God." The knowledge of God includes a factual understanding about Him, His past acts, and His promises. But in this context, the psalmist calls on the Israelites to commit themselves to the Lord and to seek His "refuge," "strength," and "fortress" (vv. 1, 7, 11). Peter Craigie sums up verse 11 this way: "Both the 'nations' and the 'earth' (v. 11), which earlier were depicted as posing a threat to orderly existence, are now harnessed in service to the exaltation of God. Hence, the people may 'relax' in appropriate confidence (v. 11a); to know that God is God is to know His Lordship of nature and history, and therefore to be aware of His total capacity as Protector" (Craigie, 345). The God of our ancestors is still the God we have today, still our refuge, our fortress!

Sources:

Barclay, William. *The Daily Study Bible: The Letter to the Hebrews. Revised ed.* Philadelphia, PA: The Westminster Press, 1976. 139.

Bible History Online. http://www.bible-history.com (accessed on September 6, 2011).

Bruce, F. F. *The Epistle to the Hebrews, Revised: New International Commentary on the New Testament.* Grand Rapids, MI: Eerdmans. Reprint, 1985.

Craigie, Peter C. *Word Biblical Commentary, Vol. 19: Psalms 1-50.* Waco, TX: Word Publishing, 1983. 345.

Dictionary.com. http://dictionary.reference.com/ (accessed September 6, 2011).

Goldingay, John. *Psalms, Vol. 2: Psalms 42-89.* Grand Rapids, MI: Baker Academic, 2007. 73.

Guthrie, Donald. *Hebrews, Tyndale New Testament Commentaries.* Grand Rapids, MI: Eerdmans, 1983.

Holman Pocket Bible Dictionary. Nashville, TN: Holman Bible Publishers, 2004. 1001, 1342-1344.

Johnson, Luke Timothy. *Hebrews: A Commentary. The New Testament Library.* Louisville, KY: Westminster John Knox Press, 2006. 259.

Keener, Craig S. The IVP Bible Background Commentary: New Testament. Downers Grove, IL: InterVarsity Press, 1993. 673-674.

Luther, Martin. "A Mighty Fortress is Our God." Composite translation by Pennsylvania Lutheran Church, 1868. Klug's Gesangbuch, 1529; http://www.lutheran-hymnal.com/lyrics/tlh262.htm (accessed Feb. 15, 2012)

Lane, William L. *Word Biblical Commentary, Vol. 47B. Hebrews 9-13.* Dallas, TX: Word Inc., 1991.

Life Application Study Bible, King James Version. Wheaton, IL: Tyndale House Publishers, Inc., 1997. 992-993, 2152-2153, 2173.

New Testament Greek Lexicon. Bible Study Tools.com. http://www.biblestudytools.com/lexicons/greek (accessed September 9, 2011).

Old Testament Hebrew Lexicon. Bible Study Tools.com. http://www.biblestudytools.com/lexicons/hebrew (accessed September 9, 2011).

Walton, John H., ed. The IVP Bible Background Commentary: Old Testament. Downers Grove, IL: InterVarsity Press, 2000. 511-518, 529.

Say It Correctly

Abel. **AY**-buhl.
Cain. **KAYN**.

Daily Bible Readings

MONDAY
The Trusting Child
(Mark 10:13–16)

TUESDAY
The Trust of the Weak
(2 Chronicles 14:2–12)

WEDNESDAY
The Prayer of Trust
(Psalm 3)

THURSDAY
The Security of Trust
(Psalm 4)

FRIDAY
The Confidence of Trust
(Psalm 27:1–6)

SATURDAY
The Patience of Trust
(Psalm 27:7–14)

SUNDAY
The Certain Refuge
(Hebrews 11:1–3, 6; Psalm 46:1–3, 8–11)

Notes

_____

_____

_____

_____

Teaching Tips

Words You Should Know

A. Witnesses (Hebrews 12:1) *martus* (Gk.)—Those who can verify a particular truth based on what they know, have seen, or heard.

B. Chastening (vv. 5, 7, 11) *paideia* (Gk.)—Education or training; by implication, it also means disciplinary correction.

Teacher Preparation

Unifying Principle—Steadfast Fortitude. The writer of Hebrews tells us to keep our eyes on Christ Jesus to grow in grace and character.

A. Study Hebrews 11 and 12.

B. Make a list of some of the struggles African Americans have had to endure to reach and enjoy the standard of living we experience today.

D. Complete the companion lesson in the *Precepts For Living Study Guide*®.

O—Open the Lesson

A. Open the class with prayer.

B. Ask the students to share some of the ways they have suffered and dealt with adversity and the lessons they learned.

C. Have the students silently read the In Focus story. Discuss.

P—Present the Scriptures

A. Use the Background and The People, Places, and Times sections to build the lesson.

B. Discuss why God allows His children to suffer for righteousness' sake.

C. Ask a student to read Hebrews 12:1-11 and then discuss it with the entire class.

E—Explore the Meaning

A. Have volunteers respond to the Discuss the Meaning questions.

B. Explain that 2 Corinthians 13:5 teaches that we are to examine ourselves to see whether we are "in the faith."

C. Ask: What can we learn from suffering for Christ's sake? Have we denied ourselves, taken up our crosses, and followed Jesus?

N—Next Steps for Application

A. Ask the students to share some of their trials and tribulations that have made them stronger in the faith with others who are in need.

B. Close with prayer.

Worship Guide

For the Superintendent or Teacher
Theme: Faith Is Endurance
Song: "I Am on the Battlefield
for My Lord"
Devotional Reading: James 5:7-11
Prayer

Faith Is Endurance

Bible Background • HEBREWS 12:1-11
Printed Text • HEBREWS 12:1-11 | Devotional Reading • JAMES 5:7-11

Aim for Change

By the end of the lesson, we will: DESCRIBE how to have enduring faith; BECOME CONVINCED that we can endure in faith; and DEVELOP a plan to utilize our faith to determine and reach spiritual goals.

In Focus

Myra had worked for a Fortune 500 company for five years. She was well liked, hardworking, and a team player; yet, she had been laid off. So many questions ran through her mind as she struggled to understand why the Lord had allowed her to lose her job. After all, she had a young child to support and bills to pay. She was distressed and disappointed and couldn't understand why she was undergoing this fiery trial.

After lamenting for a while, she remembered God's promise: "All things work together for good to them that love God, to them who are the called according to his purpose" (Romans 8:28).

She began to trust God for what direction she should take, and her faith began to increase. She decided to go back to school and get her MBA. Times were tough for her and her daughter, but they survived. She finally earned her MBA and soon found a better paying job that had more prestige and responsibility.

What do you think of when you think of leadership? In today's lesson, we see that Jesus set the perfect example as the leader who was tempted but did not give in. He endured the pain and shame of the Cross to achieve the joy and victory of eternal life with God.

Keep in Mind

"Wherefore seeing we also are compassed about with so great a cloud of witnesses, let us lay aside every weight, and the sin which doth so easily beset us, and let us run with patience the race that is set before us, Looking unto Jesus the author and finisher of our faith; who for the joy that was set before him endured the cross, despising the shame, and is set down at the right hand of the throne of God" (Hebrews 12:1-2).

"Wherefore seeing we also are compassed about with so great a cloud of witnesses, let us lay aside every weight, and the sin which doth so easily beset us, and let us run with patience the race that is set before us, Looking unto Jesus the author and finisher of our faith; who for the joy that was set before him endured the cross, despising the shame, and is set down at the right hand of the throne of God" (Hebrews 12:1-2).

Focal Verses

KJV **Hebrews 12:1** Wherefore seeing we also are compassed about with so great a cloud of witnesses, let us lay aside every weight, and the sin which doth so easily beset us, and let us run with patience the race that is set before us,

2 Looking unto Jesus the author and finisher of our faith; who for the joy that was set before him endured the cross, despising the shame, and is set down at the right hand of the throne of God.

3 For consider him that endured such contradiction of sinners against himself, lest ye be wearied and faint in your minds.

4 Ye have not yet resisted unto blood, striving against sin.

5 And ye have forgotten the exhortation which speaketh unto you as unto children, My son, despise not thou the chastening of the Lord, nor faint when thou art rebuked of him:

6 For whom the Lord loveth he chasteneth, and scourgeth every son whom he receiveth.

7 If ye endure chastening, God dealeth with you as with sons; for what son is he whom the father chasteneth not?

8 But if ye be without chastisement, whereof all are partakers, then are ye bastards, and not sons.

9 Furthermore we have had fathers of our flesh which corrected us, and we gave them reverence: shall we not much rather be in subjection unto the Father of spirits, and live?

10 For they verily for a few days chastened us after their own pleasure; but he for our profit, that we might be partakers of his holiness.

11 Now no chastening for the present seemeth to be joyous, but grievous:

NLT **Hebrews 12:1** Therefore, since we are surrounded by such a huge crowd of witnesses to the life of faith, let us strip off every weight that slows us down, especially the sin that so easily trips us up. And let us run with endurance the race God has set before us.

2 We do this by keeping our eyes on Jesus, the champion who initiates and perfects our faith. Because of the joy awaiting him, he endured the cross, disregarding its shame. Now he is seated in the place of honor beside God's throne.

3 Think of all the hostility he endured from sinful people; then you won't become weary and give up.

4 After all, you have not yet given your lives in your struggle against sin.

5 And have you forgotten the encouraging words God spoke to you as his children? He said, "My child, don't make light of the LORD's discipline, and don't give up when he corrects you.

6 For the LORD disciplines those he loves, and he punishes each one he accepts as his child."

7 As you endure this divine discipline, remember that God is treating you as his own children. Who ever heard of a child who is never disciplined by its father?

8 If God doesn't discipline you as he does all of his children, it means that you are illegitimate and are not really his children at all.

9 Since we respected our earthly fathers who disciplined us, shouldn't we submit even more to the discipline of the Father of our spirits, and live forever?

10 For our earthly fathers disciplined us for a few years, doing the best they knew how. But God's discipline is always good for us, so that we might share in his holiness.

KJV continued

nevertheless afterward it yieldeth the peaceable fruit of righteousness unto them which are exercised thereby.

NLT continued

11 No discipline is enjoyable while it is happening—it's painful! But afterward there will be a peaceful harvest of right living for those who are trained in this way.

The People, Places, and Times

Rome. As the capital city of Italy, it was the center of commerce, culture, and religion. A myriad of religions dotted the social landscape at the time this letter to the Hebrews was circulated. Although there were times when Jews and Christians were expelled from Rome, there were other times when they could worship freely.

Believers in Rome. Scholars are very unsure of the intended audience, but in Hebrews 13:24, the writer sends greetings from those of Italy. The *NIV Study Bible* notes that the writer is passing on greetings from some Italian believers. William Barclay in his *Daily Study Bible* on Hebrews suggests that it was written to a group of Jewish Christians who met in a "house–church" in Rome (Barclay, 6-7). They were a subgroup of the main Christian congregation that had been formed there years earlier. Living in a climate of other religions and cults, their faith was tested constantly. When times were hard—politically, culturally, socially, and economically—the chance was greater that they would be tempted to return to Judaism.

It was not easy nor politically correct to be a Christian at this time. Christians in Rome had to deal with the threat of persecution by the Roman authorities; although, none of them had become martyrs like Stephen and others. (This happened later under Nero, the emperor.) Because they were still alive, the writer encouraged them to continue to run their race and not give up. He reminded them that Jesus never gave up and that they shouldn't either.

Background

Some Bible commentators believe Hebrews was written to a Jewish-Christian congregation in Rome around A.D. 67-70. Others believe it was written to Jews living in Egypt or Palestine. Traditionally, authorship was attributed to the apostle Paul, but modern scholars are unsure of the true identity of the author of this epistle. Some believe Barnabas wrote it, and still others suggest Apollos, the Jew born in Alexandria, which is located in northern Africa. The author wrote the letter in response to the threat that believers might renounce Christianity and revert to Judaism. The writer wanted to inform his vacillating readers that Jesus Christ, the object of God's final revelation, is superior to the greatest of Judaism's heroes.

The writer also wanted to highlight, while reminding his audience of, the efficacy of Jesus' power of salvation. He emphasizes that whereas the Jewish legal sacrificial system was powerless to remit sins, Jesus, the eternal High Priest, "is able also to save them to the uttermost that come unto God by him, seeing he ever liveth to make intercession for them" (Hebrews 7:25). Furthermore, the writer explained the need for patient endurance amid the persecution and sufferings to which the heirs of eternal salvation are inevitably exposed.

The writer suggests that all Christians emulate Jesus' suffering and patience in anticipation of an eternal reward. One cannot help but notice the metaphors of Greek athletic terms such as "run with perseverance the race" and "a great cloud of witnesses [spectators]" (Hebrews 12:1, NIV). These Christians were to think of themselves as athletes who possessed endurance in order to ensure victory over the forces of evil. The writer also made it clear that the Christians' secret weapon, needed for victory in spite of trials and tribulations, was unwavering faith.

At-A-Glance

1. Believers Must Run the Race
   (Hebrews 12:1–2)
2. Believers Must Develop Endurance
   (vv. 3–6)
3. Believers Must Learn to Accept the
   Discipline of the Lord (vv. 7–11)

In Depth

1. Believers Must Run the Race (Hebrews 12:1–2)

The writer encourages the Christian readers to continue to "run their race" of discipleship no matter what tries to hinder them. He tells them not to get distracted by burdens or sins that are present in their lives.

Being a Christian was not an easy thing back then, and it still isn't today. It is a life-long commitment that involves peaks and valleys, good times and bad times, and sunshine and rain. Christian discipleship is not akin to a sprint; it is a marathon. That is why the author tells his audience to use "perseverance" (v. 1, NIV). Perseverance is an inner quality that allows one to continue in some course of action in spite of difficulty or opposition. To persevere is to be steadfast in a particular purpose.

Disciples of Jesus Christ must always look to Jesus as the ultimate model of perseverance. In His ministry, He suffered insults and attempts on His life. He persisted even though His hometown and relatives rejected Him. He overcame the obstinacy of His followers and betrayal by one of His own. He never faltered during the unjust criminal trial that accused Him of sedition and heresy or the beating by the Roman police force. Finally, He did not waver on the Cross at Calvary. He did all of that not only so future generations of believers would have access to a spiritual power potent enough to change the world but also to set an example of the perfect leader who was tempted but did not give in. And most importantly, He endured the Cross to carry our sins and provide the way of salvation for us.

We must also remember that we have an inspiration. We are surrounded by a "great ... cloud of witnesses," credible leaders who have fought a good fight, finished their course, kept the faith, and earned their crowns of righteousness. They are our inspiration. Our heroes of faith should inspire us to keep our faith so we can pursue a life of complete holiness and participate in kingdom work that can change our world and be a witness of the world to come. Today, we look at heroes of faith such as Dr. Martin Luther King, Jr., Mary McLeod Bethune, Frederick Douglass, Harriet Tubman, and Rosa Parks.

Therefore, as we continue to live as ambassadors of Christ, let us persevere on our jobs, in our homes, and in our communities. God demands our best in this life. No matter what hardships we go through, our history is peppered with credible leaders who have overcome greater hardships than we have ever had to imagine. We can learn from them. If they made it, surely we can make it. With God on our side and a "great ... cloud of witnesses" cheering us on, we can get through any adverse situation we face.

2. Believers Must Develop Endurance (vv. 3–6)

When life becomes unbearable and we get discouraged by some temporal circumstances, we ought to have enough of a spiritual sense to look to Jesus as our source of strength. If we think of all that Jesus endured, giving His life so we might have life, we have to thank God for the character and integrity of His Son Jesus Christ.

The writer of Hebrews encouraged the vacillating Jewish Christians, when they began to complain about the adversity they had to face, to consider Jesus' suffering. He supported his argument by testifying that they had not faced persecution to the degree that they had shed their own blood. He also let them know that trials suffered for righteousness' sake could be theologically viewed as the "chastening of the Lord," God's "disciplinary correction, instruction, and nurture."

The Lord's chastening is not arbitrary or without direction—it always has a purpose. The writer suggests that trials could be disciplinary correction and a part of God's overall plan to edify His children. Corrective discipline is always a good thing that symbolizes love. When an earthly father exercises discipline on his child, in most cases it's meant to be is beneficial to the child so that the same wrong actions will not be repeated. Our Heavenly Father operates in the same way. Because God loves us, He disciplines us so we will not commit the same sins or something worse.

Even when seemingly unprovoked trials and tribulations come into our lives, we can benefit from them. Romans 8:28 reads, "And we know that all things work together for good to them that love God, to them who are the called according to his purpose." Truly, when we try to compare what we have to go through to what Jesus endured, we see there is no comparison. He suffered much for us. The question is: What will we suffer through for Him? It is hard for us to lose, to mourn the death of a loved one, to feel the pain of a broken relationship or the discomfort of owing insurmountable debt. Trials will come in this life. Pain will be a part of our pilgrimage. But the good news is that enduring the suffering brings us into new levels of God's consciousness.

3. Believers Must Learn to Accept the Discipline of the Lord (vv. 7–11)

The writer of Hebrews presents yet another reason that believers should cheerfully bear affliction when it comes. Christians are encouraged to endure the discipline of the Lord because it is the mark of the sonship of Christ as well as the way to become more holy and righteous.

The Bible is clear that those who suffer for righteousness' sake glorify God: "Beloved, think it not strange concerning the fiery trial which is to try you, as though some strange thing happened unto you: But rejoice, inasmuch as ye are partakers of Christ's sufferings; that, when his glory shall be revealed, ye may be glad also with exceeding joy" (1 Peter 4:12–13, KJV). Second Timothy 2:12 says, "If we suffer, we shall also reign with him: if we deny him, he also will deny us." The writers insist that we must look on all the hardships of life as the discipline of God sent to work, not for our harm, but for our ultimate and highest good.

It is never pleasant to be corrected and disciplined by God, but His discipline is a sign of His deep love for us. When God corrects you, see it as proof of His love and His ability to lead you in the right direction. Then pray and ask Him what He is working to teach you.

We may respond to the Lord's discipline in several ways. First, we can accept it with resignation. Second, we can accept it with self-pity, thinking we really don't deserve it. Third, we can be angry and resentful toward God. Or, fourth, we can accept it gratefully, which is the appropriate response we owe a loving Father who cares enough about us to point us in the right direction.

Search the Scriptures

1. What should inspire Christians to hold on to their faith (Hebrews 12:1)?

2. Why is our Christianity never to be stationary or stagnant (v. 1)?

3. Who should we model ourselves after (v. 2)?

4. What is the end result of God's chastening (vv. 10–11)?

Discuss the Meaning

1. What makes Jesus a credible leader? How would you have turned out if the Lord had not chastised you? Think about your children or children you know. Imagine how they would grow up without someone to discipline them.

2. Why is it so hard for Christians to adjust to suffering? Have you been told that once you give your life to Jesus, everything will be all right? How have we been anesthetized into believing that children of God are exempt from suffering?

Lesson in Our Society

Before a professional sports team takes the field, it goes through training camp. Training camp is a fiery trial that most players hate. However, veterans and rookies alike must endure training camp in order to learn new plays, to get into shape, and, most importantly, to learn how to become a disciplined and victorious team.

If we Christians are going to be victorious, we have to endure our own version of training camp. God, our coach (leader), wants to turn us into a well-trained and well-disciplined body of believers. To do that, God allows some adversity into our lives. Christians are like tea bags. In order for our rich and robust flavor to come out, we have to be placed in hot water. The Christians in our text were being tested so that their "flavor" would come out.

Make It Happen

Many great biblical and historical characters had to endure much suffering for the causes they supported, whether it was for the spread of Christianity or in the fight for civil rights. Life is a marathon, not a sprint. If we are going to be successful, individually and collectively, we have to keep our eyes on the prize. Individually, that prize is to become like Jesus Christ; collectively, the prize is to make the kingdom of God a reality in our midst.

Commit to following Jesus' example of godly discipline even when times are tough and temptation to sin is great. Continue working toward your goals, never giving up and keeping your eyes on the prize.

Follow the Spirit

What God wants me to do:

_____

_____

_____

_____

Remember Your Thoughts

Special insights I have learned:

_____

_____

_____

_____

More Light on the Text

Hebrews 12:1-11

1 Wherefore seeing we also are compassed about with so great a cloud of witnesses, let us lay aside every weight, and the sin which doth so easily beset us, and let us run with patience the race that is set before us,

In this verse, the "great ... cloud of witnesses" is referring to those persons mentioned in chapter 11. Here, the writer is saying that those who have gone before are examples to others of living the life of faith. God has confirmed their faithfulness, and they can be seen as examples of those who endured. Therefore, in light of our inspiring audience, we must rid ourselves of "every weight" and "run with patience."

The Greek word for "patience" is *hupomone* (**hoo-po-mo-NAY**), derived from two Greek words: *hupo* (**hoo-PO**), meaning "under," and *meno* (**MEN-oh**), meaning "to remain." In other words, the Greek root suggests that by remaining under some trial, we may be molded to fit God's purposes.

2 Looking unto Jesus the author and finisher of our faith; who for the joy that was set before him endured the cross, despising the shame, and is set down at the right hand of the throne of God. 3 For consider him that endured such contradiction of sinners

against himself, lest ye be wearied and faint in your minds.**

To run the race, one must stay focused on Jesus, as implied here by the use of the Greek word *aphorao* (**ah-for-AH-oh**), translated as "looking." To *aphorao* means "to turn the eyes away from other things and fix them on something else"—namely Jesus. We do so because Jesus is the "author" (Gk. *archegos*, **ar-khay-GOSS**), meaning chief leader, and the "finisher" (Gk. *teleiotes*, **tel-i-OT-ace**), which means "perfecter" of faith. In other words, Jesus' life is the perfect example of faith.

The word "endured" comes from *hupomeno* (Gk. **hoop-om-EN-oh**), meaning "to remain or tarry." Jesus chose to remain on the Cross and bear the shame of crucifixion to save humanity. Jesus focused on the future and finished the work of our redemption, bringing many to glory (Hebrews 2:10).

4 Ye have not yet resisted unto blood, striving against sin.

Here, the readers are reminded that although they may have suffered great persecution (Hebrews 10:32–34), none have shed blood and died as Jesus did. None had yet become martyrs because of their confession of Jesus as their Messiah or Savior.

5 And ye have forgotten the exhortation that speaketh unto you as unto children, My son, despise not thou the chastening of the Lord, nor faint when thou art rebuked of him: 6 For whom the Lord loveth he chasteneth, and scourgeth every son he receiveth.

In verses 5 and 6, the author quotes Proverbs 3:11–12. The Lord disciplines those He loves. In these verses, the reader is reminded of the parent-child relationship. Undisciplined children are unloved children. In this instance, the use of the Greek word *paideia* (**pahee-DI-ah**) means "to nurture" or "give instruction." The writer is saying that one should not make light of God's instruction but welcome it as a means of spiritual growth.

7 If ye endure chastening, God dealeth with you as with sons; for what son is he whom the father chasteneth not? 8 But if ye be without chastisement, whereof all are partakers, then are ye bastards, and not sons.

Christians should view trials as a form of divine discipline. Just as a parent would discipline a child so, too, God deals with the sinner. No wise father or mother would allow his or her children to continue exhibiting bad behavior and not correct it. Therefore, receiving discipline can be viewed as a sign of God's fatherly love.

9 Furthermore we have had fathers of our flesh which corrected us, and we gave them reverence: shall we not much rather be in subjection unto the Father of spirits, and live?

God, here, is called "the Father of spirits" (an expression that occurs only here in the New Testament) in contrast to the human "fathers of our flesh." The writer makes a comparison between an earthly father and the Heavenly Father—the argument being, if earthly parents discipline us and we respect them for it over the long run, then we should respect our Heavenly Father even more.

10 For they verily for a few days chastened us after their own pleasure; but he for our profit, that we might be partakers of his holiness.

Verse 10 points out the difference between human and heavenly discipline. The Greek word for "profit" is *sumphero* (**soom-FEHR-oh**), which means "to help, to be profitable or to be expedient." Our earthly parents discipline us "for a few days," whereas God's discipline gives us an eternal benefit. Human discipline is often inconsistent and sometimes provides a temporary benefit. However, the long-range goal in God's discipline is that we might be "partakers" (Gk. *metalambano*, **me-ta-la-hm-BAHN-oh**) of His holiness. Nothing pleases God more than children who grow to emulate Him.

11 Now no chastening for the present seemeth to be joyous, but grievous: nevertheless afterward it yieldeth the peaceable fruit of righteousness unto them which are exercised thereby.

Present discipline seems painful because it is! The purpose of our pain is to produce Christ-like behavior. Sometimes we have to endure painful discipline. The Greek word for "exercised" is *gumnazo* (**goom-NAHD-zoh**), and as used here it implies exercise of the mind in order to endure persecution. God desires for His children to have fruitful lives, and often, that requires pain and sacrifice.

Sources:

Barclay, William. *The Daily Study Bible: The Letter to the Hebrews.* Edinburgh, Scotland: Saint Andrew Press, 1957. 6-7.

Dictionary.com. http://dictionary.reference.com/ (accessed September 7, 2011).

New Testament Greek Lexicon. Bible Study Tools.com. http://www.biblestudytools.com/lexicons/greek (accessed September 7, 2011).

The NIV Study Bible. Grand Rapids, MI: Zondervan Publishing House, 2002. 1916.

Say It Correctly

Beset. bih-**SET**.
Chasten. **CHEY**-suhn.
Exhortation. Eg-zawr-**TEY**-shuhn.

Daily Bible Readings

MONDAY
The Discipline of the Lord
(Job 5:8-18)

TUESDAY
The Death of Sin
(Romans 6:1-11)

WEDNESDAY
The Race for the Prize
(1 Corinthians 9:24-27)

THURSDAY
The Training for Godliness
(1 Timothy 4:6-10)

FRIDAY
The Endurance of the Faithful
(James 5:7-11)

SATURDAY
The Example of Faithfulness
(1 Peter 2:18-25)

SUNDAY
The Pioneer of Faith
(Hebrews 12:1-11)

Notes

_____

_____

_____

_____

Teaching Tips

September 23
Bible Study Guide 4

Words You Should Know

A. Voice (Hebrews 12:19, 26) *phone* (Gk.)—A sound; a tone; speech; the sound of uttered words.

B. Mediator (v. 24) *mesites* (Gk.)—One who intervenes between two others to restore peace and friendship.

Teacher Preparation

Unifying Principle—Steadfast Thanks. The writer of Hebrews says we do not have to fear death because God, in Christ Jesus, brought us forgiveness and the promise of eternal life.

A. Pray and ask God for lesson clarity and that students will seek God's forgiveness and the promise of eternal life.

B. Study and reflect on the entire lesson.

C. Complete the companion lesson in the *Precepts For Living Personal Study Guide*®.

O—Open the Lesson

A. After receiving prayer requests, open class with prayer.

B. Discuss students' fears about death and assurance of God's grace.

C. Ask for a volunteer to read the In Focus story and relate the story to today's Aim for Change.

D. Discuss expressions of God's love and forgiveness.

P—Present the Scriptures

A. Read the Keep in Mind verse collectively.

B. Ask for volunteers to read the Focal Verses.

C. Use the Background, The People, Places, and Times, and In Depth outline to expand the meaning of today's Focal Verses.

E—Explore the Meaning

A. Read and discuss the Make It Happen and Lesson in Our Society sections.

B. Ask the students to suggest ways to share God's forgiveness and the promise of eternal life.

C. Discuss the peace we have because of the assurance of God's grace.

N—Next Steps for Application

A. Instruct students to review the Daily Bible Readings to prepare for next week's class.

B. Close with prayer.

Worship Guide

For the Superintendent or Teacher
Theme: Faith Inspires Gratitude
Song: "Give Thanks with a Grateful Heart"
Devotional Reading:
2 Thessalonians 1:1-7
Prayer

Faith Inspires Gratitude

Bible Background • HEBREWS 12:14-29
Printed Text • HEBREWS 12:18-29 | Devotional Reading • 2 THESSALONIANS 1:1-7

—— Aim for Change ——

By the end of the lesson, we will: KNOW the meaning of God's forgiveness and promise of eternal life; EXPLORE our fears about death and assurances of God's grace; and REPENT for sometimes rejecting God's grace.

—— In Focus ——

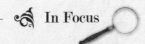

Samuel lay in the hospital bed; he couldn't remember anything. His brother, Phillip, said, "Good morning. It has been almost six days since the accident. Do you remember what happened?" Samuel shook his head.

Phillip said, "You had a stroke while you were driving. Your car just stopped on the side of the road."

Samuel became frustrated when he tried to lift his right hand. As his wife, Sabrina, hugged him, she whispered, "You are paralyzed on your right side. The doctors don't know if it is permanent." Tears ran down Samuel's face.

Each day, Sabrina prayed with Samuel, who was withdrawn. One day, Phillip visited Samuel at the rehabilitation center.

Phillip said, "You know God has His hand in your life. His grace and mercy are so evident. You could be dead, but His grace has allowed you to live. Be thankful!"

Samuel said, "I am not sure. I believe that death would be better than half a life."

Phillip said, "You are blessed with life for a purpose. God's grace has spared you."

God is gracious and merciful. When we experience difficulty in life, we should trust God. In today's lesson, we are reminded to trust God and not fear death but live each day with thankfulness as we experience God's grace.

—— Keep in Mind ——

"Wherefore we receiving a kingdom which cannot be moved, let us have grace, whereby we may serve God acceptably with reverence and godly fear" (Hebrews 12:28).

"Wherefore we receiving a kingdom which cannot be moved, let us have grace, whereby we may serve God acceptably with reverence and godly fear" (Hebrews 12:28).

Focal Verses

KJV **Hebrews 12:18** For ye are not come unto the mount that might be touched, and that burned with fire, nor unto blackness, and darkness, and tempest,

19 And the sound of a trumpet, and the voice of words; which voice they that heard intreated that the word should not be spoken to them any more:

20 (For they could not endure that which was commanded, And if so much as a beast touch the mountain, it shall be stoned, or thrust through with a dart:

21 And so terrible was the sight, that Moses said, I exceedingly fear and quake:)

22 But ye are come unto mount Sion, and unto the city of the living God, the heavenly Jerusalem, and to an innumerable company of angels,

23 To the general assembly and church of the firstborn, which are written in heaven, and to God the Judge of all, and to the spirits of just men made perfect,

24 And to Jesus the mediator of the new covenant, and to the blood of sprinkling, that speaketh better things than that of Abel.

25 See that ye refuse not him that speaketh. For if they escaped not who refused him that spake on earth, much more shall not we escape, if we turn away from him that speaketh from heaven:

26 Whose voice then shook the earth: but now he hath promised, saying, Yet once more I shake not the earth only, but also heaven.

27 And this word, Yet once more, signifieth the removing of those things that are shaken, as of things that are made, that those things which cannot be shaken may remain.

28 Wherefore we receiving a kingdom which cannot be moved, let us have grace, whereby we may serve God acceptably with reverence and godly fear:

29 For our God is a consuming fire.

NLT **Hebrews 12:18** You have not come to a physical mountain, to a place of flaming fire, darkness, gloom, and whirlwind, as the Israelites did at Mount Sinai.

19 For they heard an awesome trumpet blast and a voice so terrible that they begged God to stop speaking.

20 They staggered back under God's command: "If even an animal touches the mountain, it must be stoned to death."

21 Moses himself was so frightened at the sight that he said, "I am terrified and trembling."

22 No, you have come to Mount Zion, to the city of the living God, the heavenly Jerusalem, and to countless thousands of angels in a joyful gathering.

23 You have come to the assembly of God's firstborn children, whose names are written in heaven. You have come to God himself, who is the judge over all things. You have come to the spirits of the righteous ones in heaven who have now been made perfect.

24 You have come to Jesus, the one who mediates the new covenant between God and people, and to the sprinkled blood, which speaks of forgiveness instead of crying out for vengeance like the blood of Abel.

25 Be careful that you do not refuse to listen to the One who is speaking. For if the people of Israel did not escape when they refused to listen to Moses, the earthly messenger, we will certainly not escape if we reject the One who speaks to us from heaven!

26 When God spoke from Mount Sinai his voice shook the earth, but now he makes another promise: "Once again I will shake not only the earth but the heavens also."

27 This means that all of creation will be shaken and removed, so that only unshakable things will remain.

28 Since we are receiving a Kingdom that is unshakable, let us be thankful and please

NLT continued

God by worshiping him with holy fear and awe. **29** For our God is a devouring fire.

The People, Places, and Times

Mosaic Covenant. The Pentateuch (first five books of Old Testament) record the conditions and requirements of the Mosaic Covenant, which was given by God to Moses on Mount Sinai for God's people, the Israelites. Moses was the liaison between God and the Israelites. Moses communicated God's requirements for the covenant and pled Israel's case before God. After God revealed His power and rescued the Israelites from slavery in Egypt, the Mosaic Covenant was conditional based on Israel fulfilling its part of the covenant.

New Covenant. The New Covenant is based on Jesus Christ, the Mediator, who died for the sins of all humanity. Jesus established the New Covenant through His own death and commissioned His disciples and believers to share the Good News about the kingdom of God. Believers will dwell with God in the heavenly city of God, Mount Zion (Sion).

Mount Zion. This is a reference to the heavenly city of God and believers who will dwell with Him. The mountain is available through the blood of Jesus. It is a celebration of the Holy One where angels, believers, and righteous people dwell.

Background

The majority of the earliest believers in Christ were Jews. When Paul went to Jerusalem, he was told, "Many thousands of Jews there are which believe" (Acts 21:20). The number of Jewish Christians grew, but the church communities endured physical and social persecution from the Jews and Romans. Many people were arrested and ostracized because of their faith, and some suffered physically and experienced loss of their property because of their belief. The writer of Hebrews expressed the superiority of Christianity and urged believers to keep their eyes on Jesus. The early believers may have considered returning to Judaism to hold on to the biblical truths. The people needed to remember that Jesus was the Messiah and that He would return. The writer of Hebrews wanted the believers to hold onto their faith and look forward to Jesus' return.

As the believers at the newborn church struggled, disciples who had victoriously run the race gazed at the struggling believers. The writer urged them not to be discouraged by struggles that perfect believers. He also urged them to be very careful and guard against defiling themselves and selling their birthrights, which would result in losing the promises of God. We must remember our actions have lasting consequences. Although we repent and seek God's forgiveness, we cannot eliminate the consequences of sin.

At-A-Glance

1. The Two Mountains: Sinai and Zion
(The Heavenly City)
(Hebrews 12:18-21)
2. The Heavenly City (Zion or Sion)
(vv. 22-23)
3. The Heavenly City and Jesus,
the Mediator (v. 24)
4. Criteria for Entering the Heavenly
City (vv. 25-26)
5. Preparing for the Heavenly City
(vv. 27-29)

In Depth

1. The Two Mountains: Sinai and Zion (The Heavenly City) (Hebrews 12:18-21)

The writer of Hebrews compares the Mosaic Covenant with the New Covenant by examining two mountains: Mount Sinai and Mount Zion. God gave the Law to the Israelites at Mount Sinai with a majestic display of "thunderings, and the lightnings ... they (the people) removed (themselves) and stood afar off" (Exodus 20:18). The people came before God with fear and trembling at Mount Sinai. They feared that speaking directly to God would lead to death.

In contrast, through a New Covenant, Christian believers joyfully approached God through the blood of Jesus on Mount Zion (Sion), which is the Heavenly City of God. While God seemed distant and threatening at Mount Sinai, at Mount Zion, Jesus has made the believer's faith personal. Through Christ, we have the promise of eternal life through forgiveness of our sins. We can accept God's invitation through Christ, receive forgiveness and experience the presence of God.

2. The Heavenly City Zion (or Sion) (vv. 22-23)

Ancient custom approved special treatment for the firstborn son, who received a father's blessings, which was a double portion. In the Old Testament, Joseph received a double inheritance among the sons of Jacob instead of Reuben, who had unacceptable behavior. The firstborn son received special blessings from his earthly father. The heirs in heaven are believers, who are justified and made perfect because they are in heaven, they are "just men made perfect" (Hebrews 12:23). Through Christ, believers will inherit the Kingdom: "Ye shall receive the reward of the inheritance: for ye serve the Lord Christ" (Colossians 3:24). We have the promise of eternal life, our inheritance.

By faith, believers' names are recorded in heaven; they are written in the Lamb's Book of Life. Believers can come to God by faith through Christ, make a supplication, and receive absolution for their sins and justification. We have an eternal home with God in heaven and the blessings of the firstborn. Thus, every believer is an heir with rights and privileges of the firstborn.

3. The Heavenly City and Jesus, the Mediator (v. 24)

Jesus Christ is the mediator or "go-between" uniting two parties: God and sinful humanity. Moses was the mediator of the Mosaic Covenant; he was the liaison between God and the Israelites. Moses gave the Israelites God's Law, instruction, and the obligations for the covenant between God and the Israelites.

In the same vein, Jesus is the mediator for the New Covenant that was established through His sacrificial death on the Cross. He helps believers to remain in a covenant relationship with God. Therefore, through Jesus, humanity prays to God and receives His favor. Jesus pleads our cause before God. The New Covenant of Jesus Christ speaks forgiveness for the believer and new life through Christ, our mediator.

4. Criteria for Entering the Heavenly City (vv. 25-26)

Jesus Christ speaks to humanity and He offers forgiveness through God's grace and mercy. Because we have more knowledge of Christ and the promise of eternal life, "If we turn away from him that speaketh from heaven" we will be judged for our unbelief (Hebrews 12:25). Therefore, our faith in God should inspire our gratitude for all that He's done for us.

When Korah, a Levite who was the tabernacle assistant, instigated a rebellion against Moses and Aaron, God destroyed him. Korah and the other leaders directly challenged Moses and God. As a result, God judged and punished their unbelief. Today, God still judges unbelief. If we do not believe and accept Christ, we refuse Him.

The "whole mountain trembled violently" when God gave the Law at Mount Sinai (Exodus 19:18, NIV). When Christ returns, God will "shake not the earth only, but also heaven" (Hebrews 12:26). The entire universe will shake when the Son of God returns, but the kingdom of God will not be shaken. It will endure through eternity. The power of God will be evident, and everyone will recognize Him.

5. Preparing for the Heavenly City (vv. 27-29)

The writer of Hebrews explains that temporary things will be shaken and removed when Christ returns, while the eternal things will not be moved. The "things which cannot be shaken may remain"; they are eternal (Hebrews 12:27). Only God's kingdom will last.

Believers will endure the shaking and endure through the grace of God. We will receive the kingdom of God that will endure; it is unchanging and cannot be moved. No power on earth or hell can destroy God's kingdom.

The writer encourages believers to "have grace whereby we may serve God acceptably with reverence and godly fear" (Hebrews 12:28). Grace is the unmerited favor of God that offers the gift of salvation to humanity. We can hold to the grace we have received and trust the assurance that we have an eternal home with God. By grace, we serve God with love and respect. If you have rejected God's grace, repent and receive God's love and mercy today. Then accept the gift of His Son with gratitude.

Search the Scriptures

1. How did the blood of Jesus satisfy God's revenge (Hebrews 12:24)?

2. When Jesus returns, the heavens and earth will shake. What and who will remain amid the burning and shaking (v. 27)?

Discuss the Meaning

1. As disciples of the New Covenant, how can we share the meaning of God's forgiveness and the promise of eternal life?

2. Why do people knowingly reject Jesus Christ and God's promise of eternal life?

Lesson in Our Society

According to a recent Gallup poll, 35 percent of Americans said they attend church each week while 20 percent say they do not and 25 percent say they seldom attend. However, the number of African Americans who say they attend church is much greater—53 percent. The economic turmoil has caused an surge in church attendance. Many people turn to God because of fear, judgment, or uncertainty to find security and seek a firm foundation that the world cannot offer. When believers accept Christ, the eternal promise of new life with God outweighs their temporary fears. By faith, we focus on the assurances we have through God's grace. The firm assurances are not based upon the world but upon God's promises. Through God's grace, we can experience God's continual presence. Receive God's grace and experience His presence and His eternal promises.

Make It Happen

The news constantly reports details of natural disasters, economic hardships, and of lives that seem to have little focus on steadfast thankfulness for God. The struggles of life are not the focus in today's lesson. Instead, it is the challenge to be thankful for God's grace even when troubles shake our world. But that grace is only available to those who believe and have accepted Jesus Christ as their Savior. Have you made that decision?

Follow the Spirit

What God wants me to do:

_____

_____

_____

_____

Remember Your Thoughts

Special insights I have learned:

_____

_____

_____

_____

More Light on the Text

Hebrews 12:18-29

18 For ye are not come unto the mount that might be touched, and that burned with fire, nor unto blackness, and darkness, and tempest, 19 And the sound of a trumpet, and the voice of words; which voice they that heard intreated that the word should not be spoken to them any more: 20 (For they could not endure that which was commanded, And if so much as a beast touch the mountain, it shall be stoned, or thrust through with a dart: 21 And so terrible was the sight, that Moses said, I exceedingly fear and quake:)

Beginning from verse 18, the author of Hebrews proceeds to contrast the Jewish and Christian ways by juxtaposing the terrors associated with the giving of the law on Mount Sinai with the joys and the glory associated with Mount Zion. Although the description in verses 18–21 leaves no doubt that the writer has Sinai in mind, he makes no explicit reference to the mountain of revelation. The phenomena listed are all associated with the Sinai event (see Deuteronomy 4:11). Elsewhere, they are all linked with the presence of God: "fire" (Judges 13:20; 1 Kings 18:38), "darkness" (1 Kings 8:12), and "tempest" (Nahum 1:3); the "trumpet" (Hebrews 12:19) are all associated with the end time when God will manifest Himself (Matthew 24:31; 1 Corinthians 15:52; 1 Thessalonians 4:16). The picture is one that strikes terror in the heart. He sounds the note of warning that great privilege means great responsibility.

The Israelites were terrified by the experience. They responded to "a sound of words" by pleading that no further message be given to them (Hebrews 12:19b). The writer's statement summarizes Deuteronomy 5:23–27; it particularly reflects on Deuteronomy 5:25, where the people express the fear that they will be consumed by the fire if they continue to listen to the voice (see Exodus 20:18–19). So they asked that they should hear God's voice no more (Exodus 20:19; Deuteronomy 5:25-27). They were overcome with terror and wanted no further part in the wonderful events. The fearfulness of the giving of the law on

Sinai is brought out with reference to one of the commands laid on the people, namely, that neither man nor beast should even touch the mountain under penalty of death (Exodus 19:13). "The writer [of Hebrews 12:20] focuses upon the most stringent aspect of the command ... 'if even an animal touches the mountain, it shall be stoned,' in order to emphasize the gravity of the injunction and the peril of coming before the annihilating holiness of the divine appearing" (Lane, 463). In effect, the command that nothing touch it indicates the holiness of the mountain. Judgment for anyone who ignores the holiness of God is swift and terrible.

Hebrews 12:21 is a further indication of the awe of it all. At the time of the giving of the law, Moses was the leader of the people. He was known as one who had an especially close relationship with God (Exodus 33:11). Yet, even he was terrified. It was a scary occasion, one that affected all the people and terrified even Moses, the man of God.

22 But ye are come unto mount Sion, and unto the city of the living God, the heavenly Jerusalem, and to an innumerable company of angels, 23 To the general assembly and church of the firstborn, which are written in heaven, and to God the Judge of all, and to the spirits of just men made perfect, 24 And to Jesus the mediator of the new covenant, and to the blood of sprinkling, that speaketh better things than that of Abel.

"But" is the strong conjunction that (Gk. *alla*, **al-LAH**) and introduces a marked contrast. Christians order their lives in accordance with a different revelation. Scholar William Lane writes, "In sharp contradistinction from the scene at Sinai, every aspect of this vision provides encouragement for coming boldly into the presence of God (see 4:16). The atmosphere at Mount Zion is festive. The frightening visual imagery of blazing fire, darkness, and gloom fades before the reality of the city of the living God, heavenly Jerusalem. The cacophony of whirlwind, trumpet blast, and a sound of words is muted and replaced by the joyful praise of angels in a festal gathering. The trembling congregation of Israel ... is superseded by the assembly of those whose names are permanently inscribed in the heavenly archives. An overwhelming impression of the distant God is eclipsed in the experience of full access to the presence of God and of Jesus, the mediator of the new covenant" (Lane, 464-465).

The destination of the Christian pilgrims is described by various evocative images. First, they are "come unto" Mount Zion (Hebrews 12:22). This is to be understood not as the seat of temporal Israel but as a reference to God's eschatological rule through Christ, just as in Revelation 14:1-5. Second, Hebrews 12:22 states that they have come to the "city of the living God," a city with foundations that the patriarchs looked forward to and one that is eternal (13:14). The book of Revelation also uses this image for God's presence, when it speaks of a "holy city" (21:2; 22:19). Third, Hebrews 12:22 says they have come to the "heavenly Jerusalem" a designation that is called "new Jerusalem" in Revelation 3:12.

It does not go without notice that the city of God is filled with life and contains a more vibrant, dynamic, and powerful sort than is available on earth. Hebrews 12:22 says there are "innumerable" or "countless numbers" (Gk. *murias*, **moo-REE-as**) of angels who are present as part of the welcoming and celebratory throng. Then we have the church of the firstborn. In verse 23, the Greek word *ekklesia* (**ek-klay-SEE-ah**), translated as "church," is taken from the common civic life of the Greeks and normally refers to the official gathering of the officials or their representatives. The "firstborn" (Gk. *prototokia*, **pro-tot-OK-ee-ah**) probably refers to all those "sons" whom God is leading into glory together with Jesus (Hebrews 2:10). Understood this way, it means "the spirits of just men made perfect" (12:23), or the spirits of righteous people. It is another way of describing the same participants in the true inheritance, which is a participation in God's holiness. In summation, the city of God is filled with angels and saints. The climax is reached in verse 24 with the reference to Jesus, seen here as "the mediator of a new covenant." The author does not only affirm the humanity of Jesus and His role as mediator but also places Him definitively at God's side, a place that was His from the beginning (Hebrews 1:1-4). Jesus' blood speaks "a better word" than that of Abel (12:24, NIV). His blood opens up a way into the holiest for people (10:19).

25 See that ye refuse not him that speaketh. For if they escaped not who refused him that spake on earth, much more shall not we escape, if we turn away from him that speaketh from heaven: 26 Whose voice then shook the earth: but now he hath promised, saying, Yet once more I shake not the earth only, but also heaven. 27 And this word, Yet once more, signifieth the removing of those things that are shaken, as of things that are made, that those things which cannot be shaken may remain. 28 Wherefore we receiving a kingdom which cannot be moved, let us have grace, whereby we may serve God acceptably with reverence and godly fear: 29 For our God is a consuming fire.

The transition from exposition in Hebrews 12:18–24 to exhortation in verses 25–29 is abrupt, and the author, with a sharp change in tone, resumes the expression of urgent concern that characterizes verses 14–17. Here, the sternness of the warning is justified by the detailing of the privileged status of Christians in verses 18-24. They have a qualitatively greater responsibility than Israel did to listen attentively to the voice of God. Those who deliberately ignore the eschatological revelation of God through his Son and who show contempt for the blessings of the New Covenant cannot possibly escape judgment. The concluding paragraph consists of a sober caution to listen to what God is saying, a concentration of His word in the form of prophecy, and a final admonition to respond appropriately with gratitude and worship. A tendency toward apathy or complacency is sharply rebuked with the phrase, "Be careful that you do not refuse to listen to the One who is speaking" (12:25, NLT). The form of the statement recalls 3:12, and it connotes a deliberate and culpable refusal to listen to the one speaking. The readers must also be aware that the greater the gift, the greater the responsibility, and the greater the peril involved in its rejection.

In 12:26, the author goes on to recall the solemnity of the events at Sinai. Repeatedly, we are told that then the earth shook (Exodus 19:18; Judges 5:4-5; Psalm 68:8; 77:18; 114:4, 7). The writer of Hebrews has already spoken of the awe-inspiring nature of what happened when the law was given. Now, the reference to the shaking of the earth brings it all back. At the same time, it enables him to go on to speak of a promise that involved a further shaking that is recorded in Haggai 2:6. The prophet looked forward to something much grander than Sinai. Then God shook the earth, but Haggai foresaw a day when God would shake "not only the earth but also the heavens" (Hebrews 12:26, NLT). This will be no small event but one of cosmic grandeur. The reference to heaven and earth may be meant to hint at the concept of the new heaven and the new earth (Isaiah 66:22). At any rate, it points to the decisive intervention that God will make at the last time.

In Hebrews 12:27, the writer uses the expression "yet once more" (Gk. *eti hapax*, **ET-ee HAP-ax**) to point out the decisive significance of the things of which he is writing. There is an air of finality about it all. God is going to make a radical and final change. This is the decisive time. This physical creation can be shaken, and it is set in contrast to what cannot be shaken. These are the things that really matter, the things that have the character of permanence. The author does not go into detail about the precise nature of the ultimate rest. But whatever it may be, it will separate the things that last forever from those that do not. It is God's will for this final differentiation to be made so that only what cannot be shaken will remain. As Donald Guthrie notes, what the writer is "concerned to demonstrate is that the Christian position, unlike the era of the Mosaic law, leads to a state of absolute stability" (Guthrie, 265).

The ultimate reality of God's sovereignty is evident in verse 28. Believers have received the kingdom of God, which cannot be shaken. The Kingdom is something we "receive." It is not earned or created by believers; it is God's gift. Although undefined, like in the Gospels, the Kingdom is in stark contrast with earthly systems that can be shaken and in due course will be shaken. This is untrue of God's kingdom! The author does not simply say that it will not be shaken but that it cannot be. It has a quality found in nothing earthly. It is on the strength of this that the writer gives two exhortations:

"*let us have grace*" and "*serve God acceptably with reverence and godly fear*" (emphasis added). The exhortations could also be understood to mean, "Let us be thankful, and let us offer acceptable worship to God." The latter meaning is preferred. The appropriate response to the gift we have received is gratitude to God and acceptable worship, that is, in living a life that is pleasing to God. The qualification "with reverence and godly fear" constitutes a sober reminder of the holy character of God.

The chapter concludes with an expression apparently taken from Deuteronomy 4:24. The author of Hebrews 12 emphasizes that God is not to be trifled with. It is easy to be so taken up with the love and compassion of God that we overlook His implacable opposition to all evil. The wrath of God is not always a popular subject today, but it looms large in biblical teaching. Because God is in fact a consuming fire, we do best to come to Him on His terms.

Sources:
Bible Places.com. http://www.bibleplaces.com (accessed September 7, 2011).
Bruce, F. F. *The Epistle to the Hebrews, Revised: New International Commentary on the New Testament.* Grand Rapids, MI: Eerdmans. Reprint, 1985.
Dictionary.com. http://dictionary.reference.com/ (accessed September 7, 2011).
Guthrie, Donald. *Tyndale New Testament Commentaries: Letter to the Hebrews.* Grand Rapids, MI: Eerdmans, 1983. 265.
Johnson, Luke Timothy. *Hebrews: A Commentary. The New Testament Library.* Louisville, KY: Westminster John Knox Press, 2006.
Keener, Craig S. *The IVP Bible Background Commentary: New Testament.* Downers Grove, IL: InterVarsity Press, 1993. 599, 678-682.
Lane, William L. *Hebrews 9-13. Word Biblical Commentary, Vol. 47B.* Dallas, TX: Word Inc., 1991. 463-465.
Life Application Study Bible, King James Version. Wheaton, IL: Tyndale House Publishers, Inc., 1997. 2115-2120, 2177-2178.
New Testament Greek Lexicon. Bible Study Tools.com. http://www.biblestudytools.com/lexicons/greek (accessed September 7, 2011).
NIV Archaeological Study Bible. Grand Rapids, MI: Zondervan, 2005. 1949-1951, 1996-1998.

Say It Correctly

Moses. **MOH**-ziz, -zis.
Zion. **ZI**-uhn.

Daily Bible Readings

MONDAY
Listening to the Voice of Warning
(Ezekiel 33:1–9)

TUESDAY
Listening to the Spirit
(Revelation 3:1–13)

WEDNESDAY
Anticipating a Better Covenant
(Hebrews 8:1–7)

THURSDAY
Giving Thanks for the Faithful
(2 Thessalonians 1:1–7)

FRIDAY
Loving with God's Kind of Love
(Matthew 5:43–48)

SATURDAY
Pursuing Peace and Holiness
(Hebrews 12:12–17)

SUNDAY
Offering Acceptable Worship
(Hebrews 12:18–29)

Notes

Teaching Tips

Words You Should Know

A. Brotherly love (Hebrews 13:1) *philadelphia* (Gk.)—Mutual love.

B. Tongues (1 Corinthians 13:1, 8) *glossa* (Gk.)—Has the simple idea of "languages."

Teacher Preparation

Unifying Principle—Steadfast Love. People search for a workable and reliable definition of love. The writers of Hebrews and 1 Corinthians define love and tell us that it is greater than faith and hope.

A. Pray for your students and lesson clarity.

B. Read and study the entire lesson.

C. Pray the Aim for Change for yourself and your students.

D. Complete the companion lesson in the *Precepts For Living Study Guide*®.

E. Bring pictures or prepare a PowerPoint presentation on the many different ways that people show love.

O—Open the Lesson

A. Open the class with prayer, after receiving prayer requests.

B. Have students silently read the In Focus story. Discuss.

C. Ask: What are some of the ways that you show love? Let volunteers share.

D. Share your pictures or PowerPoint.

P—Present the Scriptures

A. Tie the Aim for Change objectives into the Unifying Principle. Discuss.

B. Have volunteers read the In Focus verses.

C. Use the Background, The People, Places, and Times, At-A-Glance outline, and In Depth to introduce the lesson.

OCT
30th

E—Explore the Meaning

A. Have volunteers respond to the Discuss the Meaning questions.

B. Summarize the type of love that Christ has for the Church and believers should have for each other (*agape*).

N—Next Steps for Application

A. Summarize the lesson.

B. Allow students to write salient points under Follow the Spirit and Remember Your Thoughts.

C. Close with prayer.

Worship Guide

For the Superintendent or Teacher
Theme: Faith Requires Mutual Love
Song: "They Will Know We Are Christians by Our Love"
Devotional Reading: John 13:31-35
Prayer

Faith Requires Mutual Love

Bible Background • HEBREWS 13:1-6; 1 CORINTHIANS 13
Printed Text • HEBREWS 13:1-3; 1 CORINTHIANS 13 | Devotional Reading • JOHN 13:31-35

Aim for Change

By the end of the lesson, we will: DEFINE Christian love and discuss its implications; REFLECT on the ways we experience Christian love in our lives; and PRACTICE love as it is rooted in our faith in Christ.

In Focus

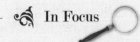

Gayle was president of the church's Usher Board. She was always on time, impeccably uniformed and knew all of the hand signals. Whenever Gayle was on duty, the members had their envelopes and fans before they requested them; she would immediately move forward when she heard crying babies—firmly removing them from their parents' arms and delivering them to the nursery so the services could proceed quietly.

As she moved about the sanctuary this morning, Gayle was clearly irritated. She had met with the pastor on Saturday afternoon, and he had been critical of her work. The pastor had complimented Gayle on her faithfulness and dedication. He had even praised her as one of his most reliable members. However, the pastor had gone on to tell her that while it appeared that she clearly enjoyed being an usher unfortunately, he was concerned that she didn't love the members.

Nothing can replace our love for others. Working on their behalf is fine, but it is meaningless unless our work is motivated by love. In today's lesson, we will see how Christian love is essential to effective ministry.

Keep in Mind

"And now abideth faith, hope, charity, these three; but the greatest of these is charity" (1 Corinthians 13:13).

"And now abideth faith, hope, charity, these three; but the greatest of these is charity" (1 Corinthians 13:13).

Focal Verses

KJV **Hebrews 13:1** Let brotherly love continue.

2 Be not forgetful to entertain strangers: for thereby some have entertained angels unawares.

3 Remember them that are in bonds, as bound with them; and them which suffer adversity, as being yourselves also in the body.

1 Corinthians 13:1 Though I speak with the tongues of men and of angels, and have not charity, I am become as sounding brass, or a tinkling cymbal.

2 And though I have the gift of prophecy, and understand all mysteries, and all knowledge; and though I have all faith, so that I could remove mountains, and have not charity, I am nothing.

3 And though I bestow all my goods to feed the poor, and though I give my body to be burned, and have not charity, it profiteth me nothing.

4 Charity suffereth long, and is kind; charity envieth not; charity vaunteth not itself, is not puffed up,

5 Doth not behave itself unseemly, seeketh not her own, is not easily provoked, thinketh no evil;

6 Rejoiceth not in iniquity, but rejoiceth in the truth;

7 Beareth all things, believeth all things, hopeth all things, endureth all things.

8 Charity never faileth: but whether there be prophecies, they shall fail; whether there be tongues, they shall cease; whether there be knowledge, it shall vanish away.

9 For we know in part, and we prophesy in part.

10 But when that which is perfect is come, then that which is in part shall be done away.

11 When I was a child, I spake as a child, I understood as a child, I thought as a child:

NLT **Hebrews 13:1** Keep on loving each other as brothers and sisters.

2 Don't forget to show hospitality to strangers, for some who have done this have entertained angels without realizing it!

3 Remember those in prison, as if you were there yourself. Remember also those being mistreated, as if you felt their pain in your own bodies.

1 Corinthians 13:1 If I could speak all the languages of earth and of angels, but didn't love others, I would only be a noisy gong or a clanging cymbal.

2 If I had the gift of prophecy, and if I understood all of God's secret plans and possessed all knowledge, and if I had such faith that I could move mountains, but didn't love others, I would be nothing.

3 If I gave everything I have to the poor and even sacrificed my body, I could boast about it; but if I didn't love others, I would have gained nothing.

4 Love is patient and kind. Love is not jealous or boastful or proud

5 or rude. It does not demand its own way. It is not irritable, and it keeps no record of being wronged.

6 It does not rejoice about injustice but rejoices whenever the truth wins out.

7 Love never gives up, never loses faith, is always hopeful, and endures through every circumstance.

8 Prophecy and speaking in unknown languages and special knowledge will become useless. But love will last forever!

9 Now our knowledge is partial and incomplete, and even the gift of prophecy reveals only part of the whole picture!

10 But when the time of perfection comes, these partial things will become useless.

KJV continued

but when I became a man, I put away childish things.

12 For now we see through a glass, darkly; but then face to face: now I know in part; but then shall I know even as also I am known.

13 And now abideth faith, hope, charity, these three; but the greatest of these is charity.

NLT continued

11 When I was a child, I spoke and thought and reasoned as a child. But when I grew up, I put away childish things.

12 Now we see things imperfectly like puzzling reflections in a mirror, but then we will see everything with perfect clarity. All that I know now is partial and incomplete, but then I will know everything completely, just as God now knows me completely.

13 Three things will last forever—faith, hope, and love—and the greatest of these is love.

The People, Places, and Times

Corinth. Located in southern Greece, about 50 miles from Athens, the Corinth of the ancient world was actually a city that had been destroyed by Rome in 146 B.C., and then rebuilt by the emperor, Julius Caesar in 46-45 B.C. A Roman colony, Corinth was the capital of the province of Achaia.

Corinth was socially, culturally, and religiously diverse. In fact, in 49 A.D. a good number of Jews who were expelled from Rome resettled in Corinth. The Christians of Corinth reflected the diversity of the city. Congregations included the wealthy, merchants, slaves, and former slaves.

Corinth was home to numerous temples dedicated to pagan gods and goddesses including Apollo, Hermes, Isis, Poseidon, and the Pantheon, which is a temple dedicated to all of the gods. When Paul arrived in Corinth (about A.D. 50) the city's reputation for immorality was widely recognized. The infamous temple of Aphrodite had fallen into ruins but was home to hundreds of "temple prostitutes," making it popular with the numerous sailors visiting the city. The Greek word *korinthiazesthai,* which means to live like a Corinthian, meant that one lived immorally.

Background

In Paul's letter to the believers in Corinth, we see the challenges that faced the early church. Corinth was a large metropolis with a diverse population. The house churches that the Corinthian Christians worshiped in reflected the city's diversity. One issue Paul addressed to the Corinthians was unity among themselves, emphasizing the importance of their relationships with one another.

At-A-Glance

1. A Plea for Brotherly Love (Hebrews 13:1-3)
2. Love Is the Basis of Our Faith (1 Corinthians 13:1-3)
3. Love Is the Proof of Our Gifts (vv. 4-7)
4. Love Is Permanent (vv. 8-13)

In Depth

1. A Plea for Brotherly Love (Hebrews 13:1-3)

The Scripture opens with "Let brotherly love continue." Our world is full of hurting people, who in turn only know how to hurt other people. As a result, our newspapers and online and TV news reports are full of stories detailing terrible murders and horrific assaults committed by and on people in every age group. Thank God that believers who have found forgiveness through the blood of Jesus Christ have a new and divine nature. Because of Christ's forgiveness, we are capable of loving others in a deeper and more spiritual way. We are now capable of loving the way that God loves us. However, this capacity to love one another must be exercised. Each day, we have to plead, "Not my will, Lord, but Thine be done" (see Matthew 26:39). It is our love for God that must be the source of our love for others.

We want to remember that verse 1 is not a request nor a mere suggestion. This reminds us that there is a possibility for our love for one another to stop. Two possible reasons are failure to ask for forgiveness when we sin and refusing to forgive someone who hurts us. In his Sermon on the Mount, Jesus taught us to ask God to "forgive us our debts, as we forgive our debtors" (Matthew 6:12).

Hebrews 13:3 hearkens to customs of the Ancient Near East. In that time, people traveled great distances on foot. It was a common practice for a family to provide a meal and night's lodging to traveling strangers. Our world is very different today, and the expectation to open one's doors to a stranger hardly seems reasonable. We can, however, ask God to provide us with opportunities to assist strangers and share with them. Hospitality is a hallmark of Christianity. We want to show the same grace and kindness toward strangers that God has shown toward us. Jesus taught that, "Inasmuch as ye have done it unto one of the least of these my brethren, ye have done it unto me" (Matthew 25:40).

Hebrews 13:3 offers yet another motivation for our Christian hospitality. The Scripture says that in doing this, we might be visited by an angel. The Old Testament has many accounts of people who were visited by angels of God. However the word "angel" translated here means a "messenger" and not necessarily a "divine" creature. While a present-day angel may never actually visit most saints, God's human messengers will most certainly visit us when we express Christian hospitality.

2. Love Is the Basis of Our Faith (1 Corinthians 13:1-3)

We want to remember that when Paul wrote this letter, he was keenly aware of the Corinthians' fascination with the "gifts of the Spirit." They were attracted to knowledge, prophecy, and speaking in tongues. Paul is teaching that these gifts were meaningless without love. When Paul speaks of "charity" we should read that word as "love." More importantly, we should know that Paul is speaking of a specific form of love. He is not talking about *eros,* or the sensuous or erotic form of love. Nor is Paul describing *philia,* which means "a brotherly affection or friendship." Rather, Paul is describing *agape,* "a commitment of the will to cherish and uphold another person." In the Bible, this is the form of love that is always used when we describe God's love. *Agape* describes our willful and deliberate decision to treat others with the utmost care and concern and allows us to esteem the best interests of our brother or sister above our own.

We must remember that this form of love is only possible when we love God first. Without this, the love toward one another is a sham, a mere imitation.

This prerequisite is demonstrated in the Scripture when we read that there are two great commandments. The first is, "Thou shalt love the Lord thy God with all thy heart, and with all thy soul, and with all thy mind, and with all thy strength." The second is, "Thou shalt love thy neighbor as thyself" (Matthew 22:37, 39; Mark 12:30-31; Luke 10:27).

When Paul speaks of "tongues of men and angels," he is not primarily describing "glossolalia," or speaking in tongues. Rather, he is saying that it is more important to act lovingly than to be able to speak all the languages of heaven or earth that definitely includes the conduct of those who practiced glossolalia. Without love, Paul is saying, the ability to communicate is useless. Similarly, Paul tells us that if he was able to explain all the mysteries of the Scriptures, but he wasn't a loving person, it would be meaningless.

3. Love Is the Proof of Our Gifts (vv. 4-7)

Contrary to what many of us believe, love is not an ethereal (heavenly) notion. Love is practical and must be put into practice on a daily basis. Christians must constantly measure their love and ask themselves, "Did I show love in that situation or toward that person?" And, more importantly, "Am I growing?" Paul shows that love can indeed be measured and that love results in characteristics that can be seen and heard.

4. Love Is Permanent (vv. 8-13)

True love will produce patience, kindness, and honesty. As Christians we have to identify and remove things from our lives that prohibit us from being able to manifest these qualities of love. Paul identifies these hindrances as jealousy, boastfulness, resentment, and ill temperament. He understood that when Jesus returned, sin and death would end. He knew that the gifts of the Spirit would no longer be needed. Paul uses two analogies to support this. First, it would be unimaginable to think that a mature adult would resort to childlike behavior. Secondly, an actual portrayal of a person could never be obtained by looking at a reflection of poor quality. Paul was teaching the Corinthians and us that when Christ returns, Christians would have direct access to Him. Our relationship with Him will be personal and intimate. Paul was trying to dispel the Corinthians' pride in temporary supernatural gifts. Much of Paul's ministry had been spent teaching about the importance of faith and hope. Now, he places love right alongside them, and in fact, elevates love above the others.

Search the Scriptures

1. According to Paul, what is necessary for any service or ministry to be of value (1 Corinthians 13:3)?

2. After our spiritual gifts cease to exist, what will remain (v. 13)?

Discuss the Meaning

If all spiritual gifts are predicated on love, why do some workers within the churches seem to believe or behave as though it is not essential to Christian ministry efforts?

Lesson in Our Society

Paul makes it clear that for the believer, love is the key. It is love that enables us to reproduce the very character of Jesus Christ in our lives and in our ministry efforts. It is only when we have love that we can access the other "fruit of the Spirit." Without love, we cannot genuinely be patient, peaceful, good, gentle, or display any of the other qualities. We may be able to imitate them, but without love, they won't be a part of our character; nor will we be able to fully embrace them in order to do the Kingdom-building work Christ has commissioned us to do.

Make It Happen

We are often frustrated in our work in the churches. Sometimes it feels as though others are not as committed as we are. Over the next week, pray and ask God to reveal to you areas where you may have failed to demonstrate love toward your co-laborers. Then, ask God what you can do to remedy the situation. Also ask Him how to show love to those who don't show it to you. It may call for you to make apologies and seek forgiveness and forgive others.

Follow the Spirit

What God wants me to do:

_____

_____

_____

_____

Remember Your Thoughts

Special insights I have learned:

_____

_____

_____

_____

More Light on the Text

Hebrews 13:1-3; 1 Corinthians 13:1-13

Hebrews 13:1 Let brotherly love continue. 2 Be not forgetful to entertain strangers: for thereby some have entertained angels unawares. 3 Remember them that are in bonds, as bound with them; and them which suffer adversity, as being yourselves also in the body.

The instructions in these verses are about life in the community and flow directly from Hebrews 12:28, which called for a giving of thanks and a worship that is acceptable to God. It is striking that the service of God is not in a vacuum but is expressed by moral dispositions and behaviors in common. "Brotherly love," or "mutual love" (Gk. *philadelphia*, **fil-ad-el-FEE-ah**), the first practice that the author enjoins in Hebrews 13:1, is an important virtue in the New Testament. It is a Christian ideal as we see in Romans 12:10; 1 Thessalonians 4:9; 1 Peter 1:22; 1 Peter 2:17. "Brotherly love" is not merely a matter of sentiment but involves a set of dispositions and practices and is intensely practical. It involves meeting the needs of others through a mutual sharing of possessions and activities. An affectionate love for fellow Christians not only restrains us from tripping them up but also prompts us to give them every encouragement possible. The author's play on words in the use of the imperative *meno* (**MEN-o**), literally, "remain" translated in Hebrews 13:1 as "continue" is insightful. As opposed to other things that will be shaken, love must remain.

To "brotherly love," the author adds "hospitality" (Gk. *philoxenia*, **fil-on-ex-NEE-ah**) or "love of strangers," a concrete expression of mutual love. It was highly esteemed in the ancient world and was certainly very important for Christians. The verse is better understood against the backdrop of itinerant preachers in the New Testament. Inns, or what we know as hotels, were expensive and had bad reputations. But as Christian preachers traveled, believers housed them and so facilitated their mission. Without hospitality in Christian homes, the spread of the faith would have been much more difficult.

The author takes an additional step concerning practical love by turning his attention to prisoners. In the early days of Christianity, many believers were unjustly jailed because of their faith in Christ. The readers were probably tempted to ignore and neglect their colleagues, who were in chains, because of the associated shame. In the first century, prisoners were not well treated, and they often depended on sympathizers, even for necessities such as food. Sometimes people withheld help for fear of identifying themselves with the prisoners and suffering similar punishment. But Christians should have compassion on those in prison "as if you were their fellow prisoners" (Hebrews 13:3, NIV). But as Paul writes, "If one part suffers, every part suffers with it" (1 Corinthians 12:26, NIV); there is something of the same thought here.

1 Corinthians 13:1 Though I speak with the tongues of men and of angels, and have not charity, I am become as sounding brass, or a tinkling cymbal. 2 And though I have the gift of prophecy, and understand all mysteries, and all knowledge; and though I have all faith, so that I could remove mountains, and have not charity, I am nothing. 3 And though I bestow all my goods to feed the poor, and though I give my body to be burned, and have not charity, it profiteth me nothing.

The Corinthian Christians were fascinated with spiritual gifts, particularly the gift of tongues, but Paul reminds them that the gifts are worthless without love. The Greek word *glossa* (**gloce-SAH**), translated "tongues" has the simple idea of "languages" in some places (Acts 2:11; Revelation 5:9). Its usage here refers to a supernatural language by which a believer communicates with God (Adewuya, 95). This is the only way the reference to "tongues ... of angels" can be understood in this context (1 Corinthians 13:1). Paul goes on to say that prophecy, knowledge, and faith to do miracles are likewise irrelevant apart from love. Giving oneself to be burnt is a barren gesture unless it is inspired by love. Paul's point is clear: The Corinthian Christians were missing the motive and the goal of the gifts, making the means to become their own end. But for Paul, love trumps all. Also, for Paul, it is not an issue of love versus the gifts; neither must it be for us. Paul is stressing the focus and end of the gifts: love, not the gifts for their own sake. For gifts to be effectual, love must guide their use.

4 Charity suffereth long, and is kind; charity envieth not; charity vaunteth not itself, is not puffed up, 5 Doth not behave itself unseemly, seeketh not her own, is not easily provoked, thinketh no evil; 6 Rejoiceth not in iniquity, but rejoiceth in the truth; 7 Beareth all things, believeth all things, hopeth all things, endureth all things.

In 1 Corinthians 13:4-7, Paul shows a life characterized by love. The word *agape* is often used of God's love, not ordinary human love. Paul's description of the characteristics of love is a matter of other-directed behavior described with action words. Love suffers long. It is the type of love that characterizes God (2 Peter 3:9). If God's love is in us, we will be longsuffering to those who annoy us and hurt us. Love is kind. Kindness is demonstrated in simple acts, such as giving a cup of water to the thirsty (Matthew 25:42).

In 1 Corinthians 13:4b-6, Paul enumerates the negative characteristics of love. Love does not envy. Whereas jealousy says, "I would like to have what you have," envy says, "I wish you did not have what you have." Envy is one of the least productive and most damaging of all sins to those who allow it. It accomplishes nothing, except to hurt the one who harbors it. But love keeps its distance from envy, and does not resent it when someone else makes progress. Love does not parade itself: Love in action can work anonymously. It does not have to have the limelight or the attention to do a good job or to be satisfied with the result. Love gives because it loves to give, not out of the sense of praise it can have from showing itself off.

Love is not puffed up. To be puffed up is to be arrogant and self-focused. It speaks of someone who has a "big head." Love does not get its head swelled; it focuses on the needs of others. Love does not behave rudely, that is, is not ill-mannered or brash. Where there is love, there will be kindness and good manners. A person who loves does not just speak his or her mind but minds his or her speech. Love does not seek its own, an idea that Paul expresses in a slightly different manner in Romans 12:10 and Philippians 2:4. This is being like Jesus in a most basic way: being an others-centered person instead of a self-centered person.

Love is not easily provoked. This is perhaps the most difficult to understand among the characteristics of love. In plain language, love is neither touchy nor irritable. Love thinks no evil. It does not store up the memory or keep an account of any wrong

it has received. It puts away the hurts of the past instead of clinging to them.

Love does not rejoice in iniquity: "I told you so," and "It serves you right," are familiar but don't reflect the language of love. Love desires the best for others and does not derive personal satisfaction from the failure of others. Instead, love rejoices in the truth.

Paul ends the discussion of the characteristics of love on a positive note, stating the things that love does. It bears all things, believes all things, hopes all things, and endures all things. The Greek word *pantos* (**PAHN-toce**), translated "all" can also be interpreted as "always" (1 Corinthians 13:7). Paul's point is that love never tires of support, never loses faith, never gives up hope, and never gives up. Most of us can bear all things and believe all things and hope all things but only for a while! The greatness of *agape* is that it keeps on bearing, believing, and hoping. It does not give up.

8 Charity never faileth: but whether there be prophecies, they shall fail; whether there be tongues, they shall cease; whether there be knowledge, it shall vanish away.

The verse begins the concluding paragraph of the chapter. Here, Paul attests to the permanence of love as he continues to put the spiritual gifts and virtues in perspective. Love never fails. Paul is addressing the over-emphasis of the Corinthian Christians on the other gifts of the Holy Spirit. He shows that they should emphasize love more than the gifts because the gifts are temporary "containers" of God's work; love is the work itself.

9 For we know in part, and we prophesy in part. 10 But when that which is perfect is come, then that which is in part shall be done away. 11 When I was a child, I spake as a child, I understood as a child, I thought as

a child: but when I became a man, I put away childish things. 12 For now we see through a glass, darkly; but then face to face: now I know in part; but then shall I know even as also I am known. 13 And now abideth faith, hope, charity, these three; but the greatest of these is charity.

Paul gives the reason why other gifts apart from love will cease. Those gifts, such as tongues, prophecy, or knowledge, are specifically meant to equip the believer to endure in this age. In due time, they will be brought to nothing. The milieu in which they operate will one day come to an end and will be superseded by a situation in which they totally become unnecessary or inappropriate. Paul likens the situation to that of growing up. There is a life appropriate to a child, which is manifested in thought, speech, and reasoning power. But when adulthood arrives, these characteristics are no longer viable and, as such, must be left behind. Tongues will cease when the Lord returns and completes His plan for Christians. Partial knowledge, such as the Corinthians and Christians now have, will be brought to nothing; not so with love. Therefore, all gifts except love can be characterized as partial.

In mistaking the part for the whole and the partial for the final, the Corinthian Christians, unlike Paul, are childish. It is wrong to suggest that verses 11-12 sees tongue speaking and prophecy as childishness, particularly considering Paul, himself, claims to do both. What Paul is saying is that there is an appropriate age to do so and that now is that age. When the completion of that age finally arrives, then it will be time to set aside what was appropriate and needful for that age. For Paul, the three great pursuits of the Christian life are not miracles, power, and gifts. Though the gifts are precious and given by the Holy Spirit,

they were never meant to be the focus or goal of our Christian lives. Instead, we must pursue faith, hope, and love.

In conclusion, it is fitting to say that Paul's discussion in the chapter is not only powerful but also heart-searching. It calls for a careful examination of our motivation for service. There is a reason Paul put this chapter in the midst of his discussion of spiritual gifts. He wants the Corinthian Christians to remember that giftedness is not the measure of maturity; the display of love is.

Sources:

Adewuya, J. Ayodeji. *A Commentary on 1 & 2 Corinthians.* London: SPCK, 2009. 95.

Bruce, F. F. *The Epistle to the Hebrews, Revised: New International Commentary on the New Testament.* Grand Rapids, MI: Eerdmans. Reprint, 1985.

"Corinth at the Time of Paul's Arrival." Global Ministries, United Methodist Women. http://gbgm-umc.org/umw/corinthians/city.stm (accessed September 13, 2011).

Dictionary.com. http://dictionary.reference.com/ (accessed September 13, 2011).

Guthrie, Donald. *Tyndale New Testament Commentaries: Letter to the Hebrews.* Grand Rapids, MI: Eerdmans, 1983.

Johnson, Luke Timothy. *Hebrews: A Commentary. The New Testament Library.* Louisville, KY: Westminster John Knox Press, 2006.

Lane, William L. *Hebrews 9-13. Word Biblical Commentary, Vol. 47B.* Dallas, TX: Word Inc., 1991.

New Testament Greek Lexicon. Bible Study Tools.com. http://www.biblestudytools.com/lexicons/greek (accessed September 13, 2011).

Padfield, David. "The Biblical City of Corinth," 2005. http://www.padfield.com/acrobat/history/corinth.pdf (accessed September 13, 2011).

Say It Correctly

Corinth. **KAWR**-inth, **KOR**-inth.
Hermes. **HUR**-meez.
Poseidon. poh-**SI**-duhn.
Pantheon. **PAN**-thee-on, -uhn

Daily Bible Readings

MONDAY
I Love You, O Lord
(Psalm 18:1–6)

TUESDAY
Faithful Love
(Deuteronomy 7:7–11)

WEDNESDAY
Obedient Love
(Deuteronomy 5:6–10)

THURSDAY
Taught to Love
(Deuteronomy 6:1–9)

FRIDAY
Love One Another
(John 13:31–35)

SATURDAY
Love Your Enemies
(Luke 6:27–36)

SUNDAY
Faith, Hope, and Love
(Hebrews 13:1–3; 1 Corinthians 13)

Notes

Teaching Tips

Words You Should Know

A. Synagogue (Acts 6:9) *sunagoge* (Gk.)—A place of worship for Jewish people.

B. Blasphemous (vv. 11, 13) *blasphemos* (Gk.)—A disrespectful attitude expressed in an act directed against God's character.

Teacher Preparation

Unifying Principle—Courage to Speak. Stephen, in the face of opposition, demonstrated the power and wisdom of the Spirit to speak the truth of Christ.

A. Read Acts 6 in several translations so you can understand the passage.

B. Read and study the entire lesson.

C. Pray the Aim for Change for yourself and your students.

D. Complete the companion lesson in the *Precepts For Living Study Guide*®.

O—Open the Lesson

A. Open the class with prayer, asking God to make us bold in witnessing for Him.

B. Have students silently read the In Focus story. Discuss.

C. Ask: Do you think there might have been another way for Calvin to witness to Jessie? What are some reasons for witnessing in situations where it is forbidden?

P—Present the Scriptures

A. Tie the Aim for Change objectives into the Unifying Principle by stating that Stephen was a bold witness for Jesus.

B. Briefly summarize the Background and The People, Places, and Times sections.

C. Discuss why God allows His children to suffer for being a witness for Him.

OCT
7th

E—Explore the Meaning

A. Have volunteers respond to the Discuss the Meaning questions.

B. Then explain that the martyrdom of Stephen meant that the Jewish Christians scattered all over the known world for that time and carried the Gospel with them.

N—Next Steps for Application

A. Divide the class by twos and role play ways to share the Gospel.

B. Close with prayer.

Worship Guide

For the Superintendent or Teacher
Theme: Stephen's Arrest and Speech
Song: "Jesus Is All the World to Me"
Devotional Reading: Proverbs 8:1-11
Prayer

Stephen's Arrest and Speech

Bible Background • ACTS 6:8—7:53
Printed Text • ACTS 6:8—7:2a | Devotional Reading • PROVERBS 8:1-11

—————— Aim for Change ——————

By the end of the lesson, we will: DISCUSS the stand that Stephen took as a response to his faith; FEEL MOTIVATED to confront principalities and powers of our day; and SEEK the power and wisdom of the Spirit in our efforts to speak truth.

————— In Focus —————

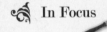

Calvin volunteered every Saturday at the city-run homeless shelter. He was a hard worker with a cheerful attitude. Ms. Martin, the supervisor, was very happy with Calvin's participation, especially because she always seemed to be short of volunteers.

But one day, she overheard Calvin telling Jessie, a man living at the shelter, that the reason for his joy was Jesus. Jessie asked him how he could get this "Jesus joy." So Calvin began explaining, "First, we tell Jesus that we are sorry for our sins. Then we thank Him for dying on the Cross to take the punishment for our sins. And lastly, we ask Jesus to save us." Right then and there, Calvin and Jessie bowed their heads, and Jessie asked Jesus to save him.

Now Calvin's joy was bubbling over so much, he felt like he could walk on air. But just as he was going back to clean up food that a child had dropped, Ms. Martin came up to him with anger written all over her face. "Calvin, don't you know this is a government-sponsored facility and you cannot come here and talk about your religion!"

How do you think Calvin will respond to Ms. Martin? What will he say? Do you think it's wise to disobey government rules? Do you think this is a government rule? Have you ever had someone challenge your Christian witness? What was your response? Today we will see how Stephen was able to witness with great power and grace.

————— Keep in Mind —————

"And Stephen, full of faith and power, did great wonders and miracles among the people" (Acts 6:8).

"And Stephen, full of faith and power, did great wonders and miracles among the people" (Acts 6:8).

Focal Verses

KJV **Acts 6:8** And Stephen, full of faith and power, did great wonders and miracles among the people.

9 Then there arose certain of the synagogue, which is called the synagogue of the Libertines, and Cyrenians, and Alexandrians, and of them of Cilicia and of Asia, disputing with Stephen.

10 And they were not able to resist the wisdom and the spirit by which he spake.

11 Then they suborned men, which said, We have heard him speak blasphemous words against Moses, and against God.

12 And they stirred up the people, and the elders, and the scribes, and came upon him, and caught him, and brought him to the council,

13 And set up false witnesses, which said, This man ceaseth not to speak blasphemous words against this holy place, and the law:

14 For we have heard him say, that this Jesus of Nazareth shall destroy this place, and shall change the customs which Moses delivered us.

15 And all that sat in the council, looking stedfastly on him, saw his face as it had been the face of an angel.

7:1 Then said the high priest, Are these things so?

2a And he said, Men, brethren, and fathers, hearken;

NLT **Acts 6:8** Stephen, a man full of God's grace and power, performed amazing miracles and signs among the people.

9 But one day some men from the Synagogue of Freed Slaves, as it was called, started to debate with him. They were Jews from Cyrene, Alexandria, Cilicia, and the province of Asia.

10 None of them could stand against the wisdom and the Spirit with which Stephen spoke.

11 So they persuaded some men to lie about Stephen, saying, "We heard him blaspheme Moses, and even God."

12 This roused the people, the elders, and the teachers of religious law. So they arrested Stephen and brought him before the high council.

13 The lying witnesses said, "This man is always speaking against the holy Temple and against the law of Moses.

14 We have heard him say that this Jesus of Nazareth will destroy the Temple and change the customs Moses handed down to us."

15 At this point everyone in the high council stared at Stephen, because his face became as bright as an angel's.

7:1 Then the high priest asked Stephen, "Are these accusations true?"

2a This was Stephen's reply: "Brothers and fathers, listen to me."

The People, Places, and Times

Synagogue of the Libertines (Freedmen). Jews who were born in the Holy Land and spent most of their lives there spoke Aramaic, which was a form of the ancient Hebrew in which our Old Testament is written. But there were other Jews born in other places who had returned to Palestine, and they did not know Aramaic or Hebrew. They only spoke Greek, which was the language of the educated people of the day. Perhaps they had been slaves in other countries, but now they were all proud to be free people. Some of them came from Cyrene, an important city in what is modern day Libya in northern Africa. Others came from Alexandria, the chief city of Egypt, and others came from Cilicia and Asia. Ephesus was a grand city located in Asia Minor. Tarsus, where Paul was born, was located in the northern part of Asia Minor in what is now known as Syria.

Pious Greek-speaking Jews attended the Synagogue of Libertines or Freedmen Paul would have attended this synagogue, and Barnabas probably did also. Among all these Greek-speaking Jews were a few Christians, but the most outspoken was Stephen. The Holy Spirit spoke through him as he reasoned, discussed, and argued for Jesus Christ.

Background

At the beginning of Acts 6, the early Christians were having problems. The Aramaic-speaking Jews were probably attending the big Temple in Jerusalem. But the early Jewish Christians, who spoke Greek, were attending the Synagogue of the Freedmen. The Jews had the wonderful custom of collecting donations for the poor among them; thus, the early Christians followed this custom and gave to needy widows. (Widows in those days had few ways to raise money to feed themselves, much less their children if they had any.)

The apostles were among the Aramaic Jews and were the early Christian leaders. They were in charge of the distribution of gifts to the widows, yet they were forgetting the Greek-speaking Christian widows. This could have been because of snobbery, because of language differences or because they just overlooked the Greek-speaking poor.

The godly solution of the apostles was to appoint Greek-speaking Jewish Christians to take charge of distributing food and money to the widows and other poor among them. The Greek-speaking Christians would know who was in need. The seven men chosen for this task were also chosen for their outstanding spirituality. Among them were Philip and Stephen, who is the focus of today's lesson.

At-A-Glance

1. Introduction of Stephen (Acts 6:8-10)
2. Opposition to Stephen (vv. 11-14)
3. Stephen's Effect on the Sanhedrin (vv. 15-7:2a)

In Depth

1. Introduction of Stephen (Acts 6:8-10)

Stephen did much more than hand out gifts to the needy. Until this time, Scripture had only mentioned the apostles performing miracles, but now we see Stephen doing great wonders. (We'll read later of the miracles that Philip performed). Scripture tells us that the reason for Stephen's ability to perform miracles is that he is full of grace and power. We would expect to hear about the power in conjunction with miracles, but maybe we are surprised by the accompaniment of grace. Grace is always an unmerited gift of God. Therefore, we see that God is working through Stephen, not because Stephen is so wonderful, but because God is wonderful and has empowered him to do these amazing things.

At this time, all Christians converted Jews and all attended synagogues. The Christian Jews were a tiny minority among the other Jews. The Jews whose primary language was Greek attended the Synagogue of the

Freedmen. As Stephen, who attended this synagogue, performed miracles in the name of Jesus, other Jewish members who did not follow Christ opposed. They debated with Stephen, but their arguments did not stand up against him for two reasons. First of all, the Holy Spirit was enabling him to use great wisdom. Secondly, the things that Stephen said concerning Jesus Christ were true.

2. Opposition to Stephen (vv. 11-14)

Those who opposed Stephen thought they were defending things that good Jews believed, but they were probably a jealous of him as well. Obviously, Stephen garnered a lot of attention from the miracles he performed and his brilliant exposition of the true meaning of Old Testament Scriptures.

Opposition spread from the Synagogue of the Freemen to the great temple in Jerusalem and to the influential Jews who had also opposed Jesus. As a result, they seized Stephen and brought him before the great Jewish religious council, the Sanhedrin. This was the same religious council that put Jesus on trial. As they had with Jesus, they also brought false witnesses against Stephen and used some of the same arguments.

They accused Stephen of speaking against the temple in Jerusalem. They said the Jesus he preached about had threatened to destroy the Temple. In John 2:19, Jesus said that if they destroyed "this Temple," meaning His body, He would raise it again in three days. We know that they were twisting the words of both Jesus and Stephen without really trying to understand the message.

In addition, they accused both Stephen and Jesus of trying to destroy the Old Testament law, again twisting their words. Jesus said He came not to abolish the Law but to fulfill it (Matthew 5:17). And because they were accusing Stephen of speaking about

the temple and the Law, they were in essence accusing him of speaking against God.

3. Stephen's Effect on the Sanhedrin (vv. 15-7:2a)

When Stephen's accusers finished what they had to say, they noticed that his face looked like that of an angel. We are sure this does not mean that he resembled the child-like pictures of angels we often see portrayed nor is it likely that he looked like some type of avenging angel. But because we have never looked into the face of an angel, we can only imagine a face that reflected the holiness of God Himself.

At that point, the high priest asked Stephen whether the charges of his accusers were true. This was probably Caiaphas, the very same man who had presided over the trial of Jesus. But that did not scare Stephen, who then launched into a history of the Jewish people, including their rejection of the prophets that God sent and finally the crucifixion of their Savior. The result of Stephen's sermon was that he was stoned and received by Jesus into heaven.

Search the Scriptures

1. How did Stephen communicate the Gospel to people (Acts 6:8-10)?

2. What did the false witnesses testify that Stephen said (v. 14)?

3. As the council looked upon Stephen's face, what did they see (v. 15)?

Discuss the Meaning

1. Stephen was mighty in both miracles and words. Do you think you must have these abilities to witness to others about Jesus Christ? What are the characteristics that we need to witness effectively concerning Jesus?

2. Stephen had wonderful spiritual gifts and he was very proactive in using them, yet it seemed that he had a

short time on earth before he died. Why do you think God would allow him to be sacrificed after such a brief time as a Christian? Acts 8:1 tells us that Saul was watching all this. Do you think Stephen's martyrdom had any influence on Saul? What other things happened as a result of Stephen's death? Acts 8:1 reveals one of those things.

Lesson in Our Society

In the days of Stephen, Jewish society was very religious. Christians retained some of good things from the religious Jews, such as collecting contributions for the poor and thus the Christians made regular gifts to the widows, the most vulnerable in their society. Unlike the context of Stephen's ministry, our society today is continuing to become increasingly secular. But even though the people of Stephen's day were very religious, they were extremely hostile to the Good News of Jesus Christ. In our society, people are seemingly becoming more hostile to the Jesus of the Bible. What are some of the things that contribute to hostility to the Christian message today? How do these things compare to the type of hostility in Stephen's day? What are some ways we can reverse this trend? Stephen, the other deacons, and the apostles demonstrated the love of Christ in the things they did for the poor. How can similar programs help prepare the way for our Christian witness?

Make It Happen

What are some times and situations when you think you could be a witness for the message of Jesus Christ? What are some of the things keeping you from speaking out? Ask God to empower you to tell people about our Lord. Ask Him to give you wisdom for the things to say and do. Before you speak up

for Christ, demonstrate your love for others in the things you do.

Follow the Spirit

What God wants me to do:

_____

_____

_____

_____

Remember Your Thoughts

Special insights I have learned:

_____

_____

_____

_____

More Light on the Text

Acts 6:8—7:2a

8 And Stephen, full of faith and power, did great wonders and miracles among the people.

By the time we get to this verse, we already know quite a bit about the character of Stephen and his spiritual gifts. Acts 6:3 tells us that the job description of the seven deacons was that they were to be full of the Spirit and wisdom. Stephen measured up so highly that after his name is a special description from which we can surmise that he is a man of deep faith, full of the Spirit, of power, and of wisdom. In Acts 6:8 the NIV substitutes the word "grace" for faith in the *King James Version*. The Greek translated "faith" in the KJV is *pistis* (**PIS-tis**). This can be translated as moral conviction, particularly reliance on Christ. This combined with power presents us with a wonderful combination of traits, leading to a strikingly Christ-like character.

Verse 8 shows us that not only was he full of faith and power but that he also did great wonders and miracles among the people. Up until this point, only the apostles demonstrated miracles, but we will soon see that not only did Stephen perform miracles, but Philip did as well (Acts 8:6). Those involved in missionary work—spreading the Good News where people have never heard it before—may have this special stamp of the Holy Spirit, in that what they are telling people is really from God.

9 Then there arose certain of the synagogue, which is called the synagogue of the Libertines, and Cyrenians, and Alexandrians, and of them of Cilicia and of Asia, disputing with Stephen. 10 And they were not able to resist the wisdom and the spirit by which he spake.

The Synagogue of the Libertines or Freedmen was composed of Jews who had been in captivity in other lands but now were back in the Promised Land. Perhaps not all of them had been slaves, but as Jews from other countries, they could not speak the Aramaic or Hebrew that the inhabitants of Israel could. And so they worshiped in a synagogue in Jerusalem, separate from the Temple. Although they came from many different countries, they all spoke Greek, the language spoken by the educated people of the Roman Empire. Some of them came from Cyrene and Alexandria, the two most prominent cities in North Africa. And some came from Cilicia and Asia, two other prominent provinces in the Roman Empire. Saul of Tarsus probably belonged to this synagogue because Tarsus was in Cilicia.

Although the men of the Freedmen's synagogue were well educated in the Greek translation of the Scripture, they did not expect that it would be so difficult to debate with Stephen. Jesus had promised His followers that He would give them words and wisdom that none of their adversaries would be able to resist or contradict (Luke 21:15).

11 Then they suborned men, which said, We have heard him speak blasphemous words against Moses, and against God.

Unable to contest Stephen's amazing presentation of the Gospel of Jesus Christ, they began a smear campaign. "Suborned" is an archaic English word meaning "bribed." The Greek for "suborned" is *hupoballo* (**hoo-po-BAL-lo**), and it means to throw in stealthily, i.e., introduce by mutual consent. We can picture this as the religious leaders gathering together for a secret meeting to conspire against Stephen. Because they could not discover any holes in Stephen's logic and exegesis of the Old Testament Scripture, they had to resort to phony charges.

Looking at the charges against Jesus and against Stephen, we see that blasphemy was not simply taking the name of God in vain. The religious scholars of that day broadened the charge to include speaking against the Temple, which was considered the throne of God, or anything that seemed to assail the Word of God or in particular the Law. We will see in the chapter to follow that Stephen was presenting Jesus as the Son of God and as the fulfillment of the Law.

12 And they stirred up the people, and the elders, and the scribes, and came upon him, and caught him, and brought him to the council,

Because the religious leaders could not logically tear apart Stephen's defense of the

Gospel, they resorted to working up the crowd with issues sure to upset the Jews of Jerusalem. As a result, before Stephen was brought to trial, everyone from the common person to the rulers of the Sanhedrin had already decided that they wanted to get rid of him. In today's legal system, this would be setting up a prejudicial attitude among the people, which any trial lawyer knows can cause a trial to be thrown out or moved to another, presumably less, prejudiced area.

13 And set up false witnesses, which said, This man ceaseth not to speak blasphemous words against this holy place, and the law: 14 For we have heard him say, that this Jesus of Nazareth shall destroy this place, and shall change the customs which Moses delivered us.

Verse 13 reveals the next step of this villainous plan, which was to bring false witnesses against Stephen. "This holy place" refers to the Temple and all the religious rites performed there. Godly Jews based their entire lives upon the Law, so the Temple and the cultic traditions would have been very dear to them. Those opposing Stephen had already incited the crowd with hot-button issues and now sought to press these issues further with witnesses paid to testify against Stephen. They were not blatantly lying; they just twisted the truth enough to get to stir up the crowd using one of the very same charges brought against Jesus.

In Matthew 26:61, two false witnesses said that Jesus declared, "'I am able to destroy the temple of God and rebuild it in three days'" (NIV). This was a shocking statement as the crowd interpreted it. It had taken 46 years for Herod's Temple to be built, but Jesus was *not* referring to Herod's temple; He was referring to *His body*. John 2:18-22 contains this statement, but John clarifies it. The religious rulers may have thought they destroyed Jesus when they hung Him on the Cross, but we know that the climax of the story is Jesus' resurrection from the dead three days later. John tells us that when Jesus rose from the dead, the disciples remembered this statement from Jesus and finally they understood and believed.

Many Scriptural passages, the prophetic ones in particular, have double meanings. In Ephesians 1:22-23, we read that the church is the body of Christ. All of us who have believed in Jesus Christ as our Savior are a part of that body. The body of Christ has gone through many trials and much persecution, sometimes even martyrdom, but the church of Christ will not be snuffed out.

15 And all that sat in the council, looking stedfastly on him, saw his face as it had been the face of an angel.

Stephen's face was shining, similar to Moses' face when he came down from Mount Sinai after receiving the Law. In Stephen's case, he demonstrated through his words and his ministry that the Law was fulfilled in Jesus. The apostles had not yet understood that although they were attending the Temple as observant Jews, this had been superseded by the sacrifice of Jesus Christ on the Cross. There was no more need to sacrifice the lives of animals to pay for their sins. Although the Ten Commandments, which is God's moral law for all human beings, is still in effect, all the rituals of the Old Testament have been superseded by the death and resurrection of Jesus. We still need to study the entire Bible, but these parts have significance primarily to demonstrate the meaning of the Cross.

7:1 Then said the high priest, Are these things so? 2a And he said, Men, brethren, and fathers, hearken.

Stephen had to respond directly to the charges leveled against him. At the first reading of his speech, we may think it's just a rehash of Old Testament history, which his listeners were well acquainted with, but it is really much more radical than even the apostles realized. Next week, we will look at part of Stephen's speech.

Sources:
Bruce, F. F. *The Epistle to the Hebrews, Revised: New International Commentary on the New Testament.* Grand Rapids, MI: Eerdmans, 1983.
Dictionary.com. http://dictionary.reference.com/ (accessed September 19, 2011).
New Testament Greek Lexicon. Bible Study Tools.com. http://www.biblestudytools.com/lexicons/greek (accessed September 19, 2011).
The NIV Study Bible. Grand Rapids, MI: Zondervan Publishing House, 1995.
Stott, John. *The Spirit, the Church, and the World: The Message of Acts.* Downers Grove, IL: InterVarsity Press, 1990

Say It Correctly

Suborn. suh-**BORN.**
Cyrenians. si-**REE**-nee-uhnz.
Alexandrians. al-ig-**ZAN**-dree-uhnz.
Libertines. **LIB**-er-teens.

Daily Bible Readings

MONDAY
Barriers between You and Your God
(Isaiah 59:1-8)

TUESDAY
Falsehood, Deceit, and Deception
(Jeremiah 8:22-9:9)

WEDNESDAY
These Things You Shall Do
(Zechariah 8:14-19)

THURSDAY
My Mouth Will Utter Truth
(Proverbs 8:1-11)

FRIDAY
Guided into All the Truth
(John 16:12-15)

SATURDAY
Full of Faith and the Spirit
(Acts 6:1-7)

SUNDAY
Full of Grace and Power
(Acts 6:8-7:2a)

Notes

_____

_____

_____

_____

Teaching Tips

Words You Should Know

A. **"Stiff-necked"** (Acts 7:51) *sklerotrachelos* (Heb.)—Stubborn, hardheaded.

B. **Witnesses** (v. 58) *martureo* (Gk.)— Those who confirm or give confirmation.

Teacher Preparation

Unifying Principle—Paying the Price. Stephen's criticism of the religious establishment and his exaltation of Christ enraged the religious leaders, so they stoned him to death.

A. Pray for your students and lesson clarity.

B. Read and study the entire lesson.

C. Complete the companion lesson in the *Precepts For Living Personal Study Guide®*.

O—Open the Lesson

A. Have a student lead the class in prayer using the Lesson Aim.

B. Ask students to share their experiences from last week's Make It Happen and tell what they learned from their Daily Bible Readings.

C. Have volunteers read the In Focus story. Discuss.

P—Present the Scriptures

A. Use the Background, The People, Places, and Times, and the At-A-Glance outline to understand the Focal Verses.

B. Refer to the Search the Scriptures questions and discuss them.

E—Explore the Meaning

A. Use the Discuss the Meaning questions to help students discuss how today's lesson applies to the practical situations they face.

B. The Lesson in Our Society section will also help students see parallels with their present-day situations.

N—Next Steps for Application

A. Summarize the lesson with the Keep in Mind verse.

B. Challenge students to follow through on the Make It Happen assignment.

C. Encourage students to read the Daily Bible Readings.

D. Close the class with prayer, thanking the Lord for the love and mercy that He has shown to the students this week.

OCT
14th

Worship Guide

For the Superintendent or Teacher
Theme: Stephen's Martyrdom
Song: "Jesus Is All the World to Me"
Devotional Reading:
Ephesians 6:13-20
Prayer

Stephen's Martyrdom

Bible Background • ACTS 7:1—8:1a
Printed Text • ACTS 7:51—8:1a | Devotional Reading • EPHESIANS 6:13-20

Aim for Change

By the end of the lesson, we will: IDENTIFY the reasons for Stephen's martyrdom, REFLECT on our reactions when our beliefs are challenged, and WITNESS peacefully and candidly for Christ regardless of the cost.

In Focus

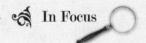

In a way it seemed like a trap, but Susan realized it was an opportunity from God. Susan was just meeting the woman who would soon become her mother-in-law. "Well, Susan," she said, "I've heard that you are one of those shoutin' type of Christians. Is that true?"

"I don't know what you mean by 'shoutin',' but I am enthusiastic about Jesus because He is my Savior and I love Him," replied Susan.

Susan was glad for the opportunity to witness, but she knew that not all of these opportunities lead to a happy ending.

"I'm glad you talked to Mom about your relationship with Jesus," said Sterling, "even though I knew what her response would be."

For years, Susan and Sterling did not hear from his mother. It hurt them both that she did not even come to their wedding.

Sometimes, even a life full of goodness and a very wise witness will not convince people. Are we ready to speak up for our Savior, no matter what the consequences will be in our lives?

Keep in Mind

"And they stoned Stephen, calling upon God, and saying, Lord Jesus, receive my spirit" (Acts 7:59).

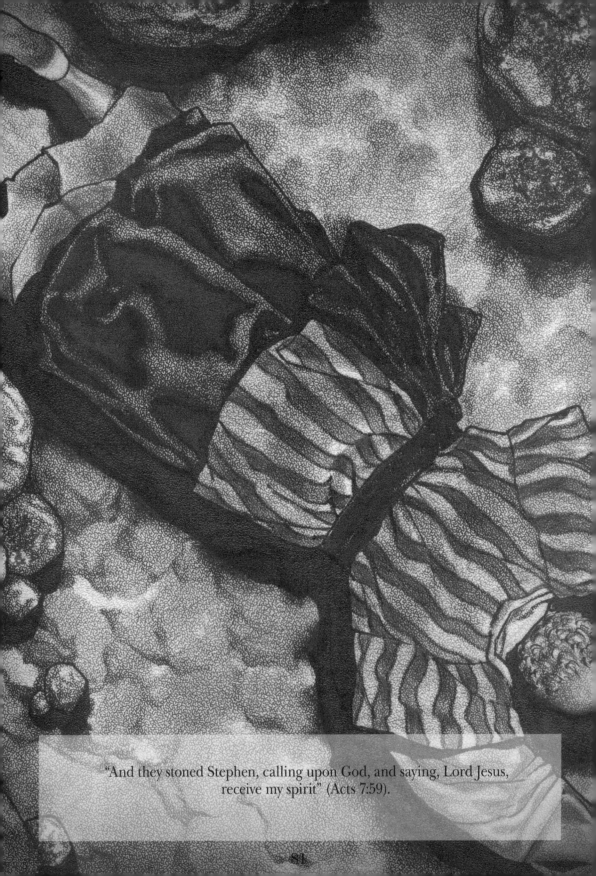

"And they stoned Stephen, calling upon God, and saying, Lord Jesus, receive my spirit" (Acts 7:59).

Focal Verses

KJV **Acts 7:51** Ye stiffnecked and uncircumcised in heart and ears, ye do always resist the Holy Ghost: as your fathers did, so do ye.

52 Which of the prophets have not your fathers persecuted? and they have slain them which shewed before of the coming of the Just One; of whom ye have been now the betrayers and murderers:

53 Who have received the law by the disposition of angels, and have not kept it.

54 When they heard these things, they were cut to the heart, and they gnashed on him with their teeth.

55 But he, being full of the Holy Ghost, looked up stedfastly into heaven, and saw the glory of God, and Jesus standing on the right hand of God,

56 And said, Behold, I see the heavens opened, and the Son of man standing on the right hand of God.

57 Then they cried out with a loud voice, and stopped their ears, and ran upon him with one accord,

58 And cast him out of the city, and stoned him: and the witnesses laid down their clothes at a young man's feet, whose name was Saul.

59 And they stoned Stephen, calling upon God, and saying, Lord Jesus, receive my spirit.

60 And he kneeled down, and cried with a loud voice, Lord, lay not this sin to their charge. And when he had said this, he fell asleep.

8:1a And Saul was consenting unto his death.

NLT **Acts 7:51** "You stubborn people! You are heathen at heart and deaf to the truth. Must you forever resist the Holy Spirit? That's what your ancestors did, and so do you!

52 Name one prophet your ancestors didn't persecute! They even killed the ones who predicted the coming of the Righteous One—the Messiah whom you betrayed and murdered.

53 You deliberately disobeyed God's law, even though you received it from the hands of angels."

54 The Jewish leaders were infuriated by Stephen's accusation, and they shook their fists at him in rage.

55 But Stephen, full of the Holy Spirit, gazed steadily into heaven and saw the glory of God, and he saw Jesus standing in the place of honor at God's right hand.

56 And he told them, "Look, I see the heavens opened and the Son of Man standing in the place of honor at God's right hand!"

57 Then they put their hands over their ears and began shouting. They rushed at him

58 and dragged him out of the city and began to stone him. His accusers took off their coats and laid them at the feet of a young man named Saul.

59 As they stoned him, Stephen prayed, "Lord Jesus, receive my spirit."

60 He fell to his knees, shouting, "Lord, don't charge them with this sin!" And with that, he died.

8:1a Saul was one of the witnesses, and he agreed completely with the killing of Stephen.

The People, Places, and Times

Blasphemy. The Greek word for "blasphemy" means "to slander" or "to speak lightly of the divine." In the New Testament, blasphemy indicated a hostile attitude toward God. In the epistle to the Romans, Paul quotes Isaiah who stated that God's name was blasphemed among the Gentiles because of the Jews (Romans 2:24, Isaiah 52:5). This confirms the importance of believers living in ways that bring praise to God rather than contempt for Him.

It is worth noting that both Jesus and Stephen were condemned to death under the false charge of blasphemy. This occurred because Jesus claimed the prerogatives that belong to God alone, and Stephen accused the unbelieving Jews of murdering the long-awaited Messiah.

Background

Jesus knew that the Gospel of the Kingdom would be preached to all nations for a witness. He knew that truth, armed with the omnipotence of the Holy Spirit, would prevail in the battle with evil and that the bloodstained banner would one day wave triumphantly over His followers.

As Christ's earthly ministry drew to a close, He knew He would soon leave His disciples to carry on the work without His personal supervision. He sought to encourage them and to prepare them for the future. He did not deceive them with false hopes. He knew He was about to be separated from them—to leave them as sheep among wolves. He knew they would suffer persecution, be cast out of the synagogues, and be thrown into prison for witnessing about Him as the Messiah. In speaking of their future, Jesus said some of them would be killed. He knew that in their coming trials they would remember His words and be strengthened

to believe in Him as the Redeemer. Are you prepared to stand up for your faith, regardless of the consequences as demonstrated by Stephen in today's lesson?

At-A-Glance

1. The Conclusion of Stephen's Defense (Acts 7:51-53)
2. The Death of Stephen (vv. 53—8:1a)

In Depth

1. The Conclusion of Stephen's Defense (Acts 7:51-53)

The beginning of Chapter 7 opens with Stephen's brilliant defense of what he believed, which was really a review of the history of the people of Israel. He begins by appealing to the memory of Abraham. He describes Abraham as a man of longtime faith who dared to change his life in obedience to God, leaving his country and even his father's house to go into a land he had never seen before. Though he was old and childless, Abram (renamed Abraham) believed God would give him descendants.

The next man on Stephen's list was Joseph. Joseph was a man of faith who obeyed God and had every letter of God's promises to him fulfilled. Stephen contrasts Joseph with members of the Sanhedrin, who refused to obey God because they feared the changes that doing so would bring in their lives and in their levels of affluence.

Next, Stephen spoke of Moses, whom they had accused him of blaspheming. Stephen argued that Moses failed when he acted according to what seemed right in his own eyes and according to his own wisdom. But when God appeared, then instructed and empowered him, Moses went back to Egypt and became a ruler and deliverer. He answers their charge by quoting Moses himself: "God will send you a prophet like me from your own people" (v. 37; see Deuteronomy 18:15, NIV). In other words, Moses himself had said things would change. God was going to raise up another prophet who, like Moses, would teach the people a whole new way of life in God. The prophet whom Moses spoke of was Jesus, the man they had put to death and were now rejecting.

Stephen answered the second charge regarding the temple by quoting from Isaiah: "'Heaven is my throne, and the earth is my footstool. What kind of house will you build for me? says the Lord. Or where will my resting place be? Has not my hand made all these things?'" (Acts 7:49-50, NIV; see Isaiah 66:1-2). No building can contain God. God is the creator of all things.

After answering their charges, Stephen levels a charge of his own: "You stiff-necked people, with uncircumcised hearts and ears! You are just like your ancestors: You always resist the Holy Spirit!" (Acts 7:51, NIV). These Jews were "stiff-necked"—they would not bow to God's will. They had "uncircumcised hearts," meaning their hearts were insensitive to the grace and glory of God; thus, they refused to repent. Just as their forefathers had persecuted and murdered the prophets who prophesied of Jesus, these Jews had betrayed and murdered the Christ.

2. The Death of Stephen (vv. 53-8:1a)

Stephen's accusers and the religious leaders were so outraged by this truth that they could not stand it. "When the members of the Sanhedrin heard this, they were furious and gnashed their teeth at him" (Acts 7:54, NIV). In contrast to his accusers, who were driven wild by their passions, Stephen continued to look to God: "But Stephen, full of the Holy Spirit, looked up to heaven and saw the glory of God, and Jesus standing at the right hand of God" (v. 55, NIV). These words are almost identical to the words Jesus had spoken to these men just a few years earlier: "'But I say to all of you: From now on you will see the Son of Man sitting at the right hand of the Mighty One and coming on the clouds of heaven'" (Matthew 26:64, NIV). When they heard this, they knew the issue was not Stephen but Jesus.

They had brought Stephen to trial and he condemned them with the very Scriptures they professed to believe. Like the men of the synagogue, they could not argue with his testimony. Consequently, these enraged Jews cried out at the top of their voices and put their hands up to their ears in a vain attempt to drown out Stephen. When confronted with the truth of Christ, one must either submit or resist. The Jewish leaders and Stephen's accusers decided to resist. Like their forefathers, instead of heeding the words of God's prophet, they would kill him. The respectable Sanhedrin turned into an unruly mob, rushed at Stephen, and dragged him outside the city gates. They threw him down into a pit and stoned him.

The reference to the "witness" (Acts 7:58) suggests that the stoning was carried out as a legal execution. The penalty for blasphemy was stoning (Leviticus 24:16). According to Jewish law, the witnesses would have to throw the first stones (Deuteronomy 17:7). Acts 7:58 says that these men took off their outer cloaks and laid them at the feet of a young Jewish Pharisee named Saul.

After the witnesses had thrown the first stones, the rest of the congregation picked up stones and hurled them at Stephen. If someone had a good aim and managed to hit Stephen in the head early on, he would lose consciousness and would not have to endure the prolonged agony. If not, his death would be long, slow, and very painful.

As the malicious and unforgiving crowd threw their stones down on Stephen, he first cried out in prayer for God to receive his spirit. Then, he dropped to his knees and uttered his final words, "'Lord, do not hold this sin against them'" (Acts 7:60, NIV). Stephen, the first Christian martyr, died at the hands of the same people who had delivered Jesus to be crucified, and he died with a similar prayer on his lips.

Scripture says that Stephen "fell asleep" (Acts 7:60; also see John 11:11). Because physical death is temporary for the believer, death is referred to as "sleep." The body sleeps, but the spirit goes to be with the Lord (1 Corinthians 15:12-19).

God never wastes the blood of His saints. The persecution that began with Stephen's murder forced many in the Church to flee Jerusalem and take the Gospel to the uttermost parts of the world. And a young man named Saul, who gave his approval to the stoning of Stephen (Acts 8:1), was so moved by Stephen's death that he never forgot it. Although Saul would become the greatest persecutor of the early Church, Stephen's death would always remain in his mind. There is little doubt that the Holy Spirit used Stephen's message and glorious death to prepare Saul for his meeting with the risen Lord on the Damascus Road (Acts 9). Saul, later called Paul, would become the single greatest evangelist the world has ever known.

Stories of martyrdom are continually written today with tales of others who are called to lay down their lives for Jesus' sake.

Search the Scriptures

1. What physical response did the Jews make that demonstrated their passionate anger with Stephen (Acts 7:54)?

2. How does Luke describe Stephen's death at the hands of his accusers (v. 60)?

Discuss the Meaning

1. After studying the life of Stephen, how do you view the responsibilities of deacons and whether their duties begin and end with the business of the local church?

2. How much responsibility do deacons have to the community they serve and to unbelievers? What might be some examples of these responsibilities?

Lesson in Our Society

Stephen is recognized as the first person to give his life to spread the Gospel. He was known as an outspoken leader and a man of great faith. He refused to compromise his beliefs and virtually spoke his own death sentence. In today's society, every day we are faced with issues that may compromise our Christian beliefs. The challenge for many Christians lies in whether we are willing to suffer persecution despite what others may think. Are we willing to stand on God's Word when it is not popular? Like Stephen, we as Christians must a have mindset that regardless of what Satan brings against us, we will tenaciously stand on the Word of God.

Make It Happen

Stephen was willing to die for the cause of Christ. Maybe God has not called you to make this kind of sacrifice, but Christianity does require something from all of us. Look for ways to make sacrifices to God for the sake of the Gospel. These offerings can be time, money, or whatever you choose. Prepare to share your experiences next week.

Follow the Spirit

What God wants me to do:

_____

_____

_____

_____

Remember Your Thoughts

Special insights I have learned:

_____

_____

_____

_____

More Light on the Text

Acts 7:51-8:1a

51 Ye stiffnecked and uncircumcised in heart and ears, ye do always resist the Holy Ghost: as your fathers did, so do ye.

Up until this verse, Stephen had been preaching on the Old Testament history of God's chosen people; now he gives the moral of the story in no uncertain terms. Stephen showed how the Jews had rejected God's many calls to them through the prophets and how the very religious Jews he preached to were just as stubborn as their ancestors had been. In Greek, "stiff-necked" is *sklerotrachelos* (**sklay-rot-RAKH-ay-los**). The Hebrew word for stiff-necked is used by God to describe His people in Exodus 33:5, and now Stephen is applying this same word to the audience before him. Stiff-necked can also be translated "stubborn." We often call a stubborn child "hardheaded."

Circumcision was the removal of the foreskin from Jewish males when they were just eight days old. This was the outward sign that these men were people of God's covenant. But Stephen was pointing out that though every male present was probably physically circumcised, their hearts were not circumcised, i.e., they lacked a spiritual relationship with God.

The third accusation was that the people were resistant to God's Spirit. Although these Jews would certainly not believe that the Holy Spirit was the third member of the Trinity, they knew that the Old Testament frequently mentioned God's Spirit. In Isaiah 48:16 the prophet says, "Come ye near unto me, hear ye this; I have not spoken in secret from the beginning; from the time that it was, there am I: and now the Lord GOD, and his Spirit, hath sent me." One can look at the mention of God's Spirit in the Old Testament and find too many references to count. To be resistant to the Holy Spirit is indeed a terrible sin.

52 Which of the prophets have not your fathers persecuted? and they have slain them which shewed before of the coming of the Just One; of whom ye have been now the betrayers and murderers:

Again Stephen reminded the people of the history of the Jewish people and how they persecuted prophets and even killed them. According to Jewish tradition, King Manasseh cut Isaiah the prophet in half, and Jeremiah was stoned by his own people. ("Shewed" is an old way of spelling "showed.") The most important accusation is that although all the prophets foretold the coming of the Just One, the people in the audience participated in His betrayal and murder. The Greek for "just" is *dikaios* (**dik-AH-yos**), which means "innocent, holy, and righteous." All these synonyms are used in the Old Testament to prophesy the coming of the Messiah. Jesus, Himself, quoted Isaiah 61:1-2a in Luke 4:16-21. These words are often referred to as Jesus' ordination speech in which He quoted from Isaiah to articulate that as the Just One, He comes to restore justice and expects us to participate in justice-seeking causes.

As we read Stephen's accusation of the crowd of Jews before him, we need to remember that not all Jews participated in the crucifixion of our Lord. In fact, Stephen himself was a Jew. Each of us, no matter what our race or other ethnic affiliation is responsible before God as to what we are going to do with Jesus today.

53 Who have received the law by the disposition of angels, and have not kept it.

They had not obeyed (Gk. *phulasso,* **foo-LAS-so**) or "kept" the law they had been specially privileged to "have received" (Gk. *lambano,* **lam-BAHN-o**). They had received the law "by the disposition of angels." The term "disposition" or "command" (Gk. *diatage,* **dee-at-ag-AY**) means "through the mediation of angels" (see Galatians 3:19; Hebrews 2:2). Therefore, they were the real lawbreakers, not Stephen. The accused had become the accuser, using the same language as Moses and the prophets (Exodus 33:5; Deuteronomy 10:16; Isaiah 48:4; Jeremiah 4:4).

54 When they heard these things, they were cut to the heart, and they gnashed on him with their teeth.

Stephen's speech made them furious, particularly his accusation about them not being true observers of the Law of Moses. They "were cut to the heart" (Gk. *diaprio,* **dee-ap-REE-o**), which literally means,

"to saw through" and denotes being infuriated and fiercely annoyed (see Acts 5:33). They "gnashed" (Gk. *brucho,* **BROO-kho**) their teeth at Stephen in a hostile sense as wild beasts leaping with rage on their prey (see Job 16:9-10; Psalm 35:16-17). They were full of hatred toward Stephen.

55 But he, being full of the Holy Ghost, looked up stedfastly into heaven, and saw the glory of God, and Jesus standing on the right hand of God,

Stephen, "being full of the Holy Ghost," had a vision of the glory of God. He saw Jesus standing at the right hand of God. Why was Jesus "standing" (Gk. *histemi,* **HIS-tay-mee**) instead of sitting at God's right hand (see Psalm 110:1; Luke 22:69; Acts 2:34-35)? It must be observed first that both expressions are symbolic of the authority given to Christ. The vision of Jesus standing evokes many possible interpretations. One is that Stephen testified that Jesus had arrived in the presence of God and had received all authority, thus fulfilling the vision of Daniel 7:13 (see also Matthew 28:18; Acts 13:33). Another is that Christ was standing either as Stephen's advocate or to welcome him into His presence. The "right hand" means the place of honor (see Matthew 20:21; 1 Kings 2:19).

56 And said, Behold, I see the heavens opened, and the Son of man standing on the right hand of God.

Stephen told them what he was seeing. He saw the heavens opened and the Son of Man standing at the right hand of God (Daniel 7:13; Mark 14:62). The expression in Acts 7:56 "Son of man" (Gk. *huios,* **hwee-OS**) is a title for Christ quoted from the book of Daniel (see Luke 6:22).

57 Then they cried out with a loud voice, and stopped their ears, and ran upon him with one accord,

They "cried out" (Gk. *krazo*, **KRAD-zo**) loudly, determined to silence him. They "stopped" or "held together" (Gk. *sunecho*, **soo-NEKH-o**) their ears so that Stephen's words, which they regarded as blasphemous, could not be heard (see Matthew 26:65). Reading the NLT of Acts 7:57, they "rushed" (Gk. *hormao*, **hor-MAH-o**) at him "with one accord." The use of the aorist tense here shows how fast things went out of control as soon as Stephen identified the figure of the Son of Man in glory as Jesus.

58 And cast him out of the city, and stoned him: and the witnesses laid down their clothes at a young man's feet, whose name was Saul.

They seized him and "cast him out" or "threw him out" (Gk. *ekballo*, **ek-BAL-lo**) of the city and began to "stone" (Gk. *lithoboleo*, **li-tho-bo-LEH-o**) him to death. Death by stoning was the punishment for blasphemy (see Leviticus 24:14). It is not clear, however, whether Stephen's death was the result of judicial action by the council or mob lynching. (Similarly, in Jesus' trial and death, the Romans had taken away the Jews' right of capital punishment; see John 18:31) The actions all happened fast: "cried aloud," "stopped," "rushed," "cast out," and "stoned," indicating a repeated and continued action. Yet, these events had some semblance of legality if the "witnesses" (Gk. *martureo*, **mar-too-REH-o**) here were the first to start the stoning as specified by law (see Deuteronomy 17:7; John 8:7).

They laid their clothes at the feet of a young man named Saul (see Acts 22:20; 26:10). Acts 7:58 is the first mention of Saul in Acts. The term "a young man" (Gk. *neanias*, **neh-an-EE-as**) gives no indication of

his age. According to Joseph Thayer's *Greek-English Lexicon of the New Testament*, *neanias* can be applied to a person up to 40 years old (see Matthew 19:20, 22).

59 And they stoned Stephen, calling upon God, and saying, Lord Jesus, receive my spirit.

As they stoned him, Stephen was "calling upon" (Gk. *epikaleomai*, **ep-ee-ka-LEH-om-ahee**) God. His prayer was very similar to Jesus' prayer on the Cross (see Luke 23:46). While Jesus committed His Spirit to the Father, Stephen committed his to Jesus. This is certainly a testimony to Christ's divinity.

60 And he kneeled down, and cried with a loud voice, Lord, lay not this sin to their charge. And when he had said this, he fell asleep.

Stephen "fell to his knees" (Gk. *tithemi*, **TITH-ay-mee**) and cried out, "Lord, do not remember this sin against them" (literally, "fix not this sin upon them," Acts 7:60, NLT; see Luke 23:34). Stephen did not pray for his own vindication. He prayed for mercy (see Matthew 5:38-48; 6:12, 14-15; James 2:13). In Acts 7:60, the phrase "he fell asleep" (Gk. *koimao*, **koy-MAH-o**) is characteristic of the New Testament expression for death (Matthew 27:52; John 11:11; Acts 13:36). The same Greek word is also used to refer to sleep, rest, lying down, or death (Gk. *koimesis*, **KOY-may-sis**).

8:1a And Saul was consenting unto his death.

Where do we get this information concerning the sermon of Stephen, the appearance of his face shining like an angel, and the keeping of the coats of his executioners? Some have thought the information came from Philip, but it is more likely that it came from Saul who was struck by Stephen's words and his appearance.

Gamaliel, Saul's teacher, advocated a soft approach toward the Christians (Acts 5:34-39). But Saul, just as Stephen did, concluded that Christianity could not exist side-by-side with traditional Judaism. At the time of this event, Saul was beginning his vigorous persecution of the Christians, but perhaps later after his conversion, the martyrdom of Stephen was in the back of his mind. Everything Stephen lived for, said, and died for was in direct opposition to the beliefs of Saul (later to be known as Paul).

Sources:
Bruce, F. F. *The Epistle to the Hebrews, Revised: New International Commentary on the New Testament.* Grand Rapids, MI: Eerdmans. Reprint, 1983.
Dictionary.com. http://dictionary.reference.com/ (accessed September 19, 2011).
New Testament Greek Lexicon. Bible Study Tools.com. http://www.biblestudytools.com/lexicons/greek (accessed September 19, 2011).
The NIV Study Bible. Grand Rapids, MI: Zondervan Publishing House, 1995.
Stott, John. *The Spirit, the Church, and the World: The Message of Acts.* Downers Grove, IL: InterVarsity Press, 1990.
Thayer, Joseph H. *A Greek-English Lexicon of the New Testament.* New York, NY: Harper & Brothers, 1889. Blue Letter Bible. org. http://www.blueletterbible.org/lang/lexicon/lexicon.cfm?strongs=G3494 (accessed September 19, 2011).

Say It Correctly

Disposition. dis-puh-**ZISH**-un.
Uncircumcised. un-**SUR**-kuhm-sized.

Daily Bible Readings

MONDAY
Equipped to Speak Boldly
(Ephesians 6:13-20)

TUESDAY
The Promised Fulfillment Draws Near
(Acts 7:17-22)

WEDNESDAY
I Have Come to Rescue Them
(Acts 7:30-34)

THURSDAY
The Rejection of Moses
(Acts 7:35-39)

FRIDAY
The Rejection of God
(Acts 7:39-43)

SATURDAY
The Inadequacy of the Temple
(Acts 7:44-50)

SUNDAY
You Are the Ones
(Acts 7:51-8:1a)

Notes

Teaching Tips

Words You Should Know

A. Used Sorcery and Bewitched (Acts 8:9) *mageuo kai existemi* (Gk.)— Practiced magic.

B. Had Regard (v. 11) *prosecho* (Gk.)— Denotes paying attention.

Teacher Preparation

Unifying Principle—Power Brokers. When Simon the magician tried to buy the power of the Holy Spirit, Peter plainly laid out the fatal consequences for those who think the Spirit can be bought or sold.

A. Pray for your students and for lesson clarity.

B. Read and study Acts 8 in its entirety.

C. Research the previous persecutions of the Christians in Jerusalem to place this particular event in context.

D. Complete the companion lesson in the *Precepts For Living Personal Study Guide®*.

O—Open the Lesson

A. Ask a student to open the class with a prayer, using the Keep in Mind verse.

B. Summarize the Background section.

C. Have the class read the Keep in Mind verse and Lesson Aim in unison.

D. Summarize the In Focus story and have the class discuss it.

P—Present the Scriptures

A. Ask several students to take turns reading the Focal Verses.

B. Use the At-A-Glance outline to explore the In Depth section.

E—Explore the Meaning

A. Allow students to work in groups of two or three to answer the questions and discuss the points in the Search the Scriptures and Discuss the Meaning sections. Have them report back to the class when they finish.

B. Discuss the Lesson in Our Society section.

N—Next Steps for Application

A. Go over the Make It Happen section.

B. Remind students to complete the Daily Bible Readings.

C. After receiving prayer requests, close with prayer.

Worship Guide

For the Superintendent or Teacher
Theme: Simon Wants to Buy Power
Song: "I Surrender All"
Devotional Reading:
1 Corinthians 1:18-25
Prayer

Simon Wants to Buy Power

Bible Background • ACTS 8:4-24
Printed Text • ACTS 8:9-24 | Devotional Reading • 1 CORINTHIANS 1:18-25

—— Aim for Change ——

By the end of the lesson, we will: DISCUSS Simon's motivation to receive the Holy Spirit; REFLECT on any selfish desires for God's power; and CREATE a list of true and sincere motives for following Christ.

——  In Focus ——

Although it was not really much of a sacrifice from his salary as a corporate lawyer, Mr. Biggs put large amounts of money in the offering. When it was time to elect members to the various church committees, Mr. Biggs thought he would easily be elected to his favorite committee: missions. After all, he gave lots to this cause. But instead of electing Mr. Biggs, the people voted for Marvin, a humble man who had already gone on a number of missions trips, including one where he dug out septic systems.

OCT 21st

Mr. Biggs was furious. "Don't these people know how much I am giving to the church, especially to the missions committee?"

What do you think is Mr. Biggs's motivation for running for member of the missions committee? Why do you think the people did not vote for him for this position? Do churches ever favor the richer people in the congregation? Can money buy a person's way into church power?

—— Keep in Mind ——

"And when Simon saw that through laying on of the apostles' hands the Holy Ghost was given, he offered them money" (Acts 8:18).

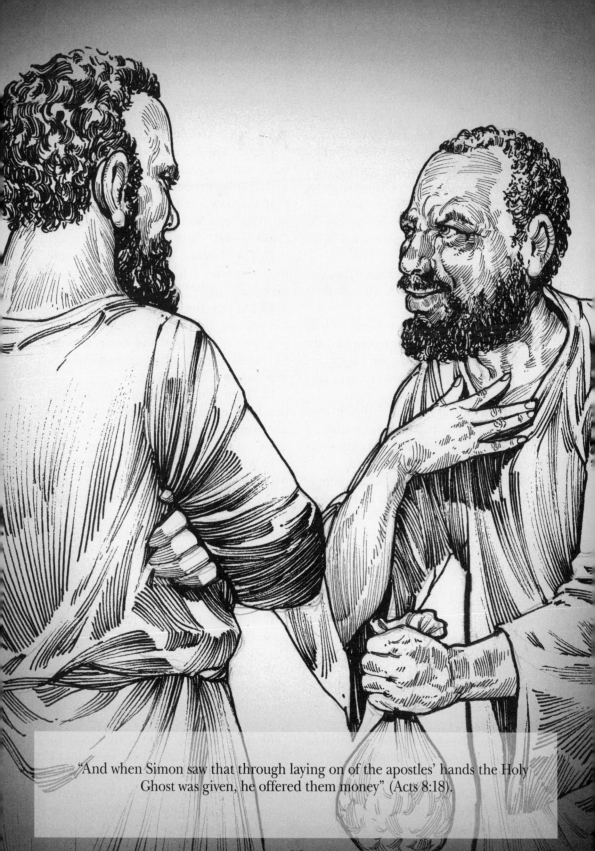

"And when Simon saw that through laying on of the apostles' hands the Holy Ghost was given, he offered them money" (Acts 8:18).

Focal Verses

KJV **Acts 8:9** But there was a certain man, called Simon, which beforetime in the same city used sorcery, and bewitched the people of Samaria, giving out that himself was some great one:

10 To whom they all gave heed, from the least to the greatest, saying, This man is the great power of God.

11 And to him they had regard, because that of long time he had bewitched them with sorceries.

12 But when they believed Philip preaching the things concerning the kingdom of God, and the name of Jesus Christ, they were baptized, both men and women.

13 Then Simon himself believed also: and when he was baptized, he continued with Philip, and wondered, beholding the miracles and signs which were done.

14 Now when the apostles which were at Jerusalem heard that Samaria had received the word of God, they sent unto them Peter and John:

15 Who, when they were come down, prayed for them, that they might receive the Holy Ghost:

16 (For as yet he was fallen upon none of them: only they were baptized in the name of the Lord Jesus.)

17 Then laid they their hands on them, and they received the Holy Ghost.

18 And when Simon saw that through laying on of the apostles' hands the Holy Ghost was given, he offered them money,

19 Saying, Give me also this power, that on whomsoever I lay hands, he may receive the Holy Ghost.

20 But Peter said unto him, Thy money perish with thee, because thou hast thought that the gift of God may be purchased with money.

NLT **Acts 8:9** A man named Simon had been a sorcerer there for many years, amazing the people of Samaria and claiming to be someone great.

10 Everyone, from the least to the greatest, often spoke of him as "the Great One—the Power of God."

11 They listened closely to him because for a long time he had astounded them with his magic.

12 But now the people believed Philip's message of Good News concerning the Kingdom of God and the name of Jesus Christ. As a result, many men and women were baptized.

13 Then Simon himself believed and was baptized. He began following Philip wherever he went, and he was amazed by the signs and great miracles Philip performed.

14 When the apostles in Jerusalem heard that the people of Samaria had accepted God's message, they sent Peter and John there.

15 As soon as they arrived, they prayed for these new believers to receive the Holy Spirit.

16 The Holy Spirit had not yet come upon any of them, for they had only been baptized in the name of the Lord Jesus.

17 Then Peter and John laid their hands upon these believers, and they received the Holy Spirit.

18 When Simon saw that the Spirit was given when the apostles laid their hands on people, he offered them money to buy this power.

19 "Let me have this power, too," he exclaimed, "so that when I lay my hands on people, they will receive the Holy Spirit!"

20 But Peter replied, "May your money be destroyed with you for thinking God's gift can be bought!"

KJV continued

21 Thou hast neither part nor lot in this matter: for thy heart is not right in the sight of God.

22 Repent therefore of this thy wickedness, and pray God, if perhaps the thought of thine heart may be forgiven thee.

23 For I perceive that thou art in the gall of bitterness, and in the bond of iniquity.

24 Then answered Simon, and said, Pray ye to the LORD for me, that none of these things which ye have spoken come upon me.

NLT continued

21 You can have no part in this, for your heart is not right with God.

22 Repent of your wickedness and pray to the Lord. Perhaps he will forgive your evil thoughts,

23 for I can see that you are full of bitter jealousy and are held captive by sin."

24 "Pray to the Lord for me," Simon exclaimed, "that these terrible things you've said won't happen to me!"

The People, Places, and Times

Sorcery. In *Unger's Bible Dictionary*, sorcery is defined as "the practice of the occult arts under the power of evil spirits or demons and has been common in all ages of the world's history" (1039). In this country, we are more familiar with a type of magic that is simply sleight of hand, using such tricks as hiding cards up the sleeve or drawing attention away from the hand doing the trick. But there is another magic that is drawn from the power of evil spirits. For example, the practitioner may actually do things that are not within the realm of the everyday laws of physics.

In today's Scripture, we will be reading about Simon the sorcerer, who called upon these occult arts to do such wonders that people held him in great awe. Simon took upon himself the title of "the great one."

In many traditional cultures in Asia, Africa, the Americas, and Europe, sorcerers scare people. If people do not sacrifice chickens and other animals and items, the sorcerer invokes fear that evil spirits might hurt them. And all along, the sorcerer is getting rich from the sacrifices. All through the Bible, magical arts are condemned because of their connection with evil spirits and because they lead people to do terrible things out of fear, including sacrificing their own children.

Background

The book of Acts is a book of history and faith. In addition to providing a transition between the Gospels and the Epistles, Luke, the writer of the book of Acts gives us the vital historical facts of how Christianity began and spread. In Acts, selected events in church history are recorded that demonstrate Christian doctrine and practice. It is clearly through the power of the Holy Spirit that the men and women of God are able to testify that Jesus is the Christ. There is great emphasis on the connection between the Old Testament, the Jews, and Christianity. There is even greater emphasis that salvation is not bound by a believer's race or ethnicity; rather, it is extended to all humankind. In Acts, it is clear that it is only Jesus, the Christ, who is able to fulfill the needs of the Gentiles and the Jews.

At-A-Glance

1. Introducing Simon the Sorcerer
(Acts 8:9-11)
2. Many Turn to Christ (vv. 12-13)
3. The Believers Receive the Holy
Spirit (vv. 14-17)
4. Simon Attempts to Buy the Power of
the Holy Spirit (vv. 18-24)

In Depth

1. Introducing Simon the Sorcerer (Acts 8:9-11)

Today's Scripture passage begins in the midst of a great evangelistic campaign in Samaria. After the stoning of Stephen, the believers, except for the apostles, scattered everywhere while spreading the Gospel. Philip, one of the deacons who was appointed along with Stephen, went to Samaria and began preaching and performing miraculous signs. Because of his witness, many came to Christ. Simon the sorcerer was among the Samaritans who heard Philip's preaching and witnessed the accompanying signs and wonders. Simon had enjoyed tremendous popularity among the Samaritans. Scripture tells us that Simon had been practicing the magical arts and had deceived many with his false claims of greatness. Simon's abilities as a magician had "bewitched the people" (Acts 8:9).

Even today, people mistakenly believe that the only difference between magic and miracles is that the latter is more impressive and is practiced by Christians. The truth is far more important. Miracles clearly point to God, while magic manipulates and points away from God. Faith comes through hearing the Word and not through just seeing miracles.

2. Many Turn to Christ (vv. 12-13)

The Samaritans had previously believed in Simon because of his magic. They had no faith in Simon; rather, their belief was predicated on his magical abilities. Through the preaching of Philip, the faith of the Samaritans was based on the Good News of Jesus, the Christ, and the kingdom of God. The Samaritans saw Philip's miracles as confirmation of the truth of the resurrection of Christ. The miracles aided—not caused—their faith. Now that faith in Jesus was the basis of their belief, they turned away from Simon. Even Simon himself believed and was baptized.

3. The Believers Receive the Holy Spirit (vv. 14-17)

When news of Philip's successful ministry in Samaria reached Jerusalem, the apostles immediately dispatched Peter and John to Samaria. That these two elder statesmen were sent to Samaria should not be misread. There was no lack of faith on the part of the church in Philip's ability to preach to salvation. This fact is apparent when we see that Peter and John did not preach in Samaria.

Instead, they prayed and laid hands on the Samaritan converts. As a result, God gave the Samaritans the gift of the Holy Spirit.

The sending of Peter and John is better understood in light of who the Samaritans were. They were a mixed-race people with some Jewish lineage but possessed an alternative style of worship. They shared some of the same beliefs as the Jews: They claimed an Abrahamic lineage, and they were also awaiting a Messiah. By sending Peter and John, the church in Jerusalem was affirming its unity with the emerging church in Samaria.

With the impartation of the Holy Spirit, this Third Person of the Trinity ensured the unity of the church. The Holy Spirit also provided a witness in the form of the apostles Peter and John. The apostles were credible and authoritative witnesses to the Jews that the acceptance of Samaritans into the church was equal to that of the Jews.

The fact that the apostles "laid their hands" on the Samaritan converts is no evidence that this was the only way for the Samaritans to receive the Holy Spirit (Acts 8:17). On the Day of Pentecost, there was no mention of laying on of hands, yet the Holy Spirit was imparted to all of the disciples who were present and believing. Additionally when Peter preached to Cornelius' household, there is no mention of laying on of hands to receive the Spirit (Acts 10:44).

There is also little Scriptural evidence that the 12 apostles were the only men empowered to impart the Holy Spirit through the laying on of hands. When Paul, formerly Saul of Tarsus, was converted, it was Ananias who laid hands on him so that Paul might be healed and receive the Holy Spirit (Acts 9:17-18). Ananias was neither an apostle nor a deacon. Instead, the laying on of hands and the receipt of the Holy Spirit by the Samaritans at the hands of the apostles marked a critical breakdown of religious and racial barriers. Philip had already baptized the believing Samaritans; thus, they were already saved. The apostles now witnessed the inclusiveness of the church. They saw that God was giving these Samaritans the exact same gift of the Holy Spirit that He had given to the apostles and disciples in Jerusalem. There was no barrier between the believing Jews and the believing Samaritans. There was one faith, one baptism, and one Spirit (see Ephesians 4:4-6).

4. Simon Attempts to Buy the Power of the Holy Spirit (vv. 18-24)

Superstitious Simon wanted to be able to impress people again with his magical powers, but he did not understand that the gift of the Holy Spirit is freely given to all who believe. Earlier, we read that Simon believed and was baptized. At this point, we wonder whether his profession of faith was genuine. When Simon saw the apostles, Peter and John, laying hands on people to receive the Holy Spirit, he wanted this same power for himself and he was ready to pay for it.

Peter saw through Simon right away. This was definitely not a genuine desire for spiritual power. In his heart was a desire to have center stage, and this is the opposite of what God desires to see in us. God wants us to give Him the preeminence. Many people today are confused about paying for spiritual blessings. God is not like the waiter who gives you better service if you tip him better. Even our good works will not open the door of heaven for us. In Ephesians 2:8-9 (NIV), we read: "For it is by grace you have been saved, through faith—and this is not from yourselves, it is the gift of God—not by works, so that no one can boast." Every gift we receive from God is just that—a gift! Even our spiritual gifts are free from our heavenly Father (Ephesians 4:7-13).

We would like to see a happy ending to this story recorded in Acts 8, but it's not there. Instead of Simon praying to God in deep repentance, he asked Peter to pray for him that the punishment for his sins would not fall on him. In other words, Simon was not sorry for his sins; he just wanted to get off the hook from the punishment.

Search the Scriptures

1. What was Simon doing to amaze the people of Samaria (Acts 8:9)?

2. How did the Samaritans respond to Philip (v. 12)?

3. What terrible thing did Simon try to do (vv. 18-19)?

Discuss the Meaning

1. Peter gave Simon a warning. Why do you think what Simon did was so terrible?

2. Name some other times when the Holy Spirit was given through the laying on of the hands. What are some similarities in these cases? What are some differences?

Lesson in Our Society

Simon reminds us of some TV preachers who seem to be in the ministry primarily for the fame and fortune. What are some signs of the authenticity or the insincerity you can see in some TV preachers?

Make It Happen

It may be easier to see false motivations in others than ourselves. Finish today's lesson by creating as a list of true and sincere motives for following Christ. Now silently examine your heart to see how you measure up, and then ask God to help form your attitudes and motives to be true and sincere.

Follow the Spirit

What God wants me to do:

_____

_____

_____

_____

Remember Your Thoughts

Special insights I have learned:

_____

_____

_____

_____

More Light on the Text

Acts 8:9-24

9 But there was a certain man, called Simon, which beforetime in the same city used sorcery, and bewitched the people of Samaria, giving out that himself was some great one:

For some time before Philip arrived in Samaria, the town had been "bewitched" (Gk. *existemi*, **ex-IS-tay-mee**) by a man named Simon. He practiced witchcraft or "sorcery" (Gk. *mageuo*, **mag-YOO-o**) literally, "the practice of magic." Simon used his magical skills to persuade the people of Samaria that he was someone great (see 5:36).

10 To whom they all gave heed, from the least to the greatest, saying, This man is the great power of God.

Everyone, "the least" (Gk. *mikros*, **mik-ROS**) and "the greatest" (Gk. *megas*, **MEG-as**) crowded around him saying that Simon was in some way the special channel of the power of God or the supreme emanation of God Himself.

11 And to him they had regard, because that of long time he had bewitched them with sorceries.

For a long time the people "had regard" (Gk. *prosecho*, **pros-EKH-o**) or were devoted to Simon because he had used witchcraft to bewitch or influence them.

12 But when they believed Philip preaching the things concerning the kingdom of God, and the name of Jesus Christ, they were baptized, both men and women.

Philip did not preach about himself. Philip was "preaching" (Gk. *euaggelizo*, **yoo-ang-ghel-ID-zo**), "the things concerning the kingdom of God, and the name of Jesus Christ." The Samaritans "believed" (Gk. *pisteuo*, **pist-YOO-o**) and "were baptized" (Gk. *baptizo*, **bap-TID-zo**).

13 Then Simon himself believed also: and when he was baptized, he continued with Philip, and wondered, beholding the miracles and signs which were done.

Simon believed and was baptized. He followed Philip everywhere, captivated by the great signs and miracles he saw. After having amazed others with his magic practice, he himself was amazed.

In view of what is said later in verse 21, we do not know whether Simon really believed. The Bible language does not always make a distinction between believing and professing to believe (see James 2:19). He may have been more taken by the healing power of Philip than by his message.

14 Now when the apostles which were at Jerusalem heard that Samaria had received the word of God, they sent unto them Peter and John:

In Acts 8:14, we read that when the "apostles" (Gk. *apostolos*, **ap-OS-tol-os**) "heard" (Gk. *akouo*, **a-KOO-o**) that Samaria "had received" (Gk. *dechomai*, **DEKH-om-ahee**) the Word of God, they sent Peter and John, two apostles, to investigate. The Greek words for "sent" (*apostello*, **a-pos-TEL-lo**) and "apostle" have the same root meaning, literally "the delegated." On one occasion, James and John had wanted to call fire down from heaven to consume a Samaritan city

(Luke 9:51-56). It was fitting that one of them should be part of the delegation that now went to welcome the people of Samaria into the church.

15 Who, when they were come down, prayed for them, that they might receive the Holy Ghost:

When they arrived, they discovered that although the people of Samaria had believed and had been baptized into the name of Jesus, they had not yet received the Holy Ghost. So they prayed for them that they might "receive" (Gk. *lambano*, **lam-BAHN-o**) the Holy Ghost.

16 (For as yet he was fallen upon none of them: only they were baptized in the name of the Lord Jesus.)

Acts 8:16 says that the Holy Ghost had not yet come "upon" (Gk. *epi*, **ep-EE**) any of the Samaritans. They had simply been baptized in the name of the Lord Jesus. This statement raises some questions that have caused much perplexity and division: How did the apostles know that the Samaritans had not received the Holy Ghost? In light of Acts 2:38, how could the Samaritans have believed and been baptized and not received the Spirit? There are two general approaches to these questions. One is that here, as in Acts 2:41 and Acts 10:44-48, Peter was using the keys of the Kingdom to open it successively to Jews, Samaritans, and Gentiles. It was a new departure in line with what Jesus said in Acts 1:8. Thus, we should see it as an abnormal rather than a normal experience of Christian life. Another view is that the Samaritan Christians' experience is a typical experience of Christian life. Becoming a Christian is a two-stage process consisting first of conversion and water baptism, and second of the gift or baptism of the Spirit. The apostle Paul argues against the latter view in Romans 8:9, NKJV. He states, "Now if anyone does not have the Spirit of Christ, he is not His." In other words, any person who is saved has the Holy Spirit.

17 Then laid they their hands on them, and they received the Holy Ghost.

In addition to praying for them, Acts 8:17 says that the apostles "laid" (Gk. *epitithemi*, **ep-ee-TITH-ay-mee**) their hands, thus identifying the people for whom they prayed with the rest of the church, particularly the mother church in Jerusalem. In answer to their prayers, the believers received the Holy Ghost.

18 And when Simon saw that through laying on of the apostles' hands the Holy Ghost was given, he offered them money, 19 Saying, Give me also this power, that on whomsoever I lay hands, he may receive the Holy Ghost.

The "Ghost" in "Holy Ghost" is *pneuma* (**PNYOO-mah)** and means a breath of air or specifically the Spirit of God, or Holy Spirit. While the KJV uses the term "Holy Ghost," all subsequent American translations use Holy Spirit instead because of the connotations with the word "ghost."

When Simon saw the apostles laying their hands on people as they received the Holy Spirit, it seemed like some very powerful religious magic. We read in verse 9 that Simon had proclaimed himself "the great one." Now he desired the power that he saw in the apostles so that he could continue to be the main practitioner of wonders. It's no doubt that he expected money when he performed his magic deeds, and he thought that he could buy the powerful "magic" that he saw in the apostles.

20 But Peter said unto him, Thy money perish with thee, because thou hast thought that the gift of God may be purchased with money. 21 Thou hast neither part nor lot in this matter: for thy heart is not right in the sight of God.

Simon completely misunderstood the power of God. It is not something that can be purchased, like the magic of the sorcerer. Because of his attempt, the term "simony" has come to mean trying to buy spiritual gifts or purchase an ecclesiastical office. We may think at first that this was just a misunderstanding, but it was showing a light into what was in Simon's heart. The reason he wanted the gift that the apostles had was because he still wanted to be the one who could perform great miracles, the one everyone looked up to. He wanted to maintain his magical power over the people.

In verse 20, the Greek word for "purchased" is *ktaomai* (**KTAH-om-ahee)** and it is defined as got, acquired, obtained, possessed, provided, or purchased. Everything we have is a gift from God and nothing is available through purchase. That Simon thought he could buy this spiritual gift revealed that he was still thinking that the gift of salvation was not truly a gift from God.

22 Repent therefore of this thy wickedness, and pray God, if perhaps the thought of thine heart may be forgiven thee. 23 For I perceive that thou art in the gall of bitterness, and in the bond of iniquity.

Peter could see that the thoughts in Simon's heart were wrong. What is "gall"? The Greek is *chole* (**khol-AY)**, and it means bile or poison. The English word has come to mean arrogance, but Peter is talking about something much worse. Bitterness is the opposite of sweetness; it is an attitude of anger, hurt, or resentment. All wrong actions are rooted in the attitudes of the heart. So Simon's request was not an innocent misunderstanding. Inside he was feeling bitterness because he would no longer be the big, important sorcerer. Now that people had the message of redemption, they would no longer be fooled by the spiritual void that the sorcerer used to his advantage.

To be bound up is literally to have shackles on. To be "in the bond of iniquity" is to be handcuffed to sin (v. 23). Simon was still not spiritually free. Peter commanded Simon to repent of the sin in his heart, but the next verse will show that he did not.

24 Then answered Simon, and said, Pray ye to the LORD for me, that none of these things which ye have spoken come upon me.

Although Simon was afraid of the judgment that Peter alluded to, he was not ready to repent. In fact, he was not even ready to pray. Instead, Simon asked Peter to pray for him—not for repentance and forgiveness but simply to pray for him that the bad things Peter talked about would not happen to him.

Sources:

Bruce, F. F. *The Epistle to the Hebrews, Revised: New International Commentary on the New Testament.* Grand Rapids, MI: Eerdmans, 1983.

Dictionary.com. http://dictionary.reference.com/ (accessed September 19, 2011).

The NIV Study Bible. Grand Rapids, MI: Zondervan Publishing House, 1995.

New Testament Greek Lexicon. Bible Study Tools.com. http://www.biblestudytools.com/lexicons/greek (accessed September 19, 2011).

Stott, John. *The Spirit, the Church, and the World: The Message of Acts.* Downers Grove, IL: InterVarsity Press, 1990.

Unger, Merrill F. *Unger's Bible Dictionary.* Chicago, IL: Moody Press, 1969. 1039.

Say It Correctly

Simony. **SI**-muh-nee.
Sorcery. **SOR**-suh-ree.

Daily Bible Readings

MONDAY
Who Can Understand God's Power?
(Job 26)

TUESDAY
Using the Name of the Lord
(Acts 19:11-20)

WEDNESDAY
Christ, the Power of God
(1 Corinthians 1:18-25)

THURSDAY
Faith Resting on God's Power
(1 Corinthians 1:26-2:5)

FRIDAY
The Works of the Flesh
(Galatians 5:16-21)

SATURDAY
The Fruit of the Spirit
(Galatians 5:22-26)

SUNDAY
What Money Cannot Buy
(Acts 8:9-24)

Teaching Tips

Words You Should Know

A. Eunuch (Acts 8:27, 34, 36, 38, 39) *eunouchos* (Gk.)—A state officer.

B. Esaias the Prophet (v. 28) *Hesaias* (Gk.)—Isaiah, an Old Testament prophet.

Teacher Preparation

Unifying Principle—Erasing the Boundary Lines. Philip's sharing of the Good News about Jesus and the baptism of the Ethiopian demonstrate the universal availability of the Gospel message.

A. Pray for your students and lesson clarity.

B. Read and study the entire lesson.

C. Complete the companion lesson in the *Precepts For Living Personal Study Guide*®.

D. Secure a Bible map of Philip's missionary route.

O—Open the Lesson

A. Ask a student to pray, focusing on the Lesson Aim.

B. Have students read the Aim for Change and Keep in Mind verse in unison and then discuss each.

C. Ask a volunteer to summarize the In Focus story. Discuss.

P—Present the Scriptures

A. Use The People, Places, and Times, Background, At-A-Glance outline, and In Depth sections to unpack the Focal Verses.

B. Allow your students five to 10 minutes to share any opportunities they had to witness in the past week.

C. Use your Bible map to show Philip's missionary route. Discuss.

E—Explore the Meaning

A. Use the Discuss the Meaning, Lesson in Our Society, and Make It Happen sections to further explore the meaning of the lesson.

B. Have students jot down salient points in the Follow the Spirit and Remember Your Thoughts sections.

N—Next Steps for Application

A. Give the students a few minutes to silently reflect on today's lesson.

B. Remind students to complete the Daily Bible Readings.

C. After receiving requests, close with prayer.

OCT
28th

Worship Guide

For the Superintendent or Teacher
Theme: Philip and the
Ethiopian Eunuch
Song: "Where He Leads Me,
I Will Follow"
Devotional Reading: Isaiah 56:1-8
Prayer

Philip and the Ethiopian Eunuch

Bible Background • ACTS 8:26-39
Printed Text • ACTS 8:26-39 | Devotional Reading • Isaiah 56:1-8

——————— Aim for Change ———————

By the end of the lesson, we will: EXPLAIN the connection between Philip's sharing of the Gospel and its universal availability; REFLECT on our openness to people who differ from us; and DEVELOP strategies to make our churches more open and inclusive.

——————— In Focus ———————

Late Saturday evening, Jessica sat at her kitchen table working on her Bible study homework. The assignment was to list several Bible verses that supported why studying Scriptures should be a daily routine. It was a good exercise for her because she had never been able to quote Scripture accurately. She wanted to make good use of this exercise, so she searched verses for hours and then she wrote the following:

1) "Thy word is a lamp unto my feet, and a light unto my path" (Psalm 119:105).

2) "But his delight is in the law of the LORD; and in his law doth he meditate day and night. And he shall be like a tree planted by the rivers of water, that bringeth forth his fruit in his season; his leaf also shall not wither; and whatsoever he doeth shall prosper" (Psalm 1:2-3).

3) "But he answered and said, It is written, Man shall not live by bread alone, but by every word that proceedeth out of the mouth of God" (Matthew 4:4).

4) "Study to shew thyself approved unto God, a workman that needeth not to be ashamed, rightly dividing the word of truth" (2 Timothy 2:15).

In our lesson this week, we will explore how Philip used the Scriptures to explain salvation to the Ethiopian eunuch.

——————— Keep in Mind ———————

"And as they went on their way, they came unto a certain water: and the eunuch said, See, here is water; what doth hinder me to be baptized?" (Acts 8:36).

"And as they went on their way, they came unto a certain water: and the eunuch said, See, here is water; what doth hinder me to be baptized?" (Acts 8:36).

Focal Verses

KJV **Acts 8:26** And the angel of the Lord spake unto Philip, saying, Arise, and go toward the south unto the way that goeth down from Jerusalem unto Gaza, which is desert.

27 And he arose and went: and, behold, a man of Ethiopia, an eunuch of great authority under Candace queen of the Ethiopians, who had the charge of all her treasure, and had come to Jerusalem for to worship,

28 Was returning, and sitting in his chariot read Esaias the prophet.

29 Then the Spirit said unto Philip, Go near, and join thyself to this chariot.

30 And Philip ran thither to *him*, and heard him read the prophet Esaias, and said, Understandest thou what thou readest?

31 And he said, How can I, except some man should guide me? And he desired Philip that he would come up and sit with him.

32 The place of the scripture which he read was this, He was led as a sheep to the slaughter; and like a lamb dumb before his shearer, so opened he not his mouth:

33 In his humiliation his judgment was taken away: and who shall declare his generation? for his life is taken from the earth.

34 And the eunuch answered Philip, and said, I pray thee, of whom speaketh the prophet this? of himself, or of some other man?

35 Then Philip opened his mouth, and began at the same scripture, and preached unto him Jesus.

36 And as they went on their way, they came unto a certain water: and the eunuch said, See, here is water; what doth hinder me to be baptized?

NLT **Acts 8:26** As for Philip, an angel of the Lord said to him, "Go south down the desert road that runs from Jerusalem to Gaza."

27 So he started out, and he met the treasurer of Ethiopia, a eunuch of great authority under the Kandake, the queen of Ethiopia. The eunuch had gone to Jerusalem to worship,

28 and he was now returning. Seated in his carriage, he was reading aloud from the book of the prophet Isaiah.

29 The Holy Spirit said to Philip, "Go over and walk along beside the carriage."

30 Philip ran over and heard the man reading from the prophet Isaiah. Philip asked, "Do you understand what you are reading?"

31 The man replied, "How can I, unless someone instructs me?" And he urged Philip to come up into the carriage and sit with him.

32 The passage of Scripture he had been reading was this: "He was led like a sheep to the slaughter. And as a lamb is silent before the shearers, he did not open his mouth.

33 He was humiliated and received no justice. Who can speak of his descendants? For his life was taken from the earth."

34 The eunuch asked Philip, "Tell me, was the prophet talking about himself or someone else?"

35 So beginning with this same Scripture, Philip told him the Good News about Jesus.

***36** As they rode along, they came to some water, and the eunuch said, "Look! There's some water! Why can't I be baptized?"

38 He ordered the carriage to stop, and they went down into the water, and Philip baptized him.

KJV continued

37 And Philip said, If thou believest with all thine heart, thou mayest. And he answered and said, I believe that Jesus Christ is the Son of God.

38 And he commanded the chariot to stand still: and they went down both into the water, both Philip and the eunuch; and he baptized him.

39 And when they were come up out of the water, the Spirit of the Lord caught away Philip, that the eunuch saw him no more: and he went on his way rejoicing.

The People, Places, and Times

Eunuchs. Throughout the Bible, there are references to royal attendants appointed by kings as official caretakers of queens, harems, and women (Esther 2:3, 12-15). Those eunuchs, who served with distinction, were able to rise in rank within the royal households. The Assyrians and the pharaohs of Egypt were known to have minor officials in their court who often served as trustees of the royal assets. While the term is often literal, referring to men who have been physically castrated, this was not always the case. The term "eunuchs" was also used to denote officials who were assigned to duties in the courts of kings. Because the Ethiopian man referenced in today's lesson was a proselyte, or Gentile who has converted to Judaism, to the Jewish religion, we may deduce that he was not castrated because the Mosaic Law would not have allowed him to become a part of the congregation of God's people (Deuteronomy 23:1).

NLT continued

39 When they came up out of the water, the Spirit of the Lord snatched Philip away. The eunuch never saw him again but went on his way rejoicing.

Background

In the book of Acts, the story of Philip's evangelistic effort serves as a transition between the ministries of Peter and Paul. The account of Paul describes how God adds to the church through his bold and relentless preaching. Philip is in the middle of the record of these two great statesmen; Philip's efforts add to the church soul by soul.

We see Philip first serving as an elected deacon in the Jerusalem church (Acts 6:5). His effective witnessing efforts are described in Acts 8:4-25, which shows how they fulfill Jesus' Great Commission to spread the Gospel from Jerusalem into Judea and Samaria to the uttermost parts of the earth.

At-A-Glance

1. Philip Obeys the Spirit (Acts 8:26-29)
2. Philip Witnesses in the Spirit (vv. 29-35)
3. The Ethiopian Confesses Christ (vv. 36-39)

In Depth

1. Philip Obeys the Spirit (Acts 8:26-29)

Acts 8 focuses on two great missionary efforts by Philip. In the first, Philip, under the direction of the Holy Spirit, has preached Christ, which led to the conversion of the Samaritans. The receipt of the Holy Spirit by the Samaritans verifies his success with spreading the Good News from Jerusalem and Judea to Samaria.

The Spirit then directs Philip on another mission. We are told that an angel of the Lord directs Philip to go down from Jerusalem to Gaza (Acts 8:26, NLT). In Acts, the writer (Luke) presupposes that Jerusalem is ground zero for church activities, implying that Philip has returned to Jerusalem from Samaria. Philip was now directed southwest into the desert. Initially, Philip was not told what to do at Gaza. However, this lack of information did not stop him. He was obedient to the word from God and immediately obeyed. We should note that while Peter and Paul are noted for their great preaching ability, Philip was outstanding in the area of obedience. Whenever the Spirit directed him, Philip heeded. Because he was so sensitive to the direction of the Holy Spirit, it is clear that prayer and the study of God's Word must have been integral parts of Philip's life. How much more effective would Christians be today if we were more sensitive and obedient to the Holy Spirit?

On the road, Philip encountered a fellow traveler. Scripture tells us four important things about this man. First, we are told that he was a man from Ethiopia. Native Ethiopians were Black people. The man was from a distant country located along the upper Nile. At this time in history, Ethiopia was located in the area we now know as the Sudan.

We then learn that he is a eunuch in the court of Candace, queen of Ethiopia, and "had the charge of all her treasure." Finally we're told that he had come to Jerusalem to worship.

Biblical scholars provide varied interpretations of what it means that the Ethiopian was a eunuch. One group takes the position that the term "eunuch" designates

that he was a government official. They also say he was a circumcised Jewish proselyte. This group uses as proof the fact that the Ethiopian was in Jerusalem to worship. Temple worship dictated both his Jewish conversion and his circumcision. Others believed that because the man was in the service of a queen, the Ethiopian had been castrated. If this second theory were correct, Mosaic Law would have prohibited him from joining "the congregation of the LORD" (Deuteronomy 23:1).

2. Philip Witnesses in the Spirit (vv. 29-35)

The Gaza road was well traveled; certainly other chariots had passed Philip. The Spirit directs Philip to "Go near, and join thyself to this chariot" (v. 29). This was no chance meeting. Philip was being purposefully led by the Holy Spirit to be with this man at this time. In this way, Philip was like Jesus. He did not mind leaving the crowds behind to deal with one lost soul. Notice Philip's zeal: He ran to the Ethiopian's chariot. Philip recognized the seriousness of his missionary work. Do we hasten to assist in the salvation of the lost?

Because the Ethiopian was reading from the book of Isaiah, we can safely assume that this man took the religion of Judaism seriously. Ethiopia was one of the areas among which the Jews were scattered after the Babylonian conquest (Isaiah 11:11). The eunuch may have had contact with Jews in Ethiopia or in nearby Egypt, where a great many Jews settled. Similarly, the fact that the Ethiopian could read Greek could be explained by the fact that from the time of Ptolemy II (306-246 B.C.), the Ethiopian kingdom had become partially Hellenized, or made to reflect Greek culture.

The custom of the time was to read Scripture aloud. Upon hearing the Ethiopian reading,

Philip asked the Ethiopian if he understood what he was reading. In Acts 8:31 he said, in effect, "How can I unless someone shows me the way?" The Ethiopian was confused by what he was reading and needed someone to explain the Scripture to him. The Ethiopian's sincerity and willingness to learn were demonstrated by his invitation to Philip to come into the chariot and sit with him. Like many people today, the Ethiopian earnestly sought the truth, but he lacked saving faith in Jesus Christ and needed someone to show him the way. We must recognize that God could have allowed an angel to explain the Scripture to the Ethiopian but instead commissioned Philip to witness to him. Similarly, Jesus has commissioned, ordered, and instructed each and every Christian to share the Gospel with others.

The Ethiopian had been reading from Isaiah 53, a passage describing the humiliation and suffering of the servant of God. The Ethiopian wanted to know, "Tell me, please, who is the prophet speaking about, himself or someone else?" (v. 34, NIV). The Holy Spirit had been preparing Philip for this very moment. Philip "opened his mouth, and ... preached unto him Jesus" (v. 35). Philip explained that the prophet Isaiah was describing Jesus, the Christ. The eunuch had no doubt heard a great deal about this Jesus while in Jerusalem.

3. The Ethiopian Confesses Christ (vv. 36-39)

During his preaching, Philip had probably talked about baptism. As soon as they came to a body of water, the eunuch asked if there was any hindrance to his being baptized right on the spot. Notice that Philip did not drill the Ethiopian on his knowledge and understanding of the Scripture. Philip simply asked him if he believed that Jesus

was the Son of God. In other words, did he have faith? Obviously, at least to Philip, there were no impediments to this man's baptism. Upon the Ethiopian's simple confession of faith, "I believe," Philip recognized that the man was prepared to be placed under the Lordship of Jesus and incorporated into the church (some early manuscripts do not have v. 37). Philip and the Ethiopian entered the water, and the Ethiopian was baptized. In this moment, another prophecy of Isaiah was being fulfilled. This prophecy spoke of strangers, eunuchs, and other outcasts who would be given an "everlasting name" and called God's people: "The Lord GOD, which gathereth the outcasts of Israel saith; Yet will I gather others to him, beside those that are gathered unto him" (Isaiah 56:8).

Search the Scriptures

1. Why was Philip on the road to Gaza (Acts 8:26)?

2. From where was the Ethiopian official returning when Stephen encountered him (v. 27)?

3. Why did Philip approach the Ethiopian (v. 29)?

4. When they reached the water, what did the Ethiopian ask Philip (v. 36)?

Discuss the Meaning

1. Read Acts 1:8. What is the role of the Holy Spirit in Philip's evangelistic efforts?

2. Why do you think Philip was able to be so sensitive to the Holy Spirit's directives?

3. It's clear that the Ethiopian's faith was sincere. Yet, in reading scripture and seeking truth, he was lost. Why?

Lesson in Our Society

When Philip then was finalizing his successful missionary work in Samaria, the Spirit ordered him to go to Gaza. Instead of dragging his feet, Philip heeded the direction of the Holy Spirit and performed a life-saving evangelistic appeal to the Ethiopian official. Today's Christians would do well to follow Philip's example and get up and go! If we are to be witnesses for the Kingdom, we will have to maintain sensitivity to the Spirit rather than follow our own course of action. We will be more effective witnesses when we allow God to order our steps in every area of our lives.

Make It Happen

Commit to daily personal devotion, prayer, and Bible study. Select a quiet time and place to do uninterrupted reading of and meditation on the Word of God. You may find that early in the morning or in the evening just before you go to bed is best. Start with five minutes of reading the first week and add three to five minutes each week. You can start with the Daily Bible Readings.

Follow the Spirit

What God wants me to do:

_____

_____

_____

_____

Remember Your Thoughts

Special insights I have learned:

_____

_____

_____

_____

More Light on the Text

Acts 8:26-39

26 And the angel of the Lord spake unto Philip, saying, Arise, and go toward the south unto the way that goeth down from Jerusalem unto Gaza, which is desert.

Angels play a critical role in the narrative of Luke and Acts (see Luke 1:11-18; 2:9-15; Acts 12:7-10; 27). Because Jerusalem was built on a hill, any departure was considered "going down" from the city. Gaza was one of the five cities occupied by the Philistines in southwest Palestine. At the time Luke writes, it was on a caravan route leading to Egypt that someone traveling from Jerusalem to Ethiopia would naturally take.

27 And he arose and went: and, behold, a man of Ethiopia, an eunuch of great authority under Candace queen of the Ethiopians, who had the charge of all her treasure, and had come to Jerusalem for to worship,

Ethiopia bordered Egypt to the South of Israel and was known in the Bible as the ancient land of Cush (Genesis 2:13; 10:6; 1 Chronicles 1:8; Isaiah 11:11; Ezekiel 38:5). The Ethiopia referred to in antiquity is now called Sudan.

Ethiopia was considered one of the most wicked nations of the world (Isaiah 20:3-5; 43:3; Ezekiel 30:1-9; Nahum 3:9; Zephaniah 2:11-12), and its people were among those foreigners who would be converted and acknowledge the true God of Israel. For example, Ethiopia figures prominently in a text of Isaiah concerning the restoration of the people (Isaiah 11:11-12; Zephaniah 3:10).

It was not uncommon for eunuchs (castrated males or government officials) to hold positions of importance in royal courts in the region. Yet, according to Deuteronomy 23:2, this condition meant a rejection of full participation in the Jewish assembly, and according to Leviticus 21:20; 22:24, an emasculated male was physically blemished and in a permanent state of ritual impurity. Some eunuchs were not castrated but were simply those set apart to serve the government. Though Isaiah prophesied that a time would come when "eunuchs [would] keep my sabbaths," "take hold of [his] covenant," and would be given a place in God's house (Isaiah 56:4-5).

The Ethiopian eunuch held a high position in the Ethiopian government. He was in charge of the entire treasury of the Candace. According to ancient writers Pliny the Elder and Callisthenes, Candace, queen of the Ethiopians, was a dynastic rather than a personal name. That is, it was used to refer to a royal line of queens over various generations (e.g., "the Candace").

The Ethiopian eunuch had come to Jerusalem to worship. The narrative does not indicate whether he was a Jew or a proselyte. He may have been a God-fearing person, i.e., a non-Jew who, although sympathetic to Judaism, did not submit to circumcision or observe the Torah in its entirety but did agree with the ethical monotheism of the Jews and sometimes attended their synagogue services. If he was a eunuch not only by position but also with a physical blemish, it would not have been possible for him to participate in the worship in the temple. In this regard, his status was like that of other foreigners who came to the Temple in spite of being excluded from it.

28 Was returning, and sitting in his chariot read Esaias the prophet. 29 Then the Spirit said unto Philip, Go near, and join thyself to this chariot. 30 And Philip ran thither to *him*, and heard him read the prophet Esaias, and said, Understandest thou what thou readest?

The angel of the Lord delivered the original message. Here, the Spirit of the Lord further instructs Philip. The point is the same: God is directly guiding Philip. When the Spirit told Philip to go and join up with the "chariot" (Gk. *harma*, **HAR-mah**), he obeyed. As he came near, he heard the eunuch reading Isaiah. It was customary in the ancient world to read aloud, even when alone. This was especially the case with lengthy scrolls where there was no separation between words; it had to be read syllable by syllable to detect the word divisions.

In Acts 8:30, Philip asks the eunuch, "Do you understand what you are reading?" Philip's question derives from the conviction that the prophetic writings contained deeper meaning for the future.

31 And he said, How can I, except some man should guide me? And he desired Philip that he would come up and sit with him.

In verse 31, NLT, the eunuch replies, "How can I (understand), unless someone instructs me?" "Guide" in the KJV (Gk. *hodegeo*, **ho-day-GEH-o**) literally means to lead along a road (see Jesus' use of the term "blind leaders" and "blind lead the blind" in Matthew 15:14). Here "guide" gains the transferred sense of "leading" in righteousness or wisdom similar to its use in passages such as Psalm 5:8; 73:24; John 16:13.

The eunuch invites Philip to get in and sit with him under the assumption that he will be able to explain the passage in Isaiah. Traditionally, the Jews applied the concepts of suffering and humiliation in Isaiah 52:13—53:12 to the nation Israel or to the unrighteous Gentile nations. Thus, the idea of a suffering Messiah was not thought of by the Jewish rabbis of the day. This passage, then, must have been unclear to the eunuch.

32 The place of the scripture which he read was this, He was led as a sheep to the slaughter; and like a lamb dumb before his shearer, so opened he not his mouth. 33 In his humiliation his judgment was taken away: and who shall declare his generation? for his life is taken from the earth.

The passage the eunuch is reading from is Isaiah 53:7-8. The Greek word for "humiliation" (*tapeinos*, **ta-pi-NOS**), used in Acts 8:33 provides a possible allusion both to Luke's theme of "humbling the haughty and exalting the humble" (Luke 1:52; 3:5; 14:11; 18:14), and to the humiliation of Jesus as described by the apostle Paul as having "made himself of no reputation" (Gk. *kenoo*, **ken-O-o**); see Philippians 2:7.

34 And the eunuch answered Philip, and said, I pray thee, of whom speaketh the prophet this? of himself, or of some other man?

The eunuch's question is the pertinent one. The traditional understanding of this passage did not address his deep spiritual hunger.

35 Then Philip opened his mouth, and began at the same scripture, and preached unto him Jesus.

After having been invited into the Ethiopian's chariot, Philip explains the Isaiah passage by beginning with the same text, and shows him that Jesus is the focus of the Scriptures. In Luke 24:13-35, the risen Jesus teaches the two on the road to Emmaus how to understand the Scriptures: "O fools, and slow of heart to believe all that the prophets have spoken: Ought not Christ to have suffered these things, and to enter into his glory? And beginning at Moses and all the prophets, he expounded unto them in all the scriptures the things concerning himself" (vv. 25b-27).

The Scripture passage in Isaiah that the eunuch is reading focused on the humiliation and exaltation of the Messiah. Similarly, Acts 8:32-33 refers to Jesus generally and to His humiliation and exaltation in particular ("his judgment was taken away," v. 33). This interpretation of the prophecy of Isaiah is also seen in other New Testament Scriptures. In Romans 10:16, Paul quotes Isaiah 53:1 and applies it to his own ministry; in John 12:38, Jesus quotes Isaiah 53:1 and applies it to His ministry.

36 And as they went on their way, they came unto a certain water: and the eunuch said, See, here is water; what doth hinder me to be baptized?

After hearing the Scripture explained and being shown how it pointed to Jesus, the eunuch asks, "What hinders me from being baptized?" "Hinder" (Gk. *koluo*, **ko-LOO-o**) is also used in Luke 11:52, where Jesus accuses the lawyers of preventing ("hindering") others from entering the Kingdom. Similar circumstances are seen later in Luke's account.

37 And Philip said, If thou believest with all thine heart, thou mayest. And he answered and said, I believe that Jesus Christ is the Son of God. 38 And he commanded the chariot to stand still: and they went down both into the water, both Philip and the eunuch; and he baptized him.

Because there was no reason for his exclusion from other followers of Jesus, the Ethiopian eunuch orders the chariot to stop; Philip and the eunuch both enter the water, and Philip baptizes him.

39 And when they were come up out of the water, the Spirit of the Lord caught away Philip, that the eunuch saw him no more: and he went on his way rejoicing.

The Old Testament often portrays the Spirit (Gk. *pneuma*, **PNYOO-mah**) moving

110

prophets around in this fashion (Ezekiel 11:24; 1 Kings 18:12; 2 Kings 2:16).

In Acts 8:39, we read that the eunuch continued on his way "rejoicing" (Gk. *chairo*, **KHAH-ee-ro**), an appropriate response to salvation. Frequently in the books of Luke and Acts, joy or rejoicing is a noted response to God's work in the world (Luke 1:14; 2:10; 6:23; 8:13; Acts 5:41).

* **Acts 8:36** Some manuscripts add verse 37, "You can," Philip answered, "if you believe with all your heart." And the eunuch replied, "I believe that Jesus Christ is the Son of God."

Sources:
Bible Gateway.com. http://www.biblegateway.com (accessed September 20, 2011).
Dictionary.com. http://dictionary.reference.com/ (accessed September 20, 2011).
New Testament Greek Lexicon. Bible Study Tools.com. http://www.biblestudytools.com/lexicons/greek (accessed September 20, 2011).
Packer, J. I. and M. C. Tenney, eds. *Illustrated Manners and Customs of the Bible.* Nashville, TN: Thomas Nelson Publishers, 1980. 324, 327.

Say It Correctly

Shewed. **SHOWED.**
Stiff-necked. **STIFF**-nekt.
Uncircumcised. uhn-**SUR**-kuhm-sized.

Daily Bible Readings

MONDAY
Blemishes That Exclude
(Leviticus 21:16-24)

TUESDAY
Lifting Up the Downtrodden
(Psalm 147:1-6)

WEDNESDAY
Gathering the Outcasts
(Isaiah 56:1-8)

THURSDAY
Changing Shame into Praise
(Zephaniah 3:14-20)

FRIDAY
A Ruler Who Seeks Justice
(Isaiah 16:1-5)

SATURDAY
A Champion for the Needy
(Job 29:2-16)

SUNDAY
The Good News about Jesus
(Acts 8:26-39)

Teaching Tips

Words You Should Know

A. Repent (Acts 26:20) *metanoeo* (Gk.)—To be sorry for sin and "turn to God."

B. Shew Light (v. 23) *kataggello* (Gk.)—To make something clear to a wide audience or over a wide area.

Teacher Preparation

Unifying Principle—Taking a Stand. It is difficult to stand by our convictions when other people think we are crazy. Confident that he spoke the truth, Paul did not back down from sharing the story of his faith in Christ.

A. Pray for your students and lesson clarity.

B. Read and study the complete lesson.

C. Research some political or civil rights figures that stood on truth and be prepared to share details about their lives.

D. Complete the companion lesson in the *Precepts For Living Personal Study Guide®*.

O—Open the Lesson

A. Ask a student to open the class with a prayer, using the Keep in Mind verse.

B. Summarize the Background and The People, Places, and Times sections.

C. Have the class read the Keep in Mind verse and Lesson Aim in unison.

D. Share information about the political or civil rights figures you selected. Discuss.

E. Summarize the In Focus story. Discuss.

P—Present the Scriptures

A. Ask several students to take turns reading the Focal Verses.

B. Use the At-A-Glance outline to explore the In Depth section.

E—Explore the Meaning

A. Allow students to work in groups of two or three to answer the questions and discuss the points in the Search the Scriptures and Discuss the Meaning sections. Have them report back to the class when they finish.

B. Discuss the Lesson in Our Society section.

N—Next Steps for Application

A. Do the Make It Happen section as a class.

B. Remind students to complete the Daily Bible Readings.

C. After receiving prayer requests, close with prayer.

Worship Guide

For the Superintendent or Teacher
Theme: Paul before King Agrippa
Song: "Standing on the
Promises of God"
Devotional Reading: Acts 23:1-11
Prayer

Paul before King Agrippa

Bible Background • ACTS 25:23—26:32
Printed Text • ACTS 26:19-32 | Devotional Reading • ACTS 23:1-11

Aim for Change

By the end of the lesson, we will: KNOW why Paul stood up for what he believed; FEEL confident in sharing our faith; and examine ways to DEFEND our faith, even in the face of rejection.

In Focus

Pat was an elementary school teacher at a local school. The parents of her students loved Pat, and her principal always complimented her on how well she controlled her classroom. Many of the teachers looked up to her and often asked her advice. Pat liked her co-workers but wasn't close to any of them. During the lunch break, she often sat in the corner of the room rather than at the table with the other teachers. Pat, a Christian and a regular church attendee, was increasingly uncomfortable with the discussions that took place in the teachers' break room.

Off-color jokes were frequently told by some of her co-workers and lately, "the church" had been the favorite butt of the jokes. Christian beliefs and practices resulted in side-splitting laughter. Pat felt that she should say something, but she was afraid that the people, who thought so highly of her, might become resentful.

Taking a stand for what you believe is never easy. Christians are not exempt. In today's lesson, we will see that God understands that His people are the objects of persecution and that He can fortify us to take a stand in Jesus' name.

NOV
4th

Keep in Mind

"But he said, I am not mad, most noble Festus; but speak forth the words of truth and soberness" (Acts 26:25).

"But he said, I am not mad, most noble Festus; but speak forth the words of truth and soberness" (Acts 26:25).

Focal Verses

KJV **Acts 26:19** Whereupon, O king Agrippa, I was not disobedient unto the heavenly vision:

20 But shewed first unto them of Damascus, and at Jerusalem, and throughout all the coasts of Judaea, and then to the Gentiles, that they should repent and turn to God, and do works meet for repentance.

21 For these causes the Jews caught me in the temple, and went about to kill me.

22 Having therefore obtained help of God, I continue unto this day, witnessing both to small and great, saying none other things than those which the prophets and Moses did say should come:

23 That Christ should suffer, and that he should be the first that should rise from the dead, and should shew light unto the people, and to the Gentiles.

24 And as he thus spake for himself, Festus said with a loud voice, Paul, thou art beside thyself; much learning doth make thee mad.

25 But he said, I am not mad, most noble Festus; but speak forth the words of truth and soberness.

26 For the king knoweth of these things, before whom also I speak freely: for I am persuaded that none of these things are hidden from him; for this thing was not done in a corner.

27 King Agrippa, believest thou the prophets? I know that thou believest.

28 Then Agrippa said unto Paul, Almost thou persuadest me to be a Christian.

29 And Paul said, I would to God, that not only thou, but also all that hear me this day, were both almost, and altogether such as I am, except these bonds.

NLT **Acts 26:19** "And so, King Agrippa, I obeyed that vision from heaven.

20 I preached first to those in Damascus, then in Jerusalem and throughout all Judea, and also to the Gentiles, that all must repent of their sins and turn to God—and prove they have changed by the good things they do.

21 Some Jews arrested me in the Temple for preaching this, and they tried to kill me.

22 But God has protected me right up to this present time so I can testify to everyone, from the least to the greatest. I teach nothing except what the prophets and Moses said would happen—

23 that the Messiah would suffer and be the first to rise from the dead, and in this way announce God's light to Jews and Gentiles alike."

24 Suddenly, Festus shouted, "Paul, you are insane. Too much study has made you crazy!"

25 But Paul replied, "I am not insane, Most Excellent Festus. What I am saying is the sober truth.

26 And King Agrippa knows about these things. I speak boldly, for I am sure these events are all familiar to him, for they were not done in a corner!

27 King Agrippa, do you believe the prophets? I know you do—"

28 Agrippa interrupted him. "Do you think you can persuade me to become a Christian so quickly?"

29 Paul replied, "Whether quickly or not, I pray to God that both you and everyone here in this audience might become the same as I am, except for these chains."

30 Then the king, the governor, Bernice, and all the others stood and left.

KJV continued

30 And when he had thus spoken, the king rose up, and the governor, and Bernice, and they that sat with them:

31 And when they were gone aside, they talked between themselves, saying, This man doeth nothing worthy of death or of bonds.

32 Then said Agrippa unto Festus, This man might have been set at liberty, if he had not appealed unto Caesar.

NLT continued

31 As they went out, they talked it over and agreed, "This man hasn't done anything to deserve death or imprisonment."

32 And Agrippa said to Festus, "He could have been set free if he hadn't appealed to Caesar."

The People, Places, and Times

King Agrippa II. He was the son of King Agrippa I, the ruler who was responsible for beheading the apostle James and who had Peter arrested. He was the grandson of the ruler who'd had John the Baptist beheaded. He was also the great-grandson of Herod the Great, who, in his attempt to kill the baby Jesus, had killed all the male Jewish children two and younger in Bethlehem.

Agrippa II's power was limited to authority over Jewish affairs, Scriptures, and conflicts. Rome appointed him as the curator of the temple, meaning he had authority over the temple treasury and to appoint high priests. Agrippa II did not have any children, and when he met the apostle Paul, he was living in an incestuous relationship with his younger sister Bernice. Agrippa's capitol was Caesarea Philippi, which he renamed Neronias in honor of Caesar Nero. Agrippa II called himself "Great King, pious Friend of Caesar and Friend of Rome." The last of the Herods, he died in A.D. 100 at age 73.

Background

When Jesus called Saul of Tarsus to be an apostle, he sent Ananias to Paul, to pray for him and to welcome him into the Christian family. The Lord prophesied, "[Saul] is a chosen vessel unto me, to bear my name before the Gentiles, and kings, and the children of Israel" (Acts 9:15). Following his conversion from persecutor to Christian, the apostle Paul was a faithful and fervent disciple. He traveled broadly, spreading the Good News and winning souls to Christ. His zeal was not without trouble. Paul frequently found himself in personal danger. Opposition to Paul often came from the Jews, who believed he was a heretic. In Acts 24, an imprisoned Paul stands before the Jewish governor, Felix, facing false accusations that he incited Christians to riot against Jews, was the ringleader of a sect of zealots intent on overthrowing the Romans, and insulted the Temple, its priests and custodians. Although Paul successfully defended himself against these charges, the Jewish authorities pressured Felix to leave him in prison where he remained for two years.

Felix is succeeded by another governor, Porcius Festus. The Jewish authorities quickly met with Festus and urged him to transport Paul to Jerusalem. Unknown to the governor, they secretly planned to have Paul assassinated during the transport. This plan was thwarted, and under God's direction, Paul wisely appeals to Festus to be tried in Rome as a Roman citizen.

Festus had no choice, and Paul was brought to Rome to appear before Caesar, thus fulfilling the Scripture.

At-A-Glance

1. Paul Declares His Apostleship
   (Acts 26:19-23)
2. Paul Declares the Truth (vv. 27-29)
3. Paul Declared Innocent (vv. 30-32)

In Depth

1. Paul Declares His Apostleship (Acts 26:19-23)

Paul begins by stating his credentials as a faithful Jew, who before his conversion had lived as a Pharisee. In spite of the fact that Agrippa was living in an incestuous relationship—he is married to his full sister, Queen Bernice—Paul is aware that King Agrippa is Jewish and is considered an expert on Jewish laws and customs. Paul makes it clear that he, like all Jews, is aware that the Jews were a "special" population, and he asserts that he is living in full expectation of God's promises to the Jewish people. Paul does not "sugar coat" the truth. He tells the whole truth, including the fact that he had formerly hated and ardently persecuted Christians. Paul explains to King Agrippa that it is only after his conversion, when he begins to be a witness to the Gentiles for Christ, that he becomes a target of the Jewish authorities. The political charges against Paul were bogus. He had never offended the sanctity of the Temple. His charges stemmed solely from his attempts to preach the Gospel, based on the Word of God. Paul freely and boldly admits preaching that Jesus had suffered; that Jesus had died and had been the first to rise from the dead, and that Jesus would one day proclaim light to the Jews and the Gentiles. Paul's assertion of Jesus' death, resurrection, and preaching to a world without particular respect to Jew or Gentile is why Jews had "tried to kill (him)" (v. 21).

2. Paul Declares the Truth (vv. 27-29)

This declaration proves to be too much to the governor, Festus, who shouts that Paul's Gospel will make people believe he is crazy. Modern-day Christians would do well to remember that when properly presented, some people will think the same thing of them. Paul taught the Corinthians, "the cross is foolishness to those who are perishing" (1 Corinthians 1:18, NIV). We must not allow such allegations to stop us from preaching to a dying world that there is a Savior in Jesus, the Christ. Our Gospel is characterized by truth and based on historical events: the crucifixion and resurrection of Jesus. Paul tells Festus that the things he has preached were based on truths and were probably known to King Agrippa. Paul now presses the challenge and asks King Agrippa whether he believes the prophets. In Acts 26:28 (NKJV), Agrippa's response is curious. He says, "You almost persuade me." One way to understand Agrippa's response is to mean that in a short time, Paul could persuade him to believe. We want to remember that there were obvious barriers to Agrippa's acceptance of the Gospel. One, seated next to him was his wife, who was also his sister. One of the hallmarks of Christianity is the willingness to turn away from sin and darkness in our lives. Here, Agrippa is openly living in an incestuous relationship. He may have been unwilling to give her up and other immoral areas in his life to embrace Christianity. Another possibility is that King Agrippa feared that others, like

Festus, would believe that he too was crazy if he embraced Christianity.

3. Paul Declared Innocent (vv. 30-32)

Paul has stated his case and now King Agrippa, his wife, and Festus go off to discuss what they have heard. It is obvious to all that Paul has done nothing wrong and is not guilty of any of the charges. As far as they are concerned, Paul is innocent. However, it appears that there is a legal problem with setting him free. Paul's initial appeal, as a Roman citizen, was to have his case heard by the "Roman" emperor. Agrippa's response seems to imply that once an appeal was made, it could not be retracted. Rather than read this as a mistake, Christians should recognize Paul's continued imprisonment as a fulfillment of God's plan. Paul will get to witness to the emperor in the same way he had just witnessed to King Agrippa and the governor. He will also fulfill a long-standing desire of Paul's to visit the Christian community already present in Rome (Acts 19:21).

Search the Scriptures

1. What were Paul's main three points of preaching (Acts 25:23)?

2. When Festus accuses Paul of being insane, what two qualities does Paul insist his testimony possess (v. 25)?

Discuss the Meaning

Why is the resurrection of Christ from the dead so essential to the Gospel?

Lesson in Our Society

This lesson clarifies that God has a plan for each of us. In it we are able to see that God knows best and that He will protect us from all things. The only things that can happen to us are what God wills. When God asks us to take a stand, we must believe He has already prepared the way. The same God that rescued Paul from the Jewish authorities promises protection to us all.

Make It Happen

Have you been guilty of remaining quiet when you hear others say negative and insulting things about Christians? Pray and ask God to give you some "holy boldness" this week and provide opportunities for you to declare your Christianity, appropriately, articulately, and with love.

Follow the Spirit

What God wants me to do:

_____

_____

_____

Remember Your Thoughts

Special insights I have learned:

_____

_____

_____

More Light on the Text

Acts 26:19-32

19 Whereupon, O king Agrippa, I was not disobedient to the heavenly vision: 20 But shewed first unto them of Damascus, and at Jerusalem, throughout all the coasts of Judea, and then to the Gentiles, that they should repent and turn to God, and do works meet for repentance.

Agrippa II, "King Agrippa" here, and his sister Bernice came from Jerusalem to Caesarea to welcome Festus as the new Roman overseer of most of Palestine (Acts 25:13). Festus had little knowledge of Judaism, had been in Caesarea only a short time, and spent less than 10 days in Jerusalem. Agrippa oversaw Galilee west of the Sea of Galilee and a thin area south of it, east of the Jordan River, Perea. In addition, Rome had assigned supervision of the Temple to him. As the great-grandson of Herod the Great, he knew Jewish beliefs well and was interested in Jewish affairs.

For that reason, even though Festus was his superior, he asked Agrippa to hear the charges against Paul and Paul's defense against them. Festus was at a loss about what charges against Paul to send for his appeal before Caesar (Acts 25:26a). Paul's appearance before Festus and Agrippa was not a trial but an examination. He uses it as an opportunity to present the experience that convinced him that Jesus was God's fulfillment of Jewish hopes (Acts 26:1-18).

In verse 19, Paul's "vision" (Gk. *optasia*, **op-tas-EE-ah**) was auditory rather visual: "I heard a voice..." A supernatural light blazed and blinded him (Acts 22:11, 13). Jesus' voice was Paul's "vision from heaven" as both the *New Living Translation* and the *New International Version* translate it.

Verse 20 describes Paul's response to God's revelation through Christ. His actions outline of how to share our faith. First, Paul goes to those closest "in Damascus" and then to those who knew him best "in Jerusalem" (26:20, NLT). As he traveled, he shared with those with whom he had a common background along "the coasts of Judea." (Rather than "coasts," Gk. *chora*, **KHO-rah**, a more accurate translation is "regions.") "The God who was nothing" to Paul became "the God who was everything."

Paul then gives one of the Bible's most important definitions of true repentance and conversion. First, genuine repentance begins with remorse for our sin and turning away from it (Gk. *metanoeo*, **me-ta-no-EH-o**). Second, characteristic of heartfelt repentance is a "turn to God" (Gk. *epistrepho*, **ep-ee-STREF-o**) through faith in Christ. Third, the confirmation of honest repentance that gives one's testimony credibility is "works meet for repentance." This phrase becomes clearer when one understands that "meet" (Gk. *axios*, **ax-EE-os**) is an outdated word that means worthy or deserving. The best proof that true repentance has occurred is that our deeds match our words.

21 For these causes the Jews caught me in the temple, and went about to kill me.

Note that Paul uses "causes"—a plural form. His arrests began when Jews from the province of Asia grabbed Paul in the Temple. Jews persecuted Paul and had him arrested repeatedly in that region (Acts 14:3-5, 19; 17:13; 20:3). The captain of Roman troops arrested Paul as a trouble-maker amid claims that he defamed the Jewish people, Jewish teaching, and the Temple. They also accused him of defiling the Temple by bringing non-Jews into it (Acts 21:27).

22 Having therefore obtained help of God, I continue unto this day, witnessing both to small and great, saying none other things than those which the prophets and Moses did say should come: 23 That Christ should suffer, and that he should be the first that should rise from the dead, and should shew light unto the people, and to the Gentiles.

Paul begins his defense by affirming God's help. That claim might seem ridiculous considering he had been in jail for two years and was about to be sent to Rome for trial (24:27; 25:26-27). But Paul felt that he'd experienced divine deliverance many times as he encountered hardship and persecution. Once he was beaten so severely that he was left for dead but survived (Acts 14:19). Repeated arrests followed, but with release each time, once with an apology (Acts 16:23-24, 35-39). A Roman captain stopped an attack on Paul, arrested him and transferred him to captivity in Caesarea. The arrest foiled a plot to seize and kill him (Acts 23:10-16). Paul saw God's hand of help in all those events.

More evidence of God's divine help was in Paul's skill in spreading Christ's message. He operated with the confident belief that God supported his success in sharing his faith. In Acts 26:22, when he says "obtained help," Paul is clear that he not working from his own power but under the leadership of God Himself. When we share our faith in Christ's message we can be assured of God's reinforcement of our efforts. Paul was.

This passage tells of an opportunity for Paul to share God's revelation in Christ to those at the pinnacle of influence in that part of the world. Their positions in Roman government made both Felix and Festus into channels for publicizing God's ultimate will and purposes through Christ. Paul understood that. He refused to let this great opportunity slip away and waste it. That was because Christ had commissioned him to proclaim God's Good News to all people (Acts 22:14-15).

"I continue unto this day ..." fails to encapsulate Paul's zeal for the task God had given him (26:22). "Continue" (Gk. *histemi*, **HIS-tay-mee**) means to stand firm, but here the form of the word is intense, adding the idea of standing fixed, unwavering, and immovable from his convictions. Paul's example teaches that even when it might be human to lose hope, we can still be witnesses because we can count on God's help.

Although the Asian Jews accused Paul of abandoning the Mosaic Law and the Jewish people (Acts 21:21, 27-28), Paul held to the orthodox expectation of a Messiah as prophesied by Moses and later prophets (Deuteronomy 18:15-18; Isaiah 53:4-9; Zechariah 12:10). As recorded in Acts 26:23, for Jesus' coming to "shew light" (Gk. *kataggello*, **ka-tang-GEL-lo**) meant to make something clear to a wide audience or over a wide area, both of which Paul did. To Paul, Christ's life, death, and resurrection were essential for making God's love understandable to humanity.

24 And as he thus spake for himself, Festus said with a loud voice, Paul, thou art beside thyself; much learning doth make thee mad. 25 But he said, I am not mad, most noble Festus; but speak forth the words of truth and soberness.

These two verses show why Paul was such an effective witness to God's revelation in Jesus Christ. Festus' outburst was not unusual. "A loud voice" means Festus bellowed, maybe in laughter in skepticism or in anger, at the ardor and certainty of Paul's faith (v. 24). Festus described Paul as "beside thyself" (Gk. *mainomai*, **MAH-ee-nom-ahee**), "crazy" in the NLT and "out of your mind" in the NIV. Christian witnesses today shouldn't be surprised when they occasionally encounter charges of, "You're crazy," "That's ridiculous," or other similar responses to our attempts to share the Gospel.

Paul's reaction wasn't to cower before rejection, resort to religious double talk, or waver from what he had said. He followed exactly Peter's counsel for sharing one's faith: "Always be prepared to give an answer to everybody who asks you to give the reason for the hope you have. But do this with gentleness and respect" (1 Peter 3:15, NIV). Paul's response in Acts 26:25 did not take an argumentative tone. Rather, his reply, "most noble Festus" showed respect for the governor's agitation as well as the authority of his powerful position. Yet, it also showed Paul's confident certainty in the trustworthy and reasonable nature of what he said. Likewise, Christians sharing their faith today should keep their confidence in God's truth strong without resorting to hurt feelings, argument, or anger.

26 For the king knoweth of these things, before whom also I speak freely: for I am persuaded that none of these are hidden from him; for this thing was not done in a corner. 27 King Agrippa, believest thou the prophets? I know that thou believest.

Although Paul was replying to Festus' loud reaction, he skillfully turns his reply to include Agrippa. He was the great-grandson of Herod the Great who attempted to kill Jesus at birth (Matthew 2:16), and the grandson of Herod Antipas who had John the Baptist beheaded (14:10). From childhood, Agrippa had been immersed in the events of Jesus' life and his interaction with the Temple and its leaders. In addition, Agrippa had an ongoing interest in Jewish affairs and religion. Although he ruled over two small areas in Palestine, the Romans had appointed him as their overseer of the Temple. So Paul accurately depicted Agrippa's knowledge of what he spoke.

His statement in Acts 26:26, "this thing was not done in a corner" was a widely known Greek saying. Also, Jesus had been crucified outside Jerusalem during Passover. Thousands of Jews from across the world were there. With this understatement, Paul emphasized Agrippa's knowledge of what was widely known.

When asked whether he believed the prophets, Paul assumed Agrippa's interest in spiritual realities. This was an effective approach to sharing his faith. Paul understood that then, as now, all people want to believe that their lives have purpose and meaning beyond their present circumstances. This should bolster Christians' confidence as we share God's Good News in Christ today.

28 Then Agrippa said unto Paul, Almost thou persuadest me to be a Christian. 29 And Paul said, I would to God, that not only thou, but also all that hear me this day, were both almost, and altogether such as I am, except these bonds.

Earlier, Festus deflected Paul's witness by questioning Paul's sanity. Here, Agrippa utilized another common ploy to sidetrack Paul's witness for Christ. He accused Paul of trying to rush him into a decision without giving needed time to think or with too little information for making a good decision. In verse 28, "almost" (Gk. *oligos*, **ol-EE-gos**) means "a little" or "slightly." Most modern translations, such as NLT, NIV, or NRSV, interpret Agrippa's words as a question. He was asking Paul, "Do you think that in a short time, or with only a few words, you can convince me to become a Christian?"

Paul again gave us a good example of effectively sharing one's faith. He responds by affirming his assurance that he saw his commitment to Christ as a good decision and as a sure path to purpose and meaning regardless of the uncertainties of his life.

30 And when he had thus spoken, the king rose up, and the governor, and Bernice, and they sat with them: 31 And when they were gone aside, they talked between themselves, saying, This doeth nothing worthy of death

or of bonds. **32 Then said Agrippa unto Festus, This man might have been set at liberty, if he had not appealed unto Caesar.**

Here we see another means of avoiding the claims of Christ—departure. Agrippa, his sister, Festus and the crowd of onlookers got up and left. Yet, all had heard a clear statement of faith in Christ and an appeal for commitment to Him.

In what most people would consider a bad situation, Paul found the opportunity to share the message of God's revelation through the life, death, and resurrection of Christ. Within two years, Festus would be dead, but he'd heard the call to follow Jesus. The Roman captain commanded one-tenth of a Roman legion—600 men. Agrippa returned to rule over two provinces. Undoubtedly, the onlookers that day were also people of privilege, wealth, and above average influence. Paul had fulfilled his commitment and Christ's will for his life (Acts 9:15; 23:11). Festus and Agrippa saw Paul's appeal to Caesar as a strategic mistake. But it was God's way, through Paul, of spreading His message in Christ to the summit of Roman power.

Sources:

Barclay, William H. *The Acts of the Apostles.* 2nd ed. Philadelphia, PA: Westminster Press, 1955.

Bible Gateway.com. http://www.biblegateway.com (accessed September 22, 2011).

Danker, Frederick William, ed. *A Greek-English Lexicon of the New Testament and Other Early Christian Literature, Based on Walter Bauer's Greek-German Edition.* 3rd ed. Translated and edited for English readers by W. F. Arndt and Walter Bauer. Chicago: University of Chicago Press, 2000.

"Herodian Dynasty." Pictorial Bible Commentary. Bibleview. http://www.bibleview.org/en/shared/HerodianDynasty.html (accessed September 22, 2011).

Merriam-Webster Online Dictionary. Merriam-Webster, Inc. http://www.merriam-webster.com (accessed September 22, 2011).

New Testament Greek Lexicon. Bible Study Tools.com. http://www.biblestudytools.com/lexicons/greek (accessed September 22, 2011).

Williams, Charles S. C. *A Commentary on The Acts of the Apostles* (*Harper's New Testament Commentaries*). New York: Harper Publishers, 1957.

Zerwick, Max; Grosvenor, Mary. *A Grammatical Analysis of the Greek New Testament.* Rome: Biblical Institute Press, 1974.

Say It Correctly

Agrippa. uh-**GRIP**-uh.
Bernice. bur-**NEES.**
Damascus. duh-**MAS**-kuhs.
Festus. **FES**-tus.
Jerusalem. jeh-**ROO**-suh-luhm.
Judea. joo-**DEE**-uh.

Daily Bible Readings

MONDAY
Appeasing Those Zealous for the Law
(Acts 21:17-26)

TUESDAY
A Stirred-Up Mob
(Acts 21:27-36)

WEDNESDAY
Taken into Custody
(Acts 22:17-24)

THURSDAY
You Must Bear Witness in Rome
(Acts 22:30-23:11)

FRIDAY
Paul's Background as a Pharisee
(Acts 26:1-8)

SATURDAY
Paul's Encounter with Christ
(Acts 26:9-18)

SUNDAY
Paul's Testimony before
Roman Authorities
(Acts 26:19-32)

Teaching Tips

Words You Should Know

A. Delivered (Acts 27:1) *paradidomi* (Gk.)—Describes handing a prisoner into someone's custody.

B. Health (v. 34) *soteria* (Gk.)—Denotes salvation or deliverance.

Teacher Preparation

Unifying Principle—Weathering the Storm. Paul's storm experience teaches that Christians can learn to respond calmly to crises, trusting God in every adverse situation.

A. Brainstorm catastrophic "storms" you have faced, and be prepared to share your responses to them.

B. Pray for students and lesson clarity.

C. Prepare a list of "storm resources"—your favorite songs and Scriptures that you use during tough times.

D. Study the entire text and complete the companion lesson in the *Precepts Personal Study Guide*®.

O—Open the Lesson

A. Open with prayer.

B. Read the Aim for Change and the Keep in Mind verse in unison.

C. Discuss recent crises in the news.

D. Ask students to share their "storms" (crises) and related responses.

E. Summarize and discuss the In Focus story.

P—Present the Scriptures

A. Invite students to read the Focal Verses.

B. Use The People, Places, and Times, Background, Search the Scriptures, the At-A-Glance outline, In Depth, and More Light on the Text to clarify the verses.

E—Explore the Meaning

A. Have volunteers summarize the Lesson in Our Society and Make It Happen sections.

B. Discuss some tools that are available to help us weather storms. Share your list.

N—Next Steps for Application

A. Invite students to share their favorite "storm resources."

B. Close in prayer.

Worship Guide

For the Superintendent or Teacher
Theme: Paul Sails for Rome
Song: "Think of His Goodness to You"
Devotional Reading: Romans 1:13-17
Prayer

NOV 11th

Paul Sails for Rome

Bible Background • ACTS 27
Printed Text • ACTS 27:1-2, 33-44 | Devotional Reading • ROMANS 1:13-17

—————————— Aim for Change ——————————

By the end of the lesson, we will: KNOW how Paul's faith in God enabled him to remain calm in the midst of a storm; APPRECIATE how our relationship with God helps us cope in a crisis; and WITNESS to others about relying on God's strength when facing crises.

———————— 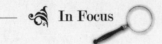 In Focus ————————

Tom and Mary stood on their porch, eagerly awaiting the ambulance that would bring their son Todd home from the military rehabilitation center. He had been there four months as he recovered from an injury suffered during military maneuvers overseas. Once strong and athletic, Todd was now paralyzed from the waist down, but they were grateful their son was alive.

Initially Tom and Mary resented the situation, but Todd's response to his disability had changed that. Over time, they came to appreciate how Todd's faith in Jesus Christ enabled him to respond to this life storm with cheerfulness instead of bitterness, and they were learning to do the same. Lately, they were attending church, hoping to experience some of the peace Todd had. The many friends, neighbors, and strangers who had donated time and resources to renovate the home in time for Todd's homecoming awed them. They knew adjusting to home life might be difficult for them all, but they were ready to accept the challenge.

How we weather life's storms reflects whether we truly have confidence in God's faithfulness. Today's lesson shows how Paul's calm response to a storm helped bring others to safety.

———————— Keep in Mind ————————

"And the rest, some on boards, and some on broken pieces of the ship. And so it came to pass, that they escaped all safe to land" (Acts 27:44).

"And the rest, some on boards, and some on broken pieces of the ship. And so it came to pass, that they escaped all safe to land" (Acts 27:44).

Focal Verses

KJV **Acts 27:1** And when it was determined that we should sail into Italy, they delivered Paul and certain other prisoners unto one named Julius, a centurion of Augustus' band.

2 And entering into a ship of Adramyttium, we launched, meaning to sail by the coasts of Asia; one Aristarchus, a Macedonian of Thessalonica, being with us.

27:33 And while the day was coming on, Paul besought them all to take meat, saying, This day is the fourteenth day that ye have tarried and continued fasting, having taken nothing.

34 Wherefore I pray you to take some meat: for this is for your health: for there shall not an hair fall from the head of any of you.

35 And when he had thus spoken, he took bread, and gave thanks to God in presence of them all: and when he had broken it, he began to eat.

36 Then were they all of good cheer, and they also took some meat.

37 And we were in all in the ship two hundred threescore and sixteen souls.

38 And when they had eaten enough, they lightened the ship, and cast out the wheat into the sea.

39 And when it was day, they knew not the land: but they discovered a certain creek with a shore, into the which they were minded, if it were possible, to thrust in the ship.

40 And when they had taken up the anchors, they committed themselves unto the sea, and loosed the rudder bands, and hoised up the mainsail to the wind, and made toward shore.

41 And falling into a place where two seas met, they ran the ship aground; and the forepart stuck fast, and remained unmoveable,

NLT **Acts 27:1** When the time came, we set sail for Italy. Paul and several other prisoners were placed in the custody of a Roman officer named Julius, a captain of the Imperial Regiment.

2 Aristarchus, a Macedonian from Thessalonica, was also with us. We left on a ship whose home port was Adramyttium on the northwest coast of the province of Asia; it was scheduled to make several stops at ports along the coast of the province.

Acts 27:33 Just as day was dawning, Paul urged everyone to eat. "You have been so worried that you haven't touched food for two weeks," he said.

34 "Please eat something now for your own good. For not a hair of your heads will perish."

35 Then he took some bread, gave thanks to God before them all, and broke off a piece and ate it.

36 Then everyone was encouraged and began to eat—

37 all 276 of us who were on board.

38 After eating, the crew lightened the ship further by throwing the cargo of wheat overboard.

39 When morning dawned, they didn't recognize the coastline, but they saw a bay with a beach and wondered if they could get to shore by running the ship aground.

40 So they cut off the anchors and left them in the sea. Then they lowered the rudders, raised the foresail, and headed toward shore.

41 But they hit a shoal and ran the ship aground too soon. The bow of the ship stuck fast, while the stern was repeatedly smashed by the force of the waves and began to break apart.

KJV continued

but the hinder part was broken with the violence of the waves.

42 And the soldiers' counsel was to kill the prisoners, lest any of them should swim out, and escape.

43 But the centurion, willing to save Paul, kept them from their purpose; and commanded that they which could swim should cast themselves first into the sea, and get to land:

44 And the rest, some on boards, and some on broken pieces of the ship. And so it came to pass, that they escaped all safe to land.

NLT continued

42 The soldiers wanted to kill the prisoners to make sure they didn't swim ashore and escape.

43 But the commanding officer wanted to spare Paul, so he didn't let them carry out their plan. Then he ordered all who could swim to jump overboard first and make for land.

44 The others held onto planks or debris from the broken ship. So everyone escaped safely to shore.

The People, Places, and Times

Book of Acts. The second of two books written by Luke, Acts highlights "the acts of the apostles." It shares accounts of how the early church fulfilled its mission to "be witnesses [of Jesus Christ] . . . in Jerusalem, and in all Judaea, and in Samaria, and unto the uttermost part of the earth" (Acts 1:8). As such, it offers a historical view of the growth of the church and the unity—or sometimes disunity—of its members. Furthermore, Luke shares the encouraging message that the Gospel is available to all people, regardless of race, class, or ethnicity.

Ships. In biblical times, ships were functional, not recreational, and used by merchants and traders in normal business dealings from spring through fall. Winter made sailing more hazardous. Soldiers, meanwhile, used ships to protect the seas from pirates and during war.

Background

Arrested after preaching the Gospel in Jerusalem, Paul exercised his right as a Roman citizen and requested a trial before Caesar. Within days of traveling there, the stormy weather made the trip dangerous. Paul warned Julius, the centurion guarding the prisoners, that, "I can see that our voyage is going to be disastrous and bring great loss to ship and cargo, and to our own lives also" (Acts 27:10, NIV). Julius ignored the warning, and the ship continued until it encountered a hurricane-like storm.

When they had given up hope and feared dying, Paul first encouraged them by sharing a vision he had in which an angel told him that no one on board would die. However, Paul warned that despite the encouraging news, they would be shipwrecked. Throughout the entire ordeal, Paul's confidence in God's faithfulness enabled him to act calmly. He believed the word of the Lord, delivered by the angel, and trusted God to fulfill His promise.

At-A-Glance

1. Calm before the Storm (Acts 27:1-2)
2. Calm in the Storm vv. 33-38)
3. Shipwrecked But Saved (vv. 39-44)

In Depth

1. Calm before the Storm (Acts 27:1-2)

On the surface, Paul's request for a trial before Caesar seemed easy to accomplish: Board a ship, travel to Rome, and speak with Caesar. But an unexpected hurricane-strength storm made the journey arduous and life threatening. Before the storm hit, Paul—and everyone else on board—was seemingly unaware of its approach. The ship's crew comprised experienced seamen familiar with navigating seas in different weather conditions. Yet, their experience was no match for the storm.

Paul's experience with the possible cyclone or hurricane-force wind mirrors how Christians often unknowingly encounter storms. One day all may be well, and on the next a catastrophic storm rages. That storm could be a spouse's plea for a divorce, a life-threatening car accident, a medical diagnosis that seems impossible to beat, or an assault by a stranger that causes great physical or emotional harm. Whatever the case, like Paul, we are not aware of what is approaching, but God knows.

2. Calm in the Storm (vv. 33-38)

How did Paul remain calm? He relied on a previously developed, sure-fire method of weathering life's storms that he had learned which allowed him to be calm. We can use calm as an acronym advising us to: Call on God during crises, Anticipate God stepping in to save us, Listen to God's instruction, and Make known God's promises.

Call on God during crises. Faith is an anchor, not a crutch. It tethers us to our Lord and Savior, who teaches us how to act calmly during storms. In faith, Paul called on God during the crises, and God answered by sending a heavenly messenger. As the days lengthened, the storm became stronger while the passengers' hope of survival diminished. They needed God's help. Calling on God during a storm is paramount for the Christian who wants to weather that storm calmly.

Anticipate God stepping in to rescue us. Initially, Paul had sensed prophetically that there would be loss of life and loss of ship. Later, however, God in His mercy sent an angel to strengthen Paul and to deliver a divine message. Thus, despite the raging seas, Paul anticipated God's salvation. He expected to live, not die. Paul's trials had taught him to surrender his will, emotions, and plans to God. We must do the same in order to weather life's storms with calm as we anticipate God's salvation.

Listen to God's instruction. In Acts 27:24, Paul was instructed to "fear not" (KJV). It is the same instruction Abram, Israel, Joshua, and many others received in the past. It is the same instruction that God whispers to His children today. He intends for Christians to go through storms without fear. Prayer, Bible study, fellowship with other believers, and a dogged determination to trust God are all necessary at such times to help defeat fear.

Make known God's promises. After Paul received instructions from the angel, he shared the vision and the inherent promise with the other passengers. He encouraged them, "[K]eep up your courage, men, for I have faith in God that it will happen just as he told me" (v. 25, NIV). Sometimes in the storms of life we are involved not for our own good but for the good of others. Through us, others can see the mercy, grace, and love of God. That Paul and all others on board the ship could go more than two weeks without eating, for example, is a testament that God alone kept them alive. That they broke their self-imposed fast by eating bread is also miraculous as most people seek liquid to ease their bodies back into eating after a prolonged fast. Furthermore, that they could still be strong to maneuver the ship, that none died from disease or starvation prove that there was another "force" battling the external situations. Finally, although they may not have realized God's presence or protection, they were comforted by His promise as shared by Paul.

3. Shipwrecked, But Saved (vv. 39-44)

Panicking neither diminishes nor stops a storm. Rather, panic hinders our ability to hear from God and to share God's promises with others. When Christians respond by staying calm, their faith shines through storms. Our friends, family members, and co-workers observe the confidence we have in God and can gain strength from us as we cope calmly with the crises. Thus, it's possible to turn storms into opportunities to share Christ and to bring others to salvation. We learn from Paul's experience that in many storms of life, we are unprepared to handle the storm without God's help. Our educational background, gifts, talents, finances, or other resources cannot provide the safe harbor we seek.

Satan is a thief that "comes only to steal and kill and destroy" (John 10:10, NIV). When storms arise, he uses them to fulfill that purpose. But God is greater than our enemy. This is an important lesson to learn because when everything else fails, when all of our systems, vehicles, plotting, and schemes fail, we can be assured that "Jesus Christ is the same yesterday and today and forever" (Hebrews 13:8, NIV). He never fails, and we can trust Him despite the thoughts that the enemy may place in our minds.

Finally, the crewmen's sneaky decision to cast out to sea with lifeboats—and later, their plot to kill the prisoners (Acts 27:30, 42)—shows how times of panic can lead us to behave irrationally. Ultimately, the ability to weather the storm was due in large part

to Paul's calm response to it. He trusted in God's faithfulness. When we respond in a similar fashion, we, too, help others draw closer to God.

Search the Scriptures

1. Why did the centurion ignore Paul's advice in Lasea (Acts 27:11-12)?

2. How did all of the passengers get to safety (v. 44)?

Discuss the Meaning

Paul's past experience with life's storms enabled him to calmly weather a natural storm. What have you learned in the past that enabled you to weather a recent storm? How did your positive response affect others?

Lesson in Our Society

Places such as Japan, Haiti, and some southern U.S. states have been hit hard recently by tumultuous weather conditions. When storms strike, how can Christians serve as beacons of calm and hope?

Make It Happen

Paul was able to provide an encouraging word to the others in the storm. Ask God to show you how to encourage others through e-mails, letters, or cards that provide hope and peace.

Follow the Spirit

What God wants me to do:

_____

_____

_____

_____

Remember Your Thoughts

Special insights I have learned:

_____

_____

_____

_____

More Light on the Text

Acts 27:1-2, 33-44

1 And when it was determined that we should sail into Italy, they delivered Paul and certain other prisoners unto one named Julius, a centurion of Augustas' band. 2 And entering into a ship of Adramyttium, we launched, meaning to sail by the coasts of Asia; one Aristarchus, a Macedonian of Thessalonica, being with us.

Paul had waited two years under house arrest in Caesarea. Two Roman governors heard his defense against groundless charges of disturbing the peace and sedition against Rome. The first wanted a bribe, but Paul had used repeated appearances before Felix to fulfill his call by God to proclaim the saving message of Christ (Acts 26:22a, 25; Romans 1:1, 14, 16). Finally, it was decided to transport Paul and some other prisoners to Rome under the supervision of a Roman officer. The officer was Julius, a member of an elite cadre of trusted, experienced soldiers.

Julius boarded his prisoners onto a ship from Adramyttium, a port city at the northeast corner of the Aegean Sea, which extends north off the Mediterranean Sea. The beginning of his respect for Paul's faith may have subtly begun when he discovered the dedication to their shared faith by one of Paul's Christian converts, Aristarchus boarded with Paul and either paid his own fare or, as a number of commentators such as William Barclay and John Stott theorize, he voluntarily boarded as Paul's slave. After an easy, 50-mile jaunt from Caesarea to Sidon, nothing went well for the rest of the voyage. After 400 miles of slow going, "because the winds were contrary," the ship docked at the coastal city of Myra (Acts 27:4).

There, Julius switched Paul and his other prisoners to another ship, a vessel full of grain that was supposedly going directly to Italy. Where the first ship had been slow, everything on the second became worse. Because of turbulent weather, most shipping on the Mediterranean Ocean ceased by November, and it was already mid-October.

Often, ships in Paul's day had a single sail, which meant a ship went in whatever direction the wind blew it. After Myra, the wind forced their ship 100 miles south past Crete, where the ship briefly put into another port. The ship's captain, its owner and Julius debated over staying docked there through the winter.

Paul was an experienced traveler on the Mediterranean. In *The Acts of the Apostles: A Commentary,* Ernst Haenchen lists 11 voyages of Paul that are recorded in the New Testament (Haenchen, 702-703). Another commentator estimates that those trips totaled more than 3,500 miles. Paul knew the dangers of winter sailing and urged staying put. His opinion was ignored.

After that, for the next 14 days, a hurricane-force wind blasted them west about 700 miles. The word Luke used in Acts 27:14 for the storm is related to our present-day word "typhoon" (Gk. *tuphonikos,* **too-fo-nee-KOS**). That is where most of today's text begins.

27:33 And while the day was coming on, Paul besought them all to take meat, saying, This day is the fourteenth day that ye have tarried and continued fasting, having taken

nothing. 34 Wherefore I pray you to take some meat: for this is for your health: for there shall not an hair fall from the head of any of you.

As daybreak approached, the storm's ferocity had not let up. Here, we see why Paul was such an effective witness for God's revelation in Jesus Christ. The sailors had just tried to desert the ship and leave its passengers to fend for themselves. Nobody had eaten for 14 days. When we speak of fasting today, we mean going without food deliberately. Here "fasting" (Gk. *asitos,* **AS-ee-tos**), refers to a lack of appetite or available food. Perhaps the waves and rain had run down into the ship's hold and soaked into its stores, spoiling most of its food. Perhaps conditions were so tempestuous that cooking became impossible in its galley. Ancient writers hardly mention seasickness, but Luke may have viewed that as a given.

For whatever reasons, when things reached their worst, God's love for others showed through in Paul's concern for those on board. The selfless action of this small-framed, accused-heretic Jew, on his way to trial before Caesar and possible execution, gave his witness with a trustworthy integrity. He "besought" (Gk. *parakaleo,* **pa-ra-ka-LEH-o**), or urges, his fellow passengers to eat because it is essential for their survival. Luke's word here described something Paul did repeatedly, not something he did once for show. In its noun form this was the same word John used in John 14:26 for the Holy Spirit, "the Comforter" (Gk. *parakletos,* **pa-RA-kleh-tos**).

This was not Paul's first effort at persuading the crew, the prisoners, and other passengers to eat. Nor was it his first assurance of their survival (Acts 27:21-26). He supports his first appeal to eat by relating the appearance of an angel from God, promising Paul's appearance before Caesar and the survival of all on board but with the ship's eventual crash upon an island. Likely, only Paul's concern for the well-being of all the others on board saved him from being thrown overboard. The apostle began that first lecture about eating by saying basically, "I told you so" (27:21). Even a godly apostle is not above times of exasperation and despair. Note Acts 27:20 where Luke admits, "... all hope that we should be saved was then taken away."

35 And when he had thus spoken, he took some bread, and gave thanks to God in the presence of them all: and when he had broken it, he began to eat. 36 Then they were all of good cheer, and they also took some meat. 37 And they were in all in the ship two hundred threescore and sixteen souls.

For two weeks from time to time, 276 other seafarers observed Paul confront their shared life-and-death struggle with the storm. The steadfast certainty of Paul's faith comforts them. While the storm rocked the ship, Paul takes bread and holds it while thanking God before eating it. His example renews the courage of his on-looking shipmates who follow his example by eating. The word "meat" (Gk. *trophe,* **tro-FAY**), here and in verses 33 and 34 can mean "animal flesh." However, it was the customary Greek word for nourishment in general.

38 And when they had eaten enough, they lightened the ship, and cast out the wheat into the sea.

When everyone's hunger was satisfied, everyone thought more clearly, including the captain and the ship's owner. The time had come to focus on saving their lives more than on saving the ship and its cargo. As Ecclesiastes 9:4 (NASB) says, "A live dog is better than a dead lion." So they lighten the ship to make it float higher in the water by throwing overboard the ship's cargo of wheat, which was doubtlessly intended for sale in Rome. By doing so, they lessen chances that the ship would run aground too far out for survivors to make it to shore. They accept Paul's prophecy that God's will was for them all to survive the ship's destruction.

39 And when it was day they knew not the land: but they discovered a certain creek with a shore, into which they were minded, if it were possible, to thrust in the ship. 40 And when they had taken up the anchors, they committed themselves unto the sea, and loosed the rudder bands, and hoised up the mainsail to the wind, and made toward shore. 41 And falling into a place where two seas met, they ran the ship aground; and the forepart stuck fast, and remained unmoveable, but the hinder part was broken with the violence of the waves.

The first compass on a ship was not known outside of China until over a century later. And the sextant was not invented until the 1700s. Consequently, in Paul's day unless the sky was in view, sailors had no way to determine where they were or in what direction they were headed. When the ship came close enough to land to see the shore through the storm, no one recognized where they were. They did, however, see a depression in the coastline. Our KJV text for Acts 27:39 says they saw a "creek" (Gk. *kolpos,* **KOL-pos**), but most modern versions, such as NLT, NIV, and NRSV, say they saw a "bay." So they decided to try and run the ship aground on its shore.

To that end, the crew cut loose the four anchors they had dropped to drag the sea's bottom and slow the ship. They had feared running aground or crashing onto boulders in the storm's blinding squall so far that survivors couldn't make it to shore (27:29). Besides releasing the anchors, they sever the top water paddles that served as the ship's primitive rudder. They then raise their one sail. Now, only God and the force of wind control the ship's movement.

Once again, events prove more difficult than they hoped. As the wind hurtles the ship toward shore, it passes over a spot where two channels, maybe rip tides, in our KJV text "two seas," forced it into a sand bank (v. 41). The front of the ship was wedged firmly in it, but its rear continued to be slapped violently by the fury of the waves.

42 And the soldiers' counsel was to kill the prisoners, lest any of them swim out, and escape. 43 But the centurion, willing to save Paul, kept them from their purposes, and commanded that they which could swim should cast themselves first into the sea, and get to land. 44 And the rest, some on boards, and some on broken pieces of the ship. And so it came to pass, that they escaped all safe to land.

As Paul had done, the soldiers helping Julius guard the prisoners foresee the coming destruction of the ship. The soldiers plan to kill them all, rather than risk that any might swim to shore and escape when the ship breaks up. The Roman penalty for allowing prisoners to escape was that their guards would receive whatever sentence the prisoners were due. It's probable that many of Paul's fellow prisoners were being sent to Rome for execution before bloodthirsty crowds in the Colosseum.

But Julius intervenes, apparently on Paul's behalf, and countermands the soldiers' plan. When KJV says in verse 43 that Julius is "willing" to save Paul, it sounds like a grudging decision to act by today's use of that word. Just the opposite is the case. The word "willing" (Gk. *boulomai,* **BOO-lom-ahee**) refers here to an action that Julius wanted and was determined to take. His desire to save Paul points to the respect he had for the apostle. Instead, he instructs that those who could swim to jump in immediately and to swim to shore. He told those who could not swim to grab onto floating planks or other pieces of the ship and hold them while paddling to shore.

Thus, the reality of the angel's appearance to Paul and his prophecy that all 276 passengers would survive the ship's destruction were confirmed. Few Christians will ever share a spiritual experience as extraordinary as Paul did. But the power of Paul's witness lay not in his private, supernatural experiences. Instead, other passengers, like the centurion, observed that Paul faced deadly peril and treated others kindly during the dangerous encounter. This observation gave witness to the credibility and authenticity of his faith. Likewise, Christians today can add power to their witness of trusting God by treating those who do not know Him with love, dignity and kindness in every situation.

Sources:

Adeyemo, Tokunboh, general ed. *Africa Bible Commentary.* 2nd edition. Grand Rapids, MI: Zondervan, 2010. 1323.

Barclay, William H. *The Acts of the Apostles.* 2nd ed. Philadelphia, PA: Westminster Press, 1955.

Beers, V. Gilbert. *The Victor Handbook of Bible Knowledge.* Wheaton, IL: Victor Books, 1981. 570.

Danker, Frederick William, ed. *A Greek-English Lexicon of the New Testament and other Early Christian Literature, based on Walter Bauer's Greek-German edition.* 3rd ed. Translated and edited by W. F. Arndt and Walter Bauer. Chicago, IL: University of Chicago Press, 2000.

Haenchen, Ernst. *The Acts of the Apostles: A Commentary.* Philadelphia, PA: Westminster Press, 1971 (translated from the 14th German edition, 1965). 702-703.

New Testament Greek Lexicon. Bible Study Tools.com. http://www.biblestudytools.com/lexicons/greek (accessed September 22, 2011).

Quest Study Bible (NIV), Revised. Grand Rapids, MI: Zondervan, 1994-2003.

Stott, John. *The Spirit, the Church, and the World: The Message of Acts.* Downers Grove, IL: InterVarsity Press, 1990.

Zerwick, Max and Mary Grosvenor. *A Grammatical Analysis of the Greek New Testament.* Rome: Biblical Institute Press, 1974.

Zodhiates, Spiros, ed. *Hebrew-Greek Key Word Study Bible (KJV), Revised.* Chattanooga, TN: AMG Publishers, 1994.

Say It Correctly

Adramyttium. ad'ruh-**MIT**-ee-uhm.
Augustus. aw-**GUHS**-tuhs.
Aristarchus. air'is-**TAHR**-kuhs.
Centurion. sen-**TOOR**-ee-uhn.
Julius. **JOOL**-yuhs.
Macedonian. mas-eh-**DOH**-nee-uhn.
Thessalonica. thes-uh-**LON**-nay-kuh.

Daily Bible Readings

MONDAY
Called to Be an Apostle
(Romans 1:1-7)

TUESDAY
Encouraged by Each Other's Faith
(Romans 1:8-12)

WEDNESDAY
Eager to Proclaim the Gospel
(Romans 1:13-17)

THURSDAY
Paul's Journey to Rome Begins
(Acts 27:3-12)

FRIDAY
A Fierce Storm Dashes Hope
(Acts 27:13-20)

SATURDAY
Keep Up Your Courage
(Acts 27:21-32)

SUNDAY
Brought Safely to Land
(Acts 27:1-2, 33-44)

Teaching Tips

Words You Should Know

A. Beast (Acts 28:4, 5) *therion* (Gk.)—A wild animal.

B. Flux (v. 8) *dusenteria* (Gk.)—A bowel sickness, such as dysentery.

Teacher Preparation

Unifying Principle—Helping One Another. Paul's character, while shipwrecked, helped others recognize something extraordinary about him.

A. Pray for students and lesson clarity.

B. Read, study, and meditate on the entire lesson.

C. Bring to class recent bulletins or church announcements that highlight volunteer opportunities.

D. Complete the companion lesson in the *Precepts for Living Study Guide®*.

O—Open the Lesson.

A. Open with prayer.

B. Have volunteers read the Aim for Change and the Keep in Mind verse.

C. Invite students to briefly share how they are using their gifts to help others in the church or community.

D. Ask students to share times they have turned away from service projects because they were overwhelmed during crises.

E. Discuss the importance of helping others during difficult times.

P—Present the Scriptures

A. Invite students to read the Focal Verses.

B. Use The People, Places, and Times, Background, Search the Scriptures, At-A-Glance outline, In Depth, and More Light on the Text sections to clarify the verses.

E—Explore the Meaning

A. Have students silently read the Devotional Reading.

B. Discuss how it relates to today's lesson on helping one another and God's help during difficult situations.

N—Next Steps for Application

A. Share the information on volunteer opportunities.

B. Discuss other service or ministry projects that students may know about.

C. Ask for prayer requests related to students' concerns about helping others or resuming ministry projects.

D. Close in prayer.

Worship Guide

For the Superintendent or Teacher
Theme: Paul Ministers in Malta
Song: "May the Work I've Done
Speak for Me"
Devotional Reading: Ezekiel 34:11-16
Prayer

Paul Ministers in Malta

Bible Background • ACTS 28:1-10
Printed Text • ACTS 28:1-10 | Devotional Reading • EZEKIEL 34:11-16

─────────────── Aim for Change ───────────────

By the end of the lesson, we will: KNOW how Paul helped people on the island of Malta; APPRECIATE the ways others minister to us; and MINISTER to those in need.

─────────── In Focus  ───────────

Demetria's car spun out of control on the slick highway. She nearly missed careening into a ditch before her car skidded to a halt. Thankfully, she was not hurt, but the car would not start. She used her cell phone to call for help but was still waiting 10 minutes later when a dark car pulled up and a man jumped out, offering his help. She was afraid to talk with him until he showed her his badge: He was an undercover detective on his way home from work. Sighing with relief, Demetria allowed him to check out the car. Although he couldn't help, he stayed with her until her emergency roadside assistance service arrived.

We sometimes forgo help from others who do not look like us or because of the situation in which we find ourselves. Helping one another becomes easier as we realize God will often send unlikely strangers to help us in our times of need. Paul was such a helper to the sick islanders.

─────────── Keep in Mind ─────────── **NOV 18th**

"And it came to pass, that the father of Publius lay sick of a fever and of a bloody flux: to whom Paul entered in, and prayed, and laid his hands on him, and healed him"
(Acts 28:8).

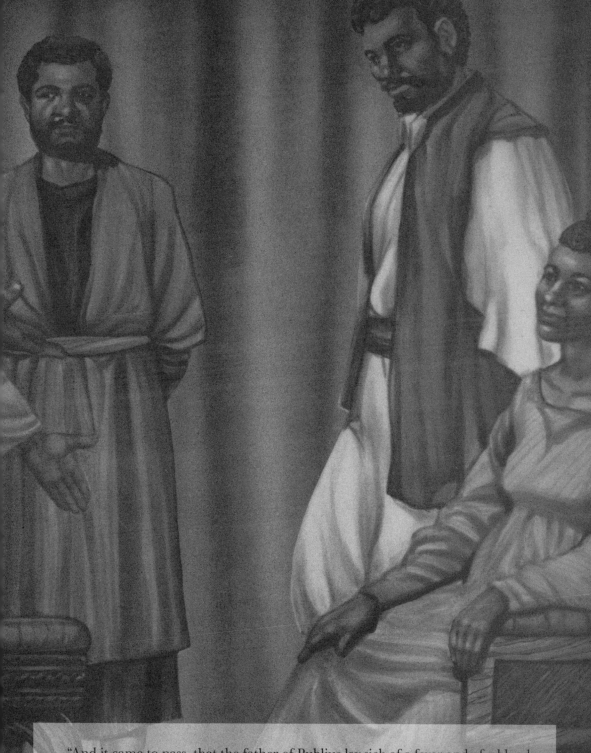

"And it came to pass, that the father of Publius lay sick of a fever and of a bloody flux: to whom Paul entered in, and prayed, and laid his hands on him, and healed him" (Acts 28:8).

Focal Verses

KJV **Acts 28:1** And when they were escaped, then they knew that the island was called Melita.

2 And the barbarous people shewed us no little kindness: for they kindled a fire, and received us every one, because of the present rain, and because of the cold.

3 And when Paul had gathered a bundle of sticks, and laid them on the fire, there came a viper out of the heat, and fastened on his hand.

4 And when the barbarians saw the venomous beast hang on his hand, they said among themselves, No doubt this man is a murderer, whom, though he hath escaped the sea, yet vengeance suffereth not to live.

5 And he shook off the beast into the fire, and felt no harm.

6 Howbeit they looked when he should have swollen, or fallen down dead suddenly: but after they had looked a great while, and saw no harm come to him, they changed their minds, and said that he was a god.

7 In the same quarters were possessions of the chief man of the island, whose name was Publius; who received us, and lodged us three days courteously.

8 And it came to pass, that the father of Publius lay sick of a fever and of a bloody flux: to whom Paul entered in, and prayed, and laid his hands on him, and healed him.

9 So when this was done, others also, which had diseases in the island, came, and were healed:

10 Who also honoured us with many honours; and when we departed, they laded us with such things as were necessary.

NLT **NLT Acts 28:1** Once we were safe on shore, we learned that we were on the island of Malta.

2 The people of the island were very kind to us. It was cold and rainy, so they built a fire on the shore to welcome us.

3 As Paul gathered an armful of sticks and was laying them on the fire, a poisonous snake, driven out by the heat, bit him on the hand.

4 The people of the island saw it hanging from his hand and said to each other, "A murderer, no doubt! Though he escaped the sea, justice will not permit him to live."

5 But Paul shook off the snake into the fire and was unharmed.

6 The people waited for him to swell up or suddenly drop dead. But when they had waited a long time and saw that he wasn't harmed, they changed their minds and decided he was a god.

7 Near the shore where we landed was an estate belonging to Publius, the chief official of the island. He welcomed us and treated us kindly for three days.

8 As it happened, Publius's father was ill with fever and dysentery. Paul went in and prayed for him, and laying his hands on him, he healed him.

9 Then all the other sick people on the island came and were healed.

10 As a result we were showered with honors, and when the time came to sail, people supplied us with everything we would need for the trip.

The People, Places, and Times

Barbarous people. The people of Malta were not barbarians as they are defined today. Rather, in biblical times, Greeks used the term for anyone who didn't speak Greek, opposed to an uncultured individual.

Malta. Also called Melita, it was an island located near both Sicily (60 miles away) and Syracuse (90 miles) and was in a strategic location for trade. It is clear that the island had an established government system and that its chief, Publius, was wealthy. He was able to lodge the 276 ship passengers at his estate (Acts 28:7).

Background

After surviving a brutal northeast storm, Paul and the other passengers either swam to the island of Malta or floated there on boards or pieces of the destroyed ship (Acts 27:44). The inhabitants warmly welcomed the strangers out of the rain and cold. Rather than resting with the others, Paul gathered firewood. As he did, a snake rose from the fire and bit him. When the islanders witnessed the biting, they believed it was divine payback for some perceived crime and waited for Paul to die. Paul, however, simply shook the snake off. The fact that he was not harmed changed the islanders opinion: They now thought he was a god.

At-A-Glance

1. Receiving Help from Strangers
   (Acts 28:1-2)
2. Divine Protection (vv. 3-6)
3. Ministering to Others (vv. 7-10)

In Depth

1. Receiving Help from Strangers (Acts 28:1-2)

While it is true that it is "more blessed to give than to receive" (Acts 20:35), it is equally true that believers must learn to receive help during difficult situations. Family, friends, co-workers, and neighbors are among those who assist in time of need. And as Paul discovered on the island of Malta, strangers also may provide timely assistance.

Paul and the other passengers found this to be true as they landed on Malta, wet from the sea during winter. They had no clothing to change into, no firewood or matches by which to warm themselves, and no food to eat. The islanders, quickly assessing the situation, came to their aid. They built a fire, offering exactly what the stranded strangers needed most. They later provided lodging and months later gave the ship's passengers needed resources to continue to Rome.

During stormy seasons of life, we learn there is no such thing as a "small blessing." Anything and everything that helps make a difficult situation easier to bear is big to the recipient. The residents of Malta built a fire. The ship's passengers were wise enough not to devalue the islanders' help or to reject it because of the givers' nationality. God recruits believers and non-believers to help Christians in distress. Learning to receive help from non-believers is especially difficult for some Christians.

It is not always how much we give or even what we give but that we are willing to be used by God to aid someone in distress. Our availability goes a long way in showing recipients God's providence and care. Using the parable of the Good Samaritan (Luke 10:25-37), Jesus taught that a neighbor is anyone in need of help, and the "good" neighbor is the person who provides help in the time of trouble. The parable teaches that we should be grateful givers and receivers. As others rush to assist you, joyfully receive their gifts of time, talent, or treasure. If you struggle with asking or receiving help from others, ask God to make you a gracious recipient.

2. Divine Protection (vv. 3-6)

Soon after surviving the tumultuous storm at sea, Paul found himself ship-wrecked on an island. Rather than sit back and allow the islanders to serve him, Paul also got involved in collecting firewood for the needed fire. As he began serving others, a viper came out of the fire and bit him. The islanders took this as a sign that Paul was a murderer who was about to reap a requisite punishment. What was Paul's response? He shook off the snake and continued his activities without any ill effects. That one action, more than any words, served to remove any doubt from the islanders' minds that Paul was a criminal.

The fact that he was able to shake off the snake is reminiscent of Jesus' teaching after His resurrection. Jesus appeared to the 11 original disciples and gave them what is commonly called the "Great Commission." During His discourse, He discussed the signs that would follow believers. Among these, He said, "They will pick up snakes with their hands; and ... they will place their hands on sick people, and they will get well" (Mark 16:18, NIV). Paul exhibited both of these miraculous signs while on Malta. He did not do so to benefit himself but to help others. The people recognized something different about Paul because of these signs, which was evidence of his faith in Christ.

3. Ministering to Others (vv. 7-10)

Paul was able to minister to others in spite of finding himself in a trying predicament. Rather than fall prey to depression and selfishness because of his circumstances, Paul continued to use his gifts and talents in executing the ministry God had given him, with signs following. When it became known that the chief's father was sick, Paul did what he knew to do. He laid hands on the man and healed him. That ability to rise above the circumstances and continue to flow in God's anointing was critical to the islanders' perception that there was something extraordinary about Paul. His example teaches that we, too, can rise above our situations to help others in need. Further, it proves that in spite of any difficulties we encounter, God's gifts and callings can still work through us if we allow them to.

Search the Scriptures

1. Why did the islanders believe Paul was a murderer (Acts 28:3-6)?

2. What critical help did Paul provide to Publius' fathers and others (vv. 8-9)?

Discuss the Meaning

News reports are filled with stories about the dangers of helping or receiving help from strangers. What strategies have you discovered to overcome fear of danger while helping others?

Lesson in Our Society

Distrust between races makes it hard for some people to receive help from people who aren't "their kind." How can God's love help believers break down barriers to communication and care for others?

Make It Happen

Paul did not allow his life storm to stop him from ministering to others. Is there an area of ministry or outreach that you have given up because of pressures from a difficult situation? If so, prayerfully ask God to help you resume using your gift to help others. Then, make an appointment with the appropriate ministry leaders to see what steps you must take to resume service.

Follow the Spirit

What God wants me to do:

_____

_____

_____

_____

Remember Your Thoughts

Special insights I have learned:

_____

_____

_____

_____

More Light on the Text

Acts 28:1-10

1 And when they were escaped, then they knew that the island was called Melita. 2 And the barbarous people shewed us no little kindness: for they kindled a fire, and received us every one, because of the present rain, and because of the cold.

Luke communicates his faith in God's care through his choice of two words in these verses. First, in verse 1 he adds an ending to a word that means we "were escaped" (Gk. *diasozo*, **dee-as-ODZE-o**), not "they" as in our KJV text. Secondly, Luke used a word here that meant to be rescued. That's why our text says, "we were escaped," instead of "we escaped." Luke clearly recognizes that the safe arrival on shore of every one of the ship's 276 passengers was solely the result of divine help. Although their ship became battered pieces on the shoreline's rocks, God confirmed Paul's prophecy from the angel's nighttime visit (Acts 27:23-24). It was not a fortunate accident by human effort but the manifestation of a promised deliverance by the God that Paul, Luke, and Aristarchus had trusted with their lives.

Gradually, the survivors learned they were on the island Melita, today called Malta, in the Mediterranean Sea, south of Sicily and Italy. In straight-line measurements, they were 1,200 miles from Caesarea where they first boarded and still more than 400 miles from Rome, their destination. In the past two weeks, the storm winds had driven more than 500 miles from Fair Havens, where Paul had urged them to stay through winter (Acts 27:8-10, 21, NIV).

Our text describes the people of Malta as "barbarous." That doesn't mean they were savage barbarians. The word simply referred to people who didn't speak Greek. Luke marveled at the loving "kindness" (Gk. *philanthropia*, **fil-an-thro-PEE-ah**) shown repeatedly by the people of Malta. "No little kindness" means the care given went far beyond what was expected. To appreciate this incident, it is crucial to remember what the conditions were.

Because of driving wind and rain, the ship crashed on the rocks. In the midst of that storm, in weather made colder by blowing torrents, the islanders came out to the shore and managed to build a fire.

Likely, they built many to accommodate 276 people. Luke notes that the island people "received us, every one."

3 And when Paul had gathered a bundle of sticks, and laid them on the fire, there came a viper, and fastened on his hand. 4 And when the barbarians saw the venomous beast hang on his hand, they said among themselves, No doubt this man is a murderer, whom, though he escaped the sea, yet vengeance suffereth not to live.

Paul was not a lazy person (Romans 12:11). Acts 28:3 says he "gathered a bundle of sticks" for the fire. One of those "sticks" could have been several inches thick, perhaps with loose bark that a little snake could slither under to hibernate during winter or maybe with a spot that had rotted away, leaving a hole where it curled up. That suggests that Paul wasn't making a show of working. Rather, he was putting real effort into helping build up the fire. The surviving crew members, and other prisoners and passengers would have seen this. Paul was a man whose example garnered respect for what he said in witness to his faith.

As Paul dropped his armful of firewood into the fire pit, the heat wakened the snake, which crawled out and latched onto Paul's hand. Although there are no poisonous snakes on present-day Malta, in verse 4 the word "viper" (Gk. *echidna*, **EKH-id-nah**), which Luke used here, usually refers to a poisonous snake. The native onlookers saw the snake hanging from Paul's hand. They instantly jumped to the conclusion that he must undoubtedly be the worst kind of desperate criminal, such as a "murderer" (Gk. *phoneus*, **fon-YOOCE**).

The Maltese thought that justice demanded retribution for the presumed criminal's evil deeds. Receiving a poisonous snakebite, after just surviving a shipwreck,

implied that to them. KJV translated Luke's word here as "vengeance" (Gk. *dike*, **DEE-kay**), but both NLT and NIV present the word to mean "justice." However, NIV capitalizes "Justice," as a reference to the Greek goddess of justice, whose name was Dike. This goddess was a companion of Zeus, the supreme Greek god. The people of Malta may have worshiped Greek gods and saw Paul's snake bite as her act of punishment.

5 And he shook off the beast into the fire, and felt no harm. 6 Howbeit they looked when he should have swollen, or fallen down dead suddenly: but after they had looked a great while, and saw no harm come to him, they changed their minds, and said that he was a god.

Undoubtedly Paul was wet and cold like all his shipmates. The description in verse 5 of his shaking the snake off his hand suggests not alarm or panic, but determination and perhaps irritation. "Shook off" (Gk. *apotinasso*, **ap-ot-in-AS-o**) is the same phrase Luke chose when quoting Jesus' command to the apostles that they should shake the dust off their feet when leaving towns where their preaching of God's kingdom was rejected (Luke 9:5).

In Acts 28, each time Paul approached the fire with more wood, the Maltese natives watched and expected him to swell up in reaction to the snake's poison or suddenly fall dead. Neither happened. Paul plainly "suffered no ill effects," as 28:5, NIV words it. In verse 6 (NIV), Paul's observers "changed" (Gk. *metaballo*, **met-ab-AL-o**) their original opinion of him. Instead, they now wrongly surmised that Paul must be a god.

7 In the same quarters were possessions of the chief man of the island, whose name was Publius; who received us and lodged us three days courteously. 8 And it came to pass, that the father of Publius lay sick of a fever and of a bloody flux: to whom Paul entered in, and prayed, and laid his hands on him, and healed him.

Near the site where the ship wrecked and those on board swam or floated to shore was the estate of "Publius" (Gk. *poplios*, **POP-lee-os**), Malta's chief magistrate and leading citizen. The Greek term meant literally "the main one," or as we say today, "the top guy." Did the gracious and caring reception that the survivors encountered in their contact with the island's residents reflect the influence of the person at the top? Publius must have been of great wealth. In verse 7, Luke says he "received us and lodged us three days courteously." "Received" did not mean to impersonally accept people's presence but to actively extend hospitality in welcoming guests. The last word in verse 7, "courteously" (Gk. *philophronos*, **fil-of-RON-oce**), means "in a friendly manner." There is no way to tell whether "us" means a few people— Paul, Luke, Aristarchus, and maybe the ship's captain, its owner, and Julius, the Roman official—as some commentators presume or all 276 stranded victims. "Lodged" (Gk. *anadechomai*, **an-ad-EKH-om-ahee**) in KJV is rendered "fed" in NLT and "entertained" in NASB. The word can be interpreted in all these ways.

Luke's point is that everyone on Malta treated the ship's survivors with exceptional care. An important lesson here for witnessing our faith is to remember, "all have sinned..." (Romans 3:23). However, people without Christ are not automatically bad people. That is why Paul admonishes in Colossians 4:6, "Let your speech be always with grace, seasoned with salt, that ye may know how ye ought to answer every man." Peter gives similar emphasis in 1 Peter 3:15, NIV: "... in your hearts revere Christ as Lord. Always be prepared to give an answer to everyone who asks you to give the reason for the hope that you have. But do this with gentleness and respect" (see also 2 Timothy 2:24). Likewise, as we saw in the previous lesson, being unapologetic and confident in sharing our faith does not mean being impolite or disrespectful.

While enjoying Publius' generosity, Paul learned that his father lay confined to his bed by recurring bouts of fever and bloody diarrhea (Acts 28:8). Paul took the initiative to visit the man as he believed he should do to support the weak (1 Thessalonians 5:14). After entering the man's room, Paul approached his bed, and as Jesus often did, laid his hands on the man and prayed (see Mark 6:5; Luke 4:40; 13:13). In Acts 28:8, Luke says what Paul did: he "healed him" (Gk. *iaomai*, **ee-AM-om-ahee**).

9 So when this was done, others also, which had diseases in the island, came, and were healed: 10 Who also honoured us with many honours: and when we departed, they laded us with such things as were necessary.

Our text, verse 9, gives no indication that Publius sought or expected Paul's miraculous intervention. It's likely that he saw his father's condition was beyond hope of recovery. Average life expectancy then was well under 40; over half of all babies died within the first year (Barclay, 188). When word got out that Publius' desperately ill father had been healed, sick people from across the island flooded to where Paul was "... and were healed" (Gk. *therapeuo*, **ther-a-PYOO-o**).

The immediate response to the father's healing would not be a surprise

(Ezekiel 34:13). What is remarkable is that although our text uses the same English word "healed" for both the father and the islanders, Luke used *iaomai* in Acts 28:8 and *therapeuo* in verse 9. That doesn't mean that the father was healed and the islanders weren't. Both were cured. The different words suggest a difference in how this happened. The father's healing described a miraculous, instant freedom from his ailments, whereas the basic meaning of the word for the others' healing is "to serve." When applied to sickness, it often referred to medical treatment.

Our text doesn't say the island's sick people came to Paul; it simply says they came. A number of commentators, including William Barclay, writes that the second word for healing applied more accurately to Luke than to Paul. Colossians 4:14, KJV, called Luke "the beloved physician" and both NLT and NIV describe him as a "beloved doctor."

The different words may well suggest two different forms of divine healing—through miraculous divine intervention when the condition is beyond human help and by Christian ministry. Barclay notes that these sections of Acts 28 may describe Luke as the first Christian medical missionary (Barclay, 189). He also notes that some medical problems are not cured either way. As an example, Paul—God's instrument for healing Publius' father—suffered unrelieved torment from a "thorn in the flesh" which God declined to heal (2 Corinthians 12:7-10; Galatians 4:13-14).

However, the Maltese people were cured; they saw loving care extended by people committed to a God who loved all people everywhere so much that He was willing to die for their sins.

Three months passed before another ship arrived when Julius could finish transporting Paul and his other prisoners on to Rome (Acts 28:11). During those three months, in verse 10 Luke says the people showered "us," not simply Paul, "with many honours" (Gk. *timao*, **tim-AH-o**). This once again supports the possibility that ministry by other Christians other than Paul is at work here. Although Luke's word could refer to things of material value or price, here, the word points to expression of affection, respect, and deep feeling. As Paul sailed away to trial in Rome, the islanders showed their esteem by loading the ship with things needed to insure a pleasant journey.

Two major lessons stand out from this passage. One concerns our attitude toward those around us who may not share our knowledge or faith in God and His revelation in Christ. While all people are sinners, that doesn't mean they cannot do commendable deeds. The image of God that we possessed in ourselves at creation has been irreparably distorted by sin but not completely blotted out. Our marred instinct toward a God-like goodness waits to be restored by our decision to trust in God's power to repair our universal spiritual brokenness.

Another lesson is the importance for each Christian to consistently make God's love visible in order to give our verbal witness an attractive credibility. It's inconceivable that Paul, the great missionary-evangelist, would allow the opportunity with such a receptive audience to slip by him. In Acts 28, Luke illustrates how making God's love real through our actions can add convicting power to what we say about God's love through Christ.

Sources:

Barclay, William H. *The Acts of the Apostles.* 2nd ed. Philadelphia, PA: Westminster Press, 1955.188-189.

"Bible Words–Phonetic Pronunciation." Better Days Are Coming com. http://www.betterdaysarecoming.com/bible/pronunciation.html (accessed September 23, 2011).

Danker, Frederick William, ed. *A Greek-English Lexicon of the New Testament and Other Early Christian Literature, Based on Walter Bauer's Greek-German Edition.* 3rd ed. Translated and edited for English readers by W. F. Arndt and Walter Bauer. Chicago: University of Chicago Press, 2000.

Haenchen, Ernst. *The Acts of the Apostles: A Commentary.* Philadelphia, PA: Westminster Press, 1971 (translated from the 14th German edition, 1965).

New Testament Greek Lexicon. Bible Study Tools.com. http://www.biblestudytools.com/lexicons/greek (accessed September 23, 2011).

Quest Study Bible (NIV), Revised. Grand Rapids, MI: Zondervan, 1994-2003.

Stott, John. *The Spirit, the Church and the World: The Message of Acts.* Downers Grove, IL: InterVarsity Press, 1990.

Zerwick, Max and Mary Grosvenor. *A Grammatical Analysis of the Greek New Testament.* Rome: Biblical Institute Press, 1974.

Zodhiates, Spiros, ed. *Hebrew-Greek Key Word Study Bible (KJV), Revised.* Chattanooga, TN: AMG Publishers, 1994.

Say It Correctly

Melita. muh-**LEE**-tuh.
Publius. **POOB**-lee-uhs.

Daily Bible Readings

MONDAY
The Failure to Minister
(Ezekiel 34:1-6)

TUESDAY
God's Ministry to the Flock
(Ezekiel 34:11-16)

WEDNESDAY
God's Judgment of the Privileged
(Ezekiel 34:17-22)

THURSDAY
Extend Hospitality to Strangers
(Romans 12:9-13)

FRIDAY
Ready for Every Good Work
(2 Timothy 2:20-26)

SATURDAY
Do Good to All
(1 Thessalonians 5:12-22)

SUNDAY
Ministering to the Sick
(Acts 28:1-10)

Teaching Tips

November 25
Bible Study Guide 13

Words You Should Know

A. Expounded (Acts 28:23) *ektithemi* (Gk.)—Set forth (used in explaining the way of God).

B. Persuading (v. 23) *peitho* (Gk.)—Prevailing upon or winning over.

Teacher Preparation

Unifying Principle—Spread the News. Even though there were many who refused to believe in the Lord Jesus Christ, Paul persevered in faith, preaching the Gospel and bringing salvation's message to those who would listen.

A. Pray for your class.

B. Read and study the entire lesson, underlining salient points.

C. Reflect on what "commitment" means and prepare to discuss it.

D. Complete the companion lesson in the *Precepts For Living Personal Study Guide*®.

O—Open the Lesson

A. Open with prayer.

B. Read the Aim for Change and Focal Verses. Explain why Paul thought his imprisonment was to serve the cause of Christ.

C. Review the Background and The People, Places, and Times sections and discuss Paul's life and commitment.

P—Present the Scriptures

A. Read the At-A-Glance outline, and use the Search the Scriptures and Discuss the Meaning questions to expound on the Focal Verses.

B. Refer the students to the Words You Should Know section as the vocabulary words arise.

E—Explore the Meaning

A. Ask a student to volunteer to read the In Focus story.

B. Discuss Ruth's difficulties and how it correlates with Paul's circumstances.

C. Highlight the Lesson in Our Society section.

N—Next Steps for Application

A. Remind the students that we find strength by looking at Jesus as our example of how to keep our commitments: God called and sustained Him through the pain and humiliation of the Cross.

B. Close with prayer.

Worship Guide

For the Superintendent or Teacher
Theme: Paul Evangelizes in Rome
Song: "Trust and Obey"
Devotional Reading:
Deuteronomy 4:32-40
Prayer

NOV
25th

Paul Evangelizes in Rome

Bible Background • ACTS 28:16-31
Printed Text • ACTS 28:23-31 | Devotional Reading • DEUTERONOMY 4:32-40

—————————— Aim for Change ——————————

By the end of the lesson, we will: SUMMARIZE the points of Paul's Gospel message; BE CONFIDENT in our ability to use Scripture to bring others to knowledge of Christ; and IDENTIFY ways we can tell resistant listeners about Christ.

—————————— In Focus ——————————

During the past year Ruth's daughter, Hope, started recognizing that her mother was becoming more and more forgetful. At first, Ruth would forget where she placed items in the house. But her memory seemed to be deteriorating. She would start teaching and get so confused the students could not understand what she was saying. Then, Ruth would get in her car to run an errand but not remember where she was headed. She also frequently put food on the stove and forgot about it. The house almost caught fire numerous times.

She visited a neurologist who took some tests. A few weeks later, the results of the tests came back. Ruth was in the early stages of dementia. The doctor told her the condition would progressively get worse over time. Ruth felt devastated over the news. How long could she continue teaching? She had served as her church's Sunday School Superintendent for more than 25 years. She was a faithful, committed worker and wondered whether to stop now or wait until things got worse.

Sometimes challenging circumstances can make it difficult to carry out our commitments. At such times, we may need to persevere in faith in spite of the difficulties we experience. In today's lesson, Paul is imprisoned but keeps his commitment to share the Gospel, which leads to souls coming to Christ.

—————————— Keep in Mind ——————————

"Be it known therefore unto you, that the salvation of God is sent unto the Gentiles, and that they will hear it" (Acts 28:28).

"Be it known therefore unto you, that the salvation of God is sent unto the Gentiles, and that they will hear it" (Acts 28:28).

Focal Verses

KJV **Acts 28:23** And when they had appointed him a day, there came many to him into his lodging; to whom he expounded and testified the kingdom of God, persuading them concerning Jesus, both out of the law of Moses, and out of the prophets, from morning till evening.

24 And some believed the things which were spoken, and some believed not.

25 And when they agreed not among themselves, they departed, after that Paul had spoken one word, Well spake the Holy Ghost by Esaias the prophet unto our fathers,

26 Saying, Go unto this people, and say, Hearing ye shall hear, and shall not understand; and seeing ye shall see, and not perceive:

27 For the heart of this people is waxed gross, and their ears are dull of hearing, and their eyes have they closed; lest they should see with their eyes, and hear with their ears, and understand with their heart, and should be converted, and I should heal them.

28 Be it known therefore unto you, that the salvation of God is sent unto the Gentiles, and that they will hear it.

29 And when he had said these words, the Jews departed, and had great reasoning among themselves.

30 And Paul dwelt two whole years in his own hired house, and received all that came in unto him,

31 Preaching the kingdom of God, and teaching those things which concern the Lord Jesus Christ, with all confidence, no man forbidding him.

NLT **Acts 28:23** So a time was set, and on that day a large number of people came to Paul's lodging. He explained and testified about the Kingdom of God and tried to persuade them about Jesus from the Scriptures. Using the law of Moses and the books of the prophets, he spoke to them from morning until evening.

24 Some were persuaded by the things he said, but others did not believe.

25 And after they had argued back and forth among themselves, they left with this final word from Paul: "The Holy Spirit was right when he said to your ancestors through Isaiah the prophet,

26 'Go and say to this people: When you hear what I say, you will not understand. When you see what I do, you will not comprehend.

27 For the hearts of these people are hardened, and their ears cannot hear, and they have closed their eyes—so their eyes cannot see, and their ears cannot hear, and their hearts cannot understand, and they cannot turn to me and let me heal them.'

28 So I want you to know that this salvation from God has also been offered to the Gentiles, and they will accept it."

30 For the next two years, Paul lived in Rome at his own expense. He welcomed all who visited him,

31 boldly proclaiming the Kingdom of God and teaching about the Lord Jesus Christ. And no one tried to stop him.

The People, Places, and Times

Rome. Rome was the capital city of the Roman Empire. Its population exceeded one million people. The city was wealthy, literate, and artistic. The Romans worshiped many pagan gods and even some of the emperors.

Jews who had come to believe apparently started the Roman church during Pentecost (Acts 2:41–47). They spread the Gospel on their return to Rome and the church grew. While in Corinth, Paul wrote a letter to the Romans to encourage the believers. After taking money to Jerusalem for the poor Christians there, he desired to visit the Roman believers on his way to Spain (Romans 15:23–28), but his visit did not happen as he had planned. Years later, Paul was taken to Rome as a prisoner.

Background

Finally, after a 2,000–mile journey that started in Caesarea, Paul arrived in Rome. He was permitted to live in his own quarters under house arrest or with a light chain. This fairly good treatment resulted from a favorable report from a Roman official, Porcius Festus, and the good will of the centurion (Acts 24:23). This proves God can grant us favor even with our enemies.

Paul called together Rome's Jewish leaders. The Jews were back; the decree of Claudius expelling them from the city had expired (18:2). Paul addressed the leaders as "my brothers" to acknowledge the common Jewish blood he shared with them (28:17, NIV). Paul wanted the leaders to feel connected to him. In doing so, they may have enough compassion toward him to try to understand the ordeal that created his unjust imprisonment. He explained to them that he was bound because of the hope of Israel, which is the Messiah. He grabbed their attention because they wanted to know more about Jesus. There was a great dispute about Jesus' claim to be the Messiah. They agreed to listen to Paul's presentation of the Gospel.

The Jewish leaders' agreement to hear the Gospel was in fulfillment of Paul's calling to share the Good News with the world, starting in Jerusalem (9:14, 28). God planned that through the seed of Abraham, He would send the Messiah into the world. Now that the Messiah had arrived in the person of Jesus Christ, the entire world needed to know about Him. That is why Paul traveled on missionary journeys during his lifetime. He wanted everyone to have the opportunity to receive Jesus Christ. In spite of the way he arrived in Rome, Paul knew God had a purpose for his imprisonment. "And we know that all things work together for good to them that love God, to them who are the called according to his purpose" (Romans 8:28, KJV). Therefore, what was intended for evil, God worked it into good in Paul's life and ministry.

At-A-Glance

1. Paul Shares the Gospel with the Jews (Acts 28:23–25a)
2. The Jews Turn Away (vv. 25b-27)
3. Paul Preaches to the Gentiles (vv. 28–31)

In Depth

1. Paul Shares the Gospel with the Jews (Acts 28:23–25a)

On the agreed-upon day, the Jewish leaders came back to the place where Paul resided with an even larger group than expected. Paul testified and taught them about the kingdom of God all day into the evening. He tried to persuade them that Jesus was the Messiah prophesied about in the

Old Testament (Acts 28:23). Romans, written some years earlier, reveals Paul's ongoing dialogue with the Jews in Rome.

Some of the Jews were persuaded while others were not. Everyone has to make a choice to either accept or reject the Gospel. The most important fact is that we share the Gospel with people no matter the circumstances in which we find ourselves. God was faithful in preserving Paul's life so he could share the Gospel in Rome. He was imprisoned but did not complain. He used the opportunity to keep his commitment to spreading the Word.

2. The Jews Turn Away (vv. 25b-27)

Verses 26 and 27 are quoted from Isaiah 6:9, 10. They are also quoted by Jesus in Matthew 13:14, 15; Mark 4:12; Luke 8:10; and John 12:40. We can picture in these verses people covering their eyes and ears so they can't hear because they are so adamantly against the message and will do what they think will stop the message from getting through. It was predicted that the majority of the Jews would not accept their Messiah, but they are also responsible because they are refusing to look and listen. But don't forget the significant number of Jews who believe, including Paul and the apostles.

3. Paul Preaches to the Gentiles (vv. 28–31)

Because the Jews rejected the message of salvation, Paul turned his attention to the Gentiles. He knew the Gentiles would listen, so he spent two years teaching, preaching, counseling, and receiving visitors (Luke, Timothy, Tychicus, Epaphroditus, and Mark) while confined. During his imprisonment, Paul wrote many of his epistles: Philemon, Colossians, Ephesians, and Philippians.

Paul did not let his imprisonment hinder him from proclaiming the Gospel. He did not worry about the outcome of his upcoming trial. Instead, he committed his life into the hands of God. For Paul, "To live is Christ, and to die is gain" (Philippians 1:21). His faithfulness was rewarded through souls coming to Christ.

Search the Scriptures

1. How did Paul preach the Gospel to the Jews (Acts 28:23)?
2. What prophet foretold the Jews not listening to God's message (v. 25)?
3. How did Paul spend his time while in prison (vv. 30-31)?

Discuss the Meaning

1. How was God's favor shown toward Paul in Rome?
2. How did Paul keep his commitment to God while imprisoned?
3. How was his faithfulness rewarded?

Lesson in Our Society

Commitment to ministry is sometimes hard. We have so many distractions and hindrances that can cause us to lapse in our responsibilities. Jesus also had a lot of adversity to deal with as He walked the Earth. However, He never allowed anything or anyone to stop Him from reaching the place He was destined to go, the Cross. If Jesus can remain faithful in spite of all He had to endure, surely we can, too. We must not allow family drama, workplace stress, or personal issues to hinder us from keeping our commitment to minister to others. The world may not understand how we can remain faithful, but we know God can and will sustain us.

Make It Happen

This week, pray God will give you the strength to keep your commitments. Always remember, God is present and in control over your circumstances. Testify to others of the faithfulness of God and how He helped you keep your commitments.

Follow the Spirit

What God wants me to do:

_____

_____

_____

_____

Remember Your Thoughts

Special insights I have learned:

_____

_____

_____

_____

More Light on the Text

Acts 28:23-31

23 And when they had appointed him a day, there came many to him into his lodging; to whom he expounded and testified the kingdom of God, persuading them concerning Jesus, both out of the law of Moses, and out of the prophets, from morning till evening.

Paul finally received his opportunity to declare the Good News in Rome. At a set time, a huge number of people gathered at Paul's house of confinement and listened as he "expounded and testified the kingdom of God" from morning until night. The word "expounded" in the Greek is *ektithemi* (**ek-TITH-ay-mee**), and means "to set forth, to declare." The word "testified" (Gk. *diamarturomai*, **dee-am-ar-TOO-rom-ahee**) means "witnessed, confirmed something by testimony." The Greek word for "kingdom" is *basileia* (**bas-il-I-ah**), which means "dominion, rule." Therefore, Paul declared and taught them, confirming the reign or rule of God and Jesus, as set forth in the five books of Moses (Genesis, Exodus, Leviticus, Numbers, and Deuteronomy) and from the Old Testament books of the prophets (Isaiah, Jeremiah, Ezekiel, Daniel, and others).

24 And some believed the things which were spoken, and some believed not.

Some of the people "believed" (Gk. *peitho*, **PIE-tho**), meaning "they were persuaded of something"—in this instance, it was God's Word—but some did not. The phrase "some believed not" in the Greek is *asumphonos* (**as-OOM-fo-nos**), and it means they spoke to one another in disagreement.

Jesus explained the importance and significance of receiving and then believing God's Word in the parable of the sower. As Jesus told a crowd: "A sower went out to sow his seed: and as he sowed, some fell by the way side; and it was trodden down, and the fowls of the air devoured it. And some fell upon a rock; and as soon as it was sprung up, it withered away, because it lacked moisture. And some fell among thorns; and the thorns sprang up with it, and choked it. And other fell on good ground, and sprang up, and bare fruit an hundredfold" (Luke 8:5–8). The apostle Paul sowed the seed, the word of God, amid his listeners, and some seeds did fall on good ground—"some believed" (Acts 28:24). However, some did not have confidence in the Word of God. It fell on deaf ears and hardened hearts. These people chose not to yield to the Word of God.

25 And when they agreed not among themselves, they departed, after that Paul had spoken one word, Well spake the Holy Ghost by Esaias the prophet unto our fathers,

For 30 years Paul preached first to the Jewish people then to Gentiles. And almost without fail, he was persecuted by them in a variety of terrible ways. But Paul loved his people and always went to them first. This is a great example of God's love for the Jews—a remnant would always believe, so Paul did not give up for all those years. But at this time, we see Paul coming to the conclusion that in God's infinite wisdom, the rejection of Jesus by the majority of the religious leaders of the Jews opened the door for the Gentiles to believe and receive. So although this final word from Paul seems very harsh, we know it really isn't.

26 Saying, Go unto this people, and say, Hearing ye shall hear, and shall not understand; and seeing ye shall see, and not perceive: 27 For the heart of this people is waxed gross, and their ears are dull of hearing, and their eyes have they closed; lest they should see with their eyes, and hear with their ears, and understand with their heart, and should be converted, and I should heal them.

When God first ordained Isaiah to go and preach to His people, this warning was given to him (Isaiah 6:9-10). Imagine how a young preacher would feel if the Lord God spoke to him at the beginning of his ministry and told him no one would listen to his message. That is just what happened to Isaiah, and some days he got pretty discouraged. Maybe you are in a difficult ministry and are finding very little response. Well, Isaiah, Paul, and Jesus all had this very same experience. This same Scripture was quoted by Jesus in Matthew 13:14-15; Mark 4:12; Luke 8:10; and John 12:39-40. Jesus had the same experience as Isaiah and Paul—all three of them had their message rejected by their own people.

28 Be it known therefore unto you, that the salvation of God is sent unto the Gentiles, and that they will hear it.

God brought His great "salvation" (Gk. *soterion*, **so-TAY-ree-on**), which means "rescue, safety, deliverance," first to His chosen people, the Jews. However, when many of them did not choose to accept Jesus Christ as the Messiah, as their Lord and Savior, His salvation then went to the Gentiles. Paul said in the affirmative that the Gentiles "will hear it." In other words, they will accept their salvation and "be grafted in."

The apostle Paul explained the concept of the Gentiles being "grafted" into this great salvation with this metaphor: "But some of these branches from Abraham's tree—some of the people of Israel—have been broken off. And you Gentiles, who were branches from a wild olive tree, have been grafted in. So now you also receive the blessing God has promised Abraham and his children, sharing in the rich nourishment from the root of God's special olive tree. But you must not brag about being grafted in to replace the branches that were broken off. You are just a branch, not the root. 'Well,' you may say, 'those branches were broken off to make room for me.' Yes, but remember— those branches [the Jews] were broken off because they didn't believe in Christ, and you are there because you do believe" (Romans 11:17–20, NLT).

In the above passage from Romans, Paul explained to Gentile Christians that they should not feel superior to the Jews because some of the Jews were rejected. Their unbelief caused them to be rejected. He explained that Abraham's faith was like the roots of a productive tree, and the Jewish people, God's chosen people, are the natural branches of that tree. Because of their unbelief, some of the Jews have been broken off from this fruitful tree. Gentile believers, who he compared to being branches from a wild olive tree, were "grafted in"—they took the place of the faithless Jews. These Gentiles were added to the family of believers based on their faith in God, and therefore they could share in the faith community's spiritual nourishment. Both the Jews and the Gentiles, then, are saved according to their faith and not because of their culture or heritage. The only way to be saved is to believe on the Lord Jesus Christ (John 3:16).

Thus, when Paul gave the word to the local Jewish leaders in Rome and some chose not to believe, they chose damnation. Those who chose to believe, chose salvation— eternal life.

29 And when he had said these words, the Jews departed, and had great reasoning among themselves.

After Paul spoke in Acts 28:28 of the salvation of the Gentiles, whom the Jews considered to be "dogs" or "heathens," they "departed, and had great reasoning among themselves" (v. 29). In the Greek, the word "reasoning" (*suzetesis*, **sood-ZAY-tay-sis**), means "mutual questioning, discussion." In essence, they left to ponder, consider, or think over among themselves the things that the apostle Paul had told them.

30 And Paul dwelt two whole years in his own hired house, and received all that came in unto him, 31 Preaching the kingdom of God, and teaching those things which concern the Lord Jesus Christ, with all confidence, no man forbidding him.

Paul preached the Good News of the Gospel in his own "hired house" (Gk. *misthoma*, **MIS-tho-mah**), which means "rented building," under house arrest for two years. However, he did not spend these years in idleness; he kept on freely preaching the Kingdom of God and teaching God's Word with all "confidence" (Gk. *parrhesia*, **par-rhay-SEE-ah**), which means "freedom in speaking, outspoken, frankness, or bluntness." He spoke with authority, under the power of the Holy Spirit—bluntly telling eternally lost humanity what it must do to be saved from never-ending damnation.

Some biblical scholars tell us that after being released from house arrest in Rome, Paul set off on a fourth missionary journey. They support this assertion with the following facts: "(1) Luke, who was such a meticulous chronicler, did not give details of Paul's trial before the Emperor Caesar; (2) the prosecutors had two years to bring Paul's case to trial and time may have just expired; (3) Paul implied in his letter to the Philippians, which was written while he was in prison in Rome, that he would soon be released and would do further travels; (4) Paul gave further information on his intended travels—places that he had not mentioned during his first three missionary journeys; and (5) early Christian literature informs of other travels of Paul" (*Life Application Study Bible*, 2211).

Paul was indeed committed to the cause of Christ, his Lord and Savior. He even used his imprisonment to bring glory to his God and to serve that cause. Because even his negative circumstances proved to be a positive witness of his faithfulness to Christ in the midst of struggles, his life was truly an example of successful Christian living.

Sources:
Bible Gateway.com. http://www.biblegateway.com (accessed September 23, 2011).
"Commentary on Acts 28." *The 1599 Geneva Study Bible.* http://www.biblestudytools.com/commentaries/geneva-study-bible/acts/acts-28.html (accessed September 23, 2011).
Dictionary.com. http://dictionary.reference.com/ (accessed September 23, 2011).
Douglas, J. D., ed. *New Bible Dictionary.* 2nd ed. Downers Grove, IL: InterVarsity Press, 1982. 1038–39, 1799, 1878.
Gill, John. "Commentary on Acts 28:30." *John Gill's Exposition of the Bible.* http://www.biblestudytools.com/commentaries/gills-exposition-of-the-bible/acts-28-30.html (accessed September 23, 2011).
Life Application Study Bible, New International Version. Wheaton, IL: Tyndale House Publishers, Inc., 2005. 1877–79; 2211.
Mears, Henrietta C. *What the Bible Is All About.* Ventura, CA: Regal Books, 1983. 428.
New Testament Greek Lexicon. Bible Study Tools.com. http://www.biblestudytools.com/lexicons/greek (accessed September 23, 2011).
"2268. Esaias." Strong's Concordance on Biblos.com. http://concordances.org/greek/2268.html (accessed September 23, 2011).
Unger, Merrill F. *Unger's Bible Dictionary.* Chicago, IL: Moody Press, 1985. 936.

Say It Correctly

Esaias. eh-sah-**EE**-as.
Expounded. ik-**SPOUND**-ed.

Daily Bible Readings

MONDAY
Will They Listen to Me?
(Exodus 6:6-13)

TUESDAY
I Told You So!
(Deuteronomy 1:41-45)

WEDNESDAY
Charged to Teach
(Deuteronomy 4:5-14)

THURSDAY
The Voice of Discipline
(Deuteronomy 4:32-40)

FRIDAY
The Word Is Very Near
(Deuteronomy 30:6-14)

SATURDAY
We Would Like to Hear
(Acts 28:16-22)

SUNDAY
Teaching Boldly and without Hindrance
(Acts 28:23-31)

Notes

_____

_____

_____

_____

Jesus Is Lord

This quarter has three units that detail the early church's teaching about Christ. These lessons from Ephesians, Philippians, and Colossians draw us toward a deeper understanding of who Christ is and what it might mean for us to imitate Christ in our lives.

UNIT 1 • VICTORY IN JESUS

This is a five-lesson study of Ephesians. The emphasis in these lessons is on the exaltation of Christ over all principalities and powers from the beginning to the end of time. The first two lessons proclaim the power of God as revealed in and through Christ. The third lesson considers the image of the Church as the body with Christ as the head. Lesson 4 focuses on Christ as the light of the world. Lesson 5 looks at another metaphor for Christ's relationship with the Church as its bridegroom.

Lesson 1: December 2, 2012
Spiritual Blessings in Jesus Christ
Ephesians 1:3–14

All people want to feel valued. The writer of Ephesians declares that, through Jesus Christ, we gain an inheritance as God's own people to become recipients of forgiveness and of salvation's redemptive power.

Lesson 2: December 9, 2012
One in Jesus Christ
Ephesians 2:11–22

Adversaries sometimes long for ways to come together. The writer of Ephesians proclaims that it is in Christ that we, once dead through our trespasses, are brought alive in Christ and that He is the one who breaks down all dividing walls and brings us together as one.

Lesson 3: December 16, 2012
Unity in the Body of Christ
Ephesians 4:1–16

The writer of Ephesians says that, although we bring different gifts, we find true unity as we grow in Christ.

Lesson 4: December 23, 2012
Live in the Light
John 1:1–5; Ephesians 5:1–2, 6–14

People sometimes think their thoughts, fears, and actions are hidden or that they're secrets from others. The writer of Ephesians tells us that as Christians, we always live in Christ's light that overcomes all kinds of darkness. The wise men received a light into their lives when they found the baby Jesus and were overwhelmed with joy.

Lesson 5: December 30, 2012
Christ's Love for the Church
Ephesians 5:21–6:4

People struggle to balance the demands of their daily lives with their need to show love for one another. The writer of Ephesians states that family members should love and care for one another just as Christ loves and cares for the Church.

UNIT 2 • EXALTING CHRIST

This is a four-lesson study of Philippians. The letter to the Philippians encourages believers to follow the pattern laid out for us in Christ and to oppose those who are enemies of Christ's Cross.

Lesson 6: January 6, 2013
Proclaiming Christ
Philippians 1:15–26

Paul says that regardless of intentions, the result was still that Christ is proclaimed in every way. Jesus used parables to teach us how to declare His message.

Lesson 7: January 13, 2013
Jesus' Humility and Exaltation
Philippians 2:5–11

Sometimes people driven by the need to succeed exploit others to get to the top. God exalted Jesus because of Christ's selflessness, obedience, servanthood, and humility. Jesus talked about the importance of finding the best surroundings in which to grow in faith and serve others.

Lesson 8: January 20, 2013
Gaining in Jesus Christ
Philippians 3:7–11

The self-worth of many people resides in the things they have accomplished. Paul believed that none of the achievements of this life are worth anything when compared to the value of knowing Christ Jesus.

Lesson 9: January 27, 2013
Stand Firm
Philippians 3:12–16

Sometimes it is difficult to sustain needed energy to achieve goals that have lasting value. Maintaining a strong bond with Christ prepares us for the relationship we will have with Him in eternity. Jesus stressed that preparation would help people reach important goals.

UNIT 3 • IMITATING JESUS

This is a four-lesson study of Colossians. These lessons have much to say about the importance of the person and work of Christ as Lord of all creation and the author of our peace with God.

Lesson 10: February 3, 2013
The Supremacy of Jesus Christ
Colossians 1:15–20

Because of the immediate availability of images of greatness, our grasp of the amazing becomes desensitized. Paul's use of metaphor strongly conveys Christ's supremacy, which helps us realize who Christ is. When Jesus called the first disciples to follow Him, their response was immediate.

Lesson 11: February 10, 2013
Full Life in Christ
Colossians 2:6–15

We regularly try but fail to live up to human expectations and traditions. Through Jesus, God forgives all our trespasses and triumphs over all earthly rulers and authorities.

Lesson 12: February 17, 2013
Clothed with Christ
Colossians 3:5–17

Our lives are guided by basic principles. Those who believe in Christ are guided by Christ's example and strive to "put on the new man," which represents acting as Christ would regardless of the situation.

Lesson 13: February 24, 2013
Spiritual Disciplines for New Life
Colossians 4:2–6

Once we commit ourselves to a new routine, it is helpful to have partners or mentors to strengthen our resolve. Paul names spiritual disciplines and faithful persons as examples of support for living a new life in Christ.

GOD: JESUS CHRIST
JESUS CHRIST IS SUPERIOR TO ...

All the angels He created to be messengers to His people

All the leaders He called to supervise His people

All the prophets He inspired to instruct and warn His people

All the priesthood He ordained to minister to/mediate for His people

JESUS CHRIST IS ...

Almighty God

The Supreme Authority

The believers' only way back to a holy God

The complete disclosure of who the One True God is

The believers' perfect example of how to please God

The perfect atoning sacrifice for our sins

The Messiah, the Son of the Living God

Source: *Life Application Study Bible*. Wheaton, IL: Tyndale House Publishers, Inc., 1996.

Because we are Believers, We are One in ⋅⋅⋅

1. *Body* (The Body is the church.)

2. *Spirit* (God's Holy Spirit dwells within us.)

3. *Hope* (Our hope is in the LORD and what He has promised.)

4. *Lord* (We all belong to Christ, who is our LORD.)

5. *Faith* (We are committed to Christ as our Lord and Savior.)

6. *Baptism* (Our sign of entry into Christ's Church.)

7. *God* (He is our only God, and He keeps us for eternity.)

(From *Life Application Study Bible, New Living Translation.* Wheaton, IL: Tyndale House Publishers, Inc., 1996. 1877.)

Ephesians

"Blessed be the God
and Father of our Lord Jesus Christ,
who hath blessed us with all spiritual blessings
in heavenly places in Christ:
According as he hath chosen us in him
before the foundation of the world,
that we should be holy
and without blame before him in love:"

(Ephesians 1:3-4, KJV)

REV. JAMES W. C. PENNINGTON

(1809–1870)
(Minister, Teacher, Orator, Abolitionist)

Even in 1855, before the Civil War began, African-American ministers in the north were protesting injustice in ways that we associate with the Civil Rights era of the last century. Rev. James W. C. Pennington was kicked off a street car in New York City for refusing to sit in the area designated for Blacks. When he complained, police briefly jailed him. After this, he along with a doctor from Scotland and Rev. Henry Highland Garnet, formed the Legal Rights Association to fight for an end to segregation in public accommodations.

Rev. Pennington spent the first 21 years of life as a slave in Maryland. Although trained to be a blacksmith, he had not learned to read or write and had no religious education. He did not even know of Jesus Christ. But when he escaped to freedom, he was shielded the first six months by Quakers who began educating him. He loved astronomy, logic, German, French, Greek, and Latin. He sat in on classes at Yale but was not allowed to enroll formally. He traveled to Paris, Brussels, and London. The University of Heidelberg in Germany conferred on him the degree of Doctor of Divinity.

But before this, while he was still in his first year of freedom, he found that he was in a different kind of slavery—to sin. He did not forget his brothers and sisters still in slavery, but he felt that he could not petition God to end slavery since his own heart was not yet right with God.

He continued in deep turmoil for several weeks, until he came into a saving relationship with God through Jesus Christ.

Rev. Pennington used his education as a teacher, advocating independently run and controlled schools and seminaries until desegregation could be achieved in the North. He was also a minister in Congregational, Presbyterian, and African Methodist Episcopal churches. As a minister, he conducted the wedding of a 21-year-old escaped slave named Frederick Douglass.

Because of the Fugitive Slave Act, even slaves who escaped to freedom in the north were in danger, so Rev. Pennington hid his enslaved past, even from his wife. But while he was in Great Britain speaking, he revealed his past, and a wealthy benefactor paid for his freedom. At this time, he began writing his autobiography, *The Fugitive Blacksmith*. He also wrote *A Text Book of the Origin and History of the Colored People*, in which he argued for African origins of western European civilization and against European claims to superiority. He also founded the Union Missionary Society, created to evangelize Africa, Jamaica, and other parts of the world.

Sources:
Durham, Dr. Joseph and Dr. C. D. Coleman. *Civil Rights*. Elgin, Ill.: David C. Cook Publishing Co., 1972.
Pennington, James W. C. *The Reluctant Blacksmith or, Events in the History of James W. C. Pennington*. London: Charles Gilpin, 5 Bishopsgate Without, second edition, 1849.

Teaching Tips

December 2
Bible Study Guide 1

Words You Should Know

A. Predestined (Ephesians 1:5) *proorizo* (Gk.)—Decided beforehand.

B. Redemption (v. 7) *apolutrosis* (Gk.)— The act of being set free from imprisonment or slavery for a ransom.

Teacher Preparation

Unifying Principle—Chosen and Claimed. The writer of Ephesians declares that, through Jesus Christ, we gain an inheritance as God's own people to become recipients of forgiveness and salvation's redemptive power.

A. Pray for your students and for lesson clarity.

B. Study the entire lesson.

C. Complete the companion *Precepts For Living Personal Study Guide*®.

O—Open the Lesson

A. Ask a volunteer to open the class with prayer.

B. Discuss the comparison between an earthly adoption and spiritual adoption into the family of God.

P—Present the Scriptures

A. Ask volunteers to read the In Focus story. Discuss.

B. Present The People, Places, and Times and Background sections. Discuss.

C. Read and discuss the Focal Verses using the At-A-Glance outline.

D. Ask for volunteers to define "predestined" and "redemption" from today's Words You Should Know. Discuss.

E—Explore the Meaning

A. Divide the class into pairs or small groups. Instruct them to complete the Search the Scriptures section together and to discuss it among themselves.

B. Bring the groups back together. Read the Lesson in Our Society section. Discuss ways that believers can enter into relationships with unbelievers with the intention of lovingly inviting them into the family of God.

N—Next Steps for Application

A. Read the Make It Happen section. Discuss.

B. Summarize the lesson.

C. Remind students to read the Daily Bible Readings.

D. Close with prayer.

Worship Guide

For the Superintendent or Teacher
Theme: Spiritual Blessings in
Jesus Christ
Song: "Wonderful Grace of Jesus"
Devotional Reading: Psalm 33:8-12
Prayer

Spiritual Blessings in Jesus Christ

Bible Background • EPHESIANS 1
Printed Text • EPHESIANS 1:3-14 | Devotional Reading • PSALM 33:8-12

—————————— Aim for Change ——————————

By the end of the lesson, we will: UNDERSTAND Paul's explanation of being adopted by God through Jesus Christ; EXPRESS humility at God's affirmation of our worthiness; and PRAISE God for the remarkable gift of His adoption of us through Jesus Christ.

—————————— In Focus 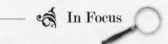 ——————————

Married for six years, Shelly and Curtis longed for a child of their own but had not been able to conceive. They decided to start the adoption process, praying God would give them a child who needed them.

Shortly after meeting with the adoption agency, Shelly began having a series of dreams. Every night for months, she dreamed of a small, dark-haired child that was always crying. Shelly would run to the child, reaching out her arms, but the child would push her away. She was deeply troubled and shared the dream with Curtis.

"Honey, I think God has a child for us," Curtis said. "Maybe it's just not the right time."

Shelly and Curtis kept praying. One night, Shelly dreamed about the child again. This time, the child reached out to her and smiled. When Shelly woke, she knew that God was answering her many prayers.

Finally, Shelly and Curtis signed adoption papers, welcoming 4-year-old Shayla into their family.

This week, we will see how God provided a way to adopt us into His family—redemption through His Son, Jesus Christ.

—————————— Keep in Mind ——————————

"Having predestinated us unto the adoption of children by Jesus Christ to himself, according to the good pleasure of his will, To the praise of the glory of his grace, wherein he hath made us accepted in the beloved" (Ephesians 1:5-6).

"Having predestinated us unto the adoption of children by Jesus Christ to himself, according to the good pleasure of his will, To the praise of the glory of his grace, wherein he hath made us accepted in the beloved" (Ephesians 1:5-6).

Focal Verses

KJV **Ephesians 1:3** Blessed be the God and Father of our Lord Jesus Christ, who hath blessed us with all spiritual blessings in heavenly places in Christ:

4 According as he hath chosen us in him before the foundation of the world, that we should be holy and without blame before him in love:

5 Having predestinated us unto the adoption of children by Jesus Christ to himself, according to the good pleasure of his will,

6 To the praise of the glory of his grace, wherein he hath made us accepted in the beloved.

7 In whom we have redemption through his blood, the forgiveness of sins, according to the riches of his grace;

8 Wherein he hath abounded toward us in all wisdom and prudence;

9 Having made known unto us the mystery of his will, according to his good pleasure which he hath purposed in himself:

10 That in the dispensation of the fulness of times he might gather together in one all things in Christ, both which are in heaven, and which are on earth; even in him:

11 In whom also we have obtained an inheritance, being predestinated according to the purpose of him who worketh all things after the counsel of his own will:

12 That we should be to the praise of his glory, who first trusted in Christ.

13 In whom ye also trusted, after that ye heard the word of truth, the gospel of your salvation: in whom also after that ye believed, ye were sealed with that holy Spirit of promise,

14 Which is the earnest of our inheritance until the redemption of the purchased possession, unto the praise of his glory.

NLT **Ephesians 1:3** All praise to God, the Father of our Lord Jesus Christ, who has blessed us with every spiritual blessing in the heavenly realms because we are united with Christ.

4 Even before he made the world, God loved us and chose us in Christ to be holy and without fault in his eyes.

5 God decided in advance to adopt us into his own family by bringing us to himself through Jesus Christ. This is what he wanted to do, and it gave him great pleasure.

6 So we praise God for the glorious grace he has poured out on us who belong to his dear Son.

7 He is so rich in kindness and grace that he purchased our freedom with the blood of his Son and forgave our sins.

8 He has showered his kindness on us, along with all wisdom and understanding.

9 God has now revealed to us his mysterious plan regarding Christ, a plan to fulfill his own good pleasure.

10 And this is the plan: At the right time he will bring everything together under the authority of Christ—everything in heaven and on earth.

11 Furthermore, because we are united with Christ, we have received an inheritance from God, for he chose us in advance, and he makes everything work out according to his plan.

12 God's purpose was that we Jews who were the first to trust in Christ would bring praise and glory to God.

13 And now you Gentiles have also heard the truth, the Good News that God saves you. And when you believed in Christ, he identified you as his own by giving you the Holy Spirit, whom he promised long ago.

NLT continued

14 The Spirit is God's guarantee that he will give us the inheritance he promised and that he has purchased us to be his own people. He did this so we would praise and glorify him.

The People, Places, and Times

The Book of Ephesians. Paul wrote the book of Ephesians while he was imprisoned (see Ephesians 3:1; 4:1; 6:20), perhaps while jailed in Rome. Most scholars agree that Ephesians was written for a wider readership than just the church at Ephesus and was probably circulated among many churches in the Roman province of Asia, where Ephesus was located.

Background

In the original Greek text, the 12 verses of Ephesians 1:3–14 were a single sentence. This is one of the most joyful and profound passages in the Bible. Like an anthem of praise, it celebrates God's eternal and glorious plan of redemption. It is broken into three stanzas, each beginning or ending with the phrase "to the praise of his glorious grace" (Ephesians 1:6, NIV) or "for" or "to the praise of his glory" (1:12, 14, NIV).

This passage examines the plan of redemption from a triune perspective: The first (1:3–6) praises the Father for choosing to redeem us from our sin; the second highlights Jesus as the Redeemer (1:7–12); and the third stanza (1:13–14) reveals the Holy Spirit as the living, divine presence to the church and the world.

In these verses, the vast plan of redemption is revealed from eternity before creation to the time of its future completion at the time of Christ's Second Advent. The focus of redemption is always Christ, and the phrase "in Christ" or "in him" occurs repeatedly throughout this passage. In fact, this expression is the key phrase of this entire epistle, or letter.

At-A-Glance

1. God Blessed Us (Ephesians 1:3-6)
2. Jesus Christ Redeemed Us (vv. 7-12)
3. The Holy Spirit Sealed Our Salvation (vv. 13-14)

In Depth

1. God Blessed Us (Ephesians 1:3-6)

Paul begins this passage with joyful praise to God the Father for His plan of redemption and He blesses Him for the blessing of Christ Jesus. Because of Christ's redemptive work, believers are beneficiaries of all the spiritual blessings of the "heavenly realms" (v. 3, NIV). These spiritual blessings come from living and abiding "in Christ."

Verse 4 tells us of the first blessing: We are chosen to be holy and blameless. God did not choose us because we are holy and blameless, but He chose us that we might become holy and blameless. Consider the implications: When we accept Christ as our Savior and Redeemer, we are accepting God's offer to make us holy and blameless. He is promising to take us unworthy sinners and make us into His very own children. And we are not only joining the family, but we are also gaining all the rights and privileges that come with the position.

In addition, we were predestined, or chosen ahead of time, to become God's children and be freely given the gift of His glorious grace. He determined beforehand what we would become or do. Some of these plans are listed in this passage of Scripture. He decided His people would be holy and blameless (v. 4), adopted as

165

His sons and daughters (v. 5), redeemed (v. 7), for the praise of His glory (vv. 11-12), recipients of the Holy Spirit (v. 13), and given an inheritance (v. 14). Verse 6 says God has freely provided for us all these blessings by His grace and through Christ Jesus. It's up to us to accept them.

2. Jesus Christ Redeemed Us (vv. 7–12)

This second stanza of Paul's hymn highlights the wonder of God's grace, revealed in the life and death of Jesus Christ. God takes sin very seriously, and it is only because of Christ's sacrifice on our behalf that we can be forgiven. But God does not forgive grudgingly. Rather, He forgives us "according to the riches of His grace" (v. 7, NKJV). God "lavished on us" His grace and forgiveness (v. 8, NIV). Just as parents love their children, God loves us. He not only adopts us into His family, but He does so in generosity and abundance.

God also promises that one day His plan for humankind will be fully accomplished. At the right time, the culmination of God's plan will come to pass, and all will be brought together under the Lordship of Jesus Christ (v. 10). In these confusing and fearful times, it is comforting to know that there will come a time when everything will come into right relationship under the leadership of Jesus.

3. The Holy Spirit Sealed Our Salvation (vv. 13-14)

In ancient times, a seal denoted ownership. In this last stanza of Paul's theological hymn, he speaks of the Holy Spirit's role in our redemption. The Holy Spirit "seals" the deal. When God adopts us into His family, He gives us the Holy Spirit as evidence that we are truly His sons and daughters (Romans 8:9) with all rights and responsibilities.

The Holy Spirit is also a promise of greater things to come—when God's entire plan is accomplished and our full redemption is realized. On that great day, when all is fulfilled, the family of God will truly be "unto the praise of his glory" (Ephesians 1:14).

Search the Scriptures

1. When and why did God choose us to become part of His family (Ephesians 1:4)?

2. How do we obtain redemption (v. 7)?

3. What role does the Holy Spirit fulfill in the redemption plan for believers (vv. 13-14)?

Discuss the Meaning

1. What are some of the benefits of being a part of God's family?

2. How do we know we are part of God's family?

Lesson in Our Society

People long for connection—a place to belong. Some search for relationships at work, at the gym, or online. Others hope for a sense of belonging within their own family. Still others move from relationship to relationship, without ever really feeling loved or accepted anywhere.

As believers, we can offer others meaningful relationships within the body of Christ. In fact, it is usually through relationships that we are able to lovingly invite others to join us in the family of God.

Make It Happen

Many people don't have a clear understanding of sin. If people do not have a clear grasp of what sin is, then they don't know that they need repentance and redemption. As believers, so that others may join us in the family of God, we must clearly point the way to the Cross. God loves every person in the world and wants him or

166

her to join His family. It's our mandated duty to extend the invitation.

Follow the Spirit

What God wants me to do:

_____

_____

_____

_____

Remember Your Thoughts

Special insights I have learned:

_____

_____

_____

_____

More Light on the Text

Ephesians 1:3–14

3 Blessed be the God and Father of our Lord Jesus Christ, who hath blessed us with all spiritual blessings in heavenly places in Christ:

The adjective "blessed" (Gk. *eulogetos*, **yoo-log-ay-TOS**) literally means "praised, well-spoken of" or "in a place of favor and benefit." Many scholars debate which meaning applies to the first word of this verse, largely because the verb "be" is not stated in the text but implied. Therefore, Paul's intended meaning could be either "God is to be praised" or "God is characterized by blessedness." The first is preferred.

The reason that Paul directs blessing toward God is because of the favor that

God has poured out on His people. The blessings here are "spiritual" (Gk. *pneumatikos*, **pnyoo-mat-ik-OS**)—related primarily to our spiritual welfare—rather than material or physical. The spiritual blessings we have received are also comprehensive; the list to follow in verses 4–14 will show us what he means by "all."

The blessings are further described as "in heavenly places" and "in Christ." "Heavenly places" (Gk. *epouranios*, **ep-oo-RAN-ee-os**) could literally be translated "heavenlies." The heavenlies are mentioned in Ephesians 1:20 as the place where Christ sat down after ascending to heaven. Then, 2:6 tells us that we are presently seated in the heavenlies with Christ (*Darby Translation*). The "heavenlies" are, therefore, the realm where God lives.

4 According as he hath chosen us in him before the foundation of the world, that we should be holy and without blame before him in love:

The word "chosen" (Gk. *eklegomai*, **ek-LEG-om-ahee**) means "picked out" or "selected." Because the Scriptures are clear that God has chosen His people, the issue that Christians debate is the basis on which He has chosen them. Christians who follow in the steps of the ancient theologian and priest St. Augustine argue that God's choice is solely based on His sovereign will. His position comes from the perspective that sin has so thoroughly corrupted man that no one is able to choose Christ unless God first regenerates his heart (John 5:21; Ephesians 2:1). Christians who follow in the footsteps of Dutch theologian Arminius believe that God's choice of individuals is based on His perfect foreknowledge (prescience) of what those individuals would do if they were left to their own free will. They hold that the prevenient grace of God makes it possible for anyone to choose to believe in Christ apart from a special regenerating work of God. This perspective emphasizes the Scripture's offer of salvation to the entire world (John 3:16) and argues that God would not offer mankind something (salvation) that we are not able to seek on our own.

The Father's work in the redemption of His people began before the foundation of the world. Other New Testament passages echo and enhance this thought. In Matthew 25:34, Jesus refers to the inheritance of the righteous as "the kingdom prepared for you from the foundation of the world." Jesus was destined for His role as our Redeemer from eternity past (John 17:24; 1 Peter 1:20), and the Lamb's Book of Life has contained the names of God's people since before the creation of the world (Revelation 13:8; 17:8).

Being chosen by God is a high privilege, but it also involves accountability. In Ephesians 1:4, the word "holy" (Gk. *hagios*, **HAG-ee-os**) means "consecrated, set apart, morally perfect." It is sometimes used in the New Testament as a noun to mean "saint" (those set apart to God). The Greek work *amomos* (**AM-o-mos**, "without blame") is a word used ceremonially to describe a sacrifice as "without blemish" (see 1 Peter 1:19). In this context, it describes a state of moral faultlessness (see Philippians 2:15; Revelation 14:5).

5 Having predestinated us unto the adoption of children by Jesus Christ to himself, according to the good pleasure of his will,

The word translated "predestinated" (Gk. *proorizo*, **pro-or-ID-zo**) means "decided upon beforehand; predetermined, foreordained." When the authors of the New Testament use this word to describe God's action in the redemption of humankind, they intend for us to understand that God did more than simply plan our redemption. He caused it to happen. God even predestined the crucifixion of Jesus (Acts 4:27-28; 1 Corinthians 2:7-8). And He has predestined not only our adoption but also our complete transformation into the image of Christ (Romans 8:29).

In Ephesians 1:5, our salvation is also described as "adoption of children" (Gk. *huiothesia*, **hwee-oth-es-EE-ah**). The predestination-to-adoption is based on the "good pleasure" (Gk. *eudokia*, **yoo-dok-EE-ah**) of God's will. *Eudokia* is used in the New Testament to mean "satisfaction, good pleasure, favor, approval." The message of the Scriptures is clear: God purposed, planned, and accomplished our redemption, not because of any obligation or compulsion but because He is merciful and compassionate. It pleases Him to save us, His people, from sin and bestow eternal blessing upon us (Luke 12:32; 1 Corinthians 1:21).

"Will" (Gk. *thelema*, **THEL-ay-mah**) in Ephesians 1:5 means "what one wishes or has determined shall be done." Until the coming of Christ, God's will for humankind's salvation was mostly hidden and only partly revealed. It was a mystery because humankind had no way of knowing exactly what God was going to do (Ephesians 3:4–5). But Christ's advent, crucifixion, and resurrection—along with the proclamation of His word—have fully revealed to us what God has "determined shall be done" (see Daniel 11:36).

6 To the praise of the glory of his grace, wherein he hath made us accepted in the beloved.

"Praise" (Gk. *epainos*, **EP-ahee-nos**) is used here and in verses 12 and 14 to refer to recognition that is due God for His work to save His people. The Lord will receive praise, thanksgiving, and honor from the redeemed for all eternity (Revelation 7:10).

"Glory" (Gk. *doxa*, **DOX-ah**) can refer to brightness, splendor, and majesty or to fame, renown, and honor. Here, the emphasis seems to be on the fame and renown of God's incredible "grace" (Gk. *charis*, **KHAR-ece**). *Charis* here refers to the favor that God has shown to His people by selecting them and orchestrating their salvation, in spite of their sin.

7 In whom we have redemption through his blood, the forgiveness of sins, according to the riches of his grace;

Paul now switches his focus from the orchestrating work of the Father to the role of the Son, who accomplished the salvation of God's people. All of the blessings of salvation are experienced "in Christ" (see comments on v. 3). "Redemption" (Gk. *apolutrosis*, **ap-ol-OO-tro-sis**) is a release from slavery or captivity brought about by the payment of a ransom, a "buying back." "Forgiveness" (Gk. *aphesis*, **AF-es-is**) is the cancellation of an obligation—namely the obligation of payment for our sin. Christ's work means that God promises to erase our sin from our record (Isaiah 43:25), to not count our sin against us (Romans 4:8), to not remember our sins any more (Hebrews 10:17), and to cleanse our conscience so that we may walk in newness of life (Hebrews 9:14; 10:22).

We experience redemption and forgiveness through the "riches" (Gk. *ploutos*, **PLOO-tos**) of God's grace. *Ploutos* can mean a literal abundance of wealth; here, the emphasis is on the fullness of the blessing experienced by believers in Christ. Furthermore, God's cleansing work is a precursor to the prosperity for which we hope (Jeremiah 33:8–9).

8 Wherein he hath abounded toward us in all wisdom and prudence;

God has "abounded" or "lavished" (Gk. *perisseuo*, **per-is-SYOO-o**) the blessings of salvation upon us. In this context, *perisseuo* means "to make extremely rich." His generosity is so great that it might cause us to question the soundness of His judgment. However, Paul uses two overlapping terms to clarify that the lavishing is deliberate and based on sound judgment. "Wisdom" (Gk. *sophia*, **sof-EE-ah**) is "the capacity to understand and function accordingly." "Prudence" (Gk. *phronesis*, **FRON-ay-sis**) is "intelligence" or "the ability to understand."

9 Having made known unto us the mystery of his will, according to his good pleasure which he hath purposed in himself:

The verb "having made known" (Gk. *gnorizo*, **gno-RID-zo**) means, "to reveal" and may indicate either the time or means of God's lavishing in verse 8. Alternate translations include "when he revealed to us" or "by revealing to us." What God revealed was the "mystery" (Gk. *musterion*, **moos-TAY-ree-on**) of His will. A biblical mystery is a secret that God has not previously disclosed. The exact nature of the mystery, however, is not necessarily the point of this passage. The point is that God has entrusted the message of His plan for the redemption of humankind with the church. We are responsible to be good stewards of that message by faithfully preserving it, guarding it from corruption, and sharing it with those who need to hear it.

The revelation of the mystery of God's will happened according to His good pleasure. The Greek word for "good pleasure," *eudokia*, was also used in verse 5 to describe the way God adopted us as His children. The word "purposed" (Gk. *protithemai*, **prot-ITH-em-ahee**) means "to set before oneself, propose to oneself." The word is used figuratively here to mean, "plan, purpose, or intend." Again, we see that God's lavish blessing of His people in Christ, although motivated by passionate love, is deliberate and carefully planned.

10 That in the dispensation of the fulness of times he might gather together in one all things in Christ, both which are in heaven, and which are on earth; even in him:

God's plan, rooted in love and guided by wisdom, concerns more than the redemption of humankind. His goal is to change or renew the order of the entire created universe by manifesting the Lordship of Christ in a powerful and dramatic way.

"Dispensation" (Gk. *oikonomia*, **oy-kon-om-EE-ah**) refers to God's plan of salvation, which He is bringing to pass in the "fulness of times." As sovereign king of the universe, God did not simply set the events of history in motion, step back, and watch to see how things would play out. He is actively involved in bringing about His intended purpose for the world He created.

"Gather together in one" (Gk. *anakephalaiomai*, **an-ak-ef-al-AH-ee-om-ahee**) could also be translated "unite" or "sum up." God's purpose is for Christ to be revealed and exalted as Redeemer and Lord of the entire universe (Ephesians 1:22; Philippians 2:9–10; Revelation 5:9). "All things" includes all people, as well as everything that Christ created when He formed the universe (John 1:3; Colossians 1:16–17). This is why the Scriptures refer to the future with terms and concepts such as "new heavens and new earth" and "the restoration of all things" (Isaiah 65:17; Acts 3:21; 2 Peter 3:13; Revelation 21:5). Jesus, who created all things in the beginning, is in the process of recreating the world, which man damaged through his sin.

11 In whom also we have obtained an inheritance, being predestinated according to the purpose of him who worketh all things after the counsel of his own will:

The benefits of our status as God's heirs (or inheritance) are not the product of chance. Paul emphasizes the determining influence of God's sovereignty with a flourish of words that repeat themes from earlier in the passage and overlap in meaning. The word "predestinated" is the same word used in verse 5 to describe God's loving act of foreordaining our adoption. "Purpose" (Gk. *prothesis*, **PROTH-es-is**) here refers to a plan or something that has been resolved. "Counsel" (Gk. *boule*, **boo-LAY**) means "plan, purpose, resolution, or decision." "Will" has already been used in verses 5 and 9.

12 That we should be to the praise of his glory, who first trusted in Christ.

The "we" of this verse is complemented by the "you" of verse 13—both of which groups are clearly composed of believers in Jesus. The "praise of his glory" is, of course, the appropriate response to God's saving grace (see v. 6). God chose and called the people of Israel to believe in the coming Messiah but revealed the salvation that He would bring through signs and symbols, such as the temple worship and the Levitical priesthood. His purpose was not to restrict salvation to the Jewish people but to make them a light for the nations of the world so that many would experience His salvation (Isaiah 49:6). Paul is among the Jewish people who heard the message of Christ and came to believe that He was the Messiah. This also means that all of the many ways in which Israel experienced both the promise and fulfillment of God's deliverance (see Romans 9:4–5) are additional grounds for praise to God.

13 In whom ye also trusted, after that ye heard the word of truth, the gospel of your salvation: in whom also after that ye believed, ye were sealed with that holy Spirit of promise,

Paul continues to point out the priceless benefits of the gospel but with special emphasis on the fact that Jews (the "we" of Ephesians 1:12) and Gentiles ("ye") have shared equally in those benefits. The experience of salvation comes from hearing the word of truth, not from being born or being circumcised as a Jew.

The Gentiles, having believed, also experienced the baptism of the Holy Spirit. Elsewhere in the New Testament, Paul and the apostles refer to the baptism of the Spirit as the fulfillment of both Old Testament prophecy (Joel 2:28) and the promise of Jesus (Luke 24:47-49). The fact that Gentiles experienced the same baptism as Jews did on the Day of Pentecost was something that many Jewish Christians found extraordinary. It served as incontrovertible evidence that Gentiles could be saved by faith in Jesus without first becoming Jews (Acts 10:44–46; 11:15–18).

"Sealed" (Gk. *sphragizo*, **sfrag-ID-zo**) means "to mark for the purpose of identification or indicating ownership." Sealing also carries with it a sense of certification—a guarantee of authenticity. The experience of Spirit baptism is, therefore, not a "second blessing" but a "down payment" toward the full benefits Christ has purchased for us.

14 Which is the earnest of our inheritance until the redemption of the purchased possession, unto the praise of his glory.

An "earnest" (Gk. *arrhabon*, **ar-hrab-OHN**) is a "first installment, deposit or down payment." We normally think of an "inheritance" (Gk. *kleronomia*, **klay-ron-om-EE-ah**) as property that changes hands at death. Even though God cannot die, the New Testament often uses this word to refer to the possessions promised by God to His children. The emphasis, therefore, is on God's incredible love for His children—that He longs to lavish everything He owns on them.

"Praise of his glory" is the same phrase used in verse 12 to describe the purpose of God's redemption of those who were first to believe. Here, the phrase applies to the salvation of all God's people. God's mighty power and incredible grace will bring Him the enduring, thankful praise of all His people, for all eternity.

Sources:

Arrington, French L.; Stronstad, Roger; eds. *Life in the Spirit New Testament Commentary.* Grand Rapids, MI: Zondervan, 1999.

Dictionary.com. http://www.dictionary.reference.com/ (accessed October 11, 2011).

Marshall, I. Howard. *Acts of the Apostles: An Introduction and Commentary. Tyndale New Testament Commentaries.* Grand Rapids, MI: William B. Eerdmans Publishing Co., 1980.

New Testament Greek Lexicon. Bible Study Tools.com. http://www.biblestudytools.com/lexicons/greek/ (accessed October 11, 2011).

Vine, W. E. *Vine's Complete Expository Dictionary of Old and New Testament Words: With Topical Index.* Edited by Merrill F. Unger and William White, Jr. Nashville, TN: Thomas Nelson Publishers, 1996.

Say It Correctly

Ephesians. ih-FEE-zhuns.
Predestinated. pre-DES-tuh-nay-ted.
Dispensation. dis-puhn-SEY-shuhn.

Daily Bible Readings

MONDAY
Blessed by God's Forgiveness
(Psalm 32:1-7)

TUESDAY
Blessed by Being Chosen
(Psalm 33:8-12)

WEDNESDAY
Blessed by God's Gift of Grace
(1 Corinthians 1:4-9)

THURSDAY
Blessed by God's Revelation
(Daniel 2:17-23)

FRIDAY
Blessed by the Word of Truth
(Colossians 1:3-8)

SATURDAY
Blessed by God's Redemption
(Luke 1:67-79)

SUNDAY
God Has Blessed Us
(Ephesians 1:3-14)

Notes

_____

_____

_____

_____

Teaching Tips

December 9
Bible Study Guide 2

Words You Should Know

A. Circumcision (Ephesians 2:11) *peritome* (Gk.)—The ritual removal of the foreskin of the Jewish male.

B. Commonwealth (v. 12) *politeia* (Gk.)—Citizenship within the community.

Teacher Preparation

Unifying Principle—Unity Not Uniformity. The writer of Ephesians proclaims that it is in Christ that we, who are dead through our trespasses, are brought alive in Christ and that Jesus Christ is the One who breaks down all dividing walls and brings us together as one.

A. Pray that your students' hearts and minds will be fertile for the planting of God's Word in their lives.

B. Prayerfully study the entire lesson.

C. Prepare the companion lesson in the *Precepts For Living Personal Study Guide*®.

O—Open the Lesson

A. After receiving prayer requests, ask a volunteer to open the class with prayer.

B. Have a volunteer read the In Focus story, and then ask the students to discuss how blending a family together is similar to blending churches full of people of diverse backgrounds.

P—Present the Scriptures

A. Ask for a few volunteers to read the Focal Verses.

B. Unpack the lesson using The People, Places, and Times and Background sections, At-A-Glance outline, and More Light on the Text.

E—Explore the Meaning

A. Discuss the Search the Scriptures questions, Discuss the Meaning, Lesson in Our Society, and Make It Happen sections.

B. Examine the salient points.

N—Next Steps for Application

A. Close with prayer.

B. Pray that your church will be a welcoming place for people of all races and economic and social classes.

Worship Guide

For the Superintendent or Teacher
Theme: One in Jesus Christ
Song: "In Christ There Is No
East or West"
Devotional Reading: Ephesians 3:14-21
Prayer

173

One in Jesus Christ

Bible Background • EPHESIANS 2—3
Printed Text • EPHESIANS 2:11-22 | Devotional Reading • EPHESIANS 3:14-21

—————————— Aim for Change ——————————

By the end of the lesson, we will: UNDERSTAND Paul's explanation of Jews and Gentiles becoming one in Christ; EXPRESS pain and sorrow over the divisions within Christ's church and joy when divisions are broken down; and BECOME acquainted with church-unifying and church-dividing issues in order to devise strategies for addressing them.

———————— In Focus  ————————

Carl and Regina held such high hopes when they married, but they could never have known that blending two families together would prove to be so difficult.

Regina's children from a previous relationship were crazy about Carl, but they seemed to resent the things he did for his children during their weekend visits. Regina felt that Carl probably was doing too much for them, trying to make up for not being with them all the time.

Last weekend was the worst! Carl and Regina had to referee what was about to become World War III. Their two daughters were arguing about what to watch on the big-screen television. Regina's daughter, Nicole, screamed at Carl's daughter Kari, "I don't care what you want! You're not really a part of this family, anyway. Your daddy lives with me!"

Carl and Regina had to explain to their children that, even though Carl's children weren't there all the time, they were both an equal and important part of their family.

Christians often have similar problems with diverse members coming together as one. What are some of the divisions in the Christian church today? In today's lesson, Paul tackles the problem of division between the Jews and Gentiles in the Ephesian congregation.

——————————— Keep in Mind ———————————

"In whom all the building fitly framed together groweth unto an holy temple in the Lord" (Ephesians 2:21).

"In whom all the building fitly framed together groweth unto an holy temple in the Lord" (Ephesians 2:21).

Focal Verses

KJV **Ephesians 2:11** Wherefore remember, that ye being in time past Gentiles in the flesh, who are called Uncircumcision by that which is called the Circumcision in the flesh made by hands;

12 That at that time ye were without Christ, being aliens from the commonwealth of Israel, and strangers from the covenants of promise, having no hope, and without God in the world:

13 But now in Christ Jesus ye who sometimes were far off are made nigh by the blood of Christ.

14 For he is our peace, who hath made both one, and hath broken down the middle wall of partition between us;

15 Having abolished in his flesh the enmity, even the law of commandments contained in ordinances; for to make in himself of twain one new man, so making peace;

16 And that he might reconcile both unto God in one body by the cross, having slain the enmity thereby:

17 And came and preached peace to you which were afar off, and to them that were nigh.

18 For through him we both have access by one Spirit unto the Father.

19 Now therefore ye are no more strangers and foreigners, but fellowcitizens with the saints, and of the household of God;

20 And are built upon the foundation of the apostles and prophets, Jesus Christ himself being the chief corner stone;

21 In whom all the building fitly framed together groweth unto an holy temple in the Lord:

22 In whom ye also are builded together for an habitation of God through the Spirit.

NLT **Ephesians 2:11** Don't forget that you Gentiles used to be outsiders. You were called "uncircumcised heathens" by the Jews, who were proud of their circumcision, even though it affected only their bodies and not their hearts.

12 In those days you were living apart from Christ. You were excluded from citizenship among the people of Israel, and you did not know the covenant promises God had made to them. You lived in this world without God and without hope.

13 But now you have been united with Christ Jesus. Once you were far away from God, but now you have been brought near to him through the blood of Christ.

14 For Christ himself has brought peace to us. He united Jews and Gentiles into one people when, in his own body on the cross, he broke down the wall of hostility that separated us.

15 He did this by ending the system of law with its commandments and regulations. He made peace between Jews and Gentiles by creating in himself one new people from the two groups.

16 Together as one body, Christ reconciled both groups to God by means of his death on the cross, and our hostility toward each other was put to death.

17 He brought this Good News of peace to you Gentiles who were far away from him, and peace to the Jews who were near.

18 Now all of us can come to the Father through the same Holy Spirit because of what Christ has done for us.

19 So now you Gentiles are no longer strangers and foreigners. You are citizens along with all of God's holy people. You are members of God's family.

NLT continued

20 Together, we are his house, built on the foundation of the apostles and the prophets. And the cornerstone is Christ Jesus himself.

21 We are carefully joined together in him, becoming a holy temple for the Lord.

22 Through him you Gentiles are also being made part of this dwelling where God lives by his Spirit.

The People, Places, and Times

The Temple. The Temple at Jerusalem was made up of many courts. Paul focuses on the outer court, but there were four different ones. The outer court was where the Gentiles had to stay. A lot of money exchanging or selling took place in the outer court. Next, there was the court of the Jewish women. The women could only go as far as this court. Next is the court of the Israelites where the Israelite men would go and offer sacrifices. The inner court is called the "Holy of Holies." No one could go into that court except the high priest; even he could go in only once a year. Before he could enter, he had to undergo a cleansing ritual. The Holy of Holies is the place where God dwelled, separated from the rest of the temple by a curtain. The Gospels report that when Jesus was crucified, the curtain was torn.

Circumcision. It is the act of removing the foreskin of the male sex organ. In ancient Israel, this act was performed as a ritual on children, natives, servants, and outsiders on the eighth day after birth. In the Jewish faith, it was an external symbol of one's total and complete allegiance and devotion to Yahweh.

Controversy arose in the early church over the circumcision of Gentile converts (Acts 15:13-18). During the A.D. first century, Jews frowned upon non-circumcision among Christians. Apostle Paul played a crucial role in settling the dispute. He determined that physical circumcision was not essential to Christian faith and fellowship. Circumcision of the heart through repentance and faith were the only requirements of the faith for non-Jewish Christians.

Background

Many barriers divided the Jews and the Gentiles in the ancient world. Paul devotes much of his attention in this portion of the letter to the essential oneness of the church. For Jews and Gentiles alike, Paul explained that keeping the law was not a requirement for salvation. Christ is the fulfillment of the law, making it complete. (Salvation cannot be earned through strict adherence to the law or by works. Nevertheless, we are not absolved of our responsibility to do what is right. Salvation by grace through faith does lead to good works; thus, no one had the right to boast about personal goodness.) There was no need for Jews and Gentiles to be divided based on Mosaic Law. Christ became and remains the peace of all believers. Therefore, there is no need for division and discord. By lessening the significance of ethnic and cultural identity, both Jews and Gentiles gained something far better and greater.

At-A-Glance

1. The Gentile's Status
(Ephesians 2:11-13)
2. Jews and Gentiles Together (vv. 14-18)
3. One Church, One Foundation
(vv. 19-22)

In Depth

1. The Gentile's Status (Ephesians 2:11-13)

Paul reminds his readers that before they were converted, they were Gentiles by birth and therefore considered outcasts by the Jews. The Jews despised them, as indicated by the fact that they were called the *Uncircumcision*. The Jews regarded their circumcised state with snobbery, as this signified that they were God's chosen people. They referred to themselves as the *Circumcision*. Paul corrects their sense of superiority by clearly stating that their circumcision was by human effort and therefore merely a physical act. What was really important, he told them, was circumcision of the heart.

While the Jews held on to a false sense of superiority about their status as the chosen, the Gentiles were without a savior altogether. The Messiah was promised to the Jews, even though Isaiah foretold that the blessing would flow to all nations. Christ was sent, "unto the lost sheep of the house of Israel" (Matthew 15:24).

The Gentiles were "aliens from the commonwealth of Israel" (Ephesians 2:12). They did not belong among God's chosen. They were strangers to His promise considering all of God's covenants had promised blessings to the Jews. For all practical purposes, the Gentiles stood on the outside looking in without hope. But because of God's love, the former establishment was done away with. When the Gentiles receive Jesus Christ as Lord and Savior, God places them in Christ and accepts them through Him. Jesus Christ has broken down the barriers that separate all people.

2. Jews and Gentiles Together (vv. 14-18)

In the first part of chapter two, Paul traces the salvation of both Jews and Gentiles. The two groups held different perceptions of what it means to be saved. Here, Paul moves forward to dissolve their nationalistic and cultural biases to affirm unity in Christ and explain the necessity for unity. Through His shed blood, Christ broke down "the middle wall of partition between us" (v. 14). The barriers that divided Jews and Gentiles are now gone. Where there were two, there is now one. There is but one Christ for both the mighty and powerful and the lowly and powerless. For every race and culture, there is only one savior.

Paul describes Christ as our peace. When Christ came to us, He "preached peace" to those near and far (v. 17). In this instance, those who were near were the Jews. They had already received a promise. Those who were afar were the Gentiles, those who had no covenant with God; they held no assurance of His presence or promise. This being the case, it is not difficult to understand why the Jews held a certain snobbery concerning their status as God's chosen people.

Peace was needed to unify two groups that were alienated from each other. As our peace, Christ has created a new people, free from the limitations of imposed human boundaries such as culture, race, gender, education, social, or economic standing. All believers now have access to the presence of God at any time. This was in stark contrast to the Old Testament, when only the high priest could go into the Holy of Holies, the place where God dwelled.

3. One Church, One Foundation (vv. 19-22)

Paul often uses the words "now therefore" when making a conclusion (see v. 19). He concludes that the Gentiles were in no way inferior to the Jews. Christ did away with all of that. The apostle lists some of the many great benefits available to all believing Gentiles, as they are no longer strangers and foreigners. Never again will they be looked upon as less than others or as outsiders. Now they are fellow citizens and equal heirs to the inheritance. Christians of Jewish ancestries have no advantage over the believing Gentiles. All believers are first-class citizens in the kingdom of heaven.

As they are now a part of the church, they have become stones, or building blocks, in the construction of a holy temple. This new temple will also have a foundation, with Christ as the "chief corner stone" that bonds the temple together. This new Temple, the church, is built upon the apostles and prophets of the New Testament. The apostles and prophets are not the foundation; Christ is the foundation. The foundation was laid in what the apostles and prophets taught about the Person and work of Jesus Christ.

Christ is more than the foundation of the church, however; He is also the chief corner-stone, joining the two walls that were once separated: Jews and Gentiles. In this new temple that Christ has created, everyone will have an equal place. When Jesus created a new covenant between God and humankind, He made a new people of God, one body—the church.

Search the Scriptures

1. What were the Gentiles called (Ephesians 2:11)?

2. How did the Jews refer to themselves (v. 11)?

3. What barrier did Christ break down (v. 14)?

Discuss the Meaning

Because it is our responsibility to care for the church of Christ and to continue to bring new stones, in what ways have we neglected our duties, both to the universal church and in local church?

Lesson in Our Society

Some believers are determined to create cultural, racial, and ethnic barriers within the church. Many arguments and divisions have arisen over doctrinal issues. Some have attacked others as being unsaved for not adhering to certain standards.

All believers should be careful to avoid ostracizing others. We should also be mindful of how what we do based on our preferences creates division. Christ desires that we engage ourselves in activities that draw us closer to Him and to one another.

Make It Happen

Think about who you are to people in your home, in your church, on your job, and in the community. Why is it important that you have good standing in all of these areas? How do you devote yourself equally to maintaining your role as a follower of Christ (not merely a church member)? How do you try to hold yourself responsible to do what Christ desires of you? Think of at least one action or step you can take to show that it is important to you to continue to live as a disciple "in good standing."

Follow the Spirit

What God wants me to do:

_____

_____

_____

_____

Remember Your Thoughts
Special insights I have learned:

_____

_____

_____

_____

More Light on the Text
Ephesians 2:11-22

11 Wherefore remember, that ye being in time past Gentiles in the flesh, who are called Uncircumcision by that which is called the Circumcision in the flesh made by hands;

Paul, for the first time, identifies those whom he is addressing in verse 11—the Gentiles. He reminds them who they were before they received Christ. He uses different terms to describe their position before their union with Christ. First, they were "Gentiles in the flesh" (Gk. *ethnos,* **ETH-nos),** heathen, non-Jewish nations by birth, which the Jews (the Circumcision) disrespectfully called the *Uncircumcision.* God had instructed Abraham in Genesis to circumcise every male child in his household, including his servants (Genesis 17:11). This practice became a visible, physical sign of the covenant between the Lord and His people. Any Jewish male who was not circumcised was to be excised from his people (Genesis 17:14) and regarded as a covenant-breaker (Exodus 4:24-26). The Jewish people took great pride in circumcision, and it became a badge of their spiritual and national superiority.

Devout Jews, in recognition of God's continuing covenant with Israel, faithfully practiced circumcision in the New Testament period. Both John the Baptist (Luke 1:59) and Jesus (Luke 2:21) were circumcised in accordance with the Jewish rite. The practice raised a spirit of exclusivity and resentment between Jews and Gentiles and later brought discord into the fellowship of the first century church (Acts 15:1; see Paul's letter to Galatians). An exaggerated importance had been placed on the rite, and each side called the other names.

Paul (especially in Galatians) seems to de-emphasize the physical rite, and he says that the so-called Jewish circumcision is only in the flesh (a purely physical mark) and something made by human hands rather than spiritual. He says in essence that the true motive behind the circumcision of the flesh is a circumcision of the heart that is spiritual instead of physical. That kind of circumcision is needed and available to both Jews and Gentiles alike (Romans 2:28-29; Colossians 2:11-13). Writing to the Philippian Christians (both Jews and Gentiles), Paul says, "For we are the true circumcision, who worship in the Spirit of God and glory in Christ Jesus and put no confidence in the flesh" (Philippians 3:3, NASB).

12 That at that time ye were without Christ, being aliens from the commonwealth of Israel, and strangers from the covenants of promise, having no hope, and without God in the world:

Acknowledging that they've been scornfully labeled, Paul calls their attention to spiritual and physical alienation. First, they are to remember that during that time ("in time past," Ephesians 2:11), they were separated from Christ ("ye were without Christ," v. 12). The word "Christ" is probably used here in the general sense of Messiah, and means they did not share in the then Jews' Messianic hope for the future. This Messianic hope is included in the Jews' privileges that Paul lists in Romans 9:4-

5. Because the Gentiles are alienated from the Messiah who is promised to and the hope of the Jews, they are also distanced from the commonwealth of Israel and therefore strangers from (and to) the covenants of promise. The word "commonwealth" (Gk. *politeia*, **pol-ee-TI-ah**) means "citizenship." Therefore, Gentiles, by the fact of their birth, are deprived of the privileges of Israel (Romans 9:4-5) and excluded from the participation in their national rights, hopes, and promise. We know from the Old Testament that this covenant is the very heart of Israel's relationship with God in which the Father solemnly pledges to be Israel's God and declares that they be called His people (Leviticus 26:12). To partake in the covenant relationship, one must have been born a Jew and be a circumcised male. Gentiles are excluded from this Old Testament covenant.

As people who are separated from the Messianic hope (without Christ), estranged from the commonwealth of Israel and its privileges, and excluded from the covenant of promise as God's people, the Gentiles have "no hope, and (are) without God in the world" (Ephesians 2:12). It is like a chain reaction. The ultimate result is that they are without God and, as such, hopeless in the world. This describes their position in their unbelief before they became Christians.

13 But now in Christ Jesus ye who sometimes were far off are made nigh by the blood of Christ. 14 For he is our peace, who hath made both one, and hath broken down the middle wall of partition between us;

After describing the apparently gloomy and hopeless situation of the Gentiles before they became Christians, Paul now moves to the present positive state brought about by their new relationship in Christ. He says, "You who once were far off have been brought near" (v. 13, NKJV). That means that they are no more aliens and strangers to the promises and covenant of God; they are no longer regarded as people without God and without hope (v. 12). They now have the same close relationship with God, which was formerly reserved for Israel alone. Israel and God are said to be near each other. "Far off" describes how separated the Gentiles were from God compared with His nearness to Israel. The separation or alienation of the Gentiles from God and from Israel is symbolized in the construction of the Temple in Jerusalem. There were partitions between the outer and inner courts. The Gentiles were only allowed entrance to the outer court; hence, its name was Court of the Gentiles. The inner court, which was closer to the court of the priests and the Holy of Holies (representing the presence of God), was reserved for Jews. Inscriptions on the outer surfaces of the Temple warned that death was the punishment for any non-Jew caught entering the inner court (*Holman Bible Dictionary*, 1326-1327). Conversely, "Solomon's dedication (of the Temple) made clear that the door was never closed to the foreigner who wished to serve the Lord (1 Kings 8:41-43)" (*Holman Bible Dictionary*, 542). This segregation and special understanding of the responsibility given to the Children of Israel figuratively and literally represented the far off position of the Gentiles from God.

Apart from symbolizing alienation from God and Israel, the partition was also a symbol of hostility between the Jews and the Gentiles. The cross is the uniting force that binds the two sides into one community.

Paul makes the unification of the two groups clear in the next verse through a profound declaration: He is our peace. The use of the pronoun "He" (Gk. *autos*, **ow-TOS**) is emphatic, which means "He Himself" or "He and He alone" is our peace. This echoes the prophecy of Isaiah 9:6, where Christ is given the title "Prince of Peace" because of His mission on earth. Christ is peace personified because only through Him are believers reconciled to God and one another. He has made both one.

15 Having abolished in his flesh the enmity, even the law of commandments contained in ordinances; for to make in himself of twain one new man, so making peace;

In addition to the separating walls of the temple, the Jews always endeavored to live separate from the rest of the world and always wanted a river or wall between them and their Gentile neighbors. Their laws and customs also separated them from the rest of the world, as did the physical walls in the temple. These were symbols of hostility between the two. Christ, through His sacrificial death, abolished the Law of Moses with its rituals, provided a new covenant that is inclusive for both Jews and Gentiles, and made them one. He brings everyone to the same level. This breakdown is literally demonstrated in the rending from top to bottom of the temple veil indicating that the way into the Holy of Holies is left open and accessible to all—to Jews and Gentiles alike.

The abolition of the law raises some questions. What does Paul mean by abolishing the law in relation to Christ's words in Matthew 5:17? There, Christ teaches that He has come not to abolish but rather to fulfill the law. Is it then a contradiction of Scriptures? In what sense was either used? The difference, as someone has suggested, seems to lie in the two types of laws: the moral law and the ceremonial law. Christ requires from His followers a more radical obedience to the moral law as compared with the Pharisees' own standards (Matthew 5:18). Paul refers to Christ's abolishment of the ceremonial law, which includes the physical ritual of circumcision (Ephesians 2:11), rather than the spiritual circumcision of the heart. This also includes some of the dietary regulations in Colossians 2:11, 16-21. These constitute barriers between the Jews and the Gentiles that Jesus has abolished through His death on the Cross, has made the two one in Himself, and has made peace between them. The unification of all believers (the church) in Christ, as we shall see later, includes the abolition of the gender, social, and racial distinctions that exist and serve to cause hatred among different people of the earth.

16 And that he might reconcile both unto God in one body by the cross, having slain the enmity thereby: 17 And came and preached peace to you which were afar off, and to them that were nigh.

Verses 16 and 17 speak to the same theme using different terms. These terms further describe what Christ has done through His blood: He has reconciled both Jews and Gentiles unto God in one body by the Cross. In verse 15, we see that the law that brought about the enmity is "abolished" (Gk. *katargeo*, **kat-arg-EH-o**), i.e., done away with, rendered idle, or destroyed. In verse 16, however, the enmity caused by the law is "slain" (Gk. *apokteino*, **ap-ok-TI-no**), i.e., inflicted a mortal death or killed. This speaks of total annihilation. In the one single act of sacrifice on the cross, Christ first abolished the ceremonial law, which for centuries separated humanity from itself and from its creator. Second, He created a new humanity where in figuratively slaying the enmity among people, making them equal to one another. Third, by this act of sacrifice, Christ reconciled this new society to God, its creator. Continuing the theme of Christ's activity in bringing near those who were far away and reconciling the two entities, uniting them into "one new man" by abolishing the law, Paul describes this same activity in a different way in verse 17. While in verse 14, Christ "is our peace" personified (i.e., the object of peace), here, he preaches "peace to you which were afar off" (the Gentiles, vv. 11-13) as well as "to them that were nigh" (the Jews). "He came and preached peace" probably refers to Christ's earthly mission and the ministry of the early church. The word "preached" (Gk. *euaggelizo,* **yoo-ang-ghel-ID-zo**) is the same Greek word translated "preach the good news" in Luke 4:17, where Jesus announced His mission in fulfillment of Isaiah's prophecy (see Isaiah 61:1-2).

18 For through him we both have access by one Spirit unto the Father. 19 Now therefore ye are no more strangers and foreigners, but fellowcitizens with the saints, and of the household of God;

Verses 18 and 19 tell us the effect of Christ's preaching. Through Him, Jews and Gentiles are now reconciled to one another and both to God. Consequently, by Him they both can approach God the Father in one Spirit. It is noteworthy to recognize a reference to the Trinity here that reveals the distinctions of the three persons in the Godhead (see 1 John 5:7). In Ephesians 2:18, the word "access" (Gk. *prosagoge,* **pros-ag-ogue-AY**) speaks of the freedom we have to approach God as our Father with boldness and assurance that we are acceptable to Him and that we shall not be turned down. There is in verse 19a, a shift in Paul's use of metaphor, from membership of a family unit to the metaphor of citizenship—nationhood. In verse 12, the Gentiles are said to be outside of the family of Israel and strangers without hope and without God. Now, they are no more "strangers and

foreigners" (Gk. *paroikos,* **PAR-oy-kos**); both terms are synonymous, meaning "one who lives in a place without the right of citizenship."

Here, Paul reminds the Gentiles that through Christ, they have become "fellow-citizens" (Gk. *sumpolites,* **soom-pol-EE-tace**) with the saints, which means with Israel in God's own kingdom.

20 And are built upon the foundation of the apostles and prophets, Jesus Christ himself being the chief corner stone;

Paul now moves from speaking of the church as God's family or community, to referring to it as a building (house) whose foundation is laid upon the apostles and prophets. The word "foundation" (Gk. *themelios,* **them-EL-ee-os**) refers to the work of the early Christian apostles and prophets who helped to grow the church through their leadership and their relationship with Christ. He is not only the builder; Christ is also the chief "corner stone" (*akrogoniaios,* **ak-rog-o-nee-AH-yos**). Peter also refers to Christ as the cornerstone (1 Peter 2:6), using the same Greek word. The stability of a house or building depends on its foundation. A house without a solid foundation would not stand the test of time. Christ's parable of the soils (Matthew 13:3-8), and His identification of Peter as the rock on which His Church would develop (16:17-19), emphasize the need for a strong foundation. In Ephesians 2:20, Paul says that Jesus is the "chief (the main) corner stone" that holds together the whole building and keeps the rest of the foundation in place, while the apostles and prophets are parts of the foundation.

21 In whom all the building fitly framed together groweth unto an holy temple in the Lord: 22 In whom ye also are builded together for an habitation of God through the Spirit.

Paul goes on to elaborate on the structural makeup of the building, which depends upon its foundation. Thus, the stability of the church is dependent upon none other than the One who is both builder and the chief cornerstone—Christ. A building does not stop at the foundation. It needs fittings and other structures before it can be called a building. Paul refocuses his picture of the whole structure to the individual stones that are used to erect a building. Peter also uses the image of a building or temple to describe the church. In the same imagery where he refers to Christ as the "chief corner stone" (1 Peter 2:6), he describes the individual members as "living stones ... being built into a spiritual house to be a holy priesthood" (1 Peter 2:4-5, NIV). Paul's picture here also sees the members of the church as the stones, which the master builder (Christ) craftily and meticulously fits together upon the chief foundation (Christ) into a magnificent edifice—a holy temple in the Lord. The phrase in Ephesians 2:22 "whom ye also are builded" refers to the Gentile Christians. The temple, as we know, represents the dwelling place and presence of God. We have also noted earlier that the temple was exclusively reserved only for the Jews. Gentiles were forbidden to enter the temple, even though an outside court was reserved for Gentiles. Here, Paul assures them that not only are they now admitted into the temple, having gained access to the Father, but they are also parts of the temple of God. This is based on their union in Christ Jesus, who is the cornerstone.

The purpose of the temple in the Old Testament was to be a dwelling place for God. This new temple serves the same purpose, namely for God's "habitation" (Gk. *katoiketerion,* **kat-oy-kay-TAY-ree-on**). We know from Scripture that God is so great that even the whole earth cannot contain Him—neither Solomon's magnificent temple nor the one rebuilt by Herod. God does not dwell in man-made houses (1 Kings 8:27; Acts 7:48-49; 17:24). He nonetheless manifested His glory and presence in the temple. However, He also makes His abode in the hearts of His followers.

Sources:

Butler, Trent, ed. *Holman Bible Dictionary*, Nashville, TN: Holman Bible Publishers, 1991. 262, 542, 1326-1327.

McCalep, George O. *Growing Up to the Head.* Lithonia, GA: Orman Press, 1997. 87-88.

New Testament Greek Lexicon. Bible Study Tools.com. http://www.biblestudytools.com/lexicons/greek/ (accessed October 18, 2011).

Say It Correctly

Circumcision. sir-kuhm-SIZH-uhn.
Enmity. EN-mi-tee.

Daily Bible Readings

MONDAY
Reviving the Humble and the Contrite
(Isaiah 57:14-19)

TUESDAY
Building on the True Foundation
(1 Corinthians 3:10-16)

WEDNESDAY
Sharing in the Promise
(Ephesians 3:1-6)

THURSDAY
Making Known the Wisdom of God
(Ephesians 3:7-13)

FRIDAY
Praying for Spiritual Power
(Ephesians 3:14-21)

SATURDAY
Discovering the Gift of Salvation
(Ephesians 2:1-10)

SUNDAY
Discovering Our Oneness in Christ
(Ephesians 2:11-22)

Notes

Teaching Tips

December 16
Bible Study Guide 3

Words You Should Know

A. Vocation (Ephesians 4:1) *klesis* (Gk.)— Invitation, calling.

B. Grace (v. 7) *charis* (Gk.)—God's divine unmerited, undeserved influence upon our hearts.

Teacher Preparation

Unifying Principle—Living Together. The writer of Ephesians says that, although each of us brings different gifts, we find true unity as we grow in Christ, who is the head of the whole body.

A. Pray for your class that God will bring lesson clarity.

B. Prepare a list of spiritual gifts, clip the items out, and place them in a container.

C. Prayerfully study the entire lesson.

D. Complete the companion Precepts For Living Personal Study Guide®.

O—Open the Lesson

A. Ask a volunteer to reword the Aim for Change as a prayer.

B. Read and discuss the In Focus story.

C. Have volunteers pull from the container of spiritual gift items and have others explain how the church can be blessed by use of the gift.

P—Present the Scriptures

A. Ask a volunteer to read aloud the Focal Verses.

B. Use the At-A-Glance outline to clarify the text.

C. Recite the Keep in Mind verse together.

E—Explore the Meaning

A. Summarize the Discuss the Meaning section.

B. Read and discuss the Lesson in Our Society.

N—Next Steps for Application

A. Summarize the Make It Happen section.

B. Summarize the salient points about spiritual gifts and how they should be used to edify the church.

C. Close with prayer.

Worship Guide

For the Superintendent or Teacher
Theme: Unity in the Body of Christ
Song: "We Are One in the Spirit"
Devotional Reading: Romans 12:3-8
Prayer

186

Unity in the Body of Christ

**DEC
16th**

Bible Background • EPHESIANS 4:1-16
Printed Text • EPHESIANS 4:1-16 | Devotional Reading • ROMANS 12:3-8

—————— Aim for Change ——————

By the end of the lesson, we will: EXPLORE characteristics of a life worthy of Christ's calling in building up the body of Christ; CELEBRATE our gifts that help build up the body of Christ; and UNDERSTAND the meaning of the statement "... one faith, one baptism, one God and Father of all" as it relates to building up the body of Christ.

——————— ✒ In Focus ———————

Stephen said a quick prayer of thanksgiving to God that he was able to walk away from Deacon Matthews without an argument. Deacon Matthews was a fine deacon, but as he advanced in age, his temperament was becoming more disagreeable. Stephen still had great respect for him, but Stephen and many of the younger members of the church sought some changes in the ministries of the church, including its business practices. Some members were frustrated because they wanted to use their gifts within the church in a more meaningful way.

Stephen laughed and said to himself, "I'm 42 years old, but 'Deac' still looks at me as one of the young folks in the church."

Deacon Matthews said he saw no need for changes. The church had operated just fine for 137 years, and it would continue to do so. That's when Stephen prayed. He knew there was a time when he would have exploded all over the elderly deacon for being so shortsighted. "By the grace of God," he thought, "I am maturing in Christ."

How can Stephen and the other younger church members use their spiritual gifts to help build up their church? Although each church has its problems, what are some of the ways you can use your gifts to build up your church? Paul helps us in today's lesson to find some answers.

—————— Keep in Mind ——————

"There is one body, and one Spirit, even as ye are called in one hope of your calling; One Lord, one faith, one baptism" (Ephesians 4:4-5).

"There is one body, and one Spirit, even as ye are called in one hope of your calling; One Lord, one faith, one baptism" (Ephesians 4:4-5).

Focal Verses

KJV **Ephesians 4:1** I therefore, the prisoner of the Lord, beseech you that ye walk worthy of the vocation wherewith ye are called,

2 With all lowliness and meekness, with longsuffering, forbearing one another in love;

3 Endeavouring to keep the unity of the Spirit in the bond of peace.

4 There is one body, and one Spirit, even as ye are called in one hope of your calling;

5 One Lord, one faith, one baptism,

6 One God and Father of all, who is above all, and through all, and in you all.

7 But unto every one of us is given grace according to the measure of the gift of Christ.

8 Wherefore he saith, When he ascended up on high, he led captivity captive, and gave gifts unto men.

9 (Now that he ascended, what is it but that he also descended first into the lower parts of the earth?

10 He that descended is the same also that ascended up far above all heavens, that he might fill all things.)

11 And he gave some, apostles; and some, prophets; and some, evangelists; and some, pastors and teachers;

12 For the perfecting of the saints, for the work of the ministry, for the edifying of the body of Christ:

13 Till we all come in the unity of the faith, and of the knowledge of the Son of God, unto a perfect man, unto the measure of the stature of the fulness of Christ:

14 That we henceforth be no more children, tossed to and fro, and carried about with every wind of doctrine, by the sleight of men, and cunning craftiness, whereby they lie in wait to deceive;

NLT **Ephesians 4:1** Therefore I, a prisoner for serving the Lord, beg you to lead a life worthy of your calling, for you have been called by God.

2 Always be humble and gentle. Be patient with each other, making allowance for each other's faults because of your love.

3 Make every effort to keep yourselves united in the Spirit, binding yourselves together with peace.

4 For there is one body and one Spirit, just as you have been called to one glorious hope for the future.

5 There is one Lord, one faith, one baptism,

6 and one God and Father, who is over all and in all and living through all.

7 However, he has given each one of us a special gift through the generosity of Christ.

8 That is why the Scriptures say, "When he ascended to the heights, he led a crowd of captives and gave gifts to his people."

9 Notice that it says "he ascended." This clearly means that Christ also descended to our lowly world.

10 And the same one who descended is the one who ascended higher than all the heavens, so that he might fill the entire universe with himself.

11 Now these are the gifts Christ gave to the church: the apostles, the prophets, the evangelists, and the pastors and teachers.

12 Their responsibility is to equip God's people to do his work and build up the church, the body of Christ.

13 This will continue until we all come to such unity in our faith and knowledge of God's Son that we will be mature in the Lord, measuring up to the full and complete standard of Christ.

KJV continued

15 But speaking the truth in love, may grow up into him in all things, which is the head, even Christ:

16 From whom the whole body fitly joined together and compacted by that which every joint supplieth, according to the effectual working in the measure of every part, maketh increase of the body unto the edifying of itself in love.

NLT continued

14 Then we will no longer be immature like children. We won't be tossed and blown about by every wind of new teaching. We will not be influenced when people try to trick us with lies so clever they sound like the truth.

15 Instead, we will speak the truth in love, growing in every way more and more like Christ, who is the head of his body, the church.

16 He makes the whole body fit together perfectly. As each part does its own special work, it helps the other parts grow, so that the whole body is healthy and growing and full of love.

The People, Places, and Times

Gifts. Spiritual gifts are the skills and abilities given to all believers by the Father through His Spirit. These gifts are for the purpose of enabling Christians to carry out His plan. Jesus promised His disciples that they also would receive the gift of the Spirit, who would guide them (Mark 13:11; Luke 11:13). His promise was fulfilled on the Day of Pentecost (Acts 2:1-47). The Spirit was given to every believer. Paul's epistles (letters to the churches) reveal that this continued in all the churches. Every believer receives gifting from the Holy Spirit (1 Corinthians 12:4-7). Spiritual gifts are for the benefit of the body of believers, not just for individual benefit or pleasure. The greatest gift, which Paul said every believer should possess, is love (1 Corinthians 12:31-13:1).

Background

In previous portions of his letter to the church at Ephesus, Paul laid the foundation concerning Christ and His church. Now, he switches his focus to a more practical purpose, setting out guidelines for his readers concerning Christian conduct. But first, he decides to give them an overview of the church's place in the world.

Paul called for the Ephesians to be true to who they are called to be in Christ and noted several truths for them to embrace: (1) it's their responsibility to be one in the body; (2) the call for unity does not mean that they should strive for a type of dull sameness; (3) the church is a living organism, made up of living beings who are expected to grow according to their use of the gifts Christ has given them; (4) Christ desires that the church reach maturity and that the people of the church be prepared to exercise their gifts; and (5) as the church grows, its members should take on the nature and character of its head, Christ Jesus.

At-A-Glance

1. The Church's Calling to Unity (Ephesians 4:1-6)
2. The Church's Gifts (vv. 7-12)
3. The Road to Maturity (vv. 13-16)

In Depth

1. The Church's Calling to Unity (Ephesians 4:1-6)

Paul considered himself a prisoner for the Lord as well as one who belonged to the Lord. Always positioning himself as the example, he issued a plea to the Ephesian Christians to walk worthy of their "vocation," or to live in a manner that is consistent with their high calling from God (v. 1). The Christian's call is the divine summons that was answered at the time of conversion. Our calling is not a hobby or a pastime. It is our life's achievement—our job.

The word "walk" is a literal translation of a Hebrew idiom for everyday conduct. The word "worthy" makes the connection between God's plan for us and our acceptance of that plan, as demonstrated in the way we live.

Paul had previously cautioned against boasting concerning good works. Now, he advises them to live out their calling with humility. He did not want them to become arrogant about their godly living. They were also to exercise patience toward the faults and failings of others and among those with different personality types and temperaments. We are to genuinely have patience for one another with love.

The reason for possessing these qualities—"lowliness and meekness, with longsuffering, forbearing"—is for unity within the body of Christ (v. 2). When Christ established the church, He abolished the greatest dividing line within humanity—the barrier that separated Jews and Gentiles. Now it was the responsibility of the early church members to try with all earnestness to avoid creating human divisions among God's people.

Arguments and dissension threaten to destroy the "bond of peace" within the body of Christ. There is but one Spirit in the church; nothing can destroy that unity. However, bickering and quarrels can destroy the peace that binds the members of the body of Christ. A healthy formula for keeping the unity is threefold: unity in those things that are essential to the faith, liberty in those matters that are nonessential or not absolute, and love in all circumstances.

In spite of the vast number of Christian churches worldwide, there is only one body of believers. The same Spirit who dwells in every believer also dwells in the body of Christ. There is but one hope in which every believer has placed his or her trust. Our one Lord is the Savior who shed His blood for our sins. We all share a common faith in that one Lord and Savior. There is one baptism by which we profess our faith in Christ. The one God and Father is supreme above all.

2. The Church's Gifts (vv. 7-12)

The unity of the church must be balanced by its odd twin, diversity. Unity is often confused with uniformity. The Christian Church is communal; every member makes a contribution. Each member of the body of Christ has been given *grace*, or a particular gift or role to fulfill. No two members are alike. No member should try to imitate the other's gifts. In other letters, Paul outlines the necessity for giving equal value to the gifts of every believer.

By His grace, He has given these gifts as He sees fit. The risen Lord bestowed these gifts by first sending His most excellent gift, the Holy Spirit. In Ephesians 4:8, Paul quotes Psalm 68:18 as a prophecy that the Messiah would ascend to heaven and conquer His foes and lead them captive. As a reward for His victory, He would receive gifts for humankind.

In Ephesians 4:9, Paul wanted to show that the prophecy could have referred only to Christ. If Jesus ascended into heaven,

He must have first come down from heaven. Paul and others understood "lower parts of the earth" to mean that Christ descended into hell. The Gospel of Luke, however, indicates that His spirit went to heaven when He died (Luke 23:43, 46). The prophecy of Psalm 68:18 was fulfilled by the birth, death, and burial of Jesus.

The ascended Christ is the giver of all gifts and the source of all blessings. He fills all things. In giving us gifts, Christ has a specific purpose in sight. All of God's saints are to be equipped with the gifts necessary to discharge their duties in the world. In Ephesians 4:10, Paul proceeds to explain the nature of some of these gifts of grace.

Apostles were those persons directly commissioned by the Lord to preach the Word and plant churches. They were those who had seen the risen Christ. *Prophets* were the mouthpieces for God. They received revelations directly from the Lord, by the aid of the Holy Spirit, and passed them on to the church.

Evangelists are those who preach the Good News. They have been divinely equipped to go out into the world and lead persons to Christ. *Pastors* are those who serve as God's under-shepherds, caring for the sheep of His flock. It is their responsibility to guide and feed the flock. The New Testament gives the impression of a number of pastors at a local church instead of one (Acts 20:17, 28; 1 Peter 5:1-2).

Teachers are persons divinely gifted to teach and explain the Bible and what it means. A Bible teacher endeavors to connect God's Word into everyday life.

The purpose of all these gifts is for leaders to enable "the perfecting (or equipping) of the saints" so that all are prepared "for the work of the ministry" and, ultimately, "for the edifying of the body of Christ" (Ephesians 4:12). These gifts should always be used to empower others to do even greater deeds for the sake of the kingdom.

3. The Road to Maturity (vv. 13-16)

At this point, Paul may have anticipated the question, "How long will this process of growing continue?" In verse 13, Paul explains that this will go on "Till we all come in the unity of the faith and of the knowledge of the Son of God."

Little can prepare the mind for the unity that exists in the afterlife. As long as we live, no matter how hard we try, we will have innumerable differences. This will continue until we are able to see Him as He truly is and to know as we are known. At that time the "unity of the faith" will occur. Until then, there will be room for growth. When we obtain full knowledge, we enter the state of "perfect man." The word "perfect," used in the King James Version, is translated "complete." Our Christian journey is done when we come to the place of full knowledge of Christ and unity of our faith.

Verses 14-15 describe the growth process in the body of Christ. As we continue toward spiritual maturity, some things will become apparent. We are no longer like "children, tossed to and fro, and carried about with every wind of doctrine" (v. 14). As we grow to be more like Him, we grow in our knowledge of Him. Our understanding is solid and sure. No one can then persuade us to change our beliefs.

All disciples are called upon to grow. Discipleship is a process. It is not a course of study from which we will earn a diploma and never revisit again. There is always room for growth, for training, for new understanding, and for enlightenment. As we grow in Christ, so do our challenges. The longer we live, if we are achieving spiritual maturity, we learn to lean on Him more, trusting more fully in His promises and His providence.

When we encounter brothers and sisters who have gone astray in their thinking and beliefs, we are commanded to speak "the truth in love," helping each other to grow toward the head, which is Christ Jesus. He is both the goal of our growth and the source of our growth. As the church receives its life from Him who supplies all of our needs, quite naturally, growth comes from Him too. But Paul adds that the church grows "toward" Christ as we as individuals grow "in" Christ.

Search the Scriptures

1. What did Paul "beseech" the Ephesian Christians to do (Ephesians 4:1)?

2. What reasons does Paul give them for exhibiting characteristics such as lowliness and meekness (v. 3)?

3. What are the seven things we are to share as one (vv. 4-6)?

4. How is the body of Christ put together through Christ (v. 16)?

Discuss the Meaning

Some Christians tend to forget that their talents and abilities are spiritual gifts from God. In what ways do believers begin to take credit for themselves? Include yourself.

Lesson in Our Society

There is a real danger among Christians to look at ourselves as having "arrived" in regard to our spiritual growth. We can never fully know God in this life; therefore, Christian discipleship is not a course of study to be completed. It is a process that causes us to change and grow continuously if we yield ourselves to the guidance of the Holy Spirit.

We are never too old to learn in matters concerning the kingdom. The oldest, most seasoned Christian can still learn about God's love from a newborn baby. A true sign of Christian maturity is in knowing there is still more to be known.

Make It Happen

Are there ways that you stunt your own spiritual growth because you are not willing to lend yourself to new challenges that are presented to you? Do you ever think, "I'm too old to be learning how to do that now," or "I've lived long enough to know what I'm talking about"? Think about an area of your life where you may be inhibiting your spiritual development, thereby building a wedge between you and the Father.

Follow the Spirit

What God wants me to do:

_____

_____

_____

_____

Remember Your Thoughts

Special insights I have learned:

_____

_____

_____

_____

More Light on the Text

Ephesians 4:1-16

1 I therefore, the prisoner of the Lord, beseech you that ye walk worthy of the vocation wherewith ye are called,

Paul starts this chapter with an appeal for us to live a Christ-filled life. Using an emphatic first person pronoun "I" (Gk. *ego,* **eg-O**), Paul begins his appeal by reintroducing himself as "the prisoner of the Lord." This probably is to assert his apostolic authority. The use of the conjunction "therefore" (Gk. *oun,* **oon**) adds the emphatic nature of the *ego*. The phrase can then be reworded in view of this (i.e., in view of the things God has done through history): I, a prisoner of the Lord, appeal to you. The phrase "the prisoner" (Gk. *desmios,* **DES-mee-os**), or captive "of the Lord" means probably that Paul regarded himself as both a prisoner of Jesus in loyal and loving obedience as an apostle and as one in custody for Christ because of his loyalty to the Gospel. Both his authority as an apostle and his personal conviction as a man under house arrest seem to motivate his appeal to believers. Paul urges them to conduct their lives in such a manner that would match their calling—their commitment in Christ. Because the Christian life is a response to God's call in one's life, he or she then has to comport oneself in a way that would show the commitment.

2 With all lowliness and meekness, with longsuffering, forbearing one another in love;

Paul gives five characteristics of the life worthy of our calling: lowliness, meekness, longsuffering (patience), mutual forbearance, and love. The unity of the church, Paul seems to imply, starts with individuals and with keeping moral qualities. To maintain unity in the church, we are to walk in "lowliness" (Gk. *tapeinophrosune,* **tap-i-nof-ros-OO-nay**), i.e., humility, which is a debasing quality and an unacceptable virtue in their contemporary society. This was especially true among people in the Greek world. The word is better translated as "lowliness of mind," a state of thinking and operating in a way that recognizes the value of others.

We are to walk in "meekness" (Gk. *praotes,* **prah-OO-tace**) or gentleness. In *Matthew Henry's Commentary on the Whole Bible,* he defines meekness in this passage: "That excellent disposition of soul which makes men unwilling to provoke others and not easily to be provoked or offended with their infirmities; and it is opposed to angry resentments and peevishness." Meekness is the gentleness of the strong one who has his strength under control. Such a person, though he or she has a certain right or authority, would decide not to lay claim to it before God or others.

The next two characteristics that will foster unity in the body of Christ also seem to go together. One of these characteristics is "longsuffering"—(Gk. *makrothumia,* **mak-roth-oo-MEE-ah**), or patience or endurance, i.e., not seeking revenge or being aggravated by others, a virtue God shows to us through Christ. Another characteristic is "forbearing one another" (Gk. *anechomai,* **an-EKH-om-ahee**), which has the idea of putting up with or enduring and bearing with someone's mistakes or attitude. It speaks of being tolerant toward others, a mutual understanding between people. These four characteristics are anchored in love, and they form the basis and foundation for unity in the church.

3 Endeavouring to keep the unity of the Spirit in the bond of peace.

In verse 3, Paul identifies the nature of the closeness among believers as the unity of the Spirit. He encourages the church in "endeavouring" (Gk. *spoudazo*, **spoo-DAD-zo**) to keep the unity of the Spirit in the bond of peace. It means "sparing no effort" or, as we idiomatically express it, leaving no stone unturned in order to maintain the unity of the Spirit. In other words, we should do our utmost to preserve harmonious fellowship. Such unity starts within the individual hearts of its members. Preserving this unity, therefore, depends on both individual and cooperative efforts of all members of the body of Christ.

4 There is one body, and one Spirit, even as ye are called in one hope of your calling; 5 One Lord, one faith, one baptism, 6 One God and Father of all, who is above all, and through all, and in you all.

Paul declares implicitly that the oneness of the church arises from the unity of the Godhead—making deliberate referral to the Trinity. First, the church is one body because there is one Spirit who created it. The unity of this body is because of the work of the Holy Spirit who also indwells it. The one Spirit unifies the body and works through it. The church with its various parts is joined to the head, who is Christ, by the Holy Spirit to function as one body. The church is called into one hope, which refers to the present reality and the future benefit of life everlasting.

Second, the reality of the Christian calling and hope is founded on the one Lord, Jesus Christ who is the object of our faith, in whom all Christians hold their belief and in whom all are baptized. One faith refers both to the Gospel, which embodies the doctrine of the Christian faith, and the gift of faith whereby all Christians are saved (see Ephesians 2:8-10). One baptism is the liturgical rite through which we profess our faith when we believe in the atoning death

and resurrection of Christ for our sin. By being baptized in the name of the Father, Son, and Holy Spirit, we declare our union with the one Lord and Savior Jesus Christ.

Third, the church is described as one family in which every believer belongs because there is only one God who is the "Father of all, who is above all, and through all, and in you all" (4:6). This cluster of phrases describes the greatness and magnitude of this one God who all Christians have in common as our Father.

7 But unto every one of us is given grace according to the measure of the gift of Christ. 8 Wherefore he saith, When he ascended up on high, he led captivity captive, and gave gifts unto men.

Although there is unity of belief and purpose, there is also diversity and uniqueness of gifts and function. In Ephesians 4:8, Paul quotes Psalm 68:18 to confirm his emphasis on the gifts through Christ. The sentence, "When he ascended up on high, he led captivity captive, and gave gifts unto men," refers to Christ's position on the right hand of the Father as conqueror over death, having defeated Satan and his agents. Some also believe that Christ liberated those who were bound and took them like captives into heaven. From there, He gives gifts to the church, which might refer to the bestowing of gifts of the Holy Spirit on the Day of Pentecost.

9 (Now that he ascended, what is it but that he also descended first into the lower parts of the earth? 10 He that descended is the same also that ascended up far above all heavens, that he might fill all things.)

Verses 9-10 in parentheses serve as support and elaboration of Christ's ascension. Paul argues in defense of the death, resurrection, and ascension of Christ that for Him to have ascended into heaven, He must also have descended from heaven. Verse 10 insists that the one who descended is the same who ascended far above everything else, that He might "fill all things." The phrase "fill all things" (Gk. *pleroo*, **play-RO-o**) means to accomplish or fulfill all things. It speaks about completing His mission. The purpose of His ascension into heaven is then to free Him to accomplish fully the purpose for which He descended. That purpose includes the distribution of gifts to the church by the Holy Spirit.

11 And he gave some, apostles; and some, prophets; and some, evangelists; and some, pastors and teachers; 12 For the perfecting of the saints, for the work of the ministry, for the edifying of the body of Christ:

Through the Holy Spirit, God equips the church with special abilities He bestows on each member for the benefit of all. In this text, there is an emphasis on gifts given to leaders of the church. The word "apostle" (Gk. *apostolos*, **ap-OS-tol-os**) is used in several ways in the New Testament. In this case, "apostle" refers to those who were eyewitnesses to the risen Lord, chosen and authorized by Christ (Acts 1:21, 22; 10:40-41; 1 Corinthians 9:1; 15:8-9). Some of these apostles were still alive during the time of the writing of Ephesians. Therefore, when used in this sense of the word, there are no apostles today.

The next gift is the "prophets" (Gk. *prophetes*, **prof-AY-tace**) with special ability from God to give guidance to the Christian community and to declare the will of God (e.g., Acts 13:1-4). Next are the "evangelists" (Gk. *euaggelistes*, **yoo-ang-ghel-is-TACE**), preachers or those who proclaim the Gospel (e.g., Philip, Acts 21:8; 2 Timothy 4:5). In the case of the use of *euaggelistes* in

Ephesians 4:11, it relates to the spreading of the Good News. Then we have the "pastors" (Gk. *poimen*, **poy-MANE**) or shepherds and teachers who give instructions.

These gifts have a twofold importance of function and purpose. The primary function is to equip or perfect the saints for the work of ministry and the other is for building up (edifying of) the body of Christ. The word translated into "perfecting" is the Greek word *katartismos* (**kat-ar-tis-MOS**), which means "equipping, preparing, or making ready." Therefore, the apostles, prophets, evangelists, pastors, and teachers' function is to prepare God's people, equipping them for the work of "ministry" (Gk. *diakonia*, **dee-ak-on-EE-ah**) or service. They are endowed with the grace of God in order to train people to do the work of service within the church community. They are "equippers" who provide others in the church with necessary tools for the ministry.

The ultimate purpose of these special gifts is to edify or build up the body of Christ. The word used here in the *King James Version* is "edifying" (Gk. *oikodome*, **oy-kod-om-AY**), with an architectural undertone. It means building a house, but used figuratively here, it refers to building up the church of Christ. We have been called to build one another up in the Lord in love.

13 Till we all come in the unity of the faith, and of the knowledge of the Son of God, unto a perfect man, unto the measure of the stature of the fulness of Christ: 14 That we henceforth be no more children, tossed to and fro, and carried about with every wind of doctrine, by the sleight of men, and cunning craftiness, whereby they lie in wait to deceive;

The church is called to unity, and this is made possible only by our spiritual knowledge of who Christ is and why He died.

196

The full unity and knowledge of the Son of God leads to maturity—"unto a perfect man" (v. 13). "Perfect" (Gk. *teleios*, **tel-I-oce**) refers to that which has reached the age of maturity or adulthood, rather than moral perfection. The proof of maturity is the unity that the church attains on the basis of its knowledge of Christ. This matured personhood or "perfect man" is measured according to Christ's standards, "unto the measure of the stature of the fulness of Christ" (v. 13). In verse 7, Christ is the measure of God's grace. He is the measure—or the yardstick—of all maturity. Although the concept of growth into maturity is corporate, the maturity of the church depends on the growth of individual members.

Children have the tendency to be easily deceived, or easily attracted to new things, but when they grow to adulthood the tendency diminishes. Maturity in the knowledge of Christ will protect the church from being misled. In verse 14, Paul illustrates this with use of the words "tossed to and fro" (Gk. *kludonizomai*, **kloo-do-NID-zom-ahee**, i.e., tossed here and there) and "carried about" (Gk. *periphero*, **per-ee-FER-o**, which means to be "driven around" or "carried around"). Such people cannot make up their minds but change from one opinion to another—"by every wind of doctrine"—according to the last teaching or the latest books they've read or information they've received. As a result, they become easy prey to people's cunning craftiness, those who lie in wait to deceive. "The sleight" (Gk. *kubeia*, **koo-BI-ah**) literally means "dice playing" and is used metaphorically here to describe the deception, trickery, and manipulation of unscrupulous men who take advantage of people's ignorance.

15 But speaking the truth in love, may grow up into him in all things, which is the head, even Christ:

Paul moves from the mark of immaturity, which is doctrinal instability, to the qualities of mature, or perfected Christianity that will promote unity and peace within the body. Truth and love are essential in the life of the body of Christ, both leading to church growth. It is important for the Christian to hold firm and be loyal to the truth on the one hand and to have loving concern for others' welfare on the other.

16 From whom the whole body fitly joined together and compacted by that which every joint supplieth, according to the effectual working in the measure of every part, maketh increase of the body unto the edifying of itself in love.

Paul then employs biological metaphors using human anatomy to describe the church's relationship with Christ. Paul compares the natural body and the Christ's mystical body, the church. As the body has many component parts, which are joined fittingly together by different ligaments to the head with each part working corporately with other parts, so it is with the church. The church has many members with various functions, joined fittingly together by the Holy Spirit unto Christ—the head. The Holy Spirit has endowed every member with various gifts and skills; each member should then work corporately with every other member in love.

Consequently, love is essential for the proper function of the church; love is the life line that keeps the church alive and united. Mutual love encourages church growth and allows the church to develop in the love of Christ.

Sources:

Butler, Trent, ed. *Holman Bible Dictionary*, Nashville, TN: Holman Bible Publishers, 1991. 1300-1301.

Dictionary.com. http://dictionary.reference.com/ (accessed October 20, 2011).

Henry, Matthew. "Ephesians 4." *Matthew Henry's Commentary on the Whole Bible. Vol. VI –Acts to Revelation.* Christian Classics Ethereal Library.org. http://www.ccel.org/ccel/henry/mhc6.Eph.html (accessed October 20, 2011).

New Testament Greek Lexicon. Bible Study Tools.com. http://www.biblestudytools.com/lexicons/greek/ (accessed October 20, 2011).

Say It Correctly

Stature. STACH-er.
Sleight. slite.

Daily Bible Readings

MONDAY
One Lord
(Zechariah 14:6-11)

TUESDAY
One Faith
(Philippians 1:27-30)

WEDNESDAY
One in Christ Jesus
(Galatians 3:23-29)

THURSDAY
One God
(Exodus 20:1-7)

FRIDAY
One Spirit
(1 Corinthians 12:4-13)

SATURDAY
One Body
(Romans 12:3-8)

SUNDAY
Building Up the Body Together
(Ephesians 4:1-16)

Notes

_____

_____

_____

_____

Teaching Tips

Words You Should Know

A.   Light (John 1:4, 5; Ephesians 5:8) *phōs* (Gk.)—The Lord Jesus as the illuminator of men—as well as Christian life—as a reflection of this light.

B. Walk (Ephesians 5:2, 8) *peripateō* (Gk.)—To make one's way, figuratively, signifying the whole round of the activities of the individual life.

Teacher Preparation

Unifying   Principle—Living   by Example. The writer of Ephesians tells us that as Christians, we always live in Christ's light that overcomes all kinds of darkness.

A. Pray and ask God to guide you through the lesson.

B. Study the entire lesson.

C. Prepare a PowerPoint presentation or handout entitled "Life in the Light" and provide various images first in darkness, a distortion, and then in light, the true image.

D. Complete the companion lesson in the Precepts For Living Personal Study Guide®.

O—Open the Lesson

A. Open with prayer and then introduce the lesson.

B. Have a volunteer read the In Focus story. Discuss.

C. Have students look at the distorted images on your handout or PowerPoint presentation and try to guess what they are before revealing the true images.

D. Have the class discuss the various attributes of light (tie this to the lesson).

DEC 23rd

P—Present the Scriptures

A. Have volunteers read the Focal Verses.

B. Use The People, Places, and Times, Background, Search the Scriptures, Discuss the Meaning, and More Light on the Text sections to clarify the text.

E—Explore the Meaning

A. Draw salient points from Lesson in Our Society and Make It Happen to further clarify the text.

B. Discuss the question: "Is it possible for a Christian to participate in sin committed by someone else? Why or why not?"

N—Next Steps for Application

A. Summarize the lesson.

B. Close with a prayer.

Worship Guide

For the Superintendent or Teacher
Theme: Live in the Light
Song: "This Little Light of Mine"
Devotional Reading: Psalm 97
Prayer

Live in the Light

Bible Background • JOHN 1:1-14; EPHESIANS 4:17—5:20
Printed Text • JOHN 1:1–5; EPHESIANS 5:1–2, 6-14 | Devotional Reading • PSALM 97

Aim for Change

By the end of the lesson, we will: KNOW the images of Jesus as light overcoming darkness; IMAGINE living in constant light where there are no secrets; and COMMIT to discovering how to live a life as the fruit of light.

 In Focus

Julia prayed every morning for the community college students she taught. Some had so many problems in their lives that their classwork suffered. They'd come in late, text during lectures, miss assignments, and have overall nasty attitudes. However Julia would continue to pray. She tried to always share Christ with her students by remaining positive and encouraging them at every step. Some days, the students were receptive. However, other times, they rejected everything she said. As Julia sat in her office after class, she began to sink into a feeling of defeat. She was deep in thought when Marcus, a former student, knocked.

"Oh, Marcus, what brings you by?"

"I just wanted to say thank you for being a great teacher. I used to be a slacker, but you really taught me to be dedicated to my education. Because of your example, I have a scholarship to a four-year university."

"Marcus, you did the work, but thank you for the good news."

The darkness of defeat left Julia, and her resolve to be a light for her students was strengthened.

As a believer, Julia knew the importance of living as a child of the light. Today's lesson tells us how to also be that light.

Keep in Mind

Be ye therefore followers of God, as dear children
(Ephesians 5:1).

"Be ye therefore followers of God, as dear children"
Ephesians 5:1).

Focal Verses

KJV **John 1:1** In the beginning was the Word, and the Word was with God, and the Word was God.

2 The same was in the beginning with God.

3 All things were made by him; and without him was not any thing made that was made.

4 In him was life; and the life was the light of men.

5 And the light shineth in darkness; and the darkness comprehended it not.

Ephesians 5:1 Be ye therefore followers of God, as dear children;

2 And walk in love, as Christ also hath loved us, and hath given himself for us an offering and a sacrifice to God for a sweetsmelling savour.

5:6 Let no man deceive you with vain words: for because of these things cometh the wrath of God upon the children of disobedience.

7 Be not ye therefore partakers with them.

8 For ye were sometimes darkness, but now are ye light in the Lord: walk as children of light:

9 (For the fruit of the Spirit is in all goodness and righteousness and truth;)

10 Proving what is acceptable unto the Lord.

11 And have no fellowship with the unfruitful works of darkness, but rather reprove them.

12 For it is a shame even to speak of those things which are done of them in secret.

13 But all things that are reproved are made manifest by the light: for whatsoever doth make manifest is light.

14 Wherefore he saith, Awake thou that sleepest, and arise from the dead, and Christ shall give thee light.

NLT **John 1:1** In the beginning the Word already existed. The Word was with God, and the Word was God.

2 He existed in the beginning with God.

3 God created everything through him, and nothing was created except through him.

4 The Word gave life to everything that was created, and his life brought light to everyone.

5 The light shines in the darkness, and the darkness can never extinguish it.

Ephesians 5:1 Imitate God, therefore, in everything you do, because you are his dear children.

2 Live a life filled with love, following the example of Christ. He loved us and offered himself as a sacrifice for us, a pleasing aroma to God.

5:6 Don't be fooled by those who try to excuse these sins, for the anger of God will fall on all who disobey him.

7 Don't participate in the things these people do.

8 For once you were full of darkness, but now you have light from the Lord. So live as people of light!

9 For this light within you produces only what is good and right and true.

10 Carefully determine what pleases the Lord.

11 Take no part in the worthless deeds of evil and darkness; instead, expose them.

12 It is shameful even to talk about the things that ungodly people do in secret.

13 But their evil intentions will be exposed when the light shines on them,

14 for the light makes everything visible. This is why it is said, "Awake, O sleeper, rise up from the dead, and Christ will give you light."

The People, Places, and Times

Ephesus. Ephesus, located on the west coast of Asia Minor, was an ancient Greek city that came under Roman rule in 133 B.C. It was the second largest city in the Roman Empire and with a population of 250,000 by 1st century B.C., it was the second largest city in the known world. Because of its great harbor and location near major trade routes, Ephesus was an affluent city. It was also politically significant because the Roman governor lived here instead of at the empire's capital, Rome. Ephesus was the worship center for the goddess Artemis, also known as Diana. Apostle Paul's longest ministry occurred here for nearly three years (Acts 19:8, 10). He came to Ephesus on his third missionary trip, beginning in A.D. 53 (*New Unger's Bible Dictionary,* 366-367, 974). While in Ephesus, Paul preached the Word of the Lord and took a stand against idol worship. As a result, more Ephesians converted to Christianity and burned their idols. Acts 19 gives an account of Demetrius, a chief silversmith who produced idols and led a riot in protest of Paul's teaching. His fellow silversmiths were losing business, and it was feared that the worship of Artemis was losing prestige in the city. When the riot ended, Paul soon left Ephesus with Timothy in charge of the church he started.

Background

According to tradition, the Apostle John was living in Ephesus when he wrote this Gospel. The purpose is to emphasize that Jesus Christ is the Messiah, the Son of God, through whom salvation is made available to those who believe (John 20:30, 31). In Jewish thought, a son is one who is obedient to his father, an apprentice of his father, and is an agent (ambassador or emissary) of his father (Thompson, 93). Jesus is, of course, all these things, but His relationship with the Father goes even deeper than this understanding of a son. Jesus also is one with the Father (10:30). John solidified this fact in the first few verses in the Gospel by proclaiming Christ's identity as the Word of God and then writing of His encounter with John the Baptist, who declares Jesus' identity (1:15).

At-A-Glance

1. The Word (John 1:1-5)
2. Children of God (Ephesians 5:1-2)
3. Living in the Light (vv. 6-14)

In Depth

1. The Word (John 1:1-5)

Particular to the Gospel of John is the use of the title *Word of God* when referring to Jesus. Matthew Henry wrote, "the Word is two-fold: *logos*—word conceived; and *logos*—word uttered" (*Henry's Commentary,* online version). The word conceived is thought, the product of the mind. Just as our thoughts are part of us, Christ as the Word is part of God. The uttered word is speech, what is spoken. Christ as the Word came to speak to us, to reveal to us, the mind of God. *Unger's Bible Dictionary* states, "Words are the vehicle for the revelation of the thoughts and intents of the mind to others" (780). Jesus is the vehicle through whom God made Himself known to humankind. Just as what we think and say are not separated from us but always with us, Christ as the Word of God has always been with the Father. If the Father is eternal, the Word of God is eternal—not made like creation. All life derives from Jesus Christ. "The Word gave life to everything that was created, and his life brought light to everyone" (John 1:4, NLT). The wise men witnessed the light that had come into the world when they found the baby Jesus, who would grow up and reveal the one true Living God to the world. Once that knowledge came, it could never be extinguished.

2. Children of God (Ephesians 5:1-2)

The phrase "Be ye therefore ..." at the beginning of Ephesians 5 indicates that the chapter continues the subject started in the previous chapter. Paul relayed in chapter 4 the characteristics of a believer's life. He ended the chapter with: "Let all bitterness, and wrath, and anger, and clamour, and evil speaking, be put away from you, with all malice: And be ye kind one to another, tenderhearted, forgiving one another, even as God for Christ's sake hath forgiven you" (Ephesians 4:31, 32). Verse 1 in chapter 5 then explains that to put aside bitterness and anger and to be kind to one another is to be a follower of God. To describe how closely a believer should follow God's ways, Paul wrote that we should follow as "dear children."

Paul uses the relationship between children and parents to show how believers, like children, are to imitate their parent, God. It is with this sentiment that Paul calls the believer to follow the ways of God because it is vital to life. In verse 2, the apostle explains that following God is to walk in love (*agape*). *Agape* not only refers to the unconditional love of God, but it is also Christian love, which "is not an impulse from the feelings." Rather, it "seeks the welfare of all" (*Vine's Complete Expository Dictionary of Old and New Testament Words*, 382). Christians are to live out this love with Christ as their example. He typified this *agape* love with the ultimate sacrifice. He "gave himself up for us as a fragrant offering and sacrifice to God" (Ephesians 5:2b, NIV).

3. Living in the Light (vv. 6-14)

In verses 3 through 5, Paul gives a list of sins that do not constitute walking in love. Verse 6 says the believer should not be deceived by those who say such sins are not offensive to God and that even if one were to engage in them, he or she could somehow escape His wrath. God's anger will come upon anyone who disobeys His command. Believers should not participate in the things these deceivers do. In fact, Christians should not even "encourage them in their sins, prompt them to sin, (but) prevent and hinder them, as far as it may be in our power to do so" (*Matthew Henry's Commentary on the Whole Bible*, online version). Now that we are no longer children of darkness, we need to exhibit the light of the Lord, the fruit of the Spirit, in our daily lives. In contrast to the list of sins, this fruit encompasses goodness, righteousness, and truth. Living in the light means we actively seek out those things that are pleasing to God: "Have nothing to do with the fruitless deeds of darkness, but rather expose them" (Ephesians 5:11, NIV). Even speaking of things that the children of darkness do in secret is shameful, but the light of the Lord exposes these secret sins. Nothing is hidden from God. Therefore, it is wise for those who are asleep in their darkness to awake and come into the light.

Search the Scriptures

1. In what way is the Word related to God (John 1:1)?

2. Why is Christ the example for walking in love (Ephesians 5:2)?

3. How should children of Light live (vv. 8-11)?

Discuss the Meaning

What are some very concrete ways we as Christians can exhibit the light of the Lord in our lives? How can we make sure we put these things into practice in our lives?

Lesson in Our Society

If we were to examine the list of the works of the flesh, we could find examples of each being implemented in our society (Galatians 5:19–21). These sinful acts are socially acceptable, and those who take a stance against them are labeled old-fashioned, out of touch, unrealistic, and unreasonable. However, as children of light, we must not waver in our goal to live a life that is pleasing to God no matter the cost.

Make It Happen

Sometimes it is hard to go against the grain, especially when it seems there are no repercussions for evil acts. This week, pray for the strength to endure and the courage to live in the light of the Lord.

Follow the Spirit

What God wants me to do:

_____

_____

_____

_____

Remember Your Thoughts

Special insights I have learned:

_____

_____

_____

_____

More Light on the Text

John 1:1-5; Ephesians 5:1-2, 6-14

John 1:1 In the beginning was the Word, and the Word was with God, and the Word was God. 2 The same was in the beginning with God.

In many aspects, John 1:1-2 echoes the creation account of Genesis 1:1, which states, "In the beginning God created the heavens and the earth." The author of the Gospel of John, the apostle John, places the "Word" (Christ Jesus, the Son) before the creation of the known universe.

There are four principles with which the reader should seek familiarity. First, the Word (Christ Jesus) was "in the beginning." The ancient Greek word for "beginning" is *arche* (**ar-KHAY**). The "beginning" probably refers to a period before Creation and the inauguration of time as we know it. This is supplied to us in verse 3 and others that we will discuss. Secondly, the Word (Christ Jesus) "was with God." Here Christ Jesus existing as the Word is not only placed before all creation but is also associated in community with God the Father, coexisting with one another. Third, Christ Jesus the Word "was God." The apostle John makes clear that Christ Jesus did not only exist with God the Father before all creation, but He Himself, too, was God. The Word is specifically recognized as deity, equal to God the Father. Lastly, in verse 2 the apostle John joins his description of the Word with another "beginning" statement, summarizing all said previously. The Word "was in the beginning with God."

3 All things were made by him; and without him was not any thing made that was made.

Verse 3 reveals a powerful and sharp revelation of the character and sovereignty of the Word (Christ Jesus). Within this verse, the apostle John directs the reader to the meaning of the phrase "in the beginning" and the specific period it is referring to. Christ Jesus (the Word) existed before all created things, and it is because of Him that all things that were created exist. John 1:3 echoes the words of apostle Paul as stated in Colossians 1:16-17, "For by Him all things were created, both in the heavens and on earth, visible and invisible, whether thrones or dominions or rulers or authorities—all things have been created through Him and for Him. He is before all things, and in Him all things hold together" (NASB). As Christians, we must continually live with a faith that consciously reminds us that we worship a God without a beginning, for He Himself was before the beginning and created the beginning itself. He is the source of everything.

4 In him was life; and the life was the light of men.

This verse makes two penetrating statements. First, in Him (Christ Jesus) "was life" (Gk. *zoe*, **dzo-AY**), meaning to live, breathe, and exist among the living. In a certain way, the apostle John continues alluding to the Creation account, where He places the Word at the beginning and establishes it as creator of the known universe along with everything in it. Life has its origins within God the Father and has residence within the Son; from them, life will continually flow and be sustained. Jesus Christ, the Word, the Son of God is the giver of life for "in Him was life." Also, the word "life" can signify a heightening or pinnacle of that which we currently have and experience. In and through Jesus, we actualize true living and authentic life. Through Him only are we able to experience the full potential of what life has to offer.

The second penetrating statement is that the life dwelling within Christ is "the light of men." The word "light" (Gk. *phos*, **foce**), meaning to shine or make manifest, can signify the revealing and transformative character and power of God. This is both who He is and how life in Him changes our whole being. As Christians, we function as agents of change, being the light of the world (Matthew 5:14), thus being imitators of Jesus Christ who is the ultimate light, which dwells in the world (John 8:12).

5 And the light shineth in darkness; and the darkness comprehended it not.

This verse provides the first mention of "darkness" (Gk. *skotia*, **skot-EE-ah**) within John's Gospel account. Every reader of the Bible must become familiar with the imagery and meanings this word brings forth. Darkness is used throughout the Bible to represent the antithesis of who and what God is. Darkness comes to represent the bad, the ugly, the corrupt, and the evil that exist. Darkness, in the New Testament, is a metaphor for evil, and those in darkness are without God and live under the rule of Satan, the evil one (Matthew 6:13). Humanity, which exists apart from God, not only lives in darkness, but the darkness dwells within it as well. This is a cyclical experience: having evil dwell within and being influenced by that same evil to create more manifestations of it throughout the world. Furthermore, through use of the Greek word *katalambano* (**kat-al-am-BAN-o,** meaning laid hold of), we read that darkness "comprehended (Light) not." On its own, the darkness can never grasp the totality of who and what Light is. Darkness cannot understand perfected light because one must be in union with and have guidance from the light itself in order to be taught the essence of that light in its entirety.

Ephesians 5:1 Be ye therefore followers of God, as dear children;

The apostle Paul displays some of the most encouraging words, aimed to inspire unity and establish the highest standard logically possible to "be imitators of God." The ancient Greek word for "imitators" is *mimetes* (**mim-ay-TACE**) and can also be translated as "followers" per the *King James Version* (1 Corinthians 4:16; 11:1; Hebrews 6:12). Paul wasn't speaking from an opinion, mere speculation, or a suggestion detached from the Word of God itself. Actually, he was reiterating a continuous biblical principle. The command "to be" or become like God is dispersed throughout the Pentateuch. God has always wanted His people to be as He is. This is first viewed within the fact that God created humanity in His image, that of the Trinity: "Then God said, 'Let Us make man in Our image, according to Our likeness'" (Genesis 1:26, NASB). Since the Fall, humanity has developed and nurtured an evil nature, severed from its relationship with God. As a result, the command to be as God is has shifted from humanity as a whole and has been placed on His chosen people (as described in the Old Testament), as well as

His children, those that accept His Son as Lord and Savior (as outlined in the New Testament).

2 And walk in love, as Christ also hath loved us, and hath given himself for us an offering and a sacrifice to God for a sweet-smelling savour.

The ancient Greek word for "walk" is *peripateo* (**per-ee-pat-EH-o**), meaning "to make one's way" to live. It is the totality of an individual's life, which encompasses his or her behavior, thoughts, and actions. For Paul, the believer's life should symbolize love but not simply a secular perspective or humanitarian ideal. The believer is to love "as Christ also loved" us all. This statement naturally draws the reader to the connection between love and sacrifice, both of which are epitomized through Christ Jesus' life, death, and resurrection. Paul describes it as "an offering and a sacrifice." When Christians live a life of sacrificial love, their hearts, thoughts, and actions become pleasing to God. Here, Paul relates the Christian's life to the life of Christ Jesus. Because of this, the Christian's life becomes "a pleasing aroma" before the presence of God the Father (v. 2, NLT).

5:6 Let no man deceive you with vain words: for because of these things cometh the wrath of God upon the children of disobedience. 7 Be not ye therefore partakers with them.

The apostle Paul begins this section with a stern warning: "Let no one deceive you with empty words" (NASB). The ancient Greek word for "deceive" is *apatao* (**ap-at-AH-o**), which denotes the trickery and cheating. This echoes another warning given by the apostle to the church in Colosse: "See to it that no one takes you captive through philosophy and empty deception, according to the tradition of men, according to the elementary principles of the world, rather than according to Christ" (Colossians 2:8, NASB). In 5:6, Paul interestingly deemed these false teachers "the children of disobedience." He mentions this phrase in two other places (Ephesians 2:2; Colossians 3:6), either in connection with the wrath of God or with the evil influence of the devil himself. Paul makes it clear that these people may be past redemption, for they have completely given themselves over to wickedness and deception. Hence the explicit command in Ephesians 5:7, "Be not ye therefore partakers with them" because only God's judgment awaits them.

8 For ye were sometimes darkness, but now are ye light in the Lord: walk as children of light: 9 (For the fruit of the Spirit is in all goodness and righteousness and truth;) 10 Proving what is acceptable unto the Lord.

Apostle Paul warned the believers of deception and in partaking with those in who are in darkness. In verses 8-10, we see a subtle allusion to the temptations of our former lifestyles in the world, symbolized by those in darkness. Our former lives are full of sin, and sin itself is very tempting. This is especially the case when we associate with it some desire for pleasure and reward from the participation in sin. "But now," says the apostle, you are "children of light" (God), and it is only by accepting His Son as Lord and Savior that this is actualized (v. 8; John 12:36). This transitional phrase is connected with a set of identifiers. Their new lives in Christ are verified by "all goodness and righteousness and truth" (Ephesians 5:9). The apostle makes a very encouraging statement in verse 10. He exhorted the Christians in Ephesus to remember that their lives in Christ were con-

tinually about "trying to learn what is pleasing to the Lord" (v. 10, NASB). Paul understood that the Christian's life was one of continual growth, always being taught by God. The children of light must always seek God to maintain the light they've received, otherwise, their lights will glow dim, increasing the threat of being consumed by darkness.

11 And have no fellowship with the unfruitful works of darkness, but rather reprove them. 12 For it is a shame even to speak of those things which are done of them in secret. 13 But all things that are reproved are made manifest by the light: for whatsoever doth make manifest is light. 14 Wherefore he saith, Awake thou that sleepest, and arise from the dead, and Christ shall give thee light.

Christian responsibility projects itself from Paul's words. Avoiding sinfulness is one part of the equation, and the alerting of sin and its practice is another. The ancient Greek word translated as "participation" is *summetochos* (**soom-met-okh-os**), describing the sharing of one thing between two or more people. *Akarpos* (**AK-ar-pos**) is the original Greek word we translate as "unfruitful." This word points toward something that produces nothing that is expected of it. This isn't the only time Paul commanded believers to "expose" (Gk. *elegcho*, **el-ENG-kho**) sin (v. 11, NLT). In 1 Timothy 5:20, we read, "Those who continue to sin, rebuke in the presence of all, so that the rest also will be fearful of sinning" (NASB). We cannot stand by as people destroy themselves and those deceived into following them. Sin must be exposed for what it is and what it does.

Sources:
Barclay, William. *The Daily Study Bible: The Gospel of John. Volume 1 and 2.* Philadelphia, PA: The Westminster Press, 1956.
Henry, Matthew. "Ephesians." *Matthew Henry's Commentary on the Whole Bible. Vol. VI –Acts to Revelation.* Christian Classics Ethereal Library.org. http://www.ccel.org/ccel/henry/mhc6. Eph.html (accessed October 20, 2011).

Henry, Matthew. "John." *Matthew Henry's Commentary on the Whole Bible. Vol. V –Matthew to John.* Christian Classics Ethereal Library.org. http://www.ccel.org/ccel/henry/mhc5.John.html (accessed October 20, 2011).

The Holy Bible, New International Version. Grand Rapids, MI: Biblica, Inc. (Zondervan), 2011. http://www.biblegateway.com/passage/?search=John%201&version=NIV,http://www.biblegateway.com/passage/?search=Ephesians%205&version=NIV (accessed October 20, 2011).

Jowett, J. H. *The Epistles of St. Peter.* London, UK: Hodder and Stoughton, 1905.

Martin, Ralph P. *Ephesians, Colossians, and Philemon. Interpretation, a Bible Commentary for Teaching and Instruction.* Atlanta, GA: John Knox Press, 1991.

New Testament Greek Lexicon. Bible Study Tools.com. http://www.biblestudytools.com/lexicons/greek/ (accessed October 20, 2011).

Patzia, Arthur G. *Ephesians, Colossians, Philemon. New International Biblical Commentary, vol. 10.* Peabody, MA: Hendrickson Publishers, 1990.

Strong, James. *Free Bible Study Tools - Strong's Concordance with Greek and Hebrew.* Tim Greenwood Ministries. http://www.tgm.org/bible.htm (accessed October 20, 2011).

Tasker, R. V. G. *The Gospel According to St. John: An Introduction and Commentary. Tyndale New Testament Commentaries.* Grand Rapids, MI: Wm. B. Eerdmans Publishing Company, 1981.

Thompson, Marianne Meye. *The God of the Gospel of John.* Grand Rapids, MI: Wm. B. Eerdmans Publishing Company, 2001. 93.

Unger, Merrill F. *The New Unger's Bible Dictionary.* Chicago, IL: Moody Press, 1988. 366-367, 780, 974.

Vine, W. E. *Vine's Complete Expository Dictionary of Old and New Testament Words: With Topical Index.* Edited by Merrill F. Unger and William White, Jr. Nashville, TN: Thomas Nelson, 1996. 369, 382, 664, 683.

Say It Correctly

Ephesians. ih-FEE-zhuhnz.
Ephesus.EF-uh-suhs, EH-fuh-suhs.

Daily Bible Readings

Monday
Light Dawns for the Righteous
(Psalm 97)

Tuesday
The Way of Darkness
(Ephesians 4:17-24)

Wednesday
Putting Away the Old Ways
(Ephesians 4:25-32)

Thursday
Be Careful How You Live
(Ephesians 5:15-20)

Friday
We Have Seen His Star
(Matthew 2:1-11)

Saturday
We Have Seen His Glory
(John 1:6-14)

Sunday
Light Shines in the Darkness
(John 1:1-5; Ephesians 5:1-2, 6-14)

Notes

Teaching Tips

December 30
Bible Study Guide 5

Words You Should Know

A. Submit (Ephesians 5:22) *hupotasso* (Gk.)—To voluntarily cooperate, assume responsibility, and carry a burden.

B. Provoke (6:4) *parorgizo* (Gk.)—To rouse to wrath, exasperation, or anger.

Teacher Preparation

Unifying Principle—Family Matters. The writer of Ephesians states that family members should love and care for one another just as Christ loves and cares for the church; the writer of 1 John says that we must put our love in action and make loving others our way of life.

A. Pray for your students and lesson clarity.

B. Prayerfully study the entire lesson.

C. Prepare the companion lesson in the *Precepts For Living Personal Study Guide®*.

D. Be prepared through your studies to discuss different "love languages"—how we show love to others and how we want others to show love to us.

O—Open the Lesson

A. Open the class with prayer.

B. Share examples of family dynamics that may cause confusion in the family.

C. Lead the class in reading the Aim for Change in unison.

D. Read the In Focus story. Discuss.

E. Share different ways that people show love to each other (love languages).

P—Present the Scriptures

A. Ask for a volunteer to read the Focal Verses.

B. Drive the discussion of the verses, utilizing the material from The People, Places, and Times, Background, and More Light on the Text sections.

E—Explore the Meaning

A. Have students complete the Search the Scriptures section in pairs. Discuss.

B. Read and answer the Discuss the Meaning questions.

N—Next Steps for Application

A. Summarize the Make It Happen section.

B. Summarize today's lesson.

C. Ask for prayer requests and end the session with prayer, thanking God for creating families.

Worship Guide

For the Superintendent or Teacher
Theme: Christ's Love for the Church
Song: "Blest Be the Tie That Binds"
Devotional Reading: John 3:16-21
Prayer

210

Christ's Love for the Church

Bible Background • EPHESIANS 5:21—6:4
Printed Text • EPHESIANS 5:21—6:4 | Devotional Reading • JOHN 3:16-21

─────────────── **Aim for Change** ───────────────

By the end of the lesson, we will: COMPARE Christ's love for the church with the relationships among family members; APPRECIATE Christ's sacrifice to show love and care for the church; and ACCEPT responsibility for showing love in the family as Christ demonstrated love for the church.

DEC 30th

─────────────── **In Focus** ───────────────

Sharinda read through her students' papers, her heart breaking. A fifth-grade teacher, Sharinda had assigned her students a paper that began, "I wish..." The students were instructed to write at least two sentences on the topic.

Sharinda expected to read things like "I wish we could go on vacation to Hawaii," or "I wish I could have a new computer." Instead, 15 out of 20 students wrote about their families:

"I wish my dad would come back."

"I wish my parents didn't fight all the time."

"I wish I could get good grades so my parents would love me."

"I wish my brother wasn't so mean."

"I wish my mom's boyfriend didn't live with us."

"I wish we could have Christmas all together for once."

Sharinda bowed her head over the papers and wept. Her students needed the love of Christ to permeate their lives and transform their families.

Strong families are built upon the foundation of Christ's love for the church. In this lesson, we will see how serving one another in love creates an atmosphere where families can grow and thrive.

─────────────── **Keep in Mind** ───────────────

"Submitting yourselves one to another in the fear of God"
(Ephesians 5:21).

"Submitting yourselves one to another in the fear of God"
(Ephesians 5:21).

Focal Verses

KJV **Ephesians 5:21** Submitting yourselves one to another in the fear of God.

22 Wives, submit yourselves unto your own husbands, as unto the Lord.

23 For the husband is the head of the wife, even as Christ is the head of the church: and he is the saviour of the body.

24 Therefore as the church is subject unto Christ, so let the wives be to their own husbands in every thing.

25 Husbands, love your wives, even as Christ also loved the church, and gave himself for it;

26 That he might sanctify and cleanse it with the washing of water by the word,

27 That he might present it to himself a glorious church, not having spot, or wrinkle, or any such thing; but that it should be holy and without blemish.

28 So ought men to love their wives as their own bodies. He that loveth his wife loveth himself.

29 For no man ever yet hated his own flesh; but nourisheth and cherisheth it, even as the Lord the church:

30 For we are members of his body, of his flesh, and of his bones.

31 For this cause shall a man leave his father and mother, and shall be joined unto his wife, and they two shall be one flesh.

32 This is a great mystery: but I speak concerning Christ and the church.

33 Nevertheless let every one of you in particular so love his wife even as himself; and the wife see that she reverence her husband.

Ephesians 6:1 Children, obey your parents in the Lord: for this is right.

2 Honour thy father and mother; which is the first commandment with promise;

NLT **Ephesians 5:21** And further, submit to one another out of reverence for Christ.

22 For wives, this means submit to your husbands as to the Lord.

23 For a husband is the head of his wife as Christ is the head of the church. He is the Savior of his body, the church.

24 As the church submits to Christ, so you wives should submit to your husbands in everything.

25 For husbands, this means love your wives, just as Christ loved the church. He gave up his life for her

26 to make her holy and clean, washed by the cleansing of God's word.

27 He did this to present her to himself as a glorious church without a spot or wrinkle or any other blemish. Instead, she will be holy and without fault.

28 In the same way, husbands ought to love their wives as they love their own bodies. For a man who loves his wife actually shows love for himself.

29 No one hates his own body but feeds and cares for it, just as Christ cares for the church.

30 And we are members of his body.

31 As the Scriptures say, "A man leaves his father and mother and is joined to his wife, and the two are united into one."

32 This is a great mystery, but it is an illustration of the way Christ and the church are one.

33 So again I say, each man must love his wife as he loves himself, and the wife must respect her husband.

Ephesians 6:1—Children, obey your parents because you belong to the Lord, for this is the right thing to do.

2 "Honor your father and mother." This is the first commandment with a promise:

KJV continued

3 That it may be well with thee, and thou mayest live long on the earth.

4 And, ye fathers, provoke not your children to wrath: but bring them up in the nurture and admonition of the Lord.

NLT continued

3 If you honor your father and mother, "things will go well for you, and you will have long life on the earth."

4 Fathers, do not provoke your children to anger by the way you treat them. Rather, bring them up with the discipline and instruction that comes from the Lord.

The People, Places, and Times

A Household Code. The verses found in Ephesians 5:21—6:4 comprise what is called a "household code." At the time Paul wrote Ephesians, many Romans were concerned that religions such as Judaism and Christianity would negatively influence traditional Roman family values. To allay these fears and show their support for these values, Christians, Jews, and other religious groups would often employ a standard form of statements.

Paul writes under the inspiration of the Holy Spirit to give God's directives for family. Also known as "household codes," the statements were often broken down into discussions of husband and wife, father and children.

Background

In Ephesians 5, Paul calls on believers to live out a life of holiness in relation to the world around them. He challenges them to live wisely, being led by the Spirit. Such a life will produce a believer who becomes more like Christ every day. As we become more like Christ, we will learn to respect and submit to others in love and humility. And the foundation of family relationships is to be modeled after Christ's love for the church.

At-A-Glance

1. Wives' Submission Should Reflect Christ's Authority Over the Church (Ephesians 5:21-24)
2. Husbands' Love for Their Wives Should Reflect Christ's Love for the Church (vv. 25-33)
3. Children Should Be Obedient and Loved (Ephesians 6:1-4)

In Depth

1. Wives' Submission Should Reflect Christ's Authority Over the Church (Ephesians 5:21-24)

Ephesians 5:21 is a general instruction to all believers to submit to one another in love. This principle is directly associated with verse 18, where Paul instructs believers to be filled with the Spirit. When we are living a Spirit-led life, God gives us the grace to live in an attitude of humility and submission to others.

Paul addresses the wives first. He instructs wives to submit to their husbands "as unto the Lord" (verse 22). The word "submit" in this verse means to yield one's rights or to cooperate. This word does not imply slavish obedience or being silent in the home. Though the household codes of ancient days often required a wife to obey her husband, Paul does not make this a requirement, as he does for children. Rather, he appeals to a wife's dedication to God as a basis for submission to her husband. In other words, when a wife honors and respects her husband, she is submits to God and His plan for the family.

In verse 23, Paul explains why a wife is to submit to her husband: because he is the "head" of the wife and family just as "Christ is the head of the church." Christ was appointed by God to be the head of the church. On the basis of this authority, the church is to submit to Him.

Some people might conclude from these verses that there is an inequality between male and female. But Paul makes clear that in Christ, all are equal (see also 1 Corinthians 11:8–12; Galatians 3:28). Within this equality, however, order and respect for authority should exist.

2. Husbands' Love for Their Wives Should Reflect Christ's Love for the Church (vv. 25-33)

Paul now turns his attention to the husbands. Interestingly, he does not stress the husband's authority or headship over the wife. Instead, Paul charges the husband to love his wife. And not only is the husband supposed to love the wife, he is to love her "even as Christ also loved the church, and gave himself for it" (v. 25).

A husband's love for his wife is to follow the pattern of Christ's love for the church. Christ's love for the church was self-sacrificing. A self-sacrificing love is unselfish love. A husband with a self-sacrificing love will demonstrate his love by seeking the best for his wife. This kind of love is committed and faithful, even through rough times. This kind of love does not depend on emotions or circumstances but strives to hold the marriage together forever.

A loving, Christ-like husband will also provide for his wife. Just as the church is the body of Christ, a wife is a part of her husband. God says that a husband should love his wife just as he loves himself. As a husband nourishes, protects, and provides for his wife, he "loves himself" (vv. 28, 29).

Christ's love for the church is a secure love. The love of a husband for his wife should be the same (verse 31). When a couple marries, they become "one flesh." Paul explains this as part of the "mystery" of marriage (v. 32). Within the security of this relationship, a wife can submit to her husband.

3. Children Should Be Obedient and Loved (Ephesians 6:1-4)

After discussing the husband-wife relationship, Paul now gives specific instructions to children. Children are exhorted to obey their parents "in the Lord," that is, in the spirit of obedience as if they were obeying God (6:1). Paul also instructs children to obey their parents because it is the right thing to do. Obedience to parents is also a commandment of God (Exodus 20:12; Deuteronomy 5:16). And according to Ephesians 6:1–3, when a child honors, respects, and obeys his parents, that child is blessed.

Just as children have a responsibility to obey their parents, parents also have responsibilities to their children. In verse 4, Paul speaks specifically to fathers as the head of the family. He first gives the fathers a negative instruction—"do not exasperate your children" (v. 4, NIV). A father's role in his child's life makes a direct impact on the child's concept of God the Father. Fathers, therefore, need to be watchful and consider how their behavior influences their children's actions. Unreasonable expectations, harsh or unfair punishment, or playing favorites will dishearten a child and can lead to disillusionment or rebellion.

Instead of these behaviors, fathers are encouraged positively to "bring them up in the nurture and admonition of the Lord" (v. 4). It is the father's responsibility to see that his children are being raised according to God's principles. Fathers are to nurture their children, which means to care for them tenderly and to lead them gently into God's ways. The word "admonition" is related to training and instructing. Therefore, parents are to give correction and instruction with the goal of developing their child's character and pointing the child toward righteousness. We give our children a great gift when we teach them how to obey God and His Word.

Search the Scriptures

1. Why are believers commanded to submit to one another (Ephesians 5:21)?

2. How are wives to submit to their husbands (v. 22)?

3. How are husbands to love their wives (v. 25)?

4. What specific instructions does Paul give to fathers (Ephesians 6:4)?

Discuss the Meaning

1. What does Paul mean when he says that wives should submit to their husbands just as the church submits to Christ (Ephesians 5:24)?

2. How can a husband love his wife "as his own body" (v. 28)? Why is this important?

Lesson in Our Society

In our post-Christian culture, we are witnessing the breakdown of the family unit. Marriages are disintegrating. Children are disobedient and disrespectful to parents and others in authority.

Families are important to God. He created them! He also laid out specific principles for a loving, harmonious family life. When we live according to these principles, a godly family is the result. And a godly, harmonious family is a living testimony to Christ's love for the church.

Make It Happen

How can we serve one another in the home in the name and Spirit of Christ? Think about your relationship with each family member. Are you following God's principles for family life? Pray that God would show you areas that need improvement, and then be willing to change and grow. Pray for your family members that they, too, would be willing to follow God's plan for your family. If possible, pray together as a family, committing to grow together in God's ways.

Follow the Spirit

What God wants me to do:

_____

_____

_____

_____

Remember Your Thoughts

Special insights I have learned:

_____

_____

_____

_____

More Light on the Text

Ephesians 5:21—6:4

5:21 Submitting yourselves one to another in the fear of God. 22 Wives, submit yourselves unto your own husbands, as unto the Lord. 23 For the husband is the head of the wife, even as Christ is the head of the church: and he is the saviour of the body. 24 Therefore as the church is subject unto Christ, so let the wives be to their own husbands in every thing.

The key word in this text is "submission" (Gk. *hupotasso*, **hoop-ot-AS-so**), and it lays a framework for a discussion on how to discharge Christian duties in dynamic relationships of mutuality in an act of true Christian spirituality. This idea, put forth in the text, suggests the potential danger that individualism poses against a true community life or fellowship. It becomes very serious when individualism is expressed without an intentional desire to willingly bear one another's burdens for the sake of Christ. Whenever there is a true submission for the sake of the Lord, it leads to a frame of heart and an attitude that is penetrated with a deep sense of obligation. True submission seeks not to repudiate or dominate others in a relationship.

It is within this context of understanding that the word "submission" sets an agenda for reverence to God and His divine principles. This is done as a means to cultivate a submissive spirit, which values and seeks to unselfishly support, love, and respect others for the sake of Christ. Thus, Paul laid this framework for his teaching regarding the marriage relationship and true harmony in the home. Paul underscored how a husband and a wife, through devotion for the sake of Christ, must dutifully exercise love and respect for each other in a marriage relationship. Paul primarily illustrated the quality of the nature of relationship that should exist between husbands and wives when he drew on the analogy of Jesus Christ and the church. The key verb, "submit," from the Greek, connotes an understanding of voluntarily placing under, or ordering oneself under, a leader or an authority source. The church, out of love, gratitude, and reverence, subjects itself to the Lord Jesus Christ as its Head. It does this in compliance with God's authority. In the same vein, wives are instructed to submit, in a marital relationship, to the husband. They should do so in acknowledgment of the fact that God ordained the husband as the leader of the household. This divine arrangement is for the sake of producing ordered household conditions, which are necessary to bring glory to God's name and also bring peace and productivity in family life. This is God's pattern of true governance or leadership.

The contextual meaning of the word "head" (Gk. *kephale*, **kef-al-AY**), in verse 23 of this passage in reference to a husband's relationship with his wife, has generated different interpretations among scholars. While some claim that "head" denotes an idea of a source, others choose to explain it as portraying leadership. The former, "source," carries an understanding of delegated authority from a higher being or power, which must be exercised with great responsibility and knowledge. In other words, it does not imply that the wife should act like a mindless person in the relationship.

The latter, "leadership," which seems to be the most probable interpretation of "head" in this context, has its foundation on ability to provide good leadership. This is accomplished by loving others who are followers. We love them by listening to and respecting them. We also love them by carrying out given responsibilities in a manner that takes into consideration the feelings of others. We assess their strengths and weaknesses. Thus a wife, out of love and humility, submits to the husband. In conjunction, the husband must seek the holistic welfare of his wife and the entire household. He does this out of reverence for God and the position God has given him. This is due to the fact that Jesus Christ, expressed as the Head of the church, exercises His pre-eminence, supremacy, and authority as the leader of the church. Jesus Christ helps the church overcome evil forces and elements, within or without, that seek to undermine God's purpose for His people.

25 Husbands, love your wives, even as Christ also loved the church, and gave himself for it; 26 That he might sanctify and cleanse it with the washing of water by the word, 27 That he might present it to himself a glorious church, not having spot, or wrinkle, or any such thing; but that it should be holy and without blemish. 28 So ought men to love their wives as their own bodies. He that loveth his wife loveth himself.

The Greek word *agapao* (**ag-ap-AH-o**), used in verse 25 for "love," is rooted in an understanding of a person who has unconditionally subordinated his or her own desires, inclinations, and personality for the benefit of others in a relationship context. It expresses an idea of an intention and activities that are based on virtues that encourage people to act by saving, building, and restoring others in love.

Jesus Christ expressed this kind of love to the church when He vicariously laid down His life so that the church could be born, developed, and expanded. In Paul's epistle to the Philippians, he states that Christ unselfishly restrained Himself from engaging in a lifestyle that would put personal glory over and above God's purpose. Christ, out of love and devotion,

had to make "himself of no reputation" (Philippians 2:7) so He could fully serve God's purpose for the church. The key motivation for His life was to fulfill God's purpose by serving the ultimate needs of God's people through a shameful, redemptive death on the Cross. In the same way, husbands are admonished to follow the example of Christ to unconditionally and sacrificially serve the holistic—spiritual, physical, psychological, emotional, economic and material—needs of their wives. This analogy or concept of how to sacrificially express love for the sake of others should not be misunderstood as a requirement for wives to over-depend on their husbands for everything. This reason is that although Christ loves the church, gave Himself for it, and still serves consistently its needs, God has also given to the church spiritual and moral responsibilities. These must be carried out with great maturity and decorum. After all, the Scriptures teach that, as a result of the grace of Christ's redemptive work of love, believers must act as "workers together with Him" (2 Corinthians 6:1, NKJV).

In Ephesians 5:26–27, the love that Christ expressed to fulfill God's divine purpose on earth is presented as being motivated by the sanctifying and cleansing of the church. Sanctification and cleansing of the Christ's church lead to its glorification and splendor in the midst of a world system characterized by sin and darkness. This implies that in a marital context, it is important to work toward values of purity and true spirituality of thoughts and actions, just as Christ purposed for the church. From this perspective, the Christian household must learn to refrain from building its hope on the foundations of material wealth, fame, and mere human legacies that gratify the flesh and oneself.

The *agape* (**ag-AH-pay**) love of Christ in the heart, and motivation to live in harmony and holiness to bring glory to God, should be the central foundation on which husbands and wives build their homes.

In verse 28, the apostle Paul re-emphasizes the basic foundations that God put in place for Adam and Eve (Genesis 2:23–25). This imagery of the marital relationship, in which Adam declared Eve as the "bone of my bones, and flesh of my flesh," proclaims forcefully a unique kind of spiritual and bodily union (2:23). It also declares an identification in which Adam's heart was prepared to love his wife despite her weaknesses and failures. This means, without any reservation, he understood that his wife was part of his own spiritual, physical, psychological, and emotional living frame. This is an application of Jesus's second greatest commandment that we love our neighbor as ourselves (Matthew 22:39). In this case, one's spouse is the closest neighbor and each one should think of the other as he or she would of himself or herself. It gives a clear picture of how Christ loved the church, His own body, and died for it.

29 For no man ever yet hated his own flesh; but nourisheth and cherisheth it, even as the Lord the church: 30 For we are members of his body, of his flesh, and of his bones.

The two key words in these verses are "nourisheth" (Gk. *ektrepho*, **ek-TREF-o**) and "cherisheth" (Gk. *thalpo*, **THAL-po**). The word "nourisheth" can be defined, in a generic sense, as providing sustenance and attending carefully to others' necessities of life. It means that the husband has been endowed with the godly responsibility of participating in the personal life of his wife. He is to meet her holistic needs in a manner that brings about progress in the marriage relationship, as ordained by God. However, this idea does not mean that the wife is socially, psychologically, or economically inferior to the husband. The author is simply emphasizing the husband's responsibility to play his role as a God-ordained leader of the family or household.

Second, by the use of the word "cherisheth," the writer is referring to a husband's promise to his wife to nurture, protect, and shelter her emotionally, physically, psychologically, and spiritually in all situations. A marriage relationship and Christian family that thrives on mutual support are informed and influenced by God's way of expressing love.

31 For this cause shall a man leave his father and mother, and shall be joined unto his wife, and they two shall be one flesh. 32 This is a great mystery: but I speak concerning Christ and the church.

Verse 31 seems to be the central and organizing phrase in the periscope of verses 22–33. These verses focus on marriage life and building an authentic relationship in a family context based on true love. The key phrases "shall a man leave," "joined unto his wife" and "shall be one flesh" are grounded on Genesis 2:24. Marriage has been presented as the fundamental relationship between a man and woman. It requires characteristics of devotion that inspire transactions of self-sacrifice, deep affection, and total commitment. The new bond and obligation that marriage involves transcend any attachment or commitment to other forms of relationships that are outside the marriage context. People must "leave" anything (except worshiping God) that stands between the love relationship between husbands and wives. The "joining," in this context, is a work of God's grace. It is also the corresponding responsibility of the man and woman, who are involved in the marriage, to mutually extend their love and personalities to each other in a special manner based on true love. This approach suggests a covenant relationship. In this covenant relationship, God's power and grace enable the two people to be bonded to each other in love. Because they have become "one flesh," they are bonded together in a corporeal relationship and are sustained by mutual respect and love for each other. Each completely needs the other.

In Ephesians 5:32, Paul connected the marriage relationship with the "great mystery" of God's plan of salvation. This plan was concealed but was later unfolded through the redemptive work of Christ and the ministry of His apostles. The Greek word used for "mystery" was *musterion* (**moos-TAY-ree-on**). Its use in this context denotes some particular deep truth about Christ's great love and concern for the church, which cannot be fully grasped by the power of the mind without the help of the Holy Spirit.

33 Nevertheless let every one of you in particular so love his wife even as himself; and the wife see that she reverence her husband.

Here, the apostle Paul summarizes the quality of marriage relationship necessary for building a healthy Christian home by once again admonishing the husband to "love his wife" and the wife to "see that she reverence her husband." This is the model that Christ laid down in the Scriptures.

Ephesians 6:1 Children, obey your parents in the Lord: for this is right. 2 Honour thy father and mother; which is the first commandment with promise; 3 That it may be well with thee, and thou mayest live long on the earth.

This new chapter opens with a shift from husband-wife relationship to a relationship between parents and children. In this context, Paul now lays out reciprocal duties and responsibilities between parents and children. First, children were instructed to obey their parents, similar to the preceding exhortation that was given to wives to submit to their husbands. This pattern of instruction seems to follow the divine structure and order that must exist within the framework of God's idea of delegated authority and leadership. This delegated authority and leadership has been structured on the heavenly framework of "ordered relationships." Children have been instructed to "honour thy father and mother" through an appeal to Old Testament Scriptures (v. 2). This appeal is to reinforce divine and ordered spiritual authority that has been structured from God's perspective (Exodus 20:12; Deuteronomy 5:16).

There are two basic elements that easily catch the attention of the reader. First, it is "right" for children to obey their parents in the Lord (Ephesians 6:1). Second, the writer reminds children that the Old Testament commandment quoted in this passage was the only one that had a promise attached to it. On one hand, the word "right," used in this discourse, was probably because it was traditionally accepted and proper behavior in that society for children to obey their parents. On the other hand, the word "promise" seems to bring encouragement to children that their obedience to parents has both personal and community implications. The personal implication emphasizes that because children listened to their parents' correction, leadership, and teachings, they are prepared to live morally and spiritually decent lives. Effectively, this line of action will prevent the children from falling prey to temptations and lifestyles that may be destructive to their future progress or well-being. In terms of community life, children's disobedience to parents may lead to a breakdown of family bonds, which foster generational continuity. The result would be a community's eventual destruction.

4 And, ye fathers, provoke not your children to wrath: but bring them up in the nurture and admonition of the Lord.

Parents have been instructed not to "provoke" (Gk. *parorgizo*, **par-org-ID-zo**) their children to anger. The etymology of the word "provoke" from the original Greek connotes an idea of a capricious, domineering, and over-stretched exercise of authority by parents on their children. Parents were instructed not to put unreasonably harsh demands or expectations on their children, to refrain from always being negative and condemning, and to treat their children fairly and without humiliating them. But parents should be intentional in training, educating, nurturing, and loving their children, by the Lord's assistance, in ways that will prepare children for success in both secular and Christian communities. Parents should realize that their children are God's gift as a heritage. Therefore, parents are responsible to love, discipline, teach, and care for their children in a way that brings glory to God.

Sources:

Arrington, French L., and Roger Stronstad, eds. *Life in the Spirit New Testament Commentary.* Grand Rapids, MI: Zondervan, 1999. 1070, 1074.

Keener, Craig S. *The IVP Bible Background Commentary: New Testament.* Downers Grove, IL: InterVarsity Press, 1993. 551.

New Testament Greek Lexicon. Bible Study Tools.com. http://www.biblestudytools.com/lexicons/greek/ (accessed October 24, 2011).

The NIV Study Bible. 10th Anniversary Edition. Grand Rapids, MI: Zondervan, 1995. 1800-1801.

Vine, W. E. *Vine's Complete Expository Dictionary of Old and New Testament Words. With Topical Index.* Edited by Merrill F. Unger and William White, Jr. Nashville, TN: Thomas Nelson Publishers, 1996.

Say It Correctly

Nurture. NUR-cher.
Admonition. ad-muh-NISH-un.

Daily Bible Readings

MONDAY
God Is Love
(1 John 4:7-12)

TUESDAY
God's Gift of Love
(John 3:16-21)

WEDNESDAY
The Proof of God's Love
(Romans 5:6-11)

THURSDAY
The Example of Jesus' Love
(John 13:1-9)

FRIDAY
Abiding in Christ's Love
(John 15:9-17)

SATURDAY
Following the Commands of Christ
(1 John 3:18-24)

SUNDAY
Following the Example of Christ
(Ephesians 5:21-6:4)

Teaching Tips

Words You Should Know

Praetorian Guard (Philippians 1:13, RSV, NAS)—Roman imperial bodyguard or member of troops that were assigned to the governors of various Roman provinces.

Teacher Preparation

Unifying Principle—Motives and Messages. In a media-driven world, we hear many messages without fully knowing what motivates the "messenger." Paul claimed that regardless of the person's intentions, the result was still that Christ is proclaimed in every way.

A. Pray for your students and lesson clarity.

B. Prayerfully study the entire lesson.

C. Complete the companion *Precepts For Living Personal Study Guide®*.

D. Bring slips of paper to class.

O—Open the Lesson

A. Open with prayer—praying the Lesson Aim.

B. Give each class member a slip of paper and ask them to do the following: Share a time when your faith was challenged.

C. Instruct them not to write their names on the papers and pass them to you. Read a few of their responses aloud and discuss them.

D. Read today's In Focus story. Discuss the fact that when faced with a life-threatening situation, our faith may be challenged.

P—Present the Scriptures

A. Ask for a volunteer to read the Focal Verses.

B. Use The People, Places, and Times, Background, At-A-Glance outline, and More Light on the Text sections to drive the discussion of the verses.

E—Explore the Meaning

A. Review the information under Search the Scriptures, Discuss the Meaning, and Lesson in Our Society. Discuss.

B. Examine why most believers gain strength through trials and suffering.

N—Next Steps for Application

A. Summarize the lesson.

B. Remind students to read the Daily Bible Readings.

C. Receive prayer requests and close with prayer.

Worship Guide

For the Superintendent or Teacher
Theme: Proclaiming Christ
Song: "Pass Me Not, O Gentle Savior"
Devotional Reading:
Psalm 119:169-176
Prayer

Proclaiming Christ

Bible Background • PHILIPPIANS 1:12-30
Printed Text • PHILIPPIANS 1:15-26 | Devotional Reading • PSALM 119:169-176

—————————— Aim for Change ——————————

By the end of the lesson, we will: COMPREHEND Paul's message of joy in the proclamation of the gospel of Jesus Christ; REFLECT on the variety of motives for proclaiming the gospel of Jesus Christ; and FASHION a personal proclamation of the gospel.

————————— In Focus —————————

JAN
6th

Carl and Brenda drove home from the doctor's office in silence. They both had a hundred thoughts passing through their heads. The doctor had actually said the word cancer.

If he were to live at all, Carl would have to undergo surgery and extensive chemotherapy. They would have to break the news to their children and grandchildren. Carl would also have to tell the church.

"Well," Carl finally broke their silence, "this will certainly put my faith to the test. Now I must live what I have preached for so long."

"Baby, don't try to deny what you are really feeling about this, not for my sake, not for the children's, and not for the church's sake, either," Brenda responded.

"It's not that," Carl said. "I know that people will be watching me. It's important to me that I will be able to praise the Lord throughout this ordeal, whether it means life or death. If I can't, I'll end up feeling like my entire life, not to mention my faith, has been just a front."

Many things come into our lives that challenge our public witness. People are watching to see if we are for real. Paul teaches us how to walk with God through the fires of life.

—————————— Keep in Mind ——————————

"What then? notwithstanding, every way, whether in pretence, or in truth, Christ is preached; and I therein do rejoice, yea, and will rejoice" (Philippians 1:18).

"What then? notwithstanding, every way, whether in pretence, or in truth, Christ is preached; and I therein do rejoice, yea, and will rejoice" (Philippians 1:18).

Focal Verses

KJV **Philippians 1:15** Some indeed preach Christ even of envy and strife; and some also of good will:

16 The one preach Christ of contention, not sincerely, supposing to add affliction to my bonds:

17 But the other of love, knowing that I am set for the defence of the gospel.

18 What then? notwithstanding, every way, whether in pretence, or in truth, Christ is preached; and I therein do rejoice, yea, and will rejoice.

19 For I know that this shall turn to my salvation through your prayer, and the supply of the Spirit of Jesus Christ,

20 According to my earnest expectation and my hope, that in nothing I shall be ashamed, but that with all boldness, as always, so now also Christ shall be magnified in my body, whether it be by life, or by death.

21 For to me to live is Christ, and to die is gain.

22 But if I live in the flesh, this is the fruit of my labour: yet what I shall choose I wot not.

23 For I am in a strait betwixt two, having a desire to depart, and to be with Christ; which is far better:

24 Nevertheless to abide in the flesh is more needful for you.

25 And having this confidence, I know that I shall abide and continue with you all for your furtherance and joy of faith;

26 That your rejoicing may be more abundant in Jesus Christ for me by my coming to you again.

NLT **Philippians 1:15** It's true that some are preaching out of jealousy and rivalry. But others preach about Christ with pure motives.

16 They preach because they love me, for they know I have been appointed to defend the Good News.

17 Those others do not have pure motives as they preach about Christ. They preach with selfish ambition, not sincerely, intending to make my chains more painful to me.

18 But that doesn't matter. Whether their motives are false or genuine, the message about Christ is being preached either way, so I rejoice. And I will continue to rejoice.

19 For I know that as you pray for me and the Spirit of Jesus Christ helps me, this will lead to my deliverance.

20 For I fully expect and hope that I will never be ashamed, but that I will continue to be bold for Christ, as I have been in the past. And I trust that my life will bring honor to Christ, whether I live or die.

21 For to me, living means living for Christ, and dying is even better.

22 But if I live, I can do more fruitful work for Christ. So I really don't know which is better.

23 I'm torn between two desires: I long to go and be with Christ, which would be far better for me.

24 But for your sakes, it is better that I continue to live.

25 Knowing this, I am convinced that I will remain alive so I can continue to help all of you grow and experience the joy of your faith.

26 And when I come to you again, you will have even more reason to take pride in Christ Jesus because of what he is doing through me.

The People, Places, and Times

Prison. During the time that the New Testament was written, people could be imprisoned for nonpayment of debt (Matthew 5:25-26), political insurrection, criminal acts (Luke 23:19, 25), and for certain religious practices (Acts 8:3). The apostle Paul was often in prison. On one occasion, he and Silas were placed under the charge of a lone jailer, who put them in an inner cell and placed their feet in stocks (Acts 16:23-24). The inner cell was probably for maximum security or solitary confinement.

In Jerusalem, Paul was detained in a Roman barracks (Acts 23:11-18). In Caesarea, Paul's confinement did allow him some freedom, and he was allowed to have visitors (Acts 23:33-35). As he awaited trial in Rome, Paul was guarded constantly under a type of house arrest (Acts 28:16-17, 30). While there, he met his own expenses, and was free to receive visitors and preach the Gospel.

Roman Empire. In the early days of the Christian movement, several emperors ruled the empire. Most of Paul's ministry is believed to have occurred under the reign of Gaius (Caligula, A.D. 37-41) and his aging uncle Claudius (A.D. 41-54). Claudius reportedly expelled some Jews from Rome because they were creating disturbances with their efforts to spread the Gospel. It is believed that both Paul and Peter were martyred during Nero's reign (A.D. 54-68), perhaps in connection with the burning of Rome in A.D. 64, an event for which Nero blamed Christians.

Background

It's interesting how some people can devote themselves to encouraging others in the midst of their own struggle. Many terminally -ill children, instead of feeling sorry for themselves, have been a source of encour-agement for the families they leave behind.

Paul was encouraging to his Christian family. Even as he sat in prison, his letter was full of love, encouragement, and instruction for those who were carrying on the work. It is very likely that his co-laborers in Christ were feeling worse about Paul's imprisonment than he was.

Paul recognized that his release from prison was uncertain. However, as he contemplated his fate, Paul did not lose faith in God. He did not become bitter or angry about his circumstances. He did not cease the work to which he had been called. Through good times and trials, Paul remained faithful to God and his task.

At-A-Glance

1. A New Effort (Philippians 1:15-18)
2. A Certain Victory (vv. 19-26)

In Depth

1. A New Effort (Philippians 1:15-18)

Paul's confinement led to many new efforts to spread the Gospel. No one particular movement could do the work. Some followers were stronger because Paul was in jail. Perhaps they felt they had to fill in the gap left by Paul's absence.

Paul called into question the motives of those who were preaching about Christ. Some were preaching out of "envy and strife" (v. 15), while others were preaching out of genuine goodwill. Some may have been jealous of the attention Paul was receiving despite his imprisonment.

This very well may have been the case in Rome where Christianity had been established prior to Paul's coming. His presence there may have posed a threat to the Christian leaders who were already there. Some were likely vying for Paul's leadership role within the Christian community, assuming he would not be released. His rivals must have felt that their success would cause Paul to become jealous, perhaps adding to his troubles. Instead, he rejoiced that others were spreading the Gospel, regardless of their motives.

Paul recognized that the Gospel is powerful enough to transcend human pettiness. If this were not so, the spread of the Gospel would have stopped at Calvary. There is no human who is truly worthy to preach the Gospel. It is fallen human nature to be affected by envy, strife, egotism, narcissism, and partisanship. From the pulpit, all kinds of motives fuel the Sunday morning sermon. Still, the Gospel is preached as people come to Christ.

Paul's solution was to continue making the Gospel known and rejoice that it came through multiple means. The Good News cannot be held hostage to human imperfection. No one can alter its power. Not even the worst example of Christianity can take away the power of the Gospel. Paul's message has many implications for the Christian community today.

2. A Certain Victory (vv. 19-26)

Paul was confident that his experience—of being both jailed and harassed by rival Christians—would lead to victory. He wrote confidently of salvation as a result of his circumstances (v. 19). Some translations refer to Paul's "deliverance," and others suggest that he was referring to salvation in its fullest sense. The latter is that full redemption would be realized through Christ.

The apostle was sure of his dependency on Christ for the impending victory. He quoted Job 13:16 (the Septuagint—the Greek translation of the Jewish Scriptures) where Job looked confidently to his ultimate vindication. There is no indication,

however, that Paul was certain of his release from prison, nor did he appear to be excessively concerned about it. Paul's primary concern was not with life or death, as determined by the outcome of his trial. He appears to have been chiefly concerned with his own constitution, that he would not be afflicted with any manner of shame. Instead, he hoped for Christ to be "magnified" (Philippians 1:20). Paul was not looking to be a hero. He was willing to meet his fate, whether life or death, so that all could see how much Christ meant to him.

Paul stood at the crossroads between life and death. The apostle found favor in either outcome. Paul had no desire to escape death in favor of life. He viewed death as portal into the greater realm of a life already filled with greatness. To Paul, life was Christ, who gave Paul's life meaning. Apart from Him, life held no meaning or purpose. Death, therefore, did not equal loss but gain. He knew that death was not final. Rather, it was an extension of his marching orders as a soldier in the army of the Lord. The life he knew in Christ would only become more magnificent through death.

Conversely, if Paul's life was spared, he viewed it as an invitation to do more fruitful work for the kingdom. His only interest in being released from jail was that it would allow him to continue his ministry. He could preach the Gospel a while longer. He could continue to encourage the churches that had become so dear to him. Through life, he could continue to live and do more for Christ.

For years, Paul had been working in the trenches as a missionary—spreading the Gospel and encouraging and guiding the faithful. His hard work was just beginning to show results. Like a farmer who has been tending to trees hoping they will bear fruit, Paul is longing to see evidence of the harvest.

He desires to stay because there is so much to be done.

The two options the apostle faced did cause some divided feelings, which he expressed in verse 23. Understandably, Paul was pulled between his two options. Not that he viewed either as negative. Instead, in his heart he longed to be with Christ. His was not a morbid desire, however. Paul probably envisioned a life with Christ too wonderful for the human spirit to totally conceive.

On the other hand, he wanted to be of service to his fellow Christians. He viewed the continuance of life as being necessary only for the sake of the Philippians (v. 24). Paul was willing for his life to be used in whatever way the Lord deemed necessary. The Philippians were openly proud of Paul, whom they, in a sense, regarded as their own special apostle. Paul lovingly reminded them that Christ, not he, must remain the subject of their boasting. If he was to return to them, they should rejoice in the works of Jesus Christ, not the apostle Paul.

The apostle Paul's ability to have hope, even in the most hopeless of circumstances, came from his own experience of being granted new life after his former life had passed on. The boldness he possessed came from his certainty that Christ would be honored by him, whether through his life or his death.

Search the Scriptures

1. For what motives were some preaching the Gospel (Philippians 1:15-17)?

2. Why were motives unimportant in preaching the Gospel (v. 18)?

3. For what reason did Paul want to remain alive (v. 25)?

4. Of what benefit would his continued life be to the Philippians (v. 26)?

Discuss the Meaning

1. Paul reached a high spiritual point that caused him to rejoice, whether the outcome of his trial meant life or death. How did he reach such a point of spiritual maturity?

2. Why were some of the Christians strengthened by Paul's imprisonment? Why did they not become fearful that the same thing might happen to them?

Lesson in Our Society

Every Christian professes belief in eternal life. Yet, very often, when we think of death, we get scared at the uncertainty of our fate. Perhaps this is because we do not feel certain about our salvation. Some may doubt Christ's promise.

Our enslaved ancestors sang often of heaven—of the streets paved with gold, the pearly gates, where the Sabbath would have no end. They longed for the day when "trouble will be no more" and every person would live in freedom and equality. Perhaps because there has been general improvement in our social and economic standing, many of us now appear to place more value on life on earth than eternal life. No matter what attainments life holds, it can never compare to the future glory of life with Christ Jesus. As Christians, we must rejoice in our assurance of eternal life and leave the matter of when we will go to heaven in the hands of God.

Make It Happen

If you were told today that you may not live much longer, what preparation would you make to insure that Christ would be glorified through your experience of passing from life to death?

Follow the Spirit

What God wants me to do:

_____

_____

_____

_____

Remember Your Thoughts

Special insights I have learned:

_____

_____

_____

_____

More Light on the Text

Philippians 1:15-26

15 Some indeed preach Christ even of envy and strife; and some also of good will: 16 The one preach Christ of contention, not sincerely, supposing to add affliction to my bonds: 17 But the other of love, knowing that I am set for the defence of the gospel.

Paul's imprisonment has yielded positive results: a) the Gospel is being made known all over the region including the official residence of the governor; b) many of the brothers are now preaching the Good News with boldness. However, Paul separates these preachers into two groups according to their motives. The first group, he says, preaches out of a wrong motive "of envy and strife." This group is prompted by "envy" (Gk. *phthonos,* **FTHON-os**), meaning jealousy or ill will, and "strife" (Gk. *eris,* **ER-is**), meaning, rivalry, or wrangling or contention. Paul goes on to illustrate in verse 16 how this

group's preaching is motivated by evil: They preach Christ out of contention, not sincerely, not with a clean motive, but rather with an ulterior motive—"to add affliction to my bonds." The word "contention" translates the Greek *eritheia* (**er-ith-I-ah**), which means, in simple terms, selfishness or a desire to put oneself forward. The word translated to mean "affliction" here is the Greek *thlipsis* (**THLIP-sis**). It can mean "burdened" (2 Corinthians 8:13), "affliction" (Mark 4:17; 13:19; Acts 7:10-11; 2 Corinthians 2:4; 4:17; 6:4), "tribulation" (Matthew 13:21; 24:21, 29; Mark 13:24; John 16:33; Acts 14:22), "persecution" (Acts 11:19), and "trouble" (1 Corinthians 7:28).

Who were these men who were preaching out of contention and selfish ambition with the intention of adding to Paul's burden? Paul does not seem as much concerned with these people and their evil plans as he was about the positive result of their preaching, as we shall see in Philippians 1:18. He does not intend to occupy himself or boggle his audience's mind with negativity. He leaves us with no answer. However, scholars have advanced a number of proposals as to who these people were. Certain preachers in Rome had attained some prominence before Paul's arrival. His presence in Rome and the spreading of his fame and the Gospel throughout the region were beginning to affect their prestige (vv. 13-14). The preachers' names seem to have been relegated to the background—not mentioned as often as before the apostle's arrival. Hence, they became envious and contentious; thus, their motive for preaching the Gospel was affected. Bear in mind that they were preaching the true Gospel with positive results, but their intentions and motives were bad and this was a source of concern for Paul, who didn't want the Philippian Christians to lose sight of the Gospel. Later in this book, Paul exhorts the

Philippians to be one in the mind of Christ, not putting oneself forward or being selfish (Philippians 2:3). Similarly, James denounces selfishness or self-promoting "in your hearts" (James 3:14).

The second group Paul refers to preached out "of good will" (Philippians 1:15b) and "love." This is evident from the phrase, "knowing that I am set for the defence of the gospel" (v. 17). This group was motivated by love for Paul and the Gospel, which he proclaimed. These people did not feel indignant about Paul because of his fame that was spreading around the region. Unlike the former group, their focus was not on themselves. They heralded Christ, out of love for Him and the Gospel, and out of concern for Paul and his tribulation. Paul prayed for them to have this type of love: "And this I pray, that your love may abound still more and more in knowledge and all discernment" (1:9, NKJV). The clause in verse 17, "knowing that I am set for the defense of the gospel," means that they are also motivated by the fact that Paul has been "set" (Gk. *keimai*, **KI-mahee**), i.e., destined or appointed. This refers either to the trial he is about to face for the sake of the Gospel or that his call or ministry is for the "defence" (Gk. *apologia*, **ap-ol-og-EE-ah**) of the Gospel for which he was imprisoned.

18 What then? notwithstanding, every way, whether in pretence, or in truth, Christ is preached; and I therein do rejoice, yea, and will rejoice.

Rather than moaning over the selfishly motivated preaching of the first group aimed at increasing Paul's burden and suffering and rather than dwelling in self-pity and attracting sympathy for such unchristian behavior toward him, Paul focused on the result of their preaching. Here he says, "What then?" or "That doesn't matter" (NLT).

It is another way of saying that what matters is the outcome of their preaching, which turned out to be positive. Whether they were preaching to hurt him is not the main concern. The most important concern is advancing the Gospel. This is clear from the statement, "Notwithstanding, every way, whether in pretence, or in truth, Christ is preached." What matters to Paul is not what the people are doing to him but rather what they are doing for the Gospel. From here, we can learn one truth: The Lord will work out His desired purpose through the Gospel without respect to how it is preached or the motive of the preachers. To Paul, it did not matter. What mattered is that in "every way"—whether in pretense, as by those with selfish motives, or "in truth" as by those who preach with sincere heart to glorify the Lord—"Christ is preached." This is true today, too.

"Pretence" (Gk. *prophasis*, **PROF-as-is**), is the same word used to describe the prayers of the scribes (Mark 12:40; also Acts 27:30): an outward show, cloak, or pretext. It is the opposite of sincerity. Regardless of the outward insincere showing in preaching, in verse 18, Paul expresses his joy found in the accompanying furtherance of the Gospel: "I therein do rejoice, yea, and will rejoice."

19 For I know that this shall turn to my salvation through your prayer, and the supply of the Spirit of Jesus Christ,

In this section, Paul expresses his confidence in the prayer of the brethren and optimism that he would be set free. This also makes him rejoice. The Greek preposition "for" (Gk. *gar*, **gar**) connects the preceding statement with the assurance of his deliverance. Paul's use of *eido* (**I-do**) means to know, to see, to perceive with the eyes or by any of the senses. It has the sense of certainty and confidence that all will turn out well for him in the end (Romans 8:28). The result will be his deliverance. Paul's expressed knowledge here does not mean he had information of his possible deliverance but rather that he had personal conviction that, through the prayers of the people and the work of the Holy Spirit, he would be set free from prison. However, some other scholars regard this as Paul's confidence of ultimate salvation. Scholar Gerald Hawthorne observes the direct similarity in Greek construction here: "This will turn out for my deliverance" (Philippians 1:19, RSV) with Job's statement (*Philippians: Word Biblical Commentary*, 39; Job 13:16, Septuagint, LXX). Paul probably sees his situation as similar to Job's, and because Job was vindicated, Paul is convinced that he would be saved and vindicated as well. Hence, he says, "I know that this shall turn to my salvation" (Philippians 1:19). Although Paul uses "salvation" in the eschatological sense of being saved at the last day, his use here of "salvation" (Gk. *soteria*, **so-tay-REE-ah**) refers to a possible immediate release from the Roman jail. Trusting the faithfulness of God, exemplified by God's deliverance of Job, coupled with the prayers of the saints and the working of the Holy Spirit, Paul is persuaded that he would be set free.

20 According to my earnest expectation and my hope, that in nothing I shall be ashamed, but that with all boldness, as always, so now also Christ shall be magnified in my body, whether it be by life, or by death. This conviction is expressed in his "earnest expectation and ... hope" based on the confidence he has in Christ. He has two convictions. The first is that whatever happens, he would not be ashamed. The Spirit will not let him down. Writing to the Romans, Paul says he is not ashamed of the

Gospel of Christ (Romans 1:16, see also Acts 5:41). The idea here is that although he is looking forward to his possible release from prison, the Spirit will not allow him an "easy way" out of his misery—by denying Christ, for example. The second conviction, contrary to the first, is that he would wax bold in proclaiming the Gospel, as he has always done, but more so now. The meaning is clear; "Christ shall be magnified" in Paul—literally, in Paul's "body" (Gk. *soma*, **SO-mah**), which means his entire personality (v. 20). Paul will continue to preach the Gospel and endure hardship, "whether it be by life," if he is released from prison, "or by death," if he is executed. His goal is that Christ would be magnified through it all. In either circumstance, he would remain faithful to the end so that Christ's name would be lifted. This is a show of courage, deeply resolute conviction, and resignation to the service of the Lord Jesus.

21 For to me to live is Christ, and to die is gain. 22 But if I live in the flesh, this is the fruit of my labour: yet what I shall choose I wot not. 23 For I am in a strait betwixt two, having a desire to depart, and to be with Christ; which is far better: Paul's conviction and courage are demonstrated in his total resignation to whatever comes his way as expressed in verses 21-23. The use of the phrase "for to me" (Gk. *gar emoi*, **gar em-OY**) is purposely put here for emphasis—to draw our attention to Paul's personal conviction regarding life and death. Paul gives new meaning to both "life" and "death." To him "living is Christ," which means, among other interpretations, "life means Christ." The essence of living is embodied in Christ Jesus; the fulfillment of life is only to be found in Christ. Paul's very existence is in Christ—whatever he does is inspired through his resolute relationship with Christ and for Him. To Paul, life would be meaningless without Christ, to whom Paul owes his existence (Romans 14:7-9). He dedicates his whole being to Christ and His cause, to love and obey Him in everything and at all times, and to trust Him in all circumstances. His resolution to live for Christ does not mean a life free from problems and difficulties. Instead, it means living for Christ and preaching the Gospel in spite of problems and difficulties: imprisonment (Philippians 1:7, 13, 16), afflictions (1:16; 4:14), suffering (1:29; 3:10), struggles (1:30), and all types of tribulation, both physical and emotional (2 Corinthians 11:23-27). It is a resolution to follow Jesus with no turning back. Paul's life and ministry were characterized by unimaginable suffering, as we can see from these and other accounts of his life.

On the one hand, for Paul to go on living means leading a dedicated and fruitful life for Christ, (Philippians 1:21a, 22a); on the other hand, for Paul "to die is gain" (v. 21b). He knows that death means an immediate experience of the presence of Christ.

Paul is so engrossed in the Gospel and in the reality of eternity that living means working and living for Christ. Dying is even more profitable because he would be with his Lord forever. This should be the hope of every believer. Paul is so confident of the reality of heaven and the assurance of resurrection that he says, "If in this life only we have hope in Christ, we are of all men most miserable" (1 Corinthians 15:19). This assurance is found in the fact of Christ's own resurrection, the first fruit of them that slept (v. 20).

Here, Paul is reiterating his total resignation to the Lord. Whatever comes his way, whether death or life, or release from prison, he has turned his life and will over to that of the Lord Jesus Christ.

24 Nevertheless to abide in the flesh is more needful for you. 25 And having this confidence, I know that I shall abide and continue with you all for your furtherance and joy of faith; 26 That your rejoicing may be more abundant in Jesus Christ for me by my coming to you again.

Paul also desires to remain alive in the flesh for the Philippians' sakes. His love for the church is so strong, and he knows that they would definitely need him, that he desires "to abide in the flesh" even though this meant he would face more persecution and suffering. It would also mean more "fruit" (Philippians 1:22) and "honor" (v. 20, NLT) for the Lord. He never allowed his subjective dream to override his objective desire. Rather, he places the needs of others above his own desires. In verse 24, the use of the particle, "nevertheless" (Gk. *de*, **deh**) —which can be translated as moreover —shows Paul's consideration of others, this time the members of the Philippian church, above his own needs and wishes. Why does he prefer to remain in the flesh for their sake? The answer can be found in Philippians 3:1-3, 19, and 4:2, where Paul writes about needs and problems facing the church. To Paul, the need to address these problems and offer further pastoral care to the believers in Philippi weighs heavier than his own desires.

This self-denial is further expressed in 1:25-26. Here, Paul expresses his confidence for his release as he writes, "Having this confidence, I know that I shall abide and continue with you all" (v. 25).

Paul speaks with absolute assurance that he would be released from prison. His release would only be useful for "your furtherance and joy of faith," that is, for their spiritual growth, which produces joy.

"Your furtherance" (Gk. *prokope*, **prok-op-AY**) or progress, means spiritual growth: in love (1:9), in knowledge (1:9), in fruitfulness (1:11), and in obedience (2:12). Such growth will give them joy in their worship and relationship with the Lord, in the faith. His release would also increase their rejoicing in the Lord Jesus Christ on his behalf. Paul's presence with them would increase their dedication to the Lord. They would realize God's grace working through Paul's vindication from prison. In Philippians 1:26, the phrase "my coming to you again" implies that Paul visited the church before (Acts 16:11-40; 20:5-6; 2 Corinthians 8:1-5). According to scholars Trent Butler and Merrill Unger, Paul's wish was granted: He was released and re-visited the church in Philippi during his third missionary journey (Butler, 1082; Unger, 968-977).

Sources:
Butler, Trent, ed. *Holman Bible Dictionary.* Nashville, TN: Holman Bible Publishers, 1991. 1082, 1138, 1139, 1207-1209.
Hawthorne, Gerald F. *Philippians: Word Biblical Commentary,* Vol. 43. Waco, TX: Word Books, 1983. 39.
New Testament Greek Lexicon. Bible Study Tools.com. http://www.biblestudytools.com/lexicons/greek/ (accessed October 25, 2011).
Unger, Merrill F. *The New Unger's Bible Dictionary.* Chicago, IL: Moody Press, 1988. 968-977.

Say It Correctly

Philippians. fi-LIP-ee-uhnz.
Praetorian. pray-TOR-ee-uhn.

Daily Bible Readings

MONDAY
Praising God in Word and Life
(Psalm 119:169-176)

TUESDAY
Giving Glory to God
(Matthew 5:13-16)

WEDNESDAY
Making the Word Fully Known
(Colossians 1:21-29)

THURSDAY
Sharing in the Gospel
(Philippians 1:1-7)

FRIDAY
Speaking the Word with Boldness
(Philippians 1:8-14)

SATURDAY
Toiling to Proclaim the Gospel
(1 Thessalonians 2:1-11)

SUNDAY
Proclaiming Christ in Every Way
(Philippians 1:15-26)

Teaching Tips

Words You Should Know

A. Exalted—(Philippians 2:9) *huperupsoo* (Gk.)—Raised up high, honored.

B. Fashion—(v. 8) *schema* (Gk.)—External appearance.

Teacher Preparation

Unifying Principle—Attitude Counts. God exalted Jesus because of Jesus' selflessness, obedience, servanthood, and humility. Jesus talked about the importance of finding the best surroundings in which to grow in faith and serve others.

A. Pray for your students and lesson clarity.

B. Prayerfully read the entire lesson.

C. Complete the companion lesson in the *Precepts For Living Personal Study Guide®*.

O—Open the Lesson

A. Think of two or three possible dilemmas, such as deciding whether to report a neighbor who embezzled money from a job. Then ask the question, "What would Jesus do?" Discuss the proper approach to each dilemma, using the mind of Christ as the standard.

B. Read the In Focus story.

C. Discuss how it is often easy for even the most devoted Christian to get caught up in selfish desires, which may cloud thinking and affect decisions.

P—Present the Scriptures

A. Ask for a volunteer to read the Focal Verses.

B. Examine the verses, utilizing The People, Places, and Times, Background, the At-A-Glance outline, and More Light on the Text sections.

E—Explore the Meaning

A. Answer the Search the Scriptures questions.

B. Summarize the Discuss the Meaning, Lesson in Our Society, and Make It Happen sections.

C. Connect them to today's theme.

N—Next Steps for Application

A. Summarize the lesson.

B. Remind students to do their Daily Bible Readings.

C. Receive prayer requests and close with prayer.

Worship Guide

For the Superintendent or Teacher
Theme: Jesus' Humility and Exaltation
Song: "He Is King of Kings"
Devotional Reading: James 3:13-18
Prayer

Jesus' Humility and Exaltation

Bible Background • PHILIPPIANS 2:1-13
Printed Text • PHILIPPIANS 2:5-11 | Devotional Reading • JAMES 3:13-18

Aim for Change

By the end of the lesson, we will: ANALYZE Paul's description of God's exaltation of Jesus based on sacrifice and selflessness rather than power; VALUE selfless behavior rather than power; and ADOPT Christ-like humility as our personal lifestyle.

In Focus

Rev. Watkins just couldn't understand why Sister Jenkins had such opposition to the new facility the church was about to purchase. In the past, she had been such a loyal supporter of the church's programs. Rev. Watkins knew he could not always have the backing of every church member, but he prayed for understanding and insight.

JAN 13th

His prayer was answered a couple of weeks later when he went to visit Mother Turner, a longtime member of the church who was not able to get to church very often.

Without mentioning Sister Jenkins' name, he talked with Mother Turner about his concern and asked her to pray for him and the church in general.

"Pastor," Mother Turner said, "I don't get out much, but I do keep up with what's going on at my church. I know Myrtle Jenkins has been opposed to the new building. She's had her mind set on opening a day care center, and she wants to use space at the church to save money. She can't use the new church because of the way it's set up."

"So that's it." Pastor Watkins shook his head. "All that fuss was about what's good for her, not what's good for the church."

Many things come into our lives that challenge our public witness. People are watching to see if we are for real. Paul advises us to have the mind of Christ.

Keep in Mind

"Let this mind be in you, which was also in Christ Jesus"
(Philippians 2:5).

"Let this mind be in you, which was also in Christ Jesus"
(Philippians 2:5).

Focal Verses

KJV **Philippians 2:5** Let this mind be in you, which was also in Christ Jesus:

6 Who, being in the form of God, thought it not robbery to be equal with God:

7 But made himself of no reputation, and took upon him the form of a servant, and was made in the likeness of men:

8 And being found in fashion as a man, he humbled himself, and became obedient unto death, even the death of the cross.

9 Wherefore God also hath highly exalted him, and given him a name which is above every name:

10 That at the name of Jesus every knee should bow, of things in heaven, and things in earth, and things under the earth;

11 And that every tongue should confess that Jesus Christ is Lord, to the glory of God the Father.

NLT **Philippians 2:5** You must have the same attitude that Christ Jesus had.

6 Though he was God, he did not think of equality with God as something to cling to.

7 Instead, he gave up his divine privileges; he took the humble position of a slave and was born as a human being. When he appeared in human form,

8 he humbled himself in obedience to God and died a criminal's death on a cross.

9 Therefore, God elevated him to the place of highest honor and gave him the name above all other names,

10 that at the name of Jesus every knee should bow, in heaven and on earth and under the earth,

11 and every tongue confess that Jesus Christ is Lord, to the glory of God the Father.

The People, Places, and Times

Philippi. A city that was located in the Roman province of Macedonia where Paul did a great deal of missionary work. Paul's first visit to Philippi took place during his second missionary journey, an outgrowth of his Macedonian vision. He and a group of companions sailed from Troas to Neapolis, located on Macedonia's eastern shore. After they docked, the group traveled a few miles inland to Philippi.

It was at Philippi that Paul was miraculously delivered from bondage and the jailer was converted. Upon discovering that Paul was a Roman citizen, the magistrates there became nervous. They pleaded with Paul to leave both the jail and the city. (See Acts 16:12-40.)

Background

Chapter two begins Paul's second appeal to the Philippians. Apparently, division was brewing within the Philippian congregation. Co-workers in the church had become openly divided. Paul had already had the experience of seeing a church riddled with controversy and dissension.

The biggest battle facing the church at Philippi was their internal battle. In the previous lesson, Paul stated his refusal to let external circumstances control his attitudes (Philippians 1:12-18). The congregation could ill afford to let internal strife afflict their witness for Christ.

Paul spoke of his imprisonment in terms of its effect on the Philippian mission. He told them that his imprisonment had special significance for them because of the nature of their relationship to the apostle. The church was kind and loyal, but its status was threatened by dissension. It was in the midst of this exhortation to be one in spirit that Paul launched into this beautiful hymn of praise to our Lord Jesus and His humility.

At-A-Glance

1. The Humility of Jesus
(Philippians 2:5-8)
2. The Exaltation of Jesus (vv. 9-11)

In Depth

1. The Humility of Jesus (Philippians 2:5-8)

From the previous chapter, we know Paul was faced with the delicate task of rebuking the congregation he had just praised. He sought to enlist the Philippians' loyalty and faithfulness against the divisions that had arisen within the church.

The concern at Philippi was not so much about instruction in right and wrong as encouragement and guidance in the right will or spirit. Paul's appeal is for unity and self-denial as exemplified in Christ. Paul was not calling for the Philippians to despise themselves. He was calling for a refusal to let personal interests or advantages govern the course of one's life. He knew that the success of his appeal was dependent upon the degree to which the Philippians abided in the Spirit of Christ. If they were united in His bond, they would seek the unity and self-denial that is essential to the Christian's existence.

If they could do this, Paul's joy would be complete in that they would be like-minded, with the same love and on one accord. Many times people misinterpret the meaning of verse five, thinking that it means there must never be a difference of opinion. It does mean, however, that the body is committed to supporting the work of the church and that the will of God is fulfilled, regardless of personal opinion.

Love would provide the incentive for the desired goal of unity, humility, and concern for others. Love (*agape*) is to do good for another regardless of the cost to self. Paul fully understood the importance of self-effacement, or self-denial. More often than anything else, it is the self that gets in the way and causes conflict. It is impossible for Christian unity to exist in an atmosphere of self-centeredness.

Paul was concerned that the Philippians give themselves over to a mindset governed by Christ. The mind was already present within them because they were believers in Christ Jesus. Paul's admonition was that they activate (or reactivate) this already present mind among themselves.

Paul wanted to address those in Philippi given to self-exaltation. He wanted them to have a true image of humility, as demonstrated in the life of Jesus Christ. In Christ, the perfect example of self-effacement can be found, having voluntarily given up His divinity for humanity. Being in the form of God, Christ "made himself of no reputation" (v. 7) and in human form humbled himself and became obedient to the Father, even to His death on the Cross.

2. The Exaltation of Jesus (vv. 9-11)

While the foregoing section dealt with total debasement of Christ to the lowest depth of humiliation, this section deals with His unprecedented exaltation to the highest point of honor. While the last segment dealt with Christ's voluntary self-humiliation, this section deals with God exalting Him. In the former, Christ is the actor, the subject of the verbs; in the latter, God is the actor and the subject of the verbs, while Christ is the object.

Peter and James echoed this same teaching in their epistles when they wrote: "Humble yourselves therefore under the mighty hand of God, that he may exalt you in due time" (1 Peter 5:6) and "Humble yourselves in the sight of the Lord, and he shall lift you up" (James 4:10).

Search the Scriptures

1. After whom did Paul advise the Philippians to model themselves (Philippians 2:5)?

2. What role did Christ choose for Himself (v. 7)?

3. To what extent did God exalt Christ (vv. 9-11)?

Discuss the Meaning

1. How can we teach young people to be proud of their ancestry and at the same time to be humble and serve one another?

2. What are some ways we can exalt Jesus today?

Lesson in Our Society

Humility is not valued or praised very much in our society. Among the rich and famous, those who have given themselves to humility and service seem to garner little attention. Conversely, those who have earned a "bad boy" reputation for arrogance or self-absorption often become media darlings.

This is all the more reason that the Christian community must understand who we are and Whose we are. Our calling, as disciples, is to follow our leader and fashion ourselves to be like Christ as much as we can. Our efforts to do this will rarely earn us human praise. It will, however, be pleasing in the eyes of the Lord.

Make It Happen

Churches tend to have personalities, just as people do. In spite of its troubles at the time Paul wrote his letter, the Philippian congregation seemed to have a loving spirit with an inclination toward obedience. The humility in today's passage is immediately followed by encouragement from Paul to move forward based on the various abilities they already possessed.

What assets, gifts, or talents do you already possess that can be polished and enhanced to make you of greater benefit to the work of God's kingdom? Ask yourself whether you are willing to be used in this manner. If so, what steps must you take to get to that point? Are you willing to, as Paul did, offer yourself as a sacrifice for the benefit of fellow Christians and those who have yet to come to know Christ?

Follow the Spirit

What God wants me to do:

_____

_____

_____

_____

Remember Your Thoughts

Special insights I have learned:

_____

_____

_____

_____

More Light on the Text

Philippians 2:5-11

5 Let this mind be in you, which was also in Christ Jesus:

The Greek verb used here is *phroneo* (**fron-EH-o,** used also in v. 2) and is translated "let this mind (or attitude) be in you." Simply put, Paul says, "Have this frame of mind in you, which was also in Christ Jesus." It should be noted here that there are limits to what examples of Christ we, as Christians, can follow. We cannot follow His redemptive acts. The sacrificial suffering and death on the Cross for our salvation and divine justice are Christ's prerogatives; no person can copy it. What we can copy is the spirit that is basic to these acts: His love, humility, and servitude to others. These are the attitudes or disposition "which was also in Christ Jesus" (v. 5).

6 Who, being in the form of God, thought it not robbery to be equal with God:

In eternity, Christ was "in the form of God" (Gk. *en morphe theos*, **en mor-FAY THEH-os**). Saying Christ existed in the form of God is probably a subtle way of affirming the divine nature of Christ, that He possessed the very nature of God, without saying plainly that Christ was God. The reason for this is ever hidden in the mind of the author and will be extremely difficult to discern.

The next clause "thought it not robbery to be equal with God" seems to corroborate the above interpretation. The expression of Christ's equality with God here is confirmed by and is consistent with John's account: "In the beginning was the Word, and the Word was with God, and the Word was God" (John 1:1). In John 10:30, Jesus said to His audience and disciples, "I and my Father are one." Writing to the Colossians concerning Christ, Paul says, "Who is the image of the invisible God, the firstborn of every creature"

(Colossians 1:15). These clearly point to the divinity of Christ and His equality with God.

In Philippians 2:6, the word "robbery" (Gk. *harpagmos*, **har-pag-MOS**) means to plunder or the act of seizing. Here, it is best interpreted that although He was equal with God in His divine nature, Christ did not think of this equality as something to be seized upon or to be held fast or held onto. That means that Christ possessed the divine nature and was by all accounts equal with God and had the right to hold tight to it and use it to His own advantage. Christ did not see His equality with the Father as a position to greedily and selfishly grasp and use for His own advantage but as "giving and spending oneself out" for others.

7 But made himself of no reputation, and took upon him the form of a servant, and was made in the likeness of men:

With the use of the conjunction "but" (Gk. *alla*, **al-LAH**), Paul clearly states the thought that rather than clinging to His divine nature and equality with God, Christ "made himself of no reputation" (Gk. *kenoo*, **ken-O-o**), i.e., He emptied or drained or gave of Himself. The use of the reflexive pronoun "himself" in the sentence is emphatic and suggests that the act of emptying by Christ was voluntary. The natural question is: What did Christ empty out of Himself? Scholars have proposed a number of suggestions. We can say that He emptied Himself of:

1. The glory He had with the Father before the foundation of the world (Matthew 16:27; John 12:23; 17:5);

2. His authority in heaven and earth; all He did on earth He attributed to the Father, and this was given back to Him after the Resurrection (Matthew 28:18; Ephesians 1:20-23; 1 Peter 3:22);

3. The independent use of His divine attributes and power; as a human He could

not perform miracles apart from the command of the Father and work of the Holy Spirit (Isaiah 11:1-2; 42:1; 61:1-2; Luke 3:21-22; 4:16-21; John 2:11; 3:34)

Some would object. As William Hendriksen put it: "'If Christ Jesus actually gave up his favorable relation to the divine law, riches, glory, and independent exercise of authority, how could he still be God?'" (*Exposition of Philippians*, 108). The answer lies in His human function. While on earth, He laid aside His consistent expression of these things, while retaining His divine nature, and operated as a man, having assumed human form (Philippians 2:7b). He was never divested of His divinity in His incarnation but "humbled himself," laying aside the independent exercise of divine attributes (v. 8).

That He retained His divinity can be seen in His teachings and miracles, which testified to His deity and dumbfounded His critics (Matthew 7:29; 21:23; John 2:1-11). He also affirmed His divinity to His disciples (John 10:30; 14:7-9).

He not only emptied Himself, but He "took upon him the form of a servant, and was made in the likeness of men" (Philippians 2:7). We notice the use of *morphe* (**mor-FAY**), "form," with the same meaning as in verse 6 used here. Taking the form of a "servant" (Gk. *doulos*, **DOO-los**), slave or bondsman, does not mean that He adopted the external appearance of a slave, neither does it mean that He pretended to be a slave or disguised Himself as a servant. Rather, it means that he adopted or "accepted" (Gk. *lambano*, **lam-BAN-o**), which refers to the disposition, characteristics, and attributes of a slave.

The word has a negative connotation in its literary sense—one under bondage and authority of another. Figuratively used,

though, the word can, at least in part, lose the sense of compulsion and have a more positive meaning. For example, *doulos* can be used to designate man's relationship to God. To some interpreters, "slave" as applied to Christ should be understood this way, especially in light of Isaiah's Suffering Servant passages (Isaiah 52:13-53:12). Christ "taking the form of a servant" means that He exactly played the part of a servant of God.

The slave had no freedom of his own, nor any personal choice or will, but was in bondage to the will of and claim of his master. Who was Christ serving—God or humankind? Christ put Himself in the place of the servant and washed His disciples' feet, and that act dramatized the call to serve one another. Thus, Paul's designation of Christ as *doulos* emphasizes the fact that in the Incarnation, Christ entered the stream of human life as a slave—that is, as a person without advantage, with no rights or privileges of his own for the express purpose of placing Himself completely to the service of all humankind (Mark 10:45; Luke 22:27). For in serving people, He was serving God, and in taking the role of a slave toward others, He was acting in obedience to the will of God.

In Philippians 2:7 Paul continues with his focus on Christ as a servant. Christ not only took on the form of a servant, He "was made in the likeness of men." The verb "was made" (Gk. *ginomai*, **GHIN-om-ahee**), gives the idea of coming into existence or to become; it is also used of men appearing in public. Here, Christ is said to come into existence "in the likeness of man," which speaks of His incarnation as a human. The word "likeness" (Gk. *homoioma*, **hom-OY-o-mah**) does not mean that "Christ only appeared to be a man" or that He seemed to resemble a man. Rather, the word should be understood as made after the likeness, image, or similarity or identity that amounts to equality. The idea here is that in all respects, both in appearance and vulnerability, Christ was like other human beings. He was born by a woman just as other men and grew up as others. He was genuinely human.

8 And being found in fashion as a man, he humbled himself, and became obedient unto death, even the death of the cross.

In verse 8, Paul continues to describe the thought of Christ's humility as shown not only by His assuming human form and the role of a servant, but by humbling Himself to such a degree of acceptance and subjecting Himself to the most humiliating type of death—on a cross. This, Paul seems to convey, is the lowest step of humility. Paul wrote, "Being found in fashion as a man," which means that He was perceived or recognized (Gk. *heurisko,* **hyoo-RIS-ko**) in every respect as an ordinary human. As if assuming the form and the role of a servant and the likeness and nature of a human being were not enough, He also "humbled himself" to the point that he "became obedient (to God, even) unto death." His obedience has no limits, the statement implies. Furthermore, Paul emphasizes the lowest extent that Christ went in His humility and obedience to God when he adds, "even the death of the cross." This act is voluntary and in absolute obedience to the will of God. Jesus says (referring to His life), "No man taketh it from me, but I lay it down of myself. I have power to lay it down, and I have power to take it again. This commandment have I received of my Father" (John 10:18). No one on earth could have gone so low, and He could not have gone lower. That was the lowest!

Death by crucifixion is said to have come from the Persians and was developed by the Romans. It was the most humiliating and cruel form of capital punishment—reserved only for the worst criminals, such as robbers, murderers, and sometimes slaves. Jews and Romans abhorred this type of death. For the Jew, death by crucifixion not only brought shame and pain, it was considered accursed by God (Deuteronomy 21:22-23; 1 Corinthians 1:23; Galatians 3:13; Hebrews 12:2).

Here, Paul reminds the Philippians that Jesus reached the lowest point of humility. He says in effect that Christ, who was in every conceivable way God (in His pre-existence) and was equal with God (an equality to which He did not think it necessary to hold tightly or to constantly assert), emptied and humbled Himself by assuming the role and attributes of a slave. He affirms that Christ came in the likeness of a mortal being and surrendered Himself totally in obedience to God, even to the point of dying—not an ordinary death, but a criminal's death—a death on the Cross. We know this was for the benefit and service to humankind. The underlying thought in verses 5-8 is that if Christ humbled Himself and went so low as to die, the Philippians, and indeed all believers, should constantly endeavor to be willing to follow their Master's example of humility and strive to achieve the spirit of oneness among themselves.

9 Wherefore God also hath highly exalted him, and given him a name which is above every name:

Verse 9 can be restated thusly: Because Christ humbled Himself to the lowest point of death, even death on the Cross, consequently "God also hath highly exalted him" to the highest point of honor. He humbled Himself, therefore He was exalted, which follows the divine order of things as taught by Christ Himself. The same rule that He laid down for others is applicable to Him, to the Philippians and indeed to all Christians of all times. This rule, stated in its various forms throughout the Scripture, simply says, "in the divine order of things, self-humbling leads inevitably to exaltation" (see Hawthorne, 90).

The Greek word used for Christ's exaltation and translated here as "highly exalted him" by most translations is *huperupsoo* (**hoop-er-oop-SO-o**). It is found only here in the New Testament. It means to exalt to the highest rank and power, as in the military or highest office, or to be elevated to the highest position. Here, Christ is exalted beyond measure—to a point after which there is nothing higher. *Huperupsoo* literally means, "to super-exalt." The use of this rare word confirms the idea that He who humbled Himself to the lowest depth is now raised to the highest heights. The same Greek word is used in the Old Testament (Septuagint, LXX) to describe Yahweh being "'exalted far above all gods'" (Psalm 97:9; see Hawthorne, 91).

Christ's super-exaltation means that He received the ultimate place of honor and majesty and is accordingly "seated at the right hand of God's throne" (Mark 16:19; Acts 2:33; 5:31; Romans 8:34; Hebrews 1:3), "far above all rule and authority and power and dominion, and every name that is named, not only in this age but also in the one to come" (Ephesians 1:21, NASB).

Paul further describes this glorious elevation of Christ by adding that God gave "him a name which is above every name" (Philippians 2:9). This statement serves as a reinforcement of the first and describes the magnitude of Christ's exaltation. He was "given" (Gk. *charizomai*, **khar-ID-zom-ahee**), i.e., God bestowed on Him the "name" (Gk. *onoma*, **ON-om-ah**) "above" (Gk. *huper*, **hoop-ER**) "... every name." The idea here is that just as He is exalted to highest position,

Christ is granted or bestowed the greatest name that surpasses every thinkable name.

In the ancient or Jewish tradition, name giving is more than merely a means of identifying, labeling, or distinguishing one person from another. In that tradition, a name usually carries a relational, spiritual, or historical significance; in many instances, it also reflects the person's character, inner being, and the true nature of the individual. A name in the Jewish tradition could also reveal God's activity on an individual. For example, God changed "Abram" to "Abraham" because He was about to make Abraham "father of many nations," which is the meaning of the new name (Genesis 17:5). Names are also given to reflect an important historical event. The angel of the Lord told Jacob after wrestling with him, "Thy name shall be called no more Jacob, but Israel: for as a prince hast thou power with God and with men, and hast prevailed" (Genesis 32:28). An angel told Joseph that Jesus would be called "Emmanuel," which is "God is with us" and reflects Christ as God who came in the flesh (Matthew 1:18-23).

We can, therefore, deduce from these passages that God not only graciously bestowed on Christ the name that is above every other name to distinguish Him from all other beings, but He bestowed on Him the name that reflects His exalted nature, a title that coincides with a new position. Some interpreters state that this name is "Lord" (Gk. *kurios*, **KOO-ree-os**), which means then that Christ not only carries both the title and the character of "Lord," He is Lord (Philippians 2:11). It is important to note that the root meaning of the term *kurios* is used in the Old Testament (LXX) to translate the personal name of God, YAHWEH, a name that denotes rulership and authority. This, therefore, means that God installed Christ to the same position, which rightly belongs to God Himself. He is now equal with God; this equality and honor Christ refused to abrogate to Himself or grasp with pride (v. 6). He now possesses the sovereign authority and rules over the entire universe. After His resurrection, Jesus declared, "All power is given unto me in heaven and in earth" (Matthew 28:18; see also Ephesians 1:20-21).

10 That at the name of Jesus every knee should bow, of things in heaven, and things in earth, and things under the earth;

Paul gives us a two-part purpose for Christ's exaltation and bestowal of the highest name. The first part, introduced by "that" — (Gk. *hina*, **HIN-ah**), which means so that or in order that — is that "at the name of Jesus every knee should bow." This clause does not say that "at the name, Jesus" every knee should bow but rather "at the name of Jesus" (meaning, the name that now belongs to Jesus or the name that He now bears). That name is *kurios* as we have discussed above. It is now bestowed to the historical Jesus, who humbled Himself to the lowest depth, who took up the role of a slave, who became human in time and space. He was crucified and died the most shameful death on the cross—the same Jesus who was rejected of all men but whom God has made both Christ and Lord (Acts 2:36). He, who was obedient even to death, is to be obeyed and worshiped.

The bowing of the knee is almost universally used as a sign of reverence to someone of higher stature or authority, such as kings and chiefs. The bending of the knee is also a symbol of worship. God says in Isaiah 45:23, "Unto me every knee shall bow, every tongue shall swear" and that such worship is reserved for Himself only (Exodus 20:5). Here, this honor is now applied to Jesus, who has been accorded the highest name ever imagined—the name Lord. Therefore,

all must fall on their knees before Christ in worship.

In Philippians 2:10, Paul goes on to declare the magnitude and sphere of the homage to Christ with a series of adjectives, "of things in heaven, and things in earth, and things under the earth." This shows that the worship of Christ is universal in nature. In other words, all creation is to worship Him. This would definitely include angels, humans, spirits, and demons, including all principalities and powers (Colossians 1:16, 20; 2:15); all would ultimately join in the act of worship to Christ. They would bow on their knees before Christ in awe and adoration. In his revelation, using the same universal phraseology, the apostle John says that he saw and heard:

"Every creature which is in heaven, and on the earth, and under the earth, and such as are in the sea, and all that are in them, ... saying, Blessing, and honour, and glory, and power, be unto him that sitteth upon the throne, and unto the Lamb for ever and ever" (Revelation 5:13).

11 And that every tongue should confess that Jesus Christ is Lord, to the glory of God the Father.

The second of Paul's two-part expression of God's purpose in exalting Christ and giving Him the highest name above every other name—is "that every tongue should confess that Jesus Christ is Lord." Here, the writer reaches the climax of the "hymn" and gives us, as we previously indicated, the name that is above other names—"Lord." The phrase "should confess" is the Greek *exomologeo* (**ex-om-ol-og-EH-o**), which is to acknowledge openly and joyfully the Lordship of Christ. The idea here is to affirm and celebrate Jesus as Lord, to praise and honor Him. Who is to acknowledge Christ as Lord? Paul says every "tongue" (Gk. *glossa*,

244

gloce-**SAH**), which literally means language, but is used here to indicate the universality of the confession—"everyone," "all," or "all peoples." *Glossa,* or "tongue," is often used in the Scriptures as a synonym for "tribe, people or nation" (Isaiah 66:18; Daniel 3:4, 7; Revelation 5:9; 7:9; 10:11). Therefore, this confession is not limited to the church but includes every being within the sphere of God's creation that will all, in fact, admit that Jesus is Lord. In Philippians 2:11, Paul concludes this hymn by saying the acknowledgment of Jesus as Lord is "to the glory of God the Father." The exaltation of Christ to the highest possible realm, the giving of the highest name imaginable, and the proclamation of Christ as Lord by all peoples, have one ultimate goal: the glory of the Father. Thus, when the Son is glorified, the Father is glorified (John 13:31-32; 14:13; 17:1).

Paul calls the Philippians to follow the example of Christ—His humility—for that is the true road to personal exaltation and to the glory of God. Here, the formula is clear: "The surest way up is by stepping down, the surest way to gain for oneself is by giving up oneself, the surest way to life is by death, the surest way to win the praise of God is by steadfastly serving others" (Hawthorne, 95).

Sources:

Butler, Trent, ed. *Holman Bible Dictionary.* Nashville, TN: Holman Bible Publishers, 1991. 1105, 1106.

Hawthorne, Gerald F. *Philippians: Word Biblical Commentary,* vol. 43, Waco, TX: Word Books, 1983. 91, 95.

Hendriksen, William. *Exposition of Philippians: New Testament Commentary.* Grand Rapids, MI: Baker Book House, 1962, 1964. 108.

New Testament Greek Lexicon. Bible Study Tools.com. http://www.biblestudytools.com/lexicons/greek/ (accessed October 25, 2011).

Say It Correctly

Philippi. fi-LIP-ahy, FIL-uh-pahy.
Philippians. fi-LIP-ee-uhnz.
Praetorian. pray-TOR-ee-uhn.

Daily Bible Readings

MONDAY
Sower, Seeds, and Soils
(Matthew 13:1-9)

TUESDAY
Hear and Understand the Word
(Matthew 13:18-23)

WEDNESDAY
Avoid Envy and Selfish Ambition
(James 3:13-18)

THURSDAY
Overcome Evil with Good
(Romans 12:14-21)

FRIDAY
Become a Servant and a Slave
(Mark 10:35-45)

SATURDAY
Look to the Interest of Others
(Philippians 2:1-4)

SUNDAY
Seek the Mind of Christ
(Philippians 2:5-11)

Teaching Tips

Words You Should Know

A. Dung—(Philippians 3:8) *skubalon* (Gk.)—Waste or excrement; something having no value.

B. Conformable—(v. 10) *summorphoo* (Gk.)—Jointly formed, similar, fashioned like unto.

Teacher Preparation

Unifying Principle—Gain and Loss. Paul believed that none of the achievements of this life are worth anything when compared to the surpassing value of knowing Christ Jesus.

A. Pray for your students and lesson clarity.

B. Read the entire lesson and meditate on the Daily Bible Readings.

C. Complete the companion lesson in the *Precepts For Living Personal Study Guide®*.

O—Open the Lesson

A. On a chalkboard, tear sheet, or using PowerPoint, write the words "World" and "Christ" in two separate columns. Ask the class to name some distinct worldly values and some distinctly Christian values. Discuss how these values are in direct opposition to one another.

B. Read today's In Focus story. Discuss.

C. Tie it in with the theme.

P—Present the Scriptures

A. Have volunteers read the Focal Verses.

B. Review the information by using The People, Places, and Times, Background, At-A-Glance outline, and More Light on the Text sections.

C. Give students an opportunity to answer the questions in Search the Scriptures. Discuss.

D. Summarize the In Depth section Discuss.

E—Explore the Meaning

A. Summarize the highlights of the Discuss the Meaning, Lesson in Our Society, and Make It Happen sections.

B. Discuss how modern day Christians can still share in Christ's suffering.

N—Next Steps for Application

A. Summarize the lesson.

B. Remind students to read and meditate on their Daily Bible Readings.

C. Solicit prayer requests and close in prayer.

Worship Guide

For the Superintendent or Teacher
Theme: Gaining in Jesus Christ
Song: "Standing on the
Promises of God"
Devotional Reading:
Matthew 13:44-46
Prayer

Gaining in Jesus Christ

Bible Background • PHILIPPIANS 3:1-11
Printed Text • PHILIPPIANS 3:7-11 | Devotional Reading • MATTHEW 13:44-46

————————— Aim for Change —————————

By the end of the lesson, we will: DISCOVER Paul's attitude about the value of knowing Christ Jesus; EXAMINE feelings of achieving honors compared to feelings of living a life in Christ; and ESTABLISH a lifelong goal of measuring our achievements against the value of knowing Jesus Christ.

In Focus

Grady really enjoyed going to his college class reunion. He'd seen a couple of his fraternity brothers and a few guys who were on the football team with him.

"Baby, that was my world 10 years ago," he told his wife, Anita. "The frat, the football team, and partying were what I lived for in those days. And, if I say so myself, I was quite popular with the girls, too."

JAN 20th

"I know what you mean," Anita chimed in. "Isn't it funny how your priorities change, especially after you marry and have children? I remember that all I wanted was to look good in a pair of jeans and have a date on Saturday night."

"I know," added Grady. "Having you and Nicole in my life means more to me than I ever thought anything could. But what really changed my life was having Jesus Christ as my Lord and Savior."

Knowing Christ changes one's life more than anything else. Have you accepted Him into your heart and life? What changes has He brought about in you? Apostle Paul teaches that we should strive to gain in Jesus Christ, not in worldly values.

————————— Keep in Mind —————————

"But what things were gain to me, those I counted loss for Christ"
(Philippians 3:7).

"But what things were gain to me, those I counted loss for Christ"
(Philippians 3:7).

Focal Verses

KJV **Philippians 3:7** But what things were gain to me, those I counted loss for Christ.

8 Yea doubtless, and I count all things but loss for the excellency of the knowledge of Christ Jesus my Lord: for whom I have suffered the loss of all things, and do count them but dung, that I may win Christ,

9 And be found in him, not having mine own righteousness, which is of the law, but that which is through the faith of Christ, the righteousness which is of God by faith:

10 That I may know him, and the power of his resurrection, and the fellowship of his sufferings, being made conformable unto his death;

11 If by any means I might attain unto the resurrection of the dead.

NLT **Philippians 3:7** I once thought these things were valuable, but now I consider them worthless because of what Christ has done.

8 Yes, everything else is worthless when compared with the infinite value of knowing Christ Jesus my Lord. For his sake I have discarded everything else, counting it all as garbage, so that I could gain Christ

9 and become one with him. I no longer count on my own righteousness through obeying the law; rather, I become righteous through faith in Christ. For God's way of making us right with himself depends on faith.

10 I want to know Christ and experience the mighty power that raised him from the dead. I want to suffer with him, sharing in his death,

11 so that one way or another I will experience the resurrection from the dead!

The People, Places, and Times

Libertine. These people who were trying to become a part of the early Christian church believed they were essentially a soul or spirit. To them, the body was only a temporary house, having no long-term value or significance. They held a dual view of life—spiritual matter is good and physical matter is evil or worthless. They believed that the body was insignificant and therefore claimed the freedom to do with it as they pleased.

Benjamin. The tribe of Benjamin occupies the smallest territory of any of the 12 Hebrew tribes. In spite of its size, however, the tribe played a significant role in Israel's history. Saul, the first ruler of Israel, was a Benjaminite. During the latter period of the judges, the Benjamin tribe practically disappeared from history when it mistreated a Levite and his concubine (Judges 19-20). But Jews were always proud when they could trace their lineage back to one of the tribes of Israel.

Background

In chapter three, Paul warned the Philippians about the dangers of a distorted religion. He railed against the problem of having confidence in the flesh versus the knowledge of Christ. With fatherly concern for the congregation, Paul warned them about people who could lead them astray.

He was also concerned about people who trusted more in themselves and their accomplishments. None, however, had reason to boast, according to Paul. For he himself had as much reason as anyone else. Paul had a background that was impressive by any standard, but especially by Hebrew qualifications. He understood from personal experience what it meant to have all the prized religious values, virtues, and achievements, only to discover that it was not the be-all and end-all of life.

Paul was born out of the tribe of Benjamin and was circumcised on the eighth day, according to the Law. Paul was a "Hebrew born of Hebrews" (Philippians 3:5). He was trained and educated as a Pharisee and used that knowledge to persecute the church. If anyone had reason to place confidence in his own ability and knowledge, it was Paul.

At-A-Glance

1. All Is Gain through Christ
(Philippians 3:7-9)
2. What It Means to Know Christ
(vv. 10-11)

In Depth

1. All Is Gain through Christ (Philippians 3:7-9)

If ever a person had reason to have confidence in himself and his intellectual abilities, it was Paul. Yet, even though Paul had impeccable credentials, which gave him standing in the Jewish hierarchy, he gave it all up when he encountered Christ. One can only give up that which one has, and one cannot give up what one does not have. Paul was able to speak with authority concerning the worthlessness of something that he once valued highly.

Paul told the Philippians about his own heritage and accomplishments (vv. 5-6). Concerning his heritage, there were four gains, which he now counted as loss for Christ's sake. First, he was circumcised on the eighth day, which meant he was born a Jew, not a proselyte, or one who has converted to Judaism. Second, he was "of the stock of Israel," meaning he was pure Hebrew, not of mixed descent as were many in Palestine during that day (v. 5, NKJV). Third, Paul was from the tribe of Benjamin, which had remained loyal to the Davidic line when the kingdom divided. Fourth, he was a "Hebrew of the Hebrews," a phrase often used to designate those who had retained the national language (v. 5, NKJV). Though settled in a Greek city, Paul's family had continued to speak the Hebrew tongue.

Concerning his expertise in the Law, Paul was a Pharisee, part of a strict sect whose life pursuit was to obey the law in every detail. In his pursuit of righteousness, Paul was no exception. He was so devoted to his way of life that he gladly and eagerly—and probably with a great sense of arrogance and superiority—persecuted those in the church.

Obviously a man of great intellectual ability, Paul came to realize that no legalistic training or adherence could save him or anyone else. Paul did give up things that were considered evil or worthless. He willingly walked away from a treasured lifestyle held in high esteem by his family and community. What he now counted as loss was not a former state of wickedness but of strict adherence to the Law. Yet, whatever advantages Paul had in his former life were nothing in light of the salvation he was now granted through the saving knowledge of Christ Jesus. Now Paul considered his former treasures to be worthless, like "dung" (excrement, v. 8).

2. What It Means to Know Christ (vv. 10-11)

Paul's surrender of legalism and self-righteousness did not cause him to go to the other extreme of libertinism. He did not understand freedom from legalism to translate into lawlessness. As it was when he was a Pharisee, righteousness remained his consuming goal. Now, however, he pursued righteousness from God, found through faith in Christ, not the self-righteousness of his previous life. Righteousness is not a human achievement; it is the work of God in someone who has the openness of faith to receive Jesus Christ as Lord and Savior.

In order to know Christ, Paul gave up the life he once held so dear. His former life became all the more meaningless with the recognition that human effort is useless in attaining the righteousness that God requires. Therefore, our righteousness can only come through our faith In Christ. Paul wanted to know Christ and the power of His resurrection.

To know Christ is not just an intellectual understanding of who He is. It is the most intimate relationship with Him. The closest example is the relationship between the husband and the wife. To know Christ is to experience His life. When we suffer, we are carrying our cross and experiencing a bit of what Christ endured for us. It is a privilege to be able to become one with Him as He hung there for you and me.

In order to live with Christ, we must die with Him. We cannot go back to the Cross of Golgotha. However, the Christ who was victorious there can come to us and allow us to be conformed to Him and His ways. In life, we can have partial knowledge of His existence. That knowledge will be made complete in the resurrection from the dead.

The resurrection of Jesus Christ is important to us for three reasons. His resurrection guarantees that our human bodies have great importance. It was in His earthly body that He died upon the Cross and in His heavenly body that He rose again. The Resurrection points to God's stamp of approval upon our physical bodies, His creation. Secondly, His resurrection is the guarantee that we shall rise again. While we don't have our beginnings in eternity, God shares His eternality with us beginning the day of our conversion. And third, His resurrection blesses us with the wonderful joy of His promise to be with us forever.

Search the Scriptures

1. Why did apostle Paul count everything a loss for Christ (Philippians 3:7-8)?

2. Apostle Paul deemed that his own righteousness would be of the _____ (v. 9).

3. The righteousness that is of God is by _____ (v. 9).

Discuss the Meaning

Apostle Paul wanted to really know the Lord—the power of His resurrection and the fellowship of His suffering. What does that mean?

Lesson in Our Society

In order to know Christ and have a personal relationship with Him, we need to be willing to make sacrifices in our lives. Sometimes, we have to give up old friends. Other times, we have to make time and take time to read and meditate on His Word, engage in prayer and fasting. So often in our fast-paced society, we have to be deliberate about making time for God. Are you determined to do so?

Make It Happen

Decide this week to spend meaningful time with God through studying His Word, meditating on it, and prayer. As you spend time with Him, ask Him to help you prioritize your time so that fellowship with Him will become first priority.

251

Follow the Spirit
What God wants me to do:

_____

_____

_____

_____

Remember Your Thoughts
Special insights I have learned:

_____

_____

_____

_____

More Light on the Text
Philippians 3:7-11

With the use of "finally" in the opening verse of chapter 3, Paul seems to indicate that he was coming to the end of his letter to the Philippians. However, in context, Paul is focusing on a different aspect of the Philippians' situation, and now he addresses it. Here, he warns them against Judaizers, who he says put much "confidence in the flesh" rather than in Christ (v. 3, NIV). He gives himself as an example of one who had by all measures reached the height of fame in the religion of Judaism and was more qualified both through birth and religious rites and tradition than any other. He was zealous about persecuting the very Church that he is now preserving and building with his suffering. The extent of his involvement is best described in his own words: "Circumcised the eighth day, of the stock of Israel, of the tribe of Benjamin, an Hebrew of the Hebrews; as touching the law, a Pharisee; Concerning zeal, persecuting the church; touching the righteousness which is in the law, blameless" (Philippians 3:5-6).

7 But what things were gain to me, those I counted loss for Christ. 8 Yea doubtless, and I count all things but loss for the excellency of the knowledge of Christ Jesus my Lord: for whom I have suffered the loss of all things, and do count them but dung, that I may win Christ,

The Pharisees were a sect of zealous self-righteous Jews, who held to the letter of their interpretation of the Law and their own traditions without regard for the effect on the Word of God. They were the most privileged and highly "respected" and "honored" people in the temple worship (see Acts 5:34). They held strongly, for example, to the physical circumcision of the flesh and equated righteousness to the keeping of the laws and the Jewish tradition. To reach that height, one must definitely be a Jew, "free born," not a proselyte, an ardent keeper of the law, and "blameless" in all aspects of the religion (Acts 22:28; Philippians 3:6). To attain the position of a Pharisee, therefore, is a very rigorous undertaking, which requires much learning and knowledge of the law. The position also comes with great advantages and privileges. As we have seen in the first six verses, Paul had reached that high echelon. Indeed, when it came to meeting every requirement of Judaism, being of pure stock, and demonstrating fanatical zeal, he had no equal (Acts 7:57-58; 8:1-3; 9:1-2; 2 Corinthians 11:22; Galatians 1:13-14).

All the things to his advantage, including honor and respect, which he possessed as a Pharisee, he "counted (as) loss for Christ," Paul says (Philippians 3:7). Here, Paul says all the positions and aspirations that every

Jewish young man dreams of and are thought to be "gain" (Gk. *kerdos*, **KER-dos**) and what he has already achieved, are now *zemia* (Gk. **dzay-MEE-ah**), a "loss" or worthless to him. *Zemia* here has the idea of loss as related to a trade or business enterprise where one incurs a material or financial loss. The loss is voluntary, where for the sake of something better and bigger, one purposely decides to take on forfeiture. One example would be throwing merchandise overboard to lighten the weight of a sinking ship to save lives (Acts 27:10, 21). The word "counted" which Paul uses here is the Greek *hegeomai* (**hayg-EH-om-ahee**), which means to consider, esteem, or deem. Paul uses business language, as intimated above, and considers all the things of his past—things gained before the Damascus encounter—as losses.

Paul considered everything lost "for Christ" (for the sake of having a relationship with Christ—for "knowing Christ," Philippians 3:8). "For Christ" should be understood as for the purpose of gaining Christ, rather than "for Christ" as though Christ were to benefit from the loss. Paul's encounter with the living Christ on the Damascus Road altered his perspective and mindset in life. He reassessed his priorities in considering access to all the worldly glory and position while being ignorant in the riches of knowing Christ on one hand and knowing Christ as Lord then gaining eternal life on the other hand.

The thought of preferring to know Christ rather than having worldly possessions and positions or basking in his past personal achievements is re-emphasized in verse 8. Paul writes, "Yea doubtless, and I count all things but loss for the excellency of the knowledge of Christ Jesus my Lord." In the Greek, "yea doubtless" is *alla menounge* (**al-LAH men-OON-geh**) and adds strength

to what he has previously said. This phrase can be interpreted as "indeed," "surely" or "definitely." Why does he consider all the worldly things as loss? It is because of "the excellency of the knowledge Christ Jesus."

The word "excellency" is the Greek *huperecho* (**hoop-er-EKH-o**), which has the idea of superiority or supremacy. Here, Paul evaluates his past—his privilege, family, religious heritage, his achievements, rise to fame as a Pharisee, power, etc.—and finds them worthless compared with his new privilege of knowing Christ. In fact, for Paul, knowing Christ is superior and supremely more valuable than all other things.

Paul did not only consider all things a loss in order to have personal knowledge of Christ, he indeed incurred the loss of everything. He says, "For whom I have suffered the loss (*zemia*) of all things," which means to sustain damage or to receive injury. Paul's quest to know Christ cost him everything, including the highest position that he had attained within Judaism. Therefore, the loss is real, rather than an ordinary cliché or empty boast. We deduce from the tense of "I have suffered" (past passive), that the "loss" occurred at a specific time. This seems to suggest that the Jewish authorities probably stripped him of all his Pharisaic privileges and advantages the very moment he declared his allegiance to Christ following his encounter with the Lord on the Damascus Road. He not only "considered" them as losses in the past, Paul says he still does "count them but dung" in the present. There is no regret at all. To him, these things he formerly cherished are now "dung" (Gk. *skubalon*, **SKOO-bal-on**), a strong word that describes Paul's attitude toward those things, compared to what he has now gained with "the knowledge of Christ" (v. 8). *Skubalon* here means garbage or what is thrown to the dogs. It is used to describe any refuse such as the excrement of animals, or things that are worthless and detestable. In order that he might "win" (Gk. *kerdaino,* **ker-DAH-ee-no**) or "gain Christ," Paul says, all things he had before became garbage to him, things that are worthless and useless (KJV, NLT).

9 And be found in him, not having mine own righteousness, which is of the law, but that which is through the faith of Christ, the righteousness which is of God by faith:

Another reason for counting all things "dung" is that he might "be found in him (Christ), not having mine own righteousness, which is of the law." Prior to his conversion, Paul attained high position by personal achievement of keeping the Law, which is the measuring stick for righteousness in Judaism. This type of self-righteousness gives rise to and is characterized by pride and arrogance (Romans 10:1-3) and contradicts the work of Christ. To him, self-righteousness (Pharisaic righteousness), based on what one could do, has no more value. Christ taught His disciples, "That except your righteousness shall exceed the righteousness of the scribes and Pharisees, ye shall in no case enter into the kingdom of heaven" (Matthew 5:20). Instead of depending on his own righteousness, Paul relies now on the "righteousness (Gk. *dikaiosune,* **dik-ah-yos-OO-nay**) which is through ... Christ" (Philippians 3:9), based not on personal merit but on the finished work of Christ (Isaiah 61:10), one appropriated by faith only.

"Righteousness," *dikaiosune,* and "justification" with its verb "to justify" were used in both Jewish and Greek communities as judicial terms, whereby a judge would either justify or condemn someone.

To justify is therefore to vindicate or to declare one right. In the Jewish religion, the criterion for being justified before God was for one to keep the Law of Moses. This amounted to being "good" or doing "good" works in order to earn God's favorable verdict, a notion Paul had. However, Paul realized after his dramatic encounter with the Lord that "by the deeds of the law there shall no flesh be justified in his sight" (Romans 3:20). This understanding conforms to the OT affirmation that no human can attain God's standards of holiness by doing good work. Man, without exception, is too sinful by nature to be able to do enough good to receive God's approval (Psalm 14:1-3; 53:1-3; 143:1-4). The only criterion for righteousness before God is by faith through Christ. Faith here simply means "trust" (see Genesis 15:6), having confidence in and accepting God's work of grace through the life and death of Christ.

10 That I may know him, and the power of his resurrection, and the fellowship of his sufferings, being made conformable unto his death;

Paul declares another goal for considering his personal advantages "dung." That is to "know (Christ), and the power of his resurrection, and the fellowship of his sufferings, and to be made conformable unto his death." To "know Christ" as Philippians 3:8 implies, is not intellectual but experiential; it involves an intimate relationship, as in the sexual intimacy between husband and wife (Genesis 4:1; Matthew 1:25). Before his encounter with Christ on the road to Damascus, Paul had intellectual knowledge of Him, but on that day, he encountered the Lord in a unique way. A special and intimate relationship was inaugurated between him and Christ—which is another dimension of knowing Christ.

Hence, he called Him "Lord" (Acts 9:5). The idea here is that he might have an ongoing relationship with Christ—more than a one-time knowledge of Him—and therefore develop a deeper relationship with the living Christ. The only obstacle was his past glory and personal advantages. These personal achievements are now rubbish, filthy and stinky garbage to him.

In Philippians 3:10, Paul qualifies this intimate knowledge of Christ with a cluster of other phrases. The first is "and the power of his resurrection." What does Paul have in mind by this phrase? Paul seems to be saying that he wants also "to know" (i.e., to experience the efficacy of the power in Christ's resurrection). The knowledge here is not separate from his knowing Christ. He wishes to experience the transforming, life-changing power with which Christ has been endowed through His resurrection. This power sustains us in Him. Christ's resurrection from the dead signifies that God has accepted the ransom He paid on our behalf (Matthew 20:28; Acts 20:28; 1 Peter 1:18), and therefore we are justified (Romans 4:25; 8:1, 16; 1 Corinthians 15:17).

The second phrase is "and the fellowship of his sufferings." That means Paul's wishes were not only to know Christ and experience the power in His resurrection but also to experience Christ by "sharing" in Christ's sufferings. This phrase poses some problems in interpretation. What does Paul mean by sharing or participating in the sufferings of Christ? Does he refer to his physical suffering—the beatings, stoning, hunger, shipwreck, imprisonment, etc. (Acts 9:15-16, 23-25; 22:22-29)? It may include all those, but it does not in any way imply that his own sufferings complement or complete Christ's suffering nor does he allude to his own

physical suffering augmenting Christ's afflictions (Colossians 1:24). Just as to know Christ and the power of His resurrection is an inward spiritual experience, to know Him in the fellowship of His suffering is also a spiritual experience expressed in terms of dying with Him (Romans 6:8; Galatians 2:19-20).

Participating in the suffering does not imply inflicting suffering on oneself, as in self-mutilation, or exposing oneself to danger in the name of Christ. When Paul says, "I am crucified with Christ" (Galatians 2:20), it does not mean literal crucifixion as some practice in the Philippines during annual Easter celebrations.

Each year on Good Friday, some Filipino Christians torture and mutilate themselves using nails in their hands and feet to hang on crosses as a sign of suffering with Christ. This is quite unbiblical and a misinterpretation of the Scriptures. Paul's view of partaking in the suffering of Christ is a total resolve to live for Christ and to serve Him under any circumstances—an intense desire to be like Him in holiness. It means dying to sin (Romans 7:9-25), and dying to self, as spoken of by Jesus Himself (Mark 8:34). With such desire and longing for complete knowledge of Christ, Paul is able to endure all physical suffering that comes his way because of his belief in and defense of the Gospel of Christ (2 Corinthians 4:7-12; Galatians 6:17; Colossians 1:24).

The last in the cluster of phrases in Philippians 3:10, "being made conformable unto his death," tends to confirm Paul's longing for holiness. "Conformable" in Greek is *summorphoo* (**soom-mor-FO-o**), and it appears once in the New Testament. It is to grant or invest in the same form, to share the likeness of, or to take on the same form. The language and idea call to mind Paul's language in his epistle (letter) to the Romans: "For if we have been planted together in the likeness of his death, we shall be also in the likeness of his resurrection ... Now if we be dead with Christ, we believe that we shall also live with him" (Romans 6:5, 8). This implies union with Christ and participation in the unique attributes of Christ, which include His humility and His unselfish love for all, which led to His sacrificial death and His righteousness (2:5), which through His death has been imparted to all believers. Indeed, Paul metaphorically describes the believer's union with Christ in the following ways: suffered with Christ (Romans 8:17), is crucified with Him (Romans 6:6), died with Him (6:8; 2 Timothy 2:11), and is buried with Him (Romans 6:4; Colossians 2:12).

Paul, by the efficacy of Christ's death on the Cross, is already dead to sin at the instance of his conversion on the road to Damascus. This was past experience. However, he strives to make the effects of this death a daily reality through his lifestyle and the conscious choices he makes daily, renouncing self with its desires and all that does not conform to the likeness of Christ.

11 If by any means I might attain unto the resurrection of the dead.

A superficial and isolated reading of verse 11 would tend to show that Paul was expressing doubt or is uncertain of his attaining the eschatological (end times) resurrection of all believers. Paul never lacked assurance of his salvation or his relationship as a child of God (Romans 8:15-17; Galatians 4:6) but often celebrates in that assurance (2 Timothy 1:12; 4:7-8). Therefore, Philippians 3:11 is to be read in context with the preceding thoughts expressed in the foregoing verses where Paul strives to live a life reflecting the life and likeness of his Savior Christ Jesus.

Sources:
Butler, Trent, ed. *Holman Bible Dictionary*. Nashville, TN: Holman Bible Publishers, 1991. 65, 210.

"In Pictures: Philippines Crucifixions." BBC News, World: Asia-Pacific. March 29, 2002. http://news.bbc.co.uk/2/hi/asia-pacific/1901095.stm (accessed October 26, 2011).
New Testament Greek Lexicon. Bible Study Tools.com. http://www.biblestudytools.com/lexicons/greek/ (accessed October 26, 2011).

Say It Correctly

Libertines. LIB-or-teens.
Proselytes. PROS-uh-lites.

Daily Bible Readings

MONDAY
The Value of Each One
(Matthew 18:10-14)

TUESDAY
You Are of More Value
(Matthew 10:26-30)

WEDNESDAY
The Value of the Spiritual
(Romans 2:17-29)

THURSDAY
The Value of the Kingdom
(Matthew 13:44-53)

FRIDAY
The True Value in Following Jesus
(Luke 9:23-27)

SATURDAY
No Value in Earthly Achievements
(Philippians 3:1-6)

SUNDAY
The Surpassing Value of
Knowing Christ
(Philippians 3:7-11)

Teaching Tips

Words You Should Know

A. Attained—(Philippians 3:12, 16) *lambano* (Gk.)—Took hold of, or received, such as having received a prize.

B. Press—(v. 14) *dioko* (Gk.)—Pursue, follow after, or press forward, work hard, do one's best.

Teacher Preparation

Unifying Principle—Gaining the Prize. Maintaining a strong relationship with Christ prepares us for the relationship we will have with Him in eternity. Jesus stressed that planning and being prepared would help people reach important goals.

A. Pray that your students will see tasks that the Lord has called them to do and will be motivated to complete them.

B. Study the entire lesson.

C. Complete the companion lesson in the *Precepts For Living Personal Study Guide®*.

O—Open the Lesson

A. Receive prayer requests and open the class with prayer.

B. Discuss some things athletes do to prepare for their games.

C. Include what happens to athletes who are not serious about competition.

D. Have a volunteer read the In Focus story and relate it to today's theme.

P—Present the Scriptures

A. Have volunteers read the Focal Verses.

B. Use The People, Places, and Times, Background, At-A-Glance outline, and More Light on the Text sections to clarify the Scripture.

C. Ask for volunteers to read and answer Search the Scriptures and Discuss the Meaning.

E—Explore the Meaning

A. Incorporate the Lesson in Our Society section and conclude with the Make It Happen section.

B. Read Discuss the Meaning and lead a conversation about the things that hinder us from running the best race we can.

N—Next Steps for Application

A. Pray silently that God will help each of you to become completely sold out to Jesus.

B. Summarize the lesson.

C. Close with prayer.

JAN 27th

Worship Guide

For the Superintendent or Teacher
Theme: Stand Firm
Song:
"I Am on the Battlefield for My Lord"
Devotional Reading:
Matthew 25:14-29
Prayer

Stand Firm

Bible Background • PHILIPPIANS 3:12—4:1
Printed Text • PHILIPPIANS 3:12-16 | Devotional Reading • MATTHEW 25:14-29

—————— Aim for Change ——————

By the end of the lesson, we will: BECOME familiar with what Paul says about living as it relates to eternity with Jesus Christ; APPRECIATE that the journey of Christian living and a quest for something eternal are demanding experiences; and PLEDGE to stand firm in Jesus Christ.

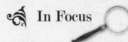

——————— In Focus ———————

One of Aesop's most enduring fables—one of many from this storyteller who became very popular in the Grecian court about 600 years before the birth of Christ—was about the tortoise (a turtle) and the hare (a rabbit). The story goes like this: One day the hare challenged the tortoise to a race. The hare thought this was going to be very easy. He could hop very fast, but the tortoise was very slow. The tortoise agreed to the race. They agreed upon the finish line just beyond a hill. Then the race began.

The hare took off like a flash of lightning, while the tortoise was plodding along at a very slow but steady pace. But when the hare got beyond the hill, he decided that because the tortoise was so far behind him, he would take a nap.

While the hare napped underneath a tree, the tortoise kept plodding along. Finally, he saw the lazy hare sleeping away. The big ol' tortoise kept plodding along until finally he crossed the finish line.

"Slow and steady wins the race!" said the triumphant tortoise.

Some people start off their Christian walk with great enthusiasm, but they soon tire and maybe move on to something else. Paul wanted to encourage the Philippians to please our Lord in their daily lives and stay in the race.

—————— Keep in Mind ——————

"Nevertheless, whereto we have already attained, let us walk by the same rule, let us mind the same thing" (Philippians 3:16).

"Nevertheless, whereto we have already attained, let us walk by the same rule, let us mind the same thing" (Philippians 3:16).

Focal Verses

KJV **Philippians 3:12** Not as though I had already attained, either were already perfect: but I follow after, if that I may apprehend that for which also I am apprehended of Christ Jesus.

13 Brethren, I count not myself to have apprehended: but this one thing I do, forgetting those things which are behind, and reaching forth unto those things which are before,

14 I press toward the mark for the prize of the high calling of God in Christ Jesus.

15 Let us therefore, as many as be perfect, be thus minded: and if in any thing ye be otherwise minded, God shall reveal even this unto you.

16 Nevertheless, whereto we have already attained, let us walk by the same rule, let us mind the same thing.

NLT **Philippians 3:12** I don't mean to say that I have already achieved these things or that I have already reached perfection. But I press on to possess that perfection for which Christ Jesus first possessed me.

13 No, dear brothers and sisters, I have not achieved it, but I focus on this one thing: Forgetting the past and looking forward to what lies ahead,

14 I press on to reach the end of the race and receive the heavenly prize for which God, through Christ Jesus, is calling us.

15 Let all who are spiritually mature agree on these things. If you disagree on some point, I believe God will make it plain to you.

16 But we must hold on to the progress we have already made.

The People, Places, and Times

Races. To the Greeks of Paul's day, races were very important. After all, this was the culture that had invented the Olympics! Beforehand, the runner spent much time in physical fitness training. A race in those days was in a straight line. The runner followed the line and raced toward the finish line. At the conclusion of the race, the herald proclaimed the winner, and the winner stepped forward to receive the prize—a palm branch and perhaps money. The race was not just a game to the Greeks; only one man could win. In Christ, however, many will win and we hope to be in that crowd.

Background

Before Paul was reaching out to grasp the prize, Jesus reached out to him and grasped him on the road to Damascus. All of us have different salvation stories. We can tell how God was reaching out to us and if we could see things from God's perspective, we would probably realize that He was calling out to us at many times and in many ways before we received Him as our Savior. But God's call to Paul (Saul, as he was called in those days) was quite different. First, God called out to him with a bright light and spoke directly to him. After this, Paul was blinded and was led to the city of Damascus.

For three days, Paul was in this city fasting and unable to see. When the Lord sent Ananias to pray with him, the Lord told Ananias that Paul would bring the name of Jesus before Gentiles, kings, and Jews. This was the task that Jesus had taken hold of Paul to do. Paul did not want to fail in the task that the Lord Jesus had for him.

The Lord has grasped each of us for different tasks. We have different things to do at different times of our lives, but we don't want to fail to do those things that the Lord has called us to do. It's a race. Will we reach the goal that He has set for us?

At-A-Glance

1. Pressing toward the Goal
(Philippians 3:12-14)
2. Putting Commitment to the Goal
into Practice (vv. 15-16)

In Depth

1. Pressing toward the Goal (Philippians 3:12-14)

After warning them about placing confidence in self, Paul proceeded to warn the Philippians about the dangers of false perfectionism. Although Paul strived with all that he had to attain this righteousness, he made no claim to having already achieved it. He emphatically rejected any claim to perfection. He knew from personal experience the dangers of legalism and its tendency to produce a false sense of righteousness.

Apparently some at the Philippian church had deluded themselves with the notion that they were perfect. Paul emphasized that resurrection from the dead was not the only goal ahead. Even the objective that may be achieved in this life still lay ahead. Paul was still running the race. He could not slow his pace; to do so would be like a runner stopping short of the finish line.

Paul does not consider his past achievements to be sufficient. He cannot rest on past accomplishments. The race is unfinished. He must continue to strive to fulfill the call of God that is given through Christ Jesus. Paul's goal is to attain the objective that Christ has set for him.

There is a danger in looking back. A runner would surely slow down and probably trip and lose the race. If we keep on looking back at the things we have accomplished, we will slow down as we admire what we have done. Some people look back and worry about the things they did and the things they didn't do. Surely, Paul could have done that. There were Christians who had suffered greatly because of him before he came to Christ. And some of us are always trying to guess whether we have done things wrong, and the worry can surely trip us up. The antidote for that is remembering that worry is the opposite of trust. Paul gives us the answer in verse 13. We need to stop looking backward and just keep our eyes ahead, looking toward Jesus who is waiting for us at the finish line.

Though unattained, perfection is Paul's goal. Admittedly, it is an ambition that one never seems to be able to grasp. Still Paul is willing to continue to press toward the goal. He has begun the race and is committed to finishing the course. The work he has done so far has been good, but it is not over. As determined as Paul is to finish, he has not yet completed the race. Therefore, he cannot afford to be slack in his efforts. In the meantime, he is concerned with avoiding the illusion of having actually gotten there.

Because Christ grasped or took hold of Paul, he, in turn, wanted to grab hold of the perfection, which is Christ's goal for him. Conversion itself represents the beginning, not the completion, of the goal. Fulfilling God's will has both a beginning and a desired end, but it is a process and a lifetime achievement.

2. Putting Commitment to the Goal into Practice (vv. 15-16)

The King James translation of the word "perfect" in verse 15 appears to be a direct contradiction to Paul's insistence that he is not perfect. What Paul meant here was the evidence of maturity—willingness to admit shortcomings, openness to correction, and willingness to be recreated in Christ Jesus. Those who possess this attitude are those who hold true to what they have attained.

The Philippians were admonished to remain true to this point of view so that they could make further progress. They must neither forget the goal nor suffer under the illusion that they have already attained it. Just as there was a danger in assuming perfection had been reached, Paul was well aware, and equally concerned, about those who treated the goal with total disregard.

Search the Scriptures

1. Why did Paul continue to pursue the goal of perfection (Philippians 3:12)?

2. What was Paul committed to doing, even though he had not yet attained the goal (v. 13)?

3. Paul pressed toward what prize (v. 14)?

4. What was Paul's advice to perfect (mature) believers (vv. 15-16)?

Discuss the Meaning

God once told Abraham that He is his exceeding great reward. So it is with us—Jesus, Himself, is the prize that we are seeking. We are running the race and Jesus stands smiling at us at the finish line. Just like a child seeking to win first place in order to please his father, we are running the race to bring joy to our Lord. What things does Paul tell us runners that we should do to win the race?

Lesson in Our Society

The picture that this Scripture paints of Paul is that he is grasping with all his might. Today, we want to make it easy to follow Jesus. We want Jesus to drop all the material blessings into our laps. We certainly don't want to suffer for Him. Is this the picture we see of Paul in these verses or anywhere else in Scripture? People in other places are suffering for Jesus, but we don't always take this as seriously as we should. How can we turn around our lazy and indifferent attitudes toward our faith in Jesus Christ?

Make It Happen

Write down on a piece of paper the things you need to do to commit your life completely to Jesus. As a reminder, post it on the refrigerator or a mirror in your bedroom.

Follow the Spirit

What God wants me to do:

_____

_____

_____

_____

Remember Your Thoughts

Special insights I have learned:

_____

_____

_____

_____

More Light on the Text
Philippians 3:12-16

12 Not as though I had already attained, either were already perfect: but I follow after, if that I may apprehend that for which also I am apprehended of Christ Jesus.

Now Paul makes it clear that the attainment of the resurrection is in the future, something he sets his eyes on but has not achieved yet. It tends to expel the notion that the resurrection of all believers is only spiritual, totally and completely achieved the moment one receives Christ as Lord. It also goes on to confirm that realization of the resurrection is not what we assume we own, without respect to the life we live. Rather, the attainment of the resurrection is something to be maintained and to strive for after receiving Christ. Paul definitely must have had this in mind when he urged the church to "work out your own salvation with fear and trembling" (2:12; 1 Corinthians 9:27; 10:12-14; Hebrews 10:26-37; 1 Peter 2:20-22).

Paul says that he has not yet "attained" (Gk. *lambano,* pronounced **lam-BAN-o**), that is, laid hold of, taken, or received in receipt of a prize. The prize is the resurrection from the dead that is still to come. He has not yet reached his goal; neither is he "already perfect." The word translated "perfect" is the Greek *teleioo* (**tel-i-O-o**) and is also translated to mean "fulfill" (Luke 2:43; John 19:28) and "finish" (John 4:34; 5:36; Acts 20:24). It has the idea of completing a given task. What kind of perfection does Paul refer to here? Is it perfection in character—meaning, Christian perfection? Alternatively, is it perfection in finishing his course?

It has been suggested that in Philippi, there were those who thought they had reached the goal of Christian perfection. Therefore, Paul wants to let them know that he neither thinks of himself as having "arrived"—reached his goal—nor does he see himself as "perfect," sinless, or holy. This does not imply that Paul was lacking in spiritual experience, that he was deficient morally, or still cleaving to his old nature. But it is another demonstration of his humility, whereby he acknowledges that in all his life, God's grace is still working. It means also that the task is not yet complete. The race is not over yet. There is still a course to finish to reach the set goal. Hence, he says, "But I follow after, if that I may apprehend that for which also I am apprehended of Christ Jesus" (Philippians 3:12).

To "follow after" (Gk. *dioko,* **dee-O-ko**) means to run swiftly to catch a person or thing. It is also translated to press on—figuratively used of one that runs swiftly in a race as in the Olympics—in order to reach the goal and win a prize. There is a definite sense of urgency and eagerness and effort exerted here. Why is he pressing so hard? He does it so that "I may apprehend" (Gk. *katalambano,* **kat-al-am-BAN-o**)—or to obtain, attain, lay hold of—"that for which also" Christ Jesus "apprehended" him. This has the sense of being seized or taking possession of.

Paul intimates that Christ had a definite purpose for taking possession of him. The first purpose is probably his call to ministry. Christ told Ananias following His encounter with Paul on the Damascus Road, "He is a chosen vessel unto me, to bear my name before the Gentiles, and kings, and the children of Israel: For I will shew him how great things he must suffer for my name's sake" (Acts 9:15-16; 22:15, 21; 26:15-18).

The second purpose is the attainment of the prize—all that Christ saved him for and wants him to be (3:12). The "prize" to which the apostle strives could not be salvation itself, because he has elsewhere stressed that salvation is a gift of God not attainable by human efforts (Romans 3:20-26;

Ephesians 2:8-9). God declares us righteous as a free gift when we exercise faith in Christ's atoning work. Again, the prize is the satisfaction of knowing he has fulfilled all that Christ saved him for and wants him to be."

13 Brethren, I count not myself to have apprehended: but this one thing I do, forgetting those things which are behind, and reaching forth unto those things which are before, 14 I press toward the mark for the prize of the high calling of God in Christ Jesus.

The content of verses 13 and 14 is more than mere repetition of what Paul has already stated. These verses add emphasis, pointing to the seriousness and the importance of the matter with loving emotion. It seems that Paul, by adding "brethren" (Gk. *adelphos,* **ad-el-FOS**), a word of endearment, is invoking his close relationship with the church and showing a deep concern that she understand the truth he is writing. The use of the word shows that he is deeply moved; he is speaking the truth and would not lie to them. They are to listen to him and take his word for it rather than listen to those who probably claim that they have already reached perfection here and now.

Again, Paul does not consider himself to have "arrived" or to have taken hold of the goal or reached the finish line (using again an athletic metaphor). Although Paul has totally given up everything for the cause of Christ, renounced his Pharisaic opportunities and advantages, and has identified himself with Christ both in His suffering and in His death, Paul does not claim that he has reached perfection. However, there is "one thing I do," he says, and that is "forgetting those things which are behind, and reaching forth unto those things which are before" (v. 13). Paul is focused on the race ahead of him and

avoiding any distraction from his past to impede his concentration on his bid for the prize. He does three things:

1. He forgets the past--the ground he has covered, or the hurdles he has scaled in the race. A good athlete does not look back when running. Otherwise, he or she would lose speed, direction and, more often than not, the race itself (1 Corinthians 9:24-27). Jesus cautioned, "No man, having put his hand to the plough, and looking back, is fit for the kingdom of God" (Luke 9:62). Literally speaking, Paul would not allow his past achievements (Philippians 3:5-7) or his failures—most of all, persecuting the church (v. 6; Acts 9:1)—to hinder him from the race. Forgetting them means he deliberately and mentally obliterates them from his focus. How easy it is for our past sins to deprive us of the joy and hope of our salvation. This is the one common weapon Satan uses against the Christian, accusing him before the throne. But we have assurance in the finished work of Christ (Romans 8:33-39).

2. He "reaches forth" (Gk. *epekteinomai,* **ep-ek-TI-nom-ahee**), meaning he stretches himself and strains every nerve and muscle, sparing no energy while using every ounce of his strength to reach the set goal. It is like running the race of one's life as if life depends totally on it. This is the attitude of every good competitive athlete. He does whatever is legally and ethically possible to win.

3. He presses on toward the mark—the finish line, the focus of every athlete's eyes and mind from start to finish. The sense here is that the ultimate prize motivates him to persevere. Paul refers to that prize here as "the high calling of God in Christ Jesus" (Philippians 3:14).

Professional sports for some athletes today are a very lucrative with a handsome reward. Apart from the gold, silver, or bronze medals, which athletes win in a race, they are rewarded with millions of dollars in salaries and product endorsements. Many take up acting careers and other endeavors that make millions more dollars. It is therefore not only the gold or the wreath of leaves or flowers, which they receive at the podium at the Olympics, for example, but the lasting benefit that follows. No wonder then that they train and try very hard to win. These rewards are earthly, perishable, and temporary. For Paul, though, the reward or prize is more than that: It is priceless and imperishable (1 Corinthians 9:25), the high calling of God in Christ Jesus, the upward call of life with Christ. "In Christ" means that Jesus is the sphere through which the invaluable prize is appropriated (Philippians 3:14). There are differences between earthly and heavenly races. In the earthly race, the prize is perishable; in the heavenly race, the prize is imperishable. In the earthly race, only one person wins the first prize (1 Corinthians 9:24); in the heavenly race, everyone who loves the appearing of Christ is a winner (2 Timothy 4:8). On earth, the fastest wins, while in heaven, whoever remains on the course, in spite of the time one starts or ends or the pace one runs, wins.

15 Let us therefore, as many as be perfect, be thus minded: and if in any thing ye be otherwise minded, God shall reveal even this unto you. 16 Nevertheless, whereto we have already attained, let us walk by the same rule, let us mind the same thing.

"Let us therefore" is language of appeal and Paul, including himself, shows again the spirit of humility that pervades this book and which he exemplifies throughout. He puts himself on the same level with the Philippines as his brethren (vv. 13, 17), and now as those who are "perfect," not in sinlessness, or complete in ethical goodness. Rather, it is perfect as in mature, or full grown, in the knowledge of Christ—not as children but as those who have been thoroughly instructed and experienced in the ways of Christ (1 Corinthians 2:6; 14:20; Ephesians 4:13; Colossians 1:28).

Paul urges them "to be thus minded" (Gk. *phroneo*, **fron-EH-o**, see Philippians 2:2-5), to set their minds on the same things as he does, imitate his example regarding the things that are behind, and stretch forward to pursue the mark for the prize. He then commits them to divine revelation and instruction. He says, "If in any thing ye be otherwise minded, God shall reveal even this unto you" (3:15). That means if any of you are in doubt of anything, are uncertain of your understanding of Christianity, or still have doubts about the Jewish ordinances, God will "reveal" the truth to you. "Reveal" in Greek is *apokalupto* (**ap-ok-al-OOP-to**), meaning to take off the cover or disclose what before was unknown. In verse 16, the Greek particle *plen* (**plane**), translated "nevertheless" here—which also means besides, moreover, or in any case—is used as a break in the sentence to emphasize an important truth. Here Paul urges them (including himself) to let their conduct be consistent with the level of understanding that they have attained. Whatever level we are, in verse 16, Paul says, "Let us walk by the same rule, let us mind the same thing," stressing the importance of harmony and mutual cooperation in spite of individual opinions on things. The phrase "let us walk," in Greek *stoicheo* (**stoy-KHEH-o**) means to march in a row or in orderly ranks as in the military, or to keep in line. That means to conform to the standards or laid down principles, which God has established.

Sources:

Butler, Trent, ed. *Holman Bible Dictionary*. Nashville, TN: Holman Bible Publishers, 1991. 165, 210.

Dictionary.com. http://dictionary.reference.com/ (accessed October 27, 2011).

Hawthorne, Gerald F. *Philippians: Word Biblical Commentary*, vol. 43. Waco, TX: Word Books, 1983.

New Testament Greek Lexicon. Bible Study Tools.com. http://www.biblestudytools.com/lexicons/greek/ (accessed October 27, 2011).

Say It Correctly

Apprehend. ap-ree-HEND.
Attained. uh-TEYND.
Whereto. hwair-TOO.

Daily Bibile Readings

MONDAY
Be Watchful
(Matthew 24:36-44)

TUESDAY
Be Prepared
(Matthew 25:1-13)

WEDNESDAY
Be Trustworthy
(Matthew 25:14-21)

THURSDAY
Be Compassionate
(Matthew 25:31-40)

FRIDAY
Be Holy
(1 Peter 1:13-21)

SATURDAY
Stand Firm
(Philippians 3:17-4:1)

SUNDAY
Hold Fast
(Philippians 3:12-16)

Notes

_____

_____

_____

Teaching Tips

February 3
Bible Study Guide 10

Words You Should Know

A. Fulness—(Colossians 1:19) *pleroma* (Gk.)—The totality of supernatural, divine powers and attributes.

B. Reconcile—(v. 20) *apokatallasso* (Gk.)—To change from hostility or enmity (hate, animosity) to friendship.

Teacher Preparation

Unifying Principle—Awed by Greatness. Paul's use of metaphor strongly conveys Christ's supremacy, which helps us realize who Christ is.

A. Pray for your students and lesson clarity.

B. Read and meditate on the entire lesson.

C. Complete the companion lesson in the *Precepts For Living Personal Study Guide®*.

D. Research who Christ is, and prepare to discuss Him and help your class make a list of His attributes.

O—Open the Lesson

A. Receive prayer requests and and open with prayer.

B. On a chalkboard or on a display ˙˙blet, allow your class to help you make a ˙ f Christ's attributes. Discuss.

˙˙ead In Focus. Discuss, tying it into ˙˙˙eme.

˙ the Scriptures

˙˙˙teers read the Focal Verses.
˙˙ple, Places, and Times,
˙˙˙-Glance outline,

and More Light on the Text sections to help clarify the verses.

C. Have volunteers answer the Search the Scriptures questions. Discuss.

E—Explore the Meaning

A. Summarize Discuss the Meaning, Lesson in Our Society, and Make It Happen.

B. Help your students draw out the significant points and encourage them to consider the questions posed at the end of More Light on the Text.

N—Next Steps for Application

A. Summarize the entire lesson.

B. Challenge students to read their Daily Bible Readings.

C. Close with prayer.

Worship Guide

For the Superintendent or Teacher
Theme: The Supremacy of Jesus Christ
Song: "He's Got the Whole World in His Hands"
Devotional Reading:
Ephesians 1:17-23
Prayer

The Supremacy of Jesus Christ

Bible Background • COLOSSIANS 1:15-20
Printed Text • **COLOSSIANS 1:15-20** | Devotional Reading • **EPHESIANS 1:17-23**

Aim for Change

By the end of the lesson, we will: UNDERSTAND Paul's description of Jesus Christ's supremacy; EXPRESS feelings of amazement at the supremacy of Jesus Christ; and DESCRIBE to others the awe-inspiring preeminence of Christ for bringing reconciliation.

In Focus

"I can't believe this," Mary said, disgusted. She threw her keys down on the kitchen table and frantically searched through her wallet for her auto club card. "I've got to make this job interview *today*!" she said, shouting to herself.

Pleading with the clerk at the auto repair shop, with more control, she said, "Can someone come by this morning? My car won't start."

"We are swamped this morning," the clerk replied, "and the computer shows you are behind in your motor club payments. We can't help you until the bill is paid."

Mary began to cry, smearing her makeup. "Lord, how can I get a job if I don't have a car to get there? How can I get a better car without a job? My life is such a mess."

As Mary laid her head on the table, a tune came to mind: "He's got the whole world in His hands." Mary had heard that song since she was a child, but today it seemed to communicate a whole new meaning. Surely, God would provide regardless of her situation.

She washed her face, prayed that somehow the Lord would work out the missed interview. She then boldly dialed the number to make another appointment.

This week's lesson gives believers a bigger picture of who Jesus is and His position in the world. Hopefully, as our view of Him increases, our perception of our personal problems will decrease.

Keep in Mind

"For it pleased the Father that in him should all fulness dwell"
(Colossians 1:19).

"For it pleased the Father that in him should all fulness dwell"
(Colossians 1:19).

Focal Verses

KJV **Colossians 1:15** Who is the image of the invisible God, the firstborn of every creature:

16 For by him were all things created, that are in heaven, and that are in earth, visible and invisible, whether they be thrones, or dominions, or principalities, or powers: all things were created by him, and for him:

17 And he is before all things, and by him all things consist.

18 And he is the head of the body, the church: who is the beginning, the firstborn from the dead; that in all things he might have the preeminence.

19 For it pleased the Father that in him should all fulness dwell;

20 And, having made peace through the blood of his cross, by him to reconcile all things unto himself; by him, I say, whether they be things in earth, or things in heaven.

NLT **Colossians 1:15** Christ is the visible image of the invisible God. He existed before anything was created and is supreme over all creation,

16 for through him God created everything in the heavenly realms and on earth. He made the things we can see and the things we can't see—such as thrones, kingdoms, rulers, and authorities in the unseen world. Everything was created through him and for him.

17 He existed before anything else, and he holds all creation together.

18 Christ is also the head of the church, which is his body. He is the beginning, supreme over all who rise from the dead. So he is first in everything.

19 For God in all his fullness was pleased to live in Christ,

20 and through him God reconciled everything to himself. He made peace with everything in heaven and on earth by means of Christ's blood on the cross.

The People, Places, and Times

Colosse. The town of Colosse (also spelled "Colossae") was located on a ridge overlooking the Lycus River Valley in the southwest corner of Asia Minor in what is now Turkey. At the time of Paul's writing, its neighboring cities, Laodicea and Hierapolis, were becoming more important, while Colosse was in decline. Epaphras and Timothy established churches in all three of these cities, but at this writing, Paul had yet to visit the believers at these churches personally. However, he did tell Philemon, a native of Colosse, that he was hoping to visit him (Philemon 1:22).

Scholars believe that Paul wrote this letter during his first imprisonment in Rome around A.D. 60. Having received a report from Epaphras of the progress being made with this budding church, he also alerted Paul to the false teachers gaining a foothold in the church.

Epaphras. Christianity came to Colossae through the work of Epaphras. He was converted and rooted in the faith by Paul during Paul's stay in Ephesus. Epaphras had established the faith in Colossae. Paul was not the founder of these congregations and never paid them a visit. He commended Epaphras for his excellent work.

Background

A heretical (false teaching) movement had started in Colossae. Before any real damage could be done, Epaphras reported to Paul the errors that were circulating among the congregation. Epaphras, under Paul's direction, was the founder of the church in Colossae. However, Paul was imprisoned at the time, probably somewhere in Rome. Paul responded by sending Tychicus with this epistle to the Colossians. Paul wrote the epistle (letter) to crush the false teaching that had arisen.

The identity of the heretics was not clear. It could have been members in the congregation pretending to be Christians or non-members from the outside, like the Judaizers, who attempted to invalidate Paul's teaching. The Colossian heretics may also have been native Jews, not members of the Colossian church, who added fancy ideas to Epaphras' teaching and fought to win members for their peculiar beliefs.

Through this brief but powerful writing, Paul completely took care of the erroneous ideas. The theme of the letter focuses on Christ's superiority. The false teachers in Colossae were attempting to reduce the significance of Christ's authority and work. Paul, therefore, set forth his case about Christ and His elevated position.

At-A-Glance

1. Christ Reigns Supreme in Creation (Colossians 1:15-17)
2. Christ Reigns Supreme in the Church (v. 18)
3. Christ Reigns Supreme in Redemption (vv. 19-20)

In Depth

1. Christ Reigns Supreme in Creation (Colossians 1:15-17)

In the earlier verses of Colossians 1, Paul gives many statements and compliments to the Colossian church. Starting in verse 15, however, his focus changes and he gives central attention to Christ. Earlier in the chapter, Christ has already been addressed as "his dear Son" (1:13). Paul continues to lift Jesus up. He gives a long report about Jesus' person, His position, and His work. These teachings about Jesus Christ are not new to the Colossians, but they are restated to combat the erroneous teachings that were being spread.

The first thing Paul emphasizes about Christ is that He is completely God and completely man. When we look at Jesus, we see who God is. Because it is beyond human understanding, this concept is difficult to comprehend. How can two natures—God's divine nature and man's nature—dwell in one man? Yet, Jesus claimed to be, and is, both God and man (John 1:1, 14). In Colossians 1:15, Paul used the word "image" to express Christ's exact likeness of God. Like the image in the reflection of a mirror, the nature and being of God are perfectly revealed in Christ.

The second major characteristic that Paul points out is that "He is the first-born Son, superior to all created things" (*Good News Translation*). Being the firstborn could mean the first child to come out of the mother's womb. It could also mean the one who is given first place (heir) of honor or authority in the family, even though he or she is not the first in the childbirth lineage. Solomon was not David's first son, but he was given the firstborn position as heir to the throne when David died. Both meanings were represented in the Colossians passage: Christ existed before all creation; He is also over all in rank and dignity.

There was an ancient custom whereby the firstborn son in a family was given rights and privileges not shared by the other offspring. He was his father's representative and heir, and the management of the household was committed to him. Following this interpretation, we understand the passage to teach that Christ is His Father's representative and heir. He has the management of everything here on Earth and in heaven.

Because Christ was the creator of the universe, He is firstborn or Lord over all creation. Creation was "through" Christ (v. 16, NLT); God spoke the words and gave the instructions. Jesus was the agent through whom it actually came into being. Because Christ is the reason all things exist, all things—that exist—are to contribute to His glory. The universe is His footstool, His throne. Thus, Christ made all things in heaven and here on Earth, visible and invisible, angelic hierarchy, or whatever supernatural powers that be. He is their Lord. Christ is before all things in time, and all things hold together because of Him. He sustains all of creation. The world would be in complete chaos if it were not for Jesus.

2. Christ Reigns Supreme in the Church (v. 18)

Paul goes on to further point out Christ's supremacy by saying, "he is the head of the body, the church." He is the source of the church's life. He guides and governs the church. Christ and Christ alone is its chief and its leader. The word "church" simply means assembly or congregation. Paul makes reference to all Christians everywhere, not just the individuals assembled in a church building.

The church is a gigantic, living, moving organism by which Christ carries out His purposes and performs His work. The church is composed of members joined vitally to one another. God gives gifts to each Christian and then places His people in His church so that they might serve Him where they are needed. Through His Word, Jesus Christ nourishes and cleanses the church.

The body of Christ cannot function without Christ, its head. He gives instructions and holds the body together. The believers carry out His mission and His purposes. It is often quoted metaphorically that, "Jesus had no eyes but our eyes, no feet but our feet, no hands but our hands." One cannot accomplish much in the way of winning the world without the other.

Christ is not only the head of the church; He is the firstborn from the dead. This does not mean He was the first to be raised from the dead because He was not. Christ is the first to be permanently resurrected from the dead, the first to be clothed with immortality, and the first to obtain and declare His victory over death. For without His resurrection, there would be no resurrection for others at the end of the age. Christ is the origin and source of the life of the church.

Paul summarized his teaching in one statement: "So that in everything he (Christ) might have the supremacy" (v. 18, NIV). Jesus alone has the first place among all and over all. He is the sole Head of all things.

The false teachers of Colossae attempted to communicate to the people that Jesus Christ was only one of many ways to God. However, the Scriptures are quite clear. Jesus emphatically said, "I am the way, the truth, and the life. No one comes to the Father *except through Me*" (John 14:6, NKJV, emphasis added). Jesus is the only entrance into heaven and the only way to know God.

3. Christ Reigns Supreme in Redemption (vv. 19-20)

Before he ends this section, Paul makes two more strong statements about Christ. The first statement is: "For it pleased the Father that in Him all the fullness should dwell" (Colossians 1:19, NKJV). God's totality has a permanent home in Christ. Not a partial part, but all of God's divine power and characteristics rest in Jesus.

The fact that God would put all that He is inside Jesus proves that Jesus is God, and because He is God, He is able to do what no mere man could ever do—reconcile lost sinners to a holy God. Paul's second strong statement in Colossians 1 is, "Through the Son, then, God decided to bring the whole universe back to himself. God made peace through his Son's blood on the cross and so brought back to himself all things, both on earth and in heaven" (1:20, *Good News*).

The Father willed that all fullness should dwell in Christ. He also willed to reconcile all things to Himself through Christ—changing the condition of man from separation to harmony with God.

Search the Scriptures

1. List as many facts as you can about Christ and creation (Colossians 1:15-18).

2. Explain the two definitions of "firstborn" and how Jesus fits them both (v. 18).

3. Explain how it is possible for sinful man to be reconciled to a holy God (v. 20).

Discuss the Meaning

1. How do the facts presented about Christ prove His supremacy over everything?

2. What does Christ's reconciling humankind to God through His death on the Cross mean to us today?

Lesson in Our Society

The assistant director of a local crisis pregnancy center had this to say about her clients. "I talk to young women all the time who call or come in and talk about the difficulties in their lives. When I ask them what they have tried to do to better themselves and their situations, many of them talk about getting a better job, better education, and job training skills. Some even mention getting out of a bad relationship. Very rarely does anyone mention turning to God as a solution."

We live in a society that habitually ignores God. And yet, God wants us to make friends with Him through His Son Jesus to personally be our guide through the difficulties of life.

Make It Happen

Make a list of personal difficulties and the way you have handled them in the past. Make another list of challenges you are facing. What changes are you going to make in your outlook? Your attitude? Your actions?

Follow the Spirit

What God wants me to do:

_____

_____

_____

Remember Your Thoughts

Special insights I have learned:

_____

_____

_____

More Light on the Text
Colossians 1:15-20

The supremacy of Christ is one of the three major themes of the book of Colossians, which Paul develops extensively in 1:15-28. Here Paul deals with the glory, preeminence, and preexistence of Christ who is the head of the church. In the previous section (1:12-14), Paul prays for the church, giving thanks to God for the spiritual inheritance, great deliverance, and redemption from sins, which He has accorded the church through His Son Jesus Christ, the source and giver of all gifts.

15 Who is the image of the invisible God, the firstborn of every creature:

The word "who," in verse 15, refers to the dear (beloved) Son into whose kingdom the church has been transferred and in whom we have redemption through His blood, even the forgiveness of sins (v. 14). The phrase in verse 15, "the image of the invisible God," is therefore a description of Jesus Christ the Son of God. "Image" (Gk. *eikon*, **i-KONE**) can be translated as "likeness or representation," and most applicable, "the replica of an object." Genesis 1:27 says that man was created in the image of God, which speaks of moral and natural faculties, rather than physical likeness. Here the word is used to describe the bodily and spiritual likeness of the Son to the Father in every aspect, in power and authority. Hebrews 1:3 describes the "express image of his person, and upholding all things by the word of his power, when he had by himself purged our sins, sat down on the right hand of the Majesty on high." John confesses that Jesus is the glory of the Father (John 1:14). To Philip and the other disciples, Jesus says, "He that hath seen me hath seen the Father" (John 14:9). The picture here is more than the picture of a son's resemblance. Christ's image of the Father can only be fully understood on the basis of Christ's preexistence. John says Christ was in the beginning, that He was with God, and that He was, in fact, God (John 1:1). Christ's incarnation is therefore a revelation of the invisible God (John 1:18; John 10:30, 38; Revelation 3:14).

Paul contends that Christ is not only the image of the Father but also "the first-born of every creature" (Colossians 1:15). This aspect of Paul's concept of Christ poses some definite theological and doctrinal problems. The major problem is in the meaning of "firstborn" (Gk. *prototokos*, **pro-tot-OK-os**) and how it relates to and is used concerning Christ here. The word is used in a number of passages in the New Testament (Matthew 1:25; Luke 2:7; Romans 8:29; Hebrews 11:28). It means "the first one to be born into a family," and is applied to Jesus as the firstborn of His earthly family. It also applies to Him as the first-born in the family of God. However, the problem is whether the word means that Christ is a part of creation, or whether, in other words, He is a created being as other creatures. How do we understand this concept of Christ? Looking at the phrase in isolation and out of context will make one tend to see Christ as a created being. Nonetheless, the context makes it clear that Christ is both the agent and creator of all creation. It then places Him above it and causes us to understand firstborn in the sense of "supreme and sovereign" rather than as "born before." Christ's sovereignty over all creation is further made clear in John 1:3 and Hebrews 1:2. The deity of Christ supports this concept.

16 For by him were all things created, that are in heaven, and that are in earth, visible and invisible, whether they be thrones, or dominions, or principalities, or powers: all things were created by him, and for him:

As we read in verse 16, the deity and preeminence of Jesus Christ are brought into focus by His creative activity. As we mentioned about the previous verse, two important things about Christ are established here. The first is that Christ is the agent of all creation; He created all things. The second is that all things belong to Him; all things were created for Him. This clarifies and substantiates what we have understood regarding verse 15—the firstborn *prototokos* does not include Christ having come into existence at a point in time; instead, He is eternal. This is supported by the conjunction "for" (Gk. *hoti*, **HOT-ee**, meaning "because" or "since"). The person we know as the historical Jesus, the only begotten of the Father, existed as an equal member of the Godhead, as the creator of all things. Paul contends that "all things" include both earthly and heavenly things, visible and invisible things; all have their beginning and existence in Christ. Nothing would exist without the sovereignty of Christ, whether visible or invisible. Everything derives its existence in Him. The "visible things" refer to the cosmic things, the earthly, material things that include humans; the "invisible things" probably refer to spirit beings such as angelic agencies. The New Testament uses different words to describe these invisible created beings but Paul applies four here: thrones, dominions, principalities, and powers. In Ephesians 1:21-22, Paul asserts that the existence of the angelic beings and the fact that they are able to exert some influence for good or for evil (Ephesians 6:12;

1 Timothy 5:21). However, Paul contends that they have neither power nor exist apart from Christ. The good angels can contribute nothing toward man's salvation, and the bad or evil angels cannot separate believers from the love of Christ (Romans 8:35-39).

17 And he is before all things, and by him all things consist.

Because He created all things for Him and they exist in Him, it then follows that He preceded all things in time, and in Him all things consist (or are held together). Both statements go further to underline the supremacy of Christ over all creation. The first statement, "he is before all things" means that He is from eternity. He is timeless. Indeed, there was no time He did not exist. This firmly establishes the preexistence of Christ, as contained in a number of New Testament passages, including John 1:1; 8:58; 17:5; Philippians 2:6; Revelation 22:13. The book of Revelation refers to Christ as the Alpha and Omega, the beginning and end, the first and last. Also, the prophet Micah says He is from everlasting (5:2). The second statement, "by him all things consist" (or "in Him all things hold together," NASB), signifies that the continuity and coherence of all creation are centered in Him and under His direction and thus speaks of His pre-eminence. Nothing, as we have already established, could exist without Him, for in Him is life. Paul, defending the Gospel at Mars Hill says to the Athenians, "For in him we live, and move, and have our being; as certain also of your own poets have said, For we are also his offspring" (Acts 17:28).

Not only is He the creator of all things (Colossians 1:16), He upholds and sustains all things, which translates the Greek word *sunistao* (**soon-is-TAH-o**). It also has the idea of consistency, to "set in the place, to put together, or to unite parts into one whole." Probably, Paul has in mind the orderliness of the universe and the harmony of the cosmic world. Although the world seems to be in chaos on the surface—wars, killings, murders by children, burglary, and all sorts of evil—beneath this seemingly chaotic nature of the world, there is order and plan. The sun comes up in the day and the moon at night; the snow comes in its season, and the summer at its time. Even the globe itself is held in balance in the vacuum with unseen gravitational force, rotating ceaselessly on its axis. Rivers run constantly into the ocean and the ocean is never filled completely. There is order in the universe. It is neither chance nor fate, nor, for that matter, the law of nature that keeps these things in place and makes them function, as some would claim. Rather, Paul, in declaring the supremacy and power of Christ, says that He holds all things and all things are by Him, who is the express image of the Father and the creator of all things (Revelation 4-5). Many scholars of Colossians 1 consider this section a hymn, which was sung in worship in ancient time but adapted by Paul to clarify the preexistence, preeminence, and superiority of Christ over all things both in heaven and on earth. It defines Christ's position in the nature of things in the created world and places Him in His rightful position in relation to the Father as the true representation.

18 And he is the head of the body, the church: who is the beginning, the firstborn from the dead; that in all things he might have the preeminence.

Hitherto, Paul has been describing Christ's preeminence in the realm of creation. He now refocuses our attention on Christ's relation to the church and deals with it in the sphere of redemption.

He says Christ is the head of the church, an assertion he also has made elsewhere, namely Ephesians (1:22, 23; 4:15) and later in the second chapter of this book (Colossians 2:19). In some of his previous letters, Paul refers to the church as the body of Christ, but the application is the relationship of the members with one another. For example, in 1 Corinthians 10:1-6; 12:12-31; and Romans 12:5, Paul describes the church as one body with many parts and functions, just as the human body has different parts—such as hands, feet, eyes, and ears—and each has different purposes. In other words, in the one organism of the church, there are gifts, talents, skills, and functions distributed among the believers, and each believer uses his or her gift for the benefit of the entire body. In these passages, Paul never expressly refers to Christ as the head of the church. However, the idea is implied, for a body cannot exist without a head. He also wrote in 1 Corinthians 11:3, "The head of every man is Christ." If Christ is the head of every man, then He is the head of the church.

Nevertheless, Paul's main emphasis to the Colossians is about Christ's preeminence and relationship with the church. In his letter to the Ephesians, Paul compares the headship of Christ to the church with the headship of the husband to his wife (5:23), and the main function of the head in relation to the body is for sustenance and growth (Colossians 2:19; Ephesians 4:15-16). The importance of a head to a body is obvious. A body without a head is dead. One can survive and lead a fruitful life with any other part of the body missing such as the eyes, legs, or hands, but have you ever seen a body moving without a head? Therefore, a church without Christ is a dead church and cannot function. Christ is not only the organic head of the church, He is also its ruling head in the sense of guidance and exercising authority, which is implied in the Ephesian passages (1:20-23; 5:23-24). Going back to the analogy of the physical body, science clearly shows that the operation of all other parts of the body comes from the head—in the brain. The brain controls and harmonizes all movements and functions of every part of the body by receiving, interpreting, transmitting, and distributing impulses from both the outside world and inside the body to all parts of the body.

In Colossians 1:18, Paul continues to explain the place of Christ within the church by describing Him as "the beginning, the firstborn from the dead." The word translated "the beginning" is the Greek word *arche* (**ar-KHAY**), which has a variety of meanings such as: "the origin by which everything begins, the first person in series, the leader in rank." All these are applicable to Christ. However, the inclination here, in view of the statement that Christ is the firstborn from the dead speaking of the Resurrection, is that He is the first person among the dead who would rise to life and signal the beginning of the end of the age. The resurrection of the body is the hope, joy, and assurance of all who believe in Christ (Colossians 3:1-17; 1 Peter 1:3). Christ is therefore the first among the many, the one who has inaugurated the principle, and causes the glorified physical resurrection of believers. He is both the author and sustainer of life and death with authority over both (Romans 8:29; 1 Corinthians 15:20; Hebrews 2:14, 15; Revelation 1:5) and the key to death and Hades. He assures His disciples, concerning His resurrection: "Because I live, ye shall live also" (John 14:19). Paul writes to Timothy that Jesus Christ has abolished death and has brought life and immortality to light through the Gospel (2 Timothy 1:10). Paul uses the same word "firstborn" in Colossians 1:18 used in verse 15

that speaks of both the aspect of creation and parallels Christ's relationship to the church, the new creation. The new creation came into existence on the same principle as the old. Tied together, all of this is the goal of supremacy—His "preeminence" (Gk. *proteuo*, **prote-YOO-o**)—His top position, esteem, and significance among all creatures.

19 For it pleased the Father that in him should all fulness dwell;

This high position of the Son is according to the Father's design and for His pleasure—and it translates into the embodiment of the fullness of God in the Son. Here, Paul says God is delighted to have His "fulness" (Gk. *pleroma*, **PLAY-ro-mah**) reside in Christ. *Pleroma* or "fullness" is used in a number of passages in the New Testament with two basic meanings: (1) something that fills or completes, such as a patch (Matthew 9:16) or love (Romans 13:10); and (2) fullness or the state of being filled, such as the completed number of saved Gentiles (Romans 11:25), or the "full measure" of Christ's blessing (Romans 15:29, NIV). First Corinthians 10:26 speaks of the earth's fullness, and Galatians 4:4 talks about the fullness of the time. In Ephesians 1:10, Paul writes about God's sovereign appointment of events in both space and time. The use of *pleroma* in Romans 11:12 refers to the completion of God's plan for the nation of Israel. Paul, in Colossians 1:19, says that the Lord Jesus Christ possesses the complete fullness of God, which likely includes God's divine nature and attributes (Colossians 1:15; Hebrews 1:3). It also says later in Colossians, "In Him (Christ) dwells all the fullness of the Godhead bodily" (Colossians 2:9, NKJV). The phrase, "all the fullness of God" (Ephesians 3:19, NIV), is used by Paul to show that Christ embodies the love of God. In Ephesians 4:13, the fullness of Christ refers to that state of Christian maturity in which believers are "no longer ... tossed to and fro and carried about with every wind of doctrine, and by the trickery of men, in the cunning and craftiness of deceitful plotting" (Ephesians 4:14, NKJV). The Father's delight in the Son was evident even before the beginning of time (Psalm 2:7-8; John 17:5; Ephesians 1:9) and manifested itself repeatedly in Christ's earthly ministry (Matthew 3:17; 17:5; John 12:28). So the fullness of God—His essence, nature, glory, and attributes and in accordance with God's own delightful pleasure from eternity—is made complete and resident in Christ, who is the creator and redeemer and in whom all things are held together. The incarnate Christ is the total and exclusive revelation of God. "If you have seen me," He says, "you have seen the Father" (see John 14:7).

20 And, having made peace through the blood of his cross, by him to reconcile all things unto himself; by him, I say, whether they be things in earth, or things in heaven.

Paul now turns our attention to the work of this exalted Son of God, in whom all the embodiment of the Godhead dwells—the reconciliation of all things through Him to Himself. The conjunction "and" (Gk. *kai*, **kahee**) denotes a continuation of the thought in verse 19 of God's pleasure in having His fullness dwell in Christ and making peace through the blood of Christ by the process of reconciliation to Himself of all things. Although Paul has stated in verse 17 that in Christ all things hold together, here, he recognizes that there is still considerable disharmony in creation, hence the necessity for reconciliation and peace. Just as He is the agent through whom all things are created (v. 16), Jesus is also the agent through whom all things are reconciled (v. 20). In both cases, "all things"

means the same. The verb "reconcile" is a translation of the Greek verb *apokatallasso* (**ap-ok-at-al-LAS-so**), which literally means, "to bring back a former state of harmony." To understand this, one has to go back to the creation story in Genesis, where sin ruined the universe and destroyed the harmony that existed between God and His creation (particularly humanity and God) and between one creature and the other. The only obstacle that separates humans and God is sin (Isaiah 59:1-2), which causes enmity between them. But through the Cross, the obstacle has been removed in principle, the work of reconciliation is accomplished (Ephesians 2:11-18; Romans 5:8-10), and peace is restored (Romans 5:1). The demands of the law have been met (Romans 3:25; Galatians 3:13) and harmony restored. The method of this reconciliation and peace is of great importance—through the blood of Christ—that is, the atoning sacrifice of the Son of God on Calvary. The importance of this process to the Apostle Paul is quite evident in the number of occasions he speaks of the blood of Christ in many portions of his letters (see Romans 3:25; 5:9; 1 Corinthians 11:25; Ephesians 1:7). It is necessary to mention the motive behind this process —the love of God for His creatures and His delighted pleasure (John 3:16; Colossians 1:19). A number of questions arise from verse 20. What does Paul mean by the phrase, "to reconcile all things ... whether they be things in earth or things in heaven"? What is included? Does it include angelic beings: good and bad angels? Are lower animals included in "all things"? These questions are meant to challenge us to reflect individually and collectively.

Sources:
"Bible Words – Phonetic Pronunciation." Better Days Are Coming.com. http://betterdaysarecoming.com/bible/pronunciation.html#e/ (accessed October 31, 2011).

New Testament Greek Lexicon. Bible Study Tools.com. biblestudytools.com/lexicons/greek/ (accessed October 31, 2011).

Say It Correctly

Colossians. co-LOSH-uhns.
Epaphras. EP-uh-fras, EP-uh-fruhs.

Daily Bible Readings

MONDAY
Christ, the Head of the Church
(Ephesians 1:17-23)

TUESDAY
Christ, the Firstborn of the Dead
(Revelation 1:1-6)

WEDNESDAY
Christ, One with the Father
(John 17:20-26)

THURSDAY
Christ, the Reconciler to God
(2 Corinthians 5:16-21)

FRIDAY
Christ, the Channel of God's Grace
(Romans 5:15-21)

SATURDAY
The Compelling Call of Christ
(Matthew 4:18:25)

SUNDAY
The Person and Work of Christ
(Colossians 1:15-20)

Notes

_____

_____

_____

_____

Teaching Tips

February 10
Bible Study Guide 11

Words You Should Know

A. Rooted (Colossians 2:7) *rhizoo* (Gk.)—Rendered firm, established.

B. Godhead (v. 9) *theotes* (Gk.)—Supreme deity, the essential being of God, the Supreme Being; the whole nature and attributes of God.

Teacher Preparation

Unifying Principle—It's a Wonderful Life! Through Jesus, God forgives all our trespasses and triumphs over all earthly rulers and authorities.

A. Use Ephesians 3:14-21 as a prayer for your students.

B. Study and meditate on the entire lesson.

C. Research the philosophies of atheism and humanism, and be prepared to biblically explore the question, "What is a wonderful life?"

D. Complete the companion lesson in the Precepts For Living Personal Study Guide®.

O—Open the Lesson

A. Receive prayer requests and open with prayer.

B. Lead a discussion of the question "What is a wonderful life?"

C. Have them read the Aim for Change and Key Verse in unison.

D. Have a volunteer summarize the In Focus story. Discuss.

P—Present the Scriptures

A. Have volunteers read the Focal Verses.

B. To examine the lesson, read and discuss The People, Places, and Times, Background, At-a-Glance outline, and More Light on the Text sections.

C. Use the Search the Scriptures and Discuss the Meaning questions to add depth to the discussion.

E—Explore the Meaning

A. Refer to the Lesson in Our Society section and discuss how this lesson is applicable to our daily lives.

B. Incorporate the Lesson in Our Society and Make It Happen sections.

C. Ask students to share how they keep Christ in His rightful position as supreme ruler and authority—as the fullness of the Godhead.

N—Next Steps for Application

A. Summarize the lesson.

B. Close with prayer.

Worship Guide

For the Superintendent or Teacher
Theme: Full Life in Christ
Song: "O, For a Thousand Tongues to Sing"
Devotional Reading: Romans 8:31-39
Prayer

Full Life in Christ

Bible Background • COLOSSIANS 2:6-15
Printed Text • COLOSSIANS 2:6-15 | Devotional Reading • ROMANS 8:31-39

——————— Aim for Change ———————

By the end of the lesson, we will: EXPLORE Paul's message describing a full life in Christ; EXPRESS thanksgiving for God's forgiveness through Jesus Christ; and REMAIN rooted in faith by continuing to pursue an understanding of life in the fullness of Jesus Christ and to be thankful to Him.

———————  In Focus ———————

Wendy heard a well-known Christian leader say that all religions lead to God and that even if you did not accept Christ into your heart and make Him the Lord of your life, you are still saved because Jesus saves everybody. At least, that's what she'd heard.

One day, Wendy was at a Bible study class at church when someone raised a question about salvation. In the midst of the discussion she said, "Everyone is saved already and no one will go to hell. Therefore, you don't have to confess Jesus as your Lord, or study the Bible, or be concerned about living for Him; just be a good person. No other religion believes in hell the way we do, so a lot of Christians must be wrong."

Her feelings emanated from the fact that sometime before, Wendy's very close friend died, and she knew that he had not accepted Christ as his Lord and Savior. Wendy had never shared her faith with her friend. Therefore, because her friend was such a good person, she refused to believe that he would not go to heaven because he had not made Jesus the Lord of his life.

In today's lesson, Paul deals head on with traditions and philosophies that threaten to unsettle the budding church in Colosse. Like this church, we, too, need to be exhorted and reminded of the fullness we have in Christ and stay rooted in the faith.

FEB
10th

——————— Keep in Mind ———————

"And ye are complete in him, which is the head of all principality and power" (Colossians 2:10).

"And ye are complete in him, which is the head of all principality and power"
(Colossians 2:10).

Focal Verses

KJV **Colossians 2:6** As ye have therefore received Christ Jesus the Lord, so walk ye in him:

7 Rooted and built up in him, and stablished in the faith, as ye have been taught, abounding therein with thanksgiving.

8 Beware lest any man spoil you through philosophy and vain deceit, after the tradition of men, after the rudiments of the world, and not after Christ.

9 For in him dwelleth all the fulness of the Godhead bodily.

10 And ye are complete in him, which is the head of all principality and power:

11 In whom also ye are circumcised with the circumcision made without hands, in putting off the body of the sins of the flesh by the circumcision of Christ:

12 Buried with him in baptism, wherein also ye are risen with him through the faith of the operation of God, who hath raised him from the dead.

13 And you, being dead in your sins and the uncircumcision of your flesh, hath he quickened together with him, having forgiven you all trespasses;

14 Blotting out the handwriting of ordinances that was against us, which was contrary to us, and took it out of the way, nailing it to his cross;

15 And having spoiled principalities and powers, he made a shew of them openly, triumphing over them in it.

NLT **Colossians 2:6** And now, just as you accepted Christ Jesus as your Lord, you must continue to follow him.

7 Let your roots grow down into him, and let your lives be built on him. Then your faith will grow strong in the truth you were taught, and you will overflow with thankfulness.

8 Don't let anyone capture you with empty philosophies and high-sounding nonsense that come from human thinking and from the spiritual powers of this world, rather than from Christ.

9 For in Christ lives all the fullness of God in a human body.

10 So you also are complete through your union with Christ, who is the head over every ruler and authority.

11 When you came to Christ, you were "circumcised," but not by a physical procedure. Christ performed a spiritual circumcision— the cutting away of your sinful nature.

12 For you were buried with Christ when you were baptized. And with him you were raised to new life because you trusted the mighty power of God, who raised Christ from the dead.

13 You were dead because of your sins and because your sinful nature was not yet cut away. Then God made you alive with Christ, for he forgave all our sins.

14 He canceled the record of the charges against us and took it away by nailing it to the cross.

15 In this way, he disarmed the spiritual rulers and authorities. He shamed them publicly by his victory over them on the cross.

The People, Places, and Times

Gnosticism. Gnosticism comes from the Greek word *gnosis,* meaning "knowledge." The Gnostics separated matter from thought. They concluded that matter was evil and formulated the idea that the possession of knowledge was the only requirement for salvation. This is why they did not want to attribute humanity to Jesus Christ because to them, material things were evil. Paul stresses that in Him (Jesus Christ as He appeared on earth) "dwelleth all the fulness of the Godhead bodily" (Colossians 2:9).

Jesus was truly God in the flesh (John 1:14). As a result of their philosophical concepts—that the body is evil, for example—the Gnostics ignored or diminished the significance of the historic facts of the ministry, death, and Resurrection of Jesus Christ because it was so apparent. To them, all the secrets of God were in the mind or only appeared within an immaterial identity.

Circumcision. Circumcision is the cutting off of the foreskin. Jewish baby boys are circumcised at 8 days old. Mosaic Law mandated this. (Leviticus 12:3). Circumcision marked males as a belonging of God, and it was supposed to be more than an outward sign, signifying complete devotion to God (Deuteronomy 10:16).

When Gentiles began turning to Jesus, a big discussion arose as to whether Gentile Christian men needed to be circumcised. Paul pointed out that uncircumcised Gentiles had come to Christ simply by grace through faith. No one came to Christ through anything else. Because no one was able to keep the law to perfection, it was obvious that the law, including circumcision, did not save anyone.

Today, many baby boys are circumcised though not necessarily for religious reasons. Studies have shown the circumcised males are less likely to get sexually transmitted diseases when exposed to them and other potential conditions. As a result, circumcision is sometimes done as a preventative measure.

Background

Throughout his ministry as the spiritual father of the Gentile church, Paul wrote letters of correction, gave instructions, and built up the faith of the body of Christ. It was especially important for him to do this in locations whose congregations had not yet met him. In the letter to the Colossians, his purpose was to refute heretical teachings (including a form of Gnosticism) that were influencing believers and thereby causing confusion. Paul's references to circumcision, food regulations, and feast days indicate that this heresy involved Judaistic tendencies. Instead of refuting the false teachings point by point, Paul gives encouragement in laying out a clear argument that all things are fulfilled in the person of Christ. He stresses that all wisdom and spiritual understanding can be found in the God-Man, Christ, who redeemed them and now holds authority over all things.

At-A-Glance

1. Warnings Against Strange Teachings (Colossians 2:6-8)
2. Fullness of Life in Christ (vv. 9-10)
3. Believers Are Complete in Christ (vv. 11-15)

In Depth

1. Warnings Against Strange Teachings (Colossians 2:6-8)

Paul warns members of this part of the family against deception: Arguments that may sound rational on the surface run counter to what they had accepted by faith in Christ. When the Colossians encounter arguments that oppose Christ, he does not want these children of God to lose heart or abandon their grounding. Therefore, Paul affirms that they have received Christ Jesus as Lord and should live their lives planted, rooted, and established in Him alone. As Paul told the church at Ephesus, their spiritual growth needs to develop so they are not "tossed to and fro ... with every wind of doctrine" (Ephesians 4:14).

As Peter does in 1 Peter 5:9-10, Paul implores the Colossian and Laodicean churches to stand firm, stick to what they have been taught, and continue to have a thankful heart. Sternly but lovingly, he warns them not to be captivated by philosophy and rhetoric fashioned in human traditions and seated in worldly ideology. Paul then alludes to what he has heard from Epaphras and Timothy concerning the messages disseminated among these congregants. The information is believed by scholars to be a mixture of Jewish tradition and Gnostic philosophy.

One of the enemy's greatest tricks is to distort the truth of God by planting a seed of doubt. If the devil, through strange doctrine and heresy, can catch members in isolation, he does his greatest damage. Thus, to help them assist in each other's spiritual growth and to stay grounded in the faith, Paul tackles the issues by encouraging believers to remain faithful and stay connected.

2. Fullness of Life in Christ (vv. 9-10)

Paul continues this discourse with his church family in Colosse by reemphasizing what he said in chapter 1 in a slightly different manner. In Colossians 1:15-20, he details that Jesus Christ is the image of the invisible God and that all things in heaven and earth were created by Him and for Him. In doing this, he emphasizes the supremacy of Christ over any other religious figure or ideology. He places Christ in His rightful position as head of the church and explains that it pleased the Father that all the fullness of God dwell in Him (1:19). Paul revisits this point in chapter 2 by informing believers that Jesus Christ came in the flesh and is fully divine (2:9). This church family is exhorted to stand firm and know that because of its faith in Jesus Christ alone and because people in that family live for His glory, they are complete in His fullness. He alone is above all rule and authority in heaven and on Earth. Because of their connection to Christ, they have access to the fullness of God the Father by the Holy Spirit. Ministry is at its best when a leader can point the way through the power of the Word to build a community of believers confident in the Son of the Living God.

3. Believers Are Complete in Christ (vv. 11-15)

Every Jewish male was circumcised to show devotion to God. But although a man may have been circumcised as a baby, he may not try to please God when he is an adult. Just as Deuteronomy 10:16 says, God desires real devotion, not just an outward sign. When we put our complete trust in Jesus Christ as Savior, Paul says we have hearts that are circumcised. Circumcision cuts off a piece of flesh, but receiving Jesus Christ as Savior means Jesus Christ has cut away our old sinful nature.

Paul says the rite of circumcision is something like baptism. When we are plunged into the water, our old sinful selves are buried with Jesus. Then we are raised to life by the power of God, through our faith in Him.

Paul says it's also like a piece of parchment containing a list of a person's debts.

When the debts are paid, the writing is erased. Again, this is just like what Jesus did for us. Imagine all of our sins written on parchment and Jesus erasing them all. In fact, the record of our sins has been nailed to the Cross and no longer exists. The physical act of baptism is not what washes the sins away, just as physical circumcision does not make a man good. Instead, it is our trust in Jesus for His death on the Cross to pay the penalty for our sins.

Colossians 2:15 gives us one more picture. When a Roman general had an especially great victory over his enemies, he had a parade. The general and all his proud soldiers marched in front. In the back, pulled by a rope, were the vanquished enemies. This is the picture that Paul paints for us. Christ, our Savior, has triumphed over His foes.

Search the Scriptures

1. "As ye have therefore received Christ Jesus the Lord, so _____ ____ ___ ___" (Colossians 2:6).

2. "_____ _____ _____ up in him, and _____ in the _____, as ye have been _____, abounding therein with thanksgiving" (v. 7).

3. "For in him _____ all the _____ of the _____ bodily" (v. 9).

Discuss the Meaning

1. What does it mean to walk in Christ Jesus as you have received Him?

2. What can we do as believers to keep ourselves from getting caught up in vain deceit and traditions that have nothing to do with Christ?

3. If Jesus is the Lord of your life, and He is acknowledged as the supreme authority in your life, what does it mean for you to be complete in Christ?

Lesson in Our Society

Jesus Christ, who is the fullness of God, put an end to all disputes of power and authority. In today's world, which is rampant with humanism, we as Christians can rest assured of our completeness in Him. We must be encouraged by the fellowship of the saints that as we are met with opposing views, we can stand on the truth of the Gospel of Jesus Christ. As a community of believers, it is incumbent on us to join with spiritual leadership in building up the body of Christ by remaining confident that Jesus is who He says He is. Also, in our hearts, we must stand guard against any attempts of the enemy of our souls to cause distractions, distortions, and confusion. We can only be effective in sharing love and winning souls for Christ by being steadfast and unmovable, always abounding in the work of the Lord.

Make It Happen

1. Seek in your own life to draw closer to the Lord by further study of what it means to be complete in Christ, who is the fullness of God.

2. God may be on your team, but do you have Him actually playing in the game of your life? Examine areas where you need to give Christ supreme authority.

Follow the Spirit

What God wants me to do:

_____

_____

_____

_____

Remember Your Thoughts

Special insights I have learned:

_____

_____

_____

_____

More Light on the Text

Colossians 2:6-15

6 As ye have therefore received Christ Jesus the Lord, so walk ye in him:

Paul's logic appears as follows: If Christ is in fact utterly sufficient for the believer, possessing all the wisdom and knowledge necessary for the church, then he or she should draw closer to Him. This should not just be for believers' entry into the church and the Christian life but also throughout their lifetimes. Paul pairs two concepts in his exhortation: "received" and "walk."

Paul's use of "received" mirrors his use of Greek word *paralambano* (**par-al-am-BAN-know**), elsewhere in his letters. In 1 Corinthians 15:3, he writes about the Gospel in this way: "For I delivered unto you first of all that which I also *received*, how that Christ died for our sins according to the scriptures" (emphasis added). In his epistle, or letter, to the people of Galatia, he uses the word "received" to describe how he came to know the truth of Christ: "For I neither received it of man, neither was I taught it, but by the revelation of Jesus Christ" (Galatians 1:12). The way to know Christ is to believe the wonderful message about Him on this basis the Holy Spirit is granted to the believer.

The word "walk" (Colossians 2:6) has to do with the believer's daily life and habits. But more specifically, when paired with the word "received," it points to a day-to-day resolve to believe the truth about Jesus as proclaimed in the Gospel. The overall sense of what Paul is saying in this verse is, "Believe what we have told you about the Lord, and continue to believe it." As we will see in verse 8, this kind of "receiving" and "walking" is the antidote to deception by those who would lead the believer away from Christ.

7 Rooted and built up in him, and stablished in the faith, as ye have been taught, abounding therein with thanksgiving.

How is the believer to "walk" in what she or he has "received" concerning Christ? The KJV translates Paul's words into three agricultural terms that paint a picture of the ongoing Christian life: "rooted," "built up," and "established."

In the Greek, the first verb "rooted" is *rhizoo* (**hrid-ZO-o**), and it means "rendered firm, fixed, established, having caused a person or thing to be firmly grounded." Other usages of this term appear in Psalm 1. This also brings to mind the seed in the parable of the sower: the plants that withered represent the person who "has no root in himself and does not endure; when trouble or persecution comes because of the word, immediately he falls away" (Matthew 13:21, NET). This is not so of the believer well founded in the truth of the gospel; his "walk" remains tied to what he received.

Essentially Paul writes that "built up" (Gk. *epoikodomeo*, **ep-oy-kod-om-EH-o**) means "to give constant increase in Christian knowledge and in a life conformed thereto." It points to how the believer's spiritual understanding develops through communion with Christ and strengthening in His Word. "Stablished" in the Greek is *bebaioo* (**beb-ah-YO-o**), and it means established, "made firm, made sure." It goes back to the "rooted" idea but adds the qualifier "in the faith," referring to the Gospel tradition passed down to and through the Colossians to us as well as the sound teaching described elsewhere as "the faith which was once delivered unto the saints" (Jude 3). Of course, rooting, building up, and establishment in the faith happen because of the gracious work of the Holy Spirit in the life of the church—as the apostle Paul made clear in another reference that combines agriculture with architecture: "Ye are God's husbandry (field), ye are God's building" (1 Corinthians 3:9b).

Then, in his letter to the Colossians, Paul puts into place the final element of what it means to walk in Christ: "abounding therein with thanksgiving" (Colossians 2:7). A heart filled with gratitude is a central theme of Paul's instructions to the Colossians, not to mention his own life. The contentment that enables the believer to remain rooted and established in Christ, rather than chasing things that seem momentarily more exciting, grows through the disciplined practice of giving thanks. The result is joy!

8 Beware lest any man spoil you through philosophy and vain deceit, after the tradition of men, after the rudiments of the world, and not after Christ.

The wording in the best manuscripts for verse 8 is not "spoil" but rather "take captive." Clearly, the danger of the false teaching that enticed the Colossian believers was that it could powerfully enslave them to a way of thinking that wasn't grounded in Christ. When Paul refers to "philosophy," he likely isn't referring to all kinds of philosophy but rather to the kind that sets itself up as a sort of "special knowledge" that one could gain without reference to the knowledge and wisdom of Christ. This sort of "philosophy" was an early version of what

was called Gnosticism, which contained the idea that knowledge of the divine could be gained by a special, individual enlightenment. The forerunners of this kind of thinking were clearly already present in Paul's day. The word "vain" in the Greek is *kenos* (**ken-OS**) and means "fruitless, of no purpose." The Greek word for "deceit" is *apate* (**ap-AT-ay**), and it means "delusion, misinformation or falsehood." Such was the "vain deceit" that undermined true Christian piety: vain because it brought forth nothing of value and deceit because it falsely convinced the believer that Christ was not necessary, or at least not enough, in the pursuit of true life.

9 For in him dwelleth all the fulness of the Godhead bodily.

The word "fulness" in Greek is *pleroma* (**PLAY-ro-mah**), and it means "that which is put in to fill up, abundance." The Greek translation of the phrase "of the God-head" is *theotes* (**theh-OT-ace**), and it means "deity." Why should it be such a tragedy for the Colossians to be "taken captive through philosophy and vain deceit" (v. 8)? In verse 9, Paul answers: Christ possesses the very fullness of God, and therefore any system of thought or worship not founded on Him has missed the very things it seeks to provide in its philosophy. This includes wisdom, virtue, access to God, and life-giving power. All of these are to be found in Jesus, for only in Him (in some profound mystery) does the very life of God dwell, joined with humanity.

We have in verse 9 also a foreshowing of the redemption that Paul has written about in verses 11-15. Christ's dual nature as God and man makes Him uniquely able to satisfy the righteousness and justice of God and uniquely able, through the Cross, to identify with fallen humankind. Thus, it is not because Paul is so concerned ultimately with philosophy that he holds up Christ as the foundation of all wisdom and truth. Rather, he cares most deeply with the redemption of the world. And for this reason also, he preaches to the Colossians the glories of Christ, considering how their captivity to a different philosophy could mean the loss of their very souls.

10 And ye are complete in him, which is the head of all principality and power:

Here is the final answer to counter the temptation to follow empty philosophies and ways of life that oppose Christ: "Ye are complete in him." What more does Paul need to say to the Colossians beyond noting that everything they are tempted to seek outside of Christ is found within Him? Paul can know this, in part, because of the full-fledged authority that the Father has given to His Son: He is "the head of all principality and power." This means that the promise of Christ's fullness is not a meaningless promise made by an impotent ruler but a real sharing between the living Lord of the universe and those who are in union with Him. In Him are all treasures of wisdom and knowledge, not hidden from His people but made known, according to the mystery of the Gospel, to all who call upon His name.

11 In whom also ye are circumcised with the circumcision made without hands, in putting off the body of the sins of the flesh by the circumcision of Christ: 12 Buried with him in baptism, wherein also ye are risen with him through the faith of the operation of God, who hath raised him from the dead.

Many Jewish men thought of circumcision as merely a mark of their ethnicity. But even from the beginning, Moses told the people that they must be circumcised in the heart as well as the flesh (Deuteronomy 30:6). This was to be a sign of complete devotion to God. But now that Gentiles were coming to Christ as Savior, the question arose as to whether they too needed to be circumcised. No, Paul said. Christ Jesus circumcised the hearts of all people when they came to Him. It did not matter whether they were circumcised in the flesh. Jesus Christ circumcised them by cutting out the sins within them. And this is what Jesus has done for us. Jesus has cut out that part of us that delights in sinning. We may still sin, but now when we do, it is very painful or uncomfortable and leaves us with guilt and perhaps regret.

Instead of circumcision, the Christian has the rite of baptism. The symbolism of going down into the water is as if we are dying, just as Jesus Christ died on the Cross. Our old sinful self is now dead. Then when we come up out of the water, we are raised with Christ. We are all brand new, sharing this experience with our risen Lord.

But no outward rite can save a person, neither can circumcision nor even baptism. Baptism is only a symbol, and we pray that the experience is true in the life of the one baptized. William Barclay paraphrases it this way: "The only true circumcision is when a man dies and rises with Christ in baptism, in such a way that it is not part of his body which is cut away but his whole sinful self which is destroyed, and he is filled with newness of life and the very holiness of God" (The Letters to the Philippians, Colossians, and Thessalonians, 140).

13 And you, being dead in your sins and the uncircumcision of your flesh, hath he quickened together with him, having forgiven you all trespasses; 14 Blotting out

the handwriting of ordinances that was against us, which was contrary to us, and took it out of the way, nailing it to his cross;

Without Jesus Christ, we are truly dead in our sins. We have no hope for eternity. We have no power to overcome sin today. And we are dead because we are punished for all the sinful things we have said, thought, and done. We were as dead as the dry bones of Ezekiel. Though we were dead in our sins, Jesus Christ has raised us up to life. He has forgiven all our sins—past, present, and even those in the future.

Now we see another picture (v. 14). A merchant might write on parchment all the debts a person owes. The Greek word for "handwriting" is *cheirographon* (**khi-ROG-raf-on**); its technical meaning is what we would call an I.O.U. All of our sins are listed on this document, and we have signed it to acknowledge that we have done everything listed. Jews had the law to show them their sins. We Gentiles have our conscience, the Holy Spirit, and the Word that show us where we have gone wrong, even if the conscience is not a perfect guide. Nevertheless, we know that we have sinned against God, and we must acknowledge this in order to be saved.

Along with "handwriting" we read the phrase "blotting out." The Greek for this is *exaleipho* (**ex-al-I-fo**). Ancient merchants often wrote on papyrus or the skin of an animal. Both were expensive, so when someone's debt was paid, the merchant usually took a sponge and wiped it away as if the debt never occurred. So it is with our sins. Because of Christ's death on the Cross for us, God in His amazing mercy wipes away the record of our sins as if they never occurred.

Then Paul gives us one more picture to show us how great is God's grace. The list of our sins is not just erased; it is nailed to the Cross. It is Jesus who has received the punishment for the wrong we've done, and we walk free.

15 And having spoiled principalities and powers, he made a shew of them openly, triumphing over them in it.

But Jesus is no longer on the Cross. He is the victor over powerful beings in the unseen world. Despite the forces that are determined to trip us up, Jesus has overcome them and triumphantly leads with the conquered beings trailing behind.

Sources:

Barclay, William. *The Daily Study Bible: The Letters to the Philippians, Colossians, and Thessalonians.* Philadelphia, PA: Westminster Press, 1975. 140.

Comment on Colossians 2. In *IVP New Testament Commentary.* BibleGateway.com. http://www.biblegateway.com/resources/commentaries/?action=getChapterSections&cid=9&source=1&schap=2 (accessed November 1, 2011).

Henry, Matthew. Comment on Colossians 2. In *Matthew Henry's Commentary on the Whole Bible, Vol. VI—Acts to Revelation.* Bible Study Guide.org. http://www.biblestudyguide.org./comment/matthew-henry/mhcc/colossians.html (accessed November 1, 2011).

Libronix Digital Library. Logos Bible Software. Bellingham, WA: Libronix. Last refreshed: July 24, 2008 (accessed January 13, 2009).

New Testament Greek Lexicon. Bible Study Tools.com. http://www.biblestudytools.com/lexicons/greek/ (accessed November 1, 2011).

Strong, James. *New Strong's Exhaustive Concordance of the Bible.* Nashville, TN: Thomas Nelson, 1990.

Zodhiates, Spiros, ed. *Hebrew-Greek Key Word Study Bible (KJV).* Chattanooga, TN: AMG, 1991. 1478, 1480.

Say It Correctly

Circumcised. sir-kuhm-sized.
Spectacle. SPEK-ta-kuhl.

Daily Bible Readings

MONDAY
Those Touched by Jesus
(Matthew 8:1-4)

TUESDAY
Those Called by God
(Acts 2:37-42)

WEDNESDAY
Those Who Are in Christ Jesus
(Romans 8:1-5)

THURSDAY
Those Who Live in the Spirit
(Romans 8:6-11)

FRIDAY
Those Who Love God
(Romans 8:26-30)

SATURDAY
Those Kept in Christ's Love
(Romans 8:31-39)

SUNDAY
Those Who Have Received Christ Jesus
(Colossians 2:6-15)

Notes

Teaching Tips

Words You Should Know

A. Anger (Colossians 3:8) *orge* (Gk.)—Feeling of discontent, displeasure, or indignation.

B. Wrath (v. 8) *thumos* (Gk.)—Sudden and passionate outburst of extreme displeasure.

C. Malice (v. 8) *kakia* (Gk.)—General feeling of evil, a vicious disposition, prompting one to injure one's neighbor.

Teacher Preparation

Unifying Principle—Breaking Bad Habits. Paul teaches how followers of Christ should behave. Holy characteristics are expressed, and believers are encouraged to do everything in the name of the Lord.

A. Read the Focal Verses. Do the exercise in the Make It Happen section and use a Bible dictionary to define the words listed.

B. Read through the entire lesson and ask God to give you insight and creative skills to make this lesson clear and practical.

C. Materials needed: Bibles, board or newsprint, and pencil and paper for each student (*optional:* a paper doll set).

O—Open the Lesson

A. If you have the paper doll set, use it to show how easily the doll can change from one outfit to another. Connect this to shedding our old life and starting a whole new life in Christ.

B. Have the class read the Aim for Change in unison and then pray about it.

C. Put the At-A-Glance outline on the board.

D. Read In Focus and the Focal Verses.

P—Present the Scriptures

A. Allow the students time to silently read the Background information and The People, Places, and Times section.

B. Read through In Depth and fill in the blanks for Search the Scriptures.

E—Explore the Meaning

A. Discuss the answers to the Discuss the Meaning questions.

B. Leave time for a brief discussion of Lesson in Our Society. Ask whether students agree.

N—Next Steps for Application

A. Give the students pencils and paper to make the two lists in Make It Happen.

B. It is important to help students understand that the old life has been discarded when they became Christians.

C. Encourage the students to read the Daily Bible Readings.

Worship Guide

For the Superintendent or Teacher
Theme: Clothed with Christ
Song: "Give Me a Clean Heart"
Devotional Reading: Psalm 107:1-9
Prayer

Clothed with Christ

Bible Background • COLOSSIANS 3:1-17
Printed Text • COLOSSIANS 3:5-17 | Devotional Reading • PSALM 107:1-9

—————————— Aim for Change ——————————

By the end of the lesson, we will: GAIN an impression of principles of living in Christ; IMAGINE how, because we follow Christ, our life principles and behavior are different from the rest of society; and EVALUATE our treatment of others and make changes where necessary as demanded by a life lived in Christ.

—————————  In Focus —————————

Most creatures in the animal kingdom shed something periodically. The most commonly known from among them are snakes. Most of us have gone to a museum and seen a snakeskin that has been shed and abandoned by the snake. It usually is hard and shaped like the snake. If the snake decided to go back into that skin, it would probably have a difficult time. Once the skin is discarded, it becomes hard and it does not fit anymore.

We can imagine a similar situation with a butterfly trying to return to its cocoon. It would likely damage its beautiful wings trying to get back into the hole of the cocoon. The butterfly no longer fits. Dogs and cats that shed usually leave their hair all over the place. It would be odd and foolish for a pet owner to gather up the hair and then attempt to paste it back on the dog or cat. That hair is dead, old, and it no longer belongs on the animal.

In our lesson today, Paul exhorts the church at Colossae to take off the old life and put on the new one in Christ. Just like the above examples, the old life no longer is appealing nor does it fit our new life in Christ.

————————— Keep in Mind —————————

FEB
17th

"And above all these things put on charity, which is the bond of perfectness"
(Colossians 3:14).

"And above all these things put on charity, which is the bond of perfectness"
(Colossians 3:14).

Focal Verses

KJV **Colossians 3:5** Mortify therefore your members which are upon the earth; fornication, uncleanness, inordinate affection, evil concupiscence, and covetousness, which is idolatry:

6 For which things' sake the wrath of God cometh on the children of disobedience:

7 In the which ye also walked some time, when ye lived in them.

8 But now ye also put off all these; anger, wrath, malice, blasphemy, filthy communication out of your mouth.

9 Lie not one to another, seeing that ye have put off the old man with his deeds;

10 And have put on the new man, which is renewed in knowledge after the image of him that created him:

11 Where there is neither Greek nor Jew, circumcision nor uncircumcision, Barbarian, Scythian, bond nor free: but Christ is all, and in all.

12 Put on therefore, as the elect of God, holy and beloved, bowels of mercies, kindness, humbleness of mind, meekness, longsuffering;

13 Forbearing one another, and forgiving one another, if any man have a quarrel against any: even as Christ forgave you, so also do ye.

14 And above all these things put on charity, which is the bond of perfectness.

15 And let the peace of God rule in your hearts, to the which also ye are called in one body; and be ye thankful.

16 Let the word of Christ dwell in you richly in all wisdom; teaching and admonishing one another in psalms and hymns and spiritual songs, singing with grace in your hearts to the Lord.

17 And whatsoever ye do in word or deed, do all in the name of the Lord Jesus, giving thanks to God and the Father by him.

NLT **Colossians 3:5** So put to death the sinful, earthly things lurking within you. Have nothing to do with sexual immorality, impurity, lust, and evil desires. Don't be greedy, for a greedy person is an idolater, worshiping the things of this world.

6 Because of these sins, the anger of God is coming.

7 You used to do these things when your life was still part of the world.

8 But now is the time to get rid of anger, rage, malicious behavior, slander, and dirty language.

9 Don't lie to each other, for you have stripped off your old sinful nature and all its wicked deeds.

10 Put on your new nature, and be renewed as you learn to know your Creator and become like him.

11 In this new life, it doesn't matter if you are Jew or Gentile, circumcised or uncircumcised, barbaric, uncivilized, slave, or free. Christ is all that matters, and he lives in all of us.

12 Since God chose you to be the holy people he loves, you must clothe yourselves with tender-hearted mercy, kindness, humility, gentleness, and patience.

13 Make allowance for each other's faults, and forgive anyone who offends you. Remember, the Lord forgave you, so you must forgive others.

14 Above all, clothe yourselves with love, which binds us all together in perfect harmony.

15 And let the peace that comes from Christ rule in your hearts. For as members of one body you are called to live in peace. And always be thankful.

16 Let the message about Christ, in all its richness, fill your lives. Teach and counsel

NLT continued

each other will all the wisdom he gives. Sing psalms and hymns and spiritual songs to God with thankful hearts.

17 And whatever you do or say, do it as a representative of the Lord Jesus, giving thanks through him to God the Father.

The People, Places, and Times

Barbarians. The Greeks used this as a term for those they deemed uneducated, that is, those who did not speak Greek or follow a Greek pattern of living. In the Old Testament, the word indicated the inhabited world in contrast to the wilderness where the nomads roamed.

Scythian. A native of Scythia, the ultimate of barbarism, a savage. The Greeks despised the Jews; a barbarian scorned a Scythian. They were the lowest of the low.

Background

In the final two chapters of Colossians, Paul challenged the Colossians to make practical application of the doctrines he had been preaching. Paul believed Christians should not just know the truth and be able to defend it but that truth must be lived out in their daily lives as well.

The pagan religions of Paul's day said little or nothing about personal morality. A worshiper could bow before an idol, put his offering on the altar, and go back to live the same old life of sin; what a person believed had no direct relationship with how he behaved. No one would attempt to correct the person for his behavior.

The Christian faith brought a whole new concept into the pagan society. Faith in Christ meant being united with Him. If Christians share His life, they must follow His example. If Christ lives in the believer, he or she cannot continue in sin. Thus, Paul concluded his letter to the Colossians with some specific instructions about Christian conduct.

At-A-Glance

1. New Life in Christ (Colossians 3:5-9)
2. Renewal Procedures (vv. 10-11)
3. Walking New (vv. 12-17)

In Depth

1. New Life in Christ (Colossians 3:5-9)

Paul speaks forthrightly about the demands of the new life and our urgent need to curb all the degrading tendencies of the old nature. The old life is dead. The believer has to let it die. We are not simply to suppress or control evil acts and attitudes; we are to wipe them out completely. Exterminate the old way of life. The action is to be undertaken decisively, with a sense of urgency. It suggests a vigorous, painful act of personal determination. Paul is calling for a slaying of evil passions, desires, and practices that root themselves in our bodies.

Paul goes on to list sins. In the *New International Version* of Colossians 3:5, "impurity" is not just physical impurity but uncleanness in thought, word, and act. "Lust" essentially means a feeling or experience from an uncontrolled desire. "Greed" suggests a ruthless desire in pursuit of material things. This attitude is identified with idolatry because it puts self-interest and material things in the place of God.

Paul warned that God's judgment would fall on the disobedient. He reminded the Colossians that this is the way they used to live. He said this ungodly life belongs to the past and that the Christian should be done with it.

Paul firmly encourages getting "rid" of this past life (v. 8, NIV). The phrase "but now" marks a new beginning. The Christian is to take off the filth of the past. Paul specifically names anger, rage (a sudden and passionate outburst of displeasure), malice, and slander (insulting talk against one's fellow man or woman). Filthy language is "bad or abusive speech, foul-mouthed abuse." The sin of falsehood is singled out. Lying is given separate treatment and given a strong exhortation: "Do not lie" (v. 9, NIV).

The Christian is to have a totally new life change in which he or she has put off the old self with its practices, habits, or characteristics and put on the new. This is like the resurrection of Christ, who pulled off the grave clothes and then left them behind in the tomb. Christians now have a new life in Christ; the old deeds and desires must be put off.

2. Renewal Procedures (vv. 10-11)

Paul talked about becoming a new creature in Christ and taking off the old self, but how can that be done? Bad habits and ungodly conduct is not simply going to fall away like dirty clothes.

Paul used the word "knowledge" to explain how a person changes (v. 10)—not through knowledge of more rules and laws but the knowledge of Christ. Our minds must be renewed. As believers grow in knowledge of the Word of God, when we learn, read, and study His Word, God's Spirit changes us. God transforms Christians by washing old thoughts, desires, and intentions out of our minds and replacing them with new ones.

Paul gives an example of this kind of mind change when he speaks about human distinctions and differences. In Christ, there are no nationalities (neither Greek nor Jew), religious differences (circumcised or non-circumcised), and no cultural differences (Barbarian or Scythian).

The Greeks considered all non-Greeks to be barbarians and the Scythians to be the lowest barbarians of all. Yet, in Jesus Christ, a person's cultural status has no advantage or disadvantage. Nor is economic or political status helpful (bond or free). Slaves should try to get their freedom, but if they do not, that does not make them any less in Christ's sight. All of these kinds of distinctions belong to the old man and the old way of thinking.

3. Walking New (vv. 12-17)

Christians are chosen, set apart, and loved by God. These are privileges God gave to His people in the Old Testament that are made available to Christians as well. Because God gave these blessings to His people, Paul encourages them to walk in compassion (a tenderness expressed toward the suffering), in kindness, goodness, graciousness (a sweet disposition), in humility (thinking humbly of oneself), in gentleness (delicate consideration for the rights and feelings of others), and in patience (self-restraint that allows one to bear injury and insult without resorting to retaliation). It also means bearing with and forgiving one another ("putting up" with things we don't like). The final word is "love" (v. 14, NIV). Love is unconditional giving and caring that goes beyond the call of duty.

Peace is another characteristic that Paul exhorts the believer to put on. Not just peace with each other but peace of mind, unruffled by difficulties and confusion. As usual,

Paul weaves an attitude of thanksgiving in this section of the letter. Thankfulness to God and to our brothers and sisters promotes inward and outward peace.

The Colossians are told to allow the word of God, the Gospel, and the messages about Christ to be a rich treasure for them that becomes so deeply implanted that it controls thinking, attitudes, and actions. When God's word is deep down in our hearts, Christ's presence causes us to conduct ourselves in a wise manner, influenced by God's insight and instruction. Paul writes that God's Word dwelling in our hearts will also cause us to sing psalms from the Old Testament and hymns and spiritual songs based on the New Testament truths.

Paul concludes with "Do all in the name of the Lord Jesus." We are to always act as Christ's representatives. Christ is to live through God's children, those who have trusted in Him for their salvation and are eternally thankful.

Search the Scriptures

1. "Mortify ... your _____ ... ; fornication, _____, inordinate affection, evil _____, and covetousness, which is _____" (Colossians 3:5).

2. "_____ not one to another" (v. 9).

3. "_____ one another, and _____ one another ... even as _____ forgave you" (v. 13).

4. "And whatsoever you do ..., do _____ in the _____ of the _____ _____" (v. 17).

Discuss the Meaning

1. How do we constantly "seek things above" when we have to live and participate in daily activities here on earth?

2. How do we get rid of old habits and lifestyles and put on new ones?

3. Why are forgiveness and love two key elements in a life that pleases God?

4. How can an attitude of thanksgiving help us in our relationship with God and with people?

Lesson in Our Society

In our society today, for many people, lying is common. Far too many people believe that if the truth is going to hurt, make you uncomfortable, ruin your reputation, get you in trouble, or cause you to pay money, then lying is OK. We justify lying or find creative ways to do it by calling it something else. In popular culture— TV, movies, politics, etc.—how does it manifest itself and how do we participate? In the midst of this kind of society, the Christian is exhorted to tell the truth. Lying in any form is considered part of our old life and needs to be discarded.

Make It Happen

Complete two lists with characteristics each from your old life and from the new as described in Colossians 3:5-17. Remember you cannot change yourself or your ways. Pray and ask God to change you in His own timing and in His own way to see positive changes in your life.

Follow the Spirit

What God wants me to do:

_____

_____

_____

_____

Remember Your Thoughts

Special insights I have learned:

_____

_____

_____

_____

More Light on the Text

Colossians 3:5-17

5 Mortify therefore your members which are upon the earth; fornication, uncleanness, inordinate affection, evil concupiscence, and covetousness, which is idolatry: 6 For which things' sake the wrath of God cometh on the children of disobedience:

In view of the foregoing paragraph of his epistle (about being united with Christ and the hope of appearing with Him in glory when He comes), Paul calls the Colossians to "mortify therefore your members which are upon the earth." The word "mortify," imperatively used here, is the active verb *nekrosate* in the Greek from *nekroo* (**nek-RO-o**), which means "put to death, to slay or to kill." "Mortify" is used metaphorically. It suggests that action should be taken and some effort should be exerted to deal a deadly blow to sinful habits.

The seeming paradox between verse 3, "Ye are dead..." and verse 5 (NKJV), "Therefore put to death your members" is obvious. On one hand, Paul is saying that the Colossians are already dead, and on the other hand, he is asking them to put their members to death. Understanding and reconciling the two seemingly contradictory statements has never been an easy task among scholars. We can best explain this by understanding the concepts of grace and working faith. The moment we acknowledge that we are

sinners, confess our sins, and accept the gift of salvation offered by grace through faith, we are forgiven. Then and there, we are dead to sin. At that moment, all of the baggage is still there and needs to be dealt with. That is the beginning. A transformative process of the inner man begins, and that is the work of the Spirit.

However, the Holy Spirit does not work in a vacuum, neither does He force Himself on anyone. He works in a heart totally yielded to the Lord and solicits our cooperation. As He works in us by making us uncomfortable in the midst of all the sinful practices and we start to obey Him, we begin to unload all the baggage of sin that easily besets us. We begin to live Christ-like lives, and all the worldly rudiments begin to dissipate. Our attitudes change, and new ways of life and behaviors begin. A change in character becomes noticeable; our desires, passions, and aspirations change. We begin to "seek ... (and) set (our) affection on things above, not on things on the earth" (vv. 1-2). This process is called sanctification and is the work of the Holy Spirit. However, conscious and deliberate self-involvement is needed— and this is working faith. Paul says to the Philippians, "Work out your own salvation with fear and trembling" (Philippians 2:12). Paul calls it putting to death "your members which are upon the earth" (Colossians 3:5).

What members of our bodies, or literally sinful characteristics, need to be slaughtered? "Fornication" (Gk. *porneia,* **por-NI-ah**) includes all manner of illicit sexual relationships and sexual intercourse outside of marriage. It embraces all types of sexual immorality, including adultery (Matthew 5:32; 19:9; 1 Corinthians 7:2; 10:8) and incest (1 Corinthians 5:1). Fornication does not apply only to single people, as some teach, but to all sorts of sexual perversion.

"Uncleanness" (Gk. *akatharsia,* **ak-ath-ar-SEE-ah**) is used in a moral sense to describe whatever is the opposite of purity, including thoughts and motives. The emphasis seems to lie on sexual immorality, which likely includes all forms of sexual seduction, homosexuality and sodomy (Matthew 23:27; Romans 1:26-27; 6:19; 2 Corinthians 12:21; Ephesians 4:19; 5:3; 1 Thessalonians 2:3; 4:7; 2 Peter 2; Jude 4). In Colossians 3:5, the phrase "inordinate affection" (Gk. *pathos,* **PATH-os**) describes the unnatural, unrestrained, and out of control passion and lust for anything (1 Thessalonians 4:5). It is called "vile affections" in Romans 1:26 where Paul writes concerning the practice and result of apostasy: "For this cause God gave them up unto vile affections: for even their women did change the natural use into that which is against nature." This refers to lesbianism, or sexual relationships between women. "Evil concupiscence" (Gk. *kakos epithumia,* **kak-OS ep-ee-thoo-MEE-ah**) is any strong or vehement desire associated mainly with evil and depraved lusts (John 8:44; Ephesians 2:3). Here again, it has the connotation of illicit sexual immorality. "Covetousness" (Gk. *pleonexia,* **pleh-on-ex-EE-ah**) is a greedy desire to have more or have what belongs to someone else.

The first four sins mentioned in Colossians 3:5 (also listed in Romans 1:24-29 and 1 Thessalonians 4:3-7) can be related to sex outside of its proper context, which is marraige. The fifth one, covetousness or greed or selfish desire, seems to be the underlying evil that summarizes the rest of the vices. It is based essentially on the worship of self (ego) rather than God and eventually replaces the Lordship of Christ. For this reason, Paul adds, it is idolatry.

Why does Paul use the phrase "your members" to describe these vices? According to William Hendriksen, John Calvin stated that these vices are called "'*members* since they adhere so closely to us'" (*Exposition of Colossians and Philemon,* 145). "Member" is a translation of the Greek word *melos* (**MEL-os**) which means "limb or a member of the human body." It is used figuratively here to describe some of the sins that have become attached to us, as limbs are attached. They have become such a part of our bodily experiences that we have become used to them as inherent parts of our being.

Paul calls on the Colossians, not only to mutilate the vices that have formed part of their being but to kill them outrightly. Having listed the evils, Paul reminds and warns the Colossians of the consequences of indulging in them. These sins attract or invoke the wrath of God against those who indulge themselves in them, i.e., the children of disobedience. God's "wrath" (Gk. *orge,* **or-GAY**) or extreme displeasure refers to the coming judgment day (see Romans 2:5-11; Ephesians 5:6; 2 Thessalonians 1:8-10; Ephesians 2:2-3).

7 In the which ye also walked some time, when ye lived in them. 8 But now ye also put off all these; anger, wrath, malice, blasphemy, filthy communication out of your mouth. 9 Lie not one to another, seeing that ye have put off the old man with his deeds;

In verses 7 and 8, Paul compares the Colossians' former lifestyle with their present disposition as those who have been raised with Christ. In their state without Christ, they walked and lived in those vices, but now they have been regenerated through the death of Christ. Therefore, those vices should be done away with. Paul now uses a different metaphor from the one used in verse 5. Instead of putting the sins to death, he urges them to put off the vices as one would do with worn-out garments or garments that no longer fit. "Put off" translates into the Greek as *apotithemi* (say **ap-ot-EETH-ay-mee**), which means "to put away, to cast off." The idea here is more serious than the language seems to convey. It is "to discard, never to be worn again."

The phrase in verse 8, "but now ye also put off all these," means that in addition to the listed vices that need to be mortified (v. 5), the believers need to discard as unfit, and unwanted garments the vices listed in verse 8: anger, wrath, malice, blasphemy, and filthy communication. Here again is a list of five vices related to attitudes toward others that the Colossians were to discard.

"Anger" is sometimes translated "wrath," and the words are used interchangeably. *The New Unger's Bible Dictionary* describes "anger" as, "The emotion of instant displeasure and indignation arising from the feeling of injury done or intended" and "wrath" as "more of an abiding and settled habit of the mind . . . with the purpose of revenge" (Unger, 62, 1373). Paul also includes "malice" (Gk. *kakia*, **kak-EE-ah**—evil or wickedness) in the list of things Colossians ought to discard. It is interesting how these sins are related. Extended anger develops into wrath, and when wrath is not dealt with, it develops into malice. When anger is allowed to develop into a grudge, and a grudge becomes hatred, it is sin. That is why Paul says in Ephesians, "Be ye angry, and sin not: let not the sun go down upon your wrath: Neither give place to the devil" (Ephesians 4:26-27).

In addition to the three vices that deal with people's attitude and disposition against others are two that relate to the use of the tongue: blasphemy and filthy communication. The first three start from the inside the heart, and manifest themselves outwardly through the mouth in the way of blasphemy (slander) and foul or abusive language. The word "blasphemy" is a direct derivation of the Greek *blasphemia*

(**blas-fay-ME-ah**), which means evil speaking. Although it is typically used exclusively in reference to evil words against God (Matthew 12:31), it also refers to speaking evil or slander against people (Ephesians 4:31). By "filthy communication" (Gk. *aischrologia*, **ahee-skhrol-og-EE-ah**), Paul refers to the use of bad or foul language or vile conversation, the same idea Paul expressed in Ephesians 4:29 and 5:4.

Lying must also be discarded. Paul imperatively says: "Lie not one to another" (Colossians 3:9). It carries the same idea as in the preceding verse and is included in the things they needed to put off. In Ephesians 4:25, Paul says, "Wherefore putting away lying, speak every man truth with his neighbour: for we are members one of another." The same reason is implicit here: Because you are members of the same body, do not "lie" (Gk. *pseudomai*, **PSYOO-dom-ahee**).

10 And have put on the new man, which is renewed in knowledge after the image of him that created him:

Continuing the clothing motif, Paul instructs the Colossians to "put on the new man" (v. 10). To "put on the new man" is to clothe oneself with the new nature, which results from our spiritual union with Christ through His death and resurrection (2 Corinthians 5:17). The "new man," Paul continues, "is renewed in knowledge after the image of him that created him" (Colossians 3:10). The phrase "is renewed" (Gk. *anakainoo*, **an-ak-ahee-NO-o**) gives the idea of growth and changing from the former corrupt state into a new kind of life.

The idea Paul portrays here is comparable to earthly relationships. When a Christian receives Christ, he begins a new relationship. As that relationship with Christ deepens, his life changes, his thought processes change, and he makes new choices patterned according to Christ's. Therefore, the standard of the renewal or the new man is God's image.

The next idea we can glean from Scripture is that God's original plan of creating man and woman in His image was for them to have the full knowledge of living according to God's moral and spiritual likeness. Humanity severely damaged the image at the Garden of Eden through sin, which we inherited. Now God renews us after His original pattern and gives us the true knowledge through the new Adam— Christ Jesus (2 Peter 1:3-13).

11 Where there is neither Greek nor Jew, circumcision nor uncircumcision, Barbarian, Scythian, bond nor free: but Christ is all, and in all.

This progressive transformation into the image of God does not distinguish between racial, religious, cultural, and social boundaries. Paul says here that in Christ, all types of people whether Jews, which he describes as "circumcision," Greeks (or Gentiles) who were regarded as uncircumcised, or slaves and free, including Barbarians, are equal. The introduction of this theme at this point indicates that Paul is aware of the scandals in his time. The partition between the Greek and Jew was practically unbreakable, especially from the Jewish end. The Jews who were circumcised would look down on the Greeks or Gentiles, the uncircumcised, as inferior and would not acknowledge them. The word "Barbarian" (Gk. *barbaros*, **BAR-bar-os**) refers to all foreigners who were non-Greeks and ignorant of the Greek language. The Greeks regarded them as the lower class in the society. Barbarians were also regarded as uncultured, crude, and rough; hence the term "barbaric" behavior

or attitude. A "Scythian" (Gk. *skuthes*, **SKOO-thace**, meaning "rude or rough,") was said to be part of the lowest class of barbarians. They were inhabitants of Scythia, probably modern day Russia.

Attitudes have not changed much, have they? Class discrimination, racial bigotry, social, sex or gender-based notions of superiority, and chauvinism remain a part of our society, including within the church. Paul condemns all of these mindsets and allows no room for such discrimination within the society of his time. The same is true within the community of believers today. How might Paul react if he were to visit our congregations today?

Paul sums it up by saying, "but Christ is all, and in all"—meaning He is all that matters. He lives in all believers, whether Greek or Jew, Barbarian or Scythian, slave or freeman. He does not discriminate based on racial, cultural, or social background or upbringing. His Spirit works in every heart yielded to Him, renewing and progressively transforming them daily "in knowledge after the image of him that created him" (v. 10).

12 Put on therefore, as the elect of God, holy and beloved, bowels of mercies, kindness, humbleness of mind, meekness, longsuffering;

Paul returns to the theme of "putting on" which he started in verse 10, with the same clothing theme: "Put on therefore, as the elect of God ..." The idea is because you have shed the old person and have put on the new person, which is being constantly and progressively renewed in knowledge of the image of God in principle, then you should act it out in practice. Paul uses a series of phrases to describe who believers become when they receive Christ. First, they are "the elect of God" (Gk. *eklektos*, **ek-lek-TOS**), which means "the chosen ones of God." Paul implicitly advances the theology of salvation based on God's choice or election. Christians are called "chosen" or "elect" of God. Secondly, they are "holy" (Gk. *hagios*, **HAG-ee-os**). It means "set apart ones, special or sacred or saints." All true believers are holy in the sight of God. Paul affirms the Colossians' position before God, a special place that they and all Christians now share with the ancient covenant people of Israel (see Isaiah 4:2-3; Hosea 2:23; 1 Peter 2:9; Romans 9:25).

After affirming who they are because of their relationship with God through Christ, Paul now enumerates the qualities expected of them—things they are to put on. It is to be noted how the list here counters the vices in Colossians 3:8, which they are to put off. While the list in verse 8 consists of sins that harm people, the list here implies a desire to care for the well being of others. While the former is self-oriented, the latter is centered on others. It is interesting, as well, to note how these qualities are paired and overlap. The first pair is "bowels of mercies" and "kindness." "Bowels of mercies" is figuratively used here and describes the spirit of compassion to reside in the heart of God's elect. The word "bowel" (Gk. *splagchnon*, **splangkh**) refers to the intestines. "Bowel" is another word for stomach or the abdomen. Used here, it means "pity," "sympathy," or "an inward affection." Bowels were regarded as the seat of more violent passions of both anger and love. For the Hebrew, it is the seat of tender affections, kindness, compassion, and benevolence, which are usually associated with the heart—hence the term tenderhearted. "Bowels" and "mercies" (Gk. *oiktirmos*, **oyk-tir-MOS**), which means "compassion" or "pity," go together. That can literally be translated as "bowels in which compassion resides."

The next word "kindness" (Gk. *chrestotes*, **khray-STOT-ace**) is essentially synonymous with bowels of mercies and expresses moral goodness and compassion. The next set of qualities the Colossians are asked to wear as garments are "humbleness of mind" (Gk. *tapeinophrosune*, **tap-i-nof-ros-OO-nay**), meaning humility or lowliness and "meekness" (Gk. *praotes*, **prah-OT-ace**). Both of these convey the spirit of gentleness and modesty. Humility is a virtue that was despised in the heathen world and is in opposition to pride, but to the Christian, it is an honorable quality to strive for and one Christ exhibited throughout His earthly ministry (Philippians 2:3).

Another quality to strive for that Paul mentions is "longsuffering" (Gk. *makrothumia*, **mak-roth-oo-MEE-ah**), which is patience or "slowness in avenging wrongs." It characterizes a person who refuses to yield to passion and rage in the face of wrongs done to him, a person who has self-control. Patience is almost exclusively associated with our relationship with other people. However, it is applied to self in relation to our attitude to the world system and life as a whole. One needs patience to succeed in life.

13 Forbearing one another, and forgiving one another, if any man have a quarrel against any: even as Christ forgave you, so also do ye.

In close association with the five virtues listed above is a pair of activities required of all believers. The first virtue, "forbearing" (Gk. *anechomai*, **an-EKH-om-ahee**), means "to hold oneself up against, to bear with or to endure." It has the idea of tolerance or putting up with something negative. Paul adds the second activity, "forgiving one another," and gives a scenario of what can constitute forgiveness, "if any man have a quarrel against any," that we should follow in the supreme example of Christ. Christ taught His disciples to pray, "And forgive us our debts, as we forgive our debtors" (Matthew 6:12), and He sets no limit on the number of times we are to forgive one another (Matthew 18:22). All virtues are apparent in Christ's life—a heart of compassion, humility, meekness, long-suffering, endurance or forbearance, and forgiveness. When a believer manifests these virtues, he has put on Christ (Romans 13:14).

14 And above all these things put on charity, which is the bond of perfectness. 15 And let the peace of God rule in your hearts, to the which also ye are called in one body; and be ye thankful.

Love is the cord that binds together all the other virtues. As William Hendriksen put it, "Love is the lubricant that enables the other virtues to function smoothly (Galatians 5:6, 13)" (*Exposition of Colossians and Philemon*, 158). Love is the essence of living. This fact is made clear in Colossians 3:14. After putting on the eight virtues above, we are to put on the outer cloak as the bond of perfectness or as the girdle. "Perfectness" (Gk. *teleiotes*, **tel-i-OT-ace**) means "completeness," and "bond" (Gk. *sundesmos*, **SOON-des-mos**) is like a joint tie or ligament by which things are bound together, especially uniting the members of the human body together.

Paul continues with his theme of unity and this peace is derived from the fact that we are forgiven of our sins and redeemed from its slavery. This peace not only brings harmony within the individual hearts, it brings harmony and oneness within the corporate body of Christ. "Let the peace of God rule in your hearts" literally means we should allow the "peace" (Gk. *eirene*, **i-RAY-nay**) of Christ, the Anointed One, "rule" (Gk. *brabeuo*, **brab-YOO-o**) or be the umpire or arbitrator who directs or controls our

hearts (v. 15). The "peace of God" means either "the peace that Christ gives" or "the peace that belongs to Christ." Paul adds that believers should "be ... thankful," an expression he used frequently throughout the epistle. A grateful heart produces a peaceful mind. Conversely, an ungrateful heart produces grudges and disharmony within oneself and overflows to others, breeding discord and quarreling within the body of Christ.

16 Let the word of Christ dwell in you richly in all wisdom; teaching and admonishing one another in psalms and hymns and spiritual songs, singing with grace in your hearts to the Lord.

The word of Christ should "dwell" (Gk. *enoikeo*, **en-oy-KEH-o**), i.e., inhabit or make its residence, within our hearts as well. The word "dwell" is used figuratively with the idea of influencing one's life and activities. While the peace of Christ should control our lives, His Word is to influence our activities, and both should make their habitation within our hearts. The Word of Christ dwelling within our hearts will produce all the wisdom we need in life. It will influence and govern our thoughts, deeds, and motivations; also, it will help us to make good and rational decisions in life. When we are abundantly equipped with all wisdom through the Word of Christ, we will be teaching and "admonishing" (Gk. *noutheteo*, **noo-thet-EH-o**), i.e., warning, cautioning or reproving each other gently through psalms and hymns and spiritual songs.

17 And whatsoever ye do in word or deed, do all in the name of the Lord Jesus, giving thanks to God and the Father by him.

"Do all in the name of the Lord Jesus" means in relation to His revealed will, in our relationship with Him, in subjection to His authority and power, and for His glory opposed to our own. Paul adds, "giving thanks to God and the Father by him." That is in appreciation for what God has accomplished for us on the basis of Christ's redemptive and atoning sacrifice, whereby we sinners receive forgiveness and are accepted by God the Father as sons and daughters. Our lives are to be motivated by the love of Christ in us with the purpose of honoring and glorifying His name. Our lives and activities must be governed by the "peace of Christ" in our hearts (v. 15, NIV), influenced by the Word of Christ dwelling richly in wisdom (v. 16), and motivated by our relationship with Christ—with eternity in view.

Sources:

Hendriksen, William. *Exposition of Colossians and Philemon: New Testament Commentary.* Grand Rapids, MI: Baker Book House, 1964. 145, 158.

Dictionary.com. http://dictionary.reference.com/ (accessed November 2, 2011).

New Testament Greek Lexicon. Bible Study Tools.com. http://www.biblestudytools.com/lexicons/greek/ (accessed November 2, 2011).

Unger, Merrill F. *The New Unger's Bible Dictionary.* Chicago, IL: Moody Press, 1988. 62, 1373.

Say It Correctly

Concupiscence. kon-KYOO-pi-sens.
Scythian. SITH-e-en.

Daily Bible Readings

MONDAY
Setting Aside Doubt
(Matthew 14:22-33)

TUESDAY
Getting Rid of the Old Ways
(Romans 6:12-19)

WEDNESDAY
Living in Love
(1 John 3:10-17)

THURSDAY
Forgiving as You Were Forgiven
(Matthew 18:21-35)

FRIDAY
Living in Peace
(John 14:25-29)

SATURDAY
Living in Gratitude
(Psalm 107:1-9)

SUNDAY
Living as God's Chosen Ones
(Colossians 3:5-17)

Teaching Tips

Words You Should Know

A. Continue (Colossians 4:2) *proskartereo* (Gk.)—To give unremitting care to a person or thing.

B. Watch (v. 2) *gregoreuo* (Gk.)—To give strict attention.

Teacher Preparation

Unifying Principle—Support through Mentoring. Apostle Paul names spiritual disciplines and faithful people as examples for living a new life in Christ.

A. Pray for your students and lesson clarity.

B. Study the entire text.

C. Provide a *Spiritual Disciplines Journal* for each student (a small memo pad) where they can write prayer requests and pray.

D. Complete the companion lesson in the *Precepts for Living Personal Study Guide®*.

O—Open the Lesson

A. After receiving prayer requests, open with prayer.

B. Introduce the subject of the lesson and have students read the Aim for Change in unison.

C. Have a volunteer read the In Focus story. Discuss.

D. To begin their journal, have the students keep an account of their prayers. In another section, they should analyze the conversations they have.

P—Present the Scriptures

A. Have volunteers read the Focal Verses.

B. Use The People, Places, and Times, Background, At-A-Glance outline, Search the Scriptures, and Discuss the Meaning sections to clarify the text.

E—Explore the Meaning

A. Ask a volunteer to read Lesson in Our Society, and ask the class to discuss: "Has there ever been a time you were not as disciplined as you should have been? How did your life change?"

B. Include the Make It Happen section to further clarify the text.

N—Next Steps for Application

A. Summarize the lesson.

B. Ask the class to continue using the *Spiritual Disciplines Journal*.

C. Close with a prayer.

Worship Guide

For the Superintendent or Teacher
Theme:
Spiritual Disciplines for New Life
Song: "What a Friend
We Have in Jesus"
Devotional Reading:
1 Corinthians 9:19-27
Prayer

Spiritual Disciplines for New Life

Bible Background • COLOSSIANS 4:2-17
Printed Text • COLOSSIANS 4:2-6 | Devotional Reading • 1 CORINTHIANS 9:19-27

―――――――――――― **Aim for Change** ――――――――――――

By the end of the lesson, we will: RECOGNIZE the importance of spiritual disciplines in maintaining a Christian life; REFLECT on people in our lives who mentor us in faith; and ACCEPT the role of mentor for a new Christians we may encounter.

―――――――――――  **In Focus** ―――――――――――

Valerie had been a believer most of her adult life. For the first few years of her Christian walk, she made a point to pray every day and to live and speak in a manner that reflected Christ. However, after taking on more responsibility at work, Valerie began to waver in her faith. Instead of maintaining her prayer life, she would often procrastinate and sometimes forget to pray altogether. Her attitude and actions began to change as well. Valerie would get angry quickly when things did not go her way. She became short with people if they disagreed with her. She was often bitter because she began to focus on what she considered broken dreams. The worst of all was that Valerie began to feel that God had abandoned her. One morning, she felt so depressed that she called her former Sunday school teacher to talk. After relaying to him how she had been feeling, he asked her how often she prayed. In that moment, Valerie realized that it was almost never. Her teacher reiterated that she must pray and be mindful of how she spoke and lived to continue to grow in the Lord.

Practicing spiritual discipline is vital to our walk with Christ. Apostle Paul emphasizes that it is a lesson we should never forget.

―――――――――――――― **Keep in Mind** ――――――――――――――

"And say to Archippus, Take heed to the ministry which thou hast received in the Lord, that thou fulfil it" (Colossians 4:17).

FEB 24th

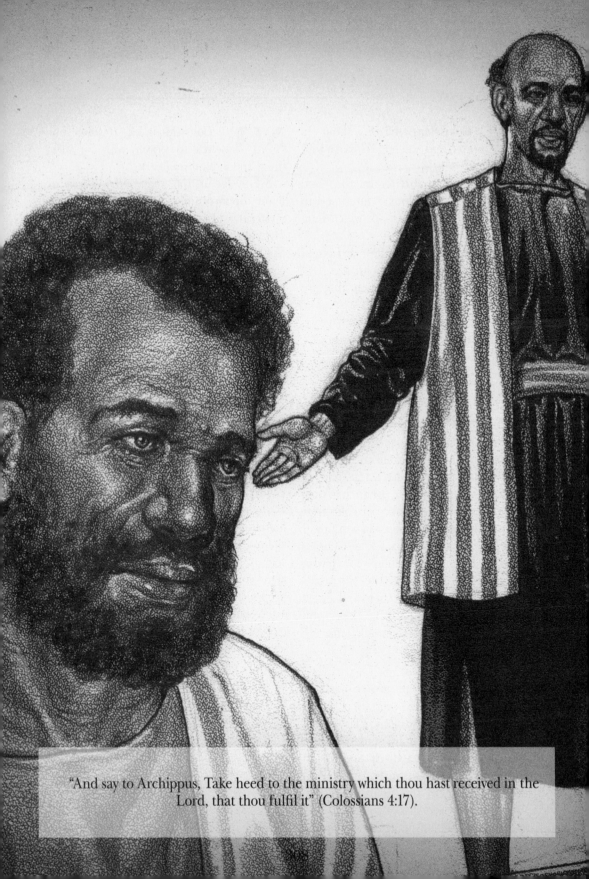

"And say to Archippus, Take heed to the ministry which thou hast received in the Lord, that thou fulfil it" (Colossians 4:17).

Focal Verses

KJV **Colossians 4:2** Continue in prayer, and watch in the same with thanksgiving;

3 Withal praying also for us, that God would open unto us a door of utterance, to speak the mystery of Christ, for which I am also in bonds:

4 That I may make it manifest, as I ought to speak.

5 Walk in wisdom toward them that are without, redeeming the time.

6 Let your speech be always with grace, seasoned with salt, that ye may know how ye ought to answer every man.

NLT **Colossians 4:2** Devote yourselves to prayer with an alert mind and a thankful heart.

3 Pray for us, too, that God will give us many opportunities to speak about his mysterious plan concerning Christ. That is why I am here in chains.

4 Pray that I will proclaim this message as clearly as I should.

5 Live wisely among those who are not believers, and make the most of every opportunity.

6 Let your conversation be gracious and attractive so that you will have the right response for everyone.

The People, Places, and Times

Colossae. Colossae (also spelled "Colosse") was a prosperous city located in the southwestern section in the Lycus River Valley in Phrygia. It was known for producing wool that had been dyed the color of colossinus, a shade of purple from the cyclamen flower. Intermarriage between Jews and Gentiles was not uncommon. Although the Jewish community was large and the Christians were thriving like their brothers and sisters in nearby Laodicea, many of the Greeks still practiced their ancient, pagan religions.

Background

Prior to writing to the Colossians, it is believed Paul had not ever visited Colossae based on Colossians 2:1 ("I want you to know how hard I am contending for you and for those at Laodicea, and for all who have not met me personally," NIV). Paul wrote his epistle to the Colossians while he was still imprisoned in Rome (A.D. 61). Christian leaders in Colossae included Archippus, Philemon, and Epaphras, who founded the Colossian church. They sought Paul's help in dealing with the heresy in the city. The Gnostics did not believe in the Incarnation, the act of Christ taking on human flesh, thus they denied His humanity. In addition, they also preached against the supremacy of Christ and His role in creation (Padfield, "The Church at Colosse in Asia Minor"). They were proponents of human logic and philosophy (Colossians 2:8). Paul sought to counter this by explaining redemption, clarifying Christ's identity, launching a polemic against the Gnostic philosophy, and describing ways to put our beliefs about the death and resurrection of Christ into practice.

At-A-Glance

1. Continue in Prayer (Colossians 4:2-4)
2. Speak with Grace (vv. 5-6)

In Depth

1. Continue in Prayer (Colossians 4:2-4)

Today's lesson text begins in the middle of Paul explaining how Christians should practice their faith. In chapter 3, he exhorts believers to make sure their lives reflect Christ and to not focus on earthly things but instead on things of God because they have a new life in Christ (vv. 1–3). He encourages them to put aside the various sins of their old selves (vv. 5–9) and embrace holiness as defined in verses 12 through 14. Perhaps to ensure that no believer be led astray by Gnostic heresy, Paul wrote: "Let the message of Christ dwell among you richly as you teach and admonish one another with all wisdom through psalms, hymns, and songs from the Spirit, singing to God with gratitude in your hearts. And whatever you do, whether in word or deed, do it all in the name of the Lord Jesus, giving thanks to God the Father through him" (3:16-17, NIV). He wanted the Colossians to learn with the Scriptures, not any outside philosophy, and to understand that in whatever they do, Jesus Christ should play an integral part. He then gives instructions for every facet of Christian society: wives, husbands, children, servants, and masters (3:18-4:1).

In verse 2 of today's text, Paul, as a mentor of faith for the Colossians, gives further instruction. Matthew Henry posited that this verse continues the duties of the Christian master but that the instruction here is practical for all believers to follow (*Matthew Henry's Commentary on the Whole Bible,* online version). Paul writes that the believers should "continue in prayer" (v. 2), giving the sense that prayer should be pursued with urgency, disciplined vigilance, and a thankful heart because prayer is essential to the Christian life. He also encourages the believers to pray for him, the ministers, and leaders in the church with the same diligence so that there would be opportunity for them to preach the gospel message. This especially involves the mystery of Christ, which is that "through the gospel the Gentiles are heirs together with Israel, members together of one body, and sharers together in the promise in Christ Jesus" (Ephesians 3:6, NIV).

Paul was imprisoned for this very same message. He asked them to pray that he have the ability to proclaim the message clearly. This was a request Paul had made often while he was imprisoned (Ephesians 6:19). We see here that even those who are the mentors in the faith need the prayers of their charges to help strengthen them in their mission.

2. Speak with Grace (vv. 5-6)

Another discipline Paul encourages the believers to practice is monitoring how they live and speak. He writes, "Live wisely among those who are not believers, and make the most of every opportunity" (Colossians 4:5, NLT). Christians should take advantage of every opportunity to display lives influenced by their faith (Ephesians 5:15–17). In fact, Paul writes that their "speech" (conversation, discourse) should be "with grace, seasoned with salt" (Colossians 4:6). The way Christians speak and the content of their conversations should suit their positions in Christ. Any kind of foolish talk, obscenities, or insults should not be a part of the Christian conversation (Ephesians 5:4). Paul uses salt, a preservative that prevents spoilage, as a metaphor for grace. "Grace is the salt which seasons our discourse, makes it savoury, and keeps it from corrupting" (*Matthew Henry's Commentary on the Whole Bible,* online version). Christians must be careful not to allow their words to be corrupted. In light of the hostile environment the

Gnostics likely created with their opposition to the Christian faith, the believers needed to be able to address any issue before them. If they were diligent in prayer and monitored their discourses, they would be ready to answer anyone appropriately.

Search the Scriptures

1. How should a Christian pray (Colossians 4:2)?

2. Why should Christians pray for their mentors (v. 3)?

3. Describe the speech of a Christian (v. 6).

Discuss the Meaning

What are some concrete ways Christians can maintain diligence in their prayer lives? If we have not already done so, how can we begin to monitor the content of our speech? How can we help new Christians learn to be disciplined in their prayer and speech?

Lesson in Our Society

In an age when most have a lot going on in our lives, sometimes we might find ourselves putting our spiritual disciplines on the back burner. However, if we are not diligent, we could compromise our Christian walk. Instead, we should pray and then look to those who encouraged us in the faith to examine how they manage to live for Christ. Once we become disciplined, we can then help new believers learn.

Make It Happen

Start a *Spiritual Disciplines* journal. In one section, you should keep an account of your prayers. In another section, analyze the conversations you have each day, being prayerful about what you should change or maintain so that eventually, you become consistent with your speech. As you become stronger in the disciplines of prayer and

conversation, share your process with others so they can begin journaling, too.

Follow the Spirit

What God wants me to do:

_____

_____

_____

_____

Remember Your Thoughts

Special insights I have learned:

_____

_____

_____

_____

More Light on the Text

Colossians 4:2-6

2 Continue in prayer, and watch in the same with thanksgiving; 3 Withal praying also for us, that God would open unto us a door of utterance, to speak the mystery of Christ, for which I am also in bonds: 4 That I may make it manifest, as I ought to speak.

Paul provides a unique emphasis throughout Colossians 4:2-6. There is a strong communication on the importance of faithful "prayer" (Gk. *proseuche*, **pros-yoo-KHAY**) and godly speech, which are ultimately pillars to one's conduct and overall discipline. For the most part, Colossians 4:2-4 can form one particular unit, and Colossians 4:5 and 4:6 can stand separately.

Colossians 4:2 focuses on prayer and attitude. There are three things Paul wishes the church of Colossae would understand and apply to their lives. First, a Christian must be devoted to prayer. Prayer is simply direct conversation with God and should be of primary importance in a believer's life. Through prayer, we share our thoughts and feelings. It is a means of seeking understanding and guidance from the very God we worship. Authentic prayer is never one-sided because it is a vital way in which God communicates directly to us. Questions are answered and guidance is given through the usage of Christian prayer. Secondly, to "watch" (Gk. *gregoreuo*, **gray-gor-YOO-o**), meaning to keep alert, must be accompanied with prayer. One should always avoid unfocused, lackadaisical prayer in which the individual or group treats it as a mere religious routine. Prayer must be intentional, focusing on what we are thinking and saying; always alert for an answer. Lastly, we must have intentionally focused prayer with a spirit of "thanksgiving" (Gk. *eucharistia*, **yoo-khar-is-TEE-ah**). Our attitude should be one of gratitude, humility, submission, and reverence toward God, not with entitlement, arrogance, or pride. Ephesians 6:18 echoes a similar idea: "With all prayer and petition, pray at all times in the Spirit, and with this in view, be on the alert with all perseverance and petition for all the saints" (NASB).

In Colossians 4:3, Paul—the apostle—displays a rather concrete faith, not only in God but in the transformative power of the Gospel message. He continues with the theme of prayer, asking the church of Colossae to lift him and his group up in prayer so that "God would open unto us a door." The word "door" comes from the Greek *thura* (**THOO-rah**), an expression in Scripture, is a metaphor for opportunities to witness

(1 Corinthians 16:9; 2 Corinthians 2:12). The Gospel message of Christ Jesus is what caused the saints' physical imprisonment (including Paul's), yet it is the sole reason for their spiritual freedom. This same Gospel message is what Paul wished to preach so that those in physical bondage could experience real spiritual freedom of life. Once again, the letter to the Ephesians complements Paul's letter to the Colossian church. Ephesians 6:19 states, "and pray on my behalf, that utterance may be given to me in the opening of my mouth, to make known with boldness the mystery of the gospel" (NASB). Paul's humility and desire for confidence is shown within this verse. He asks for prayer so that God would grant him the ability "to proclaim this message as clearly as I should" (Colossians 3:4, NLT).

Similar to when he wrote Colossians, Paul was imprisoned at the time of writing his letter to the church of Ephesus (Ephesians 6:20). This may explain the similarity between the two letters. In each, Paul speaks from a particular context in which the same emotions, thoughts, and perspectives of faith could have possibly influenced and sustained him. Philippians 1:13-18 also notes that Paul is living in a prison cell; this stemmed from his preaching the Gospel message (Philippians 1:13). In a strange twist of encouragement, Paul states that because of his imprisonment, most of the fellow believers in Christ "have far more courage to speak the word of God without fear" (Philippians 1:14, NASB). This becomes a powerful statement and principle, especially when one realizes the extent to which fear and dangerous threats have nullified the ability of some Christians to proclaim the very Gospel that has changed their lives. Our lives are powerful witnesses to everyone. A faith that isn't worth the sacrifice if one's life isn't worth following.

When the apostle Paul risked freedom and his life for the sake of the Gospel message, everyone took notice and even gleaned the encouragement to do the same.

5 Walk in wisdom toward them that are without, redeeming the time.

The manner in which we express and present ourselves is always important. Through the eyes, ears, and mind, people judge, examine, and interpret in order to acquire an understanding of things. With this in mind, Paul turns from an emphasis on prayer and speech toward overall conduct. For "wisdom" should always influence and mold our conduct. Interestingly enough, the ancient Greek word for "walk" (*peripateo*, **per-ee-pat-EH-o**) can be translated as "conduct" as well. The shift to wisdom-influenced conduct may appear out of place on the surface, but it fits neatly within this context. A life devoted to prayer, proper speech, and awareness with a heart of thanksgiving will create godly discipline and wise conduct in our lives. The discernment needed to distinguish between what is appropriate and inappropriate will develop internally.

For Paul, wise conduct is instrumental to a Christian's witnessing power. Conducting ourselves in a godly manner is beneficial not only for ourselves but for others as well. This includes individuals with whom we have a closer relationship and those who we may influence from a distance. "Enthusiasm must be accompanied by common sense and tact. Witness without wisdom often produces ill will and negative results" (Patzia, 97). The Apostle Peter makes a similar declaration in 1 Peter 3:15: "But sanctify Christ as Lord in your hearts, always being ready to make a defense to everyone who asks you to give an account for the hope that is in you, yet with gentleness and reverence" (NASB).

Inevitably, Christians will face situations and people who demand explanations for their choices in life.

6 Let your speech be alway with grace, seasoned with salt, that ye may know how ye ought to answer every man.

In Colossians 4:6, Paul returns to the importance of proper speech. Grace pervades every aspect of the Christian's life, even within one's speech. Paul makes it clear that peace, love, compassion, and other traits should guide each verbal expression we exhibit. Consider what Jesus says in Mark 7:20, "That which proceeds out of the man, that is what defiles the man" (NASB). Many people fail to realize that speech is merely an expression of the conditions of the heart and mind. We speak in a manner that symbolizes the state of our feelings, thoughts, and overall world view. Language is merely indicative of our spiritual condition. If your spirit is evil, then your speech will be the same. "The Christian who is in God's grace will demonstrate that fact by the nature of his or her speech" (Patzia, 97-98).

Sources:
"The Aegean Region." *Travel Guide to Turkey.* http://www.guide-martine.com/aegean12.asp(accessed November 4, 2011).
"Bible Words – Phonetic Pronunciation." Better Days Are Coming.com. http://betterdaysarecoming.com/bible/pronunciation.html#e/ (accessed November 4, 2011).
Browning, W. R. F. "Colossae." *A Dictionary of the Bible.* 1997. Encyclopedia.com. http://www.encyclopedia.com/topic/Colossae.aspx (accessed November 4, 2011).
"Colossae." *Catholic Encyclopedia.* http://www.newadvent.org/cathen/04131a.htm (accessed November 4, 2011).
"Colossae." Holy Land Photos.org. http://holylandphotos.org/browse.asp?s=1,3,7,23,62 (accessed November 4, 2011).
"Colossians." *The New Unger's Bible Dictionary.* Chicago: Moody Press, 1988. 247, 248.
Henry, Matthew. "Colossians." *Matthew Henry's Commentary on the Whole Bible, Vol. VI* –
Acts to Revelation. Christian Classics Ethereal Library.org. http://www.ccel.org/ccel/henry/mhc6.Col.html (accessed November 4, 2011).
Martin, Ralph P. *Ephesians, Colossians, and Philemon. Interpretation, a Bible Commentary for Teaching and Instruction.* Atlanta, GA: John Knox Press, 1991.

New Testament Greek Lexicon. Bible Study Tools.com. http://www.biblestudytools.com/lexicons/greek/ (accessed November 4, 2011).

Padfield, David. "The Church at Colosse in Asia Minor." Padfield. com, the Church of Christ in Zion, Illinois. http://www.padfield.com/2005/colosse.html (accessed November 4, 2011).

Patzia, Arthur G. *Ephesians, Colossians, Philemon. New International Biblical Commentary: Vol. 10*. Peabody, MA: Hendrickson Publishers, 1990. 96-98.

Strong, James. *Free Bible Study Tools - Strong's Concordance with Greek and Hebrew*. Tim Greenwood Ministries. http://www.tgm.org/bible.htm (accessed November 4, 2011).

Vine, W. E. *Vine's Complete Expository Dictionary of Old and New Testament Words*. Nashville, TN: Thomas Nelson, 1996. 127, 395, 562-536, 591-592.

Say It Correctly

Colossae. kuh-LOS-ee(').
Colossians. kuh-LOSH-uhnz,
-LAH-shuhnz, *also* -shee-uhnz.
Epaphras. EP-uh-fras, EP-uh-fruhs.

Daily Bible Readings

MONDAY
Following Jesus
(Matthew 20:29-34)

TUESDAY
Devoted to Prayer
(Acts 1:6-14)

WEDNESDAY
Living in Harmony
(Romans 15:1-6)

THURSDAY
Living to Please God
(1 Thessalonians 4:1-12)

FRIDAY
Guarding Your Words
(Ecclesiastes 5:1-6)

SATURDAY
Supporting Others in the Faith
(Colossians 4:7-17)

SUNDAY
Devotion and Conduct
(Colossians 4:2-6)

Notes

Beyond the Present Time

The study this quarter focuses on the theological theme of hope in both the Old and New Testament. In addition, students will consider the resurrection hope of believers, who wait for Christ's return and focus on the hope that Jesus inspires for those who are suffering.

UNIT 1 • THE KINGDOM OF GOD

This Old Testament study considers the apocalyptic view of hope found in the book of Daniel. These lessons show the connection between the hope found in Daniel's prophecy and the Christian's resurrection hope.

Lesson 1: March 3, 2013
Daniel's Vision of Change
Daniel 7:9–14

We live in the hope that the future will be better than the past. Daniel's experiences taught him to trust in God in spite of the danger he faced.

Lesson 2: March 10, 2013
Daniel's Prayer
Daniel 9:4b–14

Even though our hopes for the future are grounded in God's past actions, we are human and become fearful. What should we do when fear encroaches? Daniel went to God in prayer.

Lesson 3: March 17, 2013
Gabriel's Interpretation
Daniel 8:19–26

Hope points us toward the future. There were times when Daniel both knew and interpreted dreams, but when he did not understand his vision, Daniel received help from Gabriel to clarify its meaning.

UNIT 2 • RESURRECTION HOPE

The Scriptures under consideration are drawn from Luke, Acts, and 1 and 2 Thessalonians. On Easter Sunday, the lesson from Luke 24 remembers the empty tomb and Jesus' appearance to His disciples following His resurrection. The following week, the lesson moves to Acts and the anointing of the Holy Spirit that comes on the disciples in Jerusalem. The final two lessons of the unit draw on the letters to the church in Thessalonica and consider the resurrection hope of believers, who wait for Christ's return.

Lesson 4: March 24, 2013 (Palm Sunday)
The Lord's Supper
Luke 22:14–30

Humans seek to exaggerate their own importance. Jesus says those who serve others will eat the bread and sip the wine at the table He has set for them in heaven.

Lesson 5: March 31, 2013 (Easter)
The Lord Has Risen Indeed!
Luke 24:13–21, 28–35

Jesus opened the eyes of two followers He encountered on the road to Emmaus, and they recognized that Jesus had risen.

Lesson 6: April 7, 2013
The Lord Appears
Luke 24:36–53

People find that promises can be hard to keep. Which promises can be relied on without reservation? Through the Resurrection, Jesus kept His word and fulfilled the words of prophecy about Him.

Lesson 7: April 14, 2013
The Holy Spirit Comes
Acts 2:1–13

We often face experiences that produce dramatic changes in our lives. How can positive, lasting change be initiated? The Holy Spirit provides life-transforming power.

Lesson 8: April 21, 2013
Living with Hope
1 Thessalonians 4:13–5:11

People find themselves in situations that can be disheartening. But Paul assures us that the promise of Christ's return provides us with comfort and hope.

Lesson 9: April 28, 2013
Hope Comes from God's Grace
2 Thessalonians 2:1–3, 9–17

Information about the future comes from a variety of sources. How can we know which sources to trust? Paul warns us against the deception that can come from satanic sources.

UNIT 3 • A CALL TO HOLY LIVING

This is a four-lesson study of 1 and 2 Peter. These studies focus on the hope that Jesus inspires for those who are suffering — Jesus' life, death, and resurrection for our "new birth into a living hope" (1 Peter 1:3).

Lesson 10: May 5, 2013
A Living Hope
1 Peter 1:3–12

Life's trials and tribulations cause us to experience hopelessness. Where can one go to find new hope and reassurance for a joyous future? Peter writes that a new birth into a living hope can be found in the resurrection of Jesus Christ.

Lesson 11: May 12, 2013
Equipped with Hope
2 Peter 1:4–14

Many people feel they are ineffective, unproductive, and unable to make the right choices in life. Peter says that the inner strength needed to face life with new assurance and hope comes because of our knowledge of and faith in our Savior, Jesus Christ.

Lesson 12: May 19, 2013 (Pentecost Sunday)
Hope through Stewardship
1 Peter 4:1–11

The perilous world in which we live sometimes tempts us to accept the lifestyles and values of others in order to be successful. First Peter 4 tells us that God will strengthen us to serve as good stewards of His manifold grace.

Lesson 13: May 26, 2013
Hope in the Day of the Lord
2 Peter 3:1–15a

There have always been people who believe that what has been and what is will always be. The writer of 2 Peter urges his readers to prepare for the day of the Lord by being patient and by living holy, godly lives.

HOPE BEYOND THE PRESENT

"And there was given him dominion,
and glory, and a kingdom,
that all people, nations, and languages,
should serve him:
his dominion is an everlasting dominion,
which shall not pass away,
and his kingdom
that which shall not be destroyed"

(Daniel 7:14, KJV).

Christian Education in Action

Books	Author	Audience	Purpose	Key People
Daniel	Daniel was a young Israelite held captive in Babylon. Conviction, intelligence, and prophecies were among his gifts (Daniel 5:12).	Other captives in Babylon and to all of God's people	To give a historical account of God's chosen people in captivity and to show how God was still in control of their destiny and the nations	Daniel, Nebuchad-nezzar, Shadrach, Meshach, Abednego, Belshazzar, Darius
Luke	Luke—a doctor (Colossians 4:14), a Greek, and Gentile Christian—was a close friend and companion of Paul.	Theophilus ("one who loves God"), Gentiles, and people everywhere	To present an accurate account of the life of Christ and to present Christ as the perfect human and Savior	Jesus, Elizabeth, Zechariah, John the Baptist, Mary, the disciples, Herod the Great, Pilate, Mary Magdalene
Acts	Luke—a doctor (Colossians 4:14), a Greek, and Gentile Christian—was a close friend and companion of Paul.	Theophilus ("one who loves God"), Gentiles, and people everywhere	To accurately portray the birth and growth of the Christian church	Peter, John, James, Stephen, Philip, Paul, Barnabas, Cornelius, James (Jesus' brother), Timothy, Lydia, Silas, Titus, Apollos, Agabus, Ananias, Felix, Festus, Agrippa, Luke

Books	Author	Audience	Purpose	Key People
1 Peter 2 Peter	Peter—a fisherman heeding Christ's call as a disciple (Mark 1:17)	The church at large and all believers	To encourage suffering Christians, to warn believers about false teachers, and to exhort them to grow in the knowledge of their Lord and Savior, Jesus Christ	Peter
1 Thessalonians 2 Thessalonians	Paul—wrote most of the New Testament and was a great missionary, particularly to the Gentiles	The church at Thessalonica and all believers	To strengthen believers in their faith and to assure them of Christ's second coming; also to clear up confusion about Christ's return	Paul, Timothy, Silas

Source:

Life Application Study Bible, New Living Translation. Wheaton, IL: Tyndale House
    Publishers, Inc., 2007. 1261, 1684, 1910, 1919, 1994.

HOPE RESTORED

"And (the disciples') eyes
were opened,
and they knew him …"

(Luke 24:31, KJV).

Thomas A. Dorsey

(1899-1993)
Prolific Gospel Composer

Billowing flames destroyed the historical Pilgrim Baptist Church, a south side Chicago landmark. Destruction to the edifice, which was more than 100 years old, devastated its parishioners.

The church once had about 10,000 members and was the church home of the famous American arranger, pianist, and versatile prolific composer, Thomas A. Dorsey. Not only was Dorsey known as the "Father of Gospel Music," but he was also considered one of the most influential figures ever to make an impact on gospel music. While the fire reduced Pilgrim Baptist Church to rubble, his legacy there and elsewhere remained. He ultimately wrote more than 1,000 songs in his lifetime, and half of them were published.

A child prodigy born in Villa Rica, Ga., Dorsey taught himself to play a variety of instruments. His talents were so widely recognized that a gospel tune was called "a Dorsey" until Dorsey himself coined the name "gospel." Then his music was known as "gospel" or "gospel blues."

After moving to Chicago in 1916, Dorsey continued his musical training at the Chicago School of Composition and Arranging. He published his first composition in 1920, and to earn money, he worked as a composer and arranger for the Chicago Music Publishing Company. He also worked as a music coach for Paramount and Vocalion Records.

In 1921, after he heard W.M. Nix's inspirational singing at the National Baptist Convention, Dorsey decided to begin composing "sacred" music. He registered his first composition in 1922.

After becoming the director of music at New Hope Baptist Church, he combined his sacred music with his blues technique. This effort made him one of the progenitors of gospel blues.

In 1932, Dorsey's wife, Nettie Harper, died in childbirth and his newborn son died soon after. To console himself, he composed "Take My Hand, Precious Lord."

Elvis Presley's recording of Dorsey's second-most popular song, "Peace in the Valley," sold millions of copies. It is considered Dorsey's most widely recognized work and was a hit nationwide.

Today, Thomas A. Dorsey is revered in church history. Because of his walk with the Lord, he is celebrated as a Christian, an accomplished pianist, choir director, and a prolific composer.

Sources:
www.answers.com/topic/rev-thomas-a-dorsey
www.ourgeorgiahistory.com/chronpop/1231

Teaching Tips

March 3
Bible Study Guide 1

Words You Should Know

A. Horn (Daniel 7:11) *qeren* (Heb.)— Of an animal; metaphorically signifies strength and honor; symbolic use in visions for kings and kingdoms.

B. Beheld (vv. 9, 11) *chaza'* (Heb.)—Saw; or in a vision or dream, it means to witness.

Teacher Preparation

Unifying Principle—Better Days Ahead. Daniel's vision gives hope that the future will be better than the past.

A. Pray for your students and lesson clarity.

B. Study and meditate on the entire text.

C. Complete companion lesson in the *Precepts For Living Personal Study Guide®*.

D. Bring in a photo of a blind person and ask students how a person without sight might "see" and how a person with sight might be "blind."

O—Open the Lesson

A. Open with prayer, including the Aim for Change.

B. Have students read the Aim for Change and Keep in Mind and discuss.

C. Share the photo of the blind person.

D. Then ask, "Is there anything that God's trying to get you to see so you'll have better days ahead?"

E. Allow volunteers to share their testimonies.

F. Now have a volunteer summarize the In Focus story. Discuss.

P—Present the Scriptures

A. Have volunteers read the Focal Verses.

B. Use The People, Places, and Times; Background; Search the Scriptures; At-A-Glance outline; In Depth; and More Light on the Text to clarify the verses.

E—Explore the Meaning

A. Have volunteers summarize the Discuss the Meaning, Lesson in Our Society, and Make It Happen sections.

B. Connect these sections to the Aim for Change and the Keep in Mind verse.

N—Next Steps for Application

A. Summarize the lesson.

B. Close with prayer.

Worship Guide

For the Superintendent or Teacher
Theme: Daniel's Vision of Change
Song: "Because He Lives"
Devotional Reading: Daniel 6:25-28
Prayer

Daniel's Vision of Change

Bible Background • DANIEL 7
Printed Text • DANIEL 7:9-14 | Devotional Reading • DANIEL 6:25-28

———————— Aim for Change ————————

By the end of the lesson, we will: RECOGNIZE that God judges the just and the unjust; TRUST that He has a future in mind for His people; and COMMIT to godly living.

———————— In Focus ————————
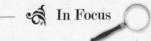

If David and Kim knew that the church-wide, 21-day financial fast would cause so many problems between them, they might not have agreed to it. First, it was the realization of how much money they spent eating out and entertaining their children. Then, it was the discovery of how little they had saved and how far behind they were. Attempts to work together to set up a budget almost did them in. One day they decided to go to their local bank and open a joint account.

Celicia, the bank representative, chuckled to herself when she sensed their apprehension. She said, "I felt like I was making the biggest mistake of my life when my husband and I opened up a joint account. It went against everything the women in my family taught me. But becoming financially intimate with my husband was the best thing I could ever have done. It has been 15 years since we started our account with $100, and today we have built more together than I could ever have on my own."

It's human nature to try to foresee the future based on past events, but the vantage point is skewed. In today's lesson, we will see a part of Daniel's dream foreshadowing better days ahead.

———————— Keep in Mind ————————

"And there was given him dominion, and glory, and a kingdom, that all people, nations, and languages, should serve him: his dominion is an everlasting dominion, which shall not pass away, and his kingdom that which shall not be destroyed" (Daniel 7:14).

"And there was given him dominion, and glory, and a kingdom, that all people, nations, and languages, should serve him: his dominion is an everlasting dominion, which shall not pass away, and his kingdom that which shall not be destroyed" (Daniel 7:14).

Focal Verses

KJV Daniel 7:9 I beheld till the thrones were cast down, and the Ancient of days did sit, whose garment was white as snow, and the hair of his head like the pure wool: his throne was like the fiery flame, and his wheels as burning fire.

10 A fiery stream issued and came forth from before him: thousand thousands ministered unto him, and ten thousand times ten thousand stood before him: the judgment was set, and the books were opened.

11 I beheld then because of the voice of the great words which the horn spake: I beheld even till the beast was slain, and his body destroyed, and given to the burning flame.

12 As concerning the rest of the beasts, they had their dominion taken away: yet their lives were prolonged for a season and time.

13 I saw in the night visions, and, behold, one like the Son of man came with the clouds of heaven, and came to the Ancient of days, and they brought him near before him.

14 And there was given him dominion, and glory, and a kingdom, that all people, nations, and languages, should serve him: his dominion is an everlasting dominion, which shall not pass away, and his kingdom that which shall not be destroyed.

NLT Daniel 7:9 I watched as thrones were put in place and the Ancient One sat down to judge. His clothing was as white as snow, his hair like purest wool. He sat on a fiery throne with wheels of blazing fire,

10 and a river of fire was pouring out, flowing from his presence. Millions of angels ministered to him; many millions stood to attend him. Then the court began its session, and the books were opened.

11 I continued to watch because I could hear the little horn's boastful speech. I kept watching until the fourth beast was killed and its body was destroyed by fire.

12 The other three beasts had their authority taken from them, but they were allowed to live a while longer.

13 As my vision continued that night, I saw someone like a son of man coming with the clouds of heaven. He approached the Ancient One and was led into his presence.

14 He was given authority, honor, and sovereignty over all the nations of the world, so that people of every race and nation and language would obey him. His rule is eternal—it will never end. His kingdom will never be destroyed.

The People, Places, and Times

Daniel. He is the fourth of the "greater prophets." His name means "judgment of God." Nothing is known about his parents, but he appears to have been of royal descent (Daniel 1:3). He was kidnapped by the Babylonians and trained for the king's service. When he refused to defile himself with the king's foods, the king's men divinely supported him—Daniel only ate fruits and vegetables, commonly known today as "the Daniel fast." He was gifted to interpret dreams and visions and was miraculously delivered from the lions' den for his faithfulness. His career spanned about 70 years, giving a time frame for the book of 605-537 B.C.

The Ancient of Days. The Aramaic words for "ancient" and "days" are `attiyq and yowm, respectively, and are translated as "aged" and "time." Together, they mean "lifetime," or "eternity." God, as judge, is called "the Ancient of days" or "the Ancient One" because He is God from everlasting to everlasting, and His reign is forever. The title is listed only three times in the Bible (Daniel 7:9, 13, 22). This same vision of God as judge was also given to the apostle John (Revelation 20:11-15).

Background

What do you do when your faith promotes you and then casts you headlong into trouble? If you asked Daniel, he'd tell you to keep being faithful. Because of his faithfulness and excellent character, Daniel was promoted in King Darius' court. Then his enemies devised a plan to get Daniel into trouble. When he chose to serve God anyway, he was thrown into a den with hungry and ferocious lions. His faith prevailed when God sent an angel to shut the lions' mouths.

Right before our lesson text, we find Daniel trying to rest after a draining night in the lions' den. He tossed and turned all evening with God-given dreams. In the lesson, we learn of these visions that speak of the Ancient of Days sitting on a throne, ruling eternally, and giving dominion and power to the Messiah.

In the verses following our lesson text, the vision is explained (Daniel 7:21-27). The horn of the beast that made war against the saints was one of 10 kings who prevailed until the Ancient of days came and judged against him in favor of the saints. Daniel's prophecy was one of hope.

At-A-Glance

1. A Vision of Judgment (Daniel 7:9-12)
2. A Vision of Hope (vv. 13-14)

In Depth

1. A Vision of Judgment (Daniel 7:9-12)

"I beheld till the thrones were cast down, and the Ancient of days did sit" (Daniel 7:9). By the way Daniel wrote the verse, one has to wonder whether he considered turning away. Perhaps he was tired after spending the night in the lions' den, but he says he watched until all thrones were put in place. Thrones were set up for everyone in power —the four beasts, men in opposition to God's kingdom, Christ, and God the father. Daniel continued to watch until the Ancient of days sat down. The Ancient of days is a name that characterizes God as a judge whose reign is eternal.

Obviously, the Ancient of days' appearance set Him apart from the others, as Daniel described His brilliant attire, woolly hair, throne of fire, and the thousands of thousands of people who stood before Him. Then court opened and while in session, two books were opened (one a book of life and the other a book of judgment). The deeds of the dead were recorded in the books, and they would be judged according to the contents.

Daniel wrote that the fourth beast was "terrible, powerful and dreadful, and ... strong ... with great iron teeth" (7:7, AMP). The beast had 10 horns. While Daniel was watching the court proceedings, a sound captured his attention. It was one of the beast's horns "boasting arrogantly" (7:8, NLT). The beast was destroyed for its defiance of heaven and burned in the burning flame of God's throne. Dominion was taken away from the other three beasts, but their lives were spared.

Matthew Henry states, "Perhaps (Daniel's vision) points at the destruction brought by the providence of God upon the empire of Syria, or that of Rome, for their tyrannizing over the people of God" (*Matthew Henry's Commentary on the Whole Bible, Vol. IV—Isaiah to Malachi,* 1072). Further, the fourth beast is likened to the Roman Empire's destruction after it began to persecute Christianity.

2. A Vision of Hope (vv. 13-14)

"I saw in the night visions, and, behold, one like the Son of man came with the clouds of heaven, and came to the Ancient of days, and they brought him near before him" (Daniel 7:13). Daniel continues to watch the vision unfold and saw the Messiah, who in the text was called "one like the Son of man" because He was made in the likeness of a human (Romans 8:3) and was found in appearance as a man (Philippians 2:8). Seeing Christ as man suggests His rulership on earth where He was given glory, dominion, and a kingdom (Daniel 7:14).

This vision brings comfort to Daniel and his friends, as it foreshadows the stripping away of power from the church's enemies and reveals that Jesus' dominion shall never pass away. The church will forever be victorious to the end of time.

Search the Scriptures

1. Why was the beast slain (Daniel 7:11)?
2. What happened to the other beasts (v. 12)?

Discuss the Meaning

What is the significance of God being called "the Ancient of days" in the text?

Lesson in Our Society

No matter how long, vivid, and disturbing Daniel's vision was, he refused to turn away. He later wrote, "the visions of my head troubled me" (Daniel 7:15). Why do you think kept Daniel watching? Was it nosiness, conviction, or compulsion? What can we learn from Daniel, as many of us find it hard to watch our own lives unfold? We've closed our eyes to our country's ongoing wars. We've refused to watch the downward spiral of our families, marriages, and economy. First Peter 4:7 advises us, "But the end of all things is at hand: be ye therefore sober, and watch unto prayer." How can we take heed to his warning?

Make It Happen

Is there something God has been trying to get you to see? This question is not hard to answer. Perhaps He's trying to bring your attention to your children, finances, relationships, community, and your emotions. Your frustration about it won't end unless you deal with it. God wants to bring you victory in the matter, but He can't if you're pretending to be blind. This week, challenge yourself to take a good look at a situation that's troubling you, and ask God to help you deal with it.

Follow the Spirit

What God wants me to do:

_____

_____

_____

_____

Remember Your Thoughts

Special insights I have learned:

_____

_____

_____

_____

More Light on the Text

Daniel 7:9–14

Introduction:

Not only is the book of Daniel referred to in the New Testament more than any other Old Testament book, it also has more fulfilled prophecy than any other. Daniel wrote at the worst time in Israel's history. The Babylonians destroyed Jerusalem, had taken the Israelites into captivity and now considered their gods superior because they had been able to bring down Yahweh's famous Temple. Because of Daniel, however, all that soon would change. Daniel's words stand as a timeless beacon of God's sovereign justice offering hope to all.

Daniel was taken hostage in 605 B.C., during the first of three major invasions of Palestine by Nebuchadnezzar, king of Babylon. He was held captive until the first year of King Cyrus the Persian in 537 B.C. (1:21). His prophetic ministry continued until the third year of Cyrus, in 535 B.C. (10:1). Through a divinely gifted ability to interpret dreams, God gave Daniel favor, first with Nebuchadnezzar then with his conqueror, Darius, the one who was tricked into throwing Daniel into the lions' den. His supernatural wisdom continued to earn him good fortune through the reign of Cyrus (6:28). Now in the first year of King Belshazzar's reign (the last Babylonian ruler before Darius and Cyrus), our passage

opens in the middle of a dream Daniel had that he wrote down when he awoke (7:1). Because Daniel himself interprets the dream right after our passage, much of the guesswork is eliminated (7:16–27). The overall flavor is typical of apocalyptic literature (warning about a disastrous future or outcome), similar to the book of Revelation (compare with Revelation 14:1–15).

Preceding this part of Daniel's dream were, in order (Daniel 7:2–8): four winds and four beasts, three of which were like a lion, a bear, and a leopard; and a special beast with iron teeth and 10 horns, out of which grew a new horn that uprooted three others, a horn with a man's eyes, and a boasting mouth. In 7:17, Daniel calls these horns or thrones "kings" (also "beasts" as per the earlier animal references) that were overpowered or "cast down" in verse 9. But commentators agree it was only their authority that was removed (see v. 12).

9 I beheld till the thrones were cast down, and the Ancient of days did sit, whose garment was white as snow, and the hair of his head like the pure wool: his throne was like the fiery flame, and his wheels as burning fire.

Into Daniel's vision comes a great, flaming throne on flaming wheels—the judgment throne of God Himself, "the Ancient of days," which in Aramaic is literally the "advanced of days" (`attiyq yowm, **at-TEEK YOME**). God sitting in judgment is a familiar Old Testament theme (see 1 Kings 22:19). The phrase "Ancient of days" is only used three times in the Old Testament, all in the seventh chapter of Daniel (7:9, 13, 22).

Fire is often used to symbolize God in the Old Testament (e.g., the burning bush, Exodus 3:2; the pillar of fire, Exodus 13:21). Fire "not only represents the blindingly brilliant manifestation of God's splendor but also the fierce heart of his judgment on sin and on all those opposed to his supreme authority" in the words of Gleason Archer (*Daniel—Minor Prophets*, 89). See also "a fire shall devour before him" (Psalm 50:3); "a fire goeth before him, and burneth up his enemies round about" (Psalm 97:3); and "God is a consuming fire" (Deuteronomy 4:24; Hebrews 12:29), which clearly implies judgment. Similarly, a "chariot of fire" came from heaven to pick up Elijah (2 Kings 2:11), and Ezekiel sees a type of chariot throne (Ezekiel 1:15–21; 10:9–17). Just as fire represents God's judgment, pure white hair and garments represent purity, wisdom, righteous judgment, or all three. Louis Hartman describes it as "symbolizing unsullied majesty" (*Anchor Bible, The Book of Daniel*, 218).

10 A fiery stream issued and came forth from before him: thousand thousands ministered unto him, and ten thousand times ten thousand stood before him: the judgment was set, and the books were opened.

A thousand thousands is a million, made plural, and 10,000 times 10,000 is 100 million, which represents an overwhelming number of celestial beings gathered to witness the events. For the Israelites, witnesses were required for a court to render judgment, and that requirement was covered by a crowd that Daniel saw. Archer writes, "This scene is a court of judgment ... for bringing the wicked and unrepentant to justice" (*Daniel—Minor Prophets*, 89). W. Sibley Towner describes the public trial scene as a "universally visible theodicy or divine self-vindication," which Daniel writes in the "most sweeping, cosmic context possible" (*Daniel*, 98, 102).

Books of record are another familiar motif throughout Scripture, but with different uses, even in Daniel. For example, the "Book of Truth" (10:21, NLT)—and the ones who will be delivered "shall be found written in the book" (12:1). This reference uses similar language to that of the "Book of Life" mentioned six times in Revelation (see also Psalm 69:28, NLT; Philippians 4:3, NLT). In Revelation 20:12, two types of books are opened, one a book of life and one a book of judgment. Such images most likely gave rise to the popular Western notion of God as a heavenly scorekeeper; this thinking puts people in charge of their own destiny, if only they can do enough good deeds to outnumber their bad deeds. The hope of Christ exists in spite of the futility of such works (Isaiah 64:6; Romans 4:6; Philippians 3:9), and in Him no works are necessary or even possible, for He alone paid the price (Romans 4:25; Hebrews 9:12; Titus 2:14).

11 I beheld then because of the voice of the great words which the horn spake: I beheld even till the beast was slain, and his body destroyed, and given to the burning flame. 12 As concerning the rest of the beasts, they had their dominion taken away: yet their lives were prolonged for a season and time.

The boasting mouth of the horn (7:8) represents the last of earth's evil rulers, called "the beast," who even though he was meeting his doom, continued his arrogant defiance of God to the bitter end. Death alone stops the mouth of the boasting beast. Daniel is privileged to foresee God's triumph over the epitome of evil.

The "rest of the beasts" (7:12), the remaining world rulers, are next to be judged, although commentators speculate about the reason their "lives were prolonged." The consensus seems to fall on the side of believing this means their judgment simply is postponed. In addition, one might speculate that these are the world's remaining superpowers, subject to the fourth horn or beast that uprooted them (7:19–21).

13 I saw in the night visions, and, behold, one like the Son of man came with the clouds of heaven, and came to the Ancient of days, and they brought him near before him.

Next, Daniel sees Jesus in His glorified state, described in a verse quoted frequently in the New Testament. W. Sibley Towner calls verses 13 and 14 "the very heart of the book of Daniel itself" (*Towner*, 102). Unlike the beasts or horns representing earth's rulers, the heavenly ruler appears as a man, "as the heavenly Sovereign incarnate" in Archer's words. In the Aramaic, the phrase "Son of man" (*bar 'enash*, **BAR en-AWSH**) refers prophetically to Jesus. Jesus confirmed this phrase as a description of Himself, personally claiming Daniel's words (see Matthew 8:20; Luke 9:58). Archer writes that Jesus regarded Daniel 7:13 as an early indication of who He was (*Daniel—Minor Prophets*, 90). Jesus also used the exact same language as Daniel for His future return to earth: "they shall see the Son of man coming in the clouds of heaven with great power and glory" (Matthew 24:30); "Hereafter shall ye see the Son of man sitting on the right hand of power, and coming in the clouds of heaven" (Matthew 26:64); "And then shall they see the Son of man coming in the clouds with great power and glory" (Mark 13:26). As well, the apostle John wrote in Revelation 1:7, "Behold, he cometh with clouds." The Old Testament uses similar language with God having "appeared in the cloud" on Mt. Sinai (Exodus 16:10), and He "maketh the clouds his chariot" (Psalm 104:3). Also, "the LORD rideth upon a swift cloud" (Isaiah 19:1), and "the clouds are the dust of his feet" (Nahum 1:3).

14 And there was given him dominion, and glory, and a kingdom, that all people, nations, and languages, should serve him: his dominion is an everlasting dominion, which shall not pass away, and his kingdom that which shall not be destroyed.

Many question why parts of Daniel are in Aramaic. C. Hassell Bullock writes that it was "the language of the Medo-Persian Empire," and also that this part of Daniel was "the ... most germane to non-Jews. Thus it was written in the language of the empire for their consumption" (*Introduction to the Old Testament Prophetic Books*, 285, 286).

Gleason Archer writes: "The messianic Son of Man is brought before the throne of the Ancient of Days" as the supreme, sovereign ruler of the Earth, and possesses "the crown of universal dominion ... (He is) ... absolute Lord and Judge by virtue of his atoning ministry as God incarnate" (*Daniel—Minor Prophets*, 91). Jesus is given authority, glory, and sovereign power, similar to His own final words on earth just preceding the Great Commission, "All power is given unto me in heaven and in earth" (Matthew 28:18). These three terms in Aramaic are *sholtan* (**shol-TAWN**), meaning dominion or sovereignty (see Daniel 4:3, 22; 6:26; 7:27); *y@qar* (**yek-AWR**), meaning honor or esteem (used only here in the sense of heavenly glory, not humankind's glory); and *malkuw* (**mal-KOO**), meaning royalty, reign, kingship, or kingdom (see Daniel 2:44; 4:34; 6:26). Here Jesus begins His earthly kingdom and all people will worship and serve Him "every knee shall bow, every tongue shall swear (confess)," as prophesied by Isaiah (45:23; see also New Testament references to the same, Romans 14:11; Philippians 2:10). Unlike every man-made kingdom and empire, Jesus' kingdom and His dominion will be eternal, never to be destroyed.

When seen through the lens of New Testament eschatology (end-time prophesies), the little horn of Daniel's vision is commonly understood to be the "son of perdition" or the Antichrist of 2 Thessalonians 2:3–4, who will appear just prior to the return of Christ. Thankfully, we have the comforting words of a prophet in exile, blessed and prospered by God to a position of great influence, similar to Joseph in ancient Egypt, whom God used to speak to all future generations of believers. Through His messenger, Daniel, God delivers a word of comfort and hope to all who have known affliction, to all who have been oppressed, and to all who have wondered if there is any justice in the world. To all who have labored tirelessly in the Lord, to all who have shed blood, sweat, and tears in service of the Kingdom, Daniel reminds us that our God is still on the throne; He will judge the wicked, and the enemy will be destroyed, never to rise again.

Sources:

Archer, Gleason L., Jr. *Daniel—Minor Prophets. The Expositor's Bible Commentary, vol.* 7. Edited by Frank E. Gaebelein. Grand Rapids, MI: Zondervan, 1985. 88–91.

BetterDaysAreComing.com.http://www.betterdaysarecoming.com (accessed April 11, 2011). Biblical Words Pronunciation Guide. http://netministries.org/Bbasics/bwords.htm (accessed November 3, 2011).

Bullock, C. Hassell. *Introduction to the Old Testament Prophetic Books.* Chicago, IL: Moody Press, 1986. 279–300.

Hartman, Louis F. *Anchor Bible, The Book of Daniel.* New York, NY: Doubleday, 1978. 217-219.

Henry, Matthew. *Matthew Henry's Commentary on the Whole Bible. Vol. IV—Isaiah to Malachi.* McLean, VA: MacDonald Publishing, nd. 1071-1074.

Old and New Testament Concordances, Lexicons, Dictionaries, Commentaries, Images, and Bible Versions. Blue Letter Bible. org. http://www.blueletterbible.org/ (accessed March 29, 2011).

Old Testament Hebrew Lexicon. http://www.biblestudytools.com/lexicons/hebrew (accessed October 29, 2011).

Smith, William. *Smith's Bible Dictionary.* Peabody, MA: Hendrickson Publishers, 2000. 135, 201.

Strong, James. *Strong's Concordance with Hebrew and Greek Lexicon.* http://www.eliyah.com/lexicon.html (accessed May 1-5, 2011).

Towner, W. Sibley. *Daniel. Interpretation: A Bible Commentary for Teaching and Preaching.* Atlanta, GA: John Knox Press, 1984. 96–104.

Word in Life Study Bible (NKJV). Nashville, TN: Thomas Nelson Publishers, 1982.

Say It Correctly

Yahweh. YAH-weh.
Nebuchadnezzar. neh-byoo-kuhd-NEHZ-er.
Belshazzar. behl-SHAZ-er.

Daily Bible Readings

MONDAY
The Lord Deals with the Mighty
(Daniel 5:13–21)

TUESDAY
The Lord Judges the Powerful
(Daniel 5:22–31)

WEDNESDAY
The Plot to Undermine Daniel
(Daniel 6:1–10)

THURSDAY
The Plot Fails
(Daniel 6:11–23)

FRIDAY
Daniel's God Is Exalted
(Daniel 6:24–28)

SATURDAY
Daniel's Vision
(Daniel 7:1–8)

SUNDAY
The Exaltation of the Coming One
(Daniel 7:9–14)

Teaching Tips

Words You Should Know

A. Trespass (Daniel 9:7) *ma'al* (Heb.)—To commit an unfaithful or treacherous act.

B. Transgress (v. 11) `*abar* (Heb.)—To go away or depart from the truth or way.

Teacher Preparation

Unifying Principle—Have Mercy! When we are afraid for our future because of our past, we should go to God in prayer.

A. Pray for lesson clarity.

B. Study and meditate on the entire text.

C. Obtain a brief article on parenting that suggests how soon discipline should occur after an offense.

D. Complete the companion lesson in the *Precepts For Living Study Guide*®.

O—Open the Lesson

A. Open with prayer, including the Aim for Change.

B. Ask a volunteer to read the Aim for Change and Keep in Mind verse. Discuss.

C. Share your article.

D. Ask, "How long should discipline occur after an offense?"

E. Challenge students to compare and contrast the article's advice with how God parents us. Emphasize God's mercifulness.

F. Now have a volunteer read the In Focus story. Discuss.

P—Present the Scriptures

A. Have volunteers read the Focal Verses.

B. Use The People, Places, and Times; Background; Search the Scriptures; At-A-Glance outline; In Depth; and More Light on the Text to clarify the verses.

E—Explore the Meaning

A. Assign one or two questions to groups to answer questions in the Discuss the Meaning, Lesson in Our Society and Make It Happen sections.

B. Have students select a representative to report their responses to the rest of the class.

N—Next Steps for Application

A. Write some take-away principles under the Follow the Spirit or Remember Your Thoughts section.

B. Close with prayer.

Worship Guide

For the Superintendent or Teacher
Theme: Daniel's Prayer
Song: "Great Is Your Mercy"
Devotional Reading: James 5:13-18
Prayer

Daniel's Prayer

Bible Background • DANIEL 9:3-19
Printed Text • DANIEL 9:4b-14 | Devotional Reading • JAMES 5:13-18

────────────── **Aim for Change** ──────────────

By the end of the lesson, we will: RECOGNIZE human sinfulness; TRUST that God forgives us of our sins; and CALL on God in times of great distress.

────────────  **In Focus** ────────────

Juanita was the only one *not* surprised that she wound up in jail. While everyone else remembered the Bible-toting, Scripture-quoting person she used to be, she remembered the day her faith changed. It was two years ago when foreclosure took the house she had prayed and believed God for.

The reality was that she could not afford her home after she was laid off. Instead of getting a job, she chose to start a business and believe God for the prosperity her pastor preached about. As her business grew, so did its expenses, and Juanita was only able to pocket enough money for gas and groceries. It seemed her telephone, electricity, and water services took turns getting disconnected.

The day her house was taken away, Juanita vowed that it was the last thing she would ever lose. She poured her heart and soul into her business and found ways to make it grow faster, bigger—illegally. Surprisingly, the day the police came to arrest her for filing fraudulent claims, she was relieved.

When things go wrong, we tend to run from God instead of going to Him. In today's lesson, we will see Daniel go to God on behalf of the people.

──────────── **Keep in Mind** ────────────

"To the Lord our God belong mercies and forgivenesses, though we have rebelled against him" (Daniel 9:9).

"To the Lord our God belong mercies and forgivenesses, though we have rebelled against him" (Daniel 9:9).

Focal Verses

KJV **Daniel 9:4b** O Lord, the great and dreadful God, keeping the covenant and mercy to them that love him, and to them that keep his commandments;

5 We have sinned, and have committed iniquity, and have done wickedly, and have rebelled, even by departing from thy precepts and from thy judgments:

6 Neither have we hearkened unto thy servants the prophets, which spake in thy name to our kings, our princes, and our fathers, and to all the people of the land.

7 O LORD, righteousness belongeth unto thee, but unto us confusion of faces, as at this day; to the men of Judah, and to the inhabitants of Jerusalem, and unto all Israel, that are near, and that are far off, through all the countries whither thou hast driven them, because of their trespass that they have trespassed against thee.

8 O Lord, to us belongeth confusion of face, to our kings, to our princes, and to our fathers, because we have sinned against thee.

9 To the Lord our God belong mercies and forgivenesses, though we have rebelled against him;

10 Neither have we obeyed the voice of the LORD our God, to walk in his laws, which he set before us by his servants the prophets.

11 Yea, all Israel have transgressed thy law, even by departing, that they might not obey thy voice; therefore the curse is poured upon us, and the oath that is written in the law of Moses the servant of God, because we have sinned against him.

12 And he hath confirmed his words, which he spake against us, and against our judges that judged us, by bringing upon us a great evil: for under the whole heaven hath not been done as hath been done upon Jerusalem.

NLT **Daniel 9:4b** "O Lord, you are a great and awesome God! You always fulfill your covenant and keep your promises of unfailing love to those who love you and obey your commands.

5 But we have sinned and done wrong. We have rebelled against you and scorned your commands and regulations.

6 We have refused to listen to your servants the prophets, who spoke on your authority to our kings and princes and ancestors and to all the people of the land.

7 "Lord, you are in the right; but as you see, our faces are covered with shame. This is true of all of us, including the people of Judah and Jerusalem and all Israel, scattered near and far, wherever you have driven us because of our disloyalty to you.

8 O LORD, we and our kings, princes, and ancestors are covered with shame because we have sinned against you.

9 But the Lord our God is merciful and forgiving, even though we have rebelled against him.

10 We have not obeyed the LORD our God, for we have not followed the instructions he gave us through his servants the prophets.

11 All Israel has disobeyed your instruction and turned away, refusing to listen to your voice. "So now the solemn curses and judgments written in the Law of Moses, the servant of God, have been poured down on us because of our sin.

12 You have kept your word and done to us and our rulers exactly as you warned. Never has there been such a disaster as happened in Jerusalem.

13 Every curse written against us in the Law of Moses has come true. Yet we have refused to seek mercy from the LORD our God by turning from our sins and recognizing his truth.

KJV continued

13 As it is written in the law of Moses, all this evil is come upon us: yet made we not our prayer before the LORD our God, that we might turn from our iniquities, and understand thy truth.

14 Therefore hath the LORD watched upon the evil, and brought it upon us: for the LORD our God is righteous in all his works which he doeth: for we obeyed not his voice.

NLT continued

14 Therefore, the LORD has brought upon us the disaster he prepared. The LORD our God was right to do all of these things, for we did not obey him.

The People, Places, and Times

Captivity of the Jews. At the time of our text, the Jews were still being held captive by the Babylonians. Based on Jeremiah's prophecy, Daniel wrote that he understood the expiration of their captivity was at hand. Jeremiah had prophesied that after 70 years of Babylonian captivity, God would release the Jews. "For thus saith the LORD, That after seventy years be accomplished at Babylon I will visit you, and perform my good word toward you, in causing you to return to this place" (Jeremiah 29:10). In our lesson text, Daniel prays for God to remember to make good on His promise of deliverance.

Background

Long before the prophets, when kings ruled Jerusalem, the Lord swore judgment upon His people for their wickedness. Manasseh, the son of King Hezekiah and king of Judah, was most wicked of all. He reigned longer than any other king in Judah's history—55 years of mixing faith in the Lord with idolatrous practices, placing heathen altars and images in the temple, and sacrificing his own sons as burnt offerings to a pagan god (2 Chronicles 33:2-9). His son, Amon, reigned after him and did no better. But his grandson, Josiah, followed the Lord (2 Kings 22:1-7) and restored the temple. Even as Josiah's repairs were being made, the Lord reiterated His intentions to allow Judah's captivity.

God's judgment came to pass during the prophet Jeremiah's reign. The Babylonians attacked Jerusalem three times, finally destroying the city in 587 B.C. Throughout the attacks, Jeremiah continued to warn his people to turn back to God, give up their idols, and to halt their alliances with foreign countries, but they ignored him. The people did not believe God would let them be captured by foreigners, and they did not think their temple would ever be destroyed. They thought their covenant with God warranted them special protection, even though they did not honor it.

During Jerusalem's siege, in 605 B.C., Daniel was deported to Babylon as a child. There he was placed in a reeducation program to prepare him for service in the very government that destroyed Jerusalem. Eventually, he became the most powerful Jew of the exile. Because he knew the prophecy of Jeremiah, he knew the 70 years of captivity was up. In our lesson text, we find him praying for God to make good on His promise to deliver the Jews.

At-A-Glance

1. A Prayer of Confession
(Daniel 9:4b-8)
2. A Prayer of Repentance (vv. 9-14)

In Depth

1. A Prayer of Confession (Daniel 9:4b-8)

Daniel's response to Jeremiah's prophecy is interesting. Instead of concerning himself with the dates of expiration for Jerusalem's captivity, he was more concerned about the hearts of the people, and he repented for them. He could have taken Jeremiah's prophecy to King Darius and told him to let them go. Or he could have simply waited, knowing they would go home soon. He simply remembered why they were captured in the first place and went to God on behalf of his people. Instead of focusing on when they would go home, he asked God if they were ready to go.

"O Lord, the great and dreadful God" does not sound like the words of a bitter man (Daniel 9:4b). Anybody else who was stripped from his royal home, thrown in a lions' den, and shown disturbing visions might be angry with God. But Daniel worshiped Him and acknowledged God for keeping His covenant with them, even when they departed from it.

Daniel was not general in his confession as some are who say, "Forgive me for what I did" or "Lord, you know my heart." Daniel specifically said, "We sinned and rebelled, we departed from thy precepts and judgments, and we did not hearken unto thy prophets" (v. 5, paraphrased). Then, he gave honor to whom it was due, "To you belongs righteousness, and to us belongs confusion." In other words he said, "You were right, God, and we were wrong."

2. A Prayer of Repentance (vv. 9-14)

Notice the transition in viewpoint in chapter 9. In verses 2-4, Daniel is writing in the first person point of view ("I Daniel understood ..." [v. 2]; "I set my face ..." [v. 3]; and "I prayed ..." [v. 4a]). Verses 4b-8 show that Daniel has shifted to a more formal viewpoint (for example, "O LORD, righteousness belongeth unto thee", [v. 7]). Here, he has used a second person point of view that has a more direct, intimate frame of reference (for example, "We have rebelled against him," v. 9). The chapter's first set of verses contains Daniel's confessions; the second set contains his standing as a representative of the people; the third set of verses indicates his willingness to join with the people in their prayers and praise of God. Perhaps we can learn from Daniel by allowing our confessions to have this combination of the personal, reverential, direct, and congregational.

The more we edify and exalt God, the smaller we should become. Our needs, desires, dreams, and thoughts should seem insignificant in the presence of a Holy God as we affirm our desire to repent. In verses 10-12, Daniel focuses on God's faithfulness to the laws He set before them through Moses. The law records the blessings of obedience and the consequences for disobedience (see Isaiah 1:2-4). Daniel acknowledges God's faithfulness for punishing Jerusalem for their disobedience according to the law (Daniel 9:13-14).

In verse 13, Daniel offers a three-step process for repentance: pray, turn from iniquity, and seek to understand God's truth.

Search the Scriptures

1. What sins did Daniel confess (Daniel 9:5-6, 9)?

2. What belongs to the Lord (vv. 7, 9)?

Discuss the Meaning

Based on Daniel's prayer, the Lord was very merciful to His people. Define mercy and use the Scripture text to identify how the Lord extended mercy to His people.

Lesson in Our Society

We take God's kindness for weakness. When we mess up, we expect immediate consequences. If punishment doesn't come quickly, then we act like we've pulled one over on God. Many of us continue sinning, as though God is OK with our actions. How can we use today's lesson to teach those in our society who are stubborn, ignorant, or hardheaded that God sees all we do, and He will judge us according to our deeds?

Make It Happen

How often do you confess your sins when you pray? Challenge yourself to pray using the ACTS acronym. The *A* stands for "adoration." Begin your prayer as Daniel did—adoring God for who He is and what He's done. *C* is for "confession." Specifically confess sins of commission (things you did) and omission (things you were supposed to do and didn't). The *T* is for "thanksgiving." Thank God for His mercy, forgiveness, and all He's done and doing in your life. Finally, the *S* is for "supplication," meaning make your requests known to God.

Follow the Spirit

What God wants me to do:

_____

_____

_____

_____

Remember Your Thoughts

Special insights I have learned:

_____

_____

_____

_____

More Light on the Text

Daniel 9:4b–14

Introduction:

The date is clear from verse 1, the first year of "Darius the Mede," who some historians say was intermediary ruler over the Babylonian Kingdom until the Persian conqueror, Cyrus, overtook the region in 538 B.C. (although many questions remain about exactly who this Darius was). In verse 2, Daniel foresees 70 weeks of desolation for Jerusalem, so he turns to God in prayer as he realizes that the time of the 70 years is drawing to a close. This is the prayer of a true disciple. Daniel is a man of integrity whose life revolves around God and His Word. Even the Babylonians recognized Daniel's impeccable character when those closest to the king convinced Darius to throw Daniel to the lions—a plan that backfired and cost the plotters their lives (6:6–24).

Daniel's prayer affirmed and endorsed the prophet Jeremiah's words about 70 years of captivity for Israel (Jeremiah 25:11–12; 29:10). The length of the exile is also confirmed in 2 Chronicles 36:20–21. Gleason Archer writes, "Daniel recognized that Jeremiah's writings were inspired by God and therefore inherently trustworthy and dependable" (*Daniel—Minor Prophets*, 107). When the Persians overtook the Babylonians, Daniel knew that the period of captivity in which he had spent most of his life was nearly over. In the 7th century, the prophet Isaiah had foretold these events in a rare type of prophecy that named Cyrus as the one who would release the captives so they could rebuild Jerusalem (see Isaiah 44:28; 45:1–2, 4, 13). Daniel recalled covenant promises and affirmations given to both Isaiah and Jeremiah in his prayer for God to release Israel as had been foretold.

4b O Lord, the great and dreadful God, keeping the covenant and mercy to them that love him, and to them that keep his commandments;

In verse 3, Daniel writes, "I set my face unto the Lord God," which versions such as ESV translate as "I turned my face"—a clear allusion to the Middle Eastern practice, still in effect, of turning toward Jerusalem to pray. Much Jewish and Christian architecture as well positioned the holiest part of their churches and synagogues facing toward Jerusalem. The first half of verse 4, which reads, "And I prayed unto the LORD my God, and made my confession," sets the tone for the whole prayer. This passage has been called "Daniel's Great Prayer," which continues to 9:19. Sibley Towner calls it a "great prose prayer of penitence" (*Daniel*, 128). Similar prayers can be found in Ezra 9:6–15 and Nehemiah 1:5–11—two examples among dozens in the Old Testament.

Also in Daniel 9:3, he had prepared himself for such a solemn prayer by fasting, mourning, and wearing sackcloth. He knew his prayer would not be based on Israel's merit, for their exile was a righteous judgment of their having utterly forsaken God. In today's language, one would say someone had worked very hard to earn such a harsh sentence, and deserved every bit of it and more. Israel's sins had included unrepentant idolatry, immorality, and martyrdom of prophets. Daniel knew that

Israel's hope lay only in the mercy and grace of God, as he saw implicit in Isaiah and Jeremiah's prophecies.

The prayer starts with a common reference to "Lord" (Heb. *yhovah*, **yeh-ho-VAW** or **ya-VAY**, depending on the Hebrew vowel points), which is God's proper name used more than 6,000 times in the Old Testament. Daniel also invokes the less common reference of "God" (Heb. *'elohiym*, **el-o-HEEM**), a plural masculine noun cited about 2,600 times in the Old Testament, which is used here and four more times in the studied portion (9:8, 10, 13, 14). Having clearly addressed the God of Israel and none other, Daniel further frames his salutation here by referencing God's transcendence ("great and dreadful God") as well as His grace ("keeping the covenant of mercy"). In so doing, he acknowledges God's unchanging, righteous character. Like a loving parent, God does not change His love for His children even when forced to discipline them. The implication, which the rest of the prayer makes clear, is that Daniel recognizes God has not acted unjustly by punishing Israel and that the people fully deserved their bitter exile.

5 We have sinned, and have committed iniquity, and have done wickedly, and have rebelled, even by departing from thy precepts and from thy judgments: 6 Neither have we hearkened unto thy servants the prophets, which spake in thy name to our kings, our princes, and our fathers, and to all the people of the land.

As the people's representative, Daniel includes himself in the confession, which also has been called a model prayer of penitence (compare with similar words in Solomon's prayer dedicating the temple in 1 Kings 8:47). His dual reference to Israel's sin matches the prior dual reference to

God in the salutation and acknowledgment of two aspects of God's character, which again is framed with a double reference to precepts and judgments. In Daniel 9:5, Israel's sin is both "iniquity" (Heb. `avah, a-VAW), which can be translated perverse or perversion (see Proverbs 12:8; Jeremiah 3:21), and "wickedness" (Heb. rasha`, raw-SHAH), which also translates and infers guilt or condemnation (see Job 10:2, "Do not condemn me"; and Psalm 94:21, "condemn the innocent blood"). These great sins violated both "precepts" (Heb. mitsvah, mits-VAW), which can mean commandments, and "judgments" (Heb. mishpat, mish-PAWT), both referring to God's laws or prohibitions.

Daniel fully professes that Israel had ignored both God and His prophets such as Isaiah and Jeremiah. Even the small remnant of faithful believers was not sufficient to ward off God's judgment. In short, the entire nation had no legs on which to stand for an appeal, such as is often the case today, where occasionally new evidence or new science surfaces and justifies a new trial. God's wrath is without blame; both God's law and His will are righteous and in harmony. In Towner's words, "The Lord is in all these things righteous. These disasters, as well as the imminent restoration, are fruits of his righteousness" (Daniel, 137).

7 O LORD, righteousness belongeth unto thee, but unto us confusion of faces, as at this day; to the men of Judah, and to the inhabitants of Jerusalem, and unto all Israel, that are near, and that are far off, through all the countries whither thou hast driven them, because of their trespass that they have trespassed against thee. 8 O Lord, to us belongeth confusion of face, to our kings, to our princes, and to our fathers, because we have sinned against thee.

There is almost a chiastic, poetic quality to this part of the prayer, which repeats the first thought in the next verse, and repeats the "confusion of faces" idea. In Hebrew, this is expressed with a single word bosheth (**BO-sheth**), which means "shame." The polarized contrast could not be more complete: righteousness for God and shame for the Israelites. Israel's former respect had turned to derision (disdain, scorn, mockery); their former glory had been decimated. All they once had was now lost—they had lost their nation, the land God had given them by promise to their forefathers, and they had even lost their freedom and dignity. A popular saying calls for losers to "pay the piper," but the biblical version is "the wages of sin is death" (Romans 6:23).

9 To the Lord our God belong mercies and forgivenesses, though we have rebelled against him;

While the Hebrew for the word "mercies" is a fairly common word racham (**RAKH-am**), the Hebrew word Daniel selected for "forgivenesses" in this verse is c@lyichah (**sel-EE-khaw**), which can mean "pardon", and it is used only three times in the Old Testament (see Nehemiah 9:17; Psalm 130:4).

In one sentence, Daniel 9:9 captures the timeless problem of humanity since the Fall. Man sins, then repents at some point, and God in His mercy forgives—then the cycle repeats again, over and over, generation after generation, century after century. No matter how faithless man is, God remains true to Himself and is continuously faithful. No matter how utterly sinful man is, God's commitment to mercy and forgiveness for those who repent is everlasting. This verse captures God's nature, His relationship with His people, and is a snapshot of the Gospel.

10 Neither have we obeyed the voice of the LORD our God, to walk in his laws, which he set before us by his servants the prophets.

Their sins were undeniable and egregious. By flagrantly disobeying God and rejecting Him, they rejected the very mercy and grace which they so desperately needed and the benefits of God's covenant too. Among the many benefits they abandoned when they turned their backs on God were His many promises, such as protection if they remained faithful, an abundance of provision, and the respect of other nations (see Deuteronomy 28:7–10). Towner notes, "this chapter is a meditation of Scripture upon earlier Scripture" (*Daniel,* 129). Readers of Daniel 9, particularly verse 10, will notice that its words and phrases are almost entirely found elsewhere in the Old Testament.

11 Yea, all Israel have transgressed thy law, even by departing, that they might not obey thy voice; therefore the curse is poured upon us, and the oath that is written in the law of Moses the servant of God, because we have sinned against him.

They were without excuse or defense. Daniel's humility was both apropos and accurate, for Israel's sins indeed were monumental. In truth, it is hard to imagine how they might have committed even more serious crimes against God—that He allowed the entire nation to be taken into captivity for what amounted to the lifespan of an average man (70 years) was self-evidence of the extent of His displeasure with the people called by His name. Towner writes, "the calamity has taken place because God is consistent and faithful to his character as Righteous One" (*Daniel,* 135).

Being just, God cannot overlook sins of such magnitude without compromising His own character and making all His prior warnings meaningless. What example would Israel then be to the world if they, in essence, could get away with such outrageous behavior? Why would anyone trust in God's covenantal faithfulness if He didn't keep His promises of blessing and curses? No other people would have any reason whatsoever to repent or follow God, much less obey His commands and trust in His righteous judgment. In a real sense, as Archer states, "... all this served to vindicate the holiness and righteousness of God and to demonstrate to all the world the sanctity of his moral law" (*Daniel—Minor Prophets,* 110).

12 And he hath confirmed his words, which he spake against us, and against our judges that judged us, by bringing upon us a great evil: for under the whole heaven hath not been done as hath been done upon Jerusalem. 13 As it is written in the law of Moses, all this evil is come upon us: yet made we not our prayer before the LORD our God, that we might turn from our iniquities, and understand thy truth. 14 Therefore hath the LORD watched upon the evil, and brought it upon us: for the LORD our God is righteous in all his works which he doeth: for we obeyed not his voice.

Daniel's only recourse was to do exactly what he was doing, which was to throw the nation of Israel on the mercy of God's court of justice (compare with Moses' prayers after Israel's idolatry with the golden calf in Exodus 32:11, 31–32). Daniel appealed to God for the future of his people, his city, and his nation. Who would speak of God; who would believe on Him if Israel were utterly destroyed and her city forgotten? This would be the greatest tragedy of all in Daniel's mind, as all the pagans from then on would believe their gods had prevailed, that the God of the Israelites was weak because He couldn't even salvage His own people or protect His own temple. Thus, Daniel leaned on the prophesied promises of restoration and pardon. As proof of Daniel's pure heart, God heard his prayer and responded through the angel Gabriel in the verses to come that their redemption already had been decreed (Daniel 9:20–27).

Verses 5–8 are part of Daniel's prayer of repentance as he makes a transition from the first person to the second person point of view, and he counts himself as one of Israel's sinners; verses 9–14 are cast as though he were preaching a sermon testifying of God's greatness and has joined with a congregation in praising God and remaining faithful. Together, the verses are a statement of understanding the experience of exile as a punishment orchestrated by a righteous God. There is a clear cause-and-effect relationship between covenant disobedience and judgment/suffering. At the same time, the prayer is a testimony of faith that in spite of the present circumstances, Daniel still has hope and faith in God's mercy. Towner writes that this classic prayer is an "example of the interim posture of the saint who can through prayer glorify God even as God points beyond the dark confines of the present era of tragedy to the bright age of reversal and renewal which lies ahead" (*Daniel,* 129).

God's dependable, steadfast love and mercy were well known (see Exodus 34:6–7; Deuteronomy 7:9, 12; 1 Kings 8:23). Just as Solomon prayed with faith in God's mercy, so Daniel held out hope for God to hear, forgive, and help (compare with 1 Kings 8:49–50). Likewise today, regardless of the seemingly hopeless condition of the planet and its billions of people, every true believer can echo the prayers of the saints of yesteryear, such as Daniel, who knew that no matter how bad things looked, faith and hope in God are always well placed and eventually will be rewarded. When all of this is cast as future, apocalyptic events, the historical principles become magnified but remain consistent—it is only through repentance that redemption comes, and this is because of God's perfect righteousness. Then, as now, as Towner words it, "God is called upon to glorify himself by saving a people in dire need" (*Daniel,* 138).

Sources:

Archer, Gleason L., Jr. *Daniel—Minor Prophets. The Expositor's Bible Commentary, vol. 7.* Edited by Frank E. Gaebelein. Grand Rapids, MI: Zondervan, 1985. 106–110.

Bullock, C. Hassell. *Introduction to the Old Testament Prophetic Books.* Chicago, IL: Moody Press, 1986. 279–300.

Hartman, Louis F. *Anchor Bible, the Book of Daniel.* New York, NY: Doubleday, 1978. 246–249.

Merriam-Webster Online Dictionary. http://www.merriam-webster.com (accessed November 3, 2011).

Old and New Testament Concordances, Lexicons, Dictionaries, Commentaries, Images, and Bible Versions. Blue Letter Bible. org. http://www.blueletterbible.org/ (accessed March 29, 2011).

Old Testament Hebrew Lexicon. http://www.biblestudytools.com/lexicons/hebrew (accessed October 29, 2011).

Towner, W. Sibley. *Daniel. Interpretation: A Bible Commentary for Teaching and Preaching.* Atlanta, GA: John Knox Press, 1984. 130–140.

Say It Correctly

Yehovah. yeh-HO-va.
Elohiym. el-o-HEEM.

Daily Bible Readings

MONDAY
Daniel's Resolve
(Daniel 1:8–15)

TUESDAY
Daniel's Recognition
(Daniel 1:16–21)

WEDNESDAY
The King's Challenge
(Daniel 2:1–11)

THURSDAY
Daniel's Intervention
(Daniel 2:12–16)

FRIDAY
Daniel's Success
(Daniel 2:36–49)

SATURDAY
Daniel's Prayer of Supplication
(Daniel 9:15–19)

SUNDAY
Daniel's Prayer of Confession
(Daniel 9:4b–14)

Notes

_____

_____

_____

_____

Teaching Tips

Words You Should Know

A. Indignation (Daniel 8:19) *za'am* (Heb.)—Anger, rage, or wrath.

B. Dark sentences (v. 23) *chiydah* (Heb.)—Enigmatic statement or question; perplexing statement.

Teacher Preparation

Unifying Principle—Dreams for a Better Tomorrow. Sometimes our hope for a better tomorrow is darkened by a lack of understanding.

A. Pray for your students and lesson clarity.

B. Study and meditate on the entire text.

C. Complete the companion lesson in the *Precepts For Living Personal Study Guide®*.

D. Prepare a brief list on how to ask for help.

O—Open the Lesson

A. Open with prayer, including the Aim for Change.

B. Have students read the Aim for Change and Keep in Mind and discuss.

C. Share your list on how to ask for help.

D. Then ask, "How many of you find it easy to ask others for help?"

E. Allow volunteers to share what enables them to ask for what they need.

F. Have a volunteer summarize the In Focus story. Discuss.

G. Ask, "What makes it hard to ask for help?" Discuss.

P—Present the Scriptures

A. Have volunteers read the Focal Verses.

B. Now use The People, Places, and Times; Background; Search the Scriptures; At-A-Glance outline; In Depth; and More Light on the Text to clarify the verses.

E—Explore the Meaning

A. Have volunteers summarize the Discuss the Meaning, Lesson in Our Society, and Make It Happen sections.

B. Connect these sections to the Aim for Change and the Keep in Mind verse.

N—Next Steps for Application

A. Summarize the lesson and write take-away principles under the Follow the Spirit or Remember Your Thoughts section.

B. Close with prayer and praise God for the victory He's won in their lives and for who He is.

Worship Guide

For the Superintendent or Teacher
Theme: Gabriel's Interpretation
Song: "Yesterday"
Devotional Reading: Psalm 91:1-12
Prayer

Gabriel's Interpretation

**MAR
17th**

**Bible Background • DANIEL 8
Printed Text • DANIEL 8:19-26 | Devotional Reading • PSALM 91:1-12**

—————— Aim for Change ——————

By the end of the lesson, we will: EXPLAIN why good decisions yield good outcomes; RECALL a time when we needed help from others; and VISUALIZE a better future in God.

———————— In Focus ————————

The reality of Gene's 40th birthday was far worse than the one he envisioned. By now, he thought he'd be married, settled financially, and established in a career. Instead he was between women and jobs, and living paycheck to paycheck.

"Man, how did I get here?" he asked his friend Mark.

"That's life. On one hand, it goes by so slow it seems like you have time to get things together. Then again, it goes so fast you can hardly keep up. Then you wake up at 40 and realize you're at the same spot you were at 20."

"Exactly. I am ashamed to be 40 and have nothing to show for it," Gene said.

"It's not too late; you just turned 40 today. You could turn things around."

"What am I going to do this year that I haven't done in the 39 before it?"

"That's the exact question you should be asking. I'm just the wrong person to pose it to," Mark said. "Go to a career counselor, a therapist, or even your pastor. If you want things to be different, you gotta do different things."

Sometimes it's hard to know what to expect when we are overwhelmed and confused. In today's lesson, we will see how Gabriel helped Daniel understand his vision.

—————— Keep in Mind ——————

"And the vision of the evening and the morning which was told is true: wherefore shut thou up the vision; for it shall be for many days" (Daniel 8:26).

"And the vision of the evening and the morning which was told is true: wherefore shut thou up the vision; for it shall be for many days" (Daniel 8:26).

Focal Verses

KJV **Daniel 8:19** And he said, Behold, I will make thee know what shall be in the last end of the indignation: for at the time appointed the end shall be.

20 The ram which thou sawest having two horns are the kings of Media and Persia.

21 And the rough goat is the king of Grecia: and the great horn that is between his eyes is the first king.

22 Now that being broken, whereas four stood up for it, four kingdoms shall stand up out of the nation, but not in his power.

23 And in the latter time of their kingdom, when the transgressors are come to the full, a king of fierce countenance, and understanding dark sentences, shall stand up.

24 And his power shall be mighty, but not by his own power: and he shall destroy wonderfully, and shall prosper, and practise, and shall destroy the mighty and the holy people.

25 And through his policy also he shall cause craft to prosper in his hand; and he shall magnify himself in his heart, and by peace shall destroy many: he shall also stand up against the Prince of princes; but he shall be broken without hand.

26 And the vision of the evening and the morning which was told is true: wherefore shut thou up the vision; for it shall be for many days.

NLT **Daniel 8:19** Then he said, "I am here to tell you what will happen later in the time of wrath. What you have seen pertains to the very end of time.

20 The two-horned ram represents the kings of Media and Persia.

21 The shaggy male goat represents the king of Greece, and the large horn between his eyes represents the first king of the Greek Empire.

22 The four prominent horns that replaced the one large horn show that the Greek Empire will break into four kingdoms, but none as great as the first.

23 "At the end of their rule, when their sin is at its height, a fierce king, a master of intrigue, will rise to power.

24 He will become very strong, but not by his own power. He will cause a shocking amount of destruction and succeed in everything he does. He will destroy powerful leaders and devastate the holy people.

25 He will be a master of deception and will become arrogant; he will destroy many without warning. He will even take on the Prince of princes in battle, but he will be broken, though not by human power.

26 "This vision about the 2,300 evenings and mornings is true. But none of these things will happen for a long time, so keep this vision a secret."

The People, Places, and Times

Gabriel. He was an angel who was sent by God to deliver messages. He announced the birth of John the Baptist to Zechariah and the birth of Jesus to Mary. In our text, he was sent to Daniel to explain his visions.

Media and Persia. The ram in Daniel's vision represents the Medo-Persian Empire.

Its two horns represent Kings Darius and Cyrus. The Persians overthrew Media under Cyrus in 558 B.C. and unlike other conquests, the Medes were appointed to stations of high honor and importance. The two nations seemed blended into one.

Background

After Daniel's vision of the four beasts, he sees another. This vision is about a ram, a goat, and a little horn. The ram had two horns on his head, one higher than the other, and was standing by the river. He pushed northward, southward, and westward and no other animal could defeat him. As Daniel was considering the vision of the ram, a goat with one horn came from the West and charged the ram. He tore the ram's two horns, making it powerless and defeating it. The goat lost his one horn and four horns grew in its place. Out of one of the four, a little horn grew toward heaven and cast down some of the angelic host. Daniel was baffled by the vision and God sent the angel Gabriel to interpret it.

At-A-Glance

1. God Sends Daniel the Help That He Needs (Daniel 8:19-22)
2. God Can and Does Interpret Dreams (vv. 23-26)

In Depth

1. God Sends Daniel the Help That He Needs (Daniel 8:19-22)

Daniel fell on his face when Gabriel arrived, thinking his end had come. But, Gabriel stood him upright and explained that Daniel's vision foretold what should happen at the end times (eschatology) of the world. With Gabriel's help, Daniel understood that the vision was one of comfort to those who live in calamitous times knowing that there should be an end to them.

Gabriel explained that the ram's two horns are the princes of Media and Persia. The horn that grew up first was shorter than the second one. The second and longest horn represented the kingdom of Persia, which rose last and was more eminent than Media. With its horns, the ram charged westward (toward Babylon, Syria, Greece, and Asia), northward (toward the Lydians, Armenians, and Scythians), and southward (toward Arabia, Ethiopia, and Egypt). The Persians launched attacks against all these nations to enlarge their dominion. The Persian Empire became so great that no one could withstand it, as the ram had in the vision.

The goat Daniel saw coming from the West represents Greece, and the horn between its eyes was Alexander the Great. In the vision, the goat did not touch the ground, and Gabriel explained that Alexander the Great had moved so lightly that he met with little or no opposition. In effect, he went to conquer the world. It is said that Alexander the Great pushed his conquests so fast and with so much fury that no one had courage enough to stand against him. He attacked Persia with three magnificent battles, killing more than 600,000 men and gaining absolute control of the Persian Empire. In the vision, the goat trampled the ram and broke its two horns.

Just as soon as the goat had become great, his horn broke and grew into four other horns. Alexander's kingdom divided itself into four parts, the kingdoms of Syria, Egypt, Asia, and Greece. But a small horn grew out of the four, and became persecutor of the church and the people of God.

2. God Can and Does Interpret Dreams (vv. 23-26)

Verses 23-25 describe the characteristics and the personality of the "small horn," which was Antiochus Epiphanes. Matthew Henry writes that Antiochus was seen as small because he "was in his original contemptible; there were others between him and the kingdom ... and (he) had been for some time a hostage and prisoner at Rome, whence he made his escape, and ... got the kingdom" (*Matthew Henry's Commentary on the Whole Bible, Vol. IV—Isaiah to Malachi,* 1079). He seized Egypt, invaded Persia and Armenia, but ran roughshod over the Jews.

According to the vision, Antiochus set himself against God, heaven, and God's people. He forbade the daily sacrifices and set his own image on the temple. It was said he would be destroyed but not by hands. He would not die in war or be killed; he would be given over to the living God. And it was so. When the Jews cast out Antiochus' image out of the temple, he vowed to make Jerusalem a burial ground. No sooner had he spoke the words, than he was struck with an incurable disease. At first, he continued to threaten the Jews. However as his illness grew worse, he tried to bargain with God to let the Jews worship freely. Finally before his death, he submitted to God and wrote letters of apology for setting himself against the Lord.

Daniel was asked to seal the vision, for it would be more useful to us who live in the last days.

Search the Scriptures

1. What do the two horns of the ram represent (Daniel 8:20)?

2. What happened to the goat's horn (v. 22)?

Discuss the Meaning

Sometimes it's hard to see clearly in the midst of so much evil. Daniel received help and support from Gabriel to increase his understanding. Who can we go to for help when our way seems dark?

Lesson in Our Society

Communities worsen when people make bad decisions or refuse to make decisions at all. Passivity robs people of the opportunity to ensure a better future for themselves and their families. Daniel was perplexed about the vision he saw, but Gabriel cleared it up for him. What can we learn from today's lesson and what we can do to ensure a better future for the residents of our communities?

Make It Happen

Do you ask others for help or always try to work things out on your own? The person who does not ask for help is either prideful, suffering from low self-esteem, afraid of rejection, or is a glutton for punishment. Asking for help is a sign of strength, not of weakness. Challenge yourself to ask someone to help you with a problem you've dealt with for too long. Consider seeking the counsel of your pastor, parents, financial adviser, friend, or licensed counselor.

Follow the Spirit

What God wants me to do:

_____

_____

_____

_____

Remember Your Thoughts

Special insights I have learned:

_____

_____

_____

_____

More Light on the Text
Daniel 8:19–26
Introduction:

Two years earlier, in chapter 7, Daniel had a dream about four beasts. Now in the third year of King Belshazzar (approximately 546 B.C.), in chapter 8, he had a vision. Both seem to predict future events, although some scholars believe the account was actually written after the events described. There is much, however, on which scholarship agrees. The essence of the vision is similar to the dream in that each involves mysterious animals, and in both instances the animals refer to kings or kingdoms of the world. Just prior to where our passage begins, three heavenly beings (two "holy ones" and Gabriel) are talking among themselves about the duration of the coming destruction (vv. 13–18). As with most prophecies, and especially apocalyptic (warning about a disastrous future or outcome) literature, commentators have a variety of views. In verse 14 (NLT), one of the angels mentions a period of "2,300 evenings and mornings" until the holy place would be restored. Some believe this refers to six years and 111 days; others believe it refers to a total of both mornings and evenings, or three years and 55 days. In this case, as Gleason Archer writes, "the preponderance of evidence seems to favor the latter interpretation" (*Daniel— Minor Prophets*, 103). See similar references in Daniel 7:25; 9:27b; 12:7.

Virtually all scholars also agree that the destruction takes place at the Temple in Jerusalem, and refers specifically to the end of sacrifices (8:13), after which the Temple is "cleansed" (v. 14) or re-consecrated, and most agree this was done by Judas Maccabeus in 164 B.C. There is also virtual unanimous agreement that it was Antiochus IV Epiphanes, ascending to power in 175 B.C., who committed the destruction and desecration in 167 B.C. (vv. 15–18). Regarding verses 23-25, Louis Hartman writes, "There is not the slightest doubt that he (Epiphanes) is the one meant, in the description of the 'small horn,' whom the angel identifies as a king 'brazen-faced and skilled in treachery'" (*Anchor Bible, the Book of Daniel*, 235).

19 And he said, Behold, I will make thee know what shall be in the last end of the indignation: for at the time appointed the end shall be.

In verse 16, just prior to our passage, Daniel hears but does not see God speaking with the "voice of a man" to the angel Gabriel in what is known as an epiphany, or pre-incarnate appearance of Christ (also called a "Christophany"). Incidentally, Gabriel is named in only four places in the KJV of Scripture (Daniel 8:16; 9:21; Luke 1:19, 26), and only Daniel names any angels in the Old Testament (see Daniel 10:13, 21; 12:1); Michael is named in the New Testament twice (Jude 1:9; Revelation 12:7).

Daniel's natural response is to fall prostrate (Daniel 8:17), like John before Jesus in Revelation 1:17, but Gabriel prefers that he stand (Daniel 8:18). The entirety of our passage consists of Gabriel's message. His words "Understand ... the vision" (v. 17), combined with "I will make thee know" in verse 19, indicate the importance of the messenger to communicate and for Daniel to grasp the message. While there are differences regarding the actual events referenced, commentators agree that these are future events (compare vv. 17, 19, 26).

In verse 19, the term "the indignation" (Heb. *za'am*, **za-AHM**) refers to Epiphanes' destruction of Jerusalem, the butchering of 80,000 Jews, and his vile desecration of the Temple, where he not only erected a statue of Zeus Olympios but sacrificed pigs on the holy altar. For Jews, all these acts were appalling, but none was a greater abomination than blasphemy in their Temple (see also Daniel 8:13; 9:27; 11:31; 12:11). Psalm 78:1–4 seems to describe this destruction.

Regarding the "time appointed the end," this term in Daniel 8:19 (Heb. *qets*, **kayts**), has generated perhaps more controversy than any other prophetic verse, Louis Hartman offers tempering wisdom, that it "is used not in the eschatological sense but in the general sense of any 'end' " (*Anchor Bible, the Book of Daniel*, 232). Compare with Habakkuk 2:3; Daniel 10:14; 11:27, 35.

20 The ram which thou sawest having two horns are the kings of Media and Persia. 21 And the rough goat is the king of Grecia: and the great horn that is between his eyes is the first king. 22 Now that being broken, whereas four stood up for it, four kingdoms shall stand up out of the nation, but not in his power.

Just as Daniel's dream was interpreted (7:16), so was his vision. Interestingly, the animals of 8:3, 5 fit their roles in history. The two-horned ram (unified kingdoms of Media and Persia) was no match (8:7) for the one-horned he-goat (kingdom of the Greeks, led by Alexander the Great). As history informs us, Alexander's rise to world domination was meteoric but short-lived as, after only 13 years in power, he died prematurely from a fever at age 32. With Greece's goat king "broken" (8:8, NKJV), his four generals divided his kingdom, but none ever approached Alexander's greatness. These four were: Ptolemy Soter, who ruled Egypt; Cassander, who ruled Macedonia and Greece; Antigonus, who ruled Asia Minor; and Seleucus III, who ruled Syria, Babylonia, and the eastern kingdoms. Seleucus' son, Antiochus IV Epiphanes, headed south to Egypt and east to Persia; during his expansion,

he also overtook Judea. Josephus records that it was in the 143rd year after Seleucus I's reign in Syria, following Alexander's death, that Epiphanes entered and crushed Jerusalem, in 168–167 B.C.

23 And in the latter time of their kingdom, when the transgressors are come to the full, a king of fierce countenance, and understanding dark sentences, shall stand up. 24 And his power shall be mighty, but not by his own power: and he shall destroy wonderfully, and shall prosper, and practise, and shall destroy the mighty and the holy people.

Epiphanes blasphemously called himself "the Illustrious God," while others called him Epimanes, which means "the Madman." His coins bore the inscription, "God Manifest." Not only did he stop sacrifices at the Temple (8:11), but also he tried to abolish Judaism by forbidding circumcision and possession of the Hebrew Scriptures by punishment of death. He knew exactly what he was doing when he erected the idolatrous Zeus statue and sacrificed unclean animals on the altar. Gleason Archer writes, "Like Nebuchadnezzar, he expected all his subjects to bow down to the great image he had set up" (*Daniel—Minor Prophets*, 104).

As with all such demonized despots in history, their evil anointing comes from Satan, the great deceiver of humankind (Genesis 3:13; John 8:44; Revelation 12:9). His closest followers are always morally corrupt, insolent rebels, without integrity, who enjoy evil. While evil may actually prosper and successfully wreak havoc temporarily, believers through the ages have gained comfort from the Scripture's clear hope that in the end every knee will bow and all will face God's judgment (Romans 14:11; Hebrews 9:27).

25 And through his policy also he shall cause craft to prosper in his hand; and he shall magnify himself in his heart, and by peace shall destroy many: he shall also stand up against the Prince of princes; but he shall be broken without hand.

Epiphanes magnifies himself, like sin itself, which is always self-centered and never God-centered. Sinclair Ferguson offers the insight that "(Epiphanes') activity is the embryonic form of an evil that all antichrists perpetrate in one form or another" (*Daniel, Communicator's Commentary*, 173). He destroys through peace because he is a master of treachery and deception, like a master con artist. Satan and his ilk are known to transform themselves into angels of light or messengers of righteousness (2 Corinthians 11:13–15), which in this use in the Greek means assuming a disguise. This is not the same Greek word as in Romans 12:2 (NIV), "Be transformed by the renewing of your mind" (Gk. *metamorphoo*, **met-am-or-FO-o**), which means to be changed or transfigured (as was Jesus in Matthew 17:2; Mark 9:2; see also 2 Corinthians 3:18), not merely disguised. Epiphanes defies God, exactly as Lucifer did (Isaiah 14:12; Luke 10:16-19), and for that he pays the ultimate and eternal price, and is broken—not by human hands, but by God directly. History informs that he died a slow and painful death. Archer describes it as an "attack of worms on his bowels, accompanied by a revolting stench," after which he died, "imploring the God of Israel to spare his life" (*Daniel—Minor Prophets*, 105). Ferguson expands the judgment aspect: "God's destruction of Antiochus will be a foretaste of His final destruction of the Antichrist ... . What is true of this Antichrist is true of all antichrists. It will also be true of the final Antichrist" (*Daniel, Communicator's Commentary*, 176).

26 And the vision of the evening and the morning which was told is true: wherefore shut thou up the vision; for it shall be for many days.

It has been said that a statement is not true because it is in Scripture, but it is in Scripture because it is true. In a similar way, God told Habakkuk in a vision that justice, detailed in a series of woes, would happen at the appointed time (Habakkuk 2:2–4). In this sense, any future time appointed by God could be an "end" (Daniel 8:17); therefore, certainly it would be true in the prophetic eschatological "end times" sense (see Daniel 10:14 referring to "latter days"; also Daniel 11:27, 35). In fact, it is reasonable that we consider the visions of Daniel, Habakkuk and others as verifiable descriptions of end times. Towner boldly states, "There is no speculation that these are future, end times events" (*Daniel*, 124).

New Testament believers are familiar with God's appointed times from incidents when Jesus told those He healed not to speak about it, for His time had not yet come (John 7:6, 8). Indeed, all believers today await the final appointed time when Jesus will return, something that will not be revealed to anyone prematurely (Mark 13:32–33). Demons, on the other hand, seem to be well aware that their time of judgment is coming, but it was not while Jesus was on the earth (Matthew 8:29). They also knew who Jesus was, but He did not permit them to speak out prior to God's timing (Mark 1:34; Luke 4:41).

Clearly, the time for God to open the seal after "many days" was in the distant future. Archer believes this "obviously refers to the crisis years (of Epiphanes' destruction and desecration) of 167–164 B.C." (*Daniel—Minor Prophets*, 105). The message was important enough to instruct Daniel to seal it up, to take measures to protect and preserve these words (compare with 12:9; Isaiah 8:16).

The great emotional strain and exhaustion Daniel experienced after receiving Gabriel's message about the coming tribulation (Daniel 8:27), prompted Daniel's great prayer of chapter 9 (see last week's lesson).

At best, prophetic and apocalyptic literature is enigmatic and problematic to decipher—especially to assign to specific events in history or developing trends. Sibley Towner writes, "The concept of a predetermined historical sequence is one of the most difficult aspects of apocalyptic literature" (*Daniel*, 121). Indeed, this is why many have made embarrassing mistakes, thinking they had accurately solved the riddle for exactly when certain events were going to happen, (e.g., the return of Jesus). Even errors like this, made with the greatest intentions, reflect badly on all believers.

Another aspect of this type of passage goes to the heart of the church's confidence in God. If God's own temple can be destroyed by an evil pagan and along with it the means of maintaining a holy relationship with him, it can create for all but the strongest believers profound questions about the security of any tangible element of faith in the world. For those truly strong in the faith, however, their security is rooted in God Himself and not in anything made by man, including His temple and holy city. In this light, especially for New Testament believers, the hope of a future, eternal Jerusalem and permanent temple, of which the former were only prototypes, is as real as the very presence of God that sustains our faith (see Revelation 11:19; 21:2, 22). Ultimately, all believers have the enduring, scriptural hope that evil will be overcome and justice will prevail, however long before it happens or however much damage the enemy does in the interim (Daniel 8:25). The hope that sustains is the core assurance that the day is coming soon when every form of evil will be completely and permanently brought to an end (Revelation 20:10, 14).

Sources:

Archer, Gleason L., Jr. *Daniel—Minor Prophets. The Expositor's Bible Commentary, vol. 7.* Edited by Frank E. Gaebelein. Grand Rapids, MI: Zondervan, 1985. 102–105.

Biblical Words Pronunciation Guide. http://netministries.org/Bbasics/bwords.htm (accessed November 3, 2011).

Ferguson, Sinclair B. *Daniel. The Communicator's Commentary, vol. 19.* Edited by Lloyd J. Ogilvie. Waco, TX: Word Books, 1988. 167–183.

Hartman, Louis F. *Anchor Bible, The Book of Daniel.* New York, NY: Doubleday, 1978. 230–237.

Henry, Matthew. *Matthew Henry's Commentary on the Whole Bible: Complete and Unabridged in One Volume.* Peabody, MA: Hendrickson Publishers, 1991. 1127-1130.

Old and New Testament Concordances, Lexicons, Dictionaries, Commentaries, Images, and Bible Versions. Blue Letter Bible.org. http://www.blueletterbible.org/ (accessed April 16, 2011).

Old Testament Hebrew Lexicon. http://www.biblestudytools.com/lexicons/hebrew (accessed October 29, 2011).

Smith, William. *Smith's Bible Dictionary.* Peabody, MA: Hendrickson Publishers, 2000. 135, 201.

Towner, Sibley W. *Daniel. Interpretation: A Bible Commentary for Teaching and Preaching.* Atlanta, GA: John Knox Press, 1984. 115–127.

Strong, James. *Strong's Concordance with Hebrew and Greek Lexicon.* http://www.eliyah.com/lexicon.html (accessed May 1-5, 2011).

Word in Life Study Bible (NKJV). Nashville, TN: Thomas Nelson Publishers, 1982.

Say It Correctly

Belshazzar. behl-SHAZ-er.
Antiochus. an-TAI-uh-kuhs.
Epiphanes. eh-PIHF-uh-neez.
Maccabeus. mak-uh-BEE-us.
Ptolemy. TAH-luh-mee.
Seleucus. seh-LOO-kuhs.

Daily Bible Readings

MONDAY
A Guide into the Future
(Exodus 23:20–25)

TUESDAY
A Messenger of Rebuke
(Judges 2:1–5)

WEDNESDAY
A Messenger with Good News
(Luke 1:8–20)

THURSDAY
A Messenger from God
(Luke 1:26–38)

FRIDAY
A Helper in Understanding
(Daniel 8:13–18)

SATURDAY
A Helper in Response to Prayer
(Daniel 9:20–27)

SUNDAY
A Helper in Facing the Future
(Daniel 8:19–26)

Notes

_____

_____

_____

_____

Teaching Tips

Words You Should Know

A. **Remembrance** (Luke 22:19) *anamnesis* (Gk.)—A recollection.

B. **Serve** (v. 26) *diakoneo* (Gk.)—To be a servant, attendant.

Teacher Preparation

Unifying Principle—The Privilege of Serving. Jesus says those who serve others will eat the bread and sip the wine at the table He has set for them in heaven.

A. Pray for your students and lesson clarity.

B. Research Luke 22 in a good commentary.

C. Complete the companion lesson in the *Precepts For Living Personal Study Guide*®.

D. Bring newspaper or magazine articles showing different types of service-oriented jobs.

O—Open the Lesson

A. Open with prayer that includes the Aim for Change.

B. Introduce today's lesson title.

C. Have your students read the Aim for Change and Keep in Mind verse together. Discuss.

D. Share your articles with the class and have students discuss them.

E. Ask, "What occupations or positions can you identify that require great sacrifice?"

F. Allow students to share their responses.

G. Tell the class to read the In Focus Story silently, then discuss it.

H. Ask, "How can we serve others?

P—Present the Scriptures

A. Have volunteers read the Focal Verses.

B. Use The People, Places, and Times; Background; Search the Scriptures; At-A-Glance outline; In Depth; and More Light on the Text to clarify the verses.

E—Explore the Meaning

A. Divide the class into groups to discuss the Discuss the Meaning, Lesson in Our Society, and Make It Happen sections. Tell the students to select a representative to report their responses.

B. Connect these sections to the Aim for Change and the Keep in Mind verse.

N—Next Steps for Application

A. Summarize the lesson.

B. Close with prayer.

Worship Guide

For the Superintendent or Teacher
Theme: The Lord's Supper
Song: "I Am Thine, O Lord"
Devotional Reading:
1 Corinthians 10:14–22
Prayer

The Lord's Supper

Bible Background • LUKE 22:14-30
Printed Text • LUKE 22:14-30 | Devotional Reading • 1 CORINTHIANS 10:14–22

Aim for Change

By the end of the lesson, we will: RECOGNIZE that even Jesus believed in service; REFLECT on the sacrificial elements of the Lord's Supper; and SHARE the sacrifices of our Lord with others.

 In Focus

Since they were in first grade, Irene and Aisha were best friends. They did everything together. When they went away to college in different states, they visited each other frequently. After graduation, they both returned home to Georgia and obtained good paying jobs.

Irene believed in volunteering and helping the needy. As a nurse, she provided free health screenings in the community and at her church. Irene thought it was important to give back considering God had blessed her with a good job. Aisha felt differently. Even though Aisha had a good job as a certified public accountant, she felt that she should get paid for everything related to the work she did. This caused a strain in Irene and Aisha's friendship.

One day, Aisha accompanied Irene to a community health screening. She was so overwhelmed when she saw how grateful the people were for the free health screenings that she volunteered to help Irene that day. A few months later, Aisha began to offer free financial advice to those who came to the community health screenings.

We all are called to be God's servants. In today's lesson, we will examine how Jesus' sacrifice on our behalf was an act of service.

Keep in Mind

"But ye shall not be so: but he that is greatest among you, let him be as the younger; and he that is chief, as he that doth serve" (Luke 22:26).

"But ye shall not be so: but he that is greatest among you, let him be as the younger; and he that is chief, as he that doth serve" (Luke 22:26).

Focal Verses

KJV **Luke 22:14** And when the hour was come, he sat down, and the twelve apostles with him.

15 And he said unto them, With desire I have desired to eat this passover with you before I suffer:

16 For I say unto you, I will not any more eat thereof, until it be fulfilled in the kingdom of God.

17 And he took the cup, and gave thanks, and said, Take this, and divide it among yourselves:

18 For I say unto you, I will not drink of the fruit of the vine, until the kingdom of God shall come.

19 And he took bread, and gave thanks, and brake it, and gave unto them, saying, This is my body which is given for you: this do in remembrance of me.

20 Likewise also the cup after supper, saying, This cup is the new testament in my blood, which is shed for you.

21 But, behold, the hand of him that betrayeth me is with me on the table.

22 And truly the Son of man goeth, as it was determined: but woe unto that man by whom he is betrayed!

23 And they began to enquire among themselves, which of them it was that should do this thing.

24 And there was also a strife among them, which of them should be accounted the greatest.

25 And he said unto them, The kings of the Gentiles exercise lordship over them; and they that exercise authority upon them are called benefactors.

26 But ye shall not be so: but he that is greatest among you, let him be as the younger; and he that is chief, as he that doth serve.

NLT **Luke 22:14** When the time came, Jesus and the apostles sat down together at the table.

15 Jesus said, "I have been very eager to eat this Passover meal with you before my suffering begins.

16 For I tell you now that I won't eat this meal again until its meaning is fulfilled in the Kingdom of God."

17 Then he took a cup of wine and gave thanks to God for it. Then he said, "Take this and share it among yourselves.

18 For I will not drink wine again until the Kingdom of God has come."

19 He took some bread and gave thanks to God for it. Then he broke it in pieces and gave it to the disciples, saying, "This is my body, which is given for you. Do this to remember me."

20 After supper he took another cup of wine and said, "This cup is the new covenant between God and his people—an agreement confirmed with my blood, which is poured out as a sacrifice for you.

21 "But here at this table, sitting among us as a friend, is the man who will betray me.

22 For it has been determined that the Son of Man must die. But what sorrow awaits the one who betrays him."

23 The disciples began to ask each other which of them would ever do such a thing.

24 Then they began to argue among themselves about who would be the greatest among them.

25 Jesus told them, "In this world the kings and great men lord it over their people, yet they are called 'friends of the people.'

26 But among you it will be different. Those who are the greatest among you should take the lowest rank, and the leader should be like a servant.

KJV continued

27 For whether is greater, he that sitteth at meat, or he that serveth? is not he that sitteth at meat? but I am among you as he that serveth.

28 Ye are they which have continued with me in my temptations.

29 And I appoint unto you a kingdom, as my Father hath appointed unto me;

30 That ye may eat and drink at my table in my kingdom, and sit on thrones judging the twelve tribes of Israel.

NLT continued

27 Who is more important, the one who sits at the table or the one who serves? The one who sits at the table, of course. But not here! For I am among you as one who serves.

28 "You have stayed with me in my time of trial.

29 And just as my Father has granted me a Kingdom, I now grant you the right

30 to eat and drink at my table in my Kingdom. And you will sit on thrones, judging the twelve tribes of Israel.

The People, Places, and Times

Jerusalem. Jerusalem was both the religious and the political seat of Palestine, and the place where the Messiah was expected to arrive. It is located 14 miles west of the Dead Sea, 33 miles east of the Mediterranean. It is 3,800 feet above the level of the Dead Sea. The temple was located there, and many Jewish families from all across the world traveled to Jerusalem during the important feasts. The temple sat on a hill overlooking the city. Solomon had built the first temple on this same site almost 1,000 years earlier (949 B.C.), but the Babylonians destroyed that temple (2 Kings 25). The temple was rebuilt in 515 B.C., and Herod the Great enlarged and remodeled it.

Jesus spent a lot of time in Jerusalem at the temple teaching and preaching. Religious leaders often challenged His authority and teachings at the temple. After the death and resurrection of Christ, Jerusalem became the focal point for most events connected with Christianity, beginning with the day of Pentecost and including much of the history contained in the Acts of the Apostles. In A.D. 70, the Romans destroyed the temple, the city, and its inhabitants with fire.

The Feast of Unleavened Bread. The Feast of the Unleavened Bread immediately followed the Passover and lasted seven days during the month of Nisan (March–April). On each of these days, after the morning sacrifice, a sacrifice in relation to the feast was presented. Unleavened bread alone was eaten and the Israelites removed all yeast from their homes (Exodus 12:15-20; 13:6-8; Leviticus 23:6; Deuteronomy 16:3-8). In the context of the exodus from Egypt, eating bread without yeast signified the haste of their preparation to depart. Moreover, yeast was not used in most grain offerings to God (Leviticus 2:11). Yeast sometimes symbolized sin. A little yeast will affect the whole loaf, just as a little sin can destroy a whole life. A holy convocation and rest from work, with the exception of preparing food, were celebrated on the first and seventh days of the feast.

Background

The Passover and Festival of Unleavened Bread were approaching. All Jewish males 12 and older had to go to Jerusalem, but the chief priests and scribes felt it would not be a good time to begin their plan to kill Jesus. They knew the large crowds, who came for the Passover, could rise up and stone them for hurting Jesus. So they tried to figure out a way to kill Him in the most secretive manner. However, they needed someone to help them. Satan entered the heart of Judas, leading Judas to conspire with the priests and scribes to betray Jesus for money, 30 pieces of silver (Luke 22:5). Waiting for the right time, he joined the disciples, who were in Bethany, preparing for Passover. Jesus arranged to celebrate Passover in the upper room of a house with the disciples. Peter and John went ahead to Jerusalem and prepared the meal for them to share.

At-A-Glance

1. Institution of the Lord's Supper
(Luke 22:14-20)
2. The Betrayal (vv. 21–23)
3. Servant Leader (vv. 24-30)

In Depth

1. Institution of the Lord's Supper (Luke 22:14-20)

Because they had put blood on their doorposts, Passover celebrated God passing over the Israelites' homes and not killing the firstborn males and animals (Exodus 12:1-13). The Passover meal began the Feast of Unleavened Bread. Peter and John secured a lamb, killed it, and prepared it for the Passover celebration. They also purchased unleavened bread, wine, and herbs. These were all necessary items for the meal. They made sure everything was ready for Jesus and the other disciples when they arrived from Bethany. Once they arrived, on the second night, Jesus and the apostles gathered together for the Passover meal. Judas was present with them. He carefully planned the best time for him to betray Jesus and turn Him over to the officials.

It had been prophesied that Jesus, the Messiah, would be betrayed (Psalm 41:9; Zechariah 11:12-13; Matthew 20:18; 26:20-25; Acts 1:16, 20). The people had offered praises of "Hosanna, Blessed is he who comes in the name of the Lord!" as He entered Jerusalem riding on a donkey. Yet, they would eventually cry out for His crucifixion. In His death and shed blood, Jesus symbolizes the slain Passover Lamb.

Jesus said to the disciples, "With desire I have desired to eat this passover with you before I suffer: For I say unto you, I will not any more eat thereof, until it be fulfilled in the kingdom of God" (Luke 22:15-16). Jesus knew it would be the last time He would share the Passover with the disciples before His death as the slain Lamb of God. His sacrifice gave all of humanity the opportunity to be forgiven and redeemed from the penalty of death and sin. After His death, Jesus would share fellowship with His believers through the Lord's Supper, until the coming of His new kingdom and the great wedding banquet (Revelation 19:9). The Lord's Supper is taken in remembrance of Christ's sacrifice of His body and blood on our behalf.

There are four cups of wine drank at the Passover. Over each cup of wine, a blessing is pronounced or the person gives thanks. This is the first cup that Jesus shares with the disciples (Luke 22:17-18). Jesus once again proclaimed that He would not drink wine with the disciples again until His kingdom comes. Afterward, Jesus "took bread, and gave thanks, and brake it, and gave unto them, saying, This is my body which is given for you: this do in remembrance of me. Likewise also the cup after supper, saying, This cup is the new testament in my blood, which is shed for you" (vv. 19-20). This passage begins the account of the Lord's Supper. It is important to note that Luke mentions two cups of wine, but Matthew and Mark mention one (Matthew 26:27-29; Mark 14:23-25).

2. The Betrayal (vv. 21-23)

After the Passover meal and Lord's Supper was over, Jesus said, "But, behold, the hand of him that betrayeth me is with me on the table. And truly the Son of man goeth, as it was determined: but woe unto that man by whom he is betrayed! And they began to enquire among themselves, which of them it was that should do this thing" (vv. 21-23). Here, Jesus let His disciples know that one amongst them, that had celebrated Passover and the Lord's Supper at the table, had betrayed Him. The disciples became suspicious about who would do this to their leader. In Matthew and John's accounts, they identify Judas Iscariot as the betrayer (Matthew 26:25; John 13:26).

Jesus knew His destiny of death on the Cross was predetermined by His Father. It was not unexpected. Jesus had come into the world to save us from sin. This could only be accomplished through His death and resurrection. Satan used Judas to fulfill God's plans. Judas realized that he was wrong for betraying Jesus, but his actions could not be reversed. Thus, he committed suicide (Matthew 27:3-5).

3. Servant Leader (vv. 24-30)

Jesus had just told His disciples about His impending death when a dispute arose among them over who was the greatest (Luke 22:24). They were only concerned about themselves. It is very easy to lose focus and start to think about ourselves as superior to others. The disciples were a group of strong-willed men who felt they were very important. This also happens in today's churches.

Jesus told the disciples the one who serves is the greatest (v. 26). We can look to Jesus as the example. Even though He could rightly claim His position as Messiah, He came into the world to minister to us because we need Him. He did not need us. Therefore, we are to bow down and serve Him. By giving His life, He exemplified servanthood. We, too, should humble ourselves and serve others as Jesus did for us. Then one day, we will sit together in God's kingdom and celebrate at the wedding feast with the Lamb of God (v. 30).

Search the Scriptures

1. What did Jesus mean when He told His disciples He was going to suffer (Luke 22:15)?

2. How does Jesus define greatness (vv. 24–27)?

Discuss the Meaning

It is very easy to think we are more important than others. The truth is God wants us to humble ourselves and serve the people around us. How does selfishness and pride separate us from God? How does Jesus' sacrifice of His body and blood exemplify servanthood?

Lesson in Our Society

There are many people who are leaders but not servants. They dictate to others what to do and demand complete obedience. God wants us to be servants. In our service, we should show humility and love to others. Jesus is our example of a servant-leader. His ministry on earth consisted of teaching, preaching, and healing the sick and other miracles. Then Jesus offered His body as a sacrifice for all humanity. He did not do these things for personal glory. Jesus wanted His Father to be glorified. Everything we do and say should be done for the glory of God.

Make It Happen

Every day and likely everywhere we go, we see people in need. Yet, we either ignore them or tell someone else to help them. Some of us would rather not humble ourselves and reach out to help. Doing something for others may ease us out of our comfort zones. Yet Jesus gave up His throne in heaven and came to earth to save us. He served without thought of Himself. What are you willing to do to make a difference in someone's life, the community, and the world? Start today by looking around your church and paying attention to what needs to be done. Commit to doing one thing every week that could make a difference in the community, in your church, and in the world.

Follow the Spirit

What God wants me to do:

_____

_____

_____

_____

Remember Your Thoughts

Special insights I have learned:

_____

_____

_____

_____

More Light on the Text
Luke 22:14–30

14 And when the hour was come, he sat down, and the twelve apostles with him.

The disciples were gathered in the guest chamber (also guest room or upper room) of a Jewish residence, the location of which Jesus had providentially selected (vv. 9–12). The Greek word for "guestchamber" in verse 11 (see also Mark 14:14) was *kataluma* (**kat-AL-oo-mah**), while "a large upper room" (see Luke 22:12) was referred to as *anogeon* (**an-OGUE-eh-on**). A *kataluma* is the same Greek word Luke chose for 2:7, referring to the already occupied guest chamber that caused Joseph and Mary to sleep downstairs with the animals at the birth of Jesus. This location is also translated "inn." (Modern inns were unknown in the 1st century).

15 And he said unto them, With desire I have desired to eat this passover with you before I suffer: 16 For I say unto you, I will not any more eat thereof, until it be fulfilled in the kingdom of God.

Jesus' statement in Luke 22:15, "With desire I have desired", which is also translated "I have eagerly desired," emphasizes the depth of His feelings. It is reinforced twice with His strong words about never again eating the bread, and in verse 18 never again drinking from the cup, until some point in the future when all would be fulfilled in His coming kingdom. The synoptic parallels of verse 18, similar to verse 16, are found in Matthew 26:29 and Mark 14:25.

New Testament believers can still relate to the disciples in the Upper Room as we continue to this day to observe the Lord's Supper "until he comes" (1 Corinthians 11:26, NIV). Jesus' enigmatic reference to the future kingdom soon was to become painfully clear to the disciples. Unlike any previous Passover, this time

Jesus' body, the spotless and unblemished Lamb of God, would replace traditional Passover lambs (1 Corinthians 5:7).

17 And he took the cup, and gave thanks, and said, Take this, and divide it among yourselves: 18 For I say unto you, I will not drink of the fruit of the vine, until the kingdom of God shall come.

Luke differs from Mark in the number and order of cups. Commentators seem to agree that the use of more than one cup, here and in verse 20 both before and after the meal, indicate the standard Passover tradition that used four cups at specific times during the ceremony. The first cup is with the opening benediction; the second cup is after explaining the Passover and singing the Hallel (Psalm 113—114); the third cup follows the meal—which primarily consisted of unleavened bread (representing the Israelites' haste to leave Egypt), lamb (from which came the lamb's blood on the doorposts), and bitter herbs (representing the bitterness of slavery); and the fourth cup follows the conclusion of the Hallel. Luke's passage records Jesus' taking the second and third cups before and after the meal but without a benediction or singing.

19 And he took bread, and gave thanks, and brake it, and gave unto them, saying, This is my body which is given for you: this do in remembrance of me. 20 Likewise also the cup after supper, saying, This cup is the new testament in my blood, which is shed for you.

To this day, Jews still celebrate Passover with the same thin, unleavened "bread," which in Greek is *artos* (**AR-tos**). Jesus' giving of thanks, which in Greek is *eucharisteo* (**yoo-khar-is-TEH-o**), is in Walter Liefeld's words, "the source of the beautiful word Eucharist" (*Matthew, Mark, Luke*, 1027).

Only Luke adds the words "given for you" for the bread, representing Jesus' body and "shed for you" for the wine representing His blood. (See also John 6:11; Acts 27:35.)

Unlike all other Passovers, with these words, Jesus ushers in the New Testament, the new covenant, ratified in blood as were all covenants between God and men (Exodus 24:8). The word here translated "testament" in the Greek is *diatheke* (**dee-ath-AY-kay**) and can mean either testament or covenant (also an arrangement, compact, disposition, or will). The KJV uniquely translates the same Greek word "covenant" when referring to Old Testament usage, and "testament" when referring to New Testament usage—with the exception of references in Hebrews 9:4; 10:16, 29. Liefeld writes, "'The new covenant' ... carried with it the assurance of forgiveness through Jesus' blood shed on the cross and the inner work of the Holy Spirit in motivating us and enabling us to fulfill our covenantal responsibility" (*Matthew, Mark, Luke*, 1027).

Jesus is well aware of His mission on earth, and soon He will ask the Father to take the "cup" (of suffering) from Him if possible (see synoptic parallels in Matthew 26:39; Mark 14:36; Luke 22:42). Liefeld writes, "The suffering motif is consistent with Jesus' understanding of his mission as the Suffering Servant" (*Matthew, Mark, Luke*, 1027). See also Isaiah 53:11.

21 But, behold, the hand of him that betrayeth me is with me on the table. 22 And truly the Son of man goeth, as it was determined: but woe unto that man by whom he is betrayed! 23 And they began to enquire among themselves, which of them it was that should do this thing.

Judas was at the Last Supper with Jesus and the disciples. The fact that it was possible for a traitor to be so close to the inner circle, even to participate in the initiation of the new covenant (even if he apparently did not finish the meal), should serve as fair warning to all that it is possible for the enemy to infiltrate the ranks of the faithful and even to "break bread" with them. Fred Craddock called this a "continuing warning" (*Luke*, 257).

Multiple scholars agree that there is a deliberate interplay with the dual mention of the Son of man being betrayed by a man, which involved two different uses in verse 22 of the Greek word for "man," *anthropos* (**ANTH-ro-pos**). That the betrayal was "determined" makes use of a Greek word, *horizo* (**hor-ID-zo**), meaning to appoint, decree, or ordain. Liefeld believes the point is that even though the events were ordained, Judas is still responsible for his role: "Divine sovereignty is balanced by human responsibility; so Jesus pronounces a 'woe' on the betrayer" (*Matthew, Mark, Luke*, 1027).

24 And there was also a strife among them, which of them should be accounted the greatest. 25 And he said unto them, The kings of the Gentiles exercise lordship over them; and they that exercise authority upon them are called benefactors.

Yet another "continuing warning" comes with Jesus' correction of the disciples' immature understanding of greatness in the kingdom of God. Any future partaker of the table would do well to take the inherent warning—certainly the church today is not immune to the temptation to love power and prestige over service and humility. Fred Craddock calls this kind of self-serving behavior an "infectious disease" (*Luke*, 257). The argument the disciples were having was about who would sit where, considering ancient seating customs put the most honored and important guests the closest to the host. The example of Jesus' own life gives

weight to His teaching on the subject—He started the meal by washing their feet, a task relegated only to servants (John 13:4-16); He has come to serve, not to be served (Matthew 20:28); and His whole purpose is to do His Father's will (John 8:28).

26 But ye shall not be so: but he that is greatest among you, let him be as the younger; and he that is chief, as he that doth serve. 27 For whether is greater, he that sitteth at meat, or he that serveth? is not he that sitteth at meat? but I am among you as he that serveth.

In the kingdom of God, true greatness doesn't seek self-veneration but is content with a lower place. In God's kingdom, everything is upside down and inside out; thus the servant, not the king, is called the benefactor. It must have been humbling for them to have their shallow argument exposed, especially when Jesus Himself had just washed their feet (John 13:12–17). As Craddock notes, "True exaltation is, therefore, God's gift to those who faithfully endure the hardships of Christ" (*Luke*, 258). Does the church truly understand and practice the lesson on service with as much reverence as they give to the Lord's Supper from which it came?

28 Ye are they which have continued with me in my temptations. 29 And I appoint unto you a kingdom, as my Father hath appointed unto me; 30 That ye may eat and drink at my table in my kingdom, and sit on thrones judging the twelve tribes of Israel.

Occasionally, some believers take the matter of being future judges too much to heart, thereby subverting the original intent. The context of Jesus' message is one of a leader about to leave His followers, and He is leaving them with final instructions, exhortations, and encouragements. The context of believers becoming judges happens only when God exalts men and women because of their humble service while on earth. The very principle is negated by present pride over future rewards for humility and service.

The symbolism of Passover could not have been more perfect for the timing of the Passion of Christ. Craddock captures the essence: "This is no unimportant detail, for the Jewish Passover not only serves as backdrop for the Christian Table of Remembrance but the celebration of liberation from slavery in Egypt provides directly and indirectly meanings for the Lord's Supper" (*Luke*, 253). In retrospect, believers today know that God planned far in advance the details of both events, including the intentional interweaving of symbolism. At the time, none of the characters on the ancient stages were fully aware of the meaning of the events occurring before their eyes. Every element of the Passover meal contained reminders of Egypt—just as the elements of the Exodus carried prototypes of Jesus' Passion. The Lord's Supper—also known as Communion (1 Corinthians 10:16) and Eucharist (Luke 22:17)—is only one of two sacraments, or ordinances, that Jesus personally instituted. Just as humans are inherently sinful, we also are inherently forgetful; thus the need for Jesus' instructions to keep this memorial alive so we will always remember His sacrifice. Far beyond the actual remembrance of Jesus' death, however, simple fellowship is often called "breaking bread" to this day. In Craddock's words, "Because of this last supper, no meal among disciples is just a meal because no loaf is just bread, no cup is just wine" (*Luke*, 255).

As well, there are futuristic meanings for the Passover, found in Jesus' prophetic words about His coming kingdom. Thus the Last Supper simultaneously looks back to the original event in Egypt when the death angel passed over Israelite homes that bore lamb's blood on the doorposts and looks ahead to the final Passover meal. That is the messianic banquet, known as "the marriage supper of the Lamb" (Revelation 19:9). Just as God once liberated His people from physical slavery and formed a covenant with them, Jesus' blood in the new covenant releases captives of sin and death from their spiritual bondage.

Sources:

Barclay, William. *The Gospel of Luke. The New Daily Study Bible.* Louisville, KY: Westminster John Knox Press, 2001. 311–318.

Bock, Darrell L. Luke. *IVP New Testament Commentary Series.* Downers Grove, IL: InterVarsity Press, 1994. 345–355.

Craddock, Fred B. Luke. *Interpretation: A Bible Commentary for Teaching and Preaching.* Louisville, KY: Westminster John Knox Press, 1990. 252–260.

Gill, John. *John Gill's Exposition of the Bible.* http://www.biblestudytools.com/commentaries/gills-exposition-of-the-bible/Luke-22.html (accessed May 6, 2011).

Liefeld, Walter L. *Matthew, Mark, Luke. The Expositor's Bible Commentary,* vol. 8. Edited by Frank E. Gaebelein. Grand Rapids, MI: Zondervan, 1984. 1025–1028.

Life Application Bible – New Revised Standard Version. Wheaton, IL: Tyndale House Publishers, 1989. 1803.

Merriam-Webster Online Dictionary. http://www.merriam-webster.com (accessed November 3, 2011).

New Testament Greek Lexicon. http://www.biblestudytools.com/lexicons/greek (accessed May 6 and October 29, 2011).

Old and New Testament Concordances, Lexicons, Dictionaries, Commentaries, Images, and Bible Versions. Blue Letter Bible. org. http://www.blueletterbible.org/ (accessed April 20, 2011).

Smith, William. *Smith's Bible Dictionary.* http://www.biblestudytools.com/dictionaries/smiths-bible-dictionary.html (accessed May 5, 2011).

Say It Correctly

Atonement. uh-TONE-muhnt.
Eucharist. yoo-kuh-rust.
Hallel. hah-LAYL.
Passover. PAS-o-ver.
Testament. teh-stuh-muhnt.

Daily Bible Readings

MONDAY
Keeping the Passover to the Lord
(Deuteronomy 16:1–8)

TUESDAY
What Does This Observance Mean?
(Exodus 12:21–27)

WEDNESDAY
Preparations for the Last Supper
(Luke 22:7–13)

THURSDAY
Partaking of the Lord's Table
(1 Corinthians 10:14–22)

FRIDAY
Showing Contempt for the Church
(1 Corinthians 11:17–22)

SATURDAY
Examine Yourselves
(1 Corinthians 11:23–32)

SUNDAY
The Last Supper
(Luke 22:14–30)

Notes

Teaching Tips

Words You Should Know

A. Opened (Luke 24:31) *dianoigo* (Gk.)—Opened the mind or soul of someone; facilitated understanding.

B. Burn (v. 32) *kaio* (Gk.)—To set on fire, light.

Teacher Preparation

Unifying Principle—Hope Restored. Jesus opened the eyes of two followers He encountered on the road to Emmaus, and they recognized that Jesus had risen.

A. Pray for your students and lesson clarity.

B. Review Luke 22-23.

C. Complete the companion lesson in the *Precepts For Living Personal Study Guide®*.

D. Bring news or magazine articles written about crime, wars, and financial crises of the world, as well as articles that express positive news.

O—Open the Lesson

A. Open with prayer, including the Aim for Change.

B. Introduce today's lesson title.

C. Have students read the Aim for Change and Keep in Mind verse.

D. Share your articles with the class.

E. Ask, "Why do we sometimes feel a sense of gloom and despair?" Discuss.

F. Have class read the In Focus Story silently, then discuss.

G. Ask, "What can give us a sense of hope?"

P—Present the Scriptures

A. Have volunteers read the Focal Verses.

B. Use The People, Places, and Times; Background; Search the Scriptures; At-A-Glance outline; In Depth; and More Light on the Text to clarify the verses.

E—Explore the Meaning

A. Divide the class into groups to discuss the Discuss the Meaning, Lesson in Our Society, and Make It Happen sections. Have students select a representative to report their responses.

B. Connect these sections to the Aim for Change and the Keep in Mind verse.

N—Next Steps for Application

A. Summarize the lesson.

B. Close with prayer and praise God that Jesus' resurrection gives us hope for the present and future.

Worship Guide

For the Superintendent or Teacher
Theme: The Lord Has Risen Indeed!
Song: "I Know My Redeemer Lives"
Devotional Reading: Luke 24:22-26
Prayer

The Lord Has Risen Indeed!

Bible Background • LUKE 24:1–35
Printed Text • LUKE 24:13–21, 28–35 | Devotional Reading • LUKE 24:22–26

—————————— Aim for Change ——————————

By the end of the lesson, we will: UNDERSTAND the power of a relationship with the Risen Christ; REFLECT on the resurrection of our Savior; and DEVELOP a desire to share the message of the Gospel.

—————————— In Focus ——————————

Lisa and Michael's son, Timothy, had been on the organ donor waiting list for five years. He was born with a heart defect and needed a transplant. His parents continually prayed for a new heart to become available. The week of Easter, the hospital staff called and said it had a new heart for Timothy. His parents rushed to the hospital and waited while the doctors operated on him.

Lisa became very upset as she thought about the parents of the child whose heart Timothy had received. She could not imagine how sad they must have felt. After 16 hours had passed, the doctor reported that the operation was a success. But until the doctor gave her the message from the other mother, Lisa still could not get those parents out of her mind. That mother wanted them to know that her daughter died but that a part of her will live on in Timothy. Immediately Lisa's despair turned to joy.

We can often get entangled in our own sense of grief and despair. In today's lesson we will learn that Jesus offers hope to us no matter the circumstances we face.

—————————— Keep in Mind ——————————

"And their eyes were opened, and they knew him; and he vanished out of their sight" (Luke 24:31).

"And their eyes were opened, and they knew him;
and he vanished out of their sight"
(Luke 24:31).

Focal Verses

KJV **Luke 24:13** And, behold, two of them went that same day to a village called Emmaus, which was from Jerusalem about threescore furlongs.

14 And they talked together of all these things which had happened.

15 And it came to pass, that, while they communed together and reasoned, Jesus himself drew near, and went with them.

16 But their eyes were holden that they should not know him.

17 And he said unto them, What manner of communications are these that ye have one to another, as ye walk, and are sad?

18 And the one of them, whose name was Cleopas, answering said unto him, Art thou only a stranger in Jerusalem, and hast not known the things which are come to pass there in these days?

19 And he said unto them, What things? And they said unto him, Concerning Jesus of Nazareth, which was a prophet mighty in deed and word before God and all the people:

20 And how the chief priests and our rulers delivered him to be condemned to death, and have crucified him.

21 But we trusted that it had been he which should have redeemed Israel: and beside all this, to day is the third day since these things were done.

24:28 And they drew nigh unto the village, whither they went: and he made as though he would have gone further.

29 But they constrained him, saying, Abide with us: for it is toward evening, and the day is far spent. And he went in to tarry with them.

30 And it came to pass, as he sat at meat with them, he took bread, and blessed it, and brake, and gave to them.

NLT **Luke 24:13** That same day two of Jesus' followers were walking to the village of Emmaus, seven miles from Jerusalem.

14 As they walked along they were talking about everything that had happened.

15 As they talked and discussed these things, Jesus himself suddenly came and began walking with them.

16 But God kept them from recognizing him.

17 He asked them, "What are you discussing so intently as you walk along?" They stopped short, sadness written across their faces.

18 Then one of them, Cleopas, replied, "You must be the only person in Jerusalem who hasn't heard about all the things that have happened there the last few days."

19 "What things?" Jesus asked. "The things that happened to Jesus, the man from Nazareth," they said. "He was a prophet who did powerful miracles, and he was a mighty teacher in the eyes of God and all the people.

20 But our leading priests and other religious leaders handed him over to be condemned to death, and they crucified him.

21 We had hoped he was the Messiah who had come to rescue Israel. This all happened three days ago.

24:28 By this time they were nearing Emmaus and the end of their journey. Jesus acted as if he were going on,

29 but they begged him, "Stay the night with us, since it is getting late." So he went home with them.

30 As they sat down to eat, he took the bread and blessed it. Then he broke it and gave it to them.

KJV continued

31 And their eyes were opened, and they knew him; and he vanished out of their sight.

32 And they said one to another, Did not our heart burn within us, while he talked with us by the way, and while he opened to us the scriptures?

33 And they rose up the same hour, and returned to Jerusalem, and found the eleven gathered together, and them that were with them,

34 Saying, The Lord is risen indeed, and hath appeared to Simon.

35 And they told what things were done in the way, and how he was known of them in breaking of bread.

NLT continued

31 Suddenly, their eyes were opened, and they recognized him. And at that moment he disappeared!

32 They said to each other, "Didn't our hearts burn within us as he talked with us on the road and explained the Scriptures to us?"

33 And within the hour they were on their way back to Jerusalem. There they found the eleven disciples and the others who had gathered with them,

34 who said, "The Lord has really risen! He appeared to Peter."

35 Then the two from Emmaus told their story of how Jesus had appeared to them as they were walking along the road, and how they had recognized him as he was breaking the bread.

The People, Places, and Times

The Resurrection. After the betrayal of Jesus by Judas for 30 pieces of silver, He was arrested and taken to trial. It was an illegal trial, and Jesus was condemned to die on the Cross. Before they nailed His hands and feet to the Cross, Jesus was beaten, mocked, and pierced by a crown of thorns. His death left His disciples sad and disappointed. Many thought He would be their new king and redeemer. Upon His death, the disciples went into hiding in Jerusalem, afraid that they, too, would be crucified as followers of Christ. Mary Magdalene, Joanna, Mary the mother of James, and other women visited the tomb where they laid Jesus' body and found it empty (Luke 24:1-11). Peter did not believe the women so he went to investigate the matter. He found the tomb empty and Jesus' burial clothes folded. The resurrected Jesus appeared to Mary Magdalene in the garden and also appeared to other women (Mark 16:9, Matthew 28:9-10). These accounts of Jesus' resurrection appearances, as well as others, confirm that He kept His promise. He had predicted three times that He would suffer, die on the cross, and be resurrected. In spite of all the evidence, some of His disciples still were hopeless and despondent.

Background

After Jesus' death, all hope seemed lost for many of His followers. They thought Jesus would become their earthly king and overthrow the government, thus providing peace for the people. When this did not happen and Jesus was crucified, they did not know where to turn or to whom for help. Two men, one named Cleopas, decided to head back to Emmaus. We do not know what they planned to do when they arrived there; we just know they were saddened by Jesus' death. However, their seven-mile journey would be interrupted by an unexpected traveler.

At-A-Glance

1. Hopelessness and Despair
   (Luke 24:13-21)
2. Restored Hope (vv. 28-35)

In Depth

1. Hopelessness and Despair (Luke 24:13-21)

On the same day that Christ rose from the dead, two of His disciples start a journey back to Emmaus. We do know the identity of one whose name is Cleopas (Luke 24:18). The other man remains unidentified. Cleopas was not a part of the first 12 disciples Jesus called.

It is unknown why the two men were headed to Emmaus, in the opposite direction of Jerusalem. It could've been that Cleopas lived there and was headed home after Passover had ended. Or, they may have been trying to escape the danger that existed in Jerusalem. All followers of Christ were under the threat of persecution. That is why the other disciples more than likely were hiding behind closed doors.

As they walked to Emmaus, they shared their experiences as disciples of Christ (v. 14). It's possible that they talked about Jesus' teachings as well as the numerous miracles and healings He performed. Perhaps they recalled Jesus' triumphant entry into Jerusalem on a donkey and the people's shouts of "Hosanna!" Yet, they had experienced that same crowd shout "Crucify Him!" His crucifixion was still fresh in their minds. After all Jesus had done for the people, He was beaten, humiliated, and nailed on a cross between two thieves. Yet, Mary Magdalene had reported the tomb where Jesus laid was empty. The two disciples still could not believe it happened. Perhaps they thought, "Who will lead us? How can we know which way to go? How can we protect ourselves?"

While the two men discussed all that happened, Jesus appeared and walked alongside them (v. 15), but they never recognized Him (v. 16). Because they were sad, their eyes were downcast. Jesus asked, "What manner of communications are these that ye have one to another, as ye walk, and are sad?" (v. 17). Christ knew what they were talking about. Yet He asked them because they did not know who He was. They could not believe He did not know what had happened (v. 18), especially considering Passover had just ended and people from far and near had come to Jerusalem. They all knew about the crucifixion of Christ.

Jesus pretended not to know what Cleopas was referring to (v. 19). Cleopas summarized the life and death of Jesus (vv. 19-21). He called Him a prophet and had respect for Jesus as a man of God, but after His death, they were reluctant to call Him Messiah. Jesus had told them of things to come, as well as His suffering, death, and resurrection. Yet Cleopas emphasized, "The chief priests and our rulers handed Jesus over to be sentenced to death, and they crucified him" (v. 20, NIV).

The disciples had hoped that Jesus would be their Redeemer (v. 21). The Israelites believed God would send the Messiah that would overthrow the Roman government and free them from bondage. But now that Jesus was dead, it seemed like their hope was gone. They did not know what to believe about the reports of the empty tomb. He did say that on the third day He would be resurrected. The two men did not realize Jesus was the Redeemer of the world that opened the way for all to be redeemed from the bondage of sin and death.

2. Restored Hope (vv. 28-35)

Because His suffering, death, and resurrection are revealed in Scripture, Jesus scolded the two men for their unbelief (vv. 25-26). He then interpreted the Old Testament and explained to them the prophecies that referred to Him (v. 27). The suffering, death, and resurrection of Jesus brought to fulfillment the prophecies of the law, of prophets, and in the writings.

As the two men and Jesus approached Emmaus, Jesus continues walking (v. 28). He was not going to continue with the two men unless invited. They urge Him to stay with them because it's late (v. 29). It is unknown whether it was their home, a friend's house, or a temporary place of rest. Jesus stays with them and continues the conversation. "And it came to pass, as he sat at meat with them, he took bread, and blessed it, and brake, and gave to them" (v. 30). The meal Jesus shared with the two men was the Lord's Supper. It is the presence of Christ, at the table opened to a stranger, that transform an ordinary meal into the Eucharist. Based on the language, we can see the similarities from previous meals (Luke 22:19). It is in the midst of Jesus taking bread, blessing and breaking it, and sharing with the men, that their eyes opened (24:31). They recognize the stranger as Christ. Then He leaves.

Jesus' teachings caused their "hearts to burn within" them (v. 32). Jeremiah 23:29a (NIV) states, "Is not my word like fire ... ?" God's Word is so powerful that it can illuminate even the darkest place of the soul. These two men had experienced sadness and hopelessness, until the Word and sacrament were shared with them. Jesus restored their hope. The two disciples returned to Jerusalem that night and witnessed to the 11 apostles and the other disciples, both men and women (Luke 24:33).

Just as the two disciples entered the place where the apostles and others had gathered, the apostles declared, "The Lord is risen indeed, and hath appeared to Simon" (v. 34). In spite of Simon Peter's denial, Jesus appears to him first to communicate His love and grace toward Him. Paul mentions in 1 Corinthians 15:5 that Jesus appeared to Cephas, Peter's Greek surname. The two disciples who had just arrived witnessed to others about their encounter with Jesus on the road to Emmaus (Luke 24:35). Their witness along with the others offered hope and encouragement to the believers.

Search the Scriptures

1. Why did the two men not recognize Jesus (Luke 24:16)?

2. How did Jesus reveal Himself to the two men on their way to Emmaus (vv. 27, 30)?

Discuss the Meaning

Once Jesus broke bread with the two men, they recognized Him. What significance does the breaking of bread (the Lord's Supper) have in helping us to remember Christ?

Lesson in Our Society

In today's society, it is very easy to become despondent over the problems of life. Many people are unemployed, houses are in foreclosure, crime is rampant, and wars and uprisings continue around the world as well. How do people react when in despair? What can we do to offer them hope?

Make It Happen

This week, we may encounter people who are experiencing difficulties in their families, financial problems, sickness, grieving the loss of a loved one, etc. We can show compassion toward others by listening to them and sharing the message of the Gospel.

The two men in our Scripture lesson went from being hopeless to hopeful. Then they returned to Jerusalem to share the news of the Resurrection with other disciples. We, too, have a message of hope for a hurting world to share wherever we go.

Follow the Spirit

What God wants me to do:

_____

_____

_____

_____

Remember Your Thoughts

Special insights I have learned:

_____

_____

_____

_____

More Light on the Text

Luke 24:13-21, 28-35

Introduction:

After the account of Jesus' ministry up to His death, Luke gives details on post-Resurrection events. Jesus died before the Sabbath and the women could not embalm His body because of the Sabbath, so they waited. Early the next morning, the women went to the tomb and found it empty. Two men (angels) dressed in white told them that Jesus arose from death. When they returned from the tomb, they reported to the 11 disciples and other followers. After the

report of the women, Peter went and witnessed the emptiness of the tomb. The disciples were mourning the death of Jesus and they were so desperate, it was hard to convince them that He has risen.

13 And, behold, two of them went that same day to a village called Emmaus, which was from Jerusalem about threescore furlongs.

After the women's report and Peter's confirmation, two of the disciples decided to go to the village of Emmaus which was about 11 kilometers ("about threescore furlongs") from Jerusalem. The precise location of Emmaus is uncertain because there are two possible sites that we know of today. The disciples' motive for going there is not known. They may have been residents of Emmaus and prevented by the Sabbath and the surrounding events from getting back to their village.

Their journey took place on the first day of the week. The phrase "that same day" indicates that this event took place on the day the women went to the tomb. Chronologically, it came after the women's visit to the tomb and probably came after Peter and John's visit to the tomb as is made clear later in the text.

14 And they talked together of all these things which had happened. 15 And it came to pass, that, while they communed together and reasoned, Jesus himself drew near, and went with them. 16 But their eyes were holden that they should not know him.

The two disciples discussed the report of the women and that of Peter. The subject of their discussions was not only on the empty tomb but also the succession of events since the betrayal of Jesus.

Jesus likely joined them early in their journey. They should have rejoiced because the one whom they were discussing has joined them and is alive. However, they were kept from recognizing Him. The Greek wording used in verse 16 says that their eyes were "holden" (*krateo*, **krat-EH-o**), meaning "restrained" from recognizing Him. This prevention is either coming from their unbelief due to their sorrow—because Mark 16:10 mentions that the disciples were mourning and weeping—or it may be that God intentionally prevented them from recognizing Him. Mark, also referring to this event, said that Jesus "appeared in another form" (Mark 16:12). It is certain that the prevention from recognizing is partly due to the disciples' unbelief and sorrow.

17 And he said unto them, What manner of communications are these that ye have one to another, as ye walk, and are sad?

Jesus' question was a probing inquiry. He knew what they were discussing. Jesus knew the thoughts of His disciples and His audience before these people even spoke (see Matthew 12:25; Mark 12:14-15; Luke 9:47). Jesus knew the subject of their discussion but more than that, He knew their state of mind. In reaction to Jesus' question, they expressed their discouragement and sorrow. Their hearts were not at peace. Jesus knew their doubts, and He wanted to provide them with healing. Jesus knows what we are going through before we even speak to Him; however, He still expects us to tell Him our concerns through prayer.

18 And the one of them, whose name was Cleopas, answering said unto him, Art thou only a stranger in Jerusalem, and hast not known the things which are come to pass there in these days?

In reply to Jesus' inquiry, one of these disciples named Cleopas was concerned. Much is not known about this disciple apart from the mention of his name. His reply to Jesus tells us the extent to which the public knew about the events concerning Jesus' trial and death. The nominal phrase "only a stranger" suggests that even strangers were informed of what went on during the Passion Week. It was therefore a surprise for these two disciples to meet someone leaving Jerusalem as they were who was not well-informed about the situation.

The "things" that happened will be told to their companion in verses 19-20. "These days" do not include this particular day. They may be referring to the day of Jesus' triumphal entry in Jerusalem up to His burial. The event of the missing body in the tomb was fresh news not yet known to the public. Matthew says that the guards went to tell the official in town, but they were bribed not to speak about it (Matthew 28:11-15).

19 And he said unto them, What things? And they said unto him, Concerning Jesus of Nazareth, which was a prophet mighty in deed and word before God and all the people: 20 And how the chief priests and our rulers delivered him to be condemned to death, and have crucified him.

Jesus asked for clarification about the things that happened. The disciples clarified their concept of things that occurred to Him: They spoke of things that happened "Concerning Jesus of Nazareth, which was a prophet" (Luke 24:19). They then gave a powerful testimony of Jesus' words and deeds. John's account includes the reinforcement from the temple guard, sent to arrest Him, who testified that no one had the speaking ability of Jesus (John 7:46). Jesus Himself, in addressing His disciples, told them that the Jews were more guilty because He had done things no one ever did among them in order to convince them (see Acts 11:15-18). Though the first part of the two disciples' summarized biography of Jesus was full of hope, Luke 24:19-20 still set a tone of despair by the usage of the past tense.

The content of verse 20 gives the disciples' reason for using the past tense. The chief priests and the rulers handed Him over to be sentenced to death. The expression "delivered him" explains the transfer of Jesus to Roman authorities by the Sanhedrin to be crucified because the Jews had no authority to put someone to death (John 18:31). Unlike Jews who carried out executions by stoning as ordered by the Law of Moses, the Roman form of capital punishment was crucifixion. The crucifixion of Jesus seems to be the end of the story for these two disciples.

21 But we trusted that it had been he which should have redeemed Israel: and beside all this, to day is the third day since these things were done.

Their hope was based on Jesus delivering Israel from Roman occupation. They misunderstood the Messianic role of Jesus. They might have been influenced by the prevailing ideas about Christ among the Jews.

"The third day" was a date Jesus gave to His disciples as the day of His resurrection from the death. Predictions have meanings when they are kept and considered faithfully. Daniel could recognize, for example, that the 70 years of the Israelites' captivity was over and decide to intercede for the people in exile (9:1-3). Here, it is possible that the disciples' sorrow has made them forget even the predictions of the Resurrection on the third day because the angels reminded the women of what Jesus had told His followers (Luke 24:6). Even with this reminder, the two disciples' situation did not allow a proper attitude of expectation like Daniel possessed. The third day was a promised day that they

should have eagerly awaited, but sorrow and distress made them forget its promise.

24:28 And they drew nigh unto the village, whither they went: and he made as though he would have gone further.

After the answer of the disciples to Jesus' question, we are now at the gate of the village of Emmaus. Before that, Jesus rebuked them and gave them a lecture on the fulfillment of Scripture concerning His life. But His explanation did not arouse their attention. When they reach Emmaus, Jesus acts as though He will continue His journey.

29 But they constrained him, saying, Abide with us: for it is toward evening, and the day is far spent. And he went in to tarry with them.

Because it was getting late, the men urged Jesus to stay the night with them. Hospitality is part of Jewish culture, as we can remember, for instance, Abraham accommodating the stranger in Genesis 18:2-5. This emphasis on hospitality is significant for our time; the practice of this virtue is rare. Individualism, mistrust, sad experiences of many hosts with their guests, fear of strangers, lack of free time, and other reasons can discourage many Christians from extending hospitality. We should be encouraged to practice hospitality with caution and by the discernment the Spirit grants to believers.

The hospitality these two disciples offered to Jesus strongly suggests that they are from Emmaus. If that were not the case, it would have been difficult for them to host someone else had they been guests themselves. One argument that favors this view is that they almost "constrained" Jesus to stay with them (Luke 24:29). Another argument that supports it forcefully comes from John 11:55, which states that many people from the villages went to Jerusalem for the Passover. The powerful way Jesus explained the Scripture to them had certainly played a role in their invitation also. They might have been willing to hear more and the sudden parting of their companion would have deprived them.

30 And it came to pass, as he sat at meat with them, he took bread, and blessed it, and brake, and gave to them.

While on the Emmaus Road, the disciples fail to recognize Jesus. Even His explanation from the Scripture and verbal rebuke could not help them. For this reason once they got indoors and were about to eat, Jesus took the responsibility of sharing the bread. This was the responsibility of the host, not the guest. It's possible that Jesus chose to break bread as an allusion to His previous act of doing so (Luke 22:19) to give the men a hint of His identity. It could also be that when Jesus was handing the bread to them, He provided further evidence though view of the scars in His hands. Whatever the case, this scene would bring them back to their senses.

31 And their eyes were opened, and they knew him; and he vanished out of their sight.

Their eyes, which had prevented them from recognizing Jesus, were enlightened now by the act of the breaking of bread. Now that they saw the resurrected Savior, they no longer needed to doubt the testimony about the empty tomb from the women or Peter. Instead, their own eyes had seen the Savior.

However, they did not enjoy His presence for long because He disappeared from their sight. This disappearance does not make Jesus' resurrected body immaterial. Had it been so, He could not have eaten with them. In addition, we know that Philip was taken away after baptizing the Ethiopian eunuch

(Acts 8:39). Though some suggest it was not a supernatural occurrence, the testimony of Jesus' different appearances and sudden disappearances testifies that it was supernatural and may be a characteristic of the resurrected body.

32 And they said one to another, Did not our heart burn within us, while he talked with us by the way, and while he opened to us the scriptures?

Now that the disciples have recognized Him, they then analyze their journey as having the companionship of a stranger who talked to them. Not only did their "heart burn within" them, but Jesus also gave them an opportunity to increase their understanding of the Scripture. His explanation of the Scriptures was progressive. Jesus probably used the scriptural prophecies, and symbols of the Old Testament related to His life and ministry to teach the two disciples. The breaking of bread was the climax of the revelation of Jesus to His unbelieving and sullen disciples.

33 And they rose up the same hour, and returned to Jerusalem, and found the eleven gathered together, and them that were with them,

Whatever their reason for coming back to Emmaus, it became secondary in comparison to the news of their encounter with Jesus. They therefore went back to Jerusalem to share the good news with the others. The same people pressured Jesus to stay with them because it was getting late.

"The eleven" were Jesus' appointed apostles; the number was no longer 12 because of Judas' betrayal of Him. It is not clear where the disciples gathered; perhaps they were assembled in the Upper Room.

34 Saying, The Lord is risen indeed, and hath appeared to Simon.

While they were bringing good news to the other disciples assembled, they probably felt an additional sense of enthusiasm because of the news they were bearing: "The Lord is risen indeed, and hath appeared to Simon (Peter)." This suggests that Peter may have gone again to the tomb. He first went there, did not find the body, and was wondering what had happened (24:12). Before leaving for Emmaus, the two disciples had Peter's first report about the empty tomb (24:24); it is therefore right to think that this appearance to Peter was later.

The disciples now recognize Jesus as who He claimed to be: the Christ. The term, "Lord" applied to Him in Greek is *Kurios* (**KOO-ree-os**), and is the rendering of the Old Testament *Yahweh*. In John 20:26-28, Thomas will be the first to clearly state, "My LORD and my God." In overcoming death, Jesus proves to be the Lord of lords, the King of kings.

35 And they told what things were done in the way, and how he was known of them in breaking of bread.

The two disciples then confirmed to the others by reporting their own encounter with Jesus with an emphasis on the breaking of bread. That Jesus has risen indeed is an expression of victory and hope.

Sources:

Barnes, Albert. *Notes on the New Testament: Luke and John*. Grand Rapids, MI: Baker Book House, 1965.

Biblical Words Pronunciation Guide. http://netministries.org/Bbasics/bwords.htm (accessed November 3, 2011).

Black, Mark C. *The College Press NIV Commentary: Luke*. Joplin, MO: College Press Publishing, 1996.

Butler, Paul T. *Bible Study Textbook Series: Gospel of Luke*. Joplin, MO: College Press Publishing, 1981.

Craddock, Fred B. *Interpretation: A Bible Commentary for Teaching and Preaching (Luke)*. Louisville, KY: John Knox Press, 1990. 279-288.

Gill, John. *John Gill's Exposition of the Bible*. http://www.biblestudytools.com/commentaries/gills-exposition-of-the-bible/Luke-24.html (accessed May 6, 2011).

Life Application Bible – New Revised Standard Version. Wheaton, IL: Tyndale House Publishers, 1989. 1811-1812.

Morris, Leon. *Tyndale New Testament Commentaries: Luke*. Grand Rapids, MI: Wm. B. Eerdmans, 1986. New Testament Greek Lexicon. http://www.biblestudytools.com/lexicons/greek (accessed May 9 and October 29, 2011).

Smith, William. *Smith's Bible Dictionary*. http://www.biblestudytools.com/dictionaries/smiths-bible-dictionary.html (accessed May 5, 2011).

Say It Correctly

Cleopas. KLEE-o-pas.
Emmaus. eh-MAY-uhs.
Jerusalem. jeh-ROO-suh-lehm.

Daily Bible Readings

MONDAY
The Trial before Pilate
(Luke 23:13–25)

TUESDAY
The Crucifixion of Jesus
(Luke 23:32–38)

WEDNESDAY
The Death of Jesus
(Luke 23:44–49)

THURSDAY
The Burial of Jesus
(Luke 23:50–56)

FRIDAY
The Messiah's Suffering
(Isaiah 53:3–9)

SATURDAY
Discovery of the Empty Tomb
(Luke 24:1–12)

SUNDAY
The Lord Has Risen Indeed!
(Luke 24:13–21, 28–35)

Notes

Teaching Tips

Words You Should Know

A. Fulfilled (Luke 24:44) *pleroo* (Gk.)—Made complete, rendered perfect.

B. Promise (v. 49) *epaggelia* (Gk.)—An announcement.

Teacher Preparation

Unifying Principle—Promises Kept. Though the Resurrection, Jesus kept His word and fulfilled the words of prophesy about Him.

A. Pray for your students and lesson clarity.

B. Study the entire text.

C. Complete the companion lesson in the *Precepts For Living Personal Study Guide®*.

D. Bring pictures of a rainbow, cross, and empty tomb.

O—Open the Lesson

A. Open with prayer, including the Aim for Change.

B. After prayer, introduce today's lesson and have students read the Aim for Change and Keep in Mind verse. Discuss.

C. Share your pictures. Then ask, "What do these biblical symbols represent?"

D. Allow students to respond. Discuss.

E. Have a volunteer summarize the In Focus story.

F. Ask, "Why is it so hard to keep promises?" Discuss.

P—Present the Scriptures

A. Have volunteers read the Focal Verses.

B. To clarify the Focal Verses, use The People, Places, and Times; Background; Search the Scriptures; At-A-Glance outline; In Depth; and More Light on the Text.

E—Explore the Meaning

A. Have volunteers answer the Discuss the Meaning questions.

B. Summarize the Lesson in Our Society and Make It Happen sections.

C. Discuss Search the Scriptures.

D. Connect these sections to the Aim for Change and the Keep in Mind verse.

N—Next Steps for Application

A. Write some take-away principles under the Follow the Spirit or Remember Your Thoughts section.

B. Close with prayer.

Worship Guide

For the Superintendent or Teacher
Theme: The Lord Appears
Song: "Standing on the Promises
of God"
Devotional Reading:
1 Corinthians 15:1-8
Prayer

The Lord Appears

Bible Background • LUKE 24:36-53
Printed Text • LUKE 24:36-53 | Devotional Reading • 1 CORINTHIANS 15:1-8

———————— Aim for Change ————————

By the end of the lesson, we will: DESCRIBE the assurance of the power of the Holy Spirit; REFLECT on the power of God displayed in Scripture; and DECIDE to seek the fulfillment of all that Jesus has promised us.

———————— In Focus  ————————

APR
7th

James and Ruth had been married for 35 years. They had two daughters and one son. Their children Jared, Michelle, and Patrice had grown up learning not to trust their father. He always promised to do things but never followed through on his promises. His focus was on hanging out and partying with his buddies. When they were young children, his broken promises always caused them to feel disappointed and sad. Now that they are adults, they do not respect their father. They also have trouble trusting other people.

One day while the family was gathered for their mother's birthday party, their father announced he had made a change. They were surprised when he told them he was now a Christian. His children had heard him say this many times only for him to continue his lying ways. Moreover, he said he wanted to become better at keeping his promises. His children rolled their eyes and laughed. He told them he would prove it. Over the next few months, their father did try to keep his promises, but he soon fell back into his old habits.

Promises made are often hard to keep. In today's lesson, we will see how Jesus kept His promises and fulfilled all Old Testament prophecies.

———————— Keep in Mind ————————

"And he said unto them, These are the words which I spake unto you, while I was yet with you, that all things must be fulfilled, which were written in the law of Moses, and in the prophets, and in the psalms, concerning me"
(Luke 24:44).

"And he said unto them, These are the words which I spake unto you, while I was yet with you, that all things must be fulfilled, which were written in the law of Moses, and in the prophets, and in the psalms, concerning me" (Luke 24:44).

Focal Verses

KJV **Luke 24:36** And as they thus spake, Jesus himself stood in the midst of them, and saith unto them, Peace be unto you.

37 But they were terrified and affrighted, and supposed that they had seen a spirit.

38 And he said unto them, Why are ye troubled? and why do thoughts arise in your hearts?

39 Behold my hands and my feet, that it is I myself: handle me, and see; for a spirit hath not flesh and bones, as ye see me have.

40 And when he had thus spoken, he shewed them his hands and his feet.

41 And while they yet believed not for joy, and wondered, he said unto them, Have ye here any meat?

42 And they gave him a piece of a broiled fish, and of an honeycomb.

43 And he took it, and did eat before them.

44 And he said unto them, These are the words which I spake unto you, while I was yet with you, that all things must be fulfilled, which were written in the law of Moses, and in the prophets, and in the psalms, concerning me.

45 Then opened he their understanding, that they might understand the scriptures,

46 And said unto them, Thus it is written, and thus it behooved Christ to suffer, and to rise from the dead the third day:

47 And that repentance and remission of sins should be preached in his name among all nations, beginning at Jerusalem.

48 And ye are witnesses of these things.

49 And, behold, I send the promise of my Father upon you: but tarry ye in the city of Jerusalem, until ye be endued with power from on high.

NLT **Luke 24:36** And just as they were telling about it, Jesus himself was suddenly standing there among them. "Peace be with you," he said.

37 But the whole group was startled and frightened, thinking they were seeing a ghost!

38 "Why are you frightened?" he asked. "Why are your hearts filled with doubt?

39 Look at my hands. Look at my feet. You can see that it's really me. Touch me and make sure that I am not a ghost, because ghosts don't have bodies, as you see that I do."

40 As he spoke, he showed them his hands and his feet.

41 Still they stood there in disbelief, filled with joy and wonder. Then he asked them, "Do you have anything here to eat?"

42 They gave him a piece of broiled fish,

43 and he ate it as they watched.

44 Then he said, "When I was with you before, I told you that everything written about me in the law of Moses and the prophets and in the Psalms must be fulfilled."

45 Then he opened their minds to understand the Scriptures.

46 And he said, "Yes, it was written long ago that the Messiah would suffer and die and rise from the dead on the third day.

47 It was also written that this message would be proclaimed in the authority of his name to all the nations, beginning in Jerusalem: 'There is forgiveness of sins for all who repent.'

48 You are witnesses of all these things.

49 "And now I will send the Holy Spirit, just as my Father promised. But stay here in the city until the Holy Spirit comes and fills you with power from heaven."

50 Then Jesus led them to Bethany, and lifting his hands to heaven, he blessed them.

KJV continued

50 And he led them out as far as to Bethany, and he lifted up his hands, and blessed them.

51 And it came to pass, while he blessed them, he was parted from them, and carried up into heaven.

52 And they worshipped him, and returned to Jerusalem with great joy:

53 And were continually in the temple, praising and blessing God. Amen.

NLT continued

51 While he was blessing them, he left them and was taken up to heaven.

52 So they worshiped him and then returned to Jerusalem filled with great joy.

53 And they spent all of their time in the Temple, praising God.

The People, Places, and Times

Jerusalem. Jerusalem was the central religious and political area for Israel. Throughout the Old Testament, Jerusalem is always the central place that the leaders, judges, prophets, and people are affiliated with in some way. This is also true of the New Testament. In the beginning of the book of Luke, he opens with a scene from the temple where Zechariah is worshiping and is told by an angel of the Lord that John the Baptist would be born (1:8-17). Immediately following that announcement, the birth of Jesus is foretold (1:26-38). Throughout the book of Luke, we are given hints that Jerusalem is where all the most important events will occur. So it is no surprise that Jesus predicted that His suffering on the Cross, death, and resurrection would occur in Jerusalem. We end the book with Jesus' followers worshiping in the temple in Jerusalem (24:52-53).

Background

On the third day after the death of Christ, two disciples encountered the resurrected Jesus on their way to Emmaus (Luke 24:13-21, 28-35). Because they were so grief stricken, they were unaware it was Jesus. He opened the Scriptures to them and revealed the Old Testament prophecies that spoke of the Messiah. After such sadness and despondency over the death of their leader, His words restored their hope. They invited Him to stay with them since it was so late when they arrived in Emmaus. They shared the Lord's Supper. Once they recognized Jesus, He disappeared. They then returned to Jerusalem to witness to the other disciples about their encounter with the resurrected Savior. Today's text tells of Jesus' appearance to the disciples and His ascension.

At-A-Glance

1. Jesus' Appearance to His Disciples
Behind Closed Doors
(Luke 24:36-43)
2. Jesus' Appearance to His Disciples in
Jerusalem (vv. 44-49)
3. Jesus' Ascension (vv. 50-53)

In Depth

1. Jesus' Appearance to His Disciples Behind Closed Doors (Luke 24:36-43)

It's very late at night when Cleopas and the other disciple arrive back in Jerusalem. Their journey from Emmaus was seven miles. And lest we forget, it is the same day that Jesus was resurrected from the dead. The

11 apostles and others assembled surely had to be surprised to see them again, especially at such a late hour. Cleopas and the other disciple felt the need to share the renewed hope they had experienced after encountering Jesus on the road to Emmaus.

In the midst of their conversation, Jesus appeared in the room (v. 36). He said, "Peace be unto you." The apostles and other disciples were behind closed doors in fear the Jews would cause harm to them (John 20:19). Moreover, it was late at night. They did not hear a knock at the door, the door open, or any footsteps. He simply appeared and greeted them. Jesus had an immortal, resurrected body, which allowed Him to appear and disappear. At the resurrection of the dead we, too, will be given new bodies (1 Corinthians 15:42-50).

They were terrified and thought Jesus was a spirit (Luke 24:37). This is in spite of the reports of the two women, Simon Peter, and the two disciples who had just arrived from Emmaus. They still did not believe it was Jesus. More than likely, the apostles thought they were seeing the dead. How else could they explain Jesus' sudden appearance?

Jesus wondered why they were so frightened and filled with doubt that it was actually Him (v. 38). After all the evidence they had that Jesus had arisen from the grave, they still doubted His promise of being resurrected on the third day. Jesus offered as evidence His nailed-pierced hands and feet for the apostles and others to see and touch (vv. 39-40). Some may not have believed it was Jesus unless they could touch His body. However as Christians, we should "walk by faith, not by sight" (2 Corinthians 5:7).

While the disciples were overjoyed at being able to see the resurrected Jesus, they still had some doubts about the reality of what they were experiencing (Luke 24:41). Once again, to prove to the believers gathered that it really was Jesus in the flesh, He ate some fish and honeycomb (vv. 42-43). This demonstrated He had a physical body that could consume food.

2. Jesus' Appearance to His Disciples in Jerusalem (vv. 44–49)

According to Acts 1:3, 40 days have passed between Jesus' resurrection (Luke 24:43) and ascension (v. 44). Jesus and His followers had traveled to Galilee and back before He returned to heaven (Matthew 28:16). In Luke 24:44–49, Jesus and His disciples were back in Jerusalem. (See comments on v. 50 in More Light on the Text.)

Jesus had to fulfill all the Old Testament prophecies concerning the Messiah (Genesis 3:15; 22:13; Isaiah 53; Psalm 16:10; 22). He opened up the minds of His disciples by the power of the Holy Spirit so they could understand the Scriptures. Jesus then reminded them that He had previously predicted His suffering, death, and resurrection on the third day (Matthew 16:21; 17:22-23; 20:18-19). There is continuity from the Old Testament through the New Testament. God is faithful and keeps His promises. The apostles and disciples were witnesses to all He did. The words that He spoke were destined to be fulfilled, even before the beginning of all creation.

The Great Commission given in Matthew 28:18-20 is repeated in Luke 24:47-48. They were told that "repentance and remission (forgiveness) of sins should be preached in his (Jesus') name"; the message should be proclaimed "among all nations, beginning in Jerusalem" (v. 47). Our response to Jesus' sacrifice should be repentance of sins. When we repent, we will be forgiven. This is the core message of the Gospel. God's plan from the very beginning has been to extend His love and mercy toward all people,

Jew or Gentile. However, the Jews had to have the first opportunity to hear the Gospel. In Jerusalem, the people involved in Christ's crucifixion needed to hear the Gospel message of repentance and forgiveness. This was accomplished at Pentecost (Acts 2). Then the message was to be shared "in all Judaea, and in Samaria, and unto the uttermost part of the earth," which they accordingly did (Acts 1:8; see also 2:30-32; 10:39-41; 20:21).

Jesus knew that His followers were not ready to preach the Gospel to all people and nations. He said, "I send the promise of my Father upon you: but tarry ye in the city of Jerusalem, until ye be endued with power from on high" (Luke 24:49). The promise was to receive power from God through the Holy Spirit. They had to wait until God decided they were ready to receive this power. God made them wait 50 days (from Easter to Pentecost). They used the time to worship and pray. The promise was fulfilled (Acts 2:4).

3. Jesus' Ascension (vv. 50-53)

Jesus led the apostles and disciples to a village on the Mount of Olives called Bethany. This Bethany is not the hometown of Jesus' friends: Mary, Martha, and Lazarus. This village was a mile away from Jerusalem and began at the Mount of Olives where Bethpage ended. It was here where Jesus chose to ascend into heaven.

Jesus "lifted up His hands and blessed them" (Luke 24:50, NKJV). The blessing is a priestly act in which Jesus places His followers in the care and favor of God. They would need to learn how to completely depend on God for all things. Most importantly, they needed God's Spirit to help them to understand the Word so as they prepare to go places and preach lives may be transformed. We all need to remember God will provide and take care of us.

While He was blessing them, Jesus started to ascend into heaven (v. 51). They watched until He could no longer be seen. Jesus returned to heaven to be with His Father, who welcomed Him. The apostles and disciples were not sad at His departure because He had promised to send the Holy Spirit to be their guide and comforter. Moreover, they knew one day they would be reunited with Jesus. They began to worship Jesus because He is the Messiah, Savior, Resurrected One, Deliverer, Healer, and so much more.

The followers returned to Jerusalem and went to the temple rejoicing for all they had experienced and what would come (vv. 52-53). They had expectations that the Holy Spirit would come just as Jesus promised. They stayed in the temple continually offering praise, prayers, and thanksgiving to God. We, too, should continually worship God and offer praise to His name for being our Savior and Lord.

Search the Scriptures

1. What evidence did Jesus offer to the disciples to prove who He really was (Luke 24:39-40, 42-43)?

2. Why did Jesus tell the disciples to remain in the city (v. 49)?

Discuss the Meaning

People make promises that they do not keep. This can cause us to doubt people when they tell us they will do certain things. What qualities make a person trustworthy?

Lesson in Our Society

We learn to trust people based on their word. Jesus proved He is trustworthy because He has fulfilled every promise made. He wants us to trust Him unconditionally and seek to live out His promises. In today's society, it can be difficult living out the promises of God. What hindrances do you face in seeking to fulfill God's promises? How can you overcome the stumbling blocks?

Make It Happen

Jesus appeared to the disciples to prove that He had been resurrected and to give reassurance to them. Sometimes we need evidence before we believe promises made by others. Jesus' life, death, and resurrection fulfilled all the prophecies of the Old Testament about the Messiah. He is trustworthy. What promises has God made to you through His Word? There is no need to delay in seeking the fulfillment of God's promises for your life. This week, write down the promises and corresponding Scriptures. Pray and ask God for guidance in the steps to take. Step out by faith and take action. Every word of God proves true.

Follow the Spirit

What God wants me to do:

_____

_____

_____

_____

Remember Your Thoughts

Special insights I have learned:

_____

_____

_____

_____

More Light on the Text

Luke 24:36-53

36 And as they thus spake, Jesus himself stood in the midst of them, and saith unto them, Peace be unto you.

The disciples needed convincing proof of the Resurrection of Christ to believe. Jesus will appear to them many times and in various circumstances and give them sufficient proofs through three important senses of human beings: seeing, hearing, and touching. When they are convinced, He will then instruct them on what to do next before His departure to His Father. It is clear from Acts that the last part of this week's Scripture text refers to the 40th day after Jesus' resurrection.

Gathered at Jerusalem in the Upper Room that would be their meeting place in the coming days (John 20:19; Acts 1:13; 2:1), the disciples were discussing Jesus' appearance to Peter and the two disciples on the road to Emmaus. Then Jesus appeared again to all of them, with the exception of Thomas. This event occurred in the evening of the first day of Jesus' resurrection. We learn from the Gospel of John that the disciples closed the door for fear of the Jews. Jesus' standing before them with the door closed is not surprising. Even before His resurrection, He demonstrated His supernatural ability. Thus, it is not strange that He could suddenly appear in their midst without opening a door or window.

Jesus greeted them in the traditional fashion in the Jews' community (Luke 24:36). "Peace be unto you" was a standard greeting that wished peace and prosperity to the recipient. Jesus was the one who could give them true peace (John 14:27). Not only does He give us peace, but He in fact is our peace (Ephesians 2:14).

37 But they were terrified and affrighted, and supposed that they had seen a spirit.

The disciples were still confused about the Resurrection. Sometimes it is not easy to convince someone about certain realities. Their fear was probably increased at the sudden appearance of Jesus in their midst in closed room. To them, only spirit beings could go through a closed door or a wall so they thought they were seeing a ghost. When Jesus walked on water in Matthew 14:25-26, the disciples thought that He was a ghost then. But as the Son of God, the image of the invisible God, and the creator of all things (Colossians 1:16b), He established the physical laws. These laws bind us, as human beings, but He is not bound by them; He subjected Himself willingly to them during the Incarnation apart from His miracles.

38 And he said unto them, Why are ye troubled? and why do thoughts arise in your hearts?

Jesus realized that they are still in a state of doubt. Even after He appeared to some of them earlier, they still remained unsure of His resurrection. Jesus' question is a reproach to them. They had grounds to believe, but they did not. The disciples on the road of Emmaus had been privileged to have a lecture from the Old Testament concerning what happened. All this was not sufficient. Repetition is a part of learning, and Jesus as a perfect teacher is patient with His disciples. He will give them other evidence to convince their doubtful hearts.

39 Behold my hands and my feet, that it is I myself: handle me, and see; for a spirit hath not flesh and bones, as ye see me have.

The eyes of the disciples could not convince them that who they saw was their risen Savior. Their ears also could not help them. For when they heard the report they were still confused, though they testified that the Lord has risen indeed and appeared to Peter. Even Jesus' own voice when He greeted them could not satisfy.

Jesus now calls on their third sense, touch. That was important. A spirit can be seen or heard, but he cannot be touched. If Jesus were not resurrected physically, there would have been no bodily resurrection at all. He invited them to touch Him for certainty that He was not a ghost, for spirits do not have flesh and blood.

40 And when he had thus spoken, he shewed them his hands and his feet.

Jesus allowed them to examine the scars of the nails on His hands and feet to confirm who He was.

41 And while they yet believed not for joy, and wondered, he said unto them, Have ye here any meat?

The experience of touching Jesus brought a response of surprise. However, their joyful amazement was still tainted with confusion about the real nature of Jesus' resurrected body. With patience again, Jesus is prepared to give them more proof. He asked them for food to eat.

42 And they gave him a piece of a broiled fish, and of an honeycomb. 43 And he took it, and did eat before them.

They had broiled fish at their disposal, and they gave Him a piece of it and He ate it while they likely watched attentively. This last evidence was convincing enough to set the stage for the Lord to teach them from the Scriptures about His life and ministry.

44 And he said unto them, These are the words which I spake unto you, while I was yet with you, that all things must be fulfilled, which were written in the law of Moses, and in the prophets, and in the psalms, concerning me.

Jesus reminded them of His earlier interaction with them where He talked about the events of His death and resurrection. The Lord told them that everything written in the Old Testament concerning His life had to be fulfilled. The Old Testament is the name given today to the combined documents He mentioned—namely the Law of Moses, the Prophets, and the Psalms.

Jesus highlights a certain difference between His former relations with them with this new phase. "While I was yet with you" refers to His ministry before His death. In addition to His teaching and miracles, He shared all the peculiarities of human life. He suffered hunger, thirst, fatigue, and pain. He expressed emotions, including weeping when Lazarus died. In view of this, He is no longer present with His disciples in the same manner; though, He is with them physically in this moment. He is no longer constrained by the laws of nature, and He has a different agenda.

45 Then opened he their understanding, that they might understand the scriptures,

Once they accepted the resurrection of the Lord, they were ready to listen to the teaching from the Scriptures, which they could now understand. This happens through the work of the Holy Spirit. With their minds opened, they could grasp the symbolism, prophecies, and archetypes that represent Jesus in the Old Testament. We need God's illuminating work through the Spirit every time we are going to His Word so He can enlighten our hearts as we read.

Similarly, the Ethiopian eunuch needed the guidance from Philip to understand the Scriptures. Intellectual ability to read or study the Word of God is not sufficient in itself. As Ephesians 1:18a (NIV) tells us, "the eyes of (our) heart" need to be enlightened to understand spiritual matters.

46 And said unto them, Thus it is written, and thus it behooved Christ to suffer, and to rise from the dead the third day:

Jesus summarized for them that the Old Testament speaks about His redemptive suffering on the Cross, His death, and His Resurrection on the third day. We should remember what Isaiah 53 says about the suffering of the Messiah. Jesus Himself referred to the snake lifted up by Moses in the desert as a symbol of His crucifixion (John 3:14-15), and He also referred to Jonah's stay in the stomach of the fish as a symbol of His stay in the tomb (Matthew 12:40). These are examples that Jesus may have used to teach His disciples.

47 And that repentance and remission of sins should be preached in his name among all nations, beginning at Jerusalem.

The goal of Jesus' death is the atonement of sins. Without the shedding of Jesus' blood on the Cross, there would be no forgiveness of sins and reconciliation with God (Hebrews 9:12, 22; Revelation 1:5; 5:9). This theme of repentance and forgiveness of sins in Jesus' name as recommended here, was used by Peter during the first preaching of the Gospel in Acts 2:38.

48 And ye are witnesses of these things.

Jesus' disciples were eyewitnesses of what happened to Him. They were involved in His earthly ministry. They witnessed His betrayal, arrest, trial, sentence, and death by crucifixion and now His Resurrection. They can go and preach with conviction concerning these things they knew.

49 And, behold, I send the promise of my Father upon you: but tarry ye in the city of Jerusalem, until ye be endued with power from on high.

In spite of all that they knew about Jesus, the disciples cannot be effective witnesses if they are not empowered by God Himself. Jesus entreats them therefore to be patient and stay in Jerusalem until the promise of the gift of the Holy Spirit is fulfilled. In John 14:16 and 16:7b, Jesus promised the disciples that after His departure, He will send the Holy Spirit. This is the promise of the Father. After they have been filled with the Holy Spirit, Peter refers to it as the fulfillment of the prophecy of Joel (Joel 2:28-32; Acts 2:21).

We know from Acts 2 that the disciples waited at Jerusalem for 10 days in the Upper Room in prayer until the Holy Spirit visited them. As soon as this happened, Peter began preaching. God was faithful to His promise, and the disciples were also faithful in keeping the commands of the Lord.

50 And he led them out as far as to Bethany, and he lifted up his hands, and blessed them.

When Jesus had finished instructing them, He led them to Bethany. This scene occurred on the 40th day after His resurrection. In this passage, it is difficult to differentiate the event that happened the first day and what happened the 40th day. However, it is probable that Jesus' eating to convince them of His identity (v. 43) happened the first day, and verse 44 could be the beginning of the narrative of the 40th day's events. Regardless, in the last earthly scene of Jesus with the disciples, He lifted up His hands and blessed them. He prayed for them, their safety in an evil world, their unity for a convincing testimony, and He blessed them to have a fruitful ministry (John 17).

It is recorded in Acts 1:12 that Jesus' ascension took place at Mount of Olives.

51 And it came to pass, while he blessed them, he was parted from them, and carried up into heaven.

As Jesus blesses them, something strange happens; the Lord is lifted up into heaven before their eyes. The One who could appear and disappear suddenly was proving to them again that He is really Lord of lords and that He rules over the physical principles of this world. A grave could not hold Him captive, and gravity could not limit Him.

52 And they worshipped him, and returned to Jerusalem with great joy:

Before the Resurrection, they referred to Jesus most often as Teacher or Master. After His appearance to Peter, they called Him by the title "Lord" (v. 34). And now they are filled with joy, ready to worship Him. They knew without a doubt that they were with the Lord of lords, the Son of God incarnate. He deserved their worship, and they will dedicate their lives to His service, even to the point of death.

However as He just recommended to them, they went back to Jerusalem to wait for the promise of the Father, the Holy Spirit. The fulfillment of the promise will be the green light for the start of their ministries.

53 And were continually in the temple, praising and blessing God. Amen.

After their return from Bethany, they were continually in the temple praising God until the Pentecost festival 10 days later.

Sources:

Barnes, Albert. *Notes on the New Testament: Luke and John.* Grand Rapids, MI: Baker Book House, 1965.

Biblical Words Pronunciation Guide. http://netministries.org/Bbasics/bwords.htm (accessed November 3, 2011).

Black, Mark C. *The College Press NIV Commentary: Luke.* Joplin, MO: College Press Publishing Company, 1996.

Butler, Paul T. *Bible Study Textbook Series: Gospel of Luke.* Joplin, MO: College Press Publishing Company, 1981.

Craddock, Fred B. *Interpretation: A Bible Commentary for Teaching and Preaching (Luke).* Louisville, KY: John Knox Press, 1990. 288-295.

Gill, John. *John Gill's Exposition of the Bible.* http://www.biblestudytools.com/commentaries/gills-exposition-of-the-bible/Luke-24.html (accessed May 9, 2011).

Life Application Bible – New Revised Standard Version. Wheaton, IL: Tyndale House Publishers, 1989. 1812-1813.

Morris, Leon. *Tyndale New Testament Commentaries: Luke.* Grand Rapids, MI: Wm. B. Eerdmans, 1986. New Testament Greek Lexicon. http://www.biblestudytools.com/lexicons/greek (accessed May 10, 2011).

Smith, William. *Smith's Bible Dictionary.* http://www.biblestudytools.com/dictionaries/smiths-bible-dictionary.html (accessed May 7, 2011).

Say It Correctly

Bethany. BETH-uh-nee.
Benjamin. BEN-juh-muhn.

Daily Bible Readings

MONDAY
Appearances of the Risen Lord
(1 Corinthians 15:1–8)

TUESDAY
The Appearance to Mary Magdalene
(John 20:11–18)

WEDNESDAY
The Appearance to Thomas
(John 20:24–29)

THURSDAY
The Appearance to Seven Disciples
(John 21:1–8)

FRIDAY
Breakfast with the Disciples
(John 21:9–14)

SATURDAY
Simon Peter Called to Follow
(John 21:15–19)

SUNDAY
You Are Witnesses of These Things
(Luke 24:36–53)

Notes

_____

_____

_____

Teaching Tips

Words You Should Know

A. Pentecost (Acts 2:1) *pentekoste* (Gk.)—A Jewish feast that marks the beginning of harvest activities. It begins on the 50th day, following Passover. For Christians it has come to be known as the day the Holy Spirit descended upon Christ's followers.

B. Holy Ghost (v. 4) *pneuma hagios* (Gk.)—The third person of the Holy Trinity, also called the Holy Spirit.

Teacher Preparation

Unifying Principle—Power to Change. The Holy Spirit provides life-transforming power.

A. Prayerfully, read the entire lesson.

B. Pray for your students and lesson clarity.

C. Consider how we can perpetuate a life led by the Holy Spirit.

D. Complete the companion lesson in the *Precepts For Living Personal Study Guide®*.

O—Open the Lesson

A. Receive prayer requests and pray. Also include the Lesson Aim.

B. Introduce the subject of the lesson, including The People, Places, and Times and the Background sections.

C. Have a volunteer read the In Focus story. Discuss, tying in the attributes of a Spirit-filled life.

P—Present the Scriptures

A. Have volunteers read the Focal Verses.

B. To clarify the Focal Verses, use The People, Places, and Times; Background; Search the Scriptures; At-A-Glance outline; In Depth; and More Light on the Text.

E—Explore the Meaning

A. Allow the students a few minutes to complete the Discuss the Meaning questions.

B. Ask for volunteers to read a Discuss the Meaning question and a corresponding verse, and share their answers.

C. Read and discuss the Lesson in Our Society and Make It Happen sections.

D. Ask students to share their thoughts and insights on these sections.

N—Next Steps for Application

A. Summarize the lesson.

B. Close with prayer.

Worship Guide

For the Superintendent or Teacher
Theme: The Holy Spirit Comes
Song: "Holy Spirit, Truth Divine"
Devotional Reading: John 15:1-7
Prayer

The Holy Spirit Comes

Bible Background • ACTS 2:1-36
Printed Text • ACTS 2:1-13 | Devotional Reading • JOHN 15:1-7

—————— Aim for Change ——————

By the end of the lesson, we will: UNDERSTAND that God wants all people to know His love; APPRECIATE the value of living by faith; and COMMIT to a closer walk with God.

—————— In Focus ——————

Gina had enjoyed the company of older people since she was a child. Now, as an adult, she worked taking care of them. She had seen so much heartache. The physical suffering was bad enough, but it was the emotional suffering of abandonment and loneliness that hurt them the most.

APR 14th

In the past year, there had been several older members in Gina's church who had succumbed to poor health and were no longer able to attend services. She genuinely missed seeing their faces in church on Sunday morning. She began to pray for them, and the more she prayed, the greater her burden became. It began to expand beyond the boundaries of her church and extended to the senior people who needed to hear the Gospel of Jesus Christ.

The Holy Spirit was at work in Gina's heart. Surely she wasn't the only one in her church who saw the need for outreach in this area. Gina spoke with her pastor, and with his prayer and support, she launched a visitation and outreach program for the older people in her community.

Today's story illustrates how the empowerment of the Holy Spirit, at work in one faithful heart, can reach out to lost, hurting souls and unite a community.

—————— Keep in Mind ——————

"And they were all filled with the Holy Ghost, and began to speak with other tongues, as the Spirit gave them utterance" (Acts 2:4).

"And they were all filled with the Holy Ghost, and began to speak with other tongues, as the Spirit gave them utterance" (Acts 2:4).

Focal Verses

KJV **Acts 2:1** And when the day of Pentecost was fully come, they were all with one accord in one place.

2 And suddenly there came a sound from heaven as of a rushing mighty wind, and it filled all the house where they were sitting.

3 And there appeared unto them cloven tongues like as of fire, and it sat upon each of them.

4 And they were all filled with the Holy Ghost, and began to speak with other tongues, as the Spirit gave them utterance.

5 And there were dwelling at Jerusalem Jews, devout men, out of every nation under heaven.

6 Now when this was noised abroad, the multitude came together, and were confounded, because that every man heard them speak in his own language.

7 And they were all amazed and marvelled, saying one to another, Behold, are not all these which speak Galilaeans?

8 And how hear we every man in our own tongue, wherein we were born?

9 Parthians, and Medes, and Elamites, and the dwellers in Mesopotamia, and in Judaea, and Cappadocia, in Pontus, and Asia,

10 Phrygia, and Pamphylia, in Egypt, and in the parts of Libya about Cyrene, and strangers of Rome, Jews and proselytes,

11 Cretes and Arabians, we do hear them speak in our tongues the wonderful works of God.

12 And they were all amazed, and were in doubt, saying one to another, What meaneth this?

13 Others mocking said, These men are full of new wine.

NLT **Acts 2:1** On the day of Pentecost all the believers were meeting together in one place.

2 Suddenly, there was a sound from heaven like the roaring of a mighty windstorm, and it filled the house where they were sitting.

3 Then, what looked like flames or tongues of fire appeared and settled on each of them.

4 And everyone present was filled with the Holy Spirit and began speaking in other languages, as the Holy Spirit gave them this ability.

5 At that time there were devout Jews from every nation living in Jerusalem.

6 When they heard the loud noise, everyone came running, and they were bewildered to hear their own languages being spoken by the believers.

7 They were completely amazed. "How can this be?" they exclaimed. "These people are all from Galilee,

8 and yet we hear them speaking in our own native languages!

9 Here we are—Parthians, Medes, Elamites, people from Mesopotamia, Judea, Cappadocia, Pontus, the province of Asia,

10 Phrygia, Pamphylia, Egypt, and the areas of Libya around Cyrene, visitors from Rome

11 (both Jews and converts to Judaism), Cretans, and Arabs. And we all hear these people speaking in our own languages about the wonderful things God has done!"

12 They stood there amazed and perplexed. "What can this mean?" they asked each other.

13 But others in the crowd ridiculed them, saying, "They're just drunk, that's all!"

The People, Places, and Times

Pentecost. The origin of Pentecost precedes the birth, death, and resurrection of Jesus Christ. It's one of the seven feasts of Jehovah and one of the three major Pilgrimage Feasts. Pentecost—also called the "Feast of Harvest" and the "Feast of First-fruits"—is celebrated 50 days after Passover on the Sabbath. God presented these holy feasts to Moses, and it was required that the Children of Israel observe them annually (Leviticus 23:5–21). Pentecost is symbolically related to the Jewish holiday Shavuot or the Feast of Weeks, which celebrates Moses receiving the Ten Commandments on Mount Sinai. In the New Testament, Pentecost takes on yet another meaning. Christians celebrate Pentecost as a commemoration of the descent of the Holy Spirit and the out-pouring of the gifts of the Spirit. The parallel between Shavuot and Pentecost is apparent in that Shavuot represents the Jews' freedom from Egyptian slavery while Pentecost represents man's freedom from slavery to sin.

Background

The celebration of Pentecost, as de-picted in the New Testament (Acts 2:1–21), was prophesied in the Old Testament in Joel 2:28–32. Some believe that the Day of Pentecost marked the beginning of the Christian church. The celebration united Jews from many nations; 16 are mentioned. Empowered by the Holy Spirit, the apostles, who were Galileans, preached the Gospel to the Jewish nations in their native languages.

At-A-Glance

1. Manifestation of the Holy Spirit (Acts 2:1–3)
2. Filled with the Holy Spirit (vv. 4–5)
3. Empowered by the Holy Spirit (vv. 6–12)
4. Doubting the Holy Spirit (v. 13)

In Depth

1. Manifestation of the Holy Spirit (Acts 2:1–3)

There are two important factors that existed on the Day of Pentecost: (1) the apostles were all gathered together in one place, and (2) they were all on one accord. They knew beforehand that this was going to happen, and they were in complete agreement with it as they anticipated the Spirit's advent. Compliance with the Holy Spirit and with each other was necessary for the success of the events that were about to unfold.

Imagine you are part of a baseball team that's about to play the tie-breaking game in the World Series. When you arrive at the stadium, you find that your team's pitcher and catcher didn't show up. The team players that are present are panicking and bickering among themselves. Can this team play a winning game? Are they going to win the support of their fans? Of course not.

The apostles were also a team, and Jesus was their leader. It was vital that God's team be on one accord in body, mind, and spirit on this history-making Day of Pentecost. The manifestation of the Holy Spirit was not a quiet, natural affair. It was rather an audacious, supernatural event. The Holy Spirit arrived with a loud sound, like that of a strong gush of wind. It was a sound so loud that it filled the place where they were sitting. Its mighty force was heard and felt by everyone present. It's likely that the surrounding area also heard the arrival of the Holy Spirit. However, to signify that this was a supernatural event, the fixation was on this particular place.

There was also visible evidence of the presence of the Holy Spirit in the form of what appeared to be flames that lit upon all of them—not consuming flames. These flames remind us of the burning bush (Exodus 3:2-5). God called to Moses out of a bush that burned but yet was not consumed. In both cases the unquenchable flames represented the presence of the Spirit of God. But at Pentecost, the flames were not untouchable as in the bush in the wilderness. At Pentecost, the flames sat on the head of each believer present. God's Spirit was coming to indwell each one.

2. Filled with the Holy Spirit (vv. 4–5)

Any person who receives salvation also receives the Holy Spirit (Romans 8:9). However, to have the indwelling of the Holy Spirit and to be filled with the Spirit are two different things. After Jesus' death and resurrection, the apostles received the Holy Spirit (John 20:22), but the filling of the Spirit would take place on Pentecost. Upon being filled with the Spirit, the apostles spoke in tongues (Acts 2:4), and it caught the attention of a multitude of Jewish people from many lands that had come for the festival. It was especially strange to them because they all heard their own languages being spoken.

The Holy Spirit guides us in our spiritual walk (John 16:13). The more we seek and follow the direction of the Holy Spirit in our life, the more He is able to use us. The Holy Spirit is necessary for us to experience sanctification. The idea of being filled with the Spirit is one of allowing God to have control. It is as though instead of holding on to the steering wheel, you handed God the keys to the car and agreed to go along for the ride. To be filled with the Spirit requires us to be in submission to God so He can direct our lives and transform us.

3. Empowered by the Holy Spirit (vv. 6–12)

When the apostles were filled with the Holy Spirit, it was then that He empowered them with the gifts of the Spirit. Gifts of the Spirit should not be confused with the fruit of the Spirit. Gifts of the Spirit enable us to serve others. The fruit of the Spirit develops and grows throughout our life. It is measured by the quality of our Christian walk. The more we delve into God's Word and apply its teachings to our lives, the more spiritual growth we experience. The more we grow, the more evident the fruit of the Spirit becomes in our life. The fruit of the Spirit is love, joy, peace, longsuffering, gentleness, goodness, faith, meekness, and temperance (Galatians 5:22–23).

On the Day of Pentecost, the apostles were graced with the gift of speaking in tongues. In this event, these Galileans preached the Gospel of Jesus Christ in the native languages of the Jewish people. This was a miracle, an unexplainable and unlikely event that amazed and confused the crowd, and led them to inquire about this strange occurrence. Perhaps we can compare it to the experience of hearing the musical performance of a child prodigy. Despite the mentality of the child, he or she can play the piano as an accomplished composer might. When we witness such a thing, we are amazed and confounded. It is simply beyond our human comprehension. So it was on the Day of Pentecost.

4. Doubting the Holy Spirit (v. 13)

Have you ever heard the saying, "there's one in every crowd"? Well, on the Day of Pentecost, there were more than one. Much like today's hecklers, the doubters in the crowd mocked the whole affair. They sought to undermine the miracle they were witnessing and explain it away by claiming that the apostles were drunk. The mockers were probably as amazed and confused as everyone else. Possibly to hide their own lack of understanding, they tried to explain a supernatural event as a human occurrence.

Search the Scriptures

1. What was the second miracle that indicated the presence of the Holy Spirit (Acts 2:3)?

2. When they heard the apostles speaking in different languages, what were the reactions of the Jewish people (vv. 6–7)?

3. In an attempt to explain away the miracle, what did the mockers in the crowds say about the apostles (v. 13)?

Discuss the Meaning

1. Why do you think the Holy Spirit made such a grand entrance (Acts 2:2–3)?

2. Do you think the miracle of tongues, on the Day of Pentecost, was in the apostles speaking in different languages or in the Jews hearing the Gospel in their own languages (vv. 4–6)?

3. In today's In Focus story, we see how the Holy Spirit at work in one heart can reach out to many for the cause of Christ. Gina could have ministered to older adults on her own rather than share her burden with the pastor and other members of her church. How successful would the ministry have been had she chosen to go it alone? Which way would you have done it and why?

Lesson in Our Society

There are so many hurting people in today's world. Poverty, illness, addiction, violence, injustice, and loneliness are just a few of the problems that plague our society. Even Christians can be overwhelmed when we look around and see all the suffering. It would be easier to stick our heads in the sand and let someone else deal with it, and many people do just that.

One news story reported that a man was beaten by a group of young people after he'd witnessed them committing a crime. The man pulled in to a convenience store across the street. The group of kids, likely fearful that he was going to call the police, beat him, causing serious injury. There were witnesses to this violent attack, but no one did a thing. No one intervened. No one even called the police. The man crawled into his car and drove home and was later admitted to the hospital. No arrests were made.

The Holy Spirit empowers us to come out of our comfort zones and to reach out and help others. If you had witnessed the above crime, what would you have done? Would you have intervened or called the police? Why? Why not?

Make It Happen

When you look around your community, what do you see? Who is hurting, who needs help, and who needs to hear the Gospel of Jesus Christ? There are so many. Are you going to answer the Holy Spirit's call to action, or are you going to leave the burden for someone else?

Follow the Spirit

What God wants me to do:

_____

_____

_____

_____

Remember Your Thoughts

Special insights I have learned:

_____

_____

_____

_____

More Light on the Text

Acts 2:1-13

1 And when the day of Pentecost was fully come, they were all with one accord in one place.

The Greek word for "Pentecost" is *pentekoste* (**pen-tay-kos-TAY**), and it literally means "50th." The Day of Pentecost was given this name because it fell on the 50th day after the Passover. This day was also referred to as the Feast of Weeks and as "the day of firstfruits" (Numbers 28:26). At the Passover feast, a sheaf from the coming grain harvest was presented and then, at Pentecost, two leavened loaves of the harvest were presented to the Lord as the firstfruits of the completed grain harvest. In later Jewish tradition, it became associated with the giving of the Law of Moses at Mount Sinai, 50 days after the exodus from Egypt.

The place where they were together is referred to as "the house" in Acts 2:2.

Perhaps this is the same place as that mentioned in 1:13, though there is no way of concluding that definitively.

2 And suddenly there came a sound from heaven as of a rushing mighty wind, and it filled all the house where they were sitting.

The Greek word for "mighty" is *biaios* (**BEE-ah-yos**) and means "violent, forcible." We are not left in doubt as to the origin of the mighty rushing wind of verse 2. It is from heaven. The Greek word for "wind" is *pnoe* (**pno-AY**) and is also translated as "breath." What took place that day was not from man; it was a supernatural and sovereign act of God. Wind is often used in the Bible in reference to the Holy Spirit, who, in light of Jesus' promise in 1:8, is represented as the mighty rushing wind that fills the house. The Spirit had come indeed to grant Christ's people what He promised: power to be His witnesses in Judea (Judaea, KJV), Samaria, and uttermost parts of the earth.

The fact that He came on Pentecost gives further significance to the event. Because God already knows the full number of those who are His in Christ, these believers and those to come are appointed as a kind of firstfruits of the full harvest of believers gathered to Christ.

3 And there appeared unto them cloven tongues like as of fire, and it sat upon each of them.

The coming of the Holy Spirit on these early Christians was both audible (the sound of a mighty rushing wind) and visible (appeared as "cloven" or divided tongues of fire). It must have been an amazing experience. The tongues rested on each one of them. No one in the house was excluded from this experience. As He is given to all who believe in the Lord Jesus Christ, the Spirit was given to them all.

4 And they were all filled with the Holy Ghost, and began to speak with other tongues, as the Spirit gave them utterance.

Being filled with the Spirit, a repeated experience, is to be distinguished though not disconnected from the baptism of the Spirit, a one-time experience. In the Scriptures, when people were filled with the Spirit, they were enabled to carry out special ministry tasks from the Lord. Here, the filling with the Spirit led to the ability of those gathered in the house to speak with "other tongues." Verse 4 does not tell us the nature of these tongues, whether they were ecstatic or not. However, the context would suggest that they were known languages, considering verse 6 reports that the people heard them speaking in their own languages. That the disciples were able to speak in these other languages was no less amazing, however, than if they had been speaking in a prayer language. The implication of the verse is that the disciples did not have knowledge of these languages of themselves but spoke in them by the power of the Holy Spirit.

5 And there were dwelling at Jerusalem Jews, devout men, out of every nation under heaven.

These Jews dwelling at Jerusalem were devout men of every nation under heaven. In the Greek, "devout" is *eulabes* (**yoo-lab-ACE**) and means "reverencing God; pious; religious." Thus, many of the Jews present during this event were pilgrims from other nations who had come to Jerusalem to celebrate Pentecost. That they were from "every nation under heaven" is a way of saying that they were from many different places.

6 Now when this was noised abroad, the multitude came together, and were confounded, because that every man heard them speak in his own language.

Evidently the noise of the arrival of the Holy Spirit was very loud and drew a great crowd from those who had come to Jerusalem for the Jewish celebration of Pentecost. The people were "confounded" (Gk. *sugcheo*, **soong-KHEH-o**) which means they were stirred up or thrown into disorder. They did not understand what was happening and they were very vocal about their confusion. Some of them understood Aramaic, the language that the disciples spoke, and others understood Greek, the language spoken by the educated people of that day. But no language speaks to us about spiritual things like the language spoken in our homes as we were growing up. And this is what the multitude heard. They came from many places and spoke many different languages, but they could hear the disciples speaking in the languages that touched their hearts.

7 And they were all amazed and marvelled, saying one to another, Behold, are not all these which speak Galilaeans? 8 And how hear we every man in our own tongue, wherein we were born?

All the apostles were from the region of Galilee, just as Jesus was. Not only were they speakers of Aramaic, but they had their own distinctive accent. Just as an American can tell a Texan from a Bostonian, so those who lived in Jerusalem could tell that the apostles were from Galilee just by listening to how they spoke Aramaic. Those from the region of Galilee were mostly village people without cosmopolitan knowledge of a variety of languages. No wonder the crowd was amazed. The Greek word for "amazed" is *existemi* (**ex-IS-tay-mee**), which means they were astounded to the point of feeling as if they were going insane.

9 Parthians, and Medes, and Elamites, and the dwellers in Mesopotamia, and in Judaea, and Cappadocia, in Pontus, and Asia, 10 Phrygia, and Pamphylia, in Egypt, and in the parts of Libya about Cyrene, and strangers of Rome, Jews and proselytes, 11 Cretes and Arabians, we do hear them speak in our tongues the wonderful works of God. 12 And they were all amazed, and were in doubt, saying one to another, What meaneth this?

Most of the people in this crowd were descendants of Jews who had been taken away when the northern kingdom (Israel) was defeated by the Assyrians and those who were taken away when the southern kingdom (Judea) was defeated by the Babylonians. The Parthians, Medes, and Elamites came from what is modern day Iran. They were also known earlier as Persians or Medo-Persians. This was the farthest east to which the Roman Empire stretched. Then to the North of Jerusalem were Cappadocia and Pontus, which were part of the Roman province of Asia (just a small part of the Asian continent). Moving to the West were Phrygia and Pamphylia. All these, except for Pamphylia, were located in the Roman province of Asia, now in modern day Turkey. However, the people in those days were not Turkish. The Turks moved in at a much later date. And then to the South of Israel is Africa. Philo, himself a Jew from Alexandria, estimated that there were a million Jews living in Alexandria alone. Jewish people from Egypt (Alexandria) and Cyrene (a city located in modern day Libya) came to participate in Pentecost. This is almost like Babel coming undone. Although these people came to Jerusalem for Pentecost, the mother tongues represented here came from east, north, west, and south. It was no accident of history that the Holy Spirit came down upon God's people in a dramatic fashion when people from everywhere known to the people of that day were gathered in Jerusalem.

Also there were proselytes in the groups, Gentiles who had been converted to Judaism. Those who were gathered were amazed to hear these people speaking in their own languages, especially in light of the fact that the speakers were all Galileans and not from any of the lands whose languages they spoke. They heard these believers speaking the mighty acts of God, which no doubt included His former acts of old and His new ones accomplished in the person and work of Jesus Christ. Such an amazing miracle needed an explanation. Thus the amazed and perplexed bystanders ask, "What does this mean?"

13 Others mocking said, These men are full of new wine.

In the Greek, the word "mocking" is *chleuazo* (**khlyoo-AD-zo**) and means "deriding, jeering." No matter how amazing the miracle, there are always skeptics, those who question the veracity of God's acts, and always those who ridicule God's work. So it was in this case. There were those who jeered at or derided the event, attributing God's miracle to the effects of alcohol. They accused those whom God had filled with the Spirit as being filled with new wine.

Sources:

Aharoni, Yohanan, and Michael Avi-Yonah. *The Macmillan Bible Atlas.* Revised edition. New York, NY: Macmillan Publishing Company, 1977.

Biblical Words Pronunciation Guide. http://netministries.org/Bbasics/bwords.htm (accessed November 3, 2011).

Bruce, F. F. *Commentary on the Book of the Acts. The New International Commentary on the New Testament.* Grand Rapids, MI: Wm. B. Eerdmans Publishing Co., 1983.

Beitzel, Barry J. *The Moody Atlas of Bible Lands.* Chicago, IL: Moody Press, 1985.

Merriam-Webster Online Dictionary. http://www.merriam-webster.com (accessed November 3, 2011).

New Testament Greek Lexicon. http://www.biblestudytools.com/lexicons/greek (accessed October 31, 2011).

Pfeiffer, Charles F., Howard F. Vos, and John Rea, eds. *Wycliffe Bible Dictionary*. Peabody, MA: Hendrickson Publishers, 2001.

Say It Correctly

Parthians. PAR-thee-uhnz.
Elamites. EE-luh-mites.
Mesopotamia. mess-o-po-TAY-mih-uh.
Cappadocia. kap-ih-DOH-shee-uh.
Phrygia. FRIH-dzih-uh.
Pamphylia. pam-FIhL-ih-uh.
Cyrene. sigh-REE-neh.
Proselytes. PRAH-suh-lites.

Daily Bible Readings

MONDAY
I Will Not Leave You Orphaned
(John 14:18-24)

TUESDAY
Abide in Me
(John 15:1-7)

WEDNESDAY
The Coming of the Advocate
(John 16:1-11)

THURSDAY
Raised Up and Freed from Death
(Acts 2:22-28)

FRIDAY
The Promise of the Spirit
(Acts 2:14-21)

SATURDAY
The Promise Received
(Acts 2:29-36)

SUNDAY
The Day of Pentecost
(Acts 2:1-13)

Notes

_____

_____

_____

_____

Teaching Tips

April 21
Bible Study Guide 8

Words You Should Know

A. Times (1 Thessalonians 5:1) *chronos* (Gk.)—A duration, which may be a point in time or a length of time.

B. Seasons (v. 1b) *kairos* (Gk.)—An opportune, set, or appointed time.

Teacher Preparation

Unifying Principle—Great Expectations. People find themselves in situations that can be destabilizing, disheartening, or despairing. Paul assures us that the promise of Christ's return provides us with comfort and hope.

A. Study and meditate on the entire lesson.

B. Consider how you would offer hope to someone who was worried about the world or even this country's current predicament.

C. Complete the companion lesson in the *Precepts For Living Personal Study Guide®*.

O—Open the Lesson

A. Receive prayer requests and pray, focusing on the Aim for Change.

B. Introduce today's subject, tying in a discussion on how you would offer hope to someone who was worried about the world or this country's current economic, social, political, and environmental situations.

C. Summarize and connect the In Focus story. Discuss.

P—Present the Scriptures

A. Ask two volunteers to read the Focal Verses according to the At-A-Glance outline.

B. Use The People, Places, and Times; Background; Search the Scriptures; At-A-Glance outline; In Depth; and More Light on the Text to clarify the lesson.

E—Explore the Meaning

A. Form two groups and assign each group a question from the Discuss the Meaning section.

B. After discussion, have each group present their conclusions to the rest of the class.

APR 21st

N—Next Steps for Application

A. Discuss The Lesson in Our Society and Make It Happen sections.

B. Challenge students to read the Daily Bible Readings.

C. Close with prayer.

Worship Guide

For the Superintendent or Teacher
Theme: Living with Hope
Song: "My Anchor Holds"
Devotional Reading: Psalm 38:9-15
Prayer

Living with Hope

Bible Background • 1 THESSALONIANS 4:13—5:11
Printed Text • 1 THESSALONIANS 4:13-5:11 | Devotional Reading • PSALM 38:9-15

—————— Aim for Change ——————

By the end of the lesson, we will: UNDERSTAND the significance of the second coming of Christ; REJOICE in our salvation; and DETERMINE to be prepared for the return of our Lord.

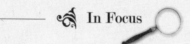

————————— In Focus —————————

Mr. and Mrs. Johnson always insisted that the house's alarm system be turned on each night when the family went to bed. But one night, Brandon and Bree decided to stay up to watch a little TV after their parents had gone to bed, and Brandon forgot to turn on the alarm.

Later that night, Brandon was awakened by what he thought was a sound in the house. He climbed out of bed, tiptoed into his parents' room, woke his dad and whispered, "Dad, someone is in the house!"

Mr. Johnson pushed a nearby panic button wired to the alarm system. A blaring alarm sounded throughout the house. The intruder ran out the back door and a car was heard screeching away. The policeman told Mr. Johnson that in his experience, thieves never showed up when people were looking for them; they always came when they were least expected.

In today's lesson, Paul explained to the Thessalonian Christians that because the Day of the Lord would come as a thief in the night, they were to live as though they expected Christ to return at any moment.

—————————— Keep in Mind ——————————

"For God hath not appointed us to wrath, but to obtain salvation
by our Lord Jesus Christ" (1 Thessalonians 5:9).

"For God hath not appointed us to wrath, but to obtain salvation by our Lord Jesus Christ" (1 Thessalonians 5:9).

Focal Verses

KJV 1 **Thessalonians 4:13** But I would not have you to be ignorant, brethren, concerning them which are asleep, that ye sorrow not, even as others which have no hope.

14 For if we believe that Jesus died and rose again, even so them also which sleep in Jesus will God bring with him.

15 For this we say unto you by the word of the Lord, that we which are alive and remain unto the coming of the Lord shall not prevent them which are asleep.

16 For the Lord himself shall descend from heaven with a shout, with the voice of the archangel, and with the trump of God: and the dead in Christ shall rise first:

17 Then we which are alive and remain shall be caught up together with them in the clouds, to meet the Lord in the air: and so shall we ever be with the Lord.

18 Wherefore comfort one another with these words.

5:1 But of the times and the seasons, brethren, ye have no need that I write unto you.

2 For yourselves know perfectly that the day of the Lord so cometh as a thief in the night.

3 For when they shall say, Peace and safety; then sudden destruction cometh upon them, as travail upon a woman with child; and they shall not escape.

4 But ye, brethren, are not in darkness, that that day should overtake you as a thief.

5 Ye are all the children of light, and the children of the day: we are not of the night, nor of darkness.

6 Therefore let us not sleep, as do others; but let us watch and be sober.

NLT 1 **Thessalonians 4:13** And now, dear brothers and sisters, we want you to know what will happen to the believers who have died so you will not grieve like people who have no hope.

14 For since we believe that Jesus died and was raised to life again, we also believe that when Jesus returns, God will bring back with him the believers who have died.

15 We tell you this directly from the Lord: We who are still living when the Lord returns will not meet him ahead of those who have died.

16 For the Lord himself will come down from heaven with a commanding shout, with the voice of the archangel, and with the trumpet call of God. First, the Christians who have died will rise from their graves.

17 Then, together with them, we who are still alive and remain on the earth will be caught up in the clouds to meet the Lord in the air. Then we will be with the Lord forever.

18 So encourage each other with these words.

5:1 Now concerning how and when all this will happen, dear brothers and sisters, we don't really need to write you.

2 For you know quite well that the day of the Lord's return will come unexpectedly, like a thief in the night.

3 When people are saying, "Everything is peaceful and secure," then disaster will fall on them as suddenly as a pregnant woman's labor pains begin. And there will be no escape.

4 But you aren't in the dark about these things, dear brothers and sisters, and you won't be surprised when the day of the Lord comes like a thief.

KJV continued

7 For they that sleep sleep in the night; and they that be drunken are drunken in the night.

8 But let us, who are of the day, be sober, putting on the breastplate of faith and love; and for an helmet, the hope of salvation.

9 For God hath not appointed us to wrath, but to obtain salvation by our Lord Jesus Christ,

10 Who died for us, that, whether we wake or sleep, we should live together with him.

11 Wherefore comfort yourselves together, and edify one another, even as also ye do.

NLT continued

5 For you are all children of the light and of the day; we don't belong to darkness and night.

6 So be on your guard, not asleep like the others. Stay alert and be clearheaded.

7 Night is the time when people sleep and drinkers get drunk.

8 But let us who live in the light be clearheaded, protected by the armor of faith and love, and wearing as our helmet the confidence of our salvation.

9 For God chose to save us through our Lord Jesus Christ, not to pour out his anger on us.

10 Christ died for us so that, whether we are dead or alive when he returns, we can live with him forever.

11 So encourage each other and build each other up, just as you are already doing.

The People, Places, and Times

The Day of the Lord. The Bible presents history as a process that will culminate in "the day of the Lord" and this current age as the final moment before the intended climax (1 Thessalonians 5:2). John saw principles of evil at work now that will be given full reign at the "last hour" (1 John 2:18, NIV). In the case of today's passage, the purpose of "that day" is to bring about the end of human history and begin the reign of Christ.

Background

Paul rejoiced with great joy that the Thessalonians had received the Gospel as the truth of God through the power of the Holy Spirit (1 Thessalonians 1:5). He then showed how deeply the Gospel's power is tied to those who proclaim and receive it, exclaiming, "So being affectionately desirous of you, we were willing to have imparted unto you, not the gospel of God

only, but also our own souls" (2:8). With this unbreakable Gospel-bond in mind, Paul spoke at length in chapter 3 about his longing to be reunited with the Thessalonian Christians. Since such a reunion had proven impossible, Paul reminded his hearers, "We sent Timothy, who is our brother and co-worker in God's service in spreading the gospel of Christ, to strengthen you and encourage you in your faith" (3:2, NIV).

At-A-Glance

1. Those Who Have Fallen Asleep
   (1 Thessalonians 4:13-18)
2. The Day of the Lord
   (1 Thessalonians 5:1–3)
3. Children of Darkness vs. Children
   of Light (vv. 4–6)
4. Walking in Readiness (vv. 7–11)

In Depth

1. Those Who Have Fallen Asleep (1 Thessalonians 4:13-18)

In this section, Paul corrected a misunderstanding about the return of Christ by the Thessalonian Christians. Apparently, at least some members of the Thessalonian church believed that only those Christians who were alive at the Second Coming would have the possibility of sharing in the kingdom of God at the time of Christ's return.

Paul referred to the dead euphemistically as "those who have fallen asleep" (4:14–15, NIV). The point he made is that they are not dead and gone; rather, their bodies are asleep awaiting the Lord's call to get up. The apostle was anxious to assure the Thessalonians that once a person is saved, he or she is guaranteed to be present when Jesus comes again. Paul wanted to comfort his readers by assuring them that in his words, Christians who are still alive "will certainly not precede those who have fallen asleep" (v. 15, NIV).

In 4:16, Paul described Christ's return to earth in a specific series of events. The Lord will descend from the heavens with a shout. The voice of the archangel and God's trumpet call will be heard. Christians will rise out of their graves and ascend into the air to meet Jesus (1 Thessalonians 4:17).

Only after the "dead in Christ" have left their graves will "we who are still alive and are left" also ascend to meet Jesus in the air (vv. 16–17, NIV). Paul appeared to have believed that he and many other Christians alive at the time of his writing would still be alive when Christ returns. Those who have ascended to be with Jesus will be with Him for all eternity when He returns to establish the kingdom of God.

2. The Day of the Lord (1 Thessalonians 5:1–3)

"The day of the Lord" (v. 2) is a term that Paul used to describe the period of judgment that culminates with the reign of Christ on earth. In His final teaching on the Mount of Olives, Jesus heard the disciples' questions about this period (Matthew 24:3). Our Lord then described a coming period of history marked by universal suffering and destruction (see 24:4–31). During this period, God will pour out His wrath and judgment (Revelation 14:6–7; 15:1).

Like many believers attempt today, the Thessalonian Christians were looking at the events of their world and pointing to them as signs of the end times. Paul cautioned them by explaining, "The day of the Lord will come like a thief in the night" (1 Thessalonians 5:2, NIV). This metaphor illustrates that the Day of the Lord will begin when it is least expected.

Rather than coming during a time of increasing trouble, Paul seemed to state that the time would occur when people are expecting "peace and safety" (v. 3). There would be calm before the storm. The unsaved world will be enjoying a period of peace and well-being. Paul compared it to a pregnant woman who anticipates a specific day of delivery, but then suddenly her water breaks and labor pains begin. The prophet Isaiah used the same illustration years earlier when he described the coming Day of the Lord (Isaiah 13:6–8).

3. Children of Darkness vs. Children of Light (vv. 4–6)

Notice here that Paul was careful to point out the difference between the unbelieving world and true believers (1 Thessalonians 5:3). Paul described the unbelieving world as living in darkness; believers as "children of the light" (v. 5). And "children of the day," i.e., believers, are not in the dark (unknowing, unable to perceive) when it comes to end-time events. We eagerly anticipate the return of Christ, and we live each day as though today will be the day. Unbelievers live as though they will never have to answer for their actions. Of them, Peter wrote: "In the last days scoffers will come, scoffing and following their own evil desires. They will say, 'Where is this 'coming' he promised? Ever since our ancestors died, everything goes on as it has since the beginning of creation'" (2 Peter 3:3–4, NIV).

Unlike those who are in darkness, "the children of the day" are awake, sensitive, alert, and prepared for that great and terrible day. Paul warned us that we must not allow anything in our lives that will deaden our moral alertness. When we allow sin in our lives, we soon are so overcome by its effects that we become oblivious to spiritual matters and unconcerned about the imminent return of Christ.

4. Walking in Readiness (vv. 7–11)

In contrast to 1 Thessalonians 5:7, Paul sets up imagery of a soldier commanded to stay alert on his post. We should do the same as Christians. Paul instructed us to put on our Christian armor and prepare for combat. First, we put on the "breastplate of faith and love" (v. 8). The breastplate, a metal piece worn defensively, is to guard our hearts. Believers must not allow the world's situations to become issues that affect our hearts. No matter what the world throws at us, be it trouble, persecution, hardship, or even the threat of death; we are more than conquerors through Christ who loves us (see Romans 8:35–37).

Next, we put on the "helmet, the hope of salvation" or better yet, hope in our salvation (1 Thessalonians 5:8). Our hope is in Christ and His promise to never leave nor forsake us.

People, institutions, and organizations all fail; but the salvation of Christ is guaranteed for eternity. God has not chosen His people "to suffer wrath but to receive salvation" through Christ who died to redeem us from God's wrath (vv. 9–10).

Search the Scriptures

1. What is the term Paul used to describe the period culminating in the return of Christ to rule and reign on the earth (1 Thessalonians 5:2)?

2. When this terrible period came upon them, what would people be expecting for the world (v. 2)?

Discuss the Meaning

Explain the difference between those who are asleep in 1 Thessalonians 5:4 and verse 11.

Lesson in Our Society

People are worried about the economy, wars, terrorism, and the general state of the world. How would you comfort someone stressed over these issues?

Make It Happen

This week, ask a couple of non-believers what they consider to be the biggest worries of the country. Then ask them how these issues affect them and their future. Use the response as a means of offering them the assurance of Christ.

Follow the Spirit

What God wants me to do:

_____

_____

_____

_____

Remember Your Thoughts

Special insights I have learned:

_____

_____

_____

_____

More Light on the Text

1 Thessalonians 4:13—5:11

13 But I would not have you to be ignorant, brethren, concerning them which are asleep, that ye sorrow not, even as others which have no hope. 14 For if we believe that Jesus died and rose again, even so them also which sleep in Jesus will God bring with him. 15 For this we say unto you by the word of the Lord, that we which are alive and remain unto the coming of the Lord shall not prevent them which are asleep.

The subject of these verses is the coming of the Lord. The Greek word for "coming" is *parousia* (**par-oo-SEE-ah**), and Christians have adopted this word to refer to the second coming of our Lord. The Thessalonians were enthusiastically anticipating the return of the Lord Jesus Christ. They expected Jesus to come any day. Yet when some died before He returned, the Thessalonians wondered what would happen to them. They considered the return of Jesus in all His glory to be something that their departed brothers and sisters would not want to miss. So this is one issue that Paul is dealing with in the epistle to the Thessalonians.

What happens to any Christian when he or she dies? We have to look at a variety of scriptural sources to get the whole picture. When we die, our physical bodies remain in the earth, slowly decaying away. But our spirits go immediately to be with the Lord. Second Corinthians 5:1-9 assures us that when we are absent from our bodies, we are present with the Lord. We do not have to sleep in the ground until the Lord returns. We go to be with Him as soon as we breathe our last breaths.

But that was not the question of the people in the church at Thessalonica. They wanted to know if those who died before the Lord returns to establish His kingdom would miss out on that glorious event. The answer here is no. If we have already died, God will raise up our bodies into glorified bodies and take us along with Jesus as He returns for all the Christians on the earth.

Although "sleep" in 1 Thessalonians 4:13-15 gives us the peaceful idea of sleeping in death, actually when we go to be with Jesus, it will be the most exciting time we have ever had. In 1 Corinthians 13:12, we discover that we will be face to face with Jesus, and we will see Him more fully than ever before.

16 For the Lord himself shall descend from heaven with a shout, with the voice of the archangel, and with the trump of God: and the dead in Christ shall rise first: 17 Then we which are alive and remain shall be caught up together with them in the clouds, to meet the Lord in the air: and so shall we ever be with the Lord. 18 Wherefore comfort one another with these words.

Jesus also spoke about this time as we read in Matthew 24:30-31, "And then shall appear the sign of the Son of man in heaven: and then shall all the tribes of the earth mourn, and they shall see the Son of man coming in the clouds of heaven with power and great glory. And he shall send his angels with a great sound of a trumpet, and they shall gather together his elect from the four winds, from one end of heaven to the other." In 1 Thessalonians 4:17, the Greek word for "meet" is *apantesis* (**ap-AN-tay-sis**) and it also includes the meaning of encounter. When Christ comes, He will meet His people in the same way as a victorious general would arrive after a battle. The citizens of God's kingdom will meet their King who has come to establish God's reign in fullness.

5:1 But of the times and the seasons, brethren, ye have no need that I write unto you.

Evidently, whether through his own preaching or through the ministry of delegates such as Timothy, Paul thoroughly versed the Thessalonians in the words of Jesus—words like, "Therefore be ye also ready: for in such an hour as ye think not the Son of man cometh" (Matthew 24:44). As Paul's words showed, the Thessalonians needed only to be reminded about Jesus' sudden and unexpected coming. But the other likely reason Paul expected the Thessalonians to know what is to come is that, in this very letter, he had just proclaimed to them again the glorious future with Christ that awaited them.

2 For yourselves know perfectly that the day of the Lord so cometh as a thief in the night.

At two other places (2:1 and 3:3), as in this verse, Paul added the Greek word *heautou* (**heh-ow-TOO**), meaning "yourselves," to show emphatically how surely the Thessalonians should recall this aspect of the Gospel. Here, like no other place in all his writings, Paul employed the Greek word *akribos* (**ak-ree-BOCE**), meaning "perfectly," "exactly," or "accurately." Because Paul had been repeatedly responding to Thessalonian questions throughout this letter (see 4:9 and 4:13), we can reasonably conclude that he used this word here because of his stated desire for them to "not grieve like people who have no hope" of when Christ would return (4:13, NIV). He followed up by saying, in effect, "You want to know accurately when Jesus will return? The only thing you can know for certain is that you can't know the time or season at all!" If the end comes "like a thief in the night," then what use is there in predicting its coming?

In talking about this anticipated day, Paul used the language of the parable found in Luke 12:39 and Matthew 24:43, but he connected the "thief" not with Jesus directly but with "the day of the Lord." This idea of the "day" or "Day of the Lord," like many repeated themes in the Bible, can refer to more than one event—often even more than one event at once. This "day" was greatly anticipated by God's people, Israel, for it held the promise that He would rescue them by destroying any and all enemies threatening to destroy them. But the prophets before the exile turned the phrase around so that on that day, God would do the unthinkable and judge His own people for covenant breaking. This "day" came about in 722 B.C. for the northern kingdom and 586 B.C. for the southern. Like many biblical images, the Day of the Lord has many fulfillments, but you might say, only one "Fulfillment," with a capital "F." So it is fitting that Paul, like Peter in 2 Peter 3:10, joined together the awesome and terrible Day of the Lord with the long-awaited second coming of Christ.

3 For when they shall say, Peace and safety; then sudden destruction cometh upon them, as travail upon a woman with child; and they shall not escape.

Paul now directed the Thessalonians to turn their gaze toward the fate of a perishing world. The *IVP Bible Background Commentary: New Testament* has this to say about the phrase "peace and safety": "Paul's readers in Thessalonica … would take his words as an attack on claims of earlier Roman emperors to have established peace and security (*pax et securitas*) throughout the empire. Teachings like this one sounded subversive and may have aroused persecution against Christians (Acts 17:7)" (594). This is not to say that Paul saw only emperors being undone by the Day of the Lord; the pronoun "they," without identification, suggests a much larger scope for his prophesy. But the picture of the Roman emperor—who exalted himself, in Paul's day, as lord and savior—would have called to mind anyone, Gentile or Jew, who would rest wholly in their own prideful complacency.

Paul's vision here brought a revolution to the Thessalonians' thinking about the end: Don't speculate about the day or the hour, Paul counsels; rather, think on your standing and that of the fallen world around you, knowing Christ will come as a reigning King.

4 But ye, brethren, are not in darkness, that that day should overtake you as a thief.

The first two words of this verse, though tiny in both English and the original Greek, exert a huge influence on the verse's meaning. The mood of the whole passage turns on the word "but" with which Paul now sets up a contrast between "they" (v. 3) and "ye" (v. 4). The Thessalonians should not respond to the promise of the King's coming with terror, but with joy and anticipation, as 4:13–18 clearly shows. After all, the Greek word *humeis* (**hoo-MICE**), translated as "ye", is placed in emphatic position at the very front of the Greek sentence so that there might be no doubt in anyone's mind about the massive canyon that separates "they" and "ye" in the mind of God.

5 Ye are all the children of light, and the children of the day: we are not of the night, nor of darkness.

We now learn further why the believer in Christ can and should welcome the day of Christ's second coming: His or her identity is forever tied to the brightness of the day and not the slumber of the night. By using the phrase "children of" to describe his hearers' relationship to "light" and "day," Paul employs a common New Testament phrase to express an unmistakable quality about a person.

As mentioned above, the meaning of "day" changes from verse 4 to verse 5; the context provided in this verse shows that Paul did not mean to say that his hearers "belong to the day of the Lord," but rather that they "belong to the day" as opposed to the night, and the light as opposed to the darkness (v. 5, GNT). The Thessalonians became part of this life-giving "day" through faith in the Gospel of Christ.

6 Therefore let us not sleep, as do others; but let us watch and be sober.

Many have accused both the Bible and sound Christian teaching of becoming a motivation for laziness and complacency. After all, if our destiny as "children of light" is so secure, what motivation could we possibly have to live lives full of holiness and love? But this way of thinking is foreign to the Bible writers; without fail, they see the possession of Christ's glorious riches as nothing less than a call to action. This is why Paul began his charge to the Thessalonians in verses 6–8 with the connector "therefore." The Christians' calling here lines up with their identity. If they are surrounded by the day and full of the light of Christ, then it makes no sense for them to sleep as if it were nighttime. Paul made it clear that there are "others" who sleep; those who have not believed the revelation of Jesus in the Gospel are truly asleep with regard to the coming Day of the Lord. However, it would be unnatural for those of the day to doze as if they could count on "peace and safety" apart from the love and mercy of Christ.

7 For they that sleep sleep in the night; and they that be drunken are drunken in the night.

The people described in this verse were doing the opposite of "watching" and "being sober." By reminding the Thessalonians of such people, Paul strengthened his appeal that they follow a different course in light of their beautifully distinct identity. As we consider this verse, it is important to keep our focus on the context of these commands, which is the hope-filled promise of Christ's return. You might say that the reigning Jesus will have one return, but that coming will be received in two different ways. To those in the day, those who are watching, the appearing will be gloriously happy. To those in the night, those sleeping, the appearing will be a terror-filled surprise.

8 But let us, who are of the day, be sober, putting on the breastplate of faith and love; and for an helmet, the hope of salvation.

Paul now included himself ("us") in his continuing call to resist the stupor of the night. Speaking in terms that would be understood both by those in Roman-occupied territory (who frequently saw centurions and other soldiers arrayed for battle), Paul spoke of a "breastplate" and "helmet," but we quickly see that these are no ordinary, literal war-related gear.

Paul referred to "the hope of salvation" as the believer's helmet. What Paul seemed to be doing here is taking Old Testament language and applying it to New Testament Christians in light of the full revelation of God in Christ. God's righteousness is worked out in faith and love and it brings hope! Thus, the believer's armor expresses the result of God's "battle" on our behalf.

Exercising faith in the Gospel of God, expressing love toward others (for this is how Paul usually used "love"—elsewhere, of course, we are told to love God), and maintaining a joyous hope are all results from someone who possesses Christ. And of course, the command regarding "putting on" these things implies that believers have such items in their wardrobe—which indeed they do—because they possess the riches of Christ.

9 For God hath not appointed us to wrath, but to obtain salvation through our Lord Jesus Christ,

The next two verses showed the heart of God's redemption for believers in Christ, and the reason that Paul could urge the Thessalonians to put on the armor of the light. Matthew Henry explains this verse by suggesting we "trace our salvation to the first cause, that is God's appointment. Those who live and die in darkness and ignorance, who sleep and are drunken as in the night, are, it is but too plain, appointed to wrath (God's punishment); but as for those who are of the day, if they watch and be sober, it is evident that they are appointed to obtain salvation" (*Matthew Henry's Commentary on the Bible, Acts to Revelation,* 788). Thus, God's amazing mercy is the subject of 1 Thessalonians 5:9. Paul mentioned "wrath" because, among other things (for example death, sin, and hell), this is exactly the thing from which the Thessalonians have been saved. But they are saved not just through God's intention ("destined") but also through God's action ("through our Lord Jesus Christ"). His atoning work on the Cross is what actually delivers salvation to those who are His, and gives them the hope to press on in their high and holy calling.

10 Who died for us, that, whether we wake or sleep, we should live together with him.

Paul now reinforced Christians' hope in their ultimate destiny by explaining the loving purpose and happy result of Jesus' death in the place of His people. The words "wake or sleep" might bring some confusion. After all, has not Paul said that those who are "asleep" when Jesus comes back will find themselves in darkness and not in the light of His merciful presence? Indeed, if the word "sleep" here referred to such people, then the apostle would have contradicted himself. But Paul was actually looking back to an earlier use of the word "sleep" (found in 4:13–18) meaning "dead." We know this because he was building on the comforting words of 5:9 and because Paul does not link Jesus' death with anyone's destruction. Jesus' death was only for redemption. Paul is again encouraging the Thessalonian believers with the knowledge that both they (who were alive at the time) and their loved ones, who had died, will be with the Lord. When will they "come to life"? It will be at the promised resurrection of all people, at the coming of Christ "like a thief," as both 4:13–18 and our passage show.

11 Wherefore comfort yourselves together, and edify one another, even as also ye do.

Just as he did in 4:18, Paul reminded the Thessalonians that the uplifting truths of the Gospel are never just for their own encouragement. A major part of "watching" for the Lord's Second Coming to come is sharing with one another the hope and glory brought about by His first coming—His incarnation, death, resurrection, and ascension on our behalf.

Sources:
Best, Ernest. *The First and Second Epistles to the Thessalonians. Black's New Testament Commentaries.* London, England: Adam and Charles Black, 1986. 205.

Biblical Words Pronunciation Guide. http://netministries.org/Bbasics/bwords.htm (accessed November 3, 2011).
Henry, Matthew. *Matthew Henry's Commentary on the Whole Bible. Vol. VI—Acts to Revelation.* McLean, VA: MacDonald Publishing, nd. 788.
Keener, Craig. *IVP Bible Background Commentary: New Testament.* Downers Grove, IL: InterVarsity Press, 1993. 594. electronic edition (accessed September 2, 2008).
New Testament Greek Lexicon. http://www.biblestudytools.com/lexicons/greek (accessed October 31, 2011).

Say It Correctly

Thessalonians. theh-suh-LO-nih-uhnz.

Daily Bible Readings

MONDAY
The Hopeless Human Situation
(Isaiah 59:9-15a)

TUESDAY
The Source of Hope
(Isaiah 59:15b-21)

WEDNESDAY
Waiting in Hope
(Psalm 38:9-15)

THURSDAY
Hoping against Hope
(Romans 4:16-25)

FRIDAY
Seizing the Hope Set before Us
(Hebrews 6:13-20)

SATURDAY
The God of Hope
(Romans 15:7-13)

SUNDAY
Encourage One Another with Hope
(1 Thessalonians 4:13-5:11)

Teaching Tips

Words You Should Know

A. Bound (2 Thessalonians 2:13) *opheilo* (Gk.)—Under obligation.

B. Salvation (v. 13) *soteria* (Gk.)—Rescue, deliverance from danger or sin.

C. Sanctification (v. 13) *hagiasmos* (Gk.)—State of purity, holiness.

Teacher Preparation

Unifying Principle—Sure Source of Hope. Paul warns us against the deception that can come from satanic sources.

A. Pray for your students and lesson clarity.

B. Study the entire text and know the problems that the church at Thessalonica faced.

C. Complete the companion lesson in the *Precepts For Living Personal Study Guide®*.

O—Open the Lesson

A. Receive prayer requests and pray, including the Aim for Change.

B. Write this question on the board: "How can we know which sources to trust?" and have the class discuss their answers.

C. Have a volunteer read the In Focus story. Discuss.

P—Present the Scriptures

A. Have students read the Aim for Change in unison.

B. Have volunteers read the Focal Verses.

C. Highlight salient points in the Focal Verses using The People, Places, and Times; Background; Search the Scriptures; At-A-Glance outline; In Depth; and More Light on the Text.

E—Explore the Meaning

A. Call attention to the Lesson in Our Society and Make it Happen sections.

B. Pull out salient points.

N—Next Steps for Application

A. Encourage your students to follow through on the Make It Happen suggestion.

B. Remind students to read the Daily Bible Readings.

C. Close with prayer.

APRIL
28th

Worship Guide

Hope Comes from God's Grace

Bible Background • 2 THESSALONIANS 2
Printed Text • 2 THESSALONIANS 2:1-3, 9-17 | Devotional Reading • TITUS 3:1-7

Aim for Change

By the end of the lesson, we will: EXPLORE the purpose for which God has called us; TRUST that God has a significant plan for our lives; and PRAY for a clear understanding of God's assignment.

In Focus

John and Mary saw that there was a lot to be done in their church, located in the heart of an inner-city neighborhood. In 25 years, they saw several pastors come and go and had witnessed firsthand the financial, personal, and spiritual struggles of the church. It was tempting for them to retreat to the beautiful suburban church closer to their home.

However, one day as John studied the Scriptures, he ran across a passage in Luke's Gospel: "But their scribes and Pharisees murmured against his disciples, saying, Why do ye eat and drink with publicans and sinners? And Jesus answering said unto them, They that are whole need not a physician; but they that are sick. I came not to call the righteous, but sinners to repentance" (Luke 5:30–32).

John felt convicted. He knew the Lord had him and Mary in their current church because there were many who were spiritually sick who could benefit from their biblical wisdom and needed to be taught God's Word. John and Mary learned that God had called them to make a needed and lasting difference in a lost and dying world—in an inner-city venue.

In today's lesson, God is calling for commitment to His agenda: saving lost souls and helping to build His kingdom.

Keep in Mind

"Now our Lord Jesus Christ himself, and God, even our Father, which hath loved us, and hath given us everlasting consolation and good hope through grace, Comfort your hearts, and stablish you in every good word and work" (2 Thessalonians 2:16-17).

"Now our Lord Jesus Christ himself, and God, even our Father, which hath loved us, and hath given us everlasting consolation and good hope through grace, Comfort your hearts, and stablish you in every good word and work" (2 Thessalonians 2:16-17).

Focal Verses

KJV **2 Thessalonians 2:1** Now we beseech you, brethren, by the coming of our Lord Jesus Christ, and by our gathering together unto him,

2 That ye be not soon shaken in mind, or be troubled, neither by spirit, nor by word, nor by letter as from us, as that the day of Christ is at hand.

3 Let no man deceive you by any means: for that day shall not come, except there come a falling away first, and that man of sin be revealed, the son of perdition;

2:9 Even him, whose coming is after the working of Satan with all power and signs and lying wonders,

10 And with all deceivableness of unrighteousness in them that perish; because they received not the love of the truth, that they might be saved.

11 And for this cause God shall send them strong delusion, that they should believe a lie:

12 That they all might be damned who believed not the truth, but had pleasure in unrighteousness.

13 But we are bound to give thanks alway to God for you, brethren beloved of the Lord, because God hath from the beginning chosen you to salvation through sanctification of the Spirit and belief of the truth:

14 Whereunto he called you by our gospel, to the obtaining of the glory of our Lord Jesus Christ.

15 Therefore, brethren, stand fast, and hold the traditions which ye have been taught, whether by word, or our epistle.

16 Now our Lord Jesus Christ himself, and God, even our Father, which hath loved us, and hath given us everlasting consolation and good hope through grace,

17 Comfort your hearts, and stablish you in every good word and work.

NLT **2 Thessalonians 2:1** Now, dear brothers and sisters, let us clarify some things about the coming of our Lord Jesus Christ and how we will be gathered to meet him.

2 Don't be so easily shaken or alarmed by those who say that the day of the Lord has already begun. Don't believe them, even if they claim to have had a spiritual vision, a revelation, or a letter supposedly from us.

3 Don't be fooled by what they say. For that day will not come until there is a great rebellion against God and the man of lawlessness is revealed—the one who brings destruction.

2:9 This man will come to do the work of Satan with counterfeit power and signs and miracles.

10 He will use every kind of evil deception to fool those on their way to destruction, because they refuse to love and accept the truth that would save them.

11 So God will cause them to be greatly deceived, and they will believe these lies.

12 Then they will be condemned for enjoying evil rather than believing the truth.

13 As for us, we can't help but thank God for you, dear brothers and sisters loved by the Lord. We are always thankful that God chose you to be among the first to experience salvation—a salvation that came through the Spirit who makes you holy and through your belief in the truth.

14 He called you to salvation when we told you the Good News; now you can share in the glory of our Lord Jesus Christ.

15 With all these things in mind, dear brothers and sisters, stand firm and keep a strong grip on the teaching we passed on to you both in person and by letter.

16 Now may our Lord Jesus Christ himself and God our Father, who loved us and by his grace gave us eternal comfort and a wonderful hope,

17 comfort you and strengthen you in every good thing you do and say.

The People, Places, and Times

Antichrist. Most Bible scholars identify the "man of sin" in today's Scripture passage as identical to an antichrist written about by Paul (2 Thessalonians 2:3). In his epistles, John describes this antichrist as denying the Incarnation (1 John 4:3; 2 John 7) and denying the deity of Christ (1 John 2:2). The Incarnation is the theological term for the Son of God becoming a human being. Deity is the truth that Jesus was and is truly God. These two truths taken together show us that Jesus was both fully human and fully God. To deny these two central truths is to be an antichrist. While there is a generic description of an antichrist, Scripture tells us that there will be a specific figure with great influence who will be the ultimate Antichrist.

In Revelation 13:1-8 the description of the beast is often equated with the Antichrist and the man of sin. Jesus also mentioned false christs (Matthew 24:24; Mark 13:22). The Antichrist is prophesied to come right before the great tribulation occurs. Some theologians interpret the antichrist symbolically, i.e., a spirit of unbelief.

Background

Paul, Silas, and Timothy founded the church at Thessalonica on Paul's second missionary journey (Acts 17:1–10), but the apostle Paul had to leave in a hurry because of the degree of persecution there. In Paul's first letter to the church, he not only comforted these struggling believers but also offered encouragement because they were still experiencing threats and other types of harassment because of their faith in God. However, false teachings were also causing problems for this infant church because incorrect information about Jesus' second coming spread and caused some to quit their jobs and become idle. Idleness bred the sinful conduct of minding other people's business. Therefore, Paul wrote this second letter to encourage the Thessalonians in their suffering of persecution and to correct the false information. In addition, he wanted to instruct them to get back to work and remind them of conduct becoming children of a Holy God set apart from sin.

At-A-Glance

1. Those Not Left Behind
(2 Thessalonians 2:1-3)
2. Those Fooled by the Man of Sin
(vv. 9-12)
3. Loved, Chosen, and Called (vv. 13-14)
4. Standing Firm in the Faith (vv. 15-17)

In Depth

1. Those Not Left Behind (2 Thessalonians 2:1-3)

Evidently, someone had forged a letter that was supposed to have come from Paul. The letter said that the day of the Lord had already come. Many novelists, so-called spiritual leaders, and even a few contemporary preachers have given people information that is contrary to what the Bible teaches concerning the second coming of our Lord. Some have even claimed to be the Messiah.

But Paul rushed in to comfort the Thessalonian Christians; Jesus has not yet returned. The Bible gives us many warning signs. Among them is the coming of the man of sin or of lawlessness, also called an antichrist, whom we can read about in Revelation 13. At this time, there will be open rebellion against God. So no, Jesus has not yet returned. And we do not need to worry about being left behind if we have accepted Jesus Christ as our Savior.

2. Those Fooled by the Man of Sin (vv. 9-12)

This Antichrist is not Satan, but Satan is the power behind him. Satan will be helping him perform all sorts of seeming miracles and evil deeds. People who did not believe in our wonder-working God will somehow believe in the "magic tricks" of the Antichrist. Human beings have a spiritual vacuum inside which can only be filled with Jesus. But those who refuse Him try to fill that vacuum with all sorts of alternatives: drugs, illicit sex, false religions, and even perfectly good deeds; but deeds without Jesus will leave people just as empty. Because these people have deliberately rejected the truth—Jesus—God will allow them to be fooled by the greatest deception of all: that the Antichrist is God.

3. Loved, Chosen, and Called (vv. 13-14)

Paul affirmed to these struggling Thessalonians that they were loved by Almighty God, Himself. In fact, this great salvation that they had received had nothing to do with their own merit but was because of God's favor. They, as we, could not earn it, but had to accept it as a gift from God. Paul reminded them that from the beginning, God chose them to be a part of His family, and through His Holy Spirit, God made them and all believers like Christ (Romans 8:29). Believers' salvation is not because they have been so good or so kind. It is because a loving God had compassion and mercy on them and chose them to be His heirs. Therefore, believers can never boast in their salvation because they all have to receive the forgiveness of sin through belief on the Lord Jesus Christ as their Lord and Savior (John 3:16). No person took Jesus' life, but as Jesus said, "I lay it down of myself. I have power to lay it down, and I have power to take it again. This commandment have I received of my Father" (John 10:18).

In today's passage, in 2 Thessalonians 2:14, Paul reiterated that God worked through Silas, Timothy, and himself to bring the Good News of salvation to the Thessalonians. Still, their salvation was all about God and His work and not about Paul and his companions, who apart from God's work are like us: "fallible, unfaithful, untrustworthy human creatures" (*Life Application Study Bible*, 1923). Yet, God can and does take fallible, unfaithful, untrustworthy human beings and uses them for His glory.

4. Standing Firm in the Faith (vv. 15-17)

Now that Paul had built up the Thessalonians by encouraging them in the faith, he moved on to encourage them to stand firm in their faith. He wanted them to commit to faithfulness to God. The apostle knew that one threat to the church was false teaching or doctrine. For the Thessalonians, believing the Second Coming was imminent had caused them to fall into the sins of idleness and being busybodies. Such a display of confusion was a negative witness for a lost and dying world. It did not represent the Holy God well. Paul, therefore, urged them to commit and hold on to the foundational truths that they had been taught from the beginning of their faith and to get back to work.

In verses 16 and 17, Paul ended this part of his letter by reminding the Thessalonians that it was God who loved them and has done so with His special favor (grace); this same God gave them "everlasting consolation" and hope through salvation by believing in Jesus Christ. According to John 10:28, Jesus said, "And I give unto them eternal life; and they shall never perish, neither shall any man pluck them out of my hand." This means

Jesus protects believers from harm forever. All believers can expect to suffer on earth. Yet we have the assurance from God Himself that Satan cannot harm our souls or take away our eternal life that Jesus paid the price for in full when He died on the Cross. Paul then prayed that this same God would both comfort the Thessalonians' hearts in the midst of their struggles as well as give them strength in everything that they did and said.

Search the Scriptures

1. What two things will happen before the day of the Lord (2 Thessalonians 2:3)?

2. Who is the power behind the man of sin (v. 9)?

Discuss the Meaning

1. Why did Paul tell the Thessalonians that first a falling away and then a man of sin would be revealed before the day of the Lord (2 Thessalonians 2:1-3)?

2. Why would God allow people to believe a delusion (vv. 9-12)?

Lesson in Our Society

Not too long ago, a rich Christian man announced via radio, billboards, etc., that the rapture was going to happen, and he gave a date for it. Many non-Christians made fun of him especially as the date passed and nothing happened. How could a careful reading of today's Scripture passage help us avoid deception by such messages? Do you know other Scriptures that would also show that this prophecy was wrong?

Make It Happen

Paul was writing to console the Thessalonians, and his words are God's words for us today. Look again at the key verses to focus on how God gives us hope through His grace. What should be the result of His comfort? Are good words and good works flowing from God's grace in our lives?

Follow the Spirit

What God wants me to do:

_____

_____

_____

_____

Remember Your Thoughts

Special insights I have learned:

_____

_____

_____

_____

More Light on the Text

2 Thessalonians 2:1-3, 9-17

1 Now we beseech you, brethren, by the coming of our Lord Jesus Christ, and by our gathering together unto him, 2 That ye be not soon shaken in mind, or be troubled, neither by spirit, nor by word, nor by letter as from us, as that the day of Christ is at hand.

In 2 Thessalonians 2:1, one Greek word is translated as two—"gathering together" (*episunagoge*, **ep-ee-soon-ag-o-GAY**), which refers to the time mentioned in 1 Thessalonians 4:17 when all believers will be raised to join our Savior when He returns to establish His kingdom. When Paul wrote his first letter to the Thessalonians, it was a time of great persecution. The second letter, which was probably written about six months later, found the Thessalonian Christians in the same situation and so shaken up that they were easily duped. It seems they had gotten a forged letter attributed to Paul, that stated that the Day of the Lord was already upon them. Or perhaps someone stood up in the church and claimed to have a divine revelation. The Thessalonians were warned to keep their heads about them, to think clearly and biblically.

3 Let no man deceive you by any means: for that day shall not come, except there come a falling away first, and that man of sin be revealed, the son of perdition;

This verse tells us that two events will happen before the coming of the Day of the Lord. The first is a falling away. "Falling away" in Greek is translated as *apostasia* (**ap-os-tas-EE-ah**) and means a defection from the truth or a religious rebellion. Theologians called it apostasy. Paul is picturing a worldwide rebellion against the authority of God.

The second thing that will happen is the appearance of the leader of this opposition to the rule of God, who is called the man of sin. Through the ages, people have tried to identify the man of sin. Some of the names suggested have been Caligula, Nero, etc. Many modern names have also been suggested as well. We need to be careful not to fall into this trap of identifying someone who personifies evil as the Antichrist.

2:9 Even him, whose coming is after the working of Satan with all power and signs and lying wonders, 10 And with all deceivableness of unrighteousness in them that perish; because they received not the love of the truth, that they might be saved.

These verses continue the conversation concerning the man of sin. Again we see that Satan is behind him. The Greek word

for "all" is *pas* (**pas**) and modifies "power and signs and lying wonders." "Lying" in Greek is *pseudos* (**PSYOO-dos**); it also means intentionally false, and here it also modifies power, signs, and wonders. The man of sin seems able to do great wonders, but they are all shams. The sad thing is that those who have rejected Jesus Christ will not be able to see how false all these wonders are. We see followers of false religions today who seem oblivious to how deceitful these religions are.

11 And for this cause God shall send them strong delusion, that they should believe a lie: 12 That they all might be damned who believed not the truth, but had pleasure in unrighteousness.

Even many well-educated Bible scholars are not sure how to interpret some of the verses in today's passage. For instance, they are not sure if the man of sin is an individual or an organization. But we do know that as powerful as Satan is, he can only do what God allows him to do. Even now he is being restrained, but shortly before the Lord returns, God will let go of the restraints, and he will be free to do more evil than we could imagine. In spite of the evil that he represents, those who have rejected the Lord will believe in him. The Greek word for "delusion" is *plane* (**PLAN-ay**), and it means fraudulence, a straying from orthodoxy or piety, delusion, deceit, or error. This delusion is the man of sin and all he will represent. However, those who follow the Lamb will not be deceived.

13 But we are bound to give thanks alway to God for you, brethren beloved of the Lord, because God hath from the beginning chosen you to salvation through sanctification of the Spirit and belief of the truth:

In this second letter to the Thessalonians, Paul reaffirmed that he and his companions

(Silas and Timothy, the founders of the church at Thessalonica) were "bound" (Gk. *opheilo,* **of-I-lo**), which means "under obligation, indebted," to always give thanks to God for these believers. They felt bound because God had from the beginning of the world "chosen" (Gk. *haireomai,* **hahee-REH-om-ahee**) these believers to become a part of His family and had used Paul, Silas, and Timothy to bring them the Good News. The word "salvation" in the Greek is *soteria* (**so-tay-REE-ah**), which means "rescue, deliverance, preservation, saving." God chose to rescue these Thessalonians from the power of sin and the penalty of sin, which is death (that is, eternal separation from a holy God). It is also God at work, through His Holy Spirit, who used "sanctification" (Gk. *hagiasmos,* **hag-ee-as-MOS**), meaning "consecration, purification," to make the Thessalonians holy as He is holy. Their salvation had been all about God doing a work in them; God, by His power, transforming them from sinners to believers. One of His attributes is He is omnipotent, or all-powerful. He used that power to bring the Thessalonians into His fold.

14 Whereunto he called you by our gospel, to the obtaining of the glory of our Lord Jesus Christ.

Paul also reaffirmed to the Thessalonians that God "called" (Gk. *kaleo,* **kal-EH-o**), or "invited, named," them out of sin to salvation. They believed in Jesus Christ and were delivered from sin and from eternal or everlasting damnation (John 3:16). Their salvation brought "glory" (Gk. *doxa,* **DOX-ah**), or "honor, praise, worship, splendor, excellence," to God. When they were saved, they, too, became a part of His kingdom that will reign forever and ever.

15 Therefore, brethren, stand fast, and hold the traditions which ye have been taught, whether by word, or our epistle.

After encouraging the Thessalonians in the faith, Paul cautioned them to "stand fast, and hold the traditions, which ye have been taught." The phrase "stand fast" in the Greek is *steko* (**STAY-ko**), meaning "to stand firm, to persevere, to persist" in the faith. They were to hold to the traditions that they had been taught when they first believed. The word "hold" in Greek is *krateo* (**krat-EH-o**), meaning, "to use strength, lay hold on, be master of." They were to hold onto, seize, and retain those fundamentals of the faith that they had been first taught. They were not to grab hold of false doctrine concerning Jesus' Second Coming and become idle in their daily living. This false doctrine contradicted the principles that Paul had taught them and that his life had embodied before them.

Because of false teachers and doctrines, it is really important that believers, even today, study God's Word in context, cross-referencing Scriptures to know what the Bible actually says or teaches. Bible study requires knowledge of context. That means we should not just read a given Scripture verse and draw our own conclusions. Instead, we should read the Scriptures surrounding the text. For example, look at the entire chapter, then consider book that contains the chapter. Finally, determine whether your interpretation of that Scripture contradicts what the Bible teaches as a whole. Also consider the people, places, and times of that Scripture. All these things bring clarity to the meaning.

16 Now our Lord Jesus Christ himself, and God, even our Father, which hath loved us, and hath given us everlasting consolation and good hope through grace,

Paul concluded this portion of his second letter to the Thessalonians with an earnest prayer for this struggling Church, recognizing two persons of the Trinity, Jesus Christ the Savior and God the Father. The apostle acknowledged what God had already done for him and them through His salvation and His unconditional love for them. God had given them "everlasting consolation and good hope through grace." The word "everlasting" in the Greek is *aionios* (**ahee-O-nee-os**), which means "eternal, forever, without beginning and end." The Greek word for "consolation" is *paraklesis* (**par-AK-lay-sis**), which means "encouragement, comfort, solace." In other words, Paul acknowledged that when God saved them through Jesus Christ, He gave them comfort that would last forever and ever. He gave believers "hope" (Gk. *elpis*, **el-PECE**), which means "joyful and confident expectation." When God saved them, He gave them confidence and an expectation that would last forever as well. He gave this to them through grace. The word "grace" in Greek is *charis* (**KHAR-ece**), meaning "favor, reward." God gave believers, therefore, comfort and expectation or hope through His grace. He favored them; they did not and could not earn these gifts.

17 Comfort your hearts, and stablish you in every good word and work.

Paul recognized that God would comfort the Thessalonian Christians' hearts, so he prayed for that comfort. The word "comfort" in the Greek is *parakaleo* (**par-ak-al-EH-o**) and it means, "to encourage and strengthen by consolation." The Greek word for "hearts" is *kardia* (**kar-DEE-ah**), meaning "the center and seat of spiritual knowledge and life." Only an omniscient, all-knowing God truly knows the heart—the core, the foundation of our spiritual life. When we are going through dire circumstances, only God can really come near to our hearts and bring His peace that surpasses all understanding. As Paul wrote, "It is a faithful saying: For if we be dead with him, we shall also live with him: If we suffer, we shall also reign with him: if we deny him, he also will deny us" (2 Timothy 2:11–12). This is the confidence and hope that the Thessalonians and all believers should have.

The apostle Paul also prayed that they might be established in the ways of God. Only God can establish us in His ways, making us firm in every good word and work so He can be honored. If we as believers commit to Him, He will establish us in every good word and work, too. He will bring about His ways in us.

Sources:

Best, Ernest. *A Commentary on the First and Second Epistles to the Thessalonians.* New York, NY: Harper and Row Publishers, 1972.

Henry, Matthew. *Commentary on the Whole Bible.* Edited by Leslie F. Church, et al. Grand Rapids, MI: Zondervan, 1961. 1884-1885.

Life Application Study Bible (New Living Translation). Wheaton, IL: Tyndale House, 1996. 1923.

Merriam-Webster Online Dictionary. http://www.merriam-webster.com (accessed November 3, 2011).

New Testament Greek Lexicon. http://www.biblestudytools.com/lexicons/greek (accessed October 31, 2011).

Vincent, Marvin R. *Word Studies in the New Testament.* Grand Rapids, MI: Wm. B. Eerdmans Publishing Co., 1957.

Say It Correctly

Perdition. per-DIH-shun.
Incarnation. in-kar-NAY-shun.
Consolation. kahn-suh-LAY-shun.

Daily Bible Readings

MONDAY
An Appointed Time
(Psalm 75)

TUESDAY
The Day Is Coming
(Malachi 4)

WEDNESDAY
No Good Thing Withheld
(Psalm 84)

THURSDAY
My Help Comes from the Lord
(Psalm 121)

FRIDAY
The Hope of Eternal Life
(Titus 3:1-7)

SATURDAY
Kept Sound and Blameless
(1 Thessalonians 5:23-28)

SUNDAY
Eternal Comfort and Good Hope
(2 Thessalonians 2:1-3, 9-17)

Notes

Teaching Tips

Words You Should Know

A. Lively hope (1 Peter 1:3) *anagennao* (Gk.)—An eternal assurance grounded in the resurrection of Christ; a new birth.

B. Inheritance (v. 4) *kleroo* (Gk.)—Something, as a quality, characteristic, or other immaterial possession, received from progenitors or predecessors.

Teacher Preparation

Unifying Principle—Hopeful Living. Peter focuses our attention on the resurrection of Jesus Christ as our hope for now and the future.

A. Pray for your students and lesson clarity.

B. Study and meditate on the entire text.

C. Complete the companion lesson in the *Precepts For Living Personal Study Guide®*.

D. Prepare a presentation or bring news clippings of historical incidents that you and others have prayed much about.

O—Open the Lesson

A. Open with prayer, including the Aim for Change.

B. After prayer, introduce today's subject, and have your students read the Aim for Change and Keep in Mind verse in unison.

C. Share your presentation.

D. Ask, "What do you hope for?"

E. Allow volunteers to share their testimonies.

F. Have a volunteer summarize the In Focus story. Discuss.

G. Ask, "Who is your source and provider?" Discuss.

P—Present the Scriptures

A. Have volunteers read the Focal Verses.

B. Now use The People, Places, and Times; Background; Search the Scriptures; At-A-Glance outline; In Depth; and More Light on the Text to clarify the verses.

E—Explore the Meaning

A. Have volunteers summarize the Discuss the Meaning, Lesson in Our Society, and Make It Happen sections.

B. Connect these sections to the Aim for Change and the Keep in Mind verse.

N—Next Steps for Application

A. Summarize the lesson.

B. Close with prayer.

Worship Guide

For the Superintendent or Teacher
Theme: A Living Hope
Song: "My Hope Is Built
on Nothing Less"
Devotional Reading:
Lamentations 3:19-24
Prayer

A Living Hope

Bible Background • 1 Peter 1:1-12
Printed Text • 1 Peter 1:3-12 | Devotional Reading • Lamentations 3:19-24

——————————— Aim for Change ———————————

By the end of the lesson, we will: KNOW how we can find meaning in life's challenges; FEEL the hope of Christ and be able to share that hope with others; and ACTIVELY turn to Christ for hope and guidance.

———————————  In Focus ———————————

Rodney had heard about rampant layoffs, plant downsizing and closings, expansion overseas, and many other reasons millions of Americans have been displaced from their workplaces. But until it happened to him, he didn't know what it felt like to be without health insurance and other benefits of the working class. What was he to do?

Often, Rodney would express that God, not his job, was his source. Now it was time to really trust Him. Especially now that his unemployment compensation had been exhausted, Rodney knew that his only hope was in Christ Jesus. He began to stand on the Scripture, "I will never leave thee, nor forsake thee" (Hebrews 13:5).

In order to make it through, Rodney knew he would need to take one day at a time. After all, he knew the Lord knows his end from his beginning. There is reason to hope.

MAY 5th

The daily struggles of life can cause us to experience hopelessness. How can we become confident and find hope for a better tomorrow? Peter writes that a new birth into a living hope can be found in the resurrection of Jesus Christ.

——————————— Keep in Mind ———————————

"Blessed be the God and Father of our Lord Jesus Christ, which according to his abundant mercy hath begotten us again unto a lively hope by the resurrection of Jesus Christ from the dead" (1 Peter 1:3).

"Blessed be the God and Father of our Lord Jesus Christ, which according to his abundant mercy hath begotten us again unto a lively hope by the resurrection of Jesus Christ from the dead" (1 Peter 1:3).

Focal Verses

KJV **1 Peter 1:3** Blessed be the God and Father of our Lord Jesus Christ, which according to his abundant mercy hath begotten us again unto a lively hope by the resurrection of Jesus Christ from the dead,

4 To an inheritance incorruptible, and undefiled, and that fadeth not away, reserved in heaven for you,

5 Who are kept by the power of God through faith unto salvation ready to be revealed in the last time.

6 Wherein ye greatly rejoice, though now for a season, if need be, ye are in heaviness through manifold temptations:

7 That the trial of your faith, being much more precious than of gold that perisheth, though it be tried with fire, might be found unto praise and honour and glory at the appearing of Jesus Christ:

8 Whom having not seen, ye love; in whom, though now ye see him not, yet believing, ye rejoice with joy unspeakable and full of glory:

9 Receiving the end of your faith, even the salvation of your souls.

10 Of which salvation the prophets have enquired and searched diligently, who prophesied of the grace that should come unto you:

11 Searching what, or what manner of time the Spirit of Christ which was in them did signify, when it testified beforehand the sufferings of Christ, and the glory that should follow.

12 Unto whom it was revealed, that not unto themselves, but unto us they did minister the things, which are now reported unto you by them that have preached the gospel unto you with the Holy Ghost sent down from heaven; which things the angels desire to look into.

NLT **1 Peter 1:3** All praise to God, the Father of our Lord Jesus Christ. It is by his great mercy that we have been born again, because God raised Jesus Christ from the dead. Now we live with great expectation,

4 and we have a priceless inheritance—an inheritance that is kept in heaven for you, pure and undefiled, beyond the reach of change and decay.

5 And through your faith, God is protecting you by his power until you receive this salvation, which is ready to be revealed on the last day for all to see.

6 So be truly glad. There is wonderful joy ahead, even though you have to endure many trials for a little while.

7 These trials will show that your faith is genuine. It is being tested as fire tests and purifies gold—though your faith is far more precious than mere gold. So when your faith remains strong through many trials, it will bring you much praise and glory and honor on the day when Jesus Christ is revealed to the whole world.

8 You love him even though you have never seen him. Though you do not see him now, you trust him; and you rejoice with a glorious, inexpressible joy.

9 The reward for trusting him will be the salvation of your souls.

10 This salvation was something even the prophets wanted to know more about when they prophesied about this gracious salvation prepared for you.

11 They wondered what time or situation the Spirit of Christ within them was talking about when he told them in advance about Christ's suffering and his great glory afterward.

NLT continued

12 They were told that their messages were not for themselves, but for you. And now this Good News has been announced to you by those who preached in the power of the Holy Spirit sent from heaven. It is all so wonderful that even the angels are eagerly watching these things happen.

The People, Places, and Times

Author, Audience, Attitude. There is little doubt that apostle Peter is the author of this epistle. He introduces himself in verse one. We also note that he is writing to strangers (perhaps Greek converts) in various regions of Asia. Whether Peter directed his letter to a specific group or not, it is encouragement for all Christians who believe on the Lord Jesus Christ, even those of us today who have accepted the truth of the death, burial, and Resurrection of Jesus our Savior. With these motivational words, we are assured there is victory over suffering.

Background

Although Peter wrote to Jewish Christians driven out of Jerusalem and scattered throughout Asia Minor, there is much that we can learn from his letter.

He wrote to encourage Christians who were under persecution. Peter himself had been beaten, jailed, and threatened often as he brought God's message to the people. He had also witnessed firsthand not only fellow Christians dying for the faith but many being scattered as they sought refuge. In the midst of his awareness of ongoing persecution and suffering, the apostle Peter sought to bring comfort and hope to Christians under duress.

At-A-Glance

1. Hope through Salvation
   (1 Peter 1:3-6)
2. Triumphant Victory (vv. 7-12)

In Depth

1. Hope through Salvation (1 Peter 1:3-6)

Abundant mercy (vv. 3-4). When Adam and Eve sinned against God in the Garden of Eden, man fell from a great estate. This did not catch God by surprise, for He had a plan of redemption already in place. As we read in these two verses, God has already established reconciliation with humankind through the death, burial, and Resurrection of our Lord and Savior Jesus Christ. It is through God's abundant mercy that we are not consumed.

The shed blood of Jesus not only brings hope of eternal life but a lively hope to all humankind. Peter writes in 1 Peter 2:5 of saints being "lively stones." This dynamic combination of a lively hope and "lively stones" allows us to have victory over the cares of this world. We have been translated into Christ's kingdom through the incorruptible inheritance we have received. All of this is accomplished by the resurrection power that is in us through the precious gift of the Holy Ghost. As believers, we have victory over suffering. We have a spiritual heritage built upon an everlasting foundation.

When the entire world is falling apart, our prayer can be: "Let your kingdom come on earth as it is in heaven." We are in this world but not of it. We serve the God of Abraham, Isaac, and Jacob. It was Abraham who searched for that city that was not made by hand. Through Jesus Christ, we have inherited the promise of His kingdom here on earth. Eternal life will not fade away for heaven belongs to His saints.

Faith works (vv. 5-6). Remember the song that many congregations used to sing Gene Martin and Richard Littlejohn? "Faith, faith, faith, just a little bit of faith. It don't take a whole lot, just use what you got, faith, faith, faith, just a little bit of faith." There is so much truth to that tune, which appeared on the 1970 "We Shall Be Like Him" album. Jesus taught that all you need is faith the size of a mustard seed for mountains to move at your command (Matthew 17:20).

Peter is encouraging the reader that although there are manifold temptations, we are kept by the power of God through faith. Salvation begins by faith, and we must hold onto faith until that day when we reach our heavenly reward. Perhaps, like Job, you have been considered by God to go through hardship. Rejoice as the fiery tests and trials engulf you. Take time to learn what the purposes of these experiences are—they exist to make us, not to break us.

2. Triumphant Victory (vv. 7-12)

In our devotional reading from the book of Lamentations, Jeremiah lets us know where to place our hope. "The LORD is my portion, saith my soul; therefore will I hope in him" (Lamentations 3:24). It seems nearly unimaginable to grasp what the world does when life's challenges happen. We as saints have the Lord as our comfort. We are privileged to be able to go to Him in prayer.

Precious trials (v. 7). Can you imagine that 24-karat gold is not worth as much as

the trials of your faith? This is what Peter is telling us. To the carnal mind, that definitely is foolishness. But to those of us who have been given the mind of Christ, how precious is this teaching! These fiery trials that we're enduring and overcoming are going to be currency with Jesus Christ in His appearing. Surely we want Him to be pleased not only then but now as well. A wise person has said it's all about attitude and perspective. How we look at a situation makes all the difference. Learn to see things as God sees them. Then the trials that seem like they're going to take you out will become precious and valuable.

Believing faith (vv. 8-9). Peter seems to echo the words of Jesus when He was speaking to Thomas: "Jesus saith unto him, Thomas, because thou hast seen me, thou hast believed: blessed are they that have not seen, and yet have believed" (John 20:29). We, too, are in that number—believing, rejoicing with unspeakable joy, and full of glory. The promise of hope has been fulfilled, and we are heirs to the promise.

Better days are coming (vv. 10-11). Throughout the Old Testament, prophets and common people alike rested in the promise of hope. They looked forward to a better day when the promised Messiah would destroy the works of man. The list is long and covers thousands of years, but these men, women, and children of faith looked to the future in hope. Present-day saints have a different vantage point. We have all these things recorded in the Word of God. We also have witness in our inner being that Jesus did just as He said. Our hope is in the glorious resurrected Christ. He has provided triumph over death and suffering. Yes, we have hope eternal.

Angelic curiosity (v. 12). "What is man, that thou art mindful of him? and the son of man, that thou visitest him? For thou hast made him a little lower than the angels, and hast crowned him with glory and honour" (Psalm 8:4-5). Man has a place of honor in God's creation. God breathed life into man and he became a living soul (Genesis 2:7). No other creature, angelic or otherwise, can boast of this status. However much the angels may be puzzled at God's decision in creation, we do know that in redemption the angels rejoice when a soul is saved (Luke 15:10).

Search the Scriptures

1. What type of inheritance do we have as saints (1 Peter 1:4)?

2. In whom does our hope lie (Lamentations 3:24)?

Discuss the Meaning

With so many catastrophes occurring in the world around us, let alone the strife among nations and individuals, from where do we draw our strength to face a world in turmoil?

Lesson in Our Society

The foundations of our society have been shaken. Everywhere a person turns there is strife, fear, and upheaval. Systems and programs that have been in place for decades such as Social Security, Medicare, college education grants and loans, and other assistance programs are in jeopardy of failing. What are some ways that the body of Christ can minister hope to the society in which we live?

Make It Happen

The church of Jesus Christ is called to be a beacon of light to a dark world. Determine ways your local church can have an impact of hope on the community in which you live.

Share the hope that you have with those who are in hopeless situations.

Follow the Spirit

What God wants me to do:

_____

_____

_____

_____

Remember Your Thoughts

Special insights I have learned:

_____

_____

_____

_____

More Light on the Text

1 Peter 1:3-12

3 Blessed be the God and Father of our Lord Jesus Christ, which according to his abundant mercy hath begotten us again unto a lively hope by the resurrection of Jesus Christ from the dead,

The apostle Peter wrote to believers living in northwestern Asia Minor, now Turkey. The bearer of the letter lists the provinces of Pontus, Galatia, Cappadocia, Asia, and Bithynia in the order of visit. Though Peter's ministry was mainly oriented to the Jews, the letter here was addressed to Christians who were largely Gentiles.

The beginning of this section, focused on thanksgiving, was a Jewish pattern of writing adopted by the Christians. While the

Jewish thanksgiving formula is limited to the mention of God, Christian thanksgiving is expanded in identifying God more specifically because of the revelation of Jesus Christ as Lord. Here Peter's praises go to God the Father of our Lord Jesus Christ. Paul uses the same template for his letters (see 2 Corinthians 1:3; Ephesians 1:3). This thanksgiving is rooted in what God has accomplished for Peter and his audience.

God in His mercy has given new birth to both Peter and the recipient of his letter. In 1 Peter 3:3, the phrase "a lively hope" translated in Greek is *anagennao* (**an-ag-en-NAH-o**), meaning new birth (or "born again," NLT). The concept of the new birth is found in John where the new birth is not dependent on the will of man but that of the Spirit (1:13; 3:6). This new birth came through God's mercy, which is the rendering of the Old Testament Hebrew word *chesed* (**KHEH-sed,** meaning loving-kindness); in Greek it is *eleos* (**EL-eh-os**). *Eleos* reminds the readers that the provision for the new birth is solely the work of God without any merit whatsoever from the receiver of the new birth. The means by which God accomplishes *anagennao* in the believer was through the Resurrection of Christ from the dead. It echoes the importance of the Resurrection for the Christian faith stated by Paul. Without it, the Christian faith is aimless and futile. All this ushered the Christian believer to a living hope.

4 To an inheritance incorruptible, and undefiled, and that fadeth not away, reserved in heaven for you,

Inheritance results from the new birth as well. The inheritance notion is found in the Old Testament with the promise of God to Abraham to give him the land of Canaan. The Children of Israel received the land through conquest by Joshua. However, their inheritance was plagued with wars, idolatry, and vices, and by the eroding effect of time.

Unlike the inheritance promised to the Israelites, which was subject to degradation because it was earthly, the inheritance God promised to Christians is not subject to these three plagues. Peter uses three qualifiers in Greek to explain the quality of this inheritance. It is first incorruptible, or permanent, and cannot suffer corruption or corrosion. Then, it is "undefiled," morally pure and cannot be tainted. Finally, it is "reserved in heaven"—set aside eternally for believers.

5 Who are kept by the power of God through faith unto salvation ready to be revealed in the last time.

The beneficiaries of God's inheritance are securely protected. The term used for "kept by the power of God" in Greek (*phroureo,* **froo-REH-o**), has military connotations. It gives a picture of defense against a military assault while those protected are in a fortress. This previews the following verse where the trials will be introduced. Indeed, Christian life is not problem free but instead is a life of trial, temptations, and assaults of all kinds. This protection from God is therefore a good assurance for Christians.

This protection has a time frame. It runs from the new birth until the "last time" where the final salvation is acquired. The Greek word used for "last time" is *kairos* (**kahee-ROS**), is different from *chronos* (**KHRON-os**), which designates time in general or a span of time. *Kairos* means a decisive point in time or an appointed time. Therefore, Christians are under God's protection until the last day appointed by God for the return of Christ and the end of the world. Proverbs 18:10 and John 17:11b give us an assurance that the name of God is a real protection.

6 Wherein ye greatly rejoice, though now for a season, if need be, ye are in heaviness through manifold temptations:

"Wherein" links this portion to the living hope described by the inheritance in heaven and the protection until the reception of the salvation ready to be revealed. This living hope is indeed a source of great joy ("So be truly glad," NLT). The anticipation of Christ's return and the glorification of saints with Him provide a real joy. Expectation of a good outcome in the future always generates joy such as Paul expressed when he projected the overflowing of the Philippians' joy in relation to his probable release from prison.

The believers' joy is challenged by the sufferings they are experiencing throughout provinces in Asia and elsewhere. But this is for a little while—"though now for a season" —because He has already set the time frame of endurance. Until Christ comes at the appointed time, the believers may go through various kinds of suffering. But Peter tells them to rejoice in partaking in Christ's suffering. The attitude they should have when they suffer for Christ could be considered as a distinct contrast to what they suffer for their own misbehavior.

7 That the trial of your faith, being much more precious than of gold that perisheth, though it be tried with fire, might be found unto praise and honour and glory at the appearing of Jesus Christ:

The sufferings in a Christian life have a purpose. The goal is to test one's faith and bring it to maturity. James gives the process of the refinement of one's faith through suffering: trials bring perseverance. When one endures these sufferings, it brings maturity in his faith (1:4-5). A mature faith will produce a testimony that will glorify the name of the Lord Jesus Christ at His Second Coming. Here again, in 1 Peter 1:7, reference is made to the last time or days.

Peter explains the purification process of believers' faith through trials by drawing a parallel with the process of purification of gold. Gold goes through this process through placement in a fire within a furnace. The aim is to remove the impurities from the mined substance and achieve pure gold. In so doing, the fire does not destroy the gold; instead, the gold's purity increases after being separated from the impurities that surround its essence. In the same way, a Christian is strengthened after going through trials successfully.

8 Whom having not seen, ye love; in whom, though now ye see him not, yet believing, ye rejoice with joy unspeakable and full of glory:

Peter has seen the Lord, and he was a participant in Jesus Christ's earthly ministry. However, his readers did not see Him physically but heard of Him through the preaching of eyewitnesses. The apostle's audience, who did not know Christ in person, did two things: They loved Him and believed in Him. Glorious, inexpressible joy is a result of their love and belief in Christ without the ability to see Him physically. It resounds like the blessing Jesus gives to those who believe without seeing (John 20:29).

9 Receiving the end of your faith, even the salvation of your souls.

The Greek word *komizomai* (**kom-ID-zo-mahee**) used for "receiving" denotes carrying off for oneself what is deserved or earned. The verb is used frequently for obtaining a prize or reward. The prize is the goal of believers' faith. Here again the notion of hope and perseverance is implicitly present. Their faith has a goal—the inheritance, the living hope. It is summed up in the salvation of their souls. "Soul" here refers to the whole person. Salvation is both present and future and relates to the whole person, not just the physical body. It starts with regeneration at new birth and is completed in glorification when Christ comes.

10 Of which salvation the prophets have enquired and searched diligently, who prophesied of the grace that should come unto you: 11 Searching what, or what manner of time the Spirit of Christ which was in them did signify, when it testified beforehand the sufferings of Christ, and the glory that should follow.

This salvation was the theme of the prophets of the Old Testament. In Luke 24:45-47, Jesus reminded the disciples of the content of the Old Testament that He summarized through His suffering, death, and Resurrection from the dead. Repentance and forgiveness was to be preached to all nations as part of this reminder. These prophets were moved by the Spirit of Christ in them. In his second letter, Peter reminds his readers that no prophecy of Scripture comes from the prophet's own will (2 Peter 1:12-21).

What the prophets receive as message was not intended for them but for the believers in Christ as is the case with Peter's audience. These prophets investigated the message to find out the time and the circumstances of the revelation they received. The revelation was centered in the sufferings of Christ and the glories that will accompany them. Part of these glories involves the resurrection of Christ from the dead and the resultant grace that came to Peter's readers and all believers in Christ Jesus.

12 Unto whom it was revealed, that not unto themselves, but unto us they did minister the things, which are now reported unto you by them that have preached the gospel unto you with the Holy Ghost sent down from heaven; which things the angels desire to look into.

The prophets were told they were not the recipients of the grace but that they were serving the believers in Christ that will come. When the prophets talked about these things, they were looking forward to the future beneficiaries. Empowered by the Holy Spirit sent by God the Father, people have preached the same message to Peter's audience. This reminds us of Jesus' commission to the disciples to go into the world and preach the Gospel after they have received the Holy Spirit (Matthew 28:18-20; Mark 16:15; Luke 24:49; Acts 1:8).

Sources:
Biblical Words Pronunciation Guide. http://netministries.org/Bbasics/bwords.htm (accessed November 3, 2011).
Davids, Peter H. *The First Epistle of Peter.* Grand Rapids, MI: Wm. B. Eerdmans, 1990. 7-9, 50-65.
Marshall, I. Howard. *1 Peter: The IVP New Testament Commentary Series.* Downers Grove, IL: InterVarsity, 1991. 32-48.
McKnight, Scot. *1 Peter: The NIV Application Commentary.* Grand Rapids, MI: Zondervan, 1996. 23-24, 67-82.
New Testament Greek Lexicon. http://www.biblestudytools.com/lexicons/greek (accessed October 31, 2011).
Selwyn, Edward G. *The First Epistle of St. Peter: The Greek Text with Introduction, Notes and Essays.* 2nd ed. Grand Rapids, MI: Baker Book House, 1947. 121-138.

Say It Correctly

Pontus. PAHN-tuhs.
Galatia. guh-LAY-shih-uh.
Cappadocia. kap-ih-DOH-shee-uh.
Bithynia. bih-THIN-ee-uh.

Daily Bible Readings

MONDAY
I Have No Help in Me
(Job 6:8-13)

TUESDAY
Days without Hope
(Job 7:1-6)

WEDNESDAY
Will Mortals Live Again?
(Job 14:7-17)

THURSDAY
My Times Are in Your Hands
(Psalm 31:9-16)

FRIDAY
The Lord Preserves the Faithful
(Psalm 31:19-24)

SATURDAY
Hope in God's Faithfulness
(Lamentations 3:19-24)

SUNDAY
New Birth into a Living Hope
(1 Peter 1:3-12)

Notes

_____

_____

_____

_____

Teaching Tips

May 12
Bible Study Guide 11

Words You Should Know

A. Corruption (2 Peter 1:4) *phthora* (Gk.)—Ruin by moral influences; depravity.

B. Temperance (v. 6) *egkrateia* (Gk.)—Holding passions in control.

C. Brotherly kindness (v. 7) *philadelphia* (Gk.)—Love of people.

D. Charity (v. 7) *agape* (Gk.)—Godly love.

Teacher Preparation

Unifying Principle—Life Worth Living. Apostle Peter says that the inner strength needed to face life with new assurance and hope comes because of our knowledge of and faith in our Savior, Jesus Christ.

A. Pray for your students and lesson clarity.

B. Study the entire lesson.

C. Complete the companion lesson in the *Precepts For Living Personal Study Guide®*.

O—Open the Lesson

A. Receive prayer requests and pray, using the Aim for Change.

B. Have the class read the Aim for Change and the Keep in Mind verse.

C. Ask for a volunteer to read the In Focus story. Discuss, tying it in with the Aim for Change.

P—Present the Scriptures

A. Have volunteers read or summarize the Focal Verses.

B. Drive the discussion of the verses using the At-A-Glance outline, In Depth, Search the Scriptures, and More Light on the Text.

E—Explore the Meaning

A. Work through the Discuss the Meaning and Lesson in Our Society sections.

B. Discuss Make It Happen, tying it into today's theme.

N—Next Steps for Application

A. Again have students read the Keep in Mind verse in unison, and ask one student to summarize.

B. Remind students of the importance of consistent Bible study.

C. Close with prayer.

Worship Guide

For the Superintendent or Teacher
Theme: Equipped with Hope
Theme Song: "Have Faith in God"
Devotional Reading: Psalm 130
Prayer

MAY 12th

437

Equipped with Hope

Bible Background • 2 PETER 1
Printed Text • 2 PETER 1:4-14 | Devotional Reading • PSALM 130

—————— Aim for Change ——————

By the end of the lesson, we will: EXPLORE biblical ways to lead a more fruitful life; FEEL empowered to live effective and fruitful lives; and DEVELOP a deeper knowledge of the Lord Jesus Christ.

—————— In Focus ——————

"I just don't understand you," Isaac complained to his wife. "I told you that I would take care of the utility bill later this week!"

They were arguing, something that seemed to occur more and more frequently these days. It seemed to Isaac that Audrey nitpicked about everything. Some of the bills were behind, but he had assured her that he would make sure they got paid. Why couldn't she just leave it alone? The bills had been delinquent before, but hadn't he always paid them?

Audrey constantly nagged him about their poor credit rating. Although she hadn't come right out and said it, Isaac felt certain that Audrey blamed him for their inability to buy a new car or move out of the apartment and into a house after eight years. Why didn't she understand that he hadn't had the time to sit down and make a plan to achieve this? Her constant reminders that a bill collector had called or another late notice had come in the mail only seemed to make things worse.

In today's lesson, we will see that faith is not equivalent to blind optimism. To live godly lives, we must not succumb to laziness; instead, we must take full advantage of the godly resources available to each of us as believers.

—————— Keep in Mind ——————

"According as his divine power hath given unto us all things that pertain unto life and godliness, through the knowledge of him that hath called us to glory and virtue" (2 Peter 1:3).

"According as his divine power hath given unto us all things that pertain unto life and godliness, through the knowledge of him that hath called us to glory and virtue" (2 Peter 1:3).

Focal Verses

KJV **2 Peter 1:4** Whereby are given unto us exceeding great and precious promises: that by these ye might be partakers of the divine nature, having escaped the corruption that is in the world through lust.

5 And beside this, giving all diligence, add to your faith virtue; and to virtue knowledge;

6 And to knowledge temperance; and to temperance patience; and to patience godliness;

7 And to godliness brotherly kindness; and to brotherly kindness charity.

8 For if these things be in you, and abound, they make you that ye shall neither be barren nor unfruitful in the knowledge of our Lord Jesus Christ.

9 But he that lacketh these things is blind, and cannot see afar off, and hath forgotten that he was purged from his old sins.

10 Wherefore the rather, brethren, give diligence to make your calling and election sure: for if ye do these things, ye shall never fall:

11 For so an entrance shall be ministered unto you abundantly into the everlasting kingdom of our Lord and Saviour Jesus Christ.

12 Wherefore I will not be negligent to put you always in remembrance of these things, though ye know them, and be established in the present truth.

13 Yea, I think it meet, as long as I am in this tabernacle, to stir you up by putting you in remembrance;

14 Knowing that shortly I must put off this my tabernacle, even as our Lord Jesus Christ hath shewed me.

NLT **2 Peter 1:4** And because of his glory and excellence, he has given us great and precious promises. These are the promises that enable you to share his divine nature and escape the world's corruption caused by human desires.

5 In view of all this, make every effort to respond to God's promises. Supplement your faith with a generous provision of moral excellence, and moral excellence with knowledge,

6 and knowledge with self-control, and self-control with patient endurance, and patient endurance with godliness,

7 and godliness with brotherly affection, and brotherly affection with love for everyone.

8 The more you grow like this, the more productive and useful you will be in your knowledge of our Lord Jesus Christ.

9 But those who fail to develop in this way are shortsighted or blind, forgetting that they have been cleansed from their old sins.

10 So, dear brothers and sisters, work hard to prove that you really are among those God has called and chosen. Do these things, and you will never fall away.

11 Then God will give you a grand entrance into the eternal Kingdom of our Lord and Savior Jesus Christ.

12 Therefore, I will always remind you about these things—even though you already know them and are standing firm in the truth you have been taught.

13 And it is only right that I should keep on reminding you as long as I live.

14 For our Lord Jesus Christ has shown me that I must soon leave this earthly life,

The People, Places, and Times

Persecution of the Christians. After the death of Jesus, His disciples became objects of hatred and persecution. Jesus' prediction that men would "kill and crucify" His disciples came to fruition (Matthew 23:34). Also after Pentecost, many believers were threatened, arrested, beaten, and killed (Acts 4:1–3, 21; 5:17–18). The mob's murder of Stephen and the subsequent wave of violent activity toward Christians caused most believers to flee from Jerusalem. While this persecution led to the scattering of the Jerusalem congregation (8:1), this scattering resulted in the rapid expansion of the church within other nations.

One of the primary persecutors of the Christians was a young man named "Saul of Tarsus." Prior to surrendering his life to Christ, Saul "made havoc" on the church, causing men and women to be thrown in prison (8:3, NKJV). Following his conversion on the Damascus Road, Saul, whose name was later changed to "Paul," became a target of persecution himself (13:50; 2 Corinthians 6:3–5; 11:23–25; Galatians 5;11).

There were other victims of 1st-century Christian persecution, including the apostle James, the brother of John. James was put to death on the orders of Herod Agrippa I. The Roman emperor Nero (A.D. 54–68) is most noted for his virulent persecution of the Christians. Historians record that Nero falsely blamed Christians for setting a great fire, which destroyed a quarter of Rome. This event marked a wave of political rather than religious persecutions. It is widely believed that it was Nero who ordered that Paul be put to death.

By the time Peter wrote this second epistle, Paul, his co-laborer in Christ, had probably been martyred, and the church was undergoing fierce persecution. Peter understood that these persecuted believers, to whom he was writing, longed for both knowledge and peace, so he mentions it in his opening salutation to them. He knows also that it is only through their intimate relationship with and personal knowledge of God and of His Son Jesus Christ that they might experience the grace and peace they sought.

Background

Apostle Peter wrote 2 Peter with a two-fold purpose: not only to warn Christians about the many false teachers who were vying to take them off the foundational truths of the faith but also to exhort them to grow in the wisdom and knowledge of Jesus Christ—to grow in their faith. At this time, Peter knew he did not have long to live and therefore, shared his heart with the saints. He wanted them to be warned about what would happen when he was no longer with them and also to remind them that the truth of God's Word is unchanging. As an overseer of the church, called by God, apostle Peter took his responsibilities very seriously.

At-A-Glance

1. Promises to Empower (2 Peter 1:4)
2. Spiritual Growth (vv. 5–9)
3. Confidence in Our Calling (vv. 10–11)
4. Remember (vv. 12–14)

In Depth

1. Promises to Empower (2 Peter 1:4)

The Bible is saturated with promises of God. Throughout the Old and New Testaments, there are constant affirmations of the promises made and kept by God. At the dedication of the temple, King Solomon reminded the people that the period of political peace they were enjoying was a result of God keeping His promises. Solomon declared, "Blessed be the LORD, that hath given rest unto his people Israel, according to all that he promised" (1 Kings 8:56).

When Peter speaks of promises in this chapter, he uses the Greek word *epaggelma*, which means a promise made voluntarily, rather than the result of a request. Here we see the connection between God's promises and God's grace.

God's promises are a result of His grace and lovingkindness, not because we deserve the blessing. Peter explains that the "exceeding great and precious promises" made to His people are a direct result of the natural goodness of God (2 Peter 1:4). Just as it is natural for us to breathe, it is natural for God to bless those He loves. God also desires that His greatest creation be "partakers" or participants in His divine nature and separate from the corrupting forces of the flesh. There is no doubt that Peter's three-year walk with Jesus had made him a personal witness to some of these promises. Peter had learned to appreciate the faithfulness of God through His Word and through personal experience. Present-day Christians can be routinely assured of the promises of God through regular and prayerful study of His Word.

2. Spiritual Growth (vv. 5–9)

Our union in Christ and our participation in His divinity provide us with the resources we need to live godly lives. This is not to say that we become gods; instead, we are confident we have the living God within us. Peter is careful to note that as Christians, we must give "all diligence" or do our part, too (v. 5). We cannot be slack or complacent about our faith walk. We must persevere and make every effort to perfect our relationship with God. Our spiritual development is an ongoing process, during which there is constant growth, shaping, and refining. The idea of planting flower seeds in a garden and then failing to tend to them is ludicrous! Left unattended, the seeds will dry up and die; or the seeds will sprout, but the tiny plants will be overtaken by weeds and strangled. Equally ludicrous is the idea that our faith, left unattended, will grow. Like the neglected flower seeds, the old habits of our former sinful nature will rise and quickly take hold of our lives.

Our faith is like the seed. Faith is what brings us to Christ in the first place. Now that we have become part of Him, we want our faith to blossom and grow so that we can reflect the very character traits of Jesus. Just as plant seeds need watering, our faith needs nurturing in the Christlike characteristics that Peter lists in verses 5-7: "virtue" (goodness), "knowledge" (understanding), "temperance" (self-control), "patience" (endurance), "godliness" (goodness), "brotherly kindness" (love toward humankind), and "charity" (godly love).

Peter's emphasis on knowledge is especially important because a great portion of this epistle addresses the false teaching that was undermining the church during this period. Peter understood that the only protection the believers had against the false doctrines cropping up was "knowledge," or a firm grasp of the truths of the life, death, and Resurrection of Jesus (vv. 3, 5–6). As we grow spiritually, so too should our knowledge of spiritual truths. The more we know about Jesus, the harder we will strive to understand how to become more like Him. Not only is knowledge critical to Christian maturity and to the development of a godly lifestyle, it is, as Paul claims, our "sword of the Spirit," an integral weapon in spiritual warfare (Ephesians 6:17).

Equally important is Peter's emphasis on "love" or "charity" (2 Peter 1:7). The Greek word used here is *agape* or godly love. This is the highest form of love and the one expressed by God Himself when He "so loved the world, that he gave his only begotten Son" (John 3:16). Love is essential to the growth, maintenance, and work of the Christian community.

3. Confidence in Our Calling (vv. 10–11)

Peter now directs his attention to exhorting believers to "give diligence to make your calling and election sure" (2 Peter 1:10). Peter is urging the believers to have confidence in their salvation. This confidence is based on living to exhibit Christlike characteristics. It should not be surprising that Christians who are not growing in faith will typically lack confidence in their choice of beliefs. It is not enough that we confess Christ. We must grow in Christ in order to gain assurance of our salvation.

Peter's reference to "an entrance ... ministered unto you abundantly" (v. 11) may be a description of the triumphal heavenly welcome that awaits believers who hold the course. Similarly, his reference to the "everlasting kingdom" reminds us that confidence in our calling encourages us to "press toward the mark for the prize of the high calling of God in Christ Jesus" (Philippians 3:14). Christians who lack confidence in their calling cannot enjoy the promise of the "prize" of a glorious and eternal life in the presence of God.

4. Remember (vv. 12–14)

Peter now turns his attention from teaching and focuses on himself. All that he has said he also has learned for himself. It is not enough that believers learn; we must be willing to share, as Peter does. Peter stresses that he "will not be negligent" in presenting these learned truths to other believers (2 Peter 1:12). The apostle is probably about 60 years old when he writes this epistle. He may be recalling the painful time in his life when he was negligent in speaking on behalf of Christ and denied even knowing Jesus. But Peter is not the spiritually immature apostle we first encountered in the Gospels. His priorities have shifted from self to Christ. In this epistle, it is a spiritually mature man who now emphasizes his solemn duty to witness and who seeks to "stir ... up" the believers (v. 13).

It is clear that Peter is thinking his death may be imminent when he writes, "shortly I must put off this my tabernacle" (v. 14). Some scholars believe Peter may have been imprisoned during the time this letter was written. Although he speaks of his death, he is more concerned that the believers be put "in remembrance" or be reminded of what he has taught them, after he is dead (v. 15). Because we know that the young disciple, John Mark, was with Peter (see 1 Peter 5:13), we may assume that Peter taught him and intended to have John Mark record these teachings. Mark's record is what we now know as the third Gospel or the Gospel of Mark. This particular theory is likely, considering Mark's Gospel includes facts about Peter that are not mentioned in any of the other Gospels.

Search the Scriptures
Fill in the blanks.

1. "According as his _____ _____ hath given unto us all things that pertain unto life and godliness, through the knowledge of him that hath called us to glory and virtue" (2 Peter 1:3).

2. "Whereby are given unto us exceeding great and _____ _____: that by these ye might be partakers of the divine nature" (v. 4).

Discuss the Meaning

1. Discuss some of the promises God has made to us that can help us win the spiritual battle against the corruption of the world.

2. Discuss the evidence that points to Christian ineffectiveness and fruitlessness. What are some of the causes? What solutions can you suggest?

Lesson in Our Society

Our spiritual growth in Christ is a constant work in progress. While God perfects us, it is His desire that we work with Him in developing spiritually. God has provided us with everything that we need, and we should use what He has given us to bring glory to Him as well help one another. We can only escape the corruption of this world and resist yielding to the flesh and falling back into our old sinful patterns by applying our spiritual power daily. As we go about our routines—conducting business, carrying out parental obligations, enjoying free time, even just running errands—remembrance is critical.

Make It Happen

Reread 2 Peter 1:1–7. Identify which of these godly characteristics are active in your life and which traits you need "to make every effort to add to your faith" (v. 5, NIV).

Follow the Spirit

What God wants me to do:

_____

_____

_____

_____

Remember Your Thoughts

Special insights I have learned:

_____

_____

_____

_____

More Light on the Text

2 Peter 1:4-14

4 Whereby are given unto us exceeding great and precious promises: that by these ye might be partakers of the divine nature, having escaped the corruption that is in the world through lust.

The purpose of God's promises is to enable us to become "partakers of the divine nature." God is at work in us to transform us so we can truly live like those who bear the divine image. God has given us His Word, which enables us to develop new life and godliness. Our Father has made great promises that lead us to a great life. Because He is a great God, He can and will keep all His promises. There are promises for eternal life, forgiveness, healing, joy, peace, and prosperity. God's greatest promise, however, was the gift of His Son, Jesus Christ. Jesus, in turn, promised that God would give the Holy Spirit to us (John 14:26).

5 And beside this, giving all diligence, add to your faith virtue; and to virtue knowledge; 6 And to knowledge temperance; and to temperance patience; and to patience godliness; 7 And to godliness brotherly kindness; and to brotherly kindness charity.

Because we are now partakers of God's divine character, we must mature spiritually. To do this, we must add to our faith. The Greek word *epichoregeo* (**ep-ee-khor-ayg-EH-o**)

444

is translated as "add" and means, "to supply generously." We develop one quality as we exercise another. These qualities grow out of our spiritual, vital relationship with Christ.

In these verses, Peter lists seven qualities of a godly life: "virtue" (Gk. *arete*, **ar-ET-ay**), which means "holy courage, strength"; "knowledge" (Gk. *gnosis*, **GNO-sis**), which means "to have discernment or to perceive"; "temperance" (Gk. *egkrateia*, **eng-KRAT-i-ah**), which means "self–control"; "patience" (Gk. *hupomone*, **hoop-om-on-AY**), which means "steadfastness, endurance," or "perseverance"; "godliness" (Gk. *eusebeia*, **yoo-SEB-i-ah**), which means "reverence" or "piety"; "brotherly kindness" (Gk. *philadelphia*, **fil-a-del-FEE-ah**), which means "love of people"; and "charity" (Gk. *agape*, **ag-AH-pay**), which means "godly love."

It is impossible for human nature to manufacture these qualities of Christian character on its own; the Spirit of God must produce them. Because Christians have a transformed nature, we can grow spiritually and develop these qualities. God wants us to be "conformed to the image of his Son" (Romans 8:29).

8 For if these things be in you, and abound, they make you that ye shall neither be barren nor unfruitful in the knowledge of our Lord Jesus Christ.

The results of adding the seven qualities mentioned earlier are that they strengthen, encourage, and improve our lives and the lives of those around us. Where these qualities are present, there will be an abundance of good works (2 Corinthians 9:8). To "abound" in good works means that we do not just sit idly. If these qualities are to exist within us, we must learn to cultivate them so that they produce fruitful results in our lives.

There is much work to do in God's kingdom. The more we become like Jesus Christ, the more the Holy Spirit can use us in witness and service. The believer who is not growing is idle—"barren (and) unfruitful" (2 Peter 1:8). As Christians, we are commanded to exhort, edify, and comfort one another, continuously building each other up in God's holy faith (1 Thessalonians 5:11; Hebrews 3:13).

9 But he that lacketh these things is blind, and cannot see afar off, and hath forgotten that he was purged from his old sins.

In 2 Peter 1:9, the phrase "cannot see afar off" denotes that one can only see those things up close. Spiritually, believers who are nearsighted can only see things they can touch. They have no vision for the future, can only see today, and are without hope for tomorrow. In addition, we often forget that Jesus died to cleanse us of our sins. Through the blood of Jesus Christ, we have been purged and forgiven. When we forget what God has done for us, when our viewpoint lacks expansive knowledge of Jesus Christ, we will not be excited to witness to others about Him.

10 Wherefore the rather, brethren, give diligence to make your calling and election sure: for if ye do these things, ye shall never fall:

Peter admonishes us to be diligent or to "make every effort" (NIV). While it is true that God must work in us before we can do His will (Philippians 2:12–23), it is also true that we must be willing to work for God and that we must cooperate with Him. Instead of following those who are spiritually blind and suffering from forgetfulness, with diligence we are to take our invitation from God and accept the benefits of salvation. Being diligent also means being obedient. Living diligently and obediently deepens our awareness of the divine power within us, which gives us all things needed for life and makes our "calling and election sure" (2 Peter 1:10).

If we, as believers, can apply the Word of God and live according to the will of God, then we will not lose faith. We must walk in righteousness and in good works; consequently, we will not fall back into sin. Because we are growing, we can look forward to an abundant life here and an entrance into heaven.

11 For so an entrance shall be ministered unto you abundantly into the everlasting kingdom of our Lord and Saviour Jesus Christ.

When we live as God wants us to, He promises us an abundant life and entrance into His kingdom. We will have riches of knowledge and holiness beyond our thoughts. Entrance into the kingdom is a gift from God through Christ Jesus, but it corresponds with diligence. We are not saved because of our works, but because we are saved, our lives should display works of obedience and diligence.

12 Wherefore I will not be negligent to put you always in remembrance of these things, though ye know them, and be established in the present truth.

Pastors, ministers, and teachers are to teach God's precepts. Here Peter was saying that it was his responsibility to always remind the people of God's goodness toward them. He realized that although they knew the precepts of God, a tendency to forget may cause them to take things for granted. By reminding them of God's divine grace, mercy, and goodness, Peter was reminding them to never forget the basis for their faith.

The Christian who consistently reads the Bible and knows what he or she believes and why will rarely be seduced by false teachers and phony doctrines. As we become established in the truth, we will not be shaken or moved by the problems we encounter in this world. We can stand on the truth—the Word of God!

13 Yea, I think it meet, as long as I am in this tabernacle, to stir you up by putting you in remembrance; 14 Knowing that shortly I must put off this my tabernacle, even as our Lord Jesus Christ hath shewed me.

Peter realized that his death was at hand. God had revealed to Peter the kind of death he would face (see John 21:18–19). In the time he had left, Peter realized that he must stimulate the knowledge of the people of God. Three times in this chapter, he asked them to always remember the things he taught them (2 Peter 1:12–13, 15). Peter indeed left behind something that would never die—the written Word of God. The epistles of 1 and 2 Peter have been ministering to the saints for centuries. People die, but the Word of God lives on!

Sources:

Merriam-Webster Online Dictionary. http://www.merriam-webster.com (accessed November 3, 2011).

New Testament Greek Lexicon. http://www.biblestudytools.com/lexicons/greek (accessed October 31, 2011).

Packer, J. I. and M. C. Tenney, eds. *Illustrated Manners and Customs of the Bible.* Nashville, TN: Thomas Nelson, 1980. 41, 537-538, 551.

Zodhiates, Spiros. *Complete Word Study Dictionary: New Testament.* Iowa Falls, IA: World Bible Publishers, 1992.

Say It Correctly

Temperance. TEM-puh-rents.
Diligence. DIH-luh-jents.
Tabernacle. TA-buhr-na-kul.

Daily Bible Readings

MONDAY
Full of Goodness and Knowledge
(Romans 15:14-21)

TUESDAY
The Beginning of Knowledge
(Proverbs 1:2-7)

WEDNESDAY
An Example in Self-Control
(Titus 1:5-9)

THURSDAY
Enduring to the End
(Matthew 24:9-14)

FRIDAY
A Life of Godliness and Dignity
(1 Timothy 2:1-7)

SATURDAY
Love for One Another
(1 Peter 3:8-12)

SUNDAY
Standing on God's Precious Promises
(2 Peter 1:4-14)

Notes

_____

_____

_____

_____

Teaching Tips

May 19
Bible Study Guide 12

Words You Should Know

A. Flesh (1 Peter 4:1) *sarx* (Gk.)—Used to denote the body (as opposed to the soul or spirit), or as the symbol of what is external; a human being.

B. Lasciviousness (v. 3) *aselgeia* (Gk.)—Depravity, iniquity, wickedness.

Teacher Preparation

Unifying Principle—Serving One Another. Jesus taught that we must be servants in order to be the greatest in His kingdom.

A. Pray for your students and lesson clarity.

B. Study and meditate on the entire text.

C. Complete the companion lesson in the *Precepts For Living Personal Study Guide®*.

D. Prepare a presentation or bring news clippings of historical incidents that you and others have prayed much about, focusing on the theme of public service.

O—Open the Lesson

A. Open with prayer, including the Aim for Change.

B. Introduce today's subject, and have students read the Aim for Change and Keep in Mind verse in unison. Discuss.

C. Share your presentation.

D. Ask, "How can we be great servants?"

E. Have a volunteer summarize the In Focus story. Discuss.

P—Present the Scriptures

A. Have volunteers read the Focal Verses.

B. Use The People, Places, and Times; Background; Search the Scriptures; At-A-Glance outline; and In Depth to clarify the verses.

E—Explore the Meaning

A. To answer questions in the Discuss the Meaning, Lesson in Our Society, and Make It Happen sections, divide the class into groups and assign one or two questions to each.

B. Have students select a representative to report their responses to the rest of the class.

N—Next Steps for Application

A. Summarize the lesson.

B. Close with prayer.

Worship Guide

For the Superintendent or Teacher
Theme: Hope through Stewardship
Song: "To Be Like Jesus"
Devotional Reading: Luke 16:10-13
Prayer

Hope through Stewardship

Bible Background • 1 Peter 4
Printed Text • 1 Peter 4:1-11 | Devotional Reading • Luke 16:10-13

—————— Aim for Change ——————

By the end of the lesson, we will: KNOW the cost of discipleship; FEEL able to recall a time when we relied on God's power; and LOOK for opportunities to serve others.

————— 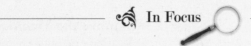 In Focus —————

Missions in other countries don't seem as popular as they were at one time. Perhaps it's because there are people from so many other places living within our communities. It may be a result of the busy lifestyle that many have taken on. Or the decline could be a result of fear brought on by terror and unrest worldwide.

All of these issues concerned Monique. However, since she was a young girl, the desire to share the Gospel in another land burned within her. She longed to be a part of the Great Commission. How could she serve the Lord in a distant place?

Monique had been faithful to her church, volunteering to serve at any opportunity. It was this eagerness that caught the attention of a visiting speaker. The speaker was from a country Monique had always wanted to visit. When the invitation to serve on a short-term mission trip came, she gladly accepted. Overwhelming joy filled her heart as she prepared to minister to the needs of others in a foreign nation.

The clarion call of Acts 1:8 is relevant today: "But ye shall receive power, after that the Holy Ghost is come upon you: and ye shall be witnesses unto me both in Jerusalem, and in all Judaea, and in Samaria, and unto the uttermost part of the earth."

—————— Keep in Mind ——————

MAY 19th

"As every man hath received the gift, even so minister the same one to another, as good stewards of the manifold grace of God" (1 Peter 4:10).

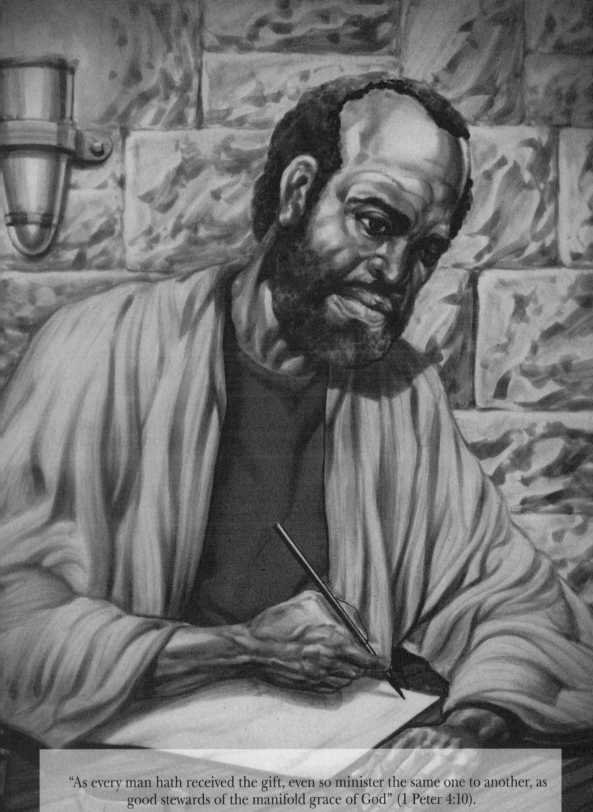

"As every man hath received the gift, even so minister the same one to another, as good stewards of the manifold grace of God" (1 Peter 4:10).

Focal Verses

KJV **1 Peter 4:1** Forasmuch then as Christ hath suffered for us in the flesh, arm yourselves likewise with the same mind: for he that hath suffered in the flesh hath ceased from sin;

2 That he no longer should live the rest of his time in the flesh to the lusts of men, but to the will of God.

3 For the time past of our life may suffice us to have wrought the will of the Gentiles, when we walked in lasciviousness, lusts, excess of wine, revellings, banquetings, and abominable idolatries:

4 Wherein they think it strange that ye run not with them to the same excess of riot, speaking evil of you:

5 Who shall give account to him that is ready to judge the quick and the dead.

6 For for this cause was the gospel preached also to them that are dead, that they might be judged according to men in the flesh, but live according to God in the spirit.

7 But the end of all things is at hand: be ye therefore sober, and watch unto prayer.

8 And above all things have fervent charity among yourselves: for charity shall cover the multitude of sins.

9 Use hospitality one to another without grudging.

10 As every man hath received the gift, even so minister the same one to another, as good stewards of the manifold grace of God.

11 If any man speak, let him speak as the oracles of God; if any man minister, let him do it as of the ability which God giveth: that God in all things may be glorified through Jesus Christ, to whom be praise and dominion for ever and ever. Amen.

NLT **1 Peter 4:1** So then, since Christ suffered physical pain, you must arm yourselves with the same attitude he had, and be ready to suffer, too. For if you have suffered physically for Christ, you have finished with sin.

2 You won't spend the rest of your lives chasing your own desires, but you will be anxious to do the will of God.

3 You have had enough in the past of the evil things that godless people enjoy—their immorality and lust, their feasting and drunkenness and wild parties, and their terrible worship of idols.

4 Of course, your former friends are surprised when you no longer plunge into the flood of wild and destructive things they do. So they slander you.

5 But remember that they will have to face God, who will judge everyone, both the living and the dead.

6 That is why the Good News was preached to those who are now dead—so although they were destined to die like all people, they now live forever with God in the Spirit.

7 The end of the world is coming soon. Therefore, be earnest and disciplined in your prayers.

8 Most important of all, continue to show deep love for each other, for love covers a multitude of sins.

9 Cheerfully share your home with those who need a meal or a place to stay.

10 God has given each of you a gift from his great variety of spiritual gifts. Use them well to serve one another.

11 Do you have the gift of speaking? Then speak as though God himself were speaking through you. Do you have the gift of helping others? Do it with all the strength and energy that God supplies. Then everything you do will bring glory to God through Jesus Christ. All glory and power to him forever and ever! Amen.

The People, Places, and Times

The Day of Pentecost. Fifty days (in the Greek, *pentekoste*) after the Passover Lamb had been slain, there were 120 of Christ's disciples gathered in an upper room, per their Master's instructions, waiting on power from on high. Secluded in this room in Jerusalem, Peter, the author of our Scripture text, initiated the selection process for replacing Judas who had betrayed Christ. Among the requirements to be a replacement were: 1) having been with Jesus from the time of John's baptism; 2) to be a witness of Jesus' resurrection; and 3) having beheld His ascension into heaven. The two men selected had been faithful followers and met these conditions. Of the two, Matthias was selected to complete the number of the 12 apostles.

Background

"And when the day of Pentecost was fully come, they were all with one accord in one place. And they were all filled with the Holy Ghost, and began to speak with other tongues as the Spirit gave them utterance" (Acts 2:1, 4). Men from every nation on earth were in Jerusalem that day and were amazed when they heard these itinerant men speaking in their own languages. This same Peter stood and preached a 3,000 souls-saving message, and many were added to the Church that day.

We should move ahead to a point many years later in Peter's life. He is filled with the Holy Spirit and has become a leader in the Church Council at Jerusalem, learning many of the things God would have the Church to accept. He was visited on a rooftop and commanded to minister to a Gentile centurion (Acts 10), along with many other vital actions in the early church. Peter points his readers to Christ, our supreme example of how to be a servant to all humankind.

At-A-Glance

1. Christ's Example (1 Peter 4:1-2)
2. Christ's Teachings: Put off the Old, Put on the New (vv. 3-6)
3. Christ's Teachings: Be Sober, Watchful, and Prayerful (vv. 7-9)
4. Christ's Teachings: Gifts of Honor (vv. 10-11)

In Depth

1. Christ's Example (1 Peter 4:1-2)

"Forasmuch then as Christ hath suffered for us in the flesh, arm yourselves likewise with the same mind: for he that hath suffered in the flesh hath ceased from sin" (1 Peter 4:1). Were Peter alive today, he may have worded this verse something like this: "Followers of Christ must put on the mind of Christ in order not to fulfill the lusts of the flesh. This is not Burger King®; you cannot have it your way. Peter knew that flesh is an enemy of the Spirit. To maintain the mind of Christ, we must cut off the old fleshly habits and desires. We must renew our minds on a daily basis."

2. Christ's Teachings: Put off the Old, Put on the New (vv. 3-6)

Think back to the time when you first got saved. To be an excellent witness of that precious gift of salvation, old friends had to go. Even though they may have ridiculed and talked about you, to be a positive witness for God, you had to suffer that separation from the old lifestyle. The Bible tells us that evil communications corrupt good manners (1 Corinthians 15:33). A choice had to be made; you had to tell yourself, "Either I'll continue in my old sinful ways, or I will change the company I keep and walk in my salvation—be sanctified and filled with the Holy Ghost."

Peter writes for us to be conscious of the judgment of Christ. It's often said that we must not fear someone who has neither heaven nor hell to put us in. Man can only do so much to you. Jesus Christ alone has the power to judge. The Gospel has the power to turn lives around that are on a collision course with death, damnation, and destruction. Praise God for the power in the blood of Jesus. As servants of humankind, we must preach this great Gospel for all to hear.

3. God's Teachings: Be Sober, Watchful, and Prayerful (vv. 7-9)

As one vintage song of the church proclaims, "In times like these, we need an anchor." We are admonished to pray without ceasing (1 Thessalonians 5:17). Jesus explained to His disciples, when asked about the end times, that there would be many signs. Among them are: deceivers of many, nations rising against nations, wars and rumors of wars, famine, pestilence, and earthquakes in many different places (Matthew 24:3-7). This, however, is only the beginning of the end. Peter admonishes the faithful to be sober and watchful in prayer.

We can all tell when another person loves us. Even little children know when they are loved. We are to love each other with a fervent love. Just think how much better it is to add energy and authenticity to the love that we share with our fellow Christians. According to Peter, this love will cover a multitude of sins. Now it may be said that there are no skeletons in your closet, but grace is sufficient for all. Use love to cover another's faults; you may need that same favor returned to you someday.

4. Christ's Teachings: Gifts of Honor (vv. 10-11)

So often, we think of stewardship and relate it to money or things of material value. Here, Peter applies stewardship to the manifold grace of God. Earlier, in 1 Peter 1, we were given the concept that our faith, through trial, is more precious then gold. Jesus said, "Seek ye first the kingdom of God and his righteousness; and all these things shall be added unto you" (Matthew 6:33). As we see God's kingdom with the mind of Christ, everything else tends to fall into place.

Gifts are given according to God's grace. These godly gifts are to be used to glorify Him and Him alone. One of the problems of walking in the flesh is that flesh has a desire to be glorified. When we take on our new nature in Christ, that attitude won't work. As the saying goes, "oil and water don't mix". The same theory applies to this subject: God's gifts and our flesh don't mix. We are accountable to God and our fellow persons to be ministers of righteousness, upholding the integrity of our calling in Christ Jesus.

Naturally, Bible scholars see the similarity and cohesion of this passage of Scripture and apostle Paul's message to the church at Corinth in 1 Corinthians 12 and other passages. The bottom line is, I need you and you need me. We are all fellow servants of our King. It is tantamount that Jesus Christ receives all the praise and glory from the service we render to Him and one another.

In the words of Jesus Christ Himself, we are made to know that "he that is greatest among you shall be your servant" (Matthew 23:11). Let us go forth, empowered to serve.

Search the Scriptures

1. Explain in your own words what it means to put on the mind of Christ (1 Peter 4:1).

2. What suggestions does Peter give for overcoming habits of the flesh to walk in the newness of life (vv. 7-11)?

Discuss the Meaning

The world of church and the world in which we live have different priorities. The person who acquires the most "toys" wins in the eyes of the world. Discuss the ways that success is measured in God's kingdom. How can we apply these successful traits while in service to others? Which of these traits would glorify God especially?

Lesson in Our Society

Sinful human nature is contrary to the nature of Christ. Prayerfully consider ways that you can minister to the body of Christ to build up and not tear down. However, let's not overlook the needs and hurts of our fellow servants. Be an encouraging, empowering, inspirational blessing to your leaders, your fellow workers in Christ, and especially the wounded soldiers that are within your sphere of influence.

Make It Happen

The American culture is one of "me first," self-reliance, and downright selfishness. Contrast how as servants of God, we can be a counter-cultural force in the world. Knowing this will not be an easy road to walk, identify ways we can minister to each other to encourage steadfastness in accomplishing the goal of impacting the world around us.

Follow the Spirit

What God wants me to do:

_____

_____

_____

_____

Remember Your Thoughts

Special insights I have learned:

_____

_____

_____

_____

More Light on the Text

1 Peter 4:1-11

1 Forasmuch then as Christ hath suffered for us in the flesh, arm yourselves likewise with the same mind: for he that hath suffered in the flesh hath ceased from sin;

Peter talked in chapter 3 about Christ's suffering and refers to it in this section. The word "therefore" links chapter 4 (NKJV) to the preceding chapter. Christ's suffering occurred in His body while on the Cross and includes emotional as well as physical suffering. Peter asks his audience in Asia Minor to arm themselves with the same attitude as Christ. The word used in Greek, *hoplizo* (**hop-LID-zo**), means to equip oneself as for a battle or "take on the same mind." Sinfulness is too serious to be neglected. There should be no compromise with sin because it brings spiritual death. When one faces a deadly enemy, one has to take every necessary action to subdue and overcome this enemy. Hebrews 12:4 suggests that the struggle against sin may require even shedding of blood.

In 1 Peter 4:1 (NIV), the statement "he who has suffered in his body is done with sin" may seem difficult to understand. The Greek word for "body" is *sarkos* (**SAR-kos**), is generally translated "flesh" (*sarx*) and is understood to refer to the sinful nature in us. It is not to say that suffering can remove sin in one's life, but rather as one commentary stated: "If anyone suffers for doing good and still faithfully obeys (God) in spite of suffering, that person has made a clean break with sin" (*Life Application Bible*, 2263). Galatians 5:16-22 talks about life in the flesh and life in the Spirit, and there Paul entreats his readers to walk according to the Spirit because life in the Spirit is opposed to life in the flesh. In 1 Corinthians 9:27, Paul says his strategy to avoid falling into sin is to "bring (his body) into subjection." He then illustrated Israel's failure in the desert resulting from immorality and idolatry.

It is obvious that these passages are not suggesting a kind of salvation by works or atonement of sins by any other means. The only lesson drawn from them is the responsibility of the believer in disciplining his life to shun evil. These disciplines can be painful sometimes.

2 That he no longer should live the rest of his time in the flesh to the lusts of men, but to the will of God.

The attitude of suffering for a life of holiness is a Christian's lifetime resolution, a determination to live in sanctification. This means a believer will not satisfy the cravings of fleshly desire. In Galatians 5:20-21, we find the list of this evil human desire. This resolution is an outcome of willingness to suffer bodily struggles—physical and emotional—as mentioned in

the passage from 1 Peter 4. Subjection of the body is a prerequisite to a life of sanctification.

The person who resolutely turns from gratifying evil human desires orients his or her life toward fulfilling what is pleasing to God. Paul stresses that the will of God is a life of holiness. The resolution to fulfill God's will will keep us away from evil human desires. The reason is that the will of God and the cravings of our heart are in opposition. We will either obey God's will or follow our own inclinations—not both at the same time.

3 For the time past of our life may suffice us to have wrought the will of the Gentiles, when we walked in lasciviousness, lusts, excess of wine, revellings, banquetings, and abominable idolatries:

The sins described here refer to idol worship. The Israelites were enticed by the Moabites to sin through their cultic practices (Numbers 25:1-3; Revelation 2:14). Baal worship and many other pagans' worship included immoral practices. In this letter, Peter mentions these vices and also names the context in which they take place. Not only should a Christian shun these sins, but the context in which these sins happen should be avoided as well.

4 Wherein they think it strange that ye run not with them to the same excess of riot, speaking evil of you:

The Christians whom Peter addresses in the letter were part of a culture and indulged in common cultural practices. When they received Christ, many gave up the reproachable customs of their former lifestyles. Their refusal to conform to their society's corrupt ways of life was noticed by their former friends and current neighbors and colleagues. These people could not understand how those who had followed them could now withdraw themselves.

Their abstention from idolatry and immoral behavior brought the fury of their former mates. In the early church, because Christians refused to take part in the worship of the king, they were portrayed as enemies of the state. It was certainly painful to bear wrongful abuse, knowing the innocence of your behavior and the righteousness of your choices. This is why Peter advised his readers to have a clear conscience and good conduct that would confuse those who spoke maliciously about them (3:16).

5 Who shall give account to him that is ready to judge the quick and the dead.

The detractors of the Christians in Asia Minor will not go unpunished. They will have to give an account to God for their false accusations and their slander. God is the judge of humankind. Those who are still alive and those who are already dead will all be judged. This judgment is a prospect of the final judgment.

6 For for this cause was the gospel preached also to them that are dead, that they might be judged according to men in the flesh, but live according to God in the spirit.

The judgment of God is done in righteousness and fairness. This could mean that those who are now dead heard about the Gospel during their lifetime. In this way, their judgment is based on their response to the Gospel while they were alive. Being "judged according to men in the flesh" refers probably to physical death, but the life "according to God in the spirit" refers to the judgment that decides the eternal fate of one's soul.

7 But the end of all things is at hand: be ye therefore sober, and watch unto prayer.

The "end of all things" reminds us of the final judgment. Peter wants his readers to be alert—because the end "is at hand"—and to focus in anticipation of the end of the world. The judgment day is getting nearer and there is a need for Christians to pray.

8 And above all things have fervent charity among yourselves: for charity shall cover the multitude of sins.

The Christian community needs to express love among its members. Love "shall cover a multitude of sins" is a citation of Proverbs 10:12. It means that when there is love ("charity" as 1 Peter 4:8 states), the brethren will forgive and overlook the sins of others; but that does not imply complacency, either. We should strive to live out the second greatest commandment: to love our neighbors as ourselves (Matthew 22:39).

As Christians, the blood of Jesus has covered our sins. God did not hold us accountable for our sins, but He forgave us in Christ. In turn, we have to forgive each other and build unity (Colossians 3:13).

9 Use hospitality one to another without grudging.

Love was also expressed in offering hospitality to fellow Christians as they traveled, particularly considering hotel-type accommodations were extremely rare. This hospitality consisted of providing shelter and food. However, a host's patience can really be tried by a guest's personality. In any circumstances, Peter urges the recipients of his letter to exercise hospitality "without grumbling" (NIV). As human beings, sometimes we abuse privileges such as hospitality and this can create difficulties in relationships. It is recorded that by A.D. 100, in Asia, guidelines had been adopted to prevent abuse. Peter Davids points out such an example in which a guest could not stay more than three days at the expense of the host (*First Epistle of Peter*, 159).

The theme of hospitality was so important that in New Testament times, it was part of the qualification for elders in the church and for enrolled widows, as noted by Davids (*First Epistle of Peter*, 159).

10 As every man hath received the gift, even so minister the same one to another, as good stewards of the manifold grace of God.

As Christians, Peter's readers received various spiritual gifts. These gifts are from the Holy Spirit. The goal of the gifts is for the service of others, not for self-gratification (1 Corinthians 12:4, 7; Ephesians 4:11-13).

The gifts should be used in faithfulness according to the purpose for which God has granted them. The appropriate use of the gifts will meet the various needs of the Christian community. God works through each Christian to fill a need in the community. There are no "ungifted" Christians.

11 If any man speak, let him speak as the oracles of God; if any man minister, let him do it as of the ability which God giveth: that God in all things may be glorified through Jesus Christ, to whom be praise and dominion for ever and ever. Amen.

Two kinds of gifts exist: the speaking gifts and that of service (Acts 6:2-6). All gifts should be exercised with the seriousness that they deserve and according to God's will. In Colossians 3:17, we are urged to do everything in the name of the Lord.

When gifts are exercised in this way, they bring God glory. The whole life of a Christian should bring glory to God. Peter ends the section by praising God with a doxology.

Sources:

Better Days Are Coming.com. http://www.betterdaysarecoming.com (accessed September 9, 2011).

Biblical Words Pronunciation Guide. http://netministries.org/Bbasics/bwords.htm (accessed November 3, 2011).

Davids, Peter H. *The First Epistle of Peter.* Grand Rapids, MI: Wm. B. Eerdmans, 1990. 147-163.

Life Application Bible, New International Version. Wheaton, IL and Grand Rapids, MI: Tyndale House Publishers and Zondervan Publishing House, 1988 and 1991. 2263.

Merriam-Webster Online Dictionary. http://www.merriam-webster.com (accessed November 3, 2011).

New Testament Greek Lexicon. http://www.biblestudytools.com/lexicons/greek (accessed October 31, 2011).

Oberst, Bruce. *First and Second Peter: Bible Study Textbook Series.* Joplin, MO: College Press Publishing, 1988.

Selwyn, Edward G. *The First Epistle of St. Peter: The Greek Text with Introduction, Notes and Essays.* 2nd ed. Grand Rapids, MI: Baker Book House, 1947.

Stibbs, Alan M., and Andrew F. Walls. *1 Peter: Tyndale New Testament Commentaries, vol. 17.* Leicester, England: InterVarsity Press, 1983. 145-157.

Say It Correctly

Lasciviousness. luh-SIV-ee-uhs-nuhs.
Pentecost. PEHN-tee-kawst.

Daily Bible Readings

MONDAY
Trust God to Provide
(Luke 12:22-28)

TUESDAY
The Unfailing Treasure
(Luke 12:29-34)

WEDNESDAY
Be Alert and Ready
(Luke 12:35-40)

THURSDAY
The Faithful and Prudent Manager
(Luke 12:41-48)

FRIDAY
The Perfect Gift from Above
(James 1:12-18)

SATURDAY
Faithful in Little and Much
(Luke 16:10-13)

SUNDAY
Good Stewards of God's Grace
(1 Peter 4:1-11)

Notes

_____

_____

_____

_____

Teaching Tips

Words You Should Know

A. Epistle (2 Peter 3:1) *epistole* (Gk.)—A letter, correspondence.

B. Scoffers (v. 3) *empaiktes* (Gk.) Mockers; denotes non-believers.

Teacher Preparation

Unifying Principle—Ready and Waiting. The writer of 2 Peter urges his readers to prepare for the day of the Lord by being patient and by living holy lives.

A. Pray for your students and lesson clarity.

B. Read the entire lesson.

C. Complete the companion lesson in the *Precepts For Living Personal Study Guide*®.

O—Open the Lesson

A. Receive prayer requests and begin the class with prayer.

B. Have a volunteer read or summarize the In Focus story.

C. Discuss, tying the In Focus story in with the Aim for Change and Keep in Mind verse.

D. Now, discuss how believers can live holy, godly lives.

P—Present the Scriptures

A. Have volunteers read the Focal Verses.

B. Work through the verses using The People, Places, and Times; Background; Search the Scriptures; At-A-Glance outline; In Depth; and More Light on the Text.

C. Review and answer the Search the Scriptures questions.

E—Explore the Meaning

A. To help students see how the lesson applies to their lives, have them answer the Discuss the Meaning questions and discuss the Lesson in Our Society section.

B. Also include the Make It Happen section.

N—Next Steps for Application

A. Summarize the lesson.

B. Remind students to do their Daily Bible Readings.

C. Close with prayer.

Worship Guide

For the Superintendent or Teacher
Theme: Hope in the Day of the Lord
Theme Song: "We Have a Hope"
Devotional Reading: John 14:1-7
Prayer

MAY
26th

Hope in the Day of the Lord

Bible Background • 2 PETER 3
Printed Text • 2 PETER 3:1-15a | Devotional Reading • JOHN 14:1-7

—————————— Aim for Change ——————————

By the end of the lesson, we will: UNDERSTAND the significance of holy living; FEEL CONFIDENT that Christ will return for His Church; and ANTICIPATE the day when God will make all things new.

———————— In Focus ————————

Willie was looking out of the window when his mother, Falicia, arrived home.

"Willie, what are you doing at the window?" she asked.

Willie did not turn to look at her. He continued to stare out of the window as he replied, "I'm waiting for my daddy to come and take me to the ball game."

Falicia walked over to Willie. "Honey, did your daddy call today?"

"Yes, ma'am," mumbled Willie. "He said that he'd pick me up around 4 o'clock."

Falicia walked away. It was already 5:30, and she did not have the heart to tell her son that his daddy probably was not coming. Falicia knew her former husband, Johnny, was not a man who kept his promises. He would simply not show up, then call a couple of weeks later with some lame excuse.

As Falicia walked to her room, she turned to look at Willie who was still staring out of the window. She knew her son was counting on his father to keep his promise. She prayed that Johnny would not let Willie down again.

A promise is a binding declaration between two or more people or institutions. Only God keeps every one of His promises. In this week's lesson, Peter confirms Christ's promise to return and to usher in the new heaven and new earth.

—————————— Keep in Mind ——————————

"The Lord is not slack concerning his promise, as some men count slackness; but is longsuffering to us-ward, not willing that any should perish, but that all should come to repentance" (2 Peter 3:9).

"The Lord is not slack concerning his promise, as some men count slackness; but is longsuffering to us-ward, not willing that any should perish, but that all should come to repentance" (2 Peter 3:9).

Focal Verses

KJV **2 Peter 3:1** This second epistle, beloved, I now write unto you; in both which I stir up your pure minds by way of remembrance:

2 That ye may be mindful of the words which were spoken before by the holy prophets, and of the commandment of us the apostles of the Lord and Saviour:

3 Knowing this first, that there shall come in the last days scoffers, walking after their own lusts,

4 And saying, Where is the promise of his coming? for since the fathers fell asleep, all things continue as they were from the beginning of the creation.

5 For this they willingly are ignorant of, that by the word of God the heavens were of old, and the earth standing out of the water and in the water:

6 Whereby the world that then was, being overflowed with water, perished:

7 But the heavens and the earth, which are now, by the same word are kept in store, reserved unto fire against the day of judgment and perdition of ungodly men.

8 But, beloved, be not ignorant of this one thing, that one day is with the Lord as a thousand years, and a thousand years as one day.

9 The Lord is not slack concerning his promise, as some men count slackness; but is longsuffering to us-ward, not willing that any should perish, but that all should come to repentance.

10 But the day of the Lord will come as a thief in the night; in the which the heavens shall pass away with a great noise, and the elements shall melt with fervent heat, the earth also and the works that are therein shall be burned up.

NLT **2 Peter 3:1** This is my second letter to you, dear friends, and in both of them I have tried to stimulate your wholesome thinking and refresh your memory.

2 I want you to remember what the holy prophets said long ago and what our Lord and Savior commanded through your apostles.

3 Most importantly, I want to remind you that in the last days scoffers will come, mocking the truth and following their own desires.

4 They will say, "What happened to the promise that Jesus is coming again? From before the times of our ancestors, everything has remained the same since the world was first created."

5 They deliberately forget that God made the heavens by the word of his command, and he brought the earth out from the water and surrounded it with water.

6 Then he used the water to destroy the ancient world with a mighty flood.

7 And by the same word, the present heavens and earth have been stored up for fire. They are being kept for the day of judgment, when ungodly people will be destroyed.

8 But you must not forget this one thing, dear friends: A day is like a thousand years to the Lord, and a thousand years is like a day.

9 The Lord isn't really being slow about his promise, as some people think. No, he is being patient for your sake. He does not want anyone to be destroyed, but wants everyone to repent.

10 But the day of the Lord will come as unexpectedly as a thief. Then the heavens will pass away with a terrible noise, and the very elements themselves will disappear in fire, and the earth and everything on it will be found to deserve judgment.

KJV continued

11 Seeing then that all these things shall be dissolved, what manner of persons ought ye to be in all holy conversation and godliness,

12 Looking for and hasting unto the coming of the day of God, wherein the heavens being on fire shall be dissolved, and the elements shall melt with fervent heat?

13 Nevertheless we, according to his promise, look for new heavens and a new earth, wherein dwelleth righteousness.

14 Wherefore, beloved, seeing that ye look for such things, be diligent that ye may be found of him in peace, without spot, and blameless.

15 And account that the longsuffering of our Lord is salvation;

NLT continued

11 Since everything around us is going to be destroyed like this, what holy and godly lives you should live,

12 looking forward to the day of God and hurrying it along. On that day, he will set the heavens on fire, and the elements will melt away in the flames.

13 But we are looking forward to the new heavens and new earth he has promised, a world filled with God's righteousness.

14 And so, dear friends, while you are waiting for these things to happen, make every effort to be found living peaceful lives that are pure and blameless in his sight.

15 And remember, our Lord's patience gives people time to be saved.

The People, Places, and Times

Day of the Lord. The Greek word is *parousia*. Theologians interpret this various ways, but it certainly is the time when Jesus returns whether in judgment for unbelievers or with everlasting joy for the followers of Christ.

Background

The apostle Peter wrote this text not only to warn Christians about false teachers but to exhort them to grow in their faith and in the knowledge of their Lord and Savior, Jesus Christ. One principle area of attack from false teachers was the return and future judgment of Christ. If there was no future judgment, then people were free to live as they chose. In the final chapter of his second epistle, Peter directly challenges this error.

He begins by admonishing the people to remember those things that he had taught them. It is important to remember the words proclaimed by anointed men and women of God. They challenge us to live holy lives, to use our gifts and talents for God, and to keep us from becoming complacent.

At-A-Glance

1. Believe God's Word (2 Peter 3:1–4)
2. Believe in God's Creation (vv. 5–9)
3. Believe God's Promise (vv. 10–13)
4. Be Spotless, Blameless, and at Peace with Him (vv. 14-15a)

In Depth

1. Believe God's Word (2 Peter 3:1–4)

Peter intended to "stir up" the people's memory (2 Peter 3:1). To "stir up" means "to fully awaken." The apostle suggests three areas where the people's memory needed awakening: the words of the holy prophets, the commandments of the apostles, and the commandments of Christ.

Peter realized that in these "last days" many people would question Christian beliefs in the Lord (3:3). These people would cause others to have doubts about the authority of God's Word. Peter called these unbelievers "scoffers" (v. 3). Scoffers are false teachers who mock the truth. The apostle had already warned the people that these scoffers would infiltrate the church with their "damnable heresies" (2:1). Some even went as far as denying the deity of Christ.

The "last days" refer to the period between the first and Second Coming of Christ. During this period, ungodly teachers will deny that Christ is coming back to execute judgment. "They will say, 'Where is this "coming" he promised? Ever since our ancestors died, everything goes on as it has since the beginning of creation'" (3:4, NIV).

It is sad that people are deceived into believing Christ is not coming again. However, Peter's message is clear: Do not listen to these scoffers and do not follow them. God's Word is true and His promises are unfailing.

2. Believe in God's Creation (vv. 5-9)

The scoffers do not believe the truth of God's Word. They portray God's truth as a moral fable. These false teachers purposely forget that God created the heavens and the earth. To refute their heresy, Peter reminds his readers of God's creative power. First he reminds them of how God, by His Word, rolled back the waters to create dry land (v. 5; Genesis 1:9–10). God used the same waters that He rolled back to destroy the old world in the days of Noah and his family (2 Peter 3:6). He did not spare the old world when His people disobeyed Him (2:5), and He will not spare the current world. God has already decided the world's fate and declared it through Christ and His apostles.

Scoffers need to be warned that God's Word is true. They think He has forgotten His creation, so they feel that they can live any way they choose. They fail to realize that God is being patient with us. Scoffers fail to understand that because His desire is to save and not destroy, God does not measure time according to human standards. "With the Lord a day is like a thousand years, and a thousand years are like a day" (3:8, NIV). God can accomplish in one day what might take 1,000 years, and He may take a 1,000 years to accomplish His will in a day.

3. Believe God's Promise (vv. 10–13)

Peter emphatically declares, "The day of the Lord will come as a thief in the night" (v. 10). According to Spiros Zodhiates—a Greek American Bible scholar and author— the "day of the Lord" represents the Second Coming of Christ and the occasion when God will actively intervene to punish sin. The term also refers to the time immediately before the creation of the new heaven and earth (*Complete Word Study Dictionary: New Testament*, 710).

Peter says that on this day, "the heavens shall pass away with a great noise" (v. 10). The Greek word translated "great noise" means "with a great crash." The apostle declares the earth will be burned up, and not only the earth, but all the "works that are therein." Everything that humanity has ever created, invented, or built will be utterly consumed in this "fervent heat."

4. Be Spotless, Blameless, and at Peace (vv. 14-15a)

The underlying theme of these verses is the second coming of the Lord. Whether our lives on earth are ended in death or whether we are alive when the Lord returns, we want to be found ready. To be found "without spot, and blameless" is to be fully like Jesus (v. 14). This thought should motivate us to examine every aspect of our lives and think about what me may be doing when we are suddenly taken to be with the Lord.

The standard is perfection, but the Lord knows our weaknesses and frailties, and the blood of Christ covers all of our sins. So we have great peace as we look forward to His return. The only reason the Lord is delaying His return is to give more people the opportunity to be saved before He returns.

Search the Scriptures

1. What three things does Peter want to remind the people of (2 Peter 3:2-4)?

2. Why is the Lord delaying His coming and the execution of judgment on the world (v. 9)?

Discuss the Meaning

1. What are some false teachings that are being spread in the church today? How do you know that these teachings are false?

2. If the "day of the Lord" is coming as a thief in the night, what characteristics can you identify in people's behavior or in institutional activities that suggest the Lord may be coming soon?

Lesson in Our Society

Many people in our society live according to a "bumper sticker" mentality. Some believe they should "live fast, die young, and make a beautiful corpse." Others believe that "the person who dies with the most toys wins."

These people live for immediate pleasure and are not concerned with the consequences. They believe they will somehow escape the consequences of their actions today and in the hereafter. They are either ignorant of or flatly deny the return of Christ and God's judgment of the rebellious. How does society perpetuate the idea of living just for the now?

Make It Happen

Read the following Scripture texts. Identify the statements said to be the will of God:

1 Thessalonians 4:3; 5:18; 2 Peter 3:9. Decide to obey God's will in these matters until Jesus comes.

Follow the Spirit

What God wants me to do:

_____

_____

_____

_____

Remember Your Thoughts

Special insights I have learned:

_____

_____

_____

_____

More Light on the Text

2 Peter 3:1-15a

1 This second epistle, beloved, I now write unto you; in both which I stir up your pure minds by way of remembrance:

"Epistle" (Gk. *epistole*, **ep-is-tol-AY**) is another word for "letter." The author identifies himself in 2 Peter 1:1 as "Simon Peter"—the fisherman turned disciple of Jesus. Peter is notable for both his fearless proclamation of Christ as Messiah (Matthew 16:16) and his cowardly denial of Christ on the night of His crucifixion (26:69–75). In Peter's second epistle, he addresses the recipients as "beloved" (Gk. *agapetos*, **ag-ap-ay-TOS**), a term of affection used by every author of the New Testament epistles.

It is impossible to know for sure if 1 Peter was the earlier epistle; many scholars speculate that there was at least one more letter that was lost to history.

Peter writes to "stir up" (Gk. *diegeiro*, **dee-eg-I-ro**)—a word that means, "to arouse completely." In chapter 1, he made it clear that he knows he will die soon—implying that this is the last letter these Christians will receive from him (1:14). His purpose is to make sure that the recipients do not forget the things he had taught them (1:15) or become lazy in their walk with Christ (1:10). In 3:1, "pure" (Gk. *heilikrines*, **i-lik-ree-NACE**), means "pertaining to being sincere, without hidden motives or pretense."

2 That ye may be mindful of the words which were spoken before by the holy prophets, and of the commandment of us the apostles of the Lord and Saviour:

"Be mindful" (Gk. *mnaomai*, **MNAH-om-ahee**), means "recall, remember." The words of the apostles and prophets were first mentioned in chapter 1. The reader should understand the words of the prophets to be the Old Testament and the words of the apostles to be the New Testament. From the time when the New Testament documents were written, they were considered as divinely inspired as the Old Testament books.

"Apostles" (Gk. *apostolos*, **ap-OS-tol-os**) means "messengers, envoys." The Greek reads literally "your apostles"—which likely means some of the apostles had ministered personally to the recipients of this letter.

Although there are many notable commandments in the New Testament, the "commandment of us the apostles" is the command to believe in Jesus for the forgiveness of sin (Acts 16:31) and live the holy life that Jesus requires (2 Peter 2:21). Most modern translations see the commandment as that which Jesus gave "through your apostles" (for example, see NIV, NLT, and AMP).

3 Knowing this first, that there shall come in the last days scoffers, walking after their own lusts,

The last days (end times) started with the first coming of Jesus (Hebrews 1:2), which initiated all of the events that had to happen for the end to come. The Greek text for 2 Peter 3:3 reads literally "scoffing scoffers will come." The repetition of the word is a way of adding emphasis. A "scoffer" is one who ridicules, mocks, or makes fun of others.

"Lusts" (Gk. *epithumia*, **ep-ee-thoo-MEE-ah**) in this context is "strong desires for something forbidden." "Walking after" could also be translated "walking according to." These scoffers discard God's revelation of the correct path through His Word and instead chart a path based on their desires.

4 And saying, Where is the promise of his coming? for since the fathers fell asleep, all things continue as they were from the beginning of the creation.

"Where is the promise of his coming?" is a literal translation of the Greek; it may also be translated "Where is His promised coming?" The word "coming" (Gk. *parousia*, **par-oo-SEE-ah**) may also be translated "appearing" and is used frequently in the New Testament to refer to Christ's return (see Matthew 24:27; 1 Thessalonians 4:15).

The argument advanced by these scoffers is that "all things continue as they were"—nothing has changed "since the fathers fell asleep" (2 Peter 3:4). The "fathers" are probably the Old Testament patriarchs. To the scoffers, the thought of the world as we know it ending is laughable.

5 For this they willingly are ignorant of, that by the word of God the heavens were of old, and the earth standing out of the water and in the water: 6 Whereby the world that then was, being overflowed with water, perished:

Because the scoffers refer to the earth's beginning, Peter's response to their argument also goes back to the beginning. He accuses them of being "willingly ... ignorant." The Greek text here is difficult to translate, but a word-for-word rendering reads something like "it escapes them willingly." The scoffers, then, deliberately fail to note that before the days of creation, the world was covered with water (Genesis 1:2). The land on which we live came out of water by God's Word alone (1:9).

The world, then, "overflowed with water" and "perished" (2 Peter 3:6). This is a clear reference to Noah's time in which the world flooded within 40 days. Peter's point here is this: It took only God's word to create the earth, and it took only another word from Him for that same earth to be destroyed.

7 But the heavens and the earth, which are now, by the same word are kept in store, reserved unto fire against the day of judgment and perdition of ungodly men.

"Kept in store" (Gk. *thesaurizo*, **thay-sow-RID-zo**) means "gathered up, stored up." The Greek text makes it clear that "fire" is the reason it has been stored. Peter will expound upon this concept in verse 10.

"Against" here means "for" or "unto." The burning by fire will not occur until the Day of Judgment. On that day, Christ will judge all people dead and living (1 Peter 4:5). Christians can face that day with confidence because judgment will mean vindication for the righteous (1 John 4:17)—and Christians, by faith, have the righteousness of Christ applied to their account (Romans 4:24). But

Peter here focuses on the fate of the wicked. In 2 Peter 3:7, "perdition" (Gk. *apoleia*, **ap-O-li-a**) means "destruction, annihilation, ruin." "Ungodly" (*asebes*, **as-eb-ACE**) means "impious, destitute of reverential awe toward God." The ungodly will receive the full measure of God's righteous wrath for their failure to honor Him as God (Romans 2:5). We have God's Word on this truth.

8 But, beloved, be not ignorant of this one thing, that one day is with the Lord as a thousand years, and a thousand years as one day.

"Be not ignorant" is the same Greek word as in the phrase "willingly ... ignorant" in verse 5. Peter instructs Christians to not make the same mistake as unbelievers who choose to neglect God's truth.

Peter alludes to Psalm 90:4: "A thousand years in thy sight are but as yesterday." The Scriptures teach that God is eternal (Deuteronomy 33:27; Job 36:26; Isaiah 40:28) —having no beginning and no end (Psalm 90:2; 1 John 2:13; Revelation 1:4). The brevity of our lifespan colors our concept of time. The Scriptures compare the human lifespan to dust and grass, which blows away and withers (Psalm 103:14–16; Isaiah 40:6–7).

9 The Lord is not slack concerning his promise, as some men count slackness; but is longsuffering to us-ward, not willing that any should perish, but that all should come to repentance.

The problem is not with God but with some people's finite, foolish perception. They forget that God is infinitely greater than they are. In their delusion, they conclude that God is too slow.

Peter goes on to reveal that the reason Jesus has not yet returned is because God is "longsuffering" (Gk. *makrothumeo*, **mak-roth-oo-MEH-o**). *Makrothumeo* means "to bear up under provocation without complaining, be patient." Ironically, those who accuse God of being late are themselves proving His patience. A harsh, vindictive god would soon lose patience with such insolence, but the God of heaven and earth does not change His mind, and He continues according to His plan. His delay, if we must call it that, is for the sake of those He came to save. God's desire is that none should "perish" (Gk. *apollumi*, **ap-OL-loo-mee**). *Apollumi* means "to be ruined or lost"—a reference to eternal, spiritual death. The Scriptures repeatedly reveal God's kindness toward the lost and His concern even for His enemies.

"Come to repentance" (2 Peter 3:9) is the alternative to perishing—repentance, therefore, is the way to life. "Repentance" (Gk. *metanoia*, **met-AN-oy-ah**) is "a change of mind, a turning around." The message of the Gospel is that all sinful people must repent—turn from their sin to God (Acts 26:20)—and put their full faith in Jesus to save them (Romans 10:9).

10 But the day of the Lord will come as a thief in the night; in the which the heavens shall pass away with a great noise, and the elements shall melt with fervent heat, the earth also and the works that are therein shall be burned up.

The "day of the Lord" is one of the Bible's many ways of referring to the day of Christ's Second Coming. It is also referred to as "the Day of Judgment" or simply "the Day." In the Old Testament, the Day of the Lord is portrayed as a day of wrath and destruction for the wicked and the enemies of Israel (Joel 1:15; Isaiah 13:6, 9). The New Testament also speaks of judgment on that day (Romans 2:5), and emphasizes that it will be a day of vindication, deliverance, and victory for the people of God (1 Corinthians 1:8; Philippians 1:6; 1 Thessalonians 5:9).

Peter describes an unprecedented devastation that will happen on the Day of the Lord. He lists three kinds: the heavens passing away with a great noise, the elements melting, and the earth burning up (along with the works thereon). Other passages in both the Old and New Testaments refer to the "passing away" of the created universe (see Matthew 24:35; Revelation 21:1), but Peter's account here is perhaps the most vivid in all of Scripture.

In 2 Peter 3:10, the Greek verb phrase that describes "the elements shall melt with fervent heat" could be translated literally as "the elements being burned up will be dissolved." The "elements" (Gk. *stoicheion*, **stoy-KHI-on**) could refer to either the material building blocks of the physical universe or the heavenly bodies.

The best, most accurate Greek manuscripts do not contain the verb "burned up"; instead, we find the verb *heurisko* (**hyoo-RIS-ko**), which means "find out, discover." The most likely meaning of the final phrase of this verse is that the earth and everything done in it will be exposed and laid bare, after which God will transform the creation—a new heavens and earth.

11 Seeing then that all these things shall be dissolved, what manner of persons ought ye to be in all holy conversation and godliness, 12 Looking for and hasting unto the coming of the day of God, wherein the heavens being on fire shall be dissolved, and the elements shall melt with fervent heat?

In verse 12, the verb "dissolved" (Gk. *luo*, **LOO-o**) is the same word used in verse 10 to describe the melting of the elements. It means "to loose, release, abolish, or destroy." "All these things" means literally everything. Christians are to live in the awareness that everything we own or accumulate will some-day pass away. The only things that will have eternal value are the things we did to serve the Lord (see 1 Corinthians 3:13–15). Furthermore, the Day of the Lord also means the revelation of all that has been done—good or evil (see comments on 2 Peter 3:10).

"Hasting" (Gk. *speudo*, **SPYOO-do**) means "to desire earnestly, to cause something to happen or come into being by exercising special effort." Jesus taught us that we can hasten His coming by praying for the coming of His kingdom (Matthew 6:10) and by spreading the Gospel to all people (24:14).

13 Nevertheless we, according to his promise, look for new heavens and a new earth, wherein dwelleth righteousness.

The new heaven and new earth (promised in Isaiah 65:17) will be perfect because all traces and effects of sin will be wiped out. Satan and his demons will be thrown into hell and no unrighteous person will gain admittance to the new heaven and new earth (1 Corinthians 6:9–10; Revelation 21:8).

In 2 Peter 3:13, "dwelleth" (Gk. *katoikeo*, **kat-oy-KEH-o**) means "reside, inhabit." It denotes permanent residency. Another Greek word (*paroikeo*, **par-oy-KEH-o**) is used in the New Testament to denote temporary residency (Luke 24:18; Hebrews 11:9). This world as we know it (under God's curse and the contaminating impact of sin) is only our temporary home; the new heaven and new earth are our permanent home.

The Greek word *kainos* (**kahee-NOS**) is used here for "new." *Kainos* is used in the New Testament to refer to newness that contrasts with the obsolete—the New Covenant, for example. The Greek word *neos* (**NEH-os**), on the other hand, is used to refer to something in the early stages of life—for instance "younger" people in 1 Peter 5:5. Peter's choice of *kainos* is consistent with the message of the rest of the Scriptures: The

new heaven and new earth will be a renewal, not a replacement, of God's good creation.

14 Wherefore, beloved, seeing that ye look for such things, be diligent that ye may be found of him in peace, without spot, and blameless. 15 And account that the longsuffering of our Lord is salvation;

Peter uses the Greek word for "look" (*prosdokao*, **pros-dok-AH-o**) once each in verses 12, 13, and 14. Whether the Lord returns first or we are taken to heaven when we die, we want to be ready to appear before Him. Although His blood covers every flaw we possess, we do not want to feel ashamed. Peter stresses again and again the connection between our belief and our behavior.

Sources:

Green, Michael. *Second Epistle General of Peter, and the General Epistle of Jude.* Grand Rapids, MI: Eerdmans, 1987.

Lucas, Richard C., and Christopher Green. *The Message of 2 Peter and Jude: The Promise of His Coming.* Downers Grove, IL: InterVarsity, 1995.

Mounce, Robert. *A Living Hope: A Commentary on 1 and 2 Peter.* Grand Rapids, MI: Eerdmans, 1982.

New Testament Greek Lexicon. http://www.biblestudytools.com/lexicons/greek (accessed October 31, 2011).

Zodhiates, Spiros. *Complete Word Study Dictionary: New Testament.* Iowa Falls, IA: World Bible Publishers, 1992. 710, 1487-1488.

Say It Correctly

Perdition. per-DIH-shun.
Scoffers. SCOF-fers.

Daily Bible Readings

MONDAY
Distressing Times Will Come
(2 Timothy 3:1-9)

TUESDAY
Warnings for False Prophets
(Jeremiah 23:23-32)

WEDNESDAY
Warnings for Rich Oppressors
(James 5:1-6)

THURSDAY
Return to the Lord
(Hosea 14:1-7)

FRIDAY
Teaching the Ways of God
(Micah 4:1-5)

SATURDAY
I Will Come Again
(John 14:1-7)

SUNDAY
The Promise of the Lord's Coming
(2 Peter 3:3-15a)

Notes

God's People Worship

This quarter has three units with a theological emphasis on worship. How does Christian worship today mirror both the pious and impious practices of the ancient world? What can we learn from God's relationship with the worshiping community in Israel that can help us honor and worship God in our communities of faith?

UNIT 1 • THE PROPHET AND PRAISE

This is a four-lesson study of worship in Jerusalem during the time of Isaiah.

Lesson 1: June 2, 2013
Holy, Holy, Holy
Isaiah 6:1–8

People seek a power beyond themselves Who is worthy of praise and worship. Isaiah, hearing the extravagant praises and worship directed to God, responded by accepting the call to become God's messenger.

Lesson 2: June 9, 2013
Give Thanks
Isaiah 12

People who experience life-saving blessings are usually grateful and speak words of thanksgiving. The prophet Isaiah gives thanks to God for salvation with joyous songs of praise.

Lesson 3: June 16, 2013
Meaningless Worship
Isaiah 29:9–16a

People sometimes ritualistically repeat words or phrases that have little or no meaning to them. However, Isaiah gives God's message that He will judge those who honor Him with their lips but not their hearts.

Lesson 4: June 23, 2013
The Glorious New Creation
Isaiah 65:17–21, 23–25

People desperately long for a time when there will be no more weeping and crying and the earth will be a place of happiness and peace. The God of truth and Creator of the earth promised through Isaiah that someday God's children would be so blessed.

UNIT 2 • WORSHIPING IN JERUSALEM (PART 1)

This is a five-lesson study of Ezra. The lessons give us a perspective on worship in Jerusalem after a remnant of Israel returns home from exile in Babylon.

Lesson 5: June 30, 2013
Joyful Worship Restored
Ezra 3:1–7

People gratefully celebrate the happy turn of events in their lives. The writer of Ezra tells of the time when God's scattered and exiled people celebrated their return with sacred festivals and worship.

Lesson 6: July 7, 2013
Temple Restored
Ezra 3:8–13

When people are separated from something they hold dear, restoration is usually a greatly anticipated goal. When the returned Israelite exiles laid the foundation stones to restore the Temple, they rejoiced and gave thanks to God with weeping, shouting, and playing of trumpets and cymbals.

Lesson 7: July 14, 2013
Dedication of the Temple
Ezra 6:13–22

People often assign great importance to specific locations. The temple was special to the Israelites because God commanded them to rebuild it and because it gave them a place to commemorate with worship their original freedom from Egyptian bondage and more recently their Babylonian exile.

Lesson 8: July 21, 2013
Fasting and Praying
Ezra 8:21–23

As people live their lives, they pause to assess their strengths and weaknesses for reaching their destinations. Ezra and his entourage stopped on their way to Jerusalem to prepare themselves by fasting and praying for God's protection on their journey.

Lesson 9: July 28, 2013
Gifts for the Temple
Ezra 8:24–30

People often make gifts to others whom they revere. As an act of worship, Ezra prepared gifts of precious metals to be carried by the priests and Levites to the house of God in Jerusalem.

UNIT 3 • WORSHIPING IN JERUSALEM AGAIN (PART 2)

The four lessons of Unit III are from the book of Nehemiah, and they are a continuation of the study begun in Unit II.

Lesson 10: August 4, 2013
Festival of Booths
Nehemiah 8:13–18

People use festivals and celebrations as observances of things most important to them in life. The festival of booths and Ezra's reading was an observation of the Israelites' wilderness exile and the giving of the law, which the people celebrated joyously, followed by solemn contemplation.

Lesson 11: August 11, 2013
Community of Confession
Nehemiah 9:2, 6–7, 9–10, 30–36

It is often hard to tell the truth about ourselves, especially our misdoings. The writer shows us that confession and repentance are necessary acts of worship because God is merciful in every generation and gives people another chance.

Lesson 12: August 18, 2013
Dedication of the Wall
Nehemiah 12:27–36, 38, 43

A sense of pride, joy, and thankfulness goes with the accomplishment of tasks. Nehemiah's portrayal of the dedication of the wall is an act of worship thanking God and celebrating a restored community.

Lesson 13: August 25, 2013
Sabbath Reforms
Nehemiah 13:15–22

People sometimes make demands of those who are breaking community rules. Keeping the Sabbath was so important to the welfare of God's community that Nehemiah ordered the gates shut to prevent the Israelites from breaking this law.

Deliberate Worship

by DeVona Alleyne

"God's People Worship" seems like a no-brainer. Obviously, those who have come to know about the goodness of God feel compelled to worship Him. But worship in general is not limited to God's people.

Worship is as automatic as breathing. Consider that God created us for Himself. That's regardless of whether we've arrived at the point of accepting Christ. He created us with a God-sized hole that only He could fill. In our quests to eliminate or fill that void, it's our human inclination to grasp whatever we naturally think will work to make us feel complete. As a result, we gravitate toward things and worship them in spite of ourselves.

Society conditions us to worship our cars, our careers, our money and even ourselves. When we worship sports teams, we proudly wear the logos, "evangelize" the merits of the team using statistics, and maintain loyalty despite losses. Once we've subscribed to the culture's idolatrous message, we then have "changed the truth of God into a lie, and worshipped and served the creature more than the Creator" (Romans 1:25). Putting those material things aside takes prayerful deliberation.

The difference in God's people is that yes, we worship, but we worship God alone and we consciously do it with purpose, discipline and focus. A worship state of mind manifests itself in our actions as we consider Him and how our lifestyles reflect an ongoing pursuit of holiness.

Worship isn't an out-of-body experience; though, doing so transcends the weight of human concerns. In focusing on God's attributes—His sovereignty, omniscience, power, wisdom, and great love for us—we focus less on our problems. We go from thinking of what He can do for us and instead concentrate solely on who God is. We then recognize and proclaim that even with our needs in front of us that "There is none holy as the LORD; for there is none beside thee; neither is there any rock like our God" (1 Samuel 2:2).

The resulting awe then spawns acts of worship. For example, we could lift our hands in the air or we could raise them to the heavens. The difference lies in the focus of our minds. In thinking and reminding ourselves of God's nature, the same movement becomes a lifting of hands in reverence to Him. When we see His greatness, we realize just how small we are and bow in unworthiness before Him. When we sing, it's an outpouring of our hearts as we thank Him for redeeming us from sin.

But worship by God's people doesn't end when the music stops. We strive to worship Him daily through holy living, or in the beauty of holiness. Our commitment to serving Him through serving others, offering forgiveness and grace, and in avoiding sin speaks to how we revere God as a matter of course.

Worshiping God is not an accident for His people. It's a purposeful lifestyle acknowledging His holiness, our sinfulness, His resulting grace and His call to do His will.

Christian Education in Action

Books	Author	Audience	Purpose	Key People
Isaiah	Isaiah, whose name means "Yahweh is salvation"; son of Amoz; some cite multiple authorship	Pre-exilic Israel, Israel during exile and return, and future generations	To explain, foreshadow the character of God, creation, judgment, redemption, and the coming Messiah	Isaiah, Judah, Ahaz, Hezekiah Shear-Jashub, Maher-Shalal-Hash-Baz, Assyrians, Samarians
Ezra	Authorship never fully resolved because it was seen as combined work with Nehemiah; attributed mostly to Ezra, scribe of the Law of Moses	Written to Jews who had returned from Babylonian exile	To establish a national identity for Jews that centers on unique worship of the God of Israel	Ezra, Cyrus, Zerubbabel, Haggai, Zechariah, Darius I, Artaxerxes
Nehemiah	Nehemiah, Artaxerxes' cupbearer, returned to the land 12 years after Ezra and became governor; parts of book attributed to Ezra	Nehemiah's personal diaries	To provide a history of the rebuilding of the Temple and of Israel's covenant relationship with God	Nehemiah, Ezra, Sanballat, Tobiah

Sources:
Evangelical Study Bible, King James Version. Wheaton, IL: World Bible Publishers, Inc., 1986.
Ross, Allen. *Introduction to the Study of the Book of Isaiah.* http://bible.org/seriespage/introduction-study-book-isaiah (accessed March 15, 2012)
Malick, David. *An Introduction to the Books of Ezra-Nehemiah.* http://bible.org/article/introduction-books-ezra-nehemiah (accessed March 15, 2012)
MacArthur, John F. *MacArthur's Quick Reference Guide to the Bible.* Thomas Nelson, Inc. 2001

Worship for a Worthy God
Revelation 4:10-11

10 The four and twenty elders fall down before him that sat on the throne, and worship him that liveth for ever and ever, and cast their crowns before the throne, saying,

11 Thou art worthy, O Lord, to receive glory and honour and power: for thou hast created all things, and for thy pleasure they are and were created.

(Revelation 4:10-11, KJV)

Lucille Clifton

1936-2010
Writer/Poet/Educator

Lucille Clifton (June 27, 1936 – February 13, 2010) was an accomplished writer, distinguished poet, and educator who has been as dubbed one of the most prolific voices of our time. Through brilliant use of colloquial vernacular and creative word images, her work carried the heart and spirit of the community.

Born Thelma Lucille Sayles, Ms. Clifton inherited her passion for writing from her mother, who wrote poetry as a hobby. Having only a grade-school education, her mother would write secretly until her husband forbade her from honing her craft. At age 12, a young Lucille witnessed the death of her mother's gift. As her mother burned her work, it fueled Ms. Clifton's ambition and passion to share her voice with the world.

Ms. Clifton's talent was first recognized by Langston Hughes, who included her poems in his anthology "The Poetry Of The Negro" in 1966. Her first poetry collection was the critically acclaimed "Good Times," published in 1969 and listed among *The New York Times'* 10 best books for that year. Her work captured the continuing struggle for equality for Blacks and women, painting the political landscape of the times while also reflecting the realities of the African-American family.

A mother of six, Ms. Clifton wrote a number of children's books, including a series featuring the beloved character Everett Anderson. These books were used to remind children of God's love, to provide a positive worldview and to help them deal with difficult situations.

Ms. Clifton won numerous literary awards, including the Ruth Lilly Poetry Prize in 2007 and the National Book Award for *Blessing the Boats: New and Selected Poems, 1988-2000* (2000). She was the first author to have two poetry books chosen as Pulitzer Prize finalists: *Good Woman: Poems and a Memoir, 1969-1980* (1987) and *Next: New Poems* (1987). In 1984, she won the Coretta Scott King Award for *Everett Anderson's Goodbye.* She also served as the state of Maryland's poet laureate from 1974 until 1985.

As an educator, Ms. Clifton began at Coppin State College as poet-in-residence (1974-79). She would later hold posts at the University of California, Santa Cruz, as professor of literature and creative writing; at St. Mary's College of Maryland as a distinguished professor of literature, then as a distinguished professor of humanities; and as a visiting professor at Columbia University School of the Arts.

Sources:
http://www.nytimes.com/2010/02/17/arts/17clifton.html (Accessed December 17, 2012)
http://www.poetryfoundation.org/bio/lucille-clifton (Accessed December 15, 2012)

Teaching Tips

June 2
Bible Study Guide 1

1. Words You Should Know

A. Train (Isaiah 6:1) *shuwl* (Heb.)— The skirt or the hem of a robe.

B. Seraphim (v. 2) *saraph* (Heb.)— Majestic beings with six wings, human hands, or voices in attendance upon God.

2. Teacher Preparation

Unifying Principle—Beyond Description. People seek a power beyond themselves worthy of praise and worship. Isaiah, hearing the passionate praises and worship directed to God, responded by accepting the call to become God's messenger.

A. Pray for lesson clarity.

B. Study and meditate on the entire lesson.

C. Complete the companion lesson in the *Precepts For Living Personal Study Guide®*.

O—Open the Lesson

A. Open with prayer, including the Aim for Change.

B. After prayer, introduce today's subject of the lesson.

C. Have your students read the Aim for Change and Keep in Mind verse in unison. Discuss.

D. Allow volunteers to share their testimonies of personal encounters with God through worship.

E. Now have a volunteer summarize the In Focus story. Discuss.

F. Then ask, "Is it ever difficult to enter into God's presence?" Discuss.

P—Present the Scriptures

A. Have volunteers read the Focal Verses.

B. Now use The People, Places, and Times; Background; Search the Scriptures; At-A-Glance outline; In Depth; and More Light on the Text to clarify the verses.

E—Explore the Meaning

A. Have volunteers summarize the Discuss the Meaning, Lesson in Our Society, and Make It Happen sections.

B. Connect these sections to the Aim for Change and the Keep in Mind verse.

N—Next Steps for Application

A. Summarize the lesson or write some take-away principles under the Follow the Spirit or Remember Your Thoughts section.

B. Close with prayer.

Worship Guide

For the Superintendent or Teacher
Theme: Holy, Holy, Holy
Song: "Only You Are Holy"
Devotional Reading: Joshua 24:14-24
Prayer

Holy, Holy, Holy

Bible Background • Isaiah 6:1-12
Printed Text • Isaiah 6:1-8 | Devotional Reading • Joshua 24:14-24

Aim for Change

By the end of the lesson, we will: RECOGNIZE that God is worthy of praise and worship; TRUST God, who is worthy of praise and worship; and COMMIT to worship God in spirit and in truth.

In Focus

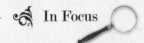

After a long day at the office, Gregory was drained from marathon meetings on what to do about the company's drop in sales. Gregory and his wife, Linda, asked the Lord for insight on how he could best help his company solve its financial woes. In the midst of this prayer, he and Linda worshiped God and voiced their complete trust in the Lord to see his company through this tough time as He had so many times before.

That night, Gregory got up out of the bed, fell prostrate on the floor, and covered his face. He felt the Lord's presence. The Lord gave Gregory ideas on how to solve his company's problem for God's glory. Gregory awoke from the dream, recognized that God had given him an extraordinary opportunity, and wrote down everything the Spirit of the Lord told him to do. Gregory met with his director to share with him the insight given from the Lord. Gregory's director asked how he knew these things; Gregory praised God for giving him the insight to solve the problem.

In today's lesson, we will study the prophet Isaiah's encounter with the holiness of God and his uncommon call.

Keep in Mind

"And one cried unto another, and said, Holy, holy, holy, is the LORD of hosts: the whole earth is full of his glory" (Isaiah 6:3).

"And one cried unto another, and said, Holy, holy, holy, is the LORD of hosts: the whole earth is full of his glory" (Isaiah 6:3).

Focal Verses

KJV **Isaiah 6:1** In the year that king Uzziah died I saw also the LORD sitting upon a throne, high and lifted up, and his train filled the temple.

2 Above it stood the seraphims: each one had six wings; with twain he covered his face, and with twain he covered his feet, and with twain he did fly.

3 And one cried unto another, and said, Holy, holy, holy, is the LORD of hosts: the whole earth is full of his glory.

4 And the posts of the door moved at the voice of him that cried, and the house was filled with smoke.

5 Then said I, Woe is me! for I am undone; because I am a man of unclean lips, and I dwell in the midst of a people of unclean lips: for mine eyes have seen the King, the LORD of hosts.

6 Then flew one of the seraphims unto me, having a live coal in his hand, which he had taken with the tongs from off the altar:

7 And he laid it upon my mouth, and said, Lo, this hath touched thy lips; and thine iniquity is taken away, and thy sin purged.

8 Also I heard the voice of the Lord, saying, Whom shall I send, and who will go for us? Then said I, Here am I; send me.

NLT **Isaiah 6:1** It was in the year King Uzziah died that I saw the Lord. He was sitting on a lofty throne, and the train of his robe filled the Temple.

2 Attending him were mighty seraphim, each having six wings. With two wings they covered their faces, with two they covered their feet, and with two they flew.

3 They were calling out to each other, "Holy, holy, holy is the LORD of Heaven's Armies! The whole earth is filled with his glory!"

4 Their voices shook the Temple to its foundations, and the entire building was filled with smoke.

5 Then I said, "It's all over! I am doomed, for I am a sinful man. I have filthy lips, and I live among a people with filthy lips. Yet I have seen the King, the LORD of Heaven's Armies."

6 Then one of the seraphim flew to me with a burning coal he had taken from the altar with a pair of tongs.

7 He touched my lips with it and said, "See, this coal has touched your lips. Now your guilt is removed, and your sins are forgiven."

8 Then I heard the Lord asking, "Whom should I send as a messenger to this people? Who will go for us?" I said, "Here I am. Send me."

The People, Places, and Times

Isaiah. He was the son of Amoz and a prophet of the southern kingdom of Judah who lived in the 8th century B.C. Isaiah lived and ministered in Jerusalem for 58 years. He prophesied during the reigns of kings Uzziah, Jotham, Ahaz, and Hezekiah. Although the Bible does not record the tribe from which Isaiah is descended, Jewish tradition suggests that Isaiah may have been related to Judah's royal family. This would explain why Isaiah enjoyed relatively easy access to the kings of Judah.

Isaiah is believed to have been the author of the biographies of King Uzziah (2 Chronicles 26:22) and King Hezekiah (2 Chronicles 32:32). At God's direction, Isaiah humbled himself and went about for three years "naked and barefoot" (Isaiah 20). No other prophet predicted the birth of the Messiah, Christ Jesus, to the extent Isaiah did. He also prophesied extensively about the ministry and the sufferings of the Messiah for the sins of humanity. While it is not certain exactly how Isaiah died, a pseudo-epigraphical work—meaning a piece falsely attributed to a biblical character—called "the Ascension of Isaiah," states that he was sawed in two with a wooden saw during the reign of Manasseh.

Background

Eighth century B.C. was a tumultuous time for the northern and southern kingdoms of Israel and Judah. This period saw the rise of four major prophets: Amos and Hosea in Israel and Isaiah and Micah in Judah. According to Isaiah 6:1 (NLT), Isaiah received his call in about 742 B.C., "the year King Uzziah died." King Uzziah, also known as Azariah, began his long reign in 783 B.C. In about 750 B.C. Jotham, his son, was made co-regent. After the death of his father, Jotham reigned seven more years. When Isaiah began his ministry, Menahem was king of Israel. Menahem was the fourth king in less than one year. Jeroboam II's death in 746, after 40 years on the throne, was followed by six kings, leading to the fall of Samaria in 721 B.C. to the Assyrians. In the southern kingdom, Jotham succeeded Ahaz and then came Hezekiah. This age was marked by the rise of Assyria to become the dominant power in the Near East. Tiglath-Pileser III ascended the throne in 745 B.C. and ruled until 727 B.C. In his second year in power, shortly before Isaiah began his ministry, he marched his army westward and occupied Israel.

As a vassal state, Israel was expected to make regular payments to the Assyrians.

After a reign of 10 years, King Menahem's son, Pekahiah, succeeded him. The next year, the Assyrian king, Tigleth-Pileser, sent his army into Palestine. Syria and Israel invaded Judah in 733 B.C. This was called the Syro-Ephramite War. Although many were killed, including the son of the king, these armies were unable to invade the capital city of Jerusalem. Rather than rely on God, King Ahaz foolishly sent a tribute of gold and silver to Tiglath-Pileser III and asked for his assistance. The Assyrians defeated the Syrian and northern kingdom's armies but very quickly Judah became a vassal state of Assyria. The combination of exile and resettlement of foreign peoples in Israel and Judah led to the creation of the people known as the Samaritans of the New Testament.

At-A-Glance

1. True Worship Recognizes God's Holiness (Isaiah 6:1–4)
2. True Worship Acknowledges Sinfulness (v. 5)
3. True Worship Receives God's Grace (vv. 6–7)
4. True Worship Responds to God's Call (v. 8)

In Depth

1. True Worship Recognizes God's Holiness (Isaiah 6:1–4)

As Isaiah began the narrative of his ministerial calling, he set the date as "in the year that king Uzziah died" (6:1). The death of King Uzziah serves as a time reference for Isaiah's vision by giving the historical context. According to Isaiah, although his body is inside the temple, his soul is taken up to heaven, and there he saw a magnificent vision of God and the heavenly hosts. Isaiah recounts seeing the Lord Himself, seated upon a throne. Here we see God's throne as the representation of God's supreme authority and power. Isaiah describes God's position as "high and lifted up." We should understand this to mean that God has no equal. He alone is the Supreme Being. Notice that the God Isaiah is viewing is neither remote nor obscure. Because Isaiah sees beyond the realm of the visible, he is able to view a God who is both majestic and wonderful. If God is to occupy the center of our lives, we, too, must not view Him as distant or mysterious. God is concerned in the affairs of humankind, especially those of His chosen people.

Isaiah continued his description of God's majesty by reporting that the robes of the Lord are so massive that the "train," or the hem of His robe, filled the entire temple. This majesty of God is shown in the behavior of the heavenly hosts. These six-winged creatures are seraphs or seraphim. Using two of their six wings, the seraphs cover their faces in reverence for God, recognizing that they are unworthy to look upon Him directly. Hiding one's face from God in reverence and in fear was also shown in the actions of Abraham, who fell on his face before the Lord (Genesis 17:3); in Moses, who hid his face from God (Exodus 3:6); and also with the prophet Elijah, who wrapped his face with his mantle (1 Kings 19:13). When Peter realized that Jesus was the Messiah, he fell to the ground and asked Jesus to go away and not look on his unworthiness (Luke 5:8).

The seraphim use another pair of their wings to cover their feet as they bow down in honor before God. This action symbolizes that their authority is derived not from them but from the God they worship. The seraphim use two wings to fly, showing that they are in constant service

to God. The holiness the angels recognize, in the presence of God, is reflected in their continuous praise: "Holy, holy, holy is the LORD of hosts" (Isaiah 6:3). The use of the word "holy" three times perhaps signifies their recognition of the plurality of God: the Father, the Son, and the Holy Spirit.

Isaiah further reported on the effectiveness of God. As the seraphs cried "holy," the doorposts of the temple shook and the temple became filled with the glory of God. As creatures created for the glory of God, how much more ought we to recognize His majesty and strive to serve Him in reverence and humility?

2. True Worship Acknowledges Sinfulness (v. 5)

God's majesty and splendor serves to point out humankind's helplessness and unworthiness. It is this realization that prompted Isaiah's response when he witnessed the tremendous heavenly scene: "Then said I, Woe is me! for I am undone; because I am a man of unclean lips, and I dwell in the midst of a people of unclean lips: for mine eyes have seen the King, the LORD of hosts" (v. 5). We have to admire Isaiah's honesty. Isaiah received a glimpse of the power and presence of God and in doing so recognized (Isaiah's) sinfulness by openly confessing it to God.

The symbolic use of the "lips" or mouth to reveal what is in our hearts is used frequently in Scripture. Jesus tells the Pharisees, "Out of the fullness ... of the heart the mouth speaks" (Matthew 12:34, AMP). Isaiah's reference to "unclean lips" may mean that his sense of unworthiness stemmed from something he may have said or perhaps something he should have said. He also refers to living among "people of unclean lips." Notice that as Isaiah viewed the majesty of

God, his immediate reaction was to view himself and those around him in a new light.

3. True Worship Receives God's Grace (vv. 6–7)

In response to God's awesome presence, Isaiah humbled himself in worship and confessed his sinfulness before God's holiness. God's response to Isaiah's confession was immediate. He dispatched one of the seraphim to take a burning hot coal and touch Isaiah's lips. Note that the hot coal was removed from the brazen altar where the sacrifices were offered. This symbolizes redemption, or the price paid to obtain forgiveness. The seraph told Isaiah, "Lo, this hath touched thy lips; and thine iniquity is taken away, and thy sin purged" (Isaiah 6:7). This action is symbolic of God's cleansing and His forgiveness. We should note that God did not chastise Isaiah. Rather, God, in response to Isaiah's humility, immediately reacted to Isaiah's need. God cleansed, forgave, and equipped Isaiah. We should be reminded how deeply God loves us and wants to be reconciled to us, His most beloved creation.

We should ask ourselves whether there are areas in our lives that need God's cleansing. If so, we must be willing to allow Him. Many times, these areas are secret. Our family and friends may be unaware that we struggle in these areas. Only God is able to reach in and cleanse us from all unrighteousness that we have hid from others.

The live coal placed in Isaiah's mouth must have been excruciatingly painful. This reminds us that God's cleansing may entail discomfort or pain. But that can't deter us from our willingness to let God into those areas that need cleansing. Are you willing to allow Him into those places that really need His touch—those places that you would rather no one know about? Are you willing to let Him take that burning coal and touch your lips with it? There is no getting around the fact that the cleansing God wants to do in our lives is hard—really hard at times—and that the process can be difficult. Despite how much it may hurt, our usefulness to God is dependent on our willingness to allow Him to cleanse and forgive us. Our call or commission from God follows His cleansing and forgiveness.

4. True Worship Responds to God's Call (v. 8)

Isaiah was being commissioned to be an instrument of God's mercy, grace, and God's prophetic words. Isaiah's response was swift and certain: "Here am I. Send me!" He told the Lord that he was ready to go wherever God wanted him to go, and he was prepared to do whatever God wanted him to do. As an act of worship, Isaiah made this commitment without even knowing what God would ask him to do. Isaiah's commitment to serve God was so sincere that he was willing to go before he knew where he would have to go!

This should make us examine our response to God's call. Our lifestyle should be an act of worship unto the Lord in response to His goodness.

How often are we quick to respond, "Use me"? Or are we fearful and reluctant? Saying "Send me" to God means giving up control of our lives. Our wishes and desires will no longer be our priority. His will and His word will be all that matters. This loss of control is frightening only if we forget that the benefits are God's blessings.

Search the Scriptures

Fill in the blanks.

1. "In the year that _____ _____ died I saw also the LORD sitting upon a throne, high and lifted up, and his train filled the temple" (Isaiah 6:1).

2. "Then said I, Woe is me! for I am undone; because I am a man of _____ lips, and I dwell in the midst of a people of _____ lips: for mine eyes have seen the King, the LORD of hosts" (v. 5).

3. "Also I heard the voice of the Lord, saying, Whom shall I send, and who will go for us? Then said I, _____ _____ ___; send me" (v. 8).

Discuss the Meaning

1. Read Joshua 5:13-15. How does Joshua's encounter with the "captain of the host of the LORD" (v. 14) compare with Isaiah's vision of God and encounter with the heavenly hosts? How are the two encounters similar? In what ways do they differ?

2. The angels Isaiah saw were crying, "Holy, holy, holy." Discuss the impact that this vision of worship should have on our corporate worship.

Lesson in Our Society

It is only when we have a proper vision of the majesty of God and His holiness that we will come to understand just how sinful and unworthy we are. Without a clear recognition of the awe of God, we may wrongly believe that we have something to boast about. Our celebrity-obsessed society can tempt us to think that boasting is a virtue and that we should strive to exalt ourselves and draw admiration from others for our appearance or achievements, real or imagined. It is only after we truly encounter God that we will see ourselves clearly and know the full measure of our unrighteousness. Only God through His Son Jesus Christ can cleanse and forgive us of our sins so we can enter into His presence and worship Him in spirit and in truth.

Make It Happen

No matter where we are (at home, in the car, at work, school, or church), we are able to set the atmosphere for worship and honor the presence of God through our praise. As the church of Jesus Christ, we have to be change agents to help the world recognize the holiness of God and how our sinfulness blocks our view of Him. However, all is not lost because through the blood of Jesus, we can be reconciled to communion with Him.

Follow the Spirit

What God wants me to do:

_____

_____

_____

_____

Remember Your Thoughts

Special insights I have learned:

_____

_____

_____

_____

More Light on the Text
Isaiah 6:1–8

1 In the year that king Uzziah died I saw also the LORD sitting upon a throne, high and lifted up, and his train filled the temple.

As a nation, Israel turned its back on God and His requirements for His chosen people. The king, having finally been struck by God with leprosy, was now dead after living in a continuous state of alienation from the people and from God (2 Chronicles 26:18-21). The people so enjoyed their sin that even the nation's prophets had been unsuccessful in guiding them away from their headlong plunge into a place devoid of God's light. Isaiah must have felt like a failure, fearfully standing alone in the highest heaven awaiting the punishment from his holy Father that he was sure would come.

For years Israel had traveled a path of its own choosing and now existed in a state of spiritual and moral darkness. The nation's leadership had aided in the people's departure from God, and now that leadership was dead. A righteous God would be justified in pronouncing the same judgment of death upon the rebellious nation and all of its inhabitants as well. This was Isaiah's state of mind as he stood observing God upon His "throne" (Heb. *kicce'*, **kis-SAY**), "high" (Heb. *ruwm*, **room**) and "lifted up" (Heb. *nasa'*, **naw-SAW**).

2 Above it stood the seraphims: each one had six wings; with twain he covered his face, and with twain he covered his feet, and with twain he did fly.

The scene is all the more frightening to Isaiah as he witnessed the "seraphims" (plural of Heb. *saraph*, **saw-RAWF**), standing in God's presence worshiping and serving Him. The Hebrew word used here for God's messengers places an emphasis on the fact that God is utterly holy and the seraphim (described as "the burning ones") must appear to Isaiah like living fire, standing above the throne waiting to serve God. With one pair of wings ("twain"), the seraphim cover their eyes lest they peer into the divine, and with another pair, they cover their feet in humble acknowledgment that they stand upon holy ground. Isaiah now sees himself all the more clearly as an unclean creature, dwelling in the midst of unclean and rebellious creatures.

3 And one cried unto another, and said, Holy, holy, holy, is the LORD of hosts: the whole earth is full of his glory. 4 And the posts of the door moved at the voice of him that cried, and the house was filled with smoke.

Every utterance of the seraphs confirms for Isaiah that God is "holy" (Heb. *qadowsh*, **kaw-DOSHE**). God is utterly transcendent; He is so far above and distinct from His created beings that none is truly worthy to be in His presence. God's holiness is central to His identity, and some scholars argue that it is His primary attribute that permeates all of the others (such as love, sovereignty, omnipotence, etc.). Amid those characteristics of God, His "glory" (Heb. *kabowd*, **kaw-BODE**) fills the whole earth, thus it is impossible to escape His presence. The scene is one that must have been overwhelming and frightening, as not only were the seraphim proclaiming God's holiness and glory, but also the temple itself shook. Then there was "smoke" (Heb. *'ashan*, **aw-SHAWN**), which may be analogous to the Shekinah cloud that represented God's presence with the Israelites in the desert. What a predicament for Isaiah, who by this time must have felt that his death was imminent. No explanation was necessary as to why he should die. Isaiah's presence, in the midst of such holiness, was sufficient for him to convict himself. As if to confirm Isaiah's sense of God's awesome power and mystery, smoke filled the chamber and once more concealed God from Isaiah's sight.

5 Then said I, Woe is me! for I am undone; because I am a man of unclean lips, and I dwell in the midst of a people of unclean lips: for mine eyes have seen the King, the LORD of hosts.

Isaiah gives voice to what he was feeling. The word "woe" in Hebrew is *'owy* (**O-ee**) and stands for a passionate cry of grief or despair. Seeing all that transpires around him, he declares himself and his people guilty before God and prepares for his death. He was "undone" (Heb. *damah*, **daw-MAW**), or on the verge of perishing in the face of this revelation of God. Faced with the unfiltered experience of God's holiness, Isaiah recognized his own sinfulness with equal clarity.

6 Then flew one of the seraphims unto me, having a live coal in his hand, which he had taken with the tongs from off the altar: 7 And he laid it upon my mouth, and said, Lo, this hath touched thy lips; and thine iniquity is taken away, and thy sin purged.

A seraph was headed in his direction, and like any awestruck human being, Isaiah may have felt that it was about to carry out God's judgment against him. Isaiah still had not realized the depth of God's commitment to His chosen people, Israel. The nation had broken faith with the only living God, but God did not break faith with them.

From within the midst of the cloud-filled chamber, Isaiah is only able to see a seraph use a pair of tongs and remove a burning coal from the altar. The living being then proceeds toward Isaiah with the coal and presses it against his mouth. For the first time, Isaiah realizes what it feels like to be fully cleansed of all sin and shame. The text here refers not only to "sin" (Heb. *chatta'ah*, **khat-taw-AW**) but also "iniquity" (Heb. *'avon*, **aw-VONE**), which refers to depravity, perversity, and the guilt from sin. Rather than the expected punishment, God has pardoned Isaiah. Rather than the deserved death (eternal separation from God), Isaiah is given life and begins to experience God's love in a way he has never understood before. He is truly and completely loved.

8 Also I heard the voice of the Lord, saying, Whom shall I send, and who will go for us? Then said I, Here am I; send me.

With the sin and shame now removed, Isaiah is now able, for the first time, to hear God speak. Isaiah hears God inquire who would be God's servant to go and carry out the mission and message He had for His covenant people. Isaiah answers the call. In accepting God's call to be a prophet to the nation, Isaiah understood that he was committing to represent God's holy authority and love on Earth. His task would be to guide the people and their leaders into right relationship with God. Isaiah's experience with God and the burning coal from the altar helps the prophet recognize that God was not interested in exacting punishment on His rebellious people. Rather, God wanted to purge the nation of the sin that separated God from His people. Isaiah commits himself to the proclamation of this message and would spend the rest of his life in this missionary enterprise.

In embracing this call from God, Isaiah would live the rest of his life set apart from the people he was to serve. The price for accepting God's assignment was loneliness and isolation. From this point on, everything in the prophet's life was secondary to God's mission. Because of the vision of God's glory, Isaiah willingly paid this price.

Sources:
Biblical Words – Pronunciation Guide. http://netministries.
org/Bbasics/bwords.htm/ (accessed January 7, 2012).
Old Testament Hebrew Lexicon. http://www.BibleStudyTools.
com/lexicons/Hebrew/kjv/ (accessed January 5, 2012).
Packer, J. I., Merrill C. Tenney, and William White, Jr., eds.
Illustrated Manners and Customs of the Bible. Nashville, TN:
Thomas Nelson Publishers, 1997, 1980.

Say It Correctly

Uzziah. yoo-ZAI-uh.
Seraphim. SEHR-uh-fihm.

Daily Bible Readings

MONDAY
Setting Yourself to Seek God
(2 Chronicles 26:1–5)

TUESDAY
From Success to Pride to Destruction
(2 Chronicles 26:16–21)

WEDNESDAY
Following a Father's Example
(2 Kings 15:32–38)

THURSDAY
People Dulled to God's Presence
(Isaiah 6:9–13)

FRIDAY
Choosing to Serve a Holy God
(Joshua 24:14–24)

SATURDAY
Seeking the Face of God
(Psalm 24)

SUNDAY
Encountering the Holy God
(Isaiah 6:1–8)

Notes

Teaching Tips

June 9
Bible Study Guide 2

Words You Should Know

A. Salvation (Isaiah 12:2, 3) *y@shuw'ah* (Heb.)—Deliverance from distress. In the spiritual sense, to be saved from the guilt and punishment of sin.

B. Name (v. 4) *shem* (Heb.)—In biblical culture more than just identity, it communicates something of the essence, character or reputation of the person.

Teacher Preparation

Unifying Principle—Sing and Shout! The prophet Isaiah gives thanks to God for salvation with joyous songs of praise.

A. Pray for your students and lesson clarity.

B. Study and meditate on the entire text.

C. Bring sacred, worshipful music.

D. Complete the companion lesson in the *Precepts For Living Study Guide®*.

O—Open the Lesson

A. As your sacred worship music is playing, open with prayer, including the Aim for Change.

B. Introduce today's subject, and have your students read the Aim for Change and Keep in Mind verse in unison. Discuss.

C. Ask, "What has God done for you that would cause you to give thanks?"

D. Share testimonies.

E. Summarize the In Focus story. Discuss.

P—Present the Scriptures

A. Have volunteers read the Focal Verses.

B. Use The People, Places, and Times; Background; At-A-Glance outline; In Depth; and More Light on the Text to clarify the verses.

E—Explore the Meaning

A. Have volunteers answer the Search the Scriptures questions. Discuss.

B. Summarize the Discuss the Meaning, Lesson in Our Society, and Make It Happen sections.

C. Connect these sections to the Aim for Change and the Keep in Mind verse.

N—Next Steps for Application

A. Summarize the lesson or write some take-away principles under the Follow the Spirit or Remember Your Thoughts section.

B. Close with prayer.

Worship Guide

For the Superintendent or Teacher
Theme: Give Thanks
Song: "Our God Reigns!"
Devotional Reading: Psalm 92:1–8
Prayer

Give Thanks

Bible Background • Isaiah 12
Printed Text • Isaiah 12 | Devotional Reading • Psalm 92:1-8

Aim for Change

By the end of the lesson, we will: UNDERSTAND that we should praise God for His mighty deeds; EXPRESS a willingness to praise God; and OFFER praises to Him for His mighty deeds.

In Focus

Isaac Watts (1674-1748) was an English pastor, preacher, poet, and hymn writer who wrote as many as 600 hymns, including the ever-popular "Joy to the World." Although this hymn—based on Psalm 98 and first published in 1719—is sung primarily during the Christmas season, a careful reading of the hymn reveals that Pastor Watts was not actually alluding to the birth of Christ in the hymn but rather the Christ's millennial reign. Consider these two of the four verses:

> Joy to the world, the Savior reigns! Let men their songs employ;
> While fields and floods, rocks, hills and plains
> Repeat the sounding joy, Repeat the sounding joy,
> Repeat, repeat, the sounding joy.

> He rules the world with truth and grace, And makes the nations prove
> The glories of His righteousness,
> And wonders of His love,
> And wonders of His love, And wonders, wonders, of His love.

In His first coming, Christ did not come to rule the world with truth and grace. He came to seek and to serve the lost. When He returns, He will rule and reign.

God gave Isaiah a vision of that time, and the prophet penned this beautiful psalm of praise that looks ahead and glorifies that great day.

Keep in Mind

"And in that day shall ye say, Praise the LORD, call upon his name, declare his doings among the people, make mention that his name is exalted" (Isaiah 12:4).

"And in that day shall ye say, Praise the LORD, call upon his name, declare his doings among the people, make mention that his name is exalted" (Isaiah 12:4).

Focal Verses

KJV Isaiah 12:1 And in that day thou shalt say, O LORD, I will praise thee: though thou wast angry with me, thine anger is turned away, and thou comfortedst me.

2 Behold, God is my salvation; I will trust, and not be afraid: for the LORD JEHOVAH is my strength and my song; he also is become my salvation.

3 Therefore with joy shall ye draw water out of the wells of salvation.

4 And in that day shall ye say, Praise the LORD, call upon his name, declare his doings among the people, make mention that his name is exalted.

5 Sing unto the LORD; for he hath done excellent things: this is known in all the earth.

6 Cry out and shout, thou inhabitant of Zion: for great is the Holy One of Israel in the midst of thee.

NLT Isaiah 12:1 In that day you will sing: "I will praise you, O Lord! You were angry with me, but not any more. Now you comfort me.

2 See, God has come to save me. I will trust in him and not be afraid. The LORD GOD is my strength and my song; he has given me victory."

3 With joy you will drink deeply from the fountain of salvation!

4 In that wonderful day you will sing: "Thank the LORD! Praise his name! Tell the nations what he has done. Let them know how mighty he is!

5 Sing to the LORD, for he has done wonderful things. Make known his praise around the world.

6 Let all the people of Jerusalem shout his praise with joy! For great is the Holy One of Israel who lives among you."

The People, Places, and Times

The Prophets. God commissioned the prophets to fulfill a particular role—to be "servants of the Lord." The prophets conveyed God's message to men and women as such, they had special abilities to carry out their tasks: As "interpreters," they explained God's acts; as "seers," they saw what was hidden from others; and as mouthpieces, they voiced God's truth.

The prophets encouraged God's people to trust in God alone and not to bow before human strength or military power. They firmly believed that God is the almighty ruler of the universe, the moral governor of the world and the covenant of Israel. He controls all things for the good of those who love Him. Therefore, God's people should obey Him and not fear the empty threats of men.

The prophets encouraged God's faithful people regarding the future. Moses had prophesied that God would cut off His people and send them into exile (Leviticus 26; Deuteronomy 28). Yet they received encouragement from God. Exile was not the end for them because God would restore His faithful people, and through them, He would send the Messiah (see, for example, Isaiah 51:11; 54:10).

Background

The great reign of Christ on earth (Revelation 20:1-6) is referred to as the "millennium," meaning a thousand years (*mille* is Latin for "thousand" and *annus* is the Latin word for "year"). Many Old Testament prophets, including Isaiah, predicted this 1,000-year period. The prophet Isaiah said,

"The government will rest on his shoulders. And he will be called: Wonderful Counselor, Mighty God, Everlasting Father, Prince of Peace" (9:6, NLT). Isaiah also prophesied: "In that wonderful day when the LORD gives his people rest from sorrow and fear, from slavery and chains" (14:3, NLT).

Of course, Isaiah was not the only prophet who was blessed with a vision of the reign of Christ on earth. The prophet Micah was given a glimpse of that time and joyfully wrote, "Everyone will live in peace and prosperity, enjoying their own grapevines and fig trees, for there will be nothing to fear. The LORD of Heaven's Armies has made this promise!" (Micah 4:4, NLT). Zechariah, another Old Testament seer who served in Jerusalem after the exile as both priest and prophet, also looked forward to that great day and wrote: "And the LORD will be king over all the earth. On that day there will be one LORD—his name alone will be worshiped" (Zechariah 14:9, NLT).

At-A-Glance

1. Praise the Lord (Isaiah 12:1-3)
2. Sing and Shout to the Lord (vv. 4-6)

In Depth

1. Praise the Lord (Isaiah 12:1-3)

Imagine a single day in which no one dies, no one gets sick, no war is waged, no crime is committed, every belly is full and all hearts are filled with joy and peace. Since the beguiling in the garden of Eden, not only has there never been one single day like this but not one single moment. Yet our Lord encourages us to anticipate not just one such day but also many glorious days. At that time all the effects of sin such as poverty and pain, death and destruction, and selfishness and sorrow will be completely eliminated. Isaiah looked at this day and his heart overflowed with song and praise for the Lord.

Isaiah compared the return of the people of Judah to the exodus experience at the end of chapter 11: "like as it was to Israel in the day that he came up out of the land of Egypt" (Isaiah 11:16). At that time, Moses and the Israelites sang a beautiful song exalting God's greatness and praising Him for His victory over their oppressors. In the future reign of Christ, God's people will again praise Him for the final restoration of Israel and unification of His divided and scattered church. "In that day" (12:1), the unified church of Jew and Gentile with one voice will say, "I will praise (Him)." Isaiah was so sure of the fulfillment of this promise from God that he composed this song of praise thousands of years before its future fulfillment.

He praises God for His great love, which causes God to turn away His anger toward disobedient people and instead bless them with divine favor. When we call out to Him in sorrow and repentance, He not only turns away from judgment; He becomes a source of comfort. His awesome power comforts those in danger. His omnipresence consoles the lonely. His infinite love is a comfort to all who seek Him, and His faithfulness comforts all that trust Him.

On that day, all God's people will say with wonder, "Behold, God is my salvation; I will trust, and not be afraid" (v. 2). He not only has saved us, but He continually rescues us from the perils of life and death through the wisdom of His Word, the indwelling presence of His Spirit and the unceasing intercession of our Great High Priest, Jesus Christ. Because we are surrounded inside and out and defended in the physical and the spiritual, we can trust and not be afraid.

Trust implies three things: security, confidence, and hope. We are secure in our knowledge of God's infinite love for us. We have absolute confidence in God's ability to meet every need, overcome every obstacle, and guide us along paths of right living. So rather than dwelling in the trials of today, we look forward in hope to the triumphs of tomorrow.

Yes, "the LORD Jehovah is my strength" (v. 2b). In all things, God's people are more than conquerors because we depend on strength greater than our own (see Romans 8:31-37). As God declared to the prophets of old, He proclaims to His people today and into all eternity, "It is not by force nor by strength, but by my Spirit" (Zechariah 4:6, NLT). Because we can depend on His strength, our hearts are merry and they burst forth, "singing psalms and hymns and spiritual songs among yourselves, making music to the Lord in your hearts" (Ephesians 5:19, NLT).

2. Sing and Shout to the Lord (vv. 4-6)

What's in a name? In today's modern Western world, people tend to be concerned with how a name sounds rather than with what it. This was not true of the ancient biblical world. In those days, parents' names for their children would reflect the future they hoped for their children, the character they desired for them, or maybe something that occurred during the birth of their children. As it is with the children of those ancient parents, the name of the Lord is packed with meaning. God's name signifies His eternality, His infinite presence and the holiness of His character.

In that day when Christ reigns on the earth, people will express their heartfelt gratitude for their deliverance from the defeated kingdom of darkness to the kingdom of His dear Son. They will express this gratitude by calling on His name, making His exploits known to the world, and proclaiming that His name is to be exalted. The Holy One's presence among His people will cause them to sing of His glorious deeds and shout for joy. What a glorious time that will be when all God's people can shout out in complete victory: "'The world has now become the Kingdom of our Lord and of His Christ, and he will reign forever and ever'" (Revelation 11:15, NLT).

Search the Scriptures

1. What two acts did God perform that caused Isaiah's heart to burst forth in praise (Isaiah 12:1)?

2. Aside from praising God with his lips, what three acts did Isaiah promise to perform in gratitude to God (v. 4)?

Discuss the Meaning

Contemplation of God's goodness to us serves two vital purposes: First, it causes us to take our minds off the things that trouble us and focus our attention on how blessed we are. Secondly, and most importantly, it brings joy and comfort to our hearts that causes us to sing and shout praises to His name.

Lesson in Our Society

How do you show your thankfulness to God? Isaiah expressed his gratitude by being both active and inactive. In his inactivity, he got alone with God, shut out the world, and thanked Him. In his activity, he sang songs of praise to God and made Him known to others. We live in a time that features an avalanche of information and activities—so much that our fast pace can distract us from taking the time to be thankful. What can you change so that you can come before God with thanksgiving?

Follow the Spirit

What God wants me to do:

_____

_____

_____

_____

Remember Your Thoughts

Special insights I have learned:

_____

_____

_____

_____

More Light on the Text

Isaiah 12

1 And in that day thou shalt say, O LORD, I will praise thee: though thou wast angry with me, thine anger is turned away, and thou comfortedst me.

The context of this hymn of praise, written by Isaiah, is climactic in that it comes on the heels of the prophetic description of the Messiah in Isaiah 11. Some scholars suggest that this short chapter is derived from two brief psalms of thanksgiving, outlined in vv. 1-2 and vv. 3-6. George Buttrick, et al., state that Isaiah 12 "forms a 'lyrical epilogue' to the first main division of the book" (253) of Isaiah (Isaiah 1-12), sometimes referred to as "First Isaiah."

It appears that this song of praise also has an echo, as Moses used some of the same phraseology when God delivered the Children of Israel from the hands of the Egyptians at the Red (or "reed") Sea (see Exodus 15). Although the date and origin of this song cannot be established, it is clear that Isaiah was thankful for the blessing of Yahweh and the power to deliver His people.

In Isaiah 12:1, the phrase "that day" comes from the Hebrew word *yowm* (**yome**) and conveys the idea of a specific point of time and history. Another way to say this would be "on the Day of the Lord." Scripture is replete with references regarding the "Day of the Lord" (see Isaiah 2:12-22; Ezekiel 13:5; 2 Peter 3:10; Revelation 16:14). Thus, it would appear that Isaiah is referring to the millennial period when God regathers His people into Zion (i.e., New Jerusalem; see Revelation 21:1-8; 22:1-5).

Notice, in Isaiah 12:1, that there shall be a declaration among God's people ("thou shalt say") to make mention of the goodness of God. Every person who has been affected by the Lord's mercy is called to tell publicly of His lovingkindness in a form of praise.

This particular Hebrew word for "praise" is *yadah* (**yaw-DAW**), and some of its meanings include: "to speak out, confess, sing, and give thanks." Essentially, *yadah* gives the idea of the acknowledgment of sin, and the public joy of the nature and work of God to deliver us from that sin. A secondary implication of this Hebrew verb is the expression of thanks to God by way of praising Him. The word "bless" would also be a good translation for *yadah*, as believers' praise should always lead to giving thanks for God's work on their behalf. Though praise is "corporate" in nature, here Isaiah affirmed that it must be an individual act of faith ("I will praise ...").

Isaiah also acknowledged that God had been annoyed and infuriated with His people because their sin was so grievous and pervasive (see Isaiah 1:2-31; also 2:5—5:30). The

Hebrew word for "angry" ('*anaph*, **aw-NAF**) illustrates anger as expressed through nostrils flared in exasperation. Indeed, a "sinning believer" would likely yield greater irritation from God, the name of Christ, and the church. Yet, Isaiah has made known to both his audience (and us) that God's compassion for His people is always evident, as His wrath and fury has subsided. God demonstrates His comfort and care for those who trust Him.

The Hebrew word for "comfort" is *nacham* (**naw-KHAM**) and some of its meanings include "having pity, compassion, and consolation." It is interesting that most of the references in the Old Testament to *nacham* speak of God "repenting" or changing His mind (for example, see Genesis 6:6-7; 1 Samuel 15:11; Jonah 3:9-10). However, a thorough understanding of *nacham* helps us see that like a mother who comforts her children (Isaiah 66:13), God also comforts His people (see Psalm 71:21). His compassion for Israel always "overflows" (see Hosea 11:8, NLT). As the church of Jesus Christ, and the "Israel of God" (see Galatians 6:16), we should thank God that we are recipients of His comfort today.

2 Behold, God is my salvation; I will trust, and not be afraid: for the LORD JEHOVAH is my strength and my song; he also is become my salvation. 3 Therefore with joy shall ye draw water out of the wells of salvation.

As we come to the second, and final, stanza of the first hymn (and the first verse of the second song), the writer decisively affirmed the nature of God as *"El Y@shuw`ah"* (**ale yesh-OO-aw**), "One who saves, delivers, provides prosperity, rescues, and destroys enemies." In both the Old and New Testaments, this phrase has a very strong spiritual meaning. As Jehovah is the God of our salvation (see Psalm 68:18-20), He brings forgiveness of sin (Luke 1:77) and the destruction of Satan's kingdom from the lives of His people (1 John 3:8).

In the New Testament, the Greek word *Y@shuw`ah* was the name given to Jesus Christ by the angel Gabriel (see Matthew 1:21; Luke 1:31) and witnesses that God and Jesus are the same. Peter declared to the religious leaders: "Neither is there salvation in any other: for there is none other name under heaven given among men, whereby we must be saved" (Acts 4:12). And, the apostle Paul made clear, "For God hath not appointed us to wrath, but to obtain salvation by our Lord Jesus Christ" (1 Thessalonians 5:9).

For Isaiah, *El Y@shuw`ah* provided two specific benefits: trust and confidence ("I will not fear ..."). The Hebrew word for "trust" (*batach*, **baw-TAKH**) literally means, "to feel safe and secure in God and depend solely upon Him for our protection" (see Isaiah 26:3), while the idea of "not (being) afraid" is "to cease from terror, dread, anxiety or fear." Why? Because we have a God who has "become" (Heb. *hayah*, **haw-yaw**) salvation for all who trust Him.

The context of 12:2 is significant because God is spoken of three times: God (*El Y@shuw`ah*); Lord Jehovah (Yahh-Yeh-ho-vah); and "become my salvation" (*hayah Y@shuw`ah*). This reveals the timelessness and self-existence of God. The key to the meaning of Jehovah/Yahweh is actually found in the verb *hayah*, as it speaks of "I AM THAT I AM" (see Exodus 3:14), or, as better translated, "I AM HE WHO IS," or "I AM HE WHO EXISTS." This is the one true God who is able to bring deliverance. No wonder Isaiah encouraged God's people to sing!

As stated earlier, this text also echoes Moses' song of deliverance as the people exited the Reed Sea (literal name), stood on the other side of the shore, and witnessed firsthand God's power to destroy Pharaoh and their Egyptian enemies (see Exodus 14:1–15:2). Moses' song confirmed the strength of God and His determination to provide salvation for Israel in its darkest hour. He has the same determination for us today. Who wouldn't want to praise a God like that?

In 12:3, Isaiah connected the two "songs" with the word "therefore." Often, this word gives the connotation "as a result" or "for this reason," and perhaps we can ascertain the basis of that connection. Just as God brought Israel from the waters of the Reed Sea through to salvation, God also makes available the "water" of salvation for those whose trust is in Him.

The image of "draw(ing) water from the wells of salvation" (Isaiah 12:3, NKJV) is intriguing. Raymond Brown, et al., suggest that this particular scene of the well is played out in Deborah's song after Jael killed Sisera and Barak pursued and destroyed Jabin, the king of Canaan (see Judges 5:11). Author Merrill Unger affirms that it points toward Israel's deliverance from the hands of Egypt (318; see Exodus 15:1–21). Adam Clarke's Commentary on the Bible concludes that the ancient Jews "seemed to have applied it to the times of Messiah. On the last day of the Feast of Tabernacles they fetched water in a golden pitcher from a fountain of Shiloah" near Mount Zion, joyful all along. "They brought it through the water gate into the Temple, mixed it with wine," and poured the mixture onto the sacrifice on the altar (Clarke, 573). They seemed to have adopted this custom as an emblem of future blessings, for it was not ordained in the Law of Moses. Although we see it in Isaiah, this song does not have a direct benefit with the Mosaic dispensation;

the characterization seems more in line with the church than with ancient Israel.

Jesus used this same word play in the New Testament as He shared with the woman at the well (see John 4:7–14) and at the Feast of Tabernacles (John 7:37–39). Jesus established that the well of living water depicts the overflowing of the Holy Spirit. When we think of the power of God's Spirit resonating through our lives and the benefits of salvation—eternal life God has guaranteed all believers whose trust and confidence is in Him, "perfect peace" in every circumstance; see Isaiah 26:1–12—we can't help but praise God!

4 And in that day shall ye say, Praise the LORD, call upon his name, declare his doings among the people, make mention that his name is exalted. 5 Sing unto the LORD; for he hath done excellent things: this is known in all the earth.

Isaiah continued his reference to "that day," an indication when all God's people shall gather (see Revelation 7:11–17); and salvation will be complete (see 2 Corinthians 6:2), as God's people pronounce "praises" to their God. Here, the Hebrew word is *yadah* (**yaw-DAW**), and it means to exult God with music, such as a song of praise, or a celebratory hymn for the glory and honor that is due Him. In the New Testament, Paul encourages us to sing and make a spontaneous melody in our hearts to the Lord (see Ephesians 5:19), and in Psalm 33, the writer David tells us that we are to sing and praise God with a new song (33:3).

Isaiah instructed those who belong to God to call upon the Lord (12:4). The Hebrew word for "call" is *qara'* (**kaw-RAW**), and there are several ideas conveyed with this definition, including: "to cry aloud, proclaim, roar, preach, summon, implore, declare a name, summon someone important, or praise and celebrate with a loud voice." As we look closely at Isaiah 12:4, all of these definitions could be inserted in this verse, as Israel is called to speak loudly and confidently of God's saving grace for His people so that His name will be lifted among the nations (see also Psalm 34:3; 145:4-6).

In what manner does Isaiah persuade the people to praise and exalt the Lord's name? First, they are told to "sing unto the Lord" (Isaiah 12:5, emphasis added). The Hebrew word for "sing" is *zamar* (**zaw-MAR**), and the idea is to celebrate something or someone with song or to be a part of continued praise with music. Thus, praising and singing to God must be a part of both our private and public lives. "Let the saints be joyful in glory; Let them sing aloud on their beds" (Psalm 149:5, NKJV). We are instructed to sing our praises, not only in our local congregation but also in the privacy of our own homes. As David declared, "I will bless the LORD at all times, His praise shall continually be in my mouth" (Psalm 34:1).

Next, Isaiah's reason for praising the Lord is based on God having done "excellent things" (12:5). The Hebrew word for "excellent" (*'addiyr*, **ad-DEER**) affirms "might, nobility, majesty, power, splendor and distinct in nature, and tells of the wonderful work God has done, chief among them."

6 Cry out and shout, thou inhabitant of Zion: for great is the Holy One of Israel in the midst of thee.

Isaiah concludes this short chapter of a praise song and thanksgiving by conferring to the people the importance of "cry(ing) out and shout(ing)" with their praise. Later, in Isaiah 54, the prophet also commanded that the people do the same: "Sing ... and cry aloud" (v. 1). The idea of crying out suggests that our praise and thanksgiving should be loud and glorious (see Psalm 66:1-2).

The prophet's original address in chapter 12 was to the "inhabitant(s) of Zion," indicating that this is a personal word for Israel regarding the mighty work of deliverance that Jehovah God has wrought for His people. In Isaiah 12:6, the phrase "Holy One of Israel" (Heb. *qadowsh*, **kaw-DOSHE**) affirms that God's majestic holiness is without equal and is completely perfect. He is the "Holy One of Israel" (Isaiah 1:4), the "holy God" (Isaiah 5:16, NIV), and the "Holy One" (Isaiah 40:25). God's "name is Holy" (Isaiah 57:15), and because He is, God is also free from the moral imperfections and failures often associated with humanity (Hosea 11:9). Thus, we can depend on God to be faithful to His promises (Psalm 22:3-5) and complete in His deliverance of His people.

In Isaiah 12:6, the prophet assures us that the Holy One of Israel wants to be "in the midst" (Heb. *qereb*, **KEH-reb**) of His people. The sense of this word is to be so intimate that one can see, speak, and touch another. Indeed, God desires that type of relationship with all of His people. That is the reason He became flesh and dwelt among humanity (John 1:14). Do we want that kind of relationship with Him?

Psalm 150:1-6 shares the importance of coming into the house of the Lord with praise and thanksgiving for God's mighty work in and through Israel (and the church). We must remember that we are "God's house" (Hebrews 3:6, NIV), and He wants to be in the midst of His people (see Revelation 1:12-13) to give divine direction to those who have a strong desire to praise His name. Indeed, praising God should be a part of our daily devotion. As David declared, our Lord "inhabitest the praises of (His people)" (Psalm 22:3). Believers certainly want to praise a God like that!

Sources:

Bible Words – Phonetic Pronunciation. http:/betterdaysarecoming .com/bible/pronunciation.html/ (accessed January 7, 2012).

Buttrick, George Arthur, et al., eds. *The Interpreter's Dictionary of the Bible, Vol. 5.* New York, NY: Abingdon Press, 1956. 253-254.

Brown, Raymond E., et al., eds. *The Jerome Biblical Commentary.* Englewood Cliffs, NJ: Prentice-Hall Publishing Company, 1968. 273.

Earle, Ralph, et al., eds. *Adam Clarke's Commentary on the Bible.* Abridged edition. Grand Rapids, MI: Baker House Books, 1967. 573.

Hayford, Jack W., Litt.D., et al., eds. *The New Spirit-Filled Life Bible, NKJV.* Nashville, TN: Thomas Nelson Publishers, 2002. 711, 733, 763, 799, 800, 1190.

Old Testament Hebrew Lexicon. http://www.BibleStudyTools. com/lexicons/Hebrew/kjv/ (accessed January 5, 2012).

Stamps, Donald C., gen. ed. *Life in the Spirit Study Bible.* Grand Rapids, MI: Zondervan Publishing, 2003. 998-100.

Strong, James, STD, LLD. *Strong's Concordance: A Concise Dictionary of the Words in the Hebrew Bible.* Nashville, TN: Thomas Nelson Publishers, 1990.

Unger, Merrill F. *Unger's Bible Handbook.* Chicago, IL: Moody Press, 1966. 318.

"Watts, Isaac." Christian Biography Resources. http://www. wholesomewords.org/biography/biorpwatts/html (accessed July 10, 2011).

Say It Correctly

Jehovah. jih-HOH-vuh.
Zion. ZI-uhn.

Daily Bible Readings

MONDAY
Giving Thanks Is Good
(Psalm 92:1-8)

TUESDAY
Coming into God's Presence with
Thanksgiving
(Psalm 95:1-7)

WEDNESDAY
Remembering God's Wonderful
Works
(1 Chronicles 16:8-13)

THURSDAY
Giving Thanks and Praise to God
(1 Chronicles 29:10-18)

FRIDAY
Receiving God's Goodness with
Thanksgiving
(1 Timothy 4:1-5)

SATURDAY
Where Are the Other Nine?
(Luke 17:11-19)

SUNDAY
Giving Thanks to the Lord
(Isaiah 12)

Notes

_____

_____

_____

Teaching Tips

June 16
Bible Study Guide 3

Words You Should Know

A. Mouth (Isaiah 29:13) *peh* (Heb.)—In reference to people, the mouth is portrayed as a manifestation of an individual's character and disposition whether good or bad.

B. Heart (v. 13) *leb* (Heb.)—Commonly used for the center of a person's inner or immaterial nature. In the Bible, the whole spectrum of human emotion is attributed to the heart, stomach, and intestines.

Teacher Preparation

Unifying Principle—More than Words. Isaiah gives God's message that He will judge those who honor Him with their lips but not their hearts.

A. Pray for your students and lesson clarity.

B. Study and meditate on the entire text.

C. Bring sacred, worshipful music.

D. Complete the companion lesson in the *Precepts For Living Study Guide®*.

O—Open the Lesson

A. As your sacred, worshipful music is playing, open with prayer, including the Aim for Change.

B. Introduce today's subject, and have your students read the Aim for Change and Keep in Mind verse in unison. Discuss.

C. Ask, "What do you think it means to worship God with all your heart?"

D. Share testimonies.

E. Summarize the In Focus story. Discuss.

P—Present the Scriptures

A. Have volunteers read the Focal Verses.

B. Now use The People, Places, and Times; Background; Search the Scriptures; At-A-Glance outline; In Depth; and More Light on the Text to clarify the verses.

E—Explore the Meaning

A. Have volunteers summarize the Discuss the Meaning, Lesson in Our Society, and Make It Happen sections.

B. Connect these sections to the Aim for Change and the Keep in Mind verse.

N—Next Steps for Application

A. Summarize the lesson or write some take-away principles under the Follow the Spirit or Remember Your Thoughts section.

B. Close with prayer.

Worship Guide

For the Superintendent or Teacher
Theme: Meaningless Worship
Song: "Lord, I Give You My Heart"
Devotional Reading: Luke 8:9-14
Prayer

Meaningless Worship

Bible Background • ISAIAH 29
Printed Text • ISAIAH 29:9–16a | Devotional Reading • LUKE 8:9–14

——————— Aim for Change ———————

By the end of the lesson, we will: KNOW that God expects worship from the heart; UNDERSTAND that God is worthy to be praised; and PRAISE God from the heart.

——————— In Focus  ———————

Have you ever heard the old English idiom about the person who can't see the forest for the trees? This proverb generally describes a person who gets so caught up in the details of a situation or life itself that he or she fails to see the complete picture. Details serve as distractions that cause us to focus our attention on the smaller, less important things in life rather than living life to its fullest.

This idiom can also apply to our relationship with God. It is so easy to get caught up in the daily burdens and blessings of life that we forget about the Life Giver. We fail to consult God about our daily decisions or even spend time with Him on a daily basis. Then, even though we faithfully attend church, our worship can become hollow. We lift our voices and sing songs without meaning, we say "Amen" to teachings we have no intention of honoring, and we fulfill our religious regulations without any thought to our righteous relationship.

Today's lesson focuses on the nation of Judea during a time when the nation's prosperity and the people's pleasures caused them to forget about God and serves as a reminder that God is always to be worshiped in spirit and in truth.

——————— Keep in Mind ———————

"Wherefore the Lord said, Forasmuch as this people draw near me with their mouth, and with their lips do honour me, but have removed their heart far from me, and their fear toward me is taught by the precept of men" (Isaiah 29:13).

"Wherefore the Lord said, Forasmuch as this people draw near me with their mouth, and with their lips do honour me, but have removed their heart far from me, and their fear toward me is taught by the precept of men" (Isaiah 29:13).

Focal Verses

KJV Isaiah 29:9 Stay yourselves, and wonder; cry ye out, and cry: they are drunken, but not with wine; they stagger, but not with strong drink.

10 For the LORD hath poured out upon you the spirit of deep sleep, and hath closed your eyes: the prophets and your rulers, the seers hath he covered.

11 And the vision of all is become unto you as the words of a book that is sealed, which men deliver to one that is learned, saying, Read this, I pray thee: and he saith, I cannot; for it is sealed:

12 And the book is delivered to him that is not learned, saying, Read this, I pray thee: and he saith, I am not learned.

13 Wherefore the Lord said, Forasmuch as this people draw near me with their mouth, and with their lips do honour me, but have removed their heart far from me, and their fear toward me is taught by the precept of men:

14 Therefore, behold, I will proceed to do a marvellous work among this people, even a marvellous work and a wonder: for the wisdom of their wise men shall perish, and the understanding of their prudent men shall be hid.

15 Woe unto them that seek deep to hide their counsel from the LORD, and their works are in the dark, and they say, Who seeth us? and who knoweth us?

16a Surely your turning of things upside down shall be esteemed as the potter's clay:

NLT Isaiah 29:9 Are you amazed and incredulous? Don't you believe it? Then go ahead and be blind. You are stupid, but not from wine! You stagger, but not from liquor!

10 For the LORD has poured out on you a spirit of deep sleep. He has closed the eyes of your prophets and visionaries.

11 All the future events in this vision are like a sealed book to them. When you give it to those who can read, they will say, "We can't read it because it is sealed."

12 When you give it to those who cannot read, they will say, "We don't know how to read."

13 And so the Lord says, "These people say they are mine. They honor me with their lips, but their hearts are far from me. And their worship of me is nothing but man-made rules learned by rote.

14 Because of this, I will once again astound these hypocrites with amazing wonders. The wisdom of the wise will pass away, and the intelligence of the intelligent will disappear."

15 What sorrow awaits those who try to hide their plans from the LORD, who do their evil deeds in the dark! "The LORD can't see us," they say. "He doesn't know what's going on!"

16a How foolish can you be? He is the Potter, and he is certainly greater than you, the clay!

The People, Places, and Times

Worship. The first clear mention of a worship act is found in Genesis 4:2-7. Previously, Adam and Eve recognized that God had given them "every herb ... and every beast" (1:29-30), so their children Cain and Abel brought simple offerings to Him. We do not know precisely where or how the offerings were made. But we are told they brought two types of offerings, and Cain's was rejected while Abel's was accepted.

The brief account in Genesis 4 tells us two very important things about worship: First, God acknowledges worship. We do not know whether God had spoken to the brothers at this particular site prior to this point. But on this day, God spoke (4:6) and acted as they were worshiping (vv. 4-5). God made this time holy for them. Second, God is the focal point of worship. Scripture does not mention an altar or any words spoken by these men. We do not know what prayers they might have offered. But we are told what God did; His action was a vital part of worship.

In the same way, God is very much involved in our worship and delights in the inner love and devotion of our hearts.

Background

Only God would dare to recruit a person for ministry by telling him he would be ineffective, but that's exactly what happened to Isaiah. When God called Isaiah into the prophetic ministry, He told him that as a result of his message, the people would harden their hearts, plug their ears, shut their eyes and not understand with their hearts (Isaiah 6:10). Given the hopelessness of the situation, the perplexed prophet asked God, "'Lord, how long will this go on?' And [God] replied, 'Until their towns are empty, their houses are deserted, and the whole country is a wasteland; until the LORD has sent everyone away, and the entire land of Israel lies deserted'" (vv. 11-12, NLT).

Years later, Isaiah told the northern kingdom of Israel—whose capital was Samaria—that its fate was set. "For the Lord will send a mighty army against it. Like a mighty hailstorm and a torrential rain, they will burst upon it like a surging flood and

smash it to the ground" (28:2, NLT). The Assyrians would utterly destroy Israel and take her inhabitants into captivity.

The destruction of Israel should have encouraged Judah, rightfully afraid of the Assyrians, to repent. However, instead of trusting the Lord to protect them, they entered into an alliance with Egypt. God told them, "I will cancel the bargain you made to cheat death and overturn your deal to dodge the grave" (v. 18, NLT). He refers to Jerusalem, the capital of Judah, as Ariel (29:1). This was a symbolic name that meant, "altar of burnt offering" referring to the altar located at the entrance to the temple. The name implied the fate of the city: "Jerusalem will become what Ariel means—an altar covered with blood" (v. 2, NLT).

The prophet foretold that the Assyrian army would surround the city and besiege it. The situation would appear to be hopeless; then suddenly, their ruthless enemies would be driven away. God Himself, not the Egyptians, would strike the Assyrians and deliver the wayward people from complete destruction. In spite of this miraculous intervention, the Judeans would still not turn their hearts to God. The people would remain rebellious, their worship would remain superficial and their leaders would continue to place their trust in things other than God.

At-A-Glance

1. Warning to the Rebellious
(Isaiah 29:9-12)
2. Warning to the Religious
(vv. 13-14)
3. Warning to Rulers
(vv. 15-16a)

In Depth

1. Warning to the Rebellious (Isaiah 29:9-12)

During the time of Isaiah's ministry, many of Judeah's citizens were drunk—not from the cup of wine but rather the cup of rebellion. God had given them Levites as priests to teach them, prophets to warn them and seers who foretold their destruction if they continued their sinful ways. However, just as alcohol dulls the physical senses to reason, the nation's prosperity and the people's pleasures had dulled their spiritual sensitivity to God. Again and again, God reached out and called out to His wayward people, and again and again they rejected Him.

A few years earlier, God had raised up the Assyrians to invade and destroy the northern nation of Israel. Now Isaiah was prophesing that God would use the Assyrians to besiege Jerusalem (Isaiah 29:1-4). Unlike Israel, God would not allow the Assyrians to destroy Judea, but His purpose was to warn them and to demonstrate His awesome power to preserve and protect them. When things apppeared at their worst, God would intervene and destroy their enemies.

This dire prophecy should have driven the people to their knees. They should have cried out to God, but instead of crying out, they rejected Him. The nation was too strong, and things were going too well, to listen to what it viewed as a tired old prophet who was too heavenly minded to be any earthly good.

This was the final straw. Instead of using the Holy Spirit to soften the people's heart to His word, God sent "the spirit of deep sleep" (v. 10) to make them even more insensitive to His calling. The people who had closed their spiritual eyes would become spiritually blind. The prophets would continue to speak, but the people would not understand. The political and religious rulers would continue to govern, but no one would seek God's direction. God's judgment against these rebellious people was to turn them over to their own hearts. There are consequences for rejecting God. That is why our Lord warns us: "'Don't harden your hearts as Israel did at Meribah'" (Psalm 95:8, NLT).

2. Warning to the Religious (vv. 13-14)

A lot of what serves as worship is nothing more than lip service. This situation is not new; it was also true of the ancient Judeans who worshiped in the temple. "These people say they are mine. They honor me with their lips, but their hearts are far from me. And their worship of me is nothing but man-made rules learned by rote" (Isaiah 29:13, NLT).

The Judeans claimed to be children of God, but they lived their lives in disobedience. Their religious ceremonies are just going through the motions. They prayed with their mouths and sang with their lips, but their hearts were far from God. They were "temple-fied." They knew how to conduct themselves in the temple. Like some of us, they knew when to sing, when to sit, when to stand, and the appropriate time to cut loose with a hearty "Amen." But this was nothing but learned robotic behavior.

Hundreds of years later, Jesus would quote this passage from Isaiah to rebuke the people of His day (Mark 7:6-7), and it still holds true for many people today. We go to church and go through the motions. There is no passion in our praise and no warmth in our worship, because during the week there has been no obedience in our observance.

According to Jesus, "A good person produces good things from the treasury of a good heart, and an evil person produces evil things from the treasury of an evil heart" (Luke 6:45, NLT). Even though the people of Judah were faithful in their religious practices, their everyday lives revealed the emptiness of their worship. They were spiritually superficial, their worship was worthless and God passed judgment on them. The wisdom of heaven ceased to flow (see James 3:15-17), and God withheld spiritual understanding.

It is so very easy to allow our personal relationship with Christ to degenerate into righteous ritual. We find ourselves going to church and going through the motions. True heartfelt worship begins with obedience, is sustained by daily communion, and bursts forth in an outpouring of public praise.

3. Warning to Rulers (vv. 15-16a)

The leaders of Judea sought advice from everyone but God. In their arrogance, they refused to accept God's protection and instead trusted in a secret alliance with Egypt (2 Kings 18:21). They thought they were scheming in secret, but Isaiah revealed to them that God was well aware of their plans. In truth, they were not revolting against Assyria; they were rebelling against God, who was using the Assyrians to accomplish His will. How could they possibly think they knew better than God or that their plans were superior to His? They were dumber than a lump of clay. Clay does not question the hands that shape it nor does the created thing think of itself as higher than its creator. However, that's exactly what the Judean rulers did. They doubted God's ability and trusted their plans over His. Their arrogance would bring them to the brink of disaster before God intervened to save them (2 Kings 18:13-19:37).

The three greatest threats to our spiritual health are rebellion, empty religion and arrogance. When we truly worship God, we submit our lives to His truth, cultivate a vibrant relationship with Him, and humble ourselves to the leading and guidance of the Holy Spirit.

Search the Scriptures

1. What was God's reaction to the people who resisted His prophets and rejected Him (Isaiah 29:10)?

2. How did Isaiah describe the empty worship the people offered up to God (v. 13)?

Discuss the Meaning

What are some "holy habits" we can build into our lives to ensure that we don't lose sight of God in our daily lives? Think of your own relationship with a holy God.

Lesson in Our Society

Unbroken fellowship with God is vital to our existence and peace of mind. Our praise and worship brings us into God's presence and protection. However, continual disobedience stirs God's wrath and puts us in a position to lose our greatest possession—a personal relationship with God.

Follow the Spirit

What God wants me to do:

_____

_____

_____

_____

Remember Your Thoughts

Special insights I have learned:

_____

_____

_____

_____

More Light on the Text

Isaiah 29:9-16a

9 Stay yourselves, and wonder; cry ye out, and cry: they are drunken, but not with wine; they stagger, but not with strong drink.

In the book of "Second Isaiah" (as Isaiah 13-55 is noted), the prophet's denunciation came because of Israel's prevalent hypocrisy and arrogance. As God's "seer" and "mouthpiece," Isaiah was given an important responsibility to cry against the nation's disobedience and false worship. Why was God angry with them? They had rejected the word of the Lord.

George Buttrick, et. al., believe that Isaiah 29:9-16a was an oracle not specifically connected to the preceding or following prophecies but a stand-alone rebuke. Though the hearers would not perceive the message's meaning, the word declared indicates that willful disobedience to God's moral and spiritual demands always destroys one's capacity to hear and respond to truth. Also, the Clarke commentary suggests that these verses literally describe the "stupidity and hypocrisy of the Jews" in the face of impending truth (Clarke, 586).

God gave Isaiah a specific command to pass on to the people: "Stay yourselves and wonder." The Hebrew word for the phrase "stay yourselves" is *mahahh* (**maw-HAH**), and it gives the idea of questioning oneself, or to be hesitant to do what is right; to be reluctant to obey what has been commanded; to linger or delay in complying with God's word. The NKJV uses the phrase "pause and wonder" and makes clear that the people were unwilling to follow God because their worship life was unhealthy.

Why did they have an unhealthy worship life? According to Isaiah 29:9, they would "cry ... out, and cry" (complacency), become blind (calloused hearts), and stagger with drunkenness (full of pleasures), but not in the physical sense. *Strong's Concordance* describes "blindness" (Heb. *canver*, **san-VARE**) in the plural form. In relation to today's Scripture text, this kind of blindness is spiritual and always occurs when we deviate from biblical truth and our hearts become desensitized to God's divine commands.

Spiritual blindness is worse than physical blindness because it always comes with deception and guile, specifically for the one who is blind. Jesus taught this principle to the Pharisees when He healed a blind man in the temple and used the event to castigate the "blind" Pharisees, who were more concerned with religious traditions than the power of God (see John 9:1-41).

Drunkenness (Heb. *raveh*, **raw-VEH**) literally means, "one who is satiated (completely satisfied and full to the brim) with intoxicating liquor." Solomon used this same image to indicate how out of control and "poisonous" one can become when he/she is under the influence of another "spirit" (see Proverbs 23:29-35). In like manner, Israel had become so totally influenced by the "spirit" of religion and tradition that their praise and worship of God had become toxic and dead to God.

10 For the LORD hath poured out upon you the spirit of deep sleep, and hath closed your eyes: the prophets and your rulers, the seers hath he covered. 11 And the vision of all is become unto you as the words of a book that is sealed, which men deliver to one that is learned, saying, Read this, I pray thee: and he saith, I cannot; for it is sealed: 12 And the book is delivered to him that is not learned, saying, Read this, I pray thee: and he saith, I am not learned.

Because Israel rejected truth and chose intoxication and spiritual blindness, God "accommodated" them two ways: (a) the spirit of deep sleep; and (b) spiritual ignorance. The text states that God "poured out ..." upon Israel (v. 10). The Hebrew word *nacak* (**naw-SAK**), is quite stunning in that it has several ideas, including "to pour out like a drink offering, to appoint, as for destruction, or to ratify like one would do a covenant." Notice the text does not say the people sought "deep sleep"; instead, it was God who initiated the sleep.

The phrase "the spirit of deep sleep" (Heb. *tardemah ruwach*, **tar-day-MAW ROO-akh**) gives the idea of the "winds of lethargy," where stupor, laziness, and slothfulness is the order of the day among God's people, including their leaders, elders, and prophets. The Hebrew words for "prophets" (*nabiy'*, **naw-BEE,** meaning inspired man or woman), "rulers" (*ro'sh*, **roshe,** meaning priest, or chief priest), and "seers" (*chozeh*, **kho-ZEH,** meaning prophet or gazer) indicate the influential of the nation. In short, those who were responsible to lead people into the presence of the Lord were themselves being turned from the Lord because of their own rebellion and spiritual lethargy. Jesus shared this same principle when He offended the Pharisees and accused them of being blind leaders who also lead blind followers (see Matthew 15:14). Israel's leaders had become a stumbling block, causing God's people to forsake true worship and turn to false and insincere worship.

Godly examples are so needed in the body of Christ. Today, the church has no shortage of sin and rebellion—even in the pulpits and among leaders. How imperative it is for those who lead the church to be irreproachable in both conduct and thought? Or should all Christians be irreproachable in both conduct and thought?

God's displeasure was clearly evident in that He closed or sealed the "book" of divine counsel so that Israel no longer had a vision of His purposes and plans. The Hebrew feminine word for "vision" is *chazuwth* (**khaw-ZOOTH**), and here the idea is a revelation or insight from God. But in this instance, the impartation of "vision" is described in the manner of one who has been handed a book and told to read it, but the words and understanding are so indistinct that it cannot be read. Raymond

Brown points out that the one who could read the book refused, and the uneducated or blind in heart and spirit were unable to read it. Thus, the "meaning of the vision is sealed in impenetrable mystery; the people were spiritually illiterate" (Brown, 278), and the stupor was self-induced by those who were being addressed.

13 Wherefore the Lord said, Forasmuch as this people draw near me with their mouth, and with their lips do honour me, but have removed their heart far from me, and their fear toward me is taught by the precept of men:

Isaiah continued his biting condemnation for God on Israel, and rebuked the people for their hypocritical and insincere worship. They were deceived to think that their religious acts and half-hearted worship was acceptable to the Lord.

One specific denunciation against Israel was that it "(drew) near to God" with mouths and lips but not with their hearts. The phrase "draw near" in Hebrew (*nagash*, **naw-GASH**) gives the idea of coming close to God but not in an intimate posture. Another meaning is to be in proximity to a person or object without ever making contact with them or it. It's tragic that our churches today are filled with people who attend every Sunday and never make intimate contact with the Lord Jesus because their worship and intimacy is extremely staid, garnered mostly by the "tradition learned by rote" (Isaiah 29:13, NASB). Jesus quoted from this same passage in Isaiah when, once again, He castigated the Pharisees for their religious "show" (see Matthew 15:7-9). Yet, Jesus knew that the religious leaders were nothing more than "smoke and mirrors," and their teaching kept Israel in spiritual ignorance and darkness. In the same manner, we should be careful not to fall prey to spiritual charlatans who substitute the Word of God with their own form of doctrine.

In Isaiah 29:13, the phrase "precept of men" in Hebrew is *mitsvah o 'enowsh* (**mits-VAW oh en-OSHE**), and the idea is a spiritual or moral law given by mortals, rather than the precise and concrete word of God. Unfortunately, churches today can be guilty of this same principle. Lest we point fingers, we need to examine our own worship and see whether we have fallen victim to following people instead of God.

14 Therefore, behold, I will proceed to do a marvellous work among this people, even a marvellous work and a wonder: for the wisdom of their wise men shall perish, and the understanding of their prudent men shall be hid.

In verse 14, the prophet came to the centerpiece of his condemnation against Israel. God would bring judgment on Israel in an extraordinary manner. The phrase used is "a marvellous work" (Heb. *pala'*, **paw-LAW**), and the idea is to be astonished, hard to fathom, and a wonder that is beyond human comprehension. *Pala'* is used primarily with God as the subject, as God does things that are beyond the bounds of human powers or reasoning. It is not the unusual act, or even the degree of astonishment that is described, but the clear-cut exhibition of God's miraculous power that is clearly evident as He brings forth His work or judgment (also see Numbers 16:1-35).

Some scholars believe that the marvelous work described by Isaiah was the judgment God would bring on the people by the hand of Sennacherib, the king of Syria (see Isaiah 36:1-22). However, another way to look at this "marvellous work" is that God would bring spiritual revival upon the "religious dead" in the form of King Hezekiah who wholly followed the Lord and sought spiritual reform for Judah (see 2 Kings 18:1-7; also see Isaiah 32:1-8). God's prerogative was to bring the people out of their spiritual lethargy into true worship. However, God would not hesitate to cleanse the land of the religious half hearted, who thought they were wise (also see Romans 1:21-22), even if they perished in the process (see Numbers 16:1-35).

15 Woe unto them that seek deep to hide their counsel from the LORD, and their works are in the dark, and they say, Who seeth us? and who knoweth us?

Isn't it interesting that human beings try to "hide" from God? How foolish can people be to try to veil their hypocritical religious practices from God, who is omniscient (knows all), omnipresent (is present everywhere), and omnipotent (all powerful)? Yet, Israel's sham and deceit were so deep that it truly believed it could bring God false worship and that He would not be the wiser.

The Bible is clear that nothing can be hidden from God (see Exodus 3:7; Psalm 33:13-14; Hebrews 4:13). However, Israel was so determined to keep its religious hypocrisy that self-deception destroyed the people. Imagine the people saying to themselves: "Who sees me? Who knows me?" It is also interesting that God delivered "woe" to the people. It gives the idea of a warning that impending judgment and destruction would come upon Israel because they chose to "hide their counsel from the LORD" (Isaiah 29:15). The Hebrew word for "counsel" is *`etsah* (**ay-TSAW**), and this feminine word gives the idea of consultation, purpose, plans, designs, and wisdom. Israel had made up its mind; the people planned to give meaningless worship to God. They were self-deluded to believe that it would be justified; however, they did not fully realize that as far as God was concerned, their worship was completely absent of faithfulness.

16a Surely your turning of things upside down shall be esteemed as the potter's clay:

The final address by God in our Scripture text reminds us of Jeremiah 18, where God told that prophet to go to the potter's house to determine how God would "reshape" Israel in the same manner the potter reshaped the vessel on the wheel. In this text, God wanted the people of Israel to know that He is God. Through their false and insincere worship, they seemed to have forgotten who called the shots in their lives. Israel's idea was to make God in its image rather than allow God to remold and shape the people in His image. However, God would teach them a very stern lesson to humble His people and bring them back to true worship.

Today, we must constantly be reminded that meaningless worship is offensive to God, and those who offer it to Him must correct it. The truest way to bring our lives in line is repentance. If we find ourselves "going through the motions," we must ask God for forgiveness so we don't fall into the same trap as Israel.

Sources:
Bible Words – Phonetic Pronunciation http: betterdaysare coming.com/bible/pronunciation.html/(accessed January 7, 2012).
Buttrick, George Arthur, et al., eds. *The Interpreter's Bible, Vol. 5.* New York, NY: Abingdon Press, 1956. 323-326.
Brown, Raymond E., et al., eds. *The Jerome Biblical Commentary.* Englewood Cliffs, NJ: Prentice-Hall Publishing Company, 1968. 278-279.
Earle, Ralph, et al., eds. *Adam Clarke's Commentary on the Bible.* Abridged edition. Grand Rapids, MI: Baker House Books, 1967. 586-587.
Hayford, Jack W., Litt.D., et al., eds. *The New Spirit-Filled Life Bible, NKJV.* Nashville, TN: Thomas Nelson Publishers, 2002. 1519, 1559, 1568, 1766.
Old Testament Hebrew Lexicon. http://www.BibleStudyTools.com/lexicons/Hebrew/kjv/ (accessed January 5, 2012).
Packer, J. I., et al., eds. *The Bible Almanac.* Nashville, TN: Thomas Nelson Publishers, 1980. 397.
Strong, James, STD, LLD. *Strong's Concordance: A Concise Dictionary of the Words in the Hebrew Bible.* Nashville, TN: Thomas Nelson Publishers, 1990.
Unger, Merrill F. *Unger's Bible Handbook.* Chicago, IL: Moody Press, 1966. 324-325.

Say It Correctly

Assyrians. uh-SIHR-ee-uhnz.
Judea. joo-DEE-uh, -DAY-uh.
Genesis. JEN-uh-sis
Samaria. suh-MER-ee-uh.

Daily Bible Readings

MONDAY
Fruitless Worship
(Isaiah 1:10-17)

TUESDAY
Worshiping Our Own Achievements
(Isaiah 2:5-17)

WEDNESDAY
Lives Untouched by Religious Observances
(Isaiah 58:1-7)

THURSDAY
Refusing to Listen
(Jeremiah 13:1-11)

FRIDAY
Tuning Out God
(Zechariah 7:8-14)

SATURDAY
Receiving the Word
(Luke 8:9-15)

SUNDAY
Hearts Far from God
(Isaiah 29:9-16a)

Teaching Tips

Words You Should Know

A. Heavens (Isaiah 65:17) *shamayim* (Heb.)—The physical realm, including the sky, where clouds float and birds fly and the universe where the celestial bodies are located; it also refers to the spiritual realm where God and the angels dwell.

B. Earth (v. 17) *'erets* (Heb.)—The planet earth including its inhabitants, land and seas.

Teacher Preparation

Unifying Principle—Nothing's Going to Be the Same. The God of truth and Creator of the earth promised through Isaiah that someday God's children would be so blessed.

A. Pray for your students and lesson clarity.

B. Study and meditate on the entire text.

C. Bring sacred worship music.

D. Complete the companion lesson in the *Precepts For Living Study Guide®*.

O—Open the Lesson

A. As your worship music is playing, open with prayer, including the Aim for Change.

B. Introduce today's subject and have your students read the Aim for Change and Keep in Mind verse in unison. Discuss.

C. Ask, "How often do you actually think about living in eternity with God?"

D. Share testimonies.

E. Summarize the In Focus story. Discuss.

P—Present the Scriptures

A. Have volunteers read the Focal Verses.

B. Now use The People, Places, and Times; Background; Search the Scriptures; At-A-Glance outline; In Depth; and More Light on the Text to clarify the verses.

E—Explore the Meaning

A. Have volunteers summarize the Discuss the Meaning, Lesson in Our Society, and Make It Happen sections.

B. Connect these sections to the Aim for Change and the Keep in Mind verse.

N—Next Steps for Application

A. Summarize the lesson or write some take-away principles under the Follow the Spirit or Remember Your Thoughts section.

B. Close with prayer.

Worship Guide

For the Superintendent or Teacher
Theme: The Glorious New Creation
Song: "When We All Get to Heaven!"
Devotional Reading: Isaiah 42:1-9
Prayer

The Glorious New Creation

Bible Background • ISAIAH 65
Printed Text • ISAIAH 65:17-21, 23-25 | Devotional Reading • ISAIAH 42:1-9

——————————— Aim for Change ———————————

By the end of the lesson, we will: KNOW that God will usher in a new heaven and a new earth; TRUST that God will keep His promise of a new heaven and a new earth; and PRAISE God that nothing is going to be the same in the new heaven and new earth.

———————  In Focus ———————

Cosmologists—scientists who study the physical universe—believe the universe is finite and has a beginning and an end. They break down the life cycle of the universe into five periods lasting trillions of years. The first began with the "Big Bang" when everything that would exist exploded out of nothing and nowhere.

The second period, the one in which we currently live, is called the Stelliferous period, or the era of starlight. At the end of this period, all the stars will burn out and release their energy into the universe. This will leave the universe with "black holes." When they have drained the remaining energy, they will cease to exist as well. This time will be the last period called the Dark period, when nothing will exist and the universe will be dead forever.

Theologians study the nature of God agree with cosmologists that the universe is finite. However, these theologians believe the end is not the end, but leads to a new beginning. At the end of time, God will create a new heaven and earth that will extend into all eternity.

Today's lesson is about how believers should look forward to a time of joyful eternal life and make the most of every witnessing opportunity because time is limited.

——————————— Keep in Mind ———————————

"For, behold, I create new heavens and a new earth: and the former shall not be remembered, nor come into mind. But be ye glad and rejoice for ever in that which I create: for, behold, I create Jerusalem a rejoicing, and her people a joy" (Isaiah 65:17-18).

"For, behold, I create new heavens and a new earth: and the former shall not be remembered, nor come into mind. But be ye glad and rejoice for ever in that which I create: for, behold, I create Jerusalem a rejoicing, and her people a joy" (Isaiah 65:17-18).

Focal Verses

KJV Isaiah 65:17 For, behold, I create new heavens and a new earth: and the former shall not be remembered, nor come into mind.

18 But be ye glad and rejoice for ever in that which I create: for, behold, I create Jerusalem a rejoicing, and her people a joy.

19 And I will rejoice in Jerusalem, and joy in my people: and the voice of weeping shall be no more heard in her, nor the voice of crying.

20 There shall be no more thence an infant of days, nor an old man that hath not filled his days: for the child shall die an hundred years old; but the sinner being an hundred years old shall be accursed.

21 And they shall build houses, and inhabit them; and they shall plant vineyards, and eat the fruit of them.

65:23 They shall not labour in vain, nor bring forth for trouble; for they are the seed of the blessed of the LORD, and their offspring with them.

24 And it shall come to pass, that before they call, I will answer; and while they are yet speaking, I will hear.

25 The wolf and the lamb shall feed together, and the lion shall eat straw like the bullock: and dust shall be the serpent's meat. They shall not hurt nor destroy in all my holy mountain, saith the LORD.

NLT Isaiah 65:17 "Look! I am creating new heavens and a new earth, and no one will even think about the old ones anymore.

18 Be glad; rejoice forever in my creation! And look! I will create Jerusalem as a place of happiness. Her people will be a source of joy.

19 I will rejoice over Jerusalem and delight in my people. And the sound of weeping and crying will be heard in it no more.

20 "No longer will babies die when only a few days old. No longer will adults die before they have lived a full life. No longer will people be considered old at one hundred! Only the cursed will die that young!

21 In those days people will live in the houses they build and eat the fruit of their own vineyards.

65:23 They will not work in vain, and their children will not be doomed to misfortune. For they are people blessed by the LORD, and their children, too, will be blessed.

24 I will answer them before they even call to me. While they are still talking about their needs, I will go ahead and answer their prayers!

25 The wolf and the lamb will feed together. The lion will eat hay like a cow. But the snakes will eat dust. In those days no one will be hurt or destroyed on my holy mountain. I, the LORD, have spoken!"

The People, Places, and Times

Jerusalem's Prophetic Destiny. The Old Testament portrays a distinctive future for Jerusalem; it will be the worship center when the promised time of renewal comes. The Messiah will take His waiting throne and the nation will be secure. This future is affirmed by most of the prophets, especially Zechariah in Zechariah chapters 12 through 14.

The New Testament introduces the concept of a heavenly Jerusalem. All that Jerusalem has been in sacred history as a political and religious center has foreshadowed what God intends to do on earth. That perfect center of political and religious life is spoken of as the heavenly or New Jerusalem (Hebrews 12:2; Revelation 3:12; 21:2, 10).

Background

In chapters 60-66, Isaiah addresses his message to the people living in exile, assuring them that they still had a future. Isaiah sees a blessed future for the nation of Israel. The apostle Paul would later add to this prophecy by revealing the mystery of God's will: to unite Jew and Gentile into one body with Christ as the head (see Ephesians 1:9-13). When that time comes, Isaiah says of Jerusalem, "'Though you were once despised and hated, with no one traveling through you, I will make you beautiful forever, a joy to all generations'" (Isaiah 60:15, NLT). He tells the people who have been taken captive into foreign lands, "'Their descendants will be recognized and honored among the nations. Everyone will realize that they are a people the LORD has blessed'" (61:9, NLT). "Jerusalem will be known as 'The Desirable Place' and 'The City No Longer Forsaken'" (62:12, NLT).

In the final chapters, the prophet describes the glorious consummation of history. In chapter 64, he pictures a God-initiated future characterized by joy, the elimination of mourning and fear, the end to death, and communion with God. Although the return from Babylonian exile to Jerusalem resulted in some measure of this blessing for the people, many contend that the full realization of this prophecy will not be fulfilled until Jesus ushers in the new age.

At-A-Glance

1. The Glorious New Creation
(Isaiah 65:17-21)
2. The Glorious New Life (vv. 23-25)

In Depth

1. The Glorious New Creation (Isaiah 65:17-21)

Very early in Israel's history, God revealed to Moses the beginning of time. Under the inspiration of the Holy Spirit, the great lawgiver penned these words: "In the beginning God created the heavens and the earth" (Genesis 1:1, NLT). This one statement is enough to drive anyone who seriously contemplates it to his knees in worship. Consider that the galaxy where we live, called the Milky Way, is only one of millions. Our galaxy is rotating at a speed of about 490,000 miles per hour, and yet it takes about 225 years to make one complete revolution. This gives you some idea of how large the galaxy and the universe is.

After creating the universe, God was pleased with His creation. Everything was virtuous, right, and beautiful. Then Adam and Eve rebelled against God, fell into sin, and all of creation suffered. The wonderful creation of God was scarred by the advent and growth of sin. As a result, God was no longer pleased with His creation. So thousands of years after Moses, God revealed to Isaiah the end of time: "'Look! I am creating new heavens and a new earth, and no one will even think about the old ones anymore'" (Isaiah 65:17, NLT). The original creation will be destroyed by fire (2 Peter 3:12). Time, space, matter, and energy will all be consumed by this great refining blaze, and God will create a new heaven to reveal His glory and a new Earth for redeemed humanity. God's creatures, created in His image, will again be able to contemplate the wonders of the creation and and appreciate His majesty (see Psalm 8:3-4). This new creation will be so beautiful and glorious that no one will even remember the original.

God will give His people cause to rejoice. Nature will fulfill its original potential for perfection: "Let the heavens be glad, and the earth rejoice! Let the sea and everything in it shout his praise! Let the fields and their crops burst out with joy! Let the trees of the forest rustle with praise" (Psalm 96:11-12, NLT). The causes of human misery will be destroyed. "Then the devil, who had deceived them, was thrown into the fiery lake of burning sulfur, joining the beast and the false prophet. ... Then death and the grave were thrown into the lake of fire" (Revelation 20:10, 14, NLT). God will rule in the midst of His people, and we will finally see His face. "No longer will there be a curse upon anything. For the throne of God and of the Lamb will be there, and His servants will worship him. And they will see his face" (Revelation 22:3-4, NLT). Not only will God's people rejoice in Him, but the Lord proclaims, "I will rejoice over Jerusalem and delight in my people" (Isaiah 65:19, NLT; see 62:5). Because death and the grave will be eliminated, people will live eternally with the Lord, and crying and weeping will never again be heard.

One day God will purify the heavens and the Earth with fire and recreate them. Don't withhold your praise until the blessed event occurs; praise Him today and thank Him for making you a new creature worthy of His new creation.

2. The Glorious New Life (vv. 23-25)

The climax of the new creation is the removal and reversal of the curse of Genesis

3. Adam and Eve's sin caused humanity to fall from grace and from God's gracious presence. Their sin affected all of creation. It caused the descendants of Adam and Eve to be born under the curse of sin. Because of the curse on nature, Adam, Eve, and their descendants experience physical hardship as they struggle through life for necessary provision (see Genesis 3:17-19). Mothers bear their children in pain, and watch in sorrow as sickness, hardship, and death affect and eventually end the lives of their offspring. In the new creation Isaiah foresees, "They will not work in vain, and their children will not be doomed to misfortune" (Isaiah 65:23, NLT). Just as God provided work for Adam in the original creation, humanity will have work to do in the new creation. However, since sin has been eliminated and the curse of sin reversed, all human effort will be fruitful and eternally significant without the worry of daily provision. In the new creation, the children of the cursed will become "blessed of the LORD, and their offspring with them" (65:23). The greatest blessing of all will be the restoration of our original fellowship with God. We will experience the loving nearness of the everlasting Father who is sensitive to our every need: "I will answer them before they even call to me. While they are still talking about their needs, I will go ahead and answer their prayers!" (v. 24, NLT).

The original order of things will return. God never intended for violence to be the rule of nature. Animals were not created to eat other animals, and men were not created to make war on or murder other men. In the new creation, the wolf and the lamb will feed in the same pasture. The mighty, flesh eating lion will eat grass like a cow. The snake, who was cursed to travel on its belly in the dust as a sign of humiliation, and the dust as its sustenance.

The advent of sin in the Earth caused changes in the planet and the rest of creation, but God never changed. He maintained His eternal love for humanity and His desire to provide a place for us. He never alters in His desire for us to have dominion over the Earth. In the end, God will recreate the world as pure, uncorrupted, and good. The redeemed of humanity will rule and reign with Christ.

Search the Scriptures

1. God promises to create a new heaven and a new Earth. What will be a key emotion in the new creation (Isaiah 65:18)?

2. How will God respond to the needs and desires of His people in the new creation (v. 24)?

Discuss the Meaning

Do you believe that the conditions of our world will get better or worse? As believers wait patiently for God to usher in the new age, what are our obligations to the present world?

Lesson in Our Society

The people of Israel received the promise of the new creation while they were in captivity as a result of turning away from God. Believers today are often just as rebellious as the ancient Israelites. We fail to share the Good News of Christ with others, reach out to the needy, and obey God's Word. We should live each day making the most of every opportunity to do all of those things.

Follow the Spirit

What God wants me to do:

_____

_____

_____

_____

Remember Your Thoughts

Special insights I have learned:

_____

_____

_____

_____

More Light on the Text

Isaiah 65:17-21, 23-25

17 For, behold, I create new heavens and a new earth: and the former shall not be remembered, nor come into mind.

Commentators differ on the specific era in mind in this passage. Some state that the passage is expressly devoted to life of the future; others suggest that the writing was ascribed to the Hellenistic era. Still others dated it with Israel's post-exilic period. In any case, there is a sense that Israel is given a pictorial description of what will happen when the Messiah sets up His rule in the new earth (also see Revelation 21:1-27). One editor of the Oxford Annotated Bible connects vv. 17-19 with vv. 1-16, where Isaiah's condemnation of false worship is presented in a contrast between the earthly politics, temple worship and "physical" Jerusalem, and between new heavens and a new Earth where the presence of the Lord will clearly be manifest.

As this text begins, we must note the primary "character:" God ("I create ..."). According to The Interpreter's Bible, the passage (vv. 17-21, 23-25) is a recollection that exceeds Isaiah's prophecies in 40-48: "The world itself will be completely transformed in the new age that God brings" (913). The word "create" is used and comes from the Hebrew *bara'* (**baw-RAW**), which gives the idea to form, produce, engrave, and create. *Bara'* emphasizes the initiation of an object, and, in its context, can only be performed by God. The Hebrew *bara'* is used in Genesis 1, where God creates from nothing, which is why Christians affirm the Latin phrase "creation ex-nihilo" —meaning "created out of nothing." However, in this instance, it appeared that the writer emphasized that the cosmos will be recreated and restored to its original intent before the fall of humanity. The context seemed to suggest that God would cleanse creation of all that has defiled it (see also Revelation 21:1-8; 22:11-15), for nothing of the former will be remembered (see Isaiah 43:18-19) or stored in one's heart. In short, paradise lost will become paradise regained when God completes His restorative work and transforms both creation and His people.

For Barton, Isaiah gives a tremendous pictorial view of the new heavens and new earth that are eternal, safe, peaceful, and abundant with all the good things God has created (see Isaiah 66:22-23; 2 Peter 3:13; Revelation 21:1). Most scholars agree that the descriptive nature of this text has not yet been fully realized; therefore, they concur it is a future prophecy with Christ as the main spokesman.

18 But be ye glad and rejoice for ever in that which I create: for, behold, I create Jerusalem a rejoicing, and her people a joy.

God encouraged His people to "be glad and rejoice." The Hebrew word for "glad" is *suws* (**soos**), while the word for "rejoice" is *giyl* (**gheel**). Both words have similar meanings; however, *suws* means to make merry and exceedingly rejoice, perhaps through dance, while *giyl* is often expressed with shouts and songs. Notice, too, that God wants the shouting, dancing, singing, and exuberant praise to continue "forever" (Heb. `*ad*, meaning into eternity). Why? God has promised to "create" Jerusalem. The Hebrew word for "create" in this instance is also *bara'*, but here God will reshape or reform the city with "existing materials," i.e., those who have clean hearts, pure motives, and a will to worship the Lord in spirit and truth (see Psalm 15:1-5; 24:3-5; John 4:23-24). Indeed, in the new earth, Jerusalem will be a place of shouting and rejoicing for all God has done in and through the life of His people.

19 And I will rejoice in Jerusalem, and joy in my people: and the voice of weeping shall be no more heard in her, nor the voice of crying.

Muilenburg suggests that a new relationship with God and Jerusalem will be established, where God will rejoice over His city and people. The time for mourning will come to an end. Coogan connects verse 19 with Isaiah 25:6-10, where the eschatological (end times) picture of a Messianic banquet is described (see also 1 Samuel 9:13; Luke 14:15-24). God's people will have no need of fear or sadness, as God will make all things new for His people. Again, the prophetic picture is also clearly seen in Revelation 22:1-5, where God will reign as the light of New Jerusalem and the leaves of the Tree of Life shall be for the healing of the nations.

20 There shall be no more thence an infant of days, nor an old man that hath not filled his days; for the child shall die a hundred years old; but the sinner being an hundred years old shall be accursed. 21 And they shall build houses, and inhabit them; and they shall plant vineyards, and eat the fruit of them.

Berlin and Brettler point out that verse 20 brings to mind those who will not enjoy the transformation. The Hebrew Bible states the verse as follows: "No more shall there be an infant or graybeard who does not live out his days. He who dies at a hundred years Shall be reckoned a youth, And he who fails to reach a hundred Shall be reckoned accursed." In short, extraordinary longevity shall return to its former days before the flood that destroyed most of humanity, when people lived well beyond 300 to 500 years (see Genesis 5:1-32). For those who are righteous, they will expect to live a long and blessed life as opposed to those who have fallen from favor with God.

Eternal prosperity is also promised for the righteous. They shall enjoy the fruit of their own labor. Contrast this verse with God's judgment on Adam, because of his rebellion and disobedience (see Genesis 3:17-19), and it is clear that this prophecy is Messianic in its scope. Also, these verses correspond to God's promise to Jerusalem that they shall gather their produce and enjoy it as they praise the Lord in the courts of His holiness (see Isaiah 62:8-9). The new millennium will bring forth from God blessing, not judgment, and will be dramatically different than the judgments spoken by the prophetic oracles in the past (see Amos 5:11; Micah 6:14-15; Zephaniah 1:12-14).

65:23 They shall not labour in vain, nor bring forth for trouble; for they are the seed of the blessed of the LORD, and their offspring with them.

The promise from God is encompassing. Not only will God's people enjoy the fruit of their work, but also that for which they labored shall bring forth an abundant harvest. The second promise is that they shall also bear children in prosperity. In this verse, Isaiah used the word "trouble," and in Hebrew it is *behalah* (**beh-haw-LAW**), which literally means, "fear, fright, sudden destruction, or the sudden terror of God brought upon disobedient Israel" (also see Jeremiah 15:8). However, unlike the judgment on the children that God spoke against Israel for disobedience (see Deuteronomy 28:41), these children shall be destined for greatness because, in the new millennium, all shall have God's stamp of approval.

24 And it shall come to pass, that before they call, I will answer; and while they are yet speaking, I will hear.

Here, the prophet described an era of peace and harmony for the people with their Creator. The silence of God, which was prevalent in the past—and tested the souls of the people—shall be broken. In both Isaiah 51:9-11 and Isaiah 63-64, the people questioned whether God listened to their prayers. God makes the declaration that not only will He answer prayer, but, in the future, God will act before they can get the words out of their mouths. For Muilenburg, God's blessing will extend even into their interior consciousness (also see Isaiah 30:19, 21; 58:9; Jeremiah 29:11-12).

In Isaiah 65:24, the Hebrew word for "answer" is `anah (aw-NAW), and by implication it means, "to pay attention, give heed, and begin to speak." Thus, God seems to indicate that before the people pay attention, or give heed to Him, He will already have paid attention to those He loves.

25 The wolf and the lamb shall feed together, and the lion shall eat straw like the bullock: and dust shall be the serpent's meat. They shall not hurt nor destroy in all my holy mountain, saith the LORD.

Berlin and Brettler state that verse 25 contains quotes from Isaiah 11: 6, 9, which speak of a new, peaceful era ushered in by an ideal Davidic king. But here, the human king is not mentioned. The prophet envisions a renewal where peace shall dwell both among humans and creatures; no human or animal will kill for food (also see Genesis 1:29-30). Thus, Jerusalem shall be a city of peace where all will reside in harmony, just as God declared before the fall of humanity.

The phrase "and dust shall be the serpent's meat" refers to Genesis 3:14, where God spoke a prophetic word against the creature Satan used to deceive both Adam and Eve. Most scholars agree that this statement may point to the idea that, unlike the garden of Eden where Satan infiltrated with this creature, there shall be no evil in the new millennium. Another reference is Micah 7:16-17, where God will destroy the nations that have risen against Israel. They, too, shall be like serpents.

In Isaiah 65:25, the Hebrew word for "hurt" (ra`a`, raw-AH), gives the idea of breaking into pieces, afflicting, dashing and destroying, doing evil, or living wickedly. Thus, ra`a` denoted any activity that is contrary to God's will and purpose. Those who seek to do malicious sin against others will not only injure themselves; God also will inflict misery and pain upon them. Thus in verse 25, God seems to reflect His final judgment on all who will be outside of New Jerusalem (His "holy mountain"). As John writes: "And there shall in no wise enter into (New Jerusalem) any thing that defileth, neither whatsoever worketh abomination, or maketh a lie: but they which are written in the Lamb's book of life" (Revelation 21:27).

For Barton, the entire prophecy "may refer to the reign of Christ on earth, because sin and death have not yet been finally destroyed" (1279; see also 1 Corinthians 15:23-28). Muilenberg suggests that this speaks of the new creation and age of peace in the Messianic community. Isaiah 65:17-25 gives the idea of the return to paradise, with no more pain and death (see Isaiah 11:1-9; Revelation 21:4).

Say It Correctly

Jerusalem.
juh-ROO-suh-luhm, -sluhm.

Sources:

Barton, Bruce B., et al., eds. *Life Application Study Bible: New International Version.* Wheaton, IL: Tyndale House Publishers, 1997. 1279.

Berlin, Adele, and Marc Brettler. *The Jewish Study Bible.* Oxford, NY: Oxford University Press, 2004. 911-913.

Bible Words – Phonetic Pronunciation. http://betterdays arecoming.html/ (accessed January 14, 2012).

Buttrick, George, Arthur, et al., eds. *The Intepreter's Bible. Vol. 5.* New York, NY: Abingdon Press, 1956. 754-757.

Coogan Michael D., et al., eds. *The New Oxford Annotated Bible, 2nd ed.* Oxford, NY: Oxford University Press, 1973. 904-905.

Fraknoi, Andrew. "How Fast Are You Moving When You Are Sitting Still." Foothill College & the Astronomical Society of the Pacific. http://www.astrosociety.org/education/publications/tnl/71/howfast.html (accessed January 27, 2012.)

Old Testament Hebrew Lexicon. http://www.BibleStudyTools. com/lexicons/hebrew/kjv/ (accessed January 11, 2012).

Richards, Lawrence O. "Jerusalem." *Expository Dictionary of Bible Words.* Grand Rapids, MI: Zondervan Publishing House, 1985. 2005. 359-360.

Wansbrough, Henry, et al., eds. *The New Jerusalem Bible.* New York, NY: Doubleday Dell Publishing Group, 1985. 1170, 1289-1291.

Daily Bible Readings

MONDAY
The Handiwork of God
(Psalm 19:1-6)

TUESDAY
The Guidance of God
(Psalm 19:7-14)

WEDNESDAY
No One Is Righteous
(Romans 3:9-20)

THURSDAY
Sin, Death, Sacrifice, and Salvation
(Romans 5:6-14)

FRIDAY
New Things Springing Forth
(Isaiah 42:1-9)

SATURDAY
God Makes All Things New
(Revelation 21:1-7)

SUNDAY
New Heavens and a New Earth
(Isaiah 65:17-21, 23-25)

Notes

Teaching Tips

Words You Should Know

A. Altar (Ezra 3:2) *mizbeach* (Heb.)—A table or flat-topped block used as the focus for a religious ritual, especially for making sacrifices or offerings to a deity.

B. Tabernacles (v. 4) *cukkah* (Heb.)— Tent sanctuaries used by Israelites during the Exodus.

Teacher Preparation

Unifying Principle—Celebrating What Is Meaningful. God's scattered and exiled people celebrated their return with sacred festivals and worship.

A. Pray for your students and lesson clarity.

B. Study and meditate on the entire text.

C. Bring sacred worship music.

D. Complete the companion lesson in the *Precepts For Living Study Guide®*.

O—Open the Lesson

A. As your music is playing, open with prayer, including the Aim for Change.

B. Introduce today's subject, and have your students read the Aim for Change and Keep in Mind verse in unison. Discuss.

C. Ask, "What has God done for you that would cause you to celebrate?"

D. Share testimonies.

E. Summarize the In Focus story. Discuss.

P—Present the Scriptures

A. Have volunteers read the Focal Verses.

B. Now use The People, Places, and Times; Background; Search the Scriptures; At-A-Glance outline; In Depth; and More Light on the Text to clarify the verses.

E—Explore the Meaning

A. Have volunteers summarize the Discuss the Meaning, Lesson in Our Society, and Make It Happen sections.

B. Connect these sections to the Aim for Change and the Keep in Mind verse.

N—Next Steps for Application

A. Summarize the lesson or write take-away principles under the Follow the Spirit or Remember Your Thoughts section.

B. Close with prayer.

Worship Guide

For the Superintendent or Teacher
Theme: Joyful Worship Restored
Song: "There Is Joy in the Lord!"
Devotional Reading:
Matthew 23:29-39
Prayer

Joyful Worship Restored

Bible Background • EZRA 1:1-3:7
Printed Text • EZRA 3:1-7 | Devotional Reading • MATTHEW 23:29-39

JUNE
30th

Aim for Change

By the end of the lesson, we will: KNOW that we should celebrate and express thanks to God for His goodness; DESIRE to praise God for His goodness; and PRAISE God for His goodness.

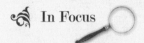

In Focus

Adam was a faithful church member who led the praise and worship portion of services. He met a woman that he liked and began to spend a lot of time with her. He sought God's approval of the relationship, though, he felt in his heart that God was not pleased.

Adam entered his place after work one evening to find his belongings gone with just a search warrant left behind. Adam had been under surveillance because of the woman he'd been dating. She'd been identified as a co-conspirator in intricately planned robberies. The warnings of the Lord came back to Adam's mind. Ashamed, Adam stopped going to church and shied away from praising and worshiping God.

Weeks later, while remembering the praise and worship services, Adam began to sing to the Lord. In tears, he called his pastor and the praise and worship leader, both who readily accepted him back. Adam gladly worshiped the Lord to prepare for the next Sunday's services. There, Adam experienced an anointing in worship like none he'd ever seen before.

Today's lesson is about how we as believers should ask God to help us maintain joyful worship of God, who is worthy to be praised.

Keep in Mind

"They kept also the feast of tabernacles, as it is written, and offered the daily burnt offerings by number, according to the custom, as the duty of every day required"
(Ezra 3:4).

"They kept also the feast of tabernacles, as it is written, and offered the daily burnt offerings by number, according to the custom, as the duty of every day required" (Ezra 3:4).

Focal Verses

KJV **Ezra 3:1** And when the seventh month was come, and the children of Israel were in the cities, the people gathered themselves together as one man to Jerusalem.

2 Then stood up Jeshua the son of Jozadak, and his brethren the priests, and Zerubbabel the son of Shealtiel, and his brethren, and builded the altar of the God of Israel, to offer burnt offerings thereon, as it is written in the law of Moses the man of God.

3 And they set the altar upon his bases; for fear was upon them because of the people of those countries: and they offered burnt offerings thereon unto the LORD, even burnt offerings morning and evening.

4 They kept also the feast of tabernacles, as it is written, and offered the daily burnt offerings by number, according to the custom, as the duty of every day required;

5 And afterward offered the continual burnt offering, both of the new moons, and of all the set feasts of the LORD that were consecrated, and of every one that willingly offered a freewill offering unto the LORD.

6 From the first day of the seventh month began they to offer burnt offerings unto the LORD. But the foundation of the temple of the LORD was not yet laid.

7 They gave money also unto the masons, and to the carpenters; and meat, and drink, and oil, unto them of Zidon, and to them of Tyre, to bring cedar trees from Lebanon to the sea of Joppa, according to the grant that they had of Cyrus king of Persia.

NLT **Ezra 3:1** In early autumn, when the Israelites had settled in their towns, all the people assembled in Jerusalem with a unified purpose.

2 Then Jeshua son of Jehozadak joined his fellow priests and Zerubbabel son of Shealtiel with his family in rebuilding the altar of the God of Israel. They wanted to sacrifice burnt offerings on it, as instructed in the Law of Moses, the man of God.

3 Even though the people were afraid of the local residents, they rebuilt the altar at its old site. Then they began to sacrifice burnt offerings on the altar to the LORD each morning and evening.

4 They celebrated the Festival of Shelters as prescribed in the Law, sacrificing the number of burnt offerings specified for each day of the festival.

5 They also offered the regular burnt offerings and the offerings required for the new moon celebrations and the annual festivals as prescribed by the LORD. The people also gave voluntary offerings to the LORD.

6 Fifteen days before the Festival of Shelters began, the priests had begun to sacrifice burnt offerings to the LORD. This was even before they had started to lay the foundation of the LORD's Temple.

7 Then the people hired masons and carpenters and bought cedar logs from the people of Tyre and Sidon, paying them with food, wine, and olive oil. The logs were brought down from the Lebanon mountains and floated along the coast of the Mediterranean Sea to Joppa, for King Cyrus had given permission for this.

The People, Places, and Times

The **Feast of Booths (or the Feast of Tabernacles** or *Sukkot*). This celebration is a harvest festival that lasts for one week. Jeshua is a descendant of Jozadak, who had been the high priest at the time Judah went into exile. Zerubbabel was appointed governor of Judah either by Darius or his predecessor, Cambyses, about 525 B.C. The altar described was built on old foundations, underscoring the continuity with the First Temple. The text notes that the reinstitution of sacrifices was not accompanied by the laying of the temple's foundations. Fear of reaction by neighboring people accounted for this delay.

Background

Throughout the history of the Children of Israel, we see a pattern where one ruler obeyed God and his successor would disobey and lead the nation into a path of unrighteousness. In the historical era prior to our lesson, King Josiah, at 8 years old, sought to cleanse and restore true worship among the people of Israel. He rebuilt the temple and led the people in obeying the Law of Moses to follow all the required feasts and sacrifices and the Passover.

After his death, his brother Jehiaham was placed over the Children of Israel, and he did evil in the sight of the Lord. The people disobeyed God, and the chief priests defiled the temple. The Lord sent prophets to warn them, but the people mocked and misused them. God's wrath against them became unquenched. The king of Chaldees came and slew them unmercifully: young, old, men, and women alike. The king took everything of value in the land and removed everything from the temple before he burned it and destroyed the wall of Jerusalem. Those who remained were taken into captivity for 70 years, the time God appointed.

At-A-Glance

1. Worship Restored (Ezra 3:1-5)
2. The Temple Restored (vv. 6-7)

In Depth

1. Worship Restored (Ezra 3:1-5)

The Children of Israel gathered in Jerusalem after their release from Babylon to find their city and temple in ruins. Jeshua and the other priests worked to restore the altar to observe the customary feasts with the people. Over time, the morale of the Children of Israel suffered after their bondage, and their spirits were in ruins like their precious Jerusalem: broken and, in many ways, desolate.

The Feast of Tabernacles, which they celebrated, is similar to our Thanksgiving. It commemorates the 40 years they worshiped in tents while in the wilderness. As with all required feasts and observances, it came with a promise and restoration of God's covenant with His people. Worshiping God is the best way to re-establish joy after emerging from a difficult time.

2. The Temple Restored (vv. 6-7)

The Temple of God represents a special place, and the things inside had a special meaning. The Children of Israel endured many transitions while serving their God. They carried the Ark of the Covenant, they served Him in a tent, and they built a beautiful temple — all so His presence could continually dwell among them.

The people were moved as they watched Jeshua and the other priests rebuild the Temple to its original order. The skilled tradesmen gave their time and skill to restore the Temple. King Cyrus of Persia preserved the pieces that belonged in the temple and returned them when the Children of Israel returned to Jerusalem. He also gave a grant to help with its completion.

More important than the dedication of the people to rebuild the physical temple was their renewed spirit, the true temple, figuratively speaking. What good is a temple if no one comes to makes sacrifices to God? The Children of Israel in the past had failed to see the significance in observing the required sacrifices and didn't for quite some time before going into captivity. After deliverance from their captors, the Children of Israel longed for those old traditions; their significance, no doubt, brought new meaning to their hearts.

It is important that we, too, recognize the significance of God and the temple where His presence dwells.

Search the Scriptures

1. What was significant in the observance of the Feast of Tabernacles among the Children of Israel (Ezra 3:4)?

2. Who granted permission to the Children of Israel to rebuild the temple (v. 7)?

Discuss the Meaning

What observances or sacrifices do we need to reinstitute to restore and rebuild our relationship with God? As you ponder this question, think of your own relationship with the holy God.

Lesson in Our Society

Unbroken fellowship with God is so vital to our existence and peace of mind in today's perilous world. Our praise and worship brings us into God's presence and protection. Our continual disobedience only stirs the wrath of God and places us in a

position to lose our greatest possession: our relationship with God—the source of our praise, worship, and more important, our joy.

Follow the Spirit

What God wants me to do:

_____

_____

_____

_____

Remember Your Thoughts

Special insights I have learned:

_____

_____

_____

_____

More Light on the Text
Ezra 3:1-7
Introduction:

There is a noticeable distance in time between Ezra chapters 2 and 3. The Children of Israel have returned home to their land, bringing a substantial amount of wealth along with them. This of course is primarily for the sole purpose of rebuilding Yahweh's Temple. We read in Ezra 2:68-70 that the people built homes for themselves before even establishing the foundation of the temple. This later ignites the rage of the prophet Haggai as the Lord commands him to rebuke Israel for their distorted priorities. "'Is it time for you yourselves to dwell in your paneled houses while this house lies desolate?'" (Haggai 1:4, NASB).

1 And when the seventh month was come, and the children of Israel were in the cities, the people gathered themselves together as one man to Jerusalem.

Ezra 3 opens with a remarkable statement. Everyone "gathered themselves together" (*'acaph,* **aw-SAF**), "as one man to Jerusalem." This is a distinct expression of unity among people of Israel. Undoubtedly, the people's unity was influenced by the permission that King Cyrus gave to people scattered throughout the land to return home to rebuild the Temple (Ezra 1:1-4). An additional factor was Haggai's prophetic message rebuking them for their selfish actions, which involved them building homes for themselves first rather than the Lord's Temple (Haggai 1:1-5). "Thus says the LORD of hosts, 'Consider your ways!'" (Haggai 1:5, NASB).

2 Then stood up Jeshua the son of Jozadak, and his brethren the priests, and Zerubbabel the son of Shealtiel, and his brethren, and builded the altar of the God of Israel, to offer burnt offerings thereon, as it is written in the law of Moses the man of God.

The individuals prominent in this verse, Jeshua and Zerubbabel represented both the priestly and royal roles of Yahweh. The divine and political authorities of Israel were not only present, but led in the construction of Yahweh's "altar" (Heb. *mizbeach,* **miz-BAY-akh**). Continuing in the spirit of being united as "one," they were accompanied by their fellow brothers of spiritual and political kin.

Even more impressive is their recognition of and return to obedience toward the Law of Moses (Pentateuch). An assumption can be made that upon reading the Pentateuch, they realized the supreme importance of the Lord's altar and the significance of the burnt offering.

3 And they set the altar upon his bases; for fear was upon them because of the people of those countries: and they offered burnt offerings thereon unto the LORD, even burnt offerings morning and evening.

Fear can cause us to do many things; some are good and some stem from bad consequences and situations. Regardless of this fact, the intense emotion in most cases will cause some form of action. In an odd set of influences, fear led to the urgent construction of the Lord's altar. The serious threats from neighboring ethnicities and cultures around them influenced a troubled and frightened nation of Israel to seek the protection of Yahweh.

It's very interesting to see the hostility from the surrounding people. This hostility could have resulted from a variety of situations and consequences. The surrounding group could have had a lasting memory of Israel when it existed as an established, unified and strong nation; interactions at the time could have varied from subtle negativity to complete disaster. Also, jealousy could have arisen from within the surrounding people, a direct result stemming from King Cyrus issuing a royal decree to allow them to return home in order to rebuild the Temple. This was an extremely important privilege that no other group enjoyed within its own contexts. As the altar was constructed, the people of God worshiped Him and sought His protection every day and night.

4 They kept also the feast of tabernacles, as it is written, and offered the daily burnt offerings by number, according to the custom, as the duty of every day required; 5 And afterward offered the continual burnt offering, both of the new moons, and of all the set feasts of the LORD that were

consecrated, and of every one that willingly offered a freewill offering unto the LORD.

The altar of the Lord being fully established brought about resurgence among the people of Israel. It encouraged them to seek the Lord and worship Him in their culturally traditional ways. "They found written in the law how the LORD had commanded through Moses that the sons of Israel should live in booths during the feast of the seventh month" (Nehemiah 8:14, NASB). The Feast of "Booths" (Heb. *cukkah*, **sook-KAW**) was a celebration of remembrance, pertaining to the time Israel had wandered in the wilderness for 40 years (Deuteronomy 2), homeless (having shelter in tents); a consequence of their rebellious disbelief in Yahweh (Deuteronomy 1). A particular observance of the burnt offerings was emphasized also. Within this offering a male ram, bull, and lamb without defect were sacrificed on the altar. Having the animal's blood sprinkled during the ceremony was a means to satisfy Yahweh, and was "a soothing aroma to the LORD" (Numbers 29:2, NASB).

As the fire within the chosen people's hearts burned to worship Yahweh, the flames and intensity were kept ablaze. We see from Ezra 3:4-5 that their participation in the various celebrations, festivals, and offerings was "continual." From the first day of their cultural month to the last day, the people of Israel realized the extreme intimate bonding and unity that could be established as they worshiped Yahweh as "one." The Hebrew word used for "freewill offering" is *n@dabah* (**ned-aw-BVAW**) and signifies that one is incited or impelled to give voluntarily. *Olah* (**o-LAW**) is the Hebrew word used that means "burnt offering." It signifies an ascent, stairway or steps, in conjunction with an offering used with fire. The imagery is of the smell rising upward toward the Lord, becoming a sweet aroma to His nostrils.

6 From the first day of the seventh month began they to offer burnt offerings unto the LORD. But the foundation of the temple of the LORD was not yet laid. 7 They gave money also unto the masons, and to the carpenters; and meat, and drink, and oil, unto them of Zidon, and to them of Tyre, to bring cedar trees from Lebanon to the sea of Joppa, according to the grant that they had of Cyrus king of Persia.

Worship of Yahweh at the altar remained constant and strong among the people of Israel. In particular, we have the burnt offering, which served as the primary sacrificial ceremony in reverence to the Lord. Another interesting addition pertains to the people groups aiding in the reconstruction of Yahweh's Temple. It must be recognized in at least the slightest sense, that non-Israelite people helped construct the Temple of God, even if they never physically worshiped there. Jeshua and Zerubbabel sought the support of the Sidonians and the Tyrians, without which obtaining the material to build the Temple would have been extremely difficult. This is simply following another pattern initiated by David and Solomon. David and Solomon both utilized the efforts of non-Israelites to construct the first Temple of God. In 1 Chronicles 22:2, we read how David gathered foreigners within the land of Israel to be stonecutters in the assisting of building the house of God. First Kings 9:20-21 depicts a more oppressive Solomon utilizing non-Israelites as slave workers in the building of the Temple. The descendants of the Jebusites, Amorites, Hittites, Hivites, and Perizzites were used as forced labor.

Sources:
DeGregorio, Scott, ed. "Footsteps of His Own: Bede's Commentary on Ezra - Nehemiah." *Innovation and Tradition in the Writings of Bede.* Morgantown, WVK: University of West Virginia Press, 2006. 143-168.
Bible Words – Phonetic Pronunciation. http://betterdays arecoming.html/ (accessed January 14, 2012).

Butler, Trent, gen. ed. *Holman Bible Dictionary.* Nashville, TN: Holman Bible Publishers, 1991. 39-40, 141-144.

McGee, J. Vernon. *Ezra, Nehemiah & Esther.* Pasadena, CA: Thru the Bible Radio Network, 1988.

Old Testament Hebrew Lexicon. http://www.BibleStudyTools.com/lexicons/Hebrew/kjv/ (accessed January 12, 2012).

Unger, Merrill F. "Erza." *The New Unger's Bible Handbook.* Revised by Gary Larson. Chicago, IL: Moody Bible Institute, Moody Publishers, 2005. 217-220.

Say It Correctly

Pentateuch. PEN-tuh-took.
Zerubbabel. zuh-RUB-uh-buhl, zuh-RUHB-uh-buhl.

Daily Bible Reading

MONDAY
Jesus' Lament over Jerusalem
(Matthew 23:29–39)

TUESDAY
The Coming Judgment
(Jeremiah 7:30—8:3)

WEDNESDAY
Jerusalem Falls to the Babylonians
(2 Kings 24:1–12)

THURSDAY
The Destruction of Jerusalem
(2 Chronicles 36:15–21)

FRIDAY
Rebuild a House for God
(Ezra 1:1–8)

SATURDAY
The People Respond
(Ezra 2:64–70)

SUNDAY
Restoring the Worship of God
(Ezra 3:1–7)

Teaching Tips

July 7
Bible Study Guide 6

Words You Should Know
A. House (Ezra 3:8, 9, 11, 12) *bayith* (Heb.)—Mansion, palace, or dwelling place.
B. Remnant (v. 8) *sh@'ar* (Heb.)—The remainder, the residue or survivors.

Teacher Preparation
Unifying Principle—Finding Joy in Restoration. When the returned Israelite exiles laid the foundation stones to restore the Temple, they rejoiced and gave thanks to God with weeping, shouting, and playing of trumpets and cymbals.
A. Pray for your students and lesson clarity.
B. Study and meditate on the entire text.
C. Prepare a PowerPoint presentation or bring news clippings of recent events where there has been restoration after damage (e.g., natural disasters, civil unrest, etc.).

O—Open the Lesson
A. Open with prayer, including the Aim for Change.
B. Introduce today's subject.
C. Read the Aim for Change and Keep in Mind verse in unison. Discuss.
D. Share your presentation.
E. Ask, "Have you experienced a moment of defeat, failure, or brokenness?"
F. Allow volunteers to share their testimonies. Discuss their restoration.
G. Have a volunteer summarize the In Focus Story. Discuss.

P—Present the Scriptures
A. Have volunteers read the Focal Verses.
B. Use The People, Places, and Times; Background; Search the Scriptures; At-A-Glance outline; In Depth; and More Light on the Text to clarify the verses.

E—Explore the Meaning
A. Summarize the Discuss the Meaning, Lesson in Our Society, and Make It Happen sections.
B. Connect these sections to the Aim for Change and the Keep in Mind verse.

N—Next Steps for Application
A. Summarize the lesson.
B. Close with prayer.

Worship Guide

For the Superintendent or Teacher
Theme: Temple Restored
Song: "Shout Unto God"
Devotional Reading: Psalm 66:1-12
Prayer

Temple Restored

Bible Background • EZRA 3:8-13
Printed Text • EZRA 3:8-13 | Devotional Reading • PSALM 66:1-12

Aim for Change

By the end of the lesson, we will: KNOW that we should find joy in restoration; FEEL joy in restoration; and PRAISE God for restoration.

In Focus

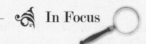

Betty thought she would never live to see this day come: an African-American inaugurated as president of the United States. At 75 years old, she had seen and lived through her share of injustices. She also recalled horrible stories of racism from her parents and foreparents who were slaves. Betty saved her money and God made special provision for her to make it to Washington, D.C., to attend the inauguration festivities. Betty took her granddaughter, Ashley, to teach her the importance of this moment in history. As the president was sworn in, Betty was overwhelmed with joy and began to cry. She reflected on the years of oppression and degradation of her people, as well as the sacrifices made to make this day possible. When the ceremony concluded, she shouted for joy and praised God for His goodness.

God's Word promises that He would cause us to triumph in His name and bring us to a place of victory. In today's lesson, we will read how God uses Jeshua, the Levitical priests, and Zerubbabel, the governor of Jerusalem, to restore the Temple of God after returning from exile in Babylon.

Keep in Mind

"And they sang together by course in praising and giving thanks unto the LORD; because he is good, for his mercy endureth for ever toward Israel. And all the people shouted with a great shout, when they praised the LORD, because the foundation of the house of the LORD was laid" (Ezra 3:11).

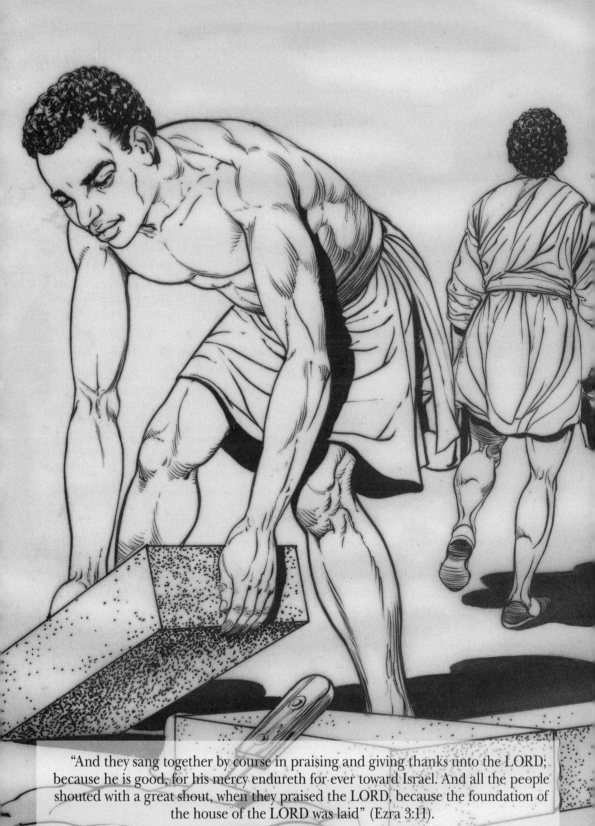

"And they sang together by course in praising and giving thanks unto the LORD; because he is good, for his mercy endureth for ever toward Israel. And all the people shouted with a great shout, when they praised the LORD, because the foundation of the house of the LORD was laid" (Ezra 3:11).

Focal Verses

KJV **Ezra 3:8** Now in the second year of their coming unto the house of God at Jerusalem, in the second month, began Zerubbabel the son of Shealtiel, and Jeshua the son of Jozadak, and the remnant of their brethren the priests and the Levites, and all they that were come out of the captivity unto Jerusalem; and appointed the Levites, from twenty years old and upward, to set forward the work of the house of the LORD.

9 Then stood Jeshua with his sons and his brethren, Kadmiel and his sons, the sons of Judah, together, to set forward the workmen in the house of God: the sons of Henadad, with their sons and their brethren the Levites.

10 And when the builders laid the foundation of the temple of the LORD, they set the priests in their apparel with trumpets, and the Levites the sons of Asaph with cymbals, to praise the LORD, after the ordinance of David king of Israel.

11 And they sang together by course in praising and giving thanks unto the LORD; because he is good, for his mercy endureth for ever toward Israel. And all the people shouted with a great shout, when they praised the LORD, because the foundation of the house of the LORD was laid.

12 But many of the priests and Levites and chief of the fathers, who were ancient men, that had seen the first house, when the foundation of this house was laid before their eyes, wept with a loud voice; and many shouted aloud for joy:

13 So that the people could not discern the noise of the shout of joy from the noise of the weeping of the people: for the people shouted with a loud shout, and the noise was heard afar off.

NLT **Ezra 3:8** The construction of the Temple of God began in midspring, during the second year after they arrived in Jerusalem. The work force was made up of everyone who had returned from exile, including Zerubbabel son of Shealtiel, Jeshua son of Jehozadak and his fellow priests, and all the Levites. The Levites who were twenty years old or older were put in charge of rebuilding the LORD's Temple.

9 The workers at the Temple of God were supervised by Jeshua with his sons and relatives, and Kadmiel and his sons, all descendants of Hodaviah. They were helped in this task by the Levites of the family of Henadad.

10 When the builders completed the foundation of the LORD's Temple, the priests put on their robes and took their places to blow their trumpets. And the Levites, descendants of Asaph, clashed their cymbals to praise the LORD, just as King David had prescribed.

11 With praise and thanks, they sang this song to the LORD: "He is so good! His faithful love for Israel endures forever!" Then all the people gave a great shout, praising the LORD because the foundation of the LORD's Temple had been laid.

12 But many of the older priests, Levites, and other leaders who had seen the first Temple wept aloud when they saw the new Temple's foundation. The others, however, were shouting for joy.

13 The joyful shouting and weeping mingled together in a loud noise that could be heard far in the distance.

The People, Places, and Times

Jeshua. A high priest of Judah, Jeshua (also called Joshua) was born during the exile of the Jews in Babylon (587-538 B.C.). Before the exile, high priests had been subordinate to the kings of Judah. But when King Cyrus of Persia permitted the Jews to return to Jerusalem and rebuild their Temple, Jeshua assumed a major leadership role along with the Jewish governor, Zerubbabel, who remained subject to the Persian ruler. Together, the pair saw to it that an altar was erected and worship restored in Jerusalem.

Levites. Descendants of Levi served as assistants to the priests in the worship system of the nation of Israel. As a Levite, Aaron and his sons and their descendants were charged with the responsibility of the priesthood, offering burnt offerings and leading the people in worship and confession.

Background

The book of Ezra is an account of Jewish history, which records their release from their 70 years of exile in Babylon as prophesied by Jeremiah (Jeremiah 25:11) and the return of the first wave of Jews in 537 B.C. through the second wave in 457-458 B.C. The first half of Ezra chronicles the rebuilding of the Temple after its destruction in 586 B.C. under the leadership of Jeshua, the high priest, and Zerubbabel, the governor of Jerusalem. One of the key tasks of these leaders in restoring the temple is to reinstitute worship according to the Law of Moses by offering up sacrifices unto God. The people were called upon to consecrate themselves and submit freewill offerings unto the Lord as well as provide the resources and talent to rebuild the Temple (Ezra 3:1-7). By the hand of God, the Jews also received favor from King Cyrus as he brought back the vessel of worship taken from the house of the Lord that King

Nebuchadnezzar stole during their conquest (Ezra 1:7). Restoring worship and honor to God was very important to accomplishing the task of rebuilding the Temple and turning the people's hearts back to God, since their captivity was a consequence of their idolatry.

At-A-Glance

1. The Temple Work Begins
(Ezra 3:8-9)
2. The Temple Work Incites Praise
(vv. 10-11)
3. The Temple Work Sparks Lament
and Joy (vv. 12-13)

In Depth

1. The Temple Work Begins (Ezra 3:8-9)

Jeshua, the the high priest, and the Levitical priesthood set the tone for the work ahead through worship—putting God in His rightful place after years of captivity. Jeshua and Zerubbabel, governor of Jerusalem under King Cyrus' rule, led the way by appointing men 20 years old and older to supervise the work of restoring the house of God. As the first wave of Jews returned from exile in Babylon, there was no question about their first task: to restore the place where the presence of the Lord dwelled. The rebuilding of the Temple was the first step in regaining their statehood as a nation again under God's protective covering.

Ezra 3:7 noted that money was given to the contractors (artisans, carpenters, and masons) and food, drink, and oil given to neighboring provinces (Tyre and Zidon) to allow for safe passage of construction materials between ports in Lebanon and Joppa. King Cyrus of Persia, who was under God's orchestration, provided authorization and gave the order. As the people worshiped, God made provision for the work of the Temple to begin; in the natural and in the spirit, the foundation was laid.

2. The Temple Work Incites Praise (vv. 10-11)

As the foundation of the temple is restored, the Levitical priesthood continues in a posture of worship by adorning their vestments; specifically, the Levitical priests and descendants of Asaph led the charge of praise as outlined by King David. The priest blew the trumpets as a signal of victory and the descendants of Asaph, who historically have been noted as musicians and singers played the cymbals (1 Chronicles 15:16-19). It was absolutely in order for worship to accompany the repair of the foundation, and as this monumental event occurred, it evoked the people's praise to God.

Taking a page from David's psalm book, they gave thanks unto the Lord for His goodness and mercy, which endures forever (Psalm 136:1, 11). As the foundation was laid, the Children of Israel were boisterous in their praise and shouted unto God with a voice of triumph. After 70 years in captivity, many who survived did not think they would ever see their homeland again; therefore, it was a joyous occasion to witness a new beginning—God's restoration at work in their lives. When we think of the goodness of the Lord and all that He has done for us, it should evoke praise in our heart as well. Throughout God's Word, we see examples of His loving-kindness to restore and redeem His people. In fact, God's very nature is one of mercy and grace. The greatest example of God's grace is His redemptive work through Jesus Christ our Lord to accomplish His original intent to commune with humanity.

3. The Temple Work Sparks Lament and Joy (vv. 12-13)

While there was great joy in the repair of the Temple's foundation, it was also met with sadness. In verse 12, the *King James Version* uses the term "ancient men" to accentuate that the tribal fathers who had seen the glory of the former house wept loudly as the foundation of the restored Temple was laid. Having witnessed the splendor of the former Temple and because of the consequences of their sins that had led them into captivity in the first place, these elders may have grieved, but at the same time they recognized the goodness of God and longed for His presence again. The praises and lamenting were intertwined and not discernable between the two because both were loud. There are times in worship where you may be in awe of the presence of God and His goodness, but also there is a realization of your sinfulness. We are bound in this realm and limited in our level of experience of God's presence. However, as our spirits yearn to be in His matchless presence, the Holy Spirit (who gives us a foretaste of what's to come) makes intercession for us with groans and moans that are too deep to discern (Romans 8:18-27). Regardless of the context of our cry, we can be confident that our Father hears our heart and cares about the cry (Psalm 34:17).

Search the Scriptures

Fill in the blanks.

1. "And when the _____ laid the _____ of the temple of the LORD, they set the priests in their _____ with trumpets ..." (Ezra 3:10).

2. "And they _____ together by course in _____ and giving

_____ unto the LORD; because he is _____, for his _____ endureth for ever toward Israel" (v. 11).

Discuss the Meaning

1. What was the significance of having men ages 20 and older supervise the restoration of the Temple?

2. Discuss the role of praise and worship in the restoration of the Temple.

3. Why do you think the ancient men wept and shouted once the foundation was laid?

Lesson in Our Society

As a nation, particularly as people of African descent, we have seen hard times and tribulation. We have known the thrill of victory and the agony of defeat, but through it all God has been and continues to be faithful. In recent history, natural disasters such as hurricanes and tornadoes have devastated the South, and most notably affected were the poor and disenfranchised. However, as we avail ourselves to God as His instruments, He has used people as an extension of His love to be a helping hand to those in need to restore lives. God has placed in all of us a resilience to overcome adversity by trusting in His faithfulness, so when we see the hand of God move on our behalf, a release of joy and gratitutde to God must be automatic.

Make It Happen

Reflect on a time in your life when you have seen God move on your behalf to restore you after a moment of defeat or failure. How did you feel? Recall your praise unto God, and as an act of worship, ask in prayer where He can use you to be a light in dark places to restore someone else in need.

Follow the Spirit

What God wants me to do:

_____

_____

_____

_____

_____

Remember Your Thoughts

Special insights I have learned:

_____

_____

_____

_____

More Light on the Text

Ezra 3:8-13

8 Now in the second year of their coming unto the house of God at Jerusalem, in the second month, began Zerubbabel the son of Shealtiel, and Jeshua the son of Jozadak, and the remnant of their brethren the priests and the Levites, and all they that were come out of the captivity unto Jerusalem; and appointed the Levites, from twenty years old and upward, to set forward the work of the house of the LORD. 9 Then stood Jeshua with his sons and his brethren, Kadmiel and his sons, the sons of Judah, together, to set forward the workmen in the house of God: the sons of Henadad, with their sons and their brethren the Levites.

After receiving clearance from King Cyrus to rebuild (Ezra 1:1-5), the work began in the second year (537 B.C.) of the second month, which according to the Hebrew calendar *Iyar* (**EE-yahr**) or *Ziv* (**zeev**), was

April-May. Zerubbabel, who was a Jew and governor of Jerusalem, represented the government's involvement in the repairing of the Temple and Jeshua, who was the high priest, represented the interest of the Temple. They worked in partnership in providing the leadership needed to bring restoration to the Children of Israel. After release from captivity, the rebuilding of the Temple marked a new beginning for the Jewish people. They had been unable to truly worship God (due to their own waywardness), but God is gracious in how He allowed them to endure captivity with the promise of their return to their own land and house of worship.

The remnant of the priests, and those from the Levite tribe ages 20 and older were called upon to supervise the work of rebuilding the temple. Because the Levitical priesthood and their brethren were keepers of the Law and servants of the temple, who better to ensure the work to rebuild the former house of God was done to specifications? The artisans, carpenters, and masons completed the manual labor and the Levites led the way and ensured that the project was funded and managed and that worship was reinstituted (Ezra 3:3-7).

10 And when the builders laid the foundation of the temple of the LORD, they set the priests in their apparel with trumpets, and the Levites the sons of Asaph with cymbals, to praise the LORD, after the ordinance of David king of Israel. 11 And they sang together by course in praising and giving thanks unto the LORD; because he is good, for his mercy endureth for ever toward Israel. And all the people shouted with a great shout, when they praised the LORD, because the foundation of the house of the LORD was laid.

As the builders laid the "foundation" (Heb. *yacad*, **yaw-SAD**), the priests and the descendants of Asaph (*'acaph*, **aw-SAWF**) brought music into this momentous occasion to restore the joy of God's people and mark that the construction of God's house was under way. The priesthood, adorned in their garments of linen, was in charge of leading the praise unto God, calling the people to assemble according to the order given by God to Moses. They blew the trumpets (Numbers 10:1-10). Children of Asaph, who were also descendants of the tribe of Levi and recorded in the Scriptures to be musicians and singers (1 Chronicles 15:16-19), were in charge of the cymbals. King David was a worshiper and knew how to get God's attention. He left his music as a legacy for ongoing acts of worship in the Temple and it remains applicable today.

Music is always used to usher in the presence of the Lord. Taking a page out of King David's hymn book, the people sang together and rejoiced in the Lord for His goodness and loving-kindness as they were now free to worship (1 Chronicles 16:34; Psalm 106:1; 107:1; 118:1; 136:1). David opened these hymns of praise unto God to acknowledge that He is always faithful. Although the Children of Israel ended up in exile for their sins (rebellion, idolatry, and waywardness) for 70 years, God remained true to His covenant promises to their forefathers Abraham, Isaac, Jacob, and David, and it was truly a celebration to return to their homeland and rebuild.

The people shouted unto God with a voice of triumph. When God brings about great deliverance, it should evoke a clamorous and rousing praise of gratitude for He inhabits the praises of His people (Psalm 22:2-4). Psalm 149:3, 5 exhorts, "Let them praise his name in the dance: let them sing praises unto him with the timbrel and harp.

Let the saints be joyful in glory: let them sing aloud upon their beds." We are to be vigilant in making a joyful noise unto the Lord and celebrate Him in good times and bad.

12 But many of the priests and Levites and chief of the fathers, who were ancient men, that had seen the first house, when the foundation of this house was laid before their eyes, wept with a loud voice; and many shouted aloud for joy: 13 So that the people could not discern the noise of the shout of joy from the noise of the weeping of the people: for the people shouted with a loud shout, and the noise was heard afar off.

Many of the priests and Levitical tribal elders, who were called "ancient (older) men," openly wept as they were overcome with mixed emotions of joy and grief. They witnessed the first version of the Temple so the reason for the grief could have been twofold: sadness over their sin, which was the result of the demise of the first Temple as well remembrance of its former glory. Solomon received everything he needed from his father, David, to build the first structure (1 Chronicles 28:10-19; 29:2-3); needless to say, the rebuilding would pale by comparison. In addition, their deliverance from captivity in Babylon and return to the land of their heritage brought shouts of great joy. The wailing and rejoicing could not be discerned, and they were loud.

Sources:
Attridge, Harold W. and Wayne A. Meeks, eds. *The Harper Collins Study Bible, New Revised Standard.* New York, NY: Harper Collins Publishers, 2006. 652.
Bible Words — Phonetic Pronunciation. http://www.betterdaysarecoming.com/bible/pronunciation.html (accessed May 24, 2011).
Old Testament Hebrew Lexicon. http://www.BibleStudyTools.com/lexicons/Hebrew/kjv/ (accessed January 12, 2012).
Strong, James. *The New Strong's Exhaustive Concordance of the Bible.* Nashville, TN: Thomas Nelson, 1990. 57.

Zodhiates, Spiros, Th.D. and Warren Baker, D.R.E., eds. *Key Word Study Bible, King James Version.* Chattanooga, TN: AMG Publishers, 1991. 625, 1602, 1663.

Say It Correctly

Jeshua. JESH-yoo-uh.
Shealtiel.
shee-AL-tee-uhl, shee-AL-tee-el.

Daily Bible Readings

MONDAY
A Great and Wonderful House
(2 Chronicles 2:1-9)

TUESDAY
Building a House for God's Name
(1 Kings 8:14-21)

WEDNESDAY
My Name Shall Be There
(1 Kings 8:22-30)

THURSDAY
A House of Prayer
(Matthew 21:10-16)

FRIDAY
Make a Joyful Noise to God
(Psalm 66:1-12)

SATURDAY
Lead Me in Your Righteousness
(Psalm 5)

SUNDAY
Tears of Joy
(Ezra 3:8-13)

Teaching Tips

Words You Should Know

A. Dedication (Ezra 6:16, 17) *chanukka'* (Heb./Aram.)—An inauguration, a dedicatory sacrifice.

B. Passover (vv. 19, 20) *pecach* (Heb.)—A sparing, an exemption, an immunity from penalty and calamity.

Teacher Preparation

Unifying Principle—Celebrating with Joy. The Temple was special to the Israelites because God commanded them to rebuild it, and because it gave them a place to commemorate with worship their original freedom from Egyptian bondage, and more recently, their Babylonian exile.

A. Read the entire lesson.

B. Pray for your students.

C. Complete the companion lesson in the *Precepts For Living Personal Study Guide®*.

O—Open the Lesson

A. Open with prayer, including the Aim for Change.

B. After prayer, introduce today's subject of the lesson.

C. Have your students read the Aim for Change and Keep in Mind verse in unison. Discuss.

D. Allow volunteers to share their testimonies of their personal encounters with God through worship.

E. Now have a volunteer summarize the In Focus story. Discuss.

F. Then ask, "Is there a physical space or place that you have dedicated to God (e.g., a walking trail, special room in your home)?" Discuss.

P—Present the Scriptures

A. Have volunteers read the Focal Verses.

B. Now use The People, Places, and Times; Background; Search the Scriptures; At-A-Glance outline; In Depth; and More Light on the Text to clarify the verses.

E—Explore the Meaning

A. Have volunteers summarize the Discuss the Meaning, Lesson in Our Society, and Make It Happen sections.

B. Connect these sections to the Aim for Change and the Keep in Mind verse.

N—Next Steps for Application

A. Summarize the lesson.

B. Close with payer.

Worship Guide

For the Superintendent or Teacher
Theme: Dedication of the Temple
Song: "You're Welcome Here"
Devotional Reading: Ezra 5:1-5
Prayer

Dedication of the Temple

Bible Background • EZRA 6
Printed Text • EZRA 6:13–22 | Devotional Reading • EZRA 5:1-5

——————— Aim for Change ———————

By the end of the lesson, we will: UNDERSTAND that we should celebrate with joy what God has done in our lives; DESIRE to celebrate God's blessings with joy; and CELEBRATE God's blessings with joy.

———————  In Focus ———————

James and Valerie have been waiting on the Lord for a new home. Valerie, in the second trimester of her pregnancy, did not want to raise their child in a tiny apartment. Valerie's dad asked James, "What are your plans, son? You're going to be a father and the baby will be here before you know it." James asked his father-in-law to agree in prayer for God's favor as they searched for a home. James found what he thought was the perfect home not too far from Valerie's parents in an area with a good school district. After fasting and prayer, James and Valerie heard from the Lord and decided to move forward. God gave them favor with the bank, and they were able to get a mortgage and purchase a new home. Not only did they have enough room for the baby, but they decided that they would make sure to always have a prayer closet that they dedicated to the Lord for His many wonderful blessings. They hosted a housewarming party, inviting family and friends over to celebrate with them; they rejoiced in the Lord for always giving them what they needed.

In today's lesson, we will study how the Children of Israel celebrated the successful rebuilding and dedication of God's Temple just in time for Passover.

JULY 14th

——————— Keep in Mind ———————

"And the children of Israel, the priests, and the Levites, and the rest of the children of the captivity, kept the dedication of this house of God with joy"
(Ezra 6:16).

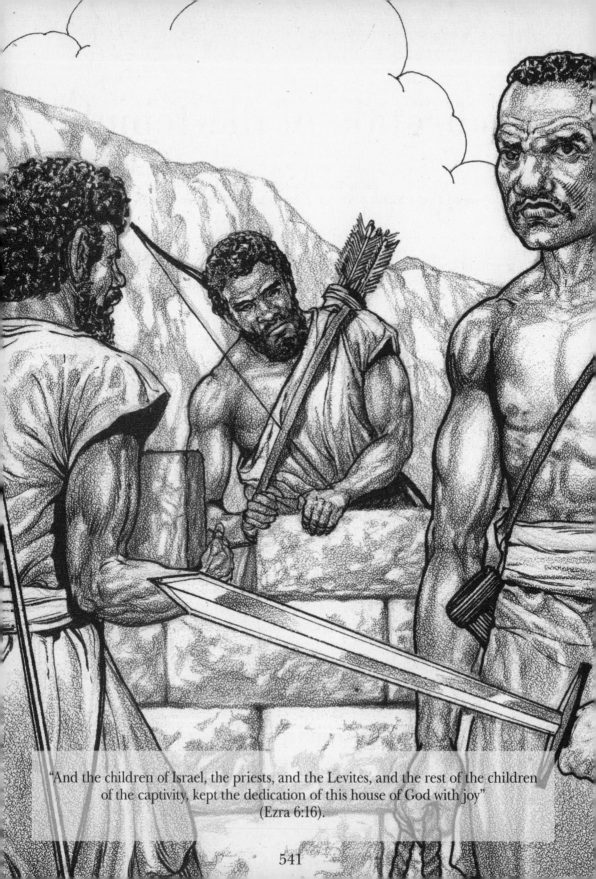

"And the children of Israel, the priests, and the Levites, and the rest of the children of the captivity, kept the dedication of this house of God with joy" (Ezra 6:16).

Focal Verses

KJV **Ezra 6:13** Then Tatnai, governor on this side the river, Shetharboznai, and their companions, according to that which Darius the king had sent, so they did speedily.

14 And the elders of the Jews builded, and they prospered through the prophesying of Haggai the prophet and Zechariah the son of Iddo. And they builded, and finished it, according to the commandment of the God of Israel, and according to the commandment of Cyrus, and Darius, and Artaxerxes king of Persia.

15 And this house was finished on the third day of the month Adar, which was in the sixth year of the reign of Darius the king.

16 And the children of Israel, the priests, and the Levites, and the rest of the children of the captivity, kept the dedication of this house of God with joy.

17 And offered at the dedication of this house of God an hundred bullocks, two hundred rams, four hundred lambs; and for a sin offering for all Israel, twelve he goats, according to the number of the tribes of Israel.

18 And they set the priests in their divisions, and the Levites in their courses, for the service of God, which is at Jerusalem; as it is written in the book of Moses.

19 And the children of the captivity kept the passover upon the fourteenth day of the first month.

20 For the priests and the Levites were purified together, all of them were pure, and killed the passover for all the children of the captivity, and for their brethren the priests, and for themselves.

NLT **Ezra 6:13** Tattenai, governor of the province west of the Euphrates River, and Shethar-bozenai and their colleagues complied at once with the command of King Darius.

14 So the Jewish elders continued their work, and they were greatly encouraged by the preaching of the prophets Haggai and Zechariah son of Iddo. The Temple was finally finished, as had been commanded by the God of Israel and decreed by Cyrus, Darius, and Artaxerxes, the kings of Persia.

15 The Temple was completed on March 12, during the sixth year of King Darius's reign.

16 The Temple of God was then dedicated with great joy by the people of Israel, the priests, the Levites, and the rest of the people who had returned from exile.

17 During the dedication ceremony for the Temple of God, 100 young bulls, 200 rams, and 400 male lambs were sacrificed. And 12 male goats were presented as a sin offering for the twelve tribes of Israel.

18 Then the priests and Levites were divided into their various divisions to serve at the Temple of God in Jerusalem, as prescribed in the Book of Moses.

19 On April 21, the returned exiles celebrated Passover.

20 The priests and Levites had purified themselves and were ceremonially clean. So they slaughtered the Passover lamb for all the returned exiles, for their fellow priests, and for themselves.

21 The Passover meal was eaten by the people of Israel who had returned from exile and by the others in the land who had turned from their immoral customs to worship the LORD, the God of Israel.

KJV continued

21 And the children of Israel, which were come again out of captivity, and all such as had separated themselves unto them from the filthiness of the heathen of the land, to seek the LORD God of Israel, did eat,

22 And kept the feast of unleavened bread seven days with joy: for the LORD had made them joyful, and turned the heart of the king of Assyria unto them, to strengthen their hands in the work of the house of God, the God of Israel.

NLT continued

22 Then they celebrated the Festival of Unleavened Bread for seven days. There was great joy throughout the land because the LORD had caused the king of Assyria to be favorable to them, so that he helped them to rebuild the Temple of God, the God of Israel.

The People, Places, and Times

King Darius. Darius the Great reigned from about 522 to 485 B.C. He was one of the most able Persian kings and is also known as Darius Hystaspes, or Darius, son of Hystaspes. Darius continued Cyrus' great policy of restoring the Jewish people to their homeland. In 520 B.C., Darius' second year as king, the Jews resumed work on the still-unfinished Temple in Jerusalem. Darius assisted with the project by ordering it to continue and even sending a generous subsidy to help restore worship in the temple. The temple was completed in 515 B.C. in the sixth year of Darius' reign.

Sin Offering. Also known as the guilt offering, it was a most holy sacrifice presented for intentional and unintentional sins of individuals as well as the priest and whole congregation (Leviticus 4-5). On the Day of Atonement, it was made with special solemnity as the priests made atonement for their sins and the sins of the people (Leviticus 16:3-11). The sin offering was representative of repentance and the appeal for divine forgiveness, and its acceptance marked continued fellowship and relationship with God.

Background

After release from captivity in Babylon for 70 years, King Cyrus issued a decree in 538 B.C., giving clearance for the Children of Israel to rebuild the temple (Ezra 1:1-4). The work was under way when the contingency was met with resistance from neighboring provinces. The foundation of the rebuilding of the Temple was laid, but the work was halted under Artaxerxes's reign between 537 to 520 B.C. (Ezra 4).

Within the second year of the reign of King Darius, he reviewed the documents issued by King Cyrus and reversed the previous ruling by King Artaxerxes (Ezra 4:24). King Darius issued a decree (Ezra 6:8, NIV): "Moreover, I hereby decree what you are to do for these elders of the Jews in the construction of this house of God."

The expenses of these men were to be fully paid out of the royal treasury. God's justice prevailed; He not only provided favor with the king to complete the work, but made sure they had more than enough to do it at someone else's expense. As we embark on today's lesson, we will study the celebration of the completed work and how the Children of Israel memorialized this God-given victory.

At-A-Glance

1. The People Dedicate the New Temple
(Ezra 6:13-16)
2. The People Offer Sacrifices to God
for the New Temple (vv. 17-18)
3. The People Celebrate Passover in the
New Temple (vv. 19-22)

In Depth

1. The People Dedicate the New Temple (Ezra 6:13-16)

After years of delays and setbacks, the Second Temple of God was finally completed! King Darius ordered that the work not only be completed, but that the neighboring provinces would provide the Children of Israel with whatever they needed. They rejoiced not because in their own strength they had accomplished something, but because of the favor of the Lord, which had been upon them as they sought to honor God by reinstituting the worship. It was a time to celebrate. To start a work and see it to completion is a sign of the grace of the Most High. How many times have we completed a task after many struggles and then got it in our heads that it is by our own strength that we were able to complete the task? How wrong-headed we humans can be!

The Temple of God was completed by God's command, not by human authority alone as He worked through humanity. From the touching of the heart of Cyrus to the decision of Darius to command the completion of the work, it was all of God. We can learn from these past people of God. Having completed the building by the power of God, it was logical to dedicate the building back to God. It was God who initiated the project by His Spirit. It was God who guided their hands to its completion. The house belonged to God. All our victories, all our accomplishments, all our celebratory possibilities are because God has favored us. The Children of Israel, the priests, and the Levites were excited and filled with joy. Rebuilding the Temple was by no means a small feat. It took unity, hard work, and dedicated people to bring it to pass. God had given the word to go forth; now it was their turn to finish the work. What a great victory—now it was time to praise God!

2. The People Offer Sacrifices to God for the New Temple (vv. 17-18)

The Children of Israel brought an offering unto God as a part of the dedication ceremony of the new Temple. Reinstituting worship was critical to their rededication as a nation to the ways of God. Following the model of how the first Temple of God was dedicated by Solomon, the Children of Israel were doing things in order and according to what was written in the books of Moses. Their sacrifices were an expression of their joy and gratitude at the grace of a God who had restored them from exile and brought them back in fellowship with Him. Sacrificial offerings in the Old Testament were a means to atone for human sins and restore people back to God. The sin offering is particularly noted because everyone from the priests to the congregation at large had to confess their sins and turn away from them as the House of God was dedicated. Jesus, the perfect sacrifice, did away with all of that when He died for us once and for all on the Cross. The Children of Israel offered what is called a "sin offering." This included the blood from bullocks, rams, lambs, and goats.

3. The People Celebrate Passover in the New Temple (vv. 19-22)

The dedication of the Temple was representative of second exodus for the Children of Israel. Having been freed from captivity and delivered from the house of exile were causes of great celebration, which was marked approximately by the Passover. The Passover as celebrated by Hebrew people is the archetype (or pattern) of divine intervention in the life of God's people. It was the 14th day of the first month, and everyone was ceremonially clean. The Levites slaughtered the Passover lamb for all the exiles, for their brothers, the priests, and for themselves.

After offering atonement for their sins, the Children of Israel and those converted to Judaism were commanded to consecrate themselves: that is, remove all filthiness and the unclean practices of their Gentile neighbors in order to seek the Lord their God. This time of consecration was very important for the abiding presence of the Lord. Therefore, they had to clear their hearts and minds from anything that would be displeasing to Him as this new edifice was dedicated in honor of Him. For seven days, they celebrated with joy the Feast of Unleavened Bread because the Lord had filled them with joy by changing the attitude of the king of Assyria, so that he assisted them in the work on the House of God, the God of Israel. The Lord is the true source of all joy, and when we have His favor, He gives peace (Proverbs 16:7). When the Lord blesses us to complete a task, included in the celebration must be a rededication of our lives to God as an act of true worship.

Search the Scriptures

Fill in the blanks.

1. "And the _____ _____ _____, the priests, and the _____, and the rest of the children of the captivity, kept the dedication of this _____

_____ _____ with joy" (Ezra 6:16).

2. "For the priests and the Levites were _____ together, all of them were _____, and killed the _____ for all the children of the captivity, and for their _____ the priests, and for themselves" (v. 20).

3. "And kept the _____ of _____ bread seven days with _____: for the Lord had made them _____" (v. 22).

Discuss the Meaning

1. What was the significance of the offerings unto the Lord, particularly the sin offering, as the new Temple was dedicated?

2. Discuss why the Passover celebration was especially meaningful as the new Temple was dedicated. Why do you think it was important to keep the Passover?

3. Why do you think the Scripture notes in Ezra 6:22 that the Lord "made them joyful"?

Lesson in Our Society

So often the picture of Christianity to the world is so solemn and devoid of joy that it does not reflect the true life the Lord Jesus came to give us. While we are to be mindful and reverent of God and His presence, this reverence does not mean that God does not want us to express His joy in our hearts at all times, especially when we experience great victory in His name. As Christians, we are to make His name great, and nothing magnifies Him more than when we celebrate with joy the wonderful things He has done for us.

Make It Happen

As we have seen in today's lesson, there is a time and place for everything as we worship the Lord as a lifestyle. Here's an opportunity to make every effort to live life in balance, remembering that by grace we are saved and not of ourselves. It is the gift of God. Therefore, we should boast in the Lord for His goodness. Practice boasting in the Lord this week with great joy, giving Him glory for everything in your life.

Follow the Spirit

What God wants me to do:

_____

_____

_____

_____

Remember Your Thoughts

Special insights I have learned:

_____

_____

_____

_____

More Light on the Text

Ezra 6:13-22

13 Then Tatnai, governor on this side the river, Shetharboznai, and their companions, according to that which Darius the king had sent, so they did speedily. 14 And the elders of the Jews builded, and they prospered through the prophesying of Haggai the prophet and Zechariah the son of Iddo. And they builded, and finished it, according to the commandment of the God of Israel, and according to the commandment of Cyrus, and Darius, and Artaxerxes king of Persia.

When the Jews originally started work on rebuilding the temple, non-Jewish settlers from neighboring provinces, possibly Samaritans as well as Assyrians, opposed them. The envoys from these provinces sent a letter to then King Artaxerxes (**ar-tuh-ZURK-seez**), informing him of the supposed danger of allowing the Jews to complete their work and noting concern that they would not pay tribute to the king. Artaxerxes agreed with these adversaries and ordered all work to come to an immediate halt. The letter that the Samaritans sent to the king was written in Aramaic. Ezra quotes the letter in the language it was written in and continues writing in Aramaic through chapter 6, verse 8. (Aramaic was the language the Jews had picked up in Persia.)

Work on the Temple stopped for 16 years until God sent His prophets Haggai and Zechariah, during the second year of the reign of Darius of Persia, to encourage the Jews to resume the rebuilding of the temple (Haggai 1:1-3; Zechariah 1:1-3). Under the leadership of Zerubbabel (a governor) and Jeshua (the high priest), the people immediately went back to work rebuilding the Temple (Ezra 5:1-2).

Tatnai and Shetharboznai complied with the king's decree and work on the temple continued and prospered through the prophesying of Haggai and Zechariah. "Prophesying" is a translation of the Aramaic *n@buw'ah* (**neb-oo-aw**) and refers to preaching, teaching, or predicting the future. This word only appears in Ezra 6:14. The phrase "through the prophesying" in verse 14 points out that this great and unexpected success was not to be credited to chance or to King Darius' kindness but to God alone. It was God acting through His prophets, who had required and encouraged the people to proceed in the work, and it was His mighty power that moved Darius' heart to allow the work to continue.

"According to the commandment," the order of various decrees to build the temple was established. Here the writer reviews the different rulers who favored the Jews in their return from captivity and the rebuilding of the Temple.

15 And this house was finished on the third day of the month Adar, which was in the sixth year of the reign of Darius the king. 16 And the children of Israel, the priests, and the Levites, and the rest of the children of the captivity, kept the dedication of this house of God with joy.

Four years later, on March 12, 515 B.C. in the sixth year of the reign of Darius, the temple was completed—20 years after the foundation had been laid during under the reign of Cyrus. The Ark of the Covenant containing the two tablets of the Law was not in the new temple. The Ark had apparently been lost or destroyed at some unknown time in the past.

The Israelites celebrated the dedication of the Temple with a great feast similar to the one that Solomon had when he dedicated the original temple (1 Kings 8:22-23). The reference in Ezra 6:16 to the "children of Israel" affirms that there were members of the northern kingdom of Israel who returned from Babylonian captivity along with the vast majority from the southern kingdom of Judah. The priests and the Levites led the temple dedication. Of the 12 tribes, the tribe of Levi was set aside for ritual religious service. Within the tribe of Levi, only those descended from the bloodline of Aaron could serve as priests. Other families from the tribe were assigned various duties linked with tabernacle or Temple worship.

17 And offered at the dedication of this house of God an hundred bullocks, two hundred rams, four hundred lambs; and for a sin offering for all Israel, twelve he goats, according to the number of the tribes of Israel.

The Hebrew/Aramaic word for "dedication" is *chanukka'* (**chan-ook-KAW**). Jews today have a different holiday called Hanukkah. The Old Testament emphasizes the dedication ceremonies that inaugurated the use of something for God's service. The sin offering at the dedication consisted of 100 male bulls, 200 rams, and 400 male lambs. Solomon offered 200 times more animals at the dedication of the original Temple, but because of their poverty the offering was accepted. Their hundreds meant much more to them than Solomon's thousands.

The "sin offering" (from the Aramaic) is the equivalent of the Hebrew *chatta'ah* (**khat-taw-AW**). The sin offering as explained in Leviticus 4:3-8 was a sacrifice made by those who committed a sin unintentionally, or out of weakness or negligence as opposed to outright rebellion against God.

18 And they set the priests in their divisions, and the Levites in their courses, for the service of God, which is at Jerusalem; as it is written in the book of Moses. 19 And the children of the captivity kept the passover upon the fourteenth day of the first month.

King David divided the descendants of Aaron, who served as priests, into 24 classes as the basis for rotating priestly duties (1 Chronicles 24:1-3, 7-19). Some of the classes died out or had to be consolidated with others, and new ones were formed to take their places. In the return from exile, only four registered classes were represented (Ezra 2:36-39). By the time of

Nehemiah's return, 22 classes had been reinstated (Nehemiah 10:2-8). The Levites were also divided into groups, or courses, corresponding to the bloodlines of Gershon, Kohath, and Merari (Exodus 6:16; Nehemiah 10:9-13). The duty of the Levites was to assist Aaron's descendants in the service of the Temple (Exodus 38:21; Numbers 3:6-7).

In Ezra 6:16, 19, the phrase "children of the captivity" is a translation of the Hebrew *ben gowlah* (**bane go-LAW**). In this case *ben* is used idiomatically to denote children or descendants. *Gowlah* refers to anyone who has been deported as a slave or taken into captivity. In this case the phrase describes the descendants of those carried into Babylonian captivity.

The Passover is called *pecach* (**PEH-sakh**) in Hebrew. This verb means "to skip or pass over, to grant exemption from penalty or calamity." The Passover is an annual feast that celebrates the day when the Lord passed over the homes of those who put lambs' blood over the door frames of their homes. On that night the firstborn male of every household that did not have the blood over the door frame was killed. This event precipitated Israel's deliverance from Egyptian bondage. The Passover lamb and the blood of the lamb point to Jesus Christ, the Lamb of God, whose blood takes away the sins of the world (John 1:29; 1 Corinthians 5:7).

20 For the priests and the Levites were purified together, all of them were pure, and killed the passover for all the children of the captivity, and for their brethren the priests, and for themselves.

"The Levites were purified together" meant that they were all on one accord and as one unit ready to observe the proper rites and ceremonies. There was no need to postpone the celebration as was prescribed by law. If circumstances made it necessary, the Passover could be postponed from the first month to the second (Numbers 9:10-11; cf. 2 Chronicles 30:3). "Purified" is a translation of the Hebrew *taher* (**taw-HARE**) and literally means "de-sinned" so as to be ceremonially clean. The word is used almost exclusively of ritual or moral purity. Those who were considered unclean were not permitted to participate in temple rituals until they were purified. Significant to this portion of the Temple celebration was this national cleansing from sin the priests and Levites as keepers of the Law and the presence of God had to first ensure their own sins were atoned for before they could represent God to the people, and thus take on the task of representing the people to God.

21 And the children of Israel, which were come again out of captivity, and all such as had separated themselves unto them from the filthiness of the heathen of the land, to seek the LORD God of Israel, did eat,

Those who had "separated themselves" refers to both ethnic Jews and the proselytes who had embraced the Jewish religion during the time of their captivity in Babylon. The proselytes are proof that the Jewish captives had maintained the principles of their religion. The unbelievers saw it, and they converted to the religion of the one true God. However, the Children of Israel and those converted had to rid themselves of heathen influences in their hearts and minds in order to receive the purity of the Passover celebration with joy.

22 And kept the feast of unleavened bread seven days with joy: for the LORD had made them joyful, and turned the heart of the king of Assyria unto them, to strengthen their hands in the work of the house of God, the God of Israel.

The Feast of Unleavened Bread was closely associated with the Passover. In fact, in preparation for the Passover, the man of the house would search through the house for leaven (yeast) and remove it.

God had given the people both causes to rejoice and hearts to rejoice. God is the Fountain from which all true joy flows. The Persian king here is called the "king of Assyria" (from two empires back). This emphatically stresses the great power and goodness of God in turning the hearts of these present Persian monarchs, whose Assyrian predecessors had formerly been the chief persecutors and cruel oppressors of God's people.

Sources:
Attridge, Harold W., and Wayne A. Meeks, eds. *The Harper Collins Study Bible, New Revised Standard.* New York, NY: Harper Collins Publishers, 2006. 652-656.
Bible Words — Phonetic Pronunciation. http://www.betterdaysarecoming.com/bible/pronunciation.html (accessed May 24, 2011).
Old Testament Hebrew Lexicon. http://www.biblestudytools.com/lexicons/hebrew/kjv (accessed May 30, 2011).
Strong, James. *The New Strong's Exhaustive Concordance of the Bible.* Nashville, TN: Thomas Nelson, 1990. 42, 51.
Zodhiates, Spiros, Th.D., and Warren Baker, D.R.E., eds. *Key Word Study Bible, King James Version.* Chattanooga, TN: AMG Publishers, 1991. 1613, 1633.

Say It Correctly

Adar. AY-dahr, AH-dahr.
Assyria. uh-SIHR-ee-uh.
Artaxerxes. Arta-ZERX-es
Shetharboznai. Sheth-R-BOZ-ny
Tetnai. TET-ny

Daily Bible Readings

MONDAY
Resistance to Rebuilding the Temple
(Ezra 4:1–5)

TUESDAY
Accusations of Sedition
(Ezra 4:11–16)

WEDNESDAY
Temple Construction Halted
(Ezra 4:17–24)

THURSDAY
The Eye of God upon Them
(Ezra 5:1–5)

FRIDAY
Who Gave You a Decree?
(Ezra 5:6–17)

SATURDAY
The Temple's Official Endorsement
(Ezra 6:1–12)

SUNDAY
The Temple's Dedication
(Ezra 6:13–22)

Teaching Tips

Words You Should Know

A. Fast (Ezra 8:21)—*tsuwm* (Heb.)—To abstain from food.

B. Intreated (v. 23)—`athar* (Heb.)—Prayed, supplicated, pleaded.

Teacher Preparation

Unifying Principle—Preparing for a Journey. As people journey through life, they pause to assess their strengths and weaknesses for reaching their destinations.

A. Pray for your students and lesson clarity.

B. Study and meditate on the entire text.

C. Complete the companion lesson in the *Precepts For Living Personal Study Guide®*.

O—Open the Lesson

A. Open with prayer, including the Aim for Change.

B. After prayer, introduce today's subject and have students read the Aim for Change and Keep in Mind verse in unison. Discuss.

C. Ask volunteers to share a time when they fasted and prayed over a dire situation.

D. Allow them to share their testimonies.

E. Now have a volunteer summarize the In Focus story. Discuss.

F. Then ask, "Why is it important to fast and pray?" Discuss.

P—Present the Scriptures

A. Have volunteers read the Focal Verses.

B. Now use The People, Places, and Times; Background; Search the Scriptures; At-A-Glance outline; In Depth; and More Light on the Text to clarify the verses.

E—Explore the Meaning

A. Have volunteers summarize the Discuss the Meaning, Lesson in Our Society, and Make It Happen sections.

B. Connect these sections to the Aim for Change and the Keep in Mind verse.

N—Next Steps for Application

A. Summarize the lesson or write some take-away principles under the Follow the Spirit or Remember Your Thoughts section.

B. Close with prayer.

JULY 21st

Worship Guide

For the Superintendent or Teacher
Theme: Fasting and Praying
Song: "When You Pray, Pray for Me!"
Devotional Reading:
2 Chronicles 7:12-18
Prayer

Fasting and Praying

Bible Background • EZRA 8:21-23
Printed Text • EZRA 8:21-23 | Devotional Reading • 2 CHRONICLES 7:12-18

—————— Aim for Change ——————

By the end of the lesson, we will: KNOW that believers can fast and pray for God's help in dire situations; DESIRE to fast and pray; and PLAN to fast and pray in times of need.

————  In Focus ————

Celeste recently graduated from college with a degree in social work. She was given a full-time position as an intern. She had to travel to unsavory neighborhoods. Some of Celeste's work surroundings made her uneasy, causing her to consider her own safety. She didn't say anything, not wanting to cause alarm while new on her post. However, her appetite had been affected; she hadn't been eating. She found herself seeking God for answers. She heard a message concerning the purpose of fasting and decided to turn her recent eating habits into a fasting sacrifice for guidance and protection.

In the weeks following Celeste's fasting, she became calm and confident of God's protection. Celeste continued to travel to her appointments faithfully. Her superiors acknowledged her dedication, and she was later reassigned to a paying position inside the main office. The clients now came to her; no more travel through unsavory neighborhoods. God made a way and showed favor to Celeste where all outcomes could be seen because of her faith, fasting and prayer.

Today's lesson discusses how fasting and praying can move God in dire situations.

———— Keep in Mind ————

"So we fasted and besought our God for this: and he was intreated of us"
(Ezra 8:23).

"So we fasted and besought our God for this: and he was intreated of us" (Ezra 8:23).

Focal Verses

KJV Ezra 8:21 Then I proclaimed a fast there, at the river of Ahava, that we might afflict ourselves before our God, to seek of him a right way for us, and for our little ones, and for all our substance.

22 For I was ashamed to require of the king a band of soldiers and horsemen to help us against the enemy in the way: because we had spoken unto the king, saying, The hand of our God is upon all them for good that seek him; but his power and his wrath is against all them that forsake him.

23 So we fasted and besought our God for this: and he was intreated of us.

NLT Ezra 8:21 And there by the Ahava Canal, I gave orders for all of us to fast and humble ourselves before our God. We prayed that he would give us a safe journey and protect us, our children, and our goods as we traveled.

22 For I was ashamed to ask the king for soldiers and horsemen to accompany us and protect us from enemies along the way. After all, we had told the king, "Our God's hand of protection is on all who worship him, but his fierce anger rages against those who abandon him."

23 So we fasted and earnestly prayed that our God would take care of us, and he heard our prayer.

The People, Places, and Times

Ezra. He was a scribe, well-versed in the Mosaic Law. He led a second group of exiles to Jerusalem from Babylon, where "Some of the people of Israel, as well as some of the priests, Levites, singers, gatekeepers, and Temple servants, traveled up to Jerusalem with him in the seventh year of King Artaxerxes' reign" (Ezra 7:7, NLT). He found that they had rebuilt the Temple; however, the people's lives were in shambles as they had intermarried with foreigners, something God forbade them to do.

Background

In today's passage, Ezra moves from a prophetic role to a leadership role. After he bragged about having God's protection, he led the people in prayer and fasting to ensure it in their return to their homeland. Typically, the Persians would have provided military escort for Ezra as they were carrying with them contributions made by the Persians.

Apparently, however, the Persian king had been convinced of God's protection for the returning exiles.

At-A-Glance

1. Why Ezra Proclaimed a Fast
(Ezra 8:21-22)
2. What Happened after the Fast
(v. 23)

In Depth

1. Why Ezra Proclaimed a Fast (Ezra 8:21-22)

The Children of Israel were released from their captors and allowed to return to their homeland with all of their belongings and the articles belonging in the Temple. They would also carry funding from the king to rebuild the Temple in Jerusalem. Ezra boasted to the king about the covering of the Lord to those who feared and obeyed Him

(v. 22). Ezra's statement made such an impact on the king that he did not send the normal emissary of protection with them. Much was at stake in this journey; there would also be women and children, so around 2,000 people were traveling. The trip was approximately 720 miles.

Many in the surrounding lands may have been aware of the journey that the people were about to embark upon; many may have been their enemies. There were those in the Persian kingdom who were against the support that was given to Ezra for the rebuilding of the temple. Understandably, the route had to be considered for the safety and welfare of all who would go with them.

Ezra understood that many obstacles could arise and hinder them on their journey. He realized if they were to have safe passage, it would only happen with the help of God. He called upon the Children of Israel to fast with him to seek God.

2. What Happened after the Fast (v. 23)

As a result of the fast, the Lord heard their prayer and supplications and showed Ezra the plan for a safe journey. He divided up the precious cargo among 12 men into equal parts. The value of that was estimated at $35 million (which is probably different today because of the changes in currency rates and the market). This is a lot to carry by caravan over 720 miles with 2,000 men, women, and children without guards as escorts. The amount itself is insignificant; what is amazing is that after their arrival in Jerusalem, they weighed and counted the precious articles and the gold and silver, and all was accounted for. Their path may not have been in a straight line or the most obvious way, but it was the way the Lord had ordained.

Search the Scriptures

1. Who proclaimed (gave orders for) a fast (Ezra 8:21)?

2. What was the most important influence on the people's safe arrival after their 720-mile journey (v. 23)?

Discuss the Meaning

1. What types of fasts are acceptable by God?

2. Why is it important to pray during a fast?

Lesson in Our Society

As we go through life, we learn that we will face things where a solution is not readily apparent. There may not be a perfect example in the Bible for us to follow for our particular situations. Often, these answers are obtained through fasting and prayer. In these instances, God affords us the opportunity to still have access to Him to help lead us through those areas in life.

Once God begins to work in our lives, it's important that we share with others His many miracles and blessings. We should understand that others will gain faith in what God can do by our testimonies.

We may have a path imagined for our lives, but only God knows what lies ahead and can direct us safely through. He awaits the call and plea of His children, wanting His guidance as yet another demonstration of His mighty effect on their lives.

Make It Happen

Set aside a few days for fasting and prayer over a situation in your own life that you know only God can deliver or supply the need. If you do not have a need at this time, consider a family member, friend, coworker, etc., for whom your testimony about God's guidance will provide support during their time of questioning or need.

Follow the Spirit
What God wants me to do:

_____

_____

_____

_____

Remember Your Thoughts
Special insights I have learned:

_____

_____

_____

_____

More Light on the Text
Ezra 8:21-23
21 Then I proclaimed a fast there, at the river of Ahava, that we might afflict ourselves before our God, to seek of him a right way for us, and for our little ones, and for all our substance.

Ezra, the priest of Yahweh, had assembled the people of Israel before continuing on their long journey. Being extremely familiar with the Word of God and having an intimate relationship with God, Ezra knew the people needed to get their hearts right with Yahweh. Ezra declared a national "fast" (Heb. *tsuwm*, **tsoom**) for Israel, one in which every single person was to participate. This spiritual fast was to restrict and deny some of the most basic human needs for the sole purpose of conditioning oneself to depend totally on Yahweh, speaking to Him through prayer and waiting for a response. This full submission and dependency carves a path and hones (refines) a person's humility.

The purpose of the people's fast was to seek God for protection on their journey. This divine protection would blanket all who traveled. Young, old, male, and female, all would be secure within the authority of Yahweh. "The little ones" (Heb. *taph*, **taf**) literally means "the weak" or "small children," but this term has also a wider scope of meaning. Scholars hold that it refers here to all the vulnerable returnees, like women, children, and the elderly. Ezra's intent on the national prayer and fast wasn't solely for protection from harm, but for protection from thievery as well.

This wasn't the first time the people of Yahweh were assembled in order to seek His protection as a unified nation. In 2 Chronicles 20:1-4, we read of a powerful army coming together from the people of Moab, Ammon and unidentified others in order to wage war against Judah and overtake the land. King Jehoshaphat, being fearful, gathered the people of Judah from all the cities of the land so that they could fast together as one nation, seeking the protection of Yahweh from their marching enemies.

22 For I was ashamed to require of the king a band of soldiers and horsemen to help us against the enemy in the way: because we had spoken unto the king, saying, The hand of our God is upon all them for good that seek him; but his power and his wrath is against all them that forsake him.

Ezra was forced to put his faith to the test after proclaiming the power of Yahweh before the king. He felt "ashamed" (Heb. *buwsh*, **boosh**) to ask for military security for their dangerous journey, and rightfully so. To ask for protection would have brought the appearance of hypocrisy upon Ezra and the people of God, and not provided an avenue where their faith in God and His divine authority could be witnessed. People would have perceived Yahweh as a weak God with cowardly followers. For the most part, what Ezra said was completely correct, and could have very well been led by the Spirit of God in proclaiming those statements. There are many occasions in our lives where the Spirit will lead us into physical situations where our faith will be tested. Whether Ezra was aware or not, he provided a powerful witness for all to follow. Sincere dedication to prayer and fasting will allow those participants to have direct communication with God. When one submits in humility to the Lord, seeking forgiveness and guidance, God tells us, "My eyes will be open and My ears attentive to the prayer offered" (2 Chronicles 7:15, NASB), and He will answer "their prayers because they trusted in Him" (1 Chronicles 5:20, NASB).

23 So we fasted and besought our God for this: and he was intreated of us.

The Lord waits for opportunities such as these, not so that He can simply flaunt His power amongst those on the earth. On the contrary, when individuals and people groups seek Him and trust in Him, they gain an invaluable opportunity to benefit from the outcomes of these situations. He desires the hearts and minds of humans submitted in humility and relying totally on His loving protection and will toward them.

We see another example of this centered on Manasseh. After rebuking him and his people, the Lord sent the Assyrian Empire to overtake him. Once he was captured and humiliated after his defeat, Manasseh turned his heart toward the Lord. The Scriptures read, "When he prayed to Him (Yahweh), He was moved by his entreaty and heard his supplication, and brought him again to Jerusalem to his kingdom. Then Manasseh knew that the LORD was God" (2 Chronicles 33:13, NASB).

God hears and attends to those that seek Him with a sincere heart and mind. Ezra was aware of this and knew that fasting and prayer would entice the attention of the Lord, because He desires this. Ezra 8:23 contains two key words related to this idea. "Besought" (Heb. *baqash*, **baw-KASH**), means "requested" or "desired," and "intreated" (Heb. `*athar*, **aw-THAR**), means "entreated, prayed, pleaded, made supplication." How many of us, after prayer and fasting come to the conclusion that God has sincerely listened to us? How many of us have sought His attention and help, with a sincere and humble heart?

Sources:
Blank, Wayne. "Ancient Empires – Babylon (Map)." *Jerusalem Fact File.* www.keyway.ca/htm2002/jerfacts.htm (accessed May 9, 2011).
Butler, Trent, gen. ed. *Holman Bible Dictionary.* Nashville, TN: Holman Bible Publishers, 1991. 1331.
Fensham, F. Charles. *Books of Ezra and Nehemiah.* Grand Rapids, MI: William B. Eerdmans Publishing Company, 1982.
Kidner, Derek. *The Tyndale Old Testament Commentaries: Ezra and Nehemiah.* Leicester, England: InterVarsity Press, 1979.
Middle Town Bible Church. *Ezra, Nehemiah, & Esther: The Three Returns to Jerusalem.* http://www.middletownbiblechurch.org/oldtesta/oldtes6.htm (accessed May 10, 2011).
Grabbe, Lester L. "'Mind the Gaps': Ezra, Nehemiah and the Judean Restoration." *Restoration: Old Testament, Jewish & Christian Perspectives.* Edited by James M. Scott. Boston, MA: Journal for the Study of Judaism, Brill, 2001. 99, 100.
Unger, Merrill F. *The New Unger's Bible Handbook, Ezra.* Revised by Gary Larson. Chicago, IL: Moody Bible Institute, Moody Publishers. 2005. 218-220.

Say It Correctly

Ahava. ah-HAY-vah, uh-HAY-vuh.
Jehoshaphat. juh-HOSH-uh-fat, jih-
HAH-suh-fat.
Manasseh. muh-NA-suh.

Daily Bible Readings

MONDAY
Humbly Calling on God
(2 Chronicles 7:12–18)

TUESDAY
Beseeching God's Answer to Prayer
(Psalm 69:9–18)

WEDNESDAY
Humble and Contrite in Spirit
(Isaiah 66:1–4)

THURSDAY
Fasting Directed to God
(Matthew 6:16–18)

FRIDAY
Studying and Keeping the Law
(Ezra 7:1–10)

SATURDAY
Securing Servants for the Temple
(Ezra 8:15–20)

SUNDAY
Praying for God's Protection
(Ezra 8:21–23)

Notes

Teaching Tips

July 28
Bible Study Guide 9

Words You Should Know

A. Ezra (book of Ezra) `ezra' (Heb.)—
A priest (descended from Aaron's son
Phinehas), who returned from exile with
Zerubbabel (Nehemiah 12:1).

B. Priests (Ezra 8:24) *kohen* (Heb.)—In
the Old Testament, priests functioned as
mediators between God and humanity.

Teacher Preparation

Unifying Principle—Generous Gifts.
As an act of worship, Ezra prepared gifts
of precious metals to be carried by the
priests and Levites to the house of God
in Jerusalem.

A. Pray for your students and lesson clarity.

B. Study and meditate on the entire text.

C. Using the widow in Mark 12:38-44 as
an example, explain how giving, especially
when we give all that we have, is one tool to
receive a blessing from God.

O—Open the Lesson

A. Open with prayer, including the Aim
for Change.

B. After prayer, introduce today's subject
of the lesson.

C. Have your students read the Aim for
Change and Keep in Mind verse in unison,
then discuss.

D. Share your presentation.

E. Ask, "Have you given a generous gift
to someone in need?"

F. Allow volunteers to share their
testimonies.

G. Now have a volunteer summarize the
In Focus story. Discuss.

P—Present the Scriptures

A. Have volunteers read the Focal Verses.

B. Now use The People, Places, and
Times; Background; Search the Scriptures;
At-A-Glance outline; In Depth; and More
Light on the Text to clarify the verses.

E—Explore the Meaning

A. Have volunteers summarize the
Discuss the Meaning, Lesson in Our
Society, and Make It Happen sections.

B. Connect these sections to the Aim for
Change and the Keep in Mind verse.

N—Next Steps for Application

A. Summarize the lesson.

B. Close with prayer.

JULY
28th

Worship Guide

For the Superintendent or Teacher
Theme: Gifts for the Temple
Song: "Count Your Blessings"
Devotional Reading: Mark 12:38-44
Prayer

558

Gifts for the Temple

Bible Background • EZRA 8:24-30
Printed Text • EZRA 8:24-30 | Devotional Reading • MARK 12:38-44

Aim for Change

By the end of the lesson, we will: KNOW that as an act of worship, we should be willing to give generously of our time and talents to the Lord; FEEL that we should give to the Lord; and GIVE to the Lord.

 In Focus

I remember what it felt like, wondering if the shelter where I slept was actually safe. I remember being hungry. I remember the kindness in the eyes of the pastor as he permitted me to sit at the church until I could check in at the shelter. Yet, I will never forget the kind words of encouragement, the shelter that provided me a safe place to sleep, or the soup kitchen that fed me. Unlike then, I now have the ability to live in a house and buy food. I am very thankful for how God kept me and still does. To express my gratitude to God, I have given back. I financially support the shelter that provided a safe place for me to sleep. I support with money the soup kitchen that fed me, and I have also paid for the badly needed repairs at the church so it may continue to be a safe haven for others.

Generously giving of our money and time is one way to worship God. When we give, we act as God's instruments to bless those who do not have. By generously giving, we show that what we have really does belong to God, and we are just stewards of those possessions. In today's lesson, we see how Ezra prepared gifts of precious metals that were to be carried by the priests and the Levites to the House of God.

Keep in Mind

"And I said unto them, Ye are holy unto the LORD; the vessels are holy also; and the silver and the gold are a freewill offering unto the LORD God of your fathers"
(Ezra 8:28).

"And I said unto them, Ye are holy unto the LORD; the vessels are holy also; and the silver and the gold are a freewill offering unto the LORD God of your fathers" (Ezra 8:28).

Focal Verses

KJV **Ezra 8:24** Then I separated twelve of the chief of the priests, Sherebiah, Hashabiah, and ten of their brethren with them,

25 And weighed unto them the silver, and the gold, and the vessels, even the offering of the house of our God, which the king, and his counsellors, and his lords, and all Israel there present, had offered:

26 I even weighed unto their hand six hundred and fifty talents of silver, and silver vessels an hundred talents, and of gold an hundred talents;

27 Also twenty basons of gold, of a thousand drams; and two vessels of fine copper, precious as gold.

28 And I said unto them, Ye are holy unto the LORD; the vessels are holy also; and the silver and the gold are a freewill offering unto the LORD God of your fathers.

29 Watch ye, and keep them, until ye weigh them before the chief of the priests and the Levites, and chief of the fathers of Israel, at Jerusalem, in the chambers of the house of the LORD.

30 So took the priests and the Levites the weight of the silver, and the gold, and the vessels, to bring them to Jerusalem unto the house of our God.

NLT **Ezra 8:24** I appointed twelve leaders of the priests—Sherebiah, Hashabiah, and ten other priests—

25 to be in charge of transporting the silver, the gold, the gold bowls, and the other items that the king, his council, his officials, and all the people of Israel had presented for the Temple of God.

26 I weighed the treasure as I gave it to them and found the totals to be as follows: 24 tons of silver, 7,500 pounds of silver articles, 7,500 pounds of gold,

27 20 gold bowls, equal in value to 1,000 gold coins, 2 fine articles of polished bronze, as precious as gold.

28 And I said to these priests, "You and these treasures have been set apart as holy to the LORD. This silver and gold is a voluntary offering to the LORD, the God of our ancestors.

29 Guard these treasures well until you present them to the leading priests, the Levites, and the leaders of Israel, who will weigh them at the storerooms of the LORD's Temple in Jerusalem."

30 So the priests and the Levites accepted the task of transporting these treasures of silver and gold to the Temple of our God in Jerusalem.

The People, Places, and Times

The Exile. The exile was the period of time when the inhabitants of the land of Israel were taken into captivity. The people of Israel consisted of the northern tribes of Israel and the southern tribes of Judah. The land of Israel was located in what is known as the Fertile Crescent and includes modern-day Egypt, Lebanon, Syria, Turkey, Jordan, Iraq, and Iran. Led by Moses, the people of Israel fled Egyptian rule and the people of the southern tribe of Judah settled in southern Palestine. At that time the southern tribes of Judah were a coalition of tribes from the people of Israel. The southern tribe of Judah was the counterpart to the northern tribe of Israel.

Ezra. A priest who descended from Aaron's son Phinehas by way of Zadok (Ezra 7:1-5) and the author of the book of Ezra and probably also of Nehemiah and 1-2 Chronicles. He returned from the exile with Zerubbabel and was skilled in the Law of Moses.

Background

The first six chapters of the book of Ezra record how the exiled people of the southern tribe of Judah returned to Jerusalem. "Now in the first year of Cyrus king of Persia, that the word of the LORD by the mouth of Jeremiah might be fulfilled, the LORD stirred up the spirit of Cyrus king of Persia, that he made a proclamation throughout all his kingdom, and put it also in writing, saying, Thus saith Cyrus king of Persia, The LORD God of heaven hath given me all the kingdoms of the earth; and he hath charged me to build him an house at Jerusalem, which is in Judah. Who is there among you of all his people? his God be with him, and let him go up to Jerusalem, which is in Judah, and build the house of the LORD God of Israel, (he is the God,) which is in Jerusalem. And whosoever remaineth in any place where he sojourneth, let the men of his place help him with silver, and with gold, and with goods, and with beasts, beside the freewill offering for the house of God that is in Jerusalem. Then rose up the chief of the fathers of Judah and Benjamin, and the priests, and the Levites, with all them whose spirit God had raised, to go up to build the house of the LORD which is in Jerusalem" (Ezra 1:1-5).

Fifty-eight years had passed between the dedication of the temple in 516 B.C. and the arrival of Ezra in Jerusalem. "Now after these things, in the reign of Artaxerxes king of Persia, Ezra ... went up from Babylon" (7:1, 6). The words, "after these" connects the completion of the building of the Temple with the arrival of Ezra in Jerusalem. Because of his skill with the Law of Moses, Ezra came to Jerusalem to deal with questions related to the Law.

After discovering no Levites were traveling with them, Ezra stopped at the Ahava Canal, sent leaders of his traveling party to approach Iddo, and made a request of Iddo that he permit some of his ministers to travel with them. Ezra then proclaimed a fast to seek protection from God while they traveled because he had refused the protection of the king. After the fast, they departed, going toward Jerusalem.

Traveling with the money given by the Persian people and the remaining Babylonian exiles, Ezra declared the money they were traveling with as holy to God. "And I said unto them, Ye are holy unto the LORD; the vessels are holy also; and the silver and the gold are a freewill offering unto the LORD God of your fathers" (8:28). The declaration to call the men and the money they carried holy transferred them from the secular realm to divine service.

At-A-Glance

1. Doing Service (Ezra 8:24-27)
2. Consecrated for Service (vv. 28-30)

In Depth

1. Doing Service (Ezra 8:24-27)

Ezra, the priest, led a second group of exiles back to Judah and Jerusalem approximately 80 years after the first group had returned. Even though he knew God had promised to protect His people, Ezra still led the people in praying and fasting before such a monumental undertaking; asking God to be with them on the journey (Ezra 8:21-23). As a priest, Ezra "knew that God's blessings are appropriated through prayer" (*Life Application Study Bible, NLT,* 735).

Now that they had done their preparatory work, it was time to carry out the service of the Lord— to get the job done. Therefore, Ezra appointed 12 leaders of the priests (Sherebiah, Hashabiah, and 10 other priests) to be in charge of transporting all the cargo— the silver, the gold, gold bowls, and the other items—that the king, his council, his leaders, and the people of Israel had presented for the Temple (vv. 24-26). They were in charge of a vast treasury that equaled "24 tons of silver, 7,500 pounds of silver utensils, 7,500 pounds of gold, 20 gold bowls, equal in value to 1,000 gold coins, 2 fine articles of polished bronze, as precious as gold" (*Life Application Study Bible, NLT,* 736). God was with Ezra (a godly leader) and this group of exiles, who traveled the dangerous route back to Judah and Jerusalem, without military escort (8:22). They arrived at their destination after several months without harm.

2. Consecrated for Service (vv. 28-30)

With his declaration, "Ye are holy unto the LORD: the vessels are holy also" (Ezra 8:28), Ezra commissioned the leaders of the priests and the offerings they carried into service for God. To consecrate simply means to be set apart for the sole purpose of service to God. Every object used in Temple service, therefore, was dedicated to God.

Ezra 1:1 demonstrates how the king of Persia obeyed and then served God. With his statement describing how the Lord stirred up his spirit, the king was being placed into position by God to set the stage for Ezra's return to Jerusalem. The king continued his declaration of obedience to God by saying, "The LORD God of heaven hath given me all the kingdoms of the earth; and he hath charge me to build him an house at Jerusalem, which is in Judah" (1:2).

Search the Scriptures

1. What was the purpose in giving an account of the offerings (Ezra 8:26, 30)?

2. Why did Ezra set the 12 leaders of the priest apart (vv. 24, 28)?

Discuss the Meaning

What God has designated for His use will always prosper. If we agree with this statement, why do we act first, before seeking guidance from God?

Lesson in Our Society

Giving is an act of worship to God. So if we truly believe in God and we truly intend to be the light in the world that God has directed us to be, we need to identify one need where we can sincerely make a contribution. Some suggestions are to volunteer at a local school; establish an after-school tutorial at our churches; volunteer at a local women or men's homeless shelter; or permit a 12-step substance-abuse program to meet at our facilities. Once we have identified the need, our next step is to commit to that need with our time and, when appropriate, our finances.

Make It Happen

As our community is experiencing unusually high rates of unemployment, underemployment, and lack of affordable health care and decent housing, the one way to show that God through His Son Jesus Christ is compassionate is to extend ourselves as believers into the community where we worship. Let's begin by helping one of our own, a family in need. After we have helped them to stabilize themselves, let's go out in our community. We can do this by giving away food or hosting a food distribution. We can also designate a portion of our benevolence offering to help those who encounter emergencies such as keeping their utilities on. As we commit to doing these acts of kindness, our satisfaction will come from the statement from our Lord, "Ye shall be holy: for the LORD your God am holy" (Leviticus 19:2). Our "holiness" comes from our obedience to God when we see the need and act on that need.

Follow the Spirit

What God wants me to do:

_____

_____

_____

_____

Remember Your Thoughts

Special insights I have learned:

_____

_____

_____

_____

More Light on the Text

Ezra 8:24-30

24 Then I separated twelve of the chief of the priests, Sherebiah, Hashabiah, and ten of their brethren with them,

The mini-story in which we find ourselves takes place in the midst of a larger story—the kind often referred to as a "return story." And a marvelous return it was: After years of exile under Babylonian and Persian rule, the Israelites embarked, in stages, on a glorious return to their homeland. Their return was a thrilling experience indeed, but also one fraught with danger. Long journeys in the Ancient Near East always involved the danger of harm from robbers or wild animals. For this reason, Ezra has just proclaimed a fast before the journey begins, "that we might afflict ourselves before our God, to seek of him a right way for us, and for our little ones, and for all our substance" (Ezra 8:21). Interestingly, Ezra notes that he was "ashamed" (verse 22) to ask Artaxerxes the Persian king for help in their journey to Jerusalem (as Nehemiah would later do; see Nehemiah 2:7-9). Ezra notes that he had already boasted to the king of God's power and goodness, and therefore he dares not imply to Artaxerxes that Israel's God needed troops and horses to accomplish His deliverance. For the modern reader, it may be difficult to tell whether Ezra's motivation was one of faith or fear; probably, like God's servants throughout all ages, he was experiencing something of both. In any case, the issue is not the fragility of man but the faithfulness of God, and in Ezra 8:23, he records that God "was intreated of us" — that is, He heard their cry.

Besides fasting and prayer, the other aspect of preparation for an important voyage, for ancient Israel, was the consecration (setting apart) of the priests. As those set apart to serve God by making sacrifices for the people, the priests were indispensable for a group of Israelites seeking God's favor. But the absence of such priests almost short-circuited the trip before it even began: "and I viewed the people, and the priests, and found there none of the sons of Levi" (8:15). As the definition of the priesthood in Leviticus 8 and 9 shows, God had commanded that Israel's priests come from the tribe of Levi. Ezra was himself a priest, but as leader of the expedition, he could hardly fulfill all the roles of an Israelite priest. Thus, when he learns of the absence of Levites among his company, he sent a message to a local leader named Iddo, who sends to Ezra priests from among his own company (Iddo's "place Casaphia" seems to have been some sort of gathering place for Jews in the midst of the Babylonian and Persian empires; see Ezra 8:17, NLT). Thus, "by the good hand of our God upon us" (8:18), Israel's voyage of holy purpose is able to continue. And the two priests mentioned by name here—Sherebiah and Hashabiah—come from the same company that God has graciously provided, through Iddo, for the journey.

25 And weighed unto them the silver, and the gold, and the vessels, even the offering of the house of our God, which the king, and his counsellors, and his lords, and all Israel there present, had offered:

This verse begins a remarkable section that shows us, through the overwhelming abundance of valuable treasures Ezra's expedition received, how powerfully God moved people's hearts to pour out generosity on this important mission. But what is probably even more significant than the amount of the riches bestowed on Israel is the *identity* of the givers. "All Israel there present," that is, the Israelites present at the time of Ezra's departure for Jerusalem, is listed last among those who poured out generosity upon Ezra's expedition. Listed before them we see the most unlikely sort of donors to the building of Yahweh's Temple: the Persian king, along with "his counselors, and his lords"!

How is it that a pagan king, who considered the Israelites a tiny and insignificant portion of his vast kingdom, would bestow vast wealth upon a small band of them returning to their homeland? One commentator has a helpful answer: "If the God of the Jews were no more than a name (he might have argued), the whole exercise was pointless; but if He existed, He would expect tangible courtesies from a king—and the scale of them should reflect the donor's power and majesty" (Kidner, 66). This explanation seems to fit the way ancient kings perceived their own glory, and how all of their public demonstrations should be in accordance with that glory. But conjecture about the king's earthly motives should in no way take away from our sense of wonder that God moved a pagan king's heart in this way, and that the king gave much more extravagantly than he likely would have felt required to do (as the next two verses show). Truly, as the Proverbs have it, "The king's heart is in the hand of the LORD, as the rivers of water: he turneth it whithersoever he will" (Proverbs 21:1). We can say that not just of God-fearing kings, but of pagan Persian kings as well!

26 I even weighed unto their hand six hundred and fifty talents of silver, and silver vessels an hundred talents, and of gold an hundred talents;

We now learn just how prodigious the offering of the Persians and Israelites was. Given that a "talent" was the equivalent of about 75 pounds, one can calculate the enormous weight that Ezra and his band of pilgrims took with them on their journey. Ezra "weighed unto their hand" the amount, and the resulting figures were no doubt an enormous encouragement both to Ezra's party of travelers and to the Jews already in Jerusalem rebuilding the Temple. The size of this offering would have no doubt funded the work of the temple and its priests for decades to come. But apart from true piety on the part of the people, these riches would have become stale, simply funding a sort of empty relic like the massive cathedrals of Europe that benefit from huge endowments but have little more than a flicker of true worship going on within them.

27 Also twenty basons of gold, of a thousand drams; and two vessels of fine copper, precious as gold.

The litany of riches continues with a description of "twenty basons of gold"—meaning 20 bowls, and probably refers to the bowls themselves being made of gold rather than being filled with gold. The King James Version translation makes the following phrase a little confusing; we might refer to the English Standard Version here, which says, "20 bowls of gold worth 1,000 darics" (about 250 ounces of coin weight). All of the ancient world's precious metals are included in the offering, demonstrating how fully the people, both Jew and Gentile, gave without holding anything back.

28 And I said unto them, Ye are holy unto the LORD; the vessels are holy also; and the silver and the gold are a freewill offering unto the LORD God of your fathers.

Ezra's words here are words of ordination. Like the priests who were ordained and set apart in Leviticus, and then in countless succeeding generations throughout the life of Israel, these priests are themselves set apart (for being "holy," in the Scriptures, always involves being set apart: consecrated for a special purpose). Also significant, though, is the fact that Ezra sets apart the offering as well: "the vessels are holy also." Being on a spiritual rather than worldly mission, Ezra does not hesitate in displaying to all present the nature of the offering that has been collected. "The gifts now belonged to the Lord and were thus changed from the profane to the divine sphere" (Fensham, 119).

29 Watch ye, and keep them, until ye weigh them before the chief of the priests and the Levites, and chief of the fathers of Israel, at Jerusalem, in the chambers of the house of the LORD.

Ezra surely did not utter the words "Watch ye, and keep them" lightly; the Israelites were about to venture on a journey of hundreds of miles through hostile territory, all while transporting riches that anyone who was not royalty would find unimaginable. Even in light of their prayers and the clear signs of God's blessings, their hearts must have trembled at what lay ahead. But Ezra speaks with the certainty of faith, assuming the people will arrive safely to the priests in Jerusalem and there display the wonder of what God has done in the hearts of both Persians and Jews. Again, Ezra speaks in the language of public ceremony; just as the first Temple was built after a massive offering from a people with stirred hearts (see 2 Chronicles 31), now the rebuilt Temple will be blessed with the people's willing offering. The connection was surely not lost on Ezra, who had set his heart to study God's commandments (7:10) and knew both the glory of Israel's history and the greatness and certainty of God's promise of restoration.

30 So took the priests and the Levites the weight of the silver, and the gold, and the vessels, to bring them to Jerusalem unto the house of our God.

A summary verse of obedience, like the one above, is common in the Scriptures. A drawn-out form of this kind of summary is found in Joshua 24, where the people repeatedly resolve to obey all that the Lord has commanded, and then are dismissed to their homes (Joshua 24:28). In this way, Ezra once again echoes a form historic and meaningful to the people of Israel, encouraging them regarding God's intention to renew and restore His people. And the precious offering they carry with them, described here again as a "weight," reminds them of the danger ahead—but also of the weightiness of God's glory among them. For He alone could have produced such an abundance by creating willing hearts among so many of those made in His image, whether they consciously worshiped Him or not!

Sources:

Bible Words – Phonetic Pronunciation. http://www.betterdays arecoming.com/bible/pronunciation.html (accessed January 21, 2012).

Fensham, F. Charles. *The Books of Ezra and Nehemiah*. Grand Rapids, MI: Eerdmans, 1982. 119.

Brand, Chad, Charles Draper, and Archie England, gen. eds. *Holman Illustrated Bible Dictionary*. Nashville, TN: Holman Bible Publishers, 2003.

Kidner, Derek. *Ezra & Nehemiah: An Introduction and Commentary*. Downers Grove, IL: InterVarsity Press, 1979. 66.

Life Application Study Bible, NLT. Wheaton, IL: Tyndale House, 2004. 735, 736.

Myers, Allen C., ed. *The Eerdmans Bible Dictionary*. Grand Rapids, MI: William B. Eerdmans Publishing Company, 1996.

The New Interpreter's Bible Volume Three. Nashville, TN: Abingdon Press, 1999.

Old Testament Hebrew Lexicon. http://www.biblestudytools. com (accessed January 20, 2012).

Rachmacher, Earl D., Th.D., gen. ed. *The Nelson Study Bible New King James Version*. Nashville, TN: Thomas Nelson Publishers, 1997.

Today's Parallel Bible, New International Version, New American Standard Bible, *Updated Edition, King James Version, New Living Translation*. Grand Rapids, MI: Zondervan Publishers, 2000.

Say It Correctly

Babylonian.
bab'uh-LOH-nee-uhn, -LOHN-yuhn.
Nehemiah. nee'(h)uh-MI-uh.
Zadok. ZAY-dok.
Zerubbabel.
zee-RUB-uh-buhl, zuh-RUHB-uh-buhl.

Daily Bible Readings

MONDAY
A Single Offering for All Time
(Hebrews 10:1-14)

TUESDAY
Stirred Hearts and Willing Spirits
(Exodus 35:20-29)

WEDNESDAY
Bring Offerings before the Lord
(Numbers 7:1-6)

THURSDAY
Contributing Tithes and Offerings
(2 Chronicles 31:2-10)

FRIDAY
More Important Than Offerings and Sacrifices
(Mark 12:28-34)

SATURDAY
The Gift of a Poor Widow
(Mark 12:28-34)

SUNDAY
The Offering for God's House
(Ezra 8:24-30)

Teaching Tips

Words You Should Know

A. **Scribe** (Nehemiah 8:13) *caphar* (Heb.)—A person with expertise at enumerating, recounting, telling, narrating, praising, and speaking to celebrate.

B. **Booths** (vv. 14-17) *cukkah* (Heb.)—Huts or arbors made of interwoven leaves and branches meant as temporary housing.

Teacher Preparation

Unifying Principle—Great Rejoicing. The Festival of Booths and Ezra's reading were observations of the Israelites' wilderness exile and the giving of the Law, which the people celebrated joyously, followed by solemn contemplation.

A. Pray for your students and lesson clarity.

B. Study and meditate on the entire text.

C. Complete the companion lesson in the *Precepts For Living Personal Study Guide®*.

O—Open the Lesson

A. Open with prayer, including the Aim for Change.

B. After prayer, introduce today's subject of the lesson.

C. Have your students read the Aim for Change and Keep in Mind verse in unison. Discuss.

D. Ask, "What are the valued traditions of your family to mark significant events?"

E. Share their testimonies.

F. Now have a volunteer summarize the In Focus Story. Discuss.

P—Present the Scriptures

A. Have volunteers read the Focal Verses.

B. Now use The People, Places, and Times; Background; Search the Scriptures; At-A-Glance outline; In Depth; and More Light on the Text to clarify the verses.

E—Explore the Meaning

A. Have volunteers summarize the Discuss the Meaning, Lesson in Our Society, and Make It Happen sections.

B. Connect these sections to the Aim for Change and the Keep in Mind verse.

N—Next Steps for Application

A. Summarize the lesson.

B. Ask class members: "If God were invited to your celebration, would He be welcomed at the festivities?"

C. Close with prayer.

AUG
4th

Worship Guide

For the Superintendent or Teacher
Theme: Festival of Booths
Song: "Again I Say Rejoice"
Devotional Reading: Exodus 23:12-17
Prayer

Festival of Booths

Bible Background • NEHEMIAH 7:73b—8:18
Printed Text • NEHEMIAH 8:13-18 | Devotional Reading • EXODUS 23:12-17

———————————— **Aim for Change** ————————————

By the end of the lesson, we will: UNDERSTAND the significance of celebrating God's blessings; REFLECT on our own attitudes toward celebrating God's blessings; and PLAN to celebrate God's blessings.

———————————— In Focus  ————————————

Olivia couldn't help smiling as she watched her grandmother move about in preparation for the family celebrations tomorrow. Standing at the bedroom door, she saw Grandma Ellis flip through old albums, some with pictures and others with tattered papers of faded handwriting.

"Ah, yes. This is the one," Grandma Ellis said out loud. Every year during the family's Juneteenth gathering, she made a point of reading a poem passed through her ancestors in commemoration of slavery's end in the United States.

"What's that?" Olivia asked, already knowing but anxious to hear the story all over again. Hearing it in her family's stories made it more real than the lectures in her African-American studies classes. She'd learned that the celebrations that began June 19th, 1865, occurred two-and-a-half years after President Abraham Lincoln's Emancipation Proclamation. Still, nothing topped the history of how her family marked knowledge of their new-found freedom over the years. Making herself comfortable on the bed, Olivia waited to hear the familiar words.

Festivals and celebrations are a great way to acknowledge and express gratitude to God for His many wonderful blessings.

———————————— **Keep in Mind** ————————————

"And all the congregation of them that were come again out of the captivity made booths, and sat under the booths: for since the days of Jeshua the son of Nun unto that day had not the children of Israel done so. And there was very great gladness" (Nehemiah 8:17).

"And all the congregation of them that were come again out of the captivity made booths, and sat under the booths: for since the days of Jeshua the son of Nun unto that day had not the children of Israel done so. And there was very great gladness" (Nehemiah 8:17).

Focal Verses

KJV Nehemiah 8:13 And on the second day were gathered together the chief of the fathers of all the people, the priests, and the Levites, unto Ezra the scribe, even to understand the words of the law.

14 And they found written in the law which the LORD had commanded by Moses, that the children of Israel should dwell in booths in the feast of the seventh month:

15 And that they should publish and proclaim in all their cities, and in Jerusalem, saying, Go forth unto the mount, and fetch olive branches, and pine branches, and myrtle branches, and palm branches, and branches of thick trees, to make booths, as it is written.

16 So the people went forth, and brought them, and made themselves booths, every one upon the roof of his house, and in their courts, and in the courts of the house of God, and in the street of the water gate, and in the street of the gate of Ephraim.

17 And all the congregation of them that were come again out of the captivity made booths, and sat under the booths: for since the days of Jeshua the son of Nun unto that day had not the children of Israel done so. And there was very great gladness.

18 Also day by day, from the first day unto the last day, he read in the book of the law of God. And they kept the feast seven days; and on the eighth day was a solemn assembly, according unto the manner.

NLT Nehemiah 8:13 On October 9 the family leaders of all the people, together with the priests and Levites, met with Ezra the scribe to go over the Law in greater detail.

14 As they studied the Law, they discovered that the LORD had commanded through Moses that the Israelites should live in shelters during the festival to be held that month

15 He had said that a proclamation should be made throughout their towns and in Jerusalem, telling the people to go to the hills to get branches from olive, wild olive, myrtle, palm, and other leafy trees. They were to use these branches to make shelters in which they would live during the festival, as prescribed in the Law.

16 So the people went out and cut branches and used them to build shelters on the roofs of their houses, in their courtyards, in the courtyards of God's Temple, or in the squares just inside the Water Gate and the Ephraim Gate.

17 So everyone who had returned from captivity lived in these shelters during the festival, and they were all filled with great joy! The Israelites had not celebrated like this since the days of Joshua son of Nun.

18 Ezra read from the Book of the Law of God on each of the seven days of the festival. Then on the eighth day they held a solemn assembly, as was required by law.

The People, Places, and Times

Levites. The Levites were chosen by God to serve in the Temple. They were descendants from the tribe of Levi and their job was to do the work in the Temple, which included preparing the materials and artifacts for worship. In the days of Moses, the Levites carried the Tabernacle in the wilderness and were responsible for setting it up at each camp (see Numbers 1:47-53). Under David, the nation regained the Ark of the Covenant and Jerusalem was the center of national worship. The Levites, who no longer had to carry the Tabernacle, continued the upkeep of the Tabernacle and the items of worship. David also engaged them as musicians and singers who led the worship of the people (see 1 Chronicles 15:14-28).

Festival of Booths. In Hebrew, *Sukkot* was instituted in Leviticus 23:33-42 by God through Moses as a celebration complete with a holy convocation and joyful celebration. This celebration commemorates God's care for the Children of Israel while they wandered in the desert as well as a harvest festival. Celebrated for seven days in the fall (September/October), Sukkot calls the people to build and "dwell" in a booth and to present burnt, grain, and drink offerings to the Lord over and beyond their regular gifts and offerings. They were to honor God by giving their best and celebrating Him to the utmost.

Background

Israel was in exile for nearly 150 years and Judah for 70 years. When Judah was conquered, the Babylonians took the scrolls from the Temple and the Temple artifacts. The captives were forced also to abandon their native language in favor of the language of the captors. Aramaic was the language of business for Babylon and later Persia. As was the case in most cultures, only the most elite in society were literate. With the scrolls of God's Word taken and a new language spoken, the people only knew God's Word through the stories of their families and other captives. They had neither seen the words given to Moses nor heard them. Their faith in God was largely based on the accounts that were kept by those who remembered the Word.

In 538 B.C., 70 years after Israel had been in exile, the first group of Israelites returned to Judah under the leadership of Zerubbabel. A number of years later, in 458 B.C., under the leadership of Ezra, a second group returned. Under Ezra's faithful teaching most of the people turned from their sins and agreed to reestablish their relationship with God and follow His will for their lives. In 444 B.C., 14 years after Ezra, Nehemiah returned and succeeded in rebuilding the walls. The book of Nehemiah overlaps the book of Ezra, as indicated in today's lesson where the covenant renewal occurs.

At-A-Glance

1. Festival of Booths Reinstated
(Nehemiah 8:13-16)
2. Festival of Booths Marks Great
Celebration (vv. 17-18)

In Depth

1. Festival of Booths Reinstated (Nehemiah 8:13-16)

In the preceding verses, Nehemiah and Ezra read aloud the books of the Law to the people while the Levitical priest taught the people and provided interpretation (Nehemiah 8:8-9). As the people heard the Law and recognized their own waywardness, they began to weep and mourn. God charged the people not to weep and mourn but to celebrate that they are back in fellowship with Him. The Lord commanded them not to be grieved on this holy day but to celebrate with great rejoicing (vv. 11-12). After this moment of silence and reverence on the second day of this momentous occasion of rededicating the Temple, a contingency representing the heads of the ancestral houses of the

Children of Israel came together to study the Law—this time concerning God's direction concerning the Festival of Booths. God originally instituted the Festival of Booths (also known as the Feast of Tabernacles) as a reminder to the Children of Israel for His goodness as He kept them during the 40 years they wandered in the wilderness.

Ezra discovered that according to the ordinance that during the seventh month (September/October), the people were to live seven days in booths: huts made of olive branches, myrtle, palm, and other leafy trees. Immediately they gathered themselves to reinstate the Festival of Booths. They realized that God had provided for them as they wandered in a strange land away from their ancestral home. The alert was sounded by messengers on foot and by the sounding of the alarm or ram's horn. Special instructions were given regarding the materials that were to be gathered for the building of the booths or temporary dwellings.

2. Festival of Booths Marks Great Celebration (vv. 17-18)

The obedience was so great that booths were built in the streets and on housetops. The people gathered before the Temple and at the gates. Their worship was not with tears but with joy, an overwhelming gladness for what God had done. They worshiped God and they celebrated His covenant. In accordance with the Law, they spent each day learning more of God's Word and purposing in their hearts to be obedient to the Law. The Festival had not been celebrated as one nation since the time of Joshua, which was several hundreds of years later.

On the eighth day, they held the "solemn assembly" as instructed by Moses (v. 18). On that day, they officially entered the covenant and offered prayers and sacrifices to God in accordance with His word. They worshiped God, the covenant giver, and determined to be covenant keepers as they carried His word in their hearts.

Search the Scriptures

1. What were the people to live in during the Festival of Booths (Nehemiah 8:14)?

2. What did the people gather in order to make the booths (v. 15)?

3. What was read to the people during this celebration, and how long did the celebration last (v. 18)?

Discuss the Meaning

1. Why is it important to celebrate significant historical/cultural events?

2. What was God's direction for the Festival of Booths?

3. Why was it important that the ancestral leaders studied the Law to execute the Festival of Booths celebration?

Lesson in Our Society

How soon we forget when we are delivered from trials and trouble. Today's lesson teaches us that God is concerned about how we receive His blessings, deliverance and restitution. The Festival of Booths was a joyous occasion, and God wanted His people to keep Him at the center of attention. It lets us know that God loves His people to have a good time. As Christians, we can have joy and celebrate life while acknowledging God as the source of every good and perfect gift. However, great celebration should also be coupled with reverent honor of God and His holiness so that He is not taken for granted and our celebrations please Him. God's Word should be at the forefront and incorporated into every celebration, not to display our self-righteousness, but with humility.

Make It Happen

When you have a celebration, is God invited? Would He be a welcomed guest? Would He attend your festivities? As you gather with family and friends, think about how you can plan to incorporate God in every aspect of your joyous occasion in a way that He would be glorified; it would be a great witness to unsaved family and friends.

Follow the Spirit

What God wants me to do:

_____

_____

_____

_____

Remember Your Thoughts

Special insights I have learned:

_____

_____

_____

_____

More Light on the Text

Nehemiah 8:13-18

13 And on the second day were gathered together the chief of the fathers of all the people, the priests, and the Levites, unto Ezra the scribe, even to understand the words of the law. 14 And they found written in the law which the LORD had commanded by Moses, that the children of Israel should dwell in booths in the feast of the seventh month:

The second review of the Law of Moses required a smaller contingency of men, most notably representative from each tribe along with the priests, Ezra and Nehemiah. The purpose was to understand exact directions on how the Festival of Booths was to be executed. All of these came before Ezra, the scribe, "to understand the words of the Law." The term "understand" used in verse 13 is from the Hebrew *sakal* (**saw-KAL**) and means to gather wisdom and instruction from the "law" (Heb. *towrah*, **to-RAW**). The leaders were there to fully comprehend the words of the Pentateuch, specifically Deuteronomy or the Mosaic Law, so that they could implement its rituals and commands in the life of the nation. They wanted to know how God wanted the Jews to behave and to conduct their affairs. They had been rejected and taken into captivity in a strange land. Having returned to their homeland, they never wanted to be faced with such a challenge again. Most importantly, they wanted to honor God with their obedience.

Now, having listened to the Word of God, they discovered something they did not know was to be done. They had built the Temple and restored the walls, but they had not been obedient to God's direction. The Feast of Tabernacles was to be celebrated on the 15th day of the seventh month, which was the month they were currently observing (see Leviticus 23:34; Deuteronomy 16:13). The Festival of Booths, which lasted for seven days, was an observance of the deliverance of Israel from Egypt and marked the time of the harvest. During this time, the Children of Israel were to leave their houses and dwell in "booths" (Heb. *cukkah*, **sook-KAW**) or temporary shelters. By doing this, they recognized God's provision for them, the same provision He had given to Moses and the Children of Israel when they were in the wilderness and which He had provided for these families when they were taken from captivity and returned to their homeland.

15 And that they should publish and proclaim in all their cities, and in Jerusalem, saying, Go forth unto the mount, and fetch olive branches, and pine branches, and myrtle branches, and palm branches, and branches of thick trees, to make booths, as it is written. 16 So the people went forth, and brought them, and made themselves booths, every one upon the roof of his house, and in their courts, and in the courts of the house of God, and in the street of the water gate, and in the street of the gate of Ephraim.

The Festival of Booths was to be celebrated by all of the people. In order to gather, there was a need to "publish" (Heb. *shama`*, **shaw-MAH**) the news. This was to be done in two ways. First, a shofar or ram's horn was to be blown throughout the nation to proclaim the observance. Secondly, messengers were sent from household to household to ensure that everyone was made aware of the coming event and that they gathered the materials for the celebration of God's provision. The people eagerly complied with the directive to dwell in booths. There were so many people who had come out of captivity and were eager to be involved in proper worship of the Lord that those who owned homes created booths on their housetops or in the courtyards of their houses. Others placed their booths in the courtyards of the Temple or in the streets before one of the gates of the city. They were truly dancing in the streets.

17 And all the congregation of them that were come again out of the captivity made booths, and sat under the booths: for since the days of Jeshua the son of Nun unto that day had not the children of Israel done so. And there was very great gladness.

18 Also day by day, from the first day unto the last day, he read in the book of the law of God. And they kept the feast seven days; and on the eighth day was a solemn assembly, according unto the manner.

Although other celebrations are noted in the Old Testament Scriptures (Judges 21:19; 1 Samuel 1:3), the outpouring was greater than the Festival of Booths had been at any time since the days of Joshua when the nation had entered the Promised Land.

They not only complied with the Law, they were excited about the Law and the opportunity to celebrate God's deliverance. Gladness permeated the entire event, which is described in verse 17 as "very" (Heb. *m@`od*, **mehe-ODE**) "great" (Heb. *gadowl*, **gaw-DOLE**) "gladness" (Heb. *simchah*, **sim-KHAW**). There was excessively intense joy. This was a serious and solemn matter, but it was also a joyous occasion. The people had been delivered from captivity and were now free to share in worship, to rebuild the celebrations of the Law and God's mercy as they recommitted themselves to their covenant relationship with Him. They rejoiced at what had been done in their lives and, no doubt, at the realization of how connected they were through the religious rituals to the ancestors of old who had been brought out of Egypt (see Leviticus 23:42-43).

The celebration of the Festival of Booths continued for the required seven days—from the 15th of the month to the 22nd of the month. Each day, Ezra read from the Book of the Law proclaiming the goodness of God. Each day they learned more about God's Law. The more they learned, the more they rejoiced over hearing the Word of God. The more they learned, the greater was their assurance that God was able to strengthen them because He had proven this time and again.

On the last day of the Festival, they kept a solemn "assembly" (Heb. `atsarah, **ats-aw-RAW**; see also Leviticus 23:36). This Hebrew term means "to gather," as on a holy day; however, the reference is followed by a call to do no servile work (labor) and to offer a sacrifice. Obviously the solemn assembly was a Sabbath day of worship and praise. The tone for this day seems to have been different from the first seven days; yet the entire experience was part of the renewal of their covenant with God.

In today's lesson, the captives have returned home and renewed their covenant with God as a result of finding the Law and obeying it. Unlike the returning Hebrew believers, we have a more secure covenant with God based on the sacrifice of Jesus Christ. By grace we are kept in covenant relationship with the Father; however, there are things that we can do to enhance our walk with God. We see also in this lesson that obedience to God's way will bring results that glorify Him. Let us examine our covenant relationship with God, apply His Word to our lives, and purpose in our hearts to renew our commitment to give Him glory.

Sources:
Abraham, A. Kenneth, ed. *The Matthew Henry Study Bible, King James Version.* Iowa Falls, IA: World Bible Publishers, 1994. 940.
Attridge, Harold W., and Wayne A. Meeks, eds. *The Harper Collins Study Bible, New Revised Standard Version.* New York, NY: Harper Collins Publishers, 2006. 651, 672.
Bible Words – Phonetic Pronunciation. http://www.betterdays arecoming.com/bible/pronunciation.html (accessed January 21, 2012).
Judaism 101: Sukkot. http://www.jewfaq.org/holiday5.htm (accessed May 30, 2011).
Old Testament Hebrew Lexicon. http://www.biblestudytools.com (accessed January 20, 2012).
Strong, James. *The New Strong's Exhaustive Concordance of the Bible.* Nashville, TN: Thomas Nelson, 1990. 99, 100.
Zodhiates, Spiros, Th.D., and Warren Baker, D.R.E., eds. *Key Word Study Bible, King James Version.* Chattanooga, TN: AMG Publishers, 1991. 1641.

Say It Correctly

Jeshua. JESH-yoo·uh.
Nun. NUHN.

Daily Bible Readings

MONDAY
Rhythms of Work and Worship
(Exodus 23:12–17)

TUESDAY
First Bring Your Offering
(Leviticus 23:9–14)

WEDNESDAY
Celebrating God's Bounty to Us
(Deuteronomy 26:1–11)

THURSDAY
Fostering the Memory of God's Deliverance
(Leviticus 23:33–44)

FRIDAY
Gathering to Hear God's Word
(Nehemiah 7:73b—8:6)

SATURDAY
Responding to God's Word
(Nehemiah 8:7b–12—the Levites)

SUNDAY
Discovering a Neglected Festival
(Nehemiah 8:13–18)

Teaching Tips

Words You Should Know

A. Confessed (Nehemiah 9:2) *yadah* (Heb.)—Made confession; cast out.

B. Iniquities (v. 2) *'avon* (Heb.)—Depravities, guilt.

Teacher Preparation

Unifying Principle—Admitting Shortcomings. Because God is merciful in every generation and gives people another chance, confession and repentance are necessary acts of worship.

A. Pray for your students and lesson clarity.

B. Study and meditate on the entire text.

C. Prepare an example of how to admit your shortcomings.

D. Complete the companion lesson in the *Precepts For Living Personal Study Guide®*.

O—Open the Lesson

A. Open with prayer, including the Aim for Change.

B. After prayer, introduce today's subject and have your students read the Aim for Change and Keep in Mind verse in unison. Discuss.

C. Share your presentation.

D. Ask: "When was the last time you confessed your shortcomings?"

E. Share their testimonies.

F. Now have a volunteer summarize the In Focus story. Discuss.

P—Present the Scriptures

A. Have volunteers read the Focal Verses.

B. Now use The People, Places, and Times; Background; Search the Scriptures; At-A-Glance outline; In Depth; and More Light on the Text to clarify the verses.

E—Explore the Meaning

A. To answer questions in the Discuss the Meaning, Lesson in Our Society, and Make It Happen sections, divide the class into groups. Assign one or two questions to each group. Select group representatives to report their responses to the rest of the class.

B. Connect these sections to the Aim for Change and the Keep in Mind verse.

N—Next Steps for Application

A. Summarize the lesson.

B. Close with prayer.

Worship Guide

For the Superintendent or Teacher
Theme: Community of Confession
Song: "Trust and Obey"
Devotional Reading: Luke 15:1-10
Prayer

Community of Confession

Bible Background • NEHEMIAH 9:1-37
Printed Text • NEHEMIAH 9:2, 6-7, 9-10, 30-36 | Devotional Reading • LUKE 15:1-10

———————— Aim for Change ————————

By the end of the lesson, we will: UNDERSTAND that confession and repentance are acts of worship; FEEL the need to confess and repent; and CONFESS and repent our shortcomings.

——————— In Focus ———————

As a retail store employee, all the training I received was from watching videos—none of it was hands-on, there was no one to show me where the items in the store belonged. Later, the opportunity arrived where I had to train someone who was from another country and did not fully understand English. Then there was the culture issue. The trainee was not used to nor did he appreciate a woman telling him how to do anything. On one particularly busy night, as we were placing the stock on the shelves, he continuously asked me how to do it. His questions confirmed to me that he really did not understand English, or so I thought.

The next week, another new person arrived. To my astonishment the person I was training volunteered to train the new arrival. I lost it and yelled at him in front of our colleagues and the store's customers. The venom that came out of my mouth scared me. I knew I had to apologize, and I had to ask God for forgiveness. After I confessed and sought repentance from God, I was able to go to my coworker and apologize.

Before seeking another chance from God, we must confess and seek repentance. As we experience God's grace and mercy, our acts of confession and repentance become another way for us to worship God.

AUG 11th

——————— Keep in Mind ———————

"And the seed of Israel separated themselves from all strangers, and stood and confessed their sins, and the iniquities of their fathers"
(Nehemiah 9:2).

"And the seed of Israel separated themselves from all strangers, and stood and confessed their sins, and the iniquities of their fathers" (Nehemiah 9:2).

Focal Verses

KJV **Nehemiah 9:2** And the seed of Israel separated themselves from all strangers, and stood and confessed their sins, and the iniquities of their fathers.

9:6 Thou, even thou, art LORD alone; thou hast made heaven, the heaven of heavens, with all their host, the earth, and all things that are therein, the seas, and all that is therein, and thou preservest them all; and the host of heaven worshippeth thee.

7 Thou art the LORD the God, who didst choose Abram, and broughtest him forth out of Ur of the Chaldees, and gavest him the name of Abraham;

9:9 And didst see the affliction of our fathers in Egypt, and heardest their cry by the Red sea;

10 And shewedst signs and wonders upon Pharaoh, and on all his servants, and on all the people of his land: for thou knewest that they dealt proudly against them. So didst thou get thee a name, as it is this day.

9:30 Yet many years didst thou forbear them, and testifiedst against them by thy spirit in thy prophets: yet would they not give ear: therefore gavest thou them into the hand of the people of the lands.

31 Nevertheless for thy great mercies' sake thou didst not utterly consume them, nor forsake them; for thou art a gracious and merciful God.

32 Now therefore, our God, the great, the mighty, and the terrible God, who keepest covenant and mercy, let not all the trouble seem little before thee, that hath come upon us, on our kings, on our princes, and on our priests, and on our prophets, and on our fathers, and on all thy people, since the time of the kings of Assyria unto this day.

33 Howbeit thou art just in all that is brought upon us; for thou hast done right, but we have done wickedly:

NLT **Nehemiah 9:2** Those of Israelite descent separated themselves from all foreigners as they confessed their own sins and the sins of their ancestors.

9:6 "You alone are the LORD. You made the skies and the heavens and all the stars. You made the earth and the seas and everything in them. You preserve them all, and the angels of heaven worship you.

7 "You are the LORD God, who chose Abram and brought him from Ur of the Chaldeans and renamed him Abraham.

9:9 "You saw the misery of our ancestors in Egypt, and you heard their cries from beside the Red Sea.

10 You displayed miraculous signs and wonders against Pharaoh, his officials, and all his people, for you knew how arrogantly they were treating our ancestors. You have a glorious reputation that has never been forgotten.

9:30 In your love, you were patient with them for many years. You sent your Spirit, who warned them through the prophets. But still they wouldn't listen! So once again you allowed the peoples of the land to conquer them.

31 But in your great mercy, you did not destroy them completely or abandon them forever. What a gracious and merciful God you are!

32 "And now, our God, the great and mighty and awesome God, who keeps his covenant of unfailing love, do not let all the hardships we have suffered seem insignificant to you. Great trouble has come upon us and upon our kings and leaders and priests and prophets and ancestors—all of your people— from the days when the kings of Assyria first triumphed over us until now.

KJV continued

34 Neither have our kings, our princes, our priests, nor our fathers, kept thy law, nor hearkened unto thy commandments and thy testimonies, wherewith thou didst testify against them.

35 For they have not served thee in their kingdom, and in thy great goodness that thou gavest them, and in the large and fat land which thou gavest before them, neither turned they from their wicked works.

36 Behold, we are servants this day, and for the land that thou gavest unto our fathers to eat the fruit thereof and the good thereof, behold, we are servants in it:

NLT continued

33 Every time you punished us you were being just. We have sinned greatly, and you gave us only what we deserved.

34 Our kings, leaders, priests, and ancestors did not obey your Law or listen to the warnings in your commands and laws.

35 Even while they had their own kingdom, they did not serve you, though you showered your goodness on them. You gave them a large, fertile land, but they refused to turn from their wickedness.

36 "So now today we are slaves in the land of plenty that you gave our ancestors for their enjoyment! We are slaves here in this good land.

The People, Places, and Times

Post-exilic. The period of time when the southern tribe returned from their exile in Babylon, returned to Jerusalem, and rebuilt the Temple.

Prayer. Dialogue or conversation between God and humankind. Prayer consists of petition, complaint, praise, thanksgiving, and confession.

Background

Led by Ezra, the people of the southern tribe returned to Jerusalem (Ezra 8:32). After offering "burnt offerings" to God for their safe travel, Ezra was told, "The people of Israel, and the priests, and the Levites, have not separated themselves from the people of the lands, doing according to their abominations ... For they have taken of their daughters for themselves, and for their sons: so that the holy seed have mingled themselves with the people of those lands" (9:1-2).

As Ezra prayed and confessed to God on behalf of the people their transgression,

Shechaniah the son of Jehiel replied to Ezra, "We have trespassed against our God, and have taken strange wives of the people of the land: yet now there is hope in Israel concerning this thing" (10:2). The "thing" Shechaniah spoke of was to divorce the foreign women the men had married.

After the men divorced their foreign wives, the Bible records the return of Nehemiah, who is immediately seen praying to God (Nehemiah 1). In his prayer to God, Nehemiah requests that God hear his confession of his sins and his confession of the sins of the people. Nehemiah asks God to remember the promise God made to the people of Israel and identifies by name the people of Israel who are to be the recipients of God's promise. Nehemiah petitions God to answer, and then asks God for the success of the rebuilding of the Temple.

After the completion of the temple, the Bible records Ezra reading the Law of Moses to the people. This reading was in response to their sins and the sins of their ancestors. In response to the reading of the Law, Nehemiah prepared the people to repent with a prayer of confession. This prayer included God's continued care for the people, God's covenant with Abraham, the people's exodus from Egypt, and God's continued grace and mercy.

At-A-Glance

1. The People Confess Their Sins (Nehemiah 9:2)
2. The People Numerate Their Sins in Their Confession (vv. 6-7, 9-10, 30-36)

In Depth

1. The People Confess Their Sins (Nehemiah 9:2)

The link between confession of one's sin and the reading and hearing of Scripture is the beginning of one's journey of faith. With the hearing and reading of Scripture, the act of forgiveness emerges as the vehicle to accept that only God can and does change. Throughout the Old Testament, the Bible records the disobedience of the people of Israel. The hearing of Scripture always preceded the link of their admission of their sin. "And all the people gathered themselves together as one man into the street that was before the water gate; and they spake unto Ezra the scribe to bring the book of the law of Moses ... before the congregation both of men and women, and all that could hear with understanding" (Nehemiah 8:1-2).

Unlike the people of Israel, we are under God's grace and mercy. With confession of our sins, our confession becomes the vehicle toward our freedom. In Romans 10, Paul explained that the people of Israel were under the law. Our confession of our sins includes our repentance and our belief in the death, burial, and resurrection of Jesus. Paul explained that our confession represents what should be in our hearts and mouths: "If you confess with your mouth that Jesus is Lord and believe in your heart that God raised him from the dead ... it is by believing in your heart that you are made right with God, and it is by confessing with your mouth that you are saved" (Romans 10:9-10, NLT). The songwriter captured the importance of confession of one's sin with the hearing and reading of the Word when he wrote, "healed by the power of His Word," for the Word of God delivers, heals, empowers, and transforms.

2. The People Numerate Their Sins in Their Confession (vv. 6-7, 9–10, 30–36)

Both Ezra and the Israelites knew that they had suffered much because of the consequences of their own sin. It was not God's fault that they went into captivity for 70 years into Babylon. They were a stiff-necked, hard-headed, ungrateful people who would not follow God's edicts, even though they promised to do so time and time again. Therefore, Ezra acknowledged before the people and God that God had been just in His punishment of them for their transgressions. "For our sins are piled higher than our heads, and our guilt has reached to the heavens" (Ezra 9:6, NLT). In other words, they did not try to excuse their transgressions or blame them on someone else. Therefore, they reviewed their past mistakes. We, too, need to do so, so we will not repeat our sins— and improve our behavior. The Israelites had been devastated by past rebellion (they had gone into bondage); but a merciful God heard their cries and delivered them.

Search the Scriptures

1. How did the people of Israel praise God (Nehemiah 9:6-7)?

2. What did the people of Israel recount to God (vv. 9-10)?

Discuss the Meaning

Again, the link between confession of one's sin and the reading and hearing of Scripture is the beginning of one's journey of faith. With the hearing and reading of Scripture, the act of forgiveness emerges as the vehicle to accept that only God can and does change or transform us.

Lesson in Our Society

Confession of one's sins is empowering because it is the introduction of faith. With faith, one accepts the plans God has for each of us. With faith, one will engage into an intimate relationship with God. With faith, one desires to please God. With faith, one will allow the Holy Spirit that dwells within each of us to lead us. With faith, nothing is impossible. With faith, one is empowered by the reading and hearing of Scripture. With faith, one will love. With faith, one will forgive.

Make It Happen

If the acceptance that the confession of one's sin and the reading and hearing of Scripture is the beginning of one's journey of faith, then one should begin with forgiving oneself. Many of us have something in our past or even present that needs to be forgiven. Once we learn to live in the generosity of God's forgiveness and also forgive ourselves, then the work of forgiving others may begin so the deliverance of past hurts may occur. With forgiveness of others, then learning to love—especially the way God loves—will

be achieved. Then, as the songwriter wrote, they will know them by their love—the love of God.

Follow the Spirit

What God wants me to do:

_____

_____

_____

_____

Remember Your Thoughts

Special insights I have learned:

_____

_____

_____

_____

More Light on the Text

Nehemiah 9:2, 6-7, 9-10, 30-36

2 And the seed of Israel separated themselves from all strangers, and stood and confessed their sins, and the iniquities of their fathers.

The occasion for the prayer of community found in chapter 9—the longest prayer in the Bible—is the rediscovery of the Book of God's Law through Ezra the scribe. Nehemiah 8 tells us that the people gathered to hear Ezra read the Book of the Law. We can only begin to imagine the power of the scene: This was the Law of Moses, the great forefather, and the community had not gathered to hear it read since before the exile to Babylon (and even then, scarcely was the Law ever read in the later, faithless years of Israel's kingdom history). We learn that the Law calls for the Feast of Tabernacles to take place, and so immediately the Israelites arise and observe it. After the feast, for reasons that the text does not make clear (but the leadership of Ezra the scribe and Nehemiah the governor were no doubt largely responsible), the people gathered once more, now garbed not in the happy raiment of feasting but in the penitential rags of sackcloth, and covered with ashes.

Why is it significant that "the seed of Israel separated themselves from all strangers" (9:2)? The answer goes all the way back to Leviticus 20:26, at the time when the covenantal community of Israel was formed: "And ye shall be holy unto me: for I the LORD am holy, and have severed you from other people, that ye should be mine." This idea lay at the heart of Israel's constitution as a nation: that they were God's chosen people drawn out from among all others to worship His name (see also Exodus 19:1-20; Deuteronomy 7:6-11). God commanded separateness from other peoples not because Israel was superior to those other peoples—quite the opposite! He knew Israel's weakness, and how quickly it would fall into idolatry if it developed deep affinities with the nations around it. And this is exactly what happened. The worship of other gods became a nauseatingly recurring narrative in the history of Israel as a nation, and led ultimately to its exile into Assyria and Babylon. And yet, despite this dismal history and the hopeful events surrounding the return to Jerusalem, we learn that many in this newly formed community at Jerusalem had already begun to intermarry and turn away from Israel's God (Nehemiah 6:17-19; 13:23-27)! The community was learning afresh the necessity of regular repentance, and this chapter is a glorious testimony to their obedience unto repentance. But before

they confessed their sins, it was necessary to separate themselves from all that hinted at idolatry, including association with the peoples around them.

Finally, we must observe that Israel does something here the modern mind might find surprising, even bizarre. The people confess not only their own sins but also "the iniquities of their fathers" (Nehemiah 9:2). If anyone wonders why the Jews felt they must apologize for their forefathers, the grim history of their people (explained in the above paragraphs) should be enough to explain it. But the answer also lies in the very nature of God's people. Briefly put, God elected for Himself not a group of worshiping individuals, but an entire covenant community. His promises and requirements (the heart of the covenant made through Abraham and Moses) were made to the people as one, and when some of the people broke the promises they had made in return, the whole community suffered (as shown in the destruction of Jerusalem and exile to Babylon, which faithful Israelites like Jeremiah had to share in with the rest). Nor is this communal understanding of God's people unique to the Old Testament. It is renewed in the new covenant through Christ (see Acts 2:38-39, for example). C. S. Lewis, in *Mere Christianity*, paints a helpful picture of this reality for us: "If you could see humanity spread out in time, as God sees it, it would not look like a lot of separate things dotted about. It would look like one single growing thing—rather like a very complicated tree. Every individual would appear connected with every other" (Lewis, 154).

9:6 Thou, even thou, art LORD alone; thou hast made heaven, the heaven of heavens, with all their host, the earth, and all things that are therein, the seas, and all that is therein, and thou preservest them all; and the host of heaven worshippeth thee.

True, vital confession springs first not from a knowledge of who we are, but from a knowledge of who God is. As one observer puts it, "The prayer is ... an example of confession in both senses of the word: *i.e.*, a confessing of God's glory and grace as well as man's ingratitude" (Kidner, 111). The first sentence, perhaps confusing in the *King James,* is probably better translated, "'You are the LORD, you alone'" (Nehemiah 9:6, ESV). In the midst of many nations and many gods, the speaker of this prayer—probably Ezra, but we don't know for sure—acknowledges that there is no God but one.

One remarkable aspect of this prayer, and a way in which it serves as a model for the prayers of God's community even today, is the way it tells a story. In this verse the story begins at creation, with God making the skies ("heavens" here probably means skies and not heaven as in God's abode, and "their host" probably refers to the stars) and the earth, along with all good things that fill both the earth and sky. Then, from the time He creates, He preserves all things that He has made, even (it might be implied) through cataclysms like the flood. The prayer also reminds all who hear that the earthly creation gives God by its very existence: "the host of heaven worshippeth thee."

7 Thou art the LORD the God, who didst choose Abram, and broughtest him forth out of Ur of the Chaldees, and gavest him the name of Abraham;

"Neither shall thy name any more be called Abram, but thy name shall be Abraham; for a father of many nations have I made thee" (Genesis 17:5). Focusing on an event mentioned by no other Old Testament passage after Genesis (Kidner, 111), the prayer in Nehemiah 9 remembers Abraham, the father of the nation of Israel. His former name, Abram, meant "exalted father," but the name God gives him means "father of many." The people are therefore reminded of their roots in that ancient place of Ur among the Chaldean people, where God made a covenant with a young man and transformed him into the covenantal father of promise. If the theme of verse 6 was "God creates and preserves," the theme of verse 7 is "God chooses and promises."

9:9 And didst see the affliction of our fathers in Egypt, and heardest their cry by the Red sea; 10 And shewedst signs and wonders upon Pharaoh, and on all his servants, and on all the people of his land: for thou knewest that they dealt proudly against them. So didst thou get thee a name, as it is this day.

Israel's exodus through the Red Sea gave an enduring shape to its community. The people remembered it every year on Passover, their national holiday, when they commemorated their harrowing escape out of slavery, across the sea that should have swallowed them but instead swallowed the Egyptians, and into freedom and nationhood in the land promised to Abraham long before. And, of course, Jews still celebrate the Passover to remember the Exodus to this day—so powerful is the resonance of an event that took place more than 3,000 years ago. And lest having such a glorious history become a source of pride in Israel, the prayer acknowledges that the Egyptians were swallowed up because "thou knewest that they dealt proudly against" Israel (Nehemiah 9:10). The pattern is clear: The one true God will humble those who seek to raise their fame to a godlike level. God alone is worthy to be remembered for His great deeds: "So didst thou get thee a name, as it to this day." So Israel's LORD, Yahweh, is not only Creator and Preserver, the One who calls and promises, but also the God who saves.

9:30 Yet many years didst thou forbear them, and testifiedst against them by thy spirit in thy prophets: yet would they not give ear: therefore gavest thou them into the hand of the people of the lands. 31 Nevertheless for thy great mercies' sake thou didst not utterly consume them, nor forsake them; for thou art a gracious and merciful God.

After reciting many of the events in Israel's history, with a focus on God's kindness and patience despite however many times the people shook their fists at Him, the prayer now summarizes these events with a reminder of why Israel went into exile. We must remember that the exile would have been a fresh wound on the consciousness of each one present, and a powerfully painful reminder of the discipline of God. The prayer acknowledges that God did right in all things, being not only perfectly just but abundantly merciful, and that the blame for the exile lies solely at the feet of the people themselves. But as has always been true for God's children, the acknowledgment of sin and rebellion is the beginning of hope for a better future. "For thy great mercies' sake thou didst not utterly consume them, nor forsake them" (v. 31); the people gathered in Jerusalem this very day were proof of that! Despite the utter despair of the exile, and the apparent loss of everything, hope was returning through God's mercy and the repentance He was granting Israel once again.

32 Now therefore, our God, the great, the mighty, and the terrible God, who keepest covenant and mercy, let not all the trouble seem little before thee, that hath come upon us, on our kings, on our princes, and on our priests, and on our prophets, and on our fathers, and on all thy people, since the time of the kings of Assyria unto this day.

The prayer's moving and significant climax brings two unshakable ideas to the forefront: first, that God is the powerful Head of His people who disciplines them for their sin, and second, that the human powers—those responsible for Israel's worship and protection—have played a central role in the aggrieving sin that led to this discipline. The people confess that God is utterly powerful, beyond them in every way, and even "terrible" (in the sense of awe-inspiring and holy, not cruel or capricious). But—and here is the beautiful mystery of biblical religion from first to last—the God so mighty beyond comprehension, so *other* and set apart, is also the God "who keepest covenant and mercy"— that is, who makes glorious promises and keeps them even when the promises made back to Him are broken. On this basis alone can the people beseech Him that their history of trouble not "seem little before thee," in the hope that the recognition of their suffering and repentance will prompt Him to mercy once again. For though their own leaders fail them again and again, the people confess their hope that their King of all kings will never fall short of His promise. And lest they appear to be blame shifting, the prayer notes that from the first exile ("the time of the kings of Assyria") to today, the guilt lies not only on the leaders but also "on our fathers, and on all thy people."

33 Howbeit thou art just in all that is brought upon us; for thou hast done right, but we have done wickedly: 34 Neither have our kings, our princes, our priests, nor our fathers, kept thy law, nor hearkened unto thy commandments and thy testimonies, wherewith thou didst testify against them.

Near the end of the book of Deuteronomy, after the detailed proclamation of God's law to Israel, the people hold an unforgettable ceremony (Deuteronomy 27:11-14). Half of

Israel's tribes stand on Mount Gerizim, to represent the blessing of God for obedience, and the other half on nearby Mount Ebal, to represent His curse for disobedience. Meanwhile, the Levites, in loud voices, declare God's curses and blessings before the people. Thus, before the people enter the Promised Land, the LORD has clearly established the basis upon which they will find the life they seek, or in fact lose it. And the people have agreed and bound themselves to the covenant. Given this history, none of these people's descendants—including those standing before God this day in a rebuilt Jerusalem—can claim to be unfairly punished. And so the prayer of confession acknowledges that the people have chosen Mount Ebal: they have chosen the curse. As a result, God has been perfectly just to carry out what He promised, while amazingly merciful in allowing a return for this faithful remnant of the people.

35 For they have not served thee in their kingdom, and in thy great goodness that thou gavest them, and in the large and fat land which thou gavest before them, neither turned they from their wicked works.

The community's prayer now brings to light another reason why God has been perfectly justified in disciplining the people. Not only did they repeatedly and egregiously break their covenantal promises to Him, but they also spurned and misused the generosity with which He lavished good things upon them. The "fat land" of their home (meaning rich with resources), the kingdom He gave them when they begged for a king to rule them (see 1 Samuel 8), and all His goodness in delivering them from both want and fear—the result of all these things is that "they have not served thee in their kingdom … neither turned they from their wicked works" (Nehemiah 9:35). This vivid contrast presents an unmistakable picture of God's righteousness and Israel's guilt.

36 Behold, we are servants this day, and for the land that thou gavest unto our fathers to eat the fruit thereof and the good thereof, behold, we are servants in it:

The prayer draws to a close with acknowledgment of a painful irony: that the Israelites, called by God to rule on His behalf over the land of Palestine, have now returned to that land, only to be servants rather than masters, small and insignificant rather than great and filled with blessings. For though this return to Israel was hopeful and merciful indeed, the nation never does gain its former glory, known under the reigns of David and Solomon. One empire replaces another in ruling over Israel: from Persia to Greece, and from Greece to Rome. Israel will be left to look for a greater King, to lead them into the true fulfillment of the Abrahamic promise. And because He came to a poor family, as an infant and then a suffering servant rather than a victorious warrior, many missed Him when He came—and still overlook Him to this day.

Sources:

Bible Words – Phonetic Pronunciation. http://www.betterdays arecoming.com/bible/pronunciation.html (accessed January 21, 2012).

Brand, Chad, Charles Draper, and Archie England, gen. eds. *Holman Illustrated Bible Dictionary*, Nashville, TN: Holman Bible Publishers, 2003.

Fensham, F. Charles. *The Books of Ezra and Nehemiah*. Grand Rapids, MI: Eerdmans, 1982.

Kidner, Derek. *Ezra & Nehemiah: An Introduction and Commentary*. Downers Grove, IL: InterVarsity Press, 1979. 111.

Lewis, C. S. *Mere Christianity*. New York, NY: MacMillan, 1981. 154.

Myers, Allen C., ed. *The Eerdmans Bible Dictionary*. Grand Rapids, MI: William B. Eerdmans Publishing Company, 1996.

The New Interpreter's Bible, Volume Three. Nashville, TN: Abingdon Press, 1999.

Old Testament Hebrew Lexicon. http://www.biblestudytools.com (accessed January 20, 2012).

Rachmacher, Earl D., Th.D., gen. ed. *The Nelson Study Bible New King James Version*. Nashville, TN: Thomas Nelson Publishers, 1997.

Today's Parallel Bible, New International Version, New American Standard Bible,

Updated Edition, King James Version, New Living Translation. Grand Rapids, MI: Zondervan Publishers, 2000.

Say It Correctly

Chaldees. KAL-dees, KAHL-.

Daily Bible Readings

MONDAY
Repent and Turn to God
(Acts 3:17-26)

TUESDAY
A Changed Mind
(Matthew 21:28-32)

WEDNESDAY
I Repent in Dust and Ashes
(Job 42:1-6)

THURSDAY
First Be Reconciled
(Matthew 5:21-26)

FRIDAY
God, Be Merciful to Me
(Luke 18:9-14)

SATURDAY
Joy in Heaven
(Luke 15:1-10)

SUNDAY
The Community Confesses Together
(Nehemiah 9:2, 6-7, 9-10, 30-36)

Notes

_____

_____

_____

_____

Teaching Tips

Words You Should Know

A. Purified (Nehemiah 12:30) *taher* (Heb.)—Cleansed and made undefiled ceremonially.

B. Rejoiced (v. 43) *samach* (Heb.)—Gladdened, made glad.

Teacher Preparation

Unifying Principle—Taking Pride in Accomplishment. Nehemiah's portrayal of the dedication of the wall is an act of worship, thanking God and celebrating a restored community.

A. Pray for your students and for lesson clarity.

B. Study and meditate on the entire text.

C. Prepare a PowerPoint presentation or other type of handout that could further bring the lesson to life.

D. Complete the companion lesson in the *Precepts For Living Personal Study Guide®*.

O—Open the Lesson

A. Open with Prayer, including the Aim for Change.

B. After prayer, introduce today's subject of the lesson.

C. Have your students read the Aim for Change and Keep in Mind verse in unison. Discuss.

D. Introduce the lesson by reviewing In Focus. Discuss.

E. Ask attendees if they have ever experienced similar situations. Discuss.

P—Present the Scriptures

A. Ask for a volunteer(s) to read the Focal Verses.

B. Go through each section: The People, Places, and Times; Background; Search the Scriptures; At-A-Glance outline; and In Depth to explain the verses.

E—Explore the Meaning

A. To answer questions in the Discuss the Meaning, Lesson in Our Society, and Make It Happen sections, divide the class into groups. Assign one or two questions to each group. Select group representatives to report their responses to the rest of the class.

B. Connect these sections to the Aim for Change and the Keep in Mind verse.

N—Next Steps for Application

A. Summarize the lesson.

B. Close with prayer.

Worship Guide

For the Superintendent or Teacher
Theme: Dedication of the Wall
Song: "Praise God from Whom All Blessings Flow"
Devotional Reading: Psalm 96
Prayer

Dedication of the Wall

Bible Background • NEHEMIAH 12:27-43
Printed Text • NEHEMIAH 12:27-36, 38, 43 | Devotional Reading • PSALM 96

———————————— Aim for Change ————————————

By the end of the lesson we will: KNOW that a part of our worship is thanking God and celebrating our restoration; RECALL times when God restored us; and THANK God for restoring us.

———————— In Focus ————————

Joan attended church with her parents as she grew up, sang in the choir throughout her childhood and participated in the church youth group. She loved the Lord and committed her life to Christ at a young age. When Joan went away to college, she found a church to attend but did not attend regularly due to a lack of transportation. In time, Joan became involved in activities unbecoming a Christian and soon found herself in a backslidden state.

When Joan went home for summer break, although she wanted to recommit herself to God, she felt ashamed and guilty for falling into a lifestyle of sin. Joan's old youth pastor saw the tug she was experiencing and reminded her from the Word about the love of God and how nothing could separate her from His love. Joan heard and embraced His Word in her heart and rededicated her life to God.

Today's lesson reminds us that no pit exists where the restoration of God's love can never find or rescue us.

———————— Keep in Mind ————————

AUG 18th

"Also that day they offered great sacrifices, and rejoiced: for God had made them rejoice with great joy: the wives also and the children rejoiced: so that the joy of Jerusalem was heard even afar off" (Nehemiah 12:43).

"Also that day they offered great sacrifices, and rejoiced: for God had made them rejoice with great joy: the wives also and the children rejoiced: so that the joy of Jerusalem was heard even afar off" (Nehemiah 12:43).

591

Focal Verses

KJV Nehemiah 12:27 And at the dedication of the wall of Jerusalem they sought the Levites out of all their places, to bring them to Jerusalem, to keep the dedication with gladness, both with thanksgivings, and with singing, with cymbals, psalteries, and with harps.

28 And the sons of the singers gathered themselves together, both out of the plain country round about Jerusalem, and from the villages of Netophathi;

29 Also from the house of Gilgal, and out of the fields of Geba and Azmaveth: for the singers had builded them villages round about Jerusalem.

30 And the priests and the Levites purified themselves, and purified the people, and the gates, and the wall.

31 Then I brought up the princes of Judah upon the wall, and appointed two great companies of them that gave thanks, whereof one went on the right hand upon the wall toward the dung gate:

32 And after them went Hoshaiah, and half of the princes of Judah,

33 And Azariah, Ezra, and Meshullam,

34 Judah, and Benjamin, and Shemaiah, and Jeremiah,

35 And certain of the priests' sons with trumpets; namely, Zechariah the son of Jonathan, the son of Shemaiah, the son of Mattaniah, the son of Michaiah, the son of Zaccur, the son of Asaph:

36 And his brethren, Shemaiah, and Azarael, Milalai, Gilalai, Maai, Nethaneel, and Judah, Hanani, with the musical instruments of David the man of God, and Ezra the scribe before them.

12:38 And the other company of them that gave thanks went over against them, and I after them, and the half of the people

NLT Nehemiah 12:27 For the dedication of the new wall of Jerusalem, the Levites throughout the land were asked to come to Jerusalem to assist in the ceremonies. They were to take part in the joyous occasion with their songs of thanksgiving and with the music of cymbals, harps, and lyres.

28 The singers were brought together from the region around Jerusalem and from the villages of the Netophathites.

29 They also came from Beth-gilgal and the rural areas near Geba and Azmaveth, for the singers had built their own settlements around Jerusalem.

30 The priests and Levites first purified themselves; then they purified the people, the gates, and the wall.

31 I led the leaders of Judah to the top of the wall and organized two large choirs to give thanks. One of the choirs proceeded southward along the top of the wall to the Dung Gate.

32 Hoshaiah and half the leaders of Judah followed them,

33 along with Azariah, Ezra, Meshullam,

34 Judah, Benjamin, Shemaiah, and Jeremiah.

35 Then came some priests who played trumpets, including Zechariah son of Jonathan, son of Shemaiah, son of Mattaniah, son of Micaiah, son of Zaccur, a descendant of Asaph.

36 And Zechariah's colleagues were Shemaiah, Azarel, Milalai, Gilalai, Maai, Nethanel, Judah, and Hanani. They used the musical instruments prescribed by David, the man of God. Ezra the scribe led this procession.

KJV continued

upon the wall, from beyond the tower of the furnaces even unto the broad wall;

12:43 Also that day they offered great sacrifices, and rejoiced: for God had made them rejoice with great joy: the wives also and the children rejoiced: so that the joy of Jerusalem was heard even afar off.

NLT continued

12:38 The second choir giving thanks went northward around the other way to meet them. I followed them, together with the other half of the people, along the top of the wall past the Tower of the Ovens to the Broad Wall,

12:43 Many sacrifices were offered on that joyous day, for God had given the people cause for great joy. The women and children also participated in the celebration, and the joy of the people of Jerusalem could be heard far away.

The People, Places, and Times

The book of Nehemiah occurs during the post-exilic history of the Children of Israel after they were in bondage to Babylon for 70 years. During their bondage, they were bound to the rulers of Babylon and Persia and no longer lived in the Promised Land, which God gave them years prior. Because of their wanton disobedience and apostasy toward God, everything they previously had was stripped and taken away. Their plight appeared hopeless and any prospect to rebuild or restore themselves looked impossible.

As the Israelites transitioned back to their land, the true plight of their low state came to light. God promised them after exile that they would return to their land and that He would restore them to fruitfulness, blessings and plenty. Any excitement or hope they left was replaced with wonder, doubt, and disappointment at the task that lay ahead for them to do. Restoration of their land, nation and status would take time.

Background

Nehemiah, an Israelite who lived in post-exilic times served the king of Persia as a cupbearer. While serving, he asked other Jews who passed through his town about Israelites who previously escaped captivity and still lived in Jerusalem. They gave a negative report: "The remnant that are left of the captivity there in the province are in great affliction and reproach: the wall of Jerusalem also is broken down, and the gates thereof are burned with fire" (Nehemiah 1:3). When Nehemiah heard this, it caused him much distress, and he fasted and prayed to hear what God thought about the situation.

Nehemiah asked God for favor so that when he went to the king to ask for help that the king would grant him his request. And God granted Nehemiah his request. He gave Nehemiah favor and Nehemiah received permission from the king to go and assist the Jews in Jerusalem with rebuilding the wall of their city. When Nehemiah sought God, he reminded Him of His Word and His promise to restore Judah from their reproach: "Remember, I beseech thee, the word that thou commandedst thy servant Moses, saying, If ye transgress, I will scatter you abroad among the nations: But if ye turn unto me, and keep my commandments, and do them; though there were of you cast out unto the uttermost part of the heaven, yet will I gather them from thence, and will bring them unto the place that I have chosen to set my name there" (Nehemiah 1:8-9).

At-A-Glance

1. Dedication and Purification
(Nehemiah 12:27-36)
2. Restoration and Thanksgiving
(vv. 38, 43)

In Depth

1. Dedication and Purification (Nehemiah 12:27-36)

Once Nehemiah received God's sanction and approval evidenced by the king's permission, he proceeded to rally the Israelites into rebuilding the wall, which they did amid great opposition. Every step of the way, their enemies ridiculed them, which added to the monumental task they faced. Here was a group of slaves, previously scattered all over, and they now began to band together as a nation to rebuild a city ravaged and completely destroyed by fire. Because of their own disobedience, apostasy, and rebellion, God had removed them from their land and taken everything from them. Now, as they turned their focus back to Him as their God, He made the way for them to return to the Promised Land. Regardless of how far the people scattered, how far they strayed or how damaged they were, Nehemiah's visit promised hope as he declared even to those who tried to stop their work: "The God of heaven, he will prosper us; therefore we his servants will arise and build: but ye have no portion, nor right, nor memorial, in Jerusalem" (Nehemiah 2:20). No longer would they be a reproach as God made a way for their restoration and reestablishing them as a nation.

With the promise of God's favor and the king's permission, the Israelites began to work toward ultimate restoration. They believed God's promise and confirmed this by declaring, "'Let us arise and build.' So they put their hands to the good work" (2:18, NASB).

Throughout the remainder of Nehemiah we see that the Israelites faced obstacle after obstacle as they tried to rebuild the wall. Ridicule, accusations, harmful plots, and other injuries hurt them and threatened to kill them. Each time, Nehemiah led the small nation to pray and seek the wisdom of God. Each time God gave them instruction of how to respond. Every time they prayed, their faith increased and strengthened even though they feared for their families and their lives. They responded in wisdom, set up guards, prepared to fight and never entangled themselves with their enemies' trouble. The Israelites remained focused on the task at hand. As a result, "the wall was completed ... When all [their] enemies heard of it, and all the nations...saw it, they lost their confidence; for they recognized that this work had been accomplished with the help of our God" (6:15-17, NASB).

Once the remnant finished the work, they also recognized that success was not based on their own hands or their own efforts but was due to the help of the Lord. Therefore, they dedicated the wall to God (12:27). A dedication refers to "a religious ceremony in which a person or a thing is set aside or consecrated to God's service" (*Nelson's New Illustrated Bible Dictionary*, 345). After experiencing God's punishment for their rebellion, the Israelites expressed their gratitude to God by first dedicating or giving back to Him what He enabled them to complete. It showed they learned from their mistakes and were now ready to move

594

forward with the next phase of their new beginning.

In addition to dedicating the wall, the priests and Levites purified themselves and purified the people (12:30). Purification referred to "the process by which an unclean person, according to the Levitical law, and thereby cut off from the sanctuary and the festivals, was restored to the enjoyment of all these privileges" (*Easton's Bible Dictionary*). Purification symbolized the washing away of their previous trespasses and gross misconduct and their renewed clean and righteous relationship with God. It demonstrated a cleansing of their association with the surrounding heathen nations and their affirmation as a people to be set apart for and by God. Dedication of the wall and of themselves represented an act of worship and celebration over their restoration.

2. Restoration and Thanksgiving (vv. 38, 43)

After a second choir sings and Nehemiah follows the remaining group in a procession to the Broad Wall (v. 38), Nehemiah 12:43 says, "that day they offered great sacrifices, and rejoiced: for God had made them rejoice with great joy: the wives also and the children rejoiced: so that the joy of Jerusalem was heard even afar off." When the Israelites rejoiced, they verbally and physically expressed gratitude to God for the blessings He allowed to occur on their behalf. This was in spite of their circumstances and the still present uphill battle they faced to rebuild their city. Despite their uncertain future and the trial of rebuilding their nation and their lives, they rejoiced at achieving and fulfilling the task of building the wall. This one task symbolized that with God all things were possible and through a restored relationship with Him, He would not only

direct the people's paths, but also allow them continued success.

The order and structure of their worship, with two choirs organized and placed in specific places around the wall and the city, demonstrated the seriousness of their experience and intentions. Not only was there much order, but also their worship was "heard from afar" (v. 43, NASB). Nations had seen the threatened demise of the Israelites, and now they would see the people's renewal and restored place of blessing and favor with God.

Search the Scriptures

1. Describe the various duties of the Levites as it pertains to worship (Nehemiah 12:27, 30).

2. How do dedication and purification lead one to restoration (12:43)?

Discuss the Meaning

If God provides forgiveness of sins and restoration to believers through repentance and faith in Jesus Christ, why do many believers live in constant condemnation and guilt over their past and their shortcomings?

Lesson in Our Society

Many times Christians tend to hold the mistakes, past and sins of other believers over their heads, even though the Bible says all sin and fall short of His glory. Why do Christians tend to condemn believers who fall or make mistakes when God Himself says, "I will forgive their iniquity, and will remember their sin no more" (Jeremiah 31:34)?

Make It Happen

As believers, we should define our forgiveness and restoration in terms of God's revelation and not our own perspective.

When we accept Christ, we accept the Lord: "The repairer of the breach, the restorer of paths to dwell in" (Isaiah 58:12). Just as God promised the nation of Judah restoration through the coming of Christ, we possess an even greater hope for experiencing fruitfulness and success because He actually lives within us. He is with and in us. He is able to repair every broken situation, fragmented relationship or disparaging circumstance, if our lives are committed to Him and if we commit these areas to Him.

Over the next week, review any areas of your life that you need the Repairer and Restorer to fix and heal. Have you prayed and given these areas to Him? Do you trust Him to fix them in spite of opposition, trials or temptations? Can you rejoice as you experience small wins? Make a commitment this week to trust God and to rejoice in who He is and what He has the power to do in your life.

Follow the Spirit

What God wants me to do:

_____

_____

_____

_____

Remember Your Thoughts

Special insights I have learned:

_____

_____

_____

_____

More Light on the Text

Nehemiah 12:27-36, 38, 43

Introduction:

This Scripture shows how God calls and uses ordinary people to do His will—to do extraordinary things. If we are willing to obey Him and follow His lead, great works can be done to help build God's kingdom. Even though Nehemiah was a cupbearer to the king of Persia and was in a foreign land, he did not forget his homeland. With God's lead and the permission of Artaxerxes, he was able to restore the dignity of his ancestral home, Jerusalem. After being appointed governor of the province surrounding Jerusalem, Nehemiah was given permission to secure the materials he needed to rebuild the fallen wall. In today's discussion, after much opposition, the work was completed. The wall was finished in 52 days, although Josephus (a leading literary scholar of the first century) used the figure of two years and four months (Wycliffe, 906-911). Now, it is time for the dedication of the wall to Almighty God who made the work possible— He brought about the success.

27 And at the dedication of the wall of Jerusalem they sought the Levites out of all their places, to bring them to Jerusalem, to keep the dedication with gladness, both with thanksgivings, and with singing, with cymbals, psalteries, and with harps.

In the Hebrew, "dedication" is *chanukkah* and is pronounced **khan-ook-KAW.** It means "consecration—set aside or consecrated to God's service." After all the hard work of rebuilding the wall with opposition from Sanballat of Samaria, Tobiah of the Ammonites, and Geshem of Arabia, who had selfish interests, the work was complete and it was time to consecrate this great work to God.

So the Levites (the priests—the descendants of Levi, specially set aside by God for His service) were asked to come to Jerusalem to assist in the consecration ceremonies. On such a momentous occasion, they were to join in songs of thanksgiving with the music of cymbals, psalteries, and harps.

28 And the sons of the singers gathered themselves together, both out of the plain country round about Jerusalem, and from the villages of Netophathi; 29 Also from the house of Gilgal, and out of the fields of Geba and Azmaveth: for the singers had builded them villages round about Jerusalem.

Israelites from surrounding villages were to join in the celebration. Many knew firsthand what mighty works God had done in their lives—leading them back to their homeland. Therefore, they recognized how far God had brought them as the wall for many years had been in disarray, and they had been vulnerable to their enemies. Now, God had brought them to a better place—a blessed place. Therefore, He deserved praise and thanksgiving.

30 And the priests and the Levites purified themselves, and purified the people, and the gates, and the wall.

The word "priests" in Hebrew is *kohen* (**ko-HANE**). This could have been the Levitical priests or Aaronic or high priest. Along with the Levites, they purified themselves, the people, the gates, and the wall. In the Hebrew "purified" is *taher* (**taw-HARE**), and it means "to be clean ceremonially." In other words, they prepared themselves to go before a holy God.

31 Then I brought up the princes of Judah upon the wall, and appointed two great companies of them that gave thanks, whereof one went on the right hand upon the wall toward the dung gate:

In Hebrew, "dung" is *'ashpoth* (**ash-POHTH**). It means "ash heap, refuse heap, dung-hill." Nehemiah appointed the positions the worshipers were to take as they gave thanks unto the Lord.

32 And after them went Hoshaiah, and half of the princes of Judah, 33 And Azariah, Ezra, and Meshullam, 34 Judah, and Benjamin, and Shemaiah, and Jeremiah, 35 And certain of the priests' sons with trumpets; namely, Zechariah the son of Jonathan, the son of Shemaiah, the son of Mattaniah, the son of Michaiah, the son of Zaccur, the son of Asaph: 36 And his brethren, Shemaiah, and Azarael, Milalai, Gilalai, Maai, Nethaneel, and Judah, Hanani, with the musical instruments of David the man of God, and Ezra the scribe before them.

A roll call was given here of who took part in the ceremony. Included in that number was Ezra the scribe who had also led a group back to Jerusalem from captivity. This was indeed a time of great celebration.

12:38 And the other company of them that gave thanks went over against them, and I after them, and the half of the people upon the wall, from beyond the tower of the furnaces even unto the broad wall;

Nehemiah showed that there was a big, important crowd of people who worshiped that day and gave thanks for what God had done. God had restored their dignity and their safety by allowing the wall to be built. In the eyes of their enemies, the Israelites were elevated because they could see that indeed God was with His people. He had not deserted them, even though God's people had deserted Him time and time again.

12:43 Also that day they offered great sacrifices, and rejoiced: for God had made them rejoice with great joy: the wives also and the children rejoiced: so that the joy of Jerusalem was heard even afar off.

The word "sacrifices" in Hebrew is *zebach* (**ZEH-bakh**), which means "thanks offering." Therefore, not only did they give thanks with offerings for all God had done, but they rejoiced as well. The word "rejoiced" in Hebrew, *samach* (**saw-MAKH**), means "gladdened, made glad." The Israelites appreciated what God had done for them. Therefore, even the wives and children were glad, and those around the Israelites saw their worship and thanksgiving. They saw what God had done for His people. Not only were the people celebrating a completed task, the wall being built, they were celebrating their restored nation—their restored Jerusalem.

Sources:
Bible Words – Phonetic Pronunciation. http://www.betterdays arecoming.com/bible/pronunciation.html (accessed January 21, 2012).
Easton, Matthew. *Easton's Bible Dictionary.* http://www.biblegateway. com/resources/dictionaries (accessed January 23, 2012).
Old Testament Hebrew Lexicon. http://www.biblestudytools.com (accessed January 20, 2012).
Online Bible Thayer's Greek Lexicon and Brown Driver & Briggs Hebrew Lexicon. Ontario, Canada: Woodside Bible Fellowship, 1993.
Pfeiffer, Charles, Howard Vos, and John Rea, eds. *Wycliffe Bible Encyclopedia, vol. 1.* Chicago, IL: Moody Press, 1975. 906-911.
Youngblood, Ronald, and Herbert Lockyer, gen. eds. *Nelson's New Illustrated Bible Dictionary.* Nashville, TN: Thomas Nelson Publishers, 1995. 345.

Say It Correctly

Azariah. az'uh-RI-uh.
Ezra. EZ-ruh.
Mattaniah. mat'uh-NI-uh.
Micaiah. muh-KI-uh, mih-KAY-yuh.
Nehemiah. nee'(h)uh-MI-uh.
Zechariah. zek'uh-RI-ah, -uh.

Daily Bible Readings

MONDAY
Celebrating God's Greatness
(Psalm 96:1-9)

TUESDAY
Celebrating the Lord's Coming
(Psalm 96:10-13)

WEDNESDAY
Celebrating God's Blessings
(Deuteronomy 12:2-7)

THURSDAY
Celebrating Freedom from Oppression
(Nahum 1:6-15)

FRIDAY
Celebrating the Restored Nation
(Jeremiah 30:18-22)

SATURDAY
Celebrating the Restored Jerusalem
(Isaiah 66:10-14)

SUNDAY
Celebrating a Completed Task
(Nehemiah 12:27-36, 38, 43)

Teaching Tips

Words You Should Know

A. Sabbath (Nehemiah 13:15) *shabbath* (Heb.)—A day of ceasing to work or a time to rest.

B. Testified (vv. 15, 21) `uwd (Heb.)— Bore witness, affirmed solemnly.

Teacher Preparation

Unifying Principle—Getting It Right. Keeping the Sabbath was so important to the welfare of God's community that Nehemiah ordered the gates shut to prevent the Israelites from breaking this law.

A. Pray for your students and lesson clarity.

B. Study and meditate on the entire text.

C. Complete the companion lesson in the *Precepts For Living Personal Study Guide*®.

O—Open the Lesson

A. Open with prayer, including the Aim for Change.

B. After prayer, introduce today's subject of the lesson.

C. Have your students read the Aim for Change and Keep in Mind verse in unison. Discuss.

D. Introduce the lesson by reviewing In Focus.

E. Ask attendees if they have ever experienced similar situations.

P—Present the Scriptures

A. Ask volunteers to read the Focal Verses.

B. Go through each section: The People, Places, and Times; Background; Search the Scriptures; At-A-Glance outline; and In Depth to explain the verses.

E—Explore the Meaning

A. To answer questions in the Discuss the Meaning, Lesson in Our Society, and Make It Happen sections, divide the class into groups. Assign one or two questions to each group. Select group representatives to report their responses to the rest of the class.

B. Connect these sections to the Aim for Change and the Keep in Mind verse.

N—Next Steps for Application

A. Summarize the lesson.

B. Close with prayer.

Worship Guide

For the Superintendent or Teacher
Theme: Sabbath Reforms
Song: "Praise Him! Praise Him!"
Devotional Reading: Mark 2:23-27
Prayer

Sabbath Reforms

Bible Background • NEHEMIAH 13:4-31
Printed Text • NEHEMIAH 13:15-22 | Devotional Reading • MARK 2:23-27

Aim for Change

By the end of the lesson we will: KNOW and UNDERSTAND that the Sabbath is to be honored; SHARE with others the importance of honoring the Sabbath; and PLAN to honor the Sabbath.

In Focus

John volunteered as a Sunday School worker at his church. He also worked full-time to support his wife and three kids. God blessed him with a promotion at his job, which required that he work beyond a normal 9-to-5 day. Sometimes he traveled to do site visits out of town, and due to the economy, his company laid off several people. John did not get laid off, but his workload increased in order to make up the shortfall in the reduction of staff.

Because of his heavy workload and travel schedule, John began to miss a lot of Sunday school. Most Sundays he was too tired to attend Sunday school, and sometimes he would miss church altogether. His wife became very concerned and discussed her feelings with John, but he refused to listen. She then turned to their pastor. When the pastor first spoke to John, he resisted and insisted that in order to keep his job, he needed to keep his current schedule. Through the prayers of his wife and pastor, John's spiritual eyes opened and he learned how to truly trust God — and that included worshiping God on Sundays.

We must always give God the firstfruits of everything He affords us, and He will in turn bless us with more—including our time. Today's lesson is about honoring the Sabbath.

Keep in Mind

"And I commanded the Levites that they should cleanse themselves, and that they should come and keep the gates, to sanctify the sabbath day. Remember me, O my God, concerning this also, and spare me according to the greatness of thy mercy" (Nehemiah 13:22).

AUG
25th

"And I commanded the Levites that they should cleanse themselves, and that they should come and keep the gates, to sanctify the sabbath day. Remember me, O my God, concerning this also, and spare me according to the greatness of thy mercy" (Nehemiah 13:22).

Focal Verses

KJV **Nehemiah 13:15** In those days saw I in Judah some treading wine presses on the sabbath, and bringing in sheaves, and lading asses; as also wine, grapes, and figs, and all manner of burdens, which they brought into Jerusalem on the sabbath day: and I testified against them in the day wherein they sold victuals.

16 There dwelt men of Tyre also therein, which brought fish, and all manner of ware, and sold on the sabbath unto the children of Judah, and in Jerusalem.

17 Then I contended with the nobles of Judah, and said unto them, What evil thing is this that ye do, and profane the sabbath day?

18 Did not your fathers thus, and did not our God bring all this evil upon us, and upon this city? yet ye bring more wrath upon Israel by profaning the sabbath.

19 And it came to pass, that when the gates of Jerusalem began to be dark before the sabbath, I commanded that the gates should be shut, and charged that they should not be opened till after the sabbath: and some of my servants set I at the gates, that there should no burden be brought in on the sabbath day.

20 So the merchants and sellers of all kind of ware lodged without Jerusalem once or twice.

21 Then I testified against them, and said unto them, Why lodge ye about the wall? if ye do so again, I will lay hands on you. From that time forth came they no more on the sabbath.

22 And I commanded the Levites that they should cleanse themselves, and that they should come and keep the gates, to sanctify the sabbath day. Remember me, O my God, concerning this also, and spare me according to the greatness of thy mercy.

NLT **Nehemiah 13:15** In those days I saw men of Judah treading out their winepresses on the Sabbath. They were also bringing in grain, loading it on donkeys, and bringing their wine, grapes, figs, and all sorts of produce to Jerusalem to sell on the Sabbath. So I rebuked them for selling their produce on that day.

16 Some men from Tyre, who lived in Jerusalem, were bringing in fish and all kinds of merchandise. They were selling it on the Sabbath to the people of Judah—and in Jerusalem at that!

17 So I confronted the nobles of Judah. "Why are you profaning the Sabbath in this evil way?" I asked.

18 "Wasn't it just this sort of thing that your ancestors did that caused our God to bring all this trouble upon us and our city? Now you are bringing even more wrath upon Israel by permitting the Sabbath to be desecrated in this way!"

19 Then I commanded that the gates of Jerusalem should be shut as darkness fell every Friday evening, not to be opened until the Sabbath ended. I sent some of my own servants to guard the gates so that no merchandise could be brought in on the Sabbath day.

20 The merchants and tradesmen with a variety of wares camped outside Jerusalem once or twice.

21 But I spoke sharply to them and said, "What are you doing out here, camping around the wall? If you do this again, I will arrest you!" And that was the last time they came on the Sabbath.

22 Then I commanded the Levites to purify themselves and to guard the gates in order to preserve the holiness of the Sabbath.

NLT continued

Remember this good deed also, O my God! Have compassion on me according to your great and unfailing love.

The People, Places, and Times

When God first established the Children of Israel as a nation, He did not just deliver them from the Egyptians and give them a land to dwell in; He provided everything they needed in order to fully function as a proper nation. From Exodus to Deuteronomy, we read how He set out a comprehensive structure, which framed the constitution of their lives. He provided laws for personal injuries, property rights, civil and criminal matters, and various other situations, as well as details regarding the people's worship. He even outlined the feasts and holidays they should celebrate. In return, God required their utter obedience to Him as their Ruler. They were to show complete submission to Him as their King and total adoration of Him as their God.

However, time and time again through history, we see their continued rebellion and disobedience to God, which eventually led to their exile. In Nehemiah, hopes existed that the Israelites would not repeat the past, but through their restoration, live an obedient, committed, and dedicated life to the ordinances of God.

Background

After the nation of Judah rebuilt the wall, the Israelites continued to slowly rebuild their nation. Rebuilding their nation required not just the physical effort of constructing houses, roads, and the Temple. Their laws, ordinances, and spiritual framework needed reshaping, too. The wall provided safety and security from outsiders and set a boundary around them as a nation. As a result,

immediately following the wall's completion, scribes read the Law aloud to inform and set the groundwork for their constitution.

Once the law was read, this motivated the remnant in Judah to confess their sins and recommit to God as a nation based on the original law He ordered. They made a covenant and set out detailed obligations, which they would comply with in order to please God. This document set the legal framework for their establishment as a nation with Nehemiah as governor over the land. He and the people voted for leaders to rule over various provinces set up across Jerusalem. In addition, the Levites were reestablished as priests, and procedures were created for the Temple such as Levitical priest service, tithes, and worship.

At-A-Glance

1. Sabbath Observance
(Nehemiah 13:15-18)
2. Keeping the Sabbath (vv. 19-22)

In Depth

1. Sabbath Observance (Nehemiah 13:15-18)

Once the Israelites accepted the law again it meant they also accepted observance of the Sabbath. "The formal institution of the Sabbath is a basic part of the Mosaic Law system. Each division of the law contains specific sections relating to the practice of the Sabbath: the moral law (the Ten Commandments), the civil law (Exodus 31:14), and the ceremonial law (Leviticus 23:3). The keeping of the Sabbath was a sign that God truly ruled Israel. To break His Sabbath law was to rebel against Him—an action meriting death (Exodus 21:14). Society was not to seek advancement outside of submission to God. Therefore, all work except acts of mercy, necessity, and worship were forbidden on the Sabbath" (*Nelson's New Illustrated Bible Dictionary*, 1106). To disobey the Sabbath meant to profane the holiness of the day, or to make it unclean or unholy.

In the newly established nation, Nehemiah observed that some Israelites did not observe the Sabbath. He found some treading wine presses, bringing in sheaves, saddling donkeys, and selling produce and goods on the Sabbath. The Israelites performed these tasks so much on the Sabbath that merchants from other nations began to come through the gates on the Sabbath to do business with the Israelites.

Nehemiah challenged the leaders of Judah regarding their conduct in how they broke the Sabbath. He reminded them that such behavior originally contributed to their demise and exile from the Promised Land. If it continued and they did not correct it, such behavior would certainly bring wrath and contribute to another downfall. Nehemiah reminded them about this; he also took corrective action by closing the gates to the city so that the Israelites could not leave the city to conduct business and outside merchants could not come into the city to conduct business. "And it came to pass, that when the gates of Jerusalem began to be dark before the sabbath, (he) commanded that the gates should be shut, and charged that they should not be opened till after the sabbath: and some of (his) servants set (he) at the gates, that there should no burden be brought in on the sabbath day" (Nehemiah 13:19).

In the Old Testament, to observe the Sabbath was a key law the Israelites needed to follow. If they broke the law and disobeyed

God, they needed to cleanse themselves. Nehemiah commanded the Levite priests to cleanse themselves in order to assist with keeping the gates as well as to sanctify the Sabbath. To "sanctify" refers to a "separation from ordinary use to a sacred purpose" (McClintock and Strong, 331). The Sabbath day was set aside for Judah to focus on God—to rest from all their daily labor and a day of obedience to Him as King and Ruler over all their lives and possessions.

2. Keeping the Sabbath (vv. 19-22)

When we compare the Old Testament with the New Testament, a number of references indicate that keeping the Sabbath refers more to a principle than strict literal observance. For example Colossians 2:16 says, "Let no man therefore judge you in meat, or in drink, or in respect of an holyday, or of the new moon, or of the sabbath days." Additionally, in Mark 3, we see Jesus healing on the Sabbath and Mark 2:27-28 (NASB) recounts, "Jesus said to them, 'The Sabbath was made for man, not man for the Sabbath. So the Son of Man is Lord even of the Sabbath.'" What God established under the law in the Old Testament was still expected in the New Testament, but in a different way.

Some denominations believe that believers are obligated to keep a formal Sabbath day to occur on either Saturday or Sunday. They feel that this is a part of the moral system as set out through the Ten Commandments, which should bind all Christians. Other denominations do not take the Sabbath observance literally, but believe it should be taken figuratively and instead "keep the Sabbath" through a worship day on Sunday, which is observed by attending church.

"The Sabbath is a means by which a person's living pattern imitates God's (Exodus 20:3-11). Work is followed by rest. This idea is expressed by the Hebrew word for Sabbath, which means 'cessation.' ... a time for God's people to think about and enjoy what God has accomplished ... (It) holds promise of the ultimate salvation that God will accomplish for His people. As certainly as He delivered them from Egypt through Moses, so will He deliver His people from sin at the end of the age through the Great Redeemer (Genesis 3:15; Hebrews 4:1) ... (Also,) the Sabbath includes the idea and practice of...a day for public convocation (Leviticus 23:3)" (*Nelson's,* 1107). On this special day, His people could gather together in public worship to signify their submission to His lordship over them and their way of living (Exodus 31:13; Ezekiel 20:12).

Regardless of one's understanding of whether the Sabbath should be formally or symbolically kept, the key purpose of why God instituted it should always be maintained. We keep a Sabbath day in order to rest from our daily jobs, conducting of business, anxiety or worry. We keep a Sabbath day in order to reflect on the goodness of God and His blessings toward us. We keep a Sabbath day in order to set aside and take time out of our week to publicly worship Him as a way to demonstrate our submission to His Lordship over our lives.

Search the Scriptures

1. What were the Israelites doing which contributed to their breaking the Sabbath (Nehemiah 13:15-20)?

2. What negative things could occur when the Israelites profaned the Sabbath (vv. 18, 21)?

Discuss the Meaning

Describe the various meanings of the Sabbath and the reasons why Christians should "keep" it, regardless of denomination.

Lesson in Our Society

Some of the biggest problems facing America is its diminishing reliance on God, decline in church attendance and reduced regard for Christian-based principles. How can believers in the United States help reverse this trend and work toward building up America, which was originally founded as a nation under God?

Make It Happen

The busyness of life can distract Christians from performing basic duties, such as reading one's Bible, praying, meditating on God's Word, and even attending church. Due to family commitments, job responsibilities, and many other tasks we must do each day, sometimes we forget or neglect to take time out for God. As you go through this week, make a point each day to spend time talking to God. If you feel as though time will not permit, try God. You will see that once you take time for Him, He will in turn give you the time required to take care of everything you need.

Follow the Spirit

What God wants me to do:

_____

_____

_____

_____

Remember Your Thoughts

Special insights I have learned:

_____

_____

_____

_____

More Light on the Text

Nehemiah 13:15-22

15 In those days saw I in Judah some treading wine presses on the sabbath, and bringing in sheaves, and lading asses; as also wine, grapes, and figs, and all manner of burdens, which they brought into Jerusalem on the sabbath day: and I testified against them in the day wherein they sold victuals.

In today's text, we see an assertive Nehemiah who refused to allow the Sabbath—the Lord's Day—to be profaned by trading, buying, and selling which was clearly disobedience to God's command. He was concerned with honoring the Sabbath. In Hebrew, "sabbath" is *shabbath* (**shab-BAWTH**); it refers to the seventh day of the week and can also mean "day of atonement." God had done so much already for the Israelites in delivering them from bondage, helping them to build the wall of Jerusalem, and also returning their dignity as a nation that Nehemiah was not going to tolerate sin in the camp. He would not tolerate them working at their vineyards, preparing loads to take to a marketplace, and otherwise carrying on with their chores as though this was just any other day. This day was set aside to worship the Lord—to bring praises and thanksgiving to Him—and nothing less would be tolerated.

16 There dwelt men of Tyre also therein, which brought fish, and all manner of ware, and sold on the sabbath unto the children of Judah, and in Jerusalem.

To add insult to injury, men from Tyre brought fish and various wares and sold them to the Israelites on the Sabbath. They had the nerve to do it in Jerusalem on the Lord's Day—the day set aside for worship—where the new wall had been built. Nehemiah found this offensive and knew that it would be offensive unto the Lord. He knew that His people had gotten in trouble with the Lord in the first place because of their disobedience. This was the major reason why they were sent into captivity for 70 years and needed deliverance. Under his watch, Nehemiah made sure that God's rules were obeyed.

17 Then I contended with the nobles of Judah, and said unto them, What evil thing is this that ye do, and profane the sabbath day?

So Nehemiah contended with the nobles of Judah. In Hebrew, the word "contended" is *riyb* (**reeb**) and it means, "strove physically, confronted, made a complaint." In other words, he went to the ones in charge and voiced his complaint—he let them know that the activities were very much out of order on the Sabbath, and something had to be done right away to alleviate the problem. In fact, he called these activities "an evil thing." The word "evil" in Hebrew is *ra`* (**rah**). It means, "bad, disagreeable, malignant, displeasing." In Nehemiah's sight, this selling and buying profaned the Sabbath. In Hebrew, "profane" is *chalal* (**khaw-LAL**), meaning, "to defile, pollute, or desecrate."

18 Did not your fathers thus, and did not our God bring all this evil upon us, and upon this city? yet ye bring more wrath upon Israel by profaning the sabbath.

Nehemiah saw the blatant disobedience as bringing more wrath upon Israel, as their fathers' disobedience had done. In Hebrew, the word "wrath," (*charown* **khaw-RONE**), means "anger, heat, burning of anger (by God)." In other words, he reminds them that it was their disobedience that brought about God's wrath before, and they would not risk this disobedience bringing His wrath again.

19 And it came to pass, that when the gates of Jerusalem began to be dark before the sabbath, I commanded that the gates should be shut, and charged that they should not be opened till after the sabbath: and some of my servants set I at the gates, that there should no burden be brought in on the sabbath day. 20 So the merchants and sellers of all kind of ware lodged without Jerusalem once or twice.

For Nehemiah, profaning of the Sabbath was so serious that he took charge and commanded that the gates be shut and that they not be opened again until after the Sabbath. He ensured that God's Day would not be violated in any way. This sent the merchants and sellers the message that it would not be business as usual on the Sabbath. This was a holy, consecrated day set aside to worship a holy God.

21 Then I testified against them, and said unto them, Why lodge ye about the wall? if ye do so again, I will lay hands on you. From that time forth came they no more on the sabbath.

Nehemiah was willing to lay hands on anyone who did not heed his words. It was so important that they not disobey God's commands that he was willing to take anyone to task who did not clear their wares from around the wall.

22 And I commanded the Levites that they should cleanse themselves, and that they should come and keep the gates, to sanctify the sabbath day. Remember me, O my God, concerning this also, and spare me according to the greatness of thy mercy.

The next step was a time of purification. Again, Nehemiah showed his great leadership by commanding the Levites (those set aside by God to do special work for Him) to cleanse themselves—to sanctify the Sabbath day. In Hebrew, "sanctify" is *qadash* (**kaw-DASH**), and it means "to be set apart, to be consecrated, to be hallowed." The Sabbath is to be a holy day because our God is holy. Nehemiah recognized this and in no way was he willing to violate God's commands. After restoring the sanctity of the Sabbath, Nehemiah then asked God to remember him and show mercy toward him. In other words, Nehemiah did not want God to bring punishment like Israel experienced in the past, and he wanted to be remembered when God was passing out His blessings.

Sources:

Bible Words – Phonetic Pronunciation. http://www.betterdays arecoming.com/bible/pronunciation.html (accessed January 21, 2012).

McClintock, John, and James Strong. *Encyclopedia of Biblical, Theological and Ecclesiastical Literature, Vol. IX.* New York, NY: Harper & Brothers Publishers, 1891. 331.

Old Testament Hebrew Lexicon. http://www.biblestudytools.com (accessed January 20, 2012).

Youngblood, Ronald, and Herbert Lockyer, gen. eds. *Nelson's New Illustrated Bible Dictionary.* Nashville, TN: Thomas Nelson Publishers, 1995. 1106, 1107.

Say It Correctly

Deuteronomy. doo'tuh-RON-uh-mee.
Nehemiah. nee'(h)uh-MI-uh.
Sabbath. SAB-uhth, SA-buhth.

Daily Bible Readings

MONDAY
A Sabbath to the Lord
(Exodus 16:13–26)

TUESDAY
Keep the Sabbath Holy
(Exodus 31:12-18)

WEDNESDAY
Honoring the Sabbath
(Isaiah 58:9c-14)

THURSDAY
The Lord of the Sabbath
(Mark 2:23-27)

FRIDAY
Doing Good on the Sabbath
(Mark 3:1-6)

SATURDAY
Restoring the Sanctity of the Temple
(Nehemiah 13:4-14)

SUNDAY
Restoring the Sanctity of the Sabbath
(Nehemiah 13:15-22)

Notes

_____

_____

_____

_____

A

Abomination: A foul and detestable thing

Affliction: Anguish, burden, persecution, tribulation, or trouble

Angels: God's messengers; they are not eternal or all-knowing, and are sometimes referred to as winged creatures known as "cherubim" and "seraphim"

Atonement: To "propitiate" (to satisfy the demands of an offended holy God) or "atone" (being reconciled to a holy God) because of sin

Avenger: One who takes revenge, one who punishes

B

Be Baptized: To dip repeatedly, to immerse, to submerge

Blameless: Irreproachable, faultless, flawless

Blessedness: Happiness, joy, prosperity. It is not based on circumstance but is rooted in the deep abiding hope shared by all who have received salvation through Jesus Christ.

Bless the Lord: To simply speak well of Him

Blood of the Lamb: The blood that Jesus shed on the Cross of Calvary when He suffered and died for humanity's sin

Bowels: The place of emotions, distress, or love

C

Called: Appointed or commissioned by God to fulfill a task

Charge: Admonish, order, command

Chosen: To be elected or selected

Christ: The Anointed One

Commandments: God's mandates; the entire body of Laws issued by God to Moses for Israel

Conduct: Manner of living

Confess: To acknowledge or to fully agree

Consider: To determine, make out

Covenant: An agreement with God based on God's character, strength, and grace; an agreement and promise between God and humankind

Crucifixion: Jesus suffered and died on the Cross

D

Decalogue: The Ten Commandments; the words translated "Ten Commandments" literally mean "ten words"

Desolation: Making something deserted or uninhabited

Disciples: Learners, students, followers

Dominion: Rule or reign

Dwelling place: A location that is a person's refuge, home

E

El: The Hebrew word for "god" or "mighty one"

Even from everlasting to everlasting: "Indefinite or unending future, eternity" (Strong)

Evil: To do "bad, unpleasant, displeasing" things

Evil doer: A malefactor, wrongdoer, criminal, troublemaker

Evil spirits: Messengers and ministers of the devil

Exalt: To raise up; to raise to the highest degree possible

Exhortation: Giving someone motivation to change his or her behavior; It can imply either rebuke or encouragement.

F

Faithfulness: Steadfastness, steadiness

Fear of the Lord: Reverence or awe of who God is

G

Gittith: A musical instrument resembling a Spanish guitar that, in ancient times, provided a musical tune or tempo during a ceremony or festival

Glory: Splendor, unparalleled honor, dignity, or distinction; to honor, praise, and worship

God called: To commission, appoint, endow

God's Bride: The Church

God's own hand: God's strength, power

God's protection: Conveys the idea of staying in God's abode, staying constantly in His presence, getting completely acquainted or connected with Him, and resting permanently in Him

Gospel: "The glad tidings of the kingdom of God soon to be set up, and later also of Jesus the Messiah, the founder of this kingdom" (Strong).

Graven image: An idol or likeness cut from stone, wood, or metal and then worshiped as a god

Great Tribulation: A time of great suffering (Daniel 12:1, Revelation 6–18)

H

Hallowed: Consecrated, dedicated, or set apart

Hear: Listen to, yield to, to be obedient

Hearken: Pay attention to, give attention to

Heart: The place, figuratively, where our emotions and passions exist

Heathen: Literally means "nations" and is used in the Old Testament to refer to the Gentiles, all those who are not a part of the people of God

Holy: Anything consecrated and set aside for sacred use; the place made sacred because of God's presence; set apart from sin

Honor: To revere, value

Hosts: Those which go forth; armies

I

Idolatry: The worship of anything other than God, our Creator

Infidel: One who is unfaithful, unbelieving, not to be trusted

Iniquities: Perversity, depravity, guilt

In vain: A waste, a worthless thing, or simply emptiness

J

Jesus' ascension: Forty days after Jesus' death, burial, and Resurrection, He ascended or went back to heaven to sit at the right hand of the Father (Acts 1:9–11).

Jesus' transfiguration: While on the Mount of Olives with His closest disciples—Peter, James, and John—Jesus changed into another form. His face shone with the brightness like the sun and His raiment was white as snow (Matthew 17:2; Mark 9:2; Luke 9:29).

Just: A word often rendered as "righteous"; that which is right and fair

Justice: Righteousness in government

K

Kingdom of Christ: It is the same as the "Kingdom of Heaven (Matthew 18:1–4); it is where Jesus reigns in "glory" (i.e., in "dignity or honor").

Know: To ascertain by seeing, have understanding, to acknowledge

Knowledge: Discernment, understanding, wisdom

L

Labor: To toil to the point of exhaustion or weariness

Logos (LOG-os): The entire Word of God

M

"Make a joyful noise": A command that literally means "shout"

Manna: Food from heaven

Messiah: The Promised One; the Anointed One

Minister: "A servant, an attendant, one who executes the commands of another" (Strong)

O

Omnipotent: All powerful

Omnipresent: All present, present everywhere

Omniscient: All knowing

Ordained: Established and founded by God; founded, fixed, appointed, or established

P

Parousia (par-oo-SEE-ah): Christ's Second Coming

Path: Connotes an ongoing process of taking dynamic steps toward an expected end

Peace: Denotes "wholeness, quietness, contentment, health, prosperity" (Strong); it is far more than an absence of conflict or problems, but that every part of life would be blessed.

Pentateuch: The Mosaic Law or Divine Law; The first five books of the Old Testament, as well as the Old Testament as a whole, reveal the entire set of legal and religious instructions which God gave, through Moses, for God's people. Terms that are synonymous for "Law" include commandments, ordinances, statutes, legal regulations, authoritative instructions, and teachings.

People(s): Most English versions translate "people" as "peoples." The New Living Translation goes even further: "Let the whole world bless our God."

Power: Boldness, might, strength, especially God's

Prophets: They were filled with the Spirit of God and under the authority and command of God, pleaded God's cause and urged humanity to be saved

Profit: To gain, benefit, avail

Prosperous: To make progress, to succeed, especially in spiritual things. It often did not refer to personal profit. Rather it meant "to move forward or succeed" in one's efforts.

Proved: Examined, tested, and tried

Psalm: A Hebrew title that means "praise"

Purity: "Sinless of life" (Strong)

R

Ransom: To redeem (buy back) from, to pay a price for a person. It is commonly used as a purchase price to free slaves.

Redeemed: Ransomed, purchased.

Refuge: Place of shelter; stronghold or fortress—a place to which we can run when the enemy threatens and be secure; a shelter from rain, storm, or danger

Repent: To change (be transformed) or turn back from sin and turn to God in faith

Righteous: To be declared "not guilty"

Righteousness: God's justness and rightness, which He works as a gift also in His people; refers to the right way to live as opposed to a lifestyle that treats others unfairly or unjustly

S

Sabbath: In Hebrew, *shabbath* means "ceasing from work." A day set aside to worship God.

Sanctuary: A word that means "holy" when used as an adjective. The "holy place" of which David speaks is the tabernacle, the portable temple built under Moses' leadership after the Exodus from Egypt

Salvation: Rescue, safety, deliverance

Satan: An adversary or devil

Savior: A defender, rescuer, deliverer

Scribes: They were secretaries, recorders, men skilled in the law

Secret place: A refuge, place of safety and a covering from all forms of destructive elements that seek to attack or destroy the children of God and to prevent us from experiencing the fullness of God's blessings, peace, and divine providence

See: To behold, consider, discern, perceive

Selah: This Hebrew expression (**SEH-lah**) is found almost exclusively in the book of Psalms. Some believe that Selah denotes a pause or a suspension in singing of the psalm or recitation, and the insertion of an instrumental musical interlude. The Greek Septuagint renders the word *dia'psalma*, meaning "a musical interlude." Still others think that the word *Selah* signaled a holding back of singing and allowed for silent meditation.

Septuagint: It means "seventy," and it is the ancient Greek translation of the Hebrew Old Testament by 70 Jewish scholars.

Servant: A slave, subject, worshiper

Shalom: Means "peace"

Shekinah Glory: The awesome presence of the Lord; His honor, fame, and reputation

Shofar (sho-FAR): Means "ram's horn" and was used in celebration as well as in signaling armies or large groups of people in civil assembly

Soul: Refers to the immaterial part of the human being (what leaves the body when death occurs), or to the whole being—the self, one's life

Stiffnecked: Obstinate and difficult

Strengthen: To secure, make firm, make strong

Strive: To struggle, to exert oneself

Supplications: Seeking, asking, entreating, pleading, imploring, and petitioning God

T

Tabernacles: Literally means "dwelling places," the name of the portable temple constructed by Moses and the people of Israel

Teaching: Instruction in Christian living

Tetragrammaton: Hebrew name for God (YHWH)

Torah: The Law, which means "instrument" or "direction"; the first five books of the Old Testament (Genesis, Exodus, Leviticus, Numbers, and Deuteronomy)

Transfigured: To change or transform

Transgressions: Include sins, rebellion, breaking God's Law

Tried: Smelted or refined, purified

Trumpet: A ram's horn that was used in celebration as well as in signaling armies or large groups of people in civil assembly

U

Understand: To consider, have wisdom

W

Wisdom: "Prudence, an understanding of ethics" (Strong)

Woe: An exclamation of grief

Worship: Bow down deeply, show obeisance and reverence

Wrath: "Burning anger, rage" (Strong)

Y

Yahweh: Many scholars simply use the Hebrew spelling with consonants only, *YHWH*, which is God's name.

Source:

Strong, James. *New Exhaustive Strong's Numbers and Concordance with Expanded Greek-Hebrew Dictionary.* Seattle, WA: Biblesoft, and International Bible Translators, 1994. 2003.